The Child with Disabling Illness

Principles of Rehabilitation

edited by

John A. Downey, M.D., D. Phil. (Oxon.)

Professor of Rehabilitation Medicine,
College of Physicians and Surgeons,
Columbia University

and

Niels L. Low, M.D.

Associate Professor of Clinical Neurology and Clinical Pediatrics,
College of Physicians and Surgeons,
Columbia University

1974   W. B. SAUNDERS COMPANY

Philadelphia, London, Toronto

W. B. Saunders Company: West Washington Square
Philadelphia, Pa. 19105

12 Dyott Street
London, WC1A   1DB

833 Oxford Street
Toronto, Ontario M8Z 5T9, Canada

The Child with Disabling Illness:
Principles of Rehabilitation   ISBN 0-7216-3183-5

Print No.:   9   8   7   6   5   4   3   2   1

DEDICATION

To our children
Richard, Susan, Robert, and Jennifer Downey
and
Roger and Judith Low

Contributors

PETER BLOS, JR., M.D.

Assistant Professor of Psychiatry, University of Michigan Medical Center, Youth Services, Children's Division, Ann Arbor, Michigan.

PETER W. CARMEL, M.D., SC.D. (MED.)

Assistant Professor of Neurological Surgery, College of Physicians and Surgeons, Columbia University, New York, New York. Assistant Attending Neurological Surgeon, Presbyterian Hospital, New York, New York; Neurosurgical Consultant, Blythedale Children's Hospital, Valhalla, New York.

SIDNEY CARTER, M.D.

Professor of Neurology and Pediatrics, College of Physicians and Surgeons, Columbia University, New York, New York. Attending Physician, Presbyterian Hospital, New York, New York; Chief of Neurology, Blythedale Children's Hospital, Valhalla, New York.

YASOMA B. CHALLENOR, M.D.

Assistant Clinical Professor of Rehabilitation Medicine, College of Physicians and Surgeons, Columbia University, New York, New York. Director, Department of Rehabilitation Medicine, Blythedale Children's Hospital, Valhalla, New York; Assistant Rehabilitation Physician, Presbyterian Hospital, and Director, Electrodiagnosis Unit, Harlem Hospital Center, New York, New York.

ABE M. CHUTORIAN, M.D.

Associate Professor of Clinical Neurology and Clinical Pediatrics, College of Physicians and Surgeons, Columbia University, New York, New York. Associate Attending Neurologist, Presbyterian Hospital, New York, New York; Visiting Neurologist, Blythedale Children's Hospital, Valhalla, New York.

FRANCES P. CONNOR, ED.D.

Professor and Chairman, Department of Special Education, Teachers College, Columbia University, New York, New York.

BARD COSMAN, M.D.

Associate Professor of Clinical Surgery, College of Physicians and Surgeons, Columbia University, New York, New York. Associate Attending Surgeon, Presbyterian Hospital, New York, New York; Visiting Attending Surgeon, Francis Delafield Hospital, New York, New York; Associate Attending Plastic Surgeon, St. Elizabeth–St. Clare's Medical Center, New York, New York; Consultant, Blythedale Children's Hospital, Valhalla, New York.

ROBERT C. DARLING, M.D.

Professor Emeritus of Rehabilitation Medicine, College of Physicians and Surgeons, Columbia University, New York, New York. Consultant, Presbyterian Hospital, New York, New York; Consultant, Blythedale Children's Hospital, Valhalla, New York.

MARTHA BRIDGE DENCKLA, M.D.

Associate in Neurology, College of Physicians and Surgeons, Columbia University, New York, New York; Visiting Lecturer in Special Education, Teachers' College, Columbia University, New York, New York. Assistant Attending Neurologist, Presbyterian Hospital, New York, New York.

PAUL A. DI SANT'AGNESE, M.D., SC.D. (MED.), DR. MED. (HON.)

Clinical Professor of Pediatrics, Georgetown University School of Medicine, Washington, District of Columbia. Chief, Pediatric Metabolism Branch, National Institute of Arthritis, Metabolism, and Digestive Diseases, National Institutes of Health, Bethesda, Maryland. Consultant, Children's Hospital of the District of Columbia, Washington, District of Columbia.

JOHN A. DOWNEY, M.D., D. Phil. (OXON.)

Professor of Rehabilitation Medicine, College of Physicians and Surgeons, Columbia University, New York, New York. Attending Physician, Department of Rehabilitation Medicine, Presbyterian Hospital, New York, New York; Attending Physician, Department of Rehabilitation Medicine, Blythedale Children's Hospital, Valhalla, New York.

GRACE FIELDS, M.S.S.

Director of Social Service, Blythedale Children's Hospital, Valhalla, New York.

STUART M. FINCH, M.D.

Lecturer in Psychiatry, University of Arizona Medical Center, Tucson, Arizona.

ARNOLD P. GOLD, M.D.

Associate Professor of Clinical Neurology and Clinical Pediatrics, College of Physicians and Surgeons, Columbia University, New York, New York. Associate Attending Pediatrician and Associate Attending Neurologist, Presbyterian Hospital, New York, New York; Visiting Neurologist, Blythedale Children's Hospital, Valhalla, New York.

A. DAVID GUREWITSCH, M.D.

Formerly Clinical Professor of Rehabilitation Medicine, College of Physicians and Surgeons, Columbia University, New York, New York. Consultant, Presbyterian Hospital, New York, New York; Medical Director Emeritus, Blythedale Children's Hospital, Valhalla, New York.

EDWARD J. HART, M.D.

Instructor of Neurology and Pediatrics, College of Physicians and Surgeons, Columbia University, New York, New York. Assistant Neurologist, Presbyterian Hospital, New York, New York; Visiting Neurologist, Blythedale Children's Hospital, Valhalla, New York.

JERRY C. JACOBS, M.D.

Associate Clinical Professor of Pediatrics, College of Physicians and Surgeons, Columbia University. Pediatrician-in-Chief, The Edward Daniels Faulkner Arthritis

Clinic, Associate Attending Pediatrician, Babies Hospital, the Children's Medical and Surgical Center at the Columbia–Presbyterian Medical Center, New York, New York.

ROSAMOND KANE, M.D.

Assistant Clinical Professor of Orthopedic Surgery, College of Physicians and Surgeons, Columbia University, New York, New York. Assistant Attending Surgeon, Presbyterian Hospital (The New York Orthopedic Hospital), New York, New York.

JACOB F. KATZ, M.D.

Professor of Clinical Orthopedics, Mt. Sinai School of Medicine, City University of New York, New York, New York. Attending Orthopedic Surgeon, Mt. Sinai Hospital, New York, New York; Chief of Orthopedics, Blythedale Children's Hospital, Valhalla, New York.

WILFRED KROM, M.D.

Instructor of Orthopedic Surgery, College of Physicians and Surgeons, Columbia University, New York, New York. Assistant Attending Surgeon, Presbyterian Hospital (The New York Orthopedic Hospital), New York, New York.

NIELS L. LOW, M.D.

Associate Professor of Clinical Neurology and Clinical Pediatrics, College of Physicians and Surgeons, Columbia University, New York, New York. Clinical Director, Blythedale Children's Hospital, Valhalla, New York; Associate Attending Neurologist, Presbyterian Hospital, New York, New York.

ARMOND V. MASCIA, M.D.

Assistant Clinical Professor of Pediatrics, College of Physicians and Surgeons, Columbia University, New York, New York. Attending Pediatric Allergist, Blythedale Children's Hospital, Valhalla, New York; Director Pediatric Allergy, Grasslands Hospital, Valhalla, New York; Associate Director, Asthmatic Children's Foundation Residential Treatment Center, Ossining, New York.

STANLEY J. MYERS, M.D.

Assistant Professor of Rehabilitation Medicine, College of Physicians and Surgeons, Columbia University, New York, New York. Assistant Attending Physician (Rehabilitation Medicine), Presbyterian Hospital, New York, New York.

SOLOMON N. ROSENSTEIN, D.D.S.

Professor of Dentistry and Director, Division of Pedodontics, School of Dental and Oral Surgery, Columbia University, New York, New York. Attending Dental Surgeon (Pedodontics), Presbyterian Hospital, New York, New York; Consultant in Pedodontics, Blythedale Children's Hospital, Valhalla, New York.

ROBERT STONE, M.S.

Instructor of Rehabilitation Medicine, College of Physicians and Surgeons, Columbia University, New York, New York. Executive Director, Blythedale Children's Hospital, Valhalla, New York.

ROBERT L. STUBBLEFIELD, M.D.

Clinical Professor of Psychiatry, University of Colorado School of Medicine, Denver, Colorado. Director, Division of Mental Health and Related Areas, Western Interstate Commission of Higher Education, Boulder, Colorado.

WILLIAM M. USDANE, PH.D.

Assistant Commissioner for Program Development, Rehabilitation Services Administration, Social and Rehabilitation Service, Department of Health, Education, and Welfare, Washington, District of Columbia.

JAMES A. WOLFF, M.D.

Professor of Pediatrics, College of Physicians and Surgeons, Columbia University, New York, New York. Attending Pediatrician, Babies Hospital at Presbyterian Hospital, New York, New York.

Acknowledgments

The editors wish to acknowledge their indebtedness to many teachers, colleagues, and students, but especially to Dr. Sidney Carter and Dr. Robert C. Darling, who have been our chiefs of Child Neurology and Rehabilitation Medicine, respectively, during much of our professional lives. They, as pioneers in their fields, have not only guided and helped us but have influenced many other physicians in the scientific and humanitarian practice of our specialties. The College of Physicians and Surgeons of Columbia University and Presbyterian Hospital and Blythedale Children's Hospital have provided a fertile environment for the work and experience of the editors and many of the authors.

One of us (J.A.D.) also wishes to acknowledge his deep debt of gratitude to Dr. A. D. Gurewitsch, formerly Clinical Professor of Rehabilitation Medicine (now Consultant) at Columbia—Presbyterian Medical Center and Medical Director at Blythedale Children's Hospital, who is a leader in rehabilitation of both adults and children and also a personal friend, and to Dr. William B. Snow, Professor of Physical Medicine (Emeritus), who was the originator and leader in the practice of what is now Rehabilitation Medicine at this Medical Center.

The other editor (N.L.L.) has been exposed to and stimulated by many teachers and friends in pediatrics and neurology. Among the physicians who influenced him most to become a pediatric neurologist were Dr. M. G. Peterman of Milwaukee and Dr. Douglas Buchanan of Chicago. The greatest thanks are due four outstanding teachers, Drs. Frederic A. Gibbs, James F. Bosma, Sidney Carter, and H. Houston Merritt, and the three men who taught and showed the need for rehabilitation of children, Drs. Robert C. Darling and John A. Downey and Mr. Robert Stone.

We both are grateful for editorial help and advice from Dr. Derek B. Frewin, Visiting Professor, Columbia University College of Physicians and Surgeons, and Mr. John L. Dusseau, Vice President and Editor, W. B. Saunders Company. We also wish to thank Ms. Rosemary Bleha for secretarial, editorial, and organizational help and Ms. Claire Stone for assistance with typing.

J.A.D.
N.L.L.

Contents

1

Introduction

"Childhood is health"*—would that this aphorism were always true. Those who profess an interest in the care of the chronically ill must look to the child as the challenging problem. Most childhood illnesses are brief and self-limited, but any illness that cannot be completely cured is perforce of greater significance and often of greater complexity in a child than in an adult because of the child's potential longevity. The ramifications of the illness lead not only into the complex medical problem of caring for a growing patient but also into myriad other concerns that are difficult enough for a normal child.

The rehabilitation of a child with long-standing or chronic illness starts with the accurate diagnosis of the disorder and the institution of appropriate medical care; however, the care must deal with the whole family complex and involve recognition of the importance of family interaction that can add to or detract from the rehabilitation. Prognostic implication of the illness for the child's future must be part of the management plan from the beginning. In some instances it may be relatively easy to predict the future, but in other situations it may be very difficult owing to the child's age or the variable or unknown course of his disease. Therefore, management must combine realistic hope and possibly even an overestimation of the potential of some in order to prevent underachievement in those others who may surprise us. The final outcome will depend on many things, including the personality and intellectual potential of the child prior to the illness, the family, the social-environmental and therapeutic facilities available, as well as the physical and emotional residual of the child. The opportunity to be involved in all aspects of a child's care throughout an often prolonged, frustrating, and troublesome period of life is a challenging privilege for the truly concerned physician.

This book does not cover all chronic and disabling illness of children but, rather, arbitrarily selects a number of disorders that reflect the interests and experience of the editors and authors and at the same time includes those

---

*George Herbert (1593–1633), *The Temple*, "Holy Baptism."

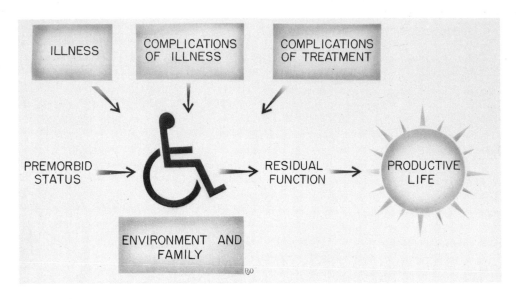

disorders that are at present common problems and about which there is ongoing research and clinical interest. The inclusion of psychiatric, social, educational, and vocational chapters is intended to highlight the great importance of these areas in the care of the chronically ill child and to point to the need for further study.

A. David Gurewitsch, M.D.

section one

Selected Chronic Medical Illnesses

Chapter 2

Juvenile Rheumatoid Arthritis

by *Jerry C. Jacobs, M.D.,*
and *John A. Downey, M.D.*

Rheumatoid arthritis is so common in adults that even in medical circles it is not thought of as one of the most frequently seen chronic diseases of childhood. With the development of pediatric rheumatology as a subspecialty, there is an increased awareness of and concern for these children. Recognition of more cases may avoid unnecessary and even harmful procedures.

A search of inpatient hospital records in New York City in 1959 suggested an incidence of juvenile rheumatoid arthritis of 1:20,000 school children. However, the disorder is much more frequent than this, since most patients are never hospitalized, and in some children it remains misdiagnosed for years. In a recent study in Erie County, New York, the cumulative prevalence rate among children under age 16 was 1:5000. Girls are afflicted slightly more frequently than boys.

SIGNS AND SYMPTOMS

The onset is usually insidious, with swelling of one or more joints, sometimes without complaints or signs of systemic illness. About 40 per cent of patients have a monoarticular onset and, of these, half begin with only one swollen knee; most who are going to develop polyarthritis will have done so within a year.

In most series, including our own, the peak year of onset in the age group under 16 is the second year of life. Half of all affected children develop symptoms by age five (Figs. 2–1 and 2–2), and fewer new cases are found between 5 and 10 than from birth to five years or from age 10 to 15 years. This particular

5

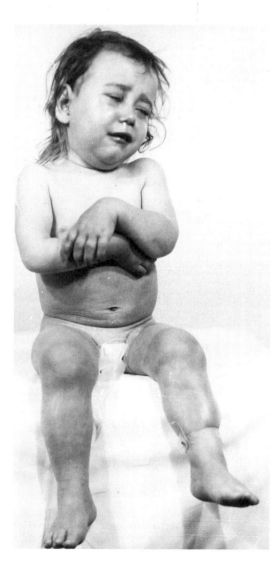

Figure 2–1   C. L., age three years. Onset of juvenile rheumatoid arthritis at three months of age, course complicated by pneumococcal septicemia and pneumatosis intestinalis.

age incidence, the frequency of permanent remissions, the occurrence of uveitis, and the almost consistent absence of rheumatoid factor in the serum, suggest that the etiology and perhaps the pathogenesis differ from the adult variety of rheumatoid arthritis.

No certain information exists regarding susceptibility. Many youngsters have a history of trauma just prior to onset. Children so often fall, however, especially those in the most commonly affected age group, that this feature may be coincidental. Since every large children's arthritis clinic has in its register affected sisters or mother-daughter pairs, family history is sometimes significant. At least five sets of monozygotic twins have been reported concurrently affected. It is not known whether the increased family incidence is due to heritable or environmental causes. Parents often inquire about the chance of another of their children becoming affected, but in spite of the rare family

Figure 2-2 C. L., age 11 years, climbing the school steps to her regular class.

with more than one arthritic member, they may be reassured that having two arthritic children is very, very rare.

Since the arthritis may involve from one to nearly all joints, some physicians have tried to divide the patient population into monoarticular, pauciarticular, polyarticular, and acute febrile types. While such an effort may have some validity, patients change from one category to another, making it impossible to predict the final outcome from the mode of onset. Some of the sickest recover completely, while some of the most troublesome residua may be found in those who are never very sick but whose disease persists for a long time. Persistent polyarticular disease without remission has the poorest prognosis.

A few children have fever as the sole presenting manifestation. The diagnosis may be suspected but cannot be made on this criterion alone, although in this group the fever tends to be intermittent with daily spikes as high as 105°F to 106°F, falling to 99°F when aspirin is given. The children usually do not look as ill as youngsters with weeks of such high fever from other causes. Some of these youngsters develop a characteristic evanescent salmon pink rash, the individual spots coming and going almost as you watch. The rash tends to come out with temperature elevations, may overlie joints, and is occasionally pruritic. The experienced observer may make an earlier diagnosis by recognizing the exanthem.

Hepatosplenomegaly or generalized lymphadenopathy or both may be striking. However, their presence is not diagnostic of juvenile rheumatoid ar-

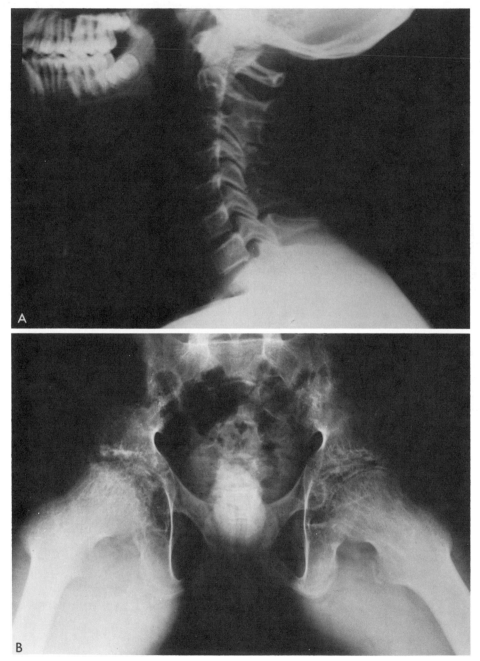

Figure 2–3 W. F., age 15 years. *A.* Lateral radiographs of the neck revealed fusion at the C2–C3 zygoapophyseal joints, which, in this youngster with bilateral hip destruction and fusion, *B,* but without other clinical evidences of old juvenile rheumatoid arthritis, makes the diagnosis.

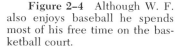

Figure 2-4 Although W. F. also enjoys baseball he spends most of his free time on the basketball court.

thritis and requires careful exclusion of other conditions. Inflammation in the anterior chamber of the eye may be visible as cells and protein accumulation seen on slit lamp examination by an experienced ophthalmologist. Most rheumatoid children with uveitis do not have complaints or visible signs until late, after irreparable damage to the eyes has occurred. Therefore, slit lamp examination is part of the diagnostic work-up and should be repeated at six month intervals. Neck pain, sometimes with torticollis, may be an early or presenting symptom, but x-ray evidence of cervical spine arthritis is not seen until much later unless the patient has had long-standing but previously unrecognized disease (Figs. 2-3 and 2-4).

Occasional patients have pericarditis as a part of their acute illness. Some have pericarditis, cardiac tamponade, myocarditis, and congestive heart failure with only minimal clinical evidence of arthritis, or even with none at all. The pericarditis differs from that seen in acute rheumatic fever because there is no evidence of concomitant valvular disease. Pleurisy and occasionally interstitial pneumonia may also occur.

Classic rheumatoid nodules are rare in children and are almost invariably seen only in late, severe cases. However, small transient nodules overlying extensor finger tendons are not uncommon, but are usually not seen early enough to aid in prompt diagnosis. Some children are referred because of "rheumatoid nodules" without any other sign of disease. These "nodules" are subcutaneous masses noted on the extensor surfaces of the legs. Biopsy

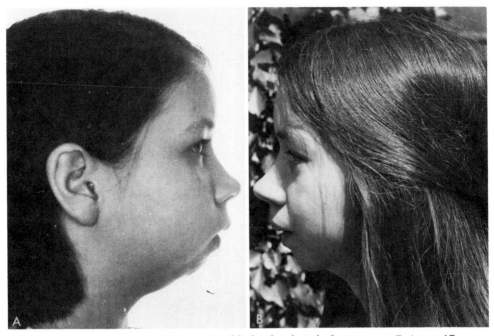

Figure 2-5 A. A. J., age 16 years. Mandibular dysplasia before surgery. *B.* At age 17 years, surgical correction had improved both the mandible and her self-image. A small correction in the mandible yielded a large correction in ego of this teenaged girl.

reveals pathological changes generally indistinguishable from rheumatoid nodule. Such patients are not known to have ever developed any systemic disease, and recognition of this syndrome is necessary to avoid repeated biopsies or harmful procedures and treatment.

Morning stiffness or "gelling" is common, but may be difficult to elicit, as the parent may not be aware of it. An older sibling occasionally reports that the affected youngster crawls to the bathroom in the morning but is improved by the time mother arises.

Tenosynovitis may accompany the arthritis and is occasionally mistaken for lymphangitis. As time goes on, flexion contractures become a sine qua non of the disease. While one usually thinks of arthritis in terms of swelling, erythema, heat, and tenderness, patients who have had unrecognized smoldering disease for some time may present with flexion contractures and sometimes synovial pouches on the dorsa of the wrists without any of these other signs. Examination of joint mobility is not a standard part of the routine pediatric examination and significant pathological changes may be missed.

Growth disturbances from earlier undiagnosed attacks (a disproportionately large toe or finger or mandibular dysplasia [Fig. 2-5]) sometimes suggest the nature of a fresh attack of polyarthritis or uveitis.

DIFFERENTIAL DIAGNOSIS

Trauma and infection are the most important diagnoses to think about in patients with monarticular onset. Joint fluid may be aspirated for examination and culture. Needle biopsy of the synovium of the knee may be easily performed in children, and a satisfactory specimen for pathological examination obtained. Except for research efforts aimed at securing specimens for tissue culture, or in cases in which tuberculosis or sarcoid are serious considerations, the authors have found little use for the procedure. Open synovial biopsy has not been useful in diagnosis in children whose tuberculin skin tests are negative and should be avoided as the immobilization after surgery may produce loss of motion and permanent deformity.

In youngsters presenting with migrating polyarthritis, rheumatic fever should be the admitting diagnosis. Rheumatoid arthritis is a chronic disease in which definite diagnosis is generally possible only after several weeks of persistent arthritis. While patients may have brief self-limited attacks before developing definite signs of disease, diagnostic accuracy is usually not possible during these episodes. The arthritis of rheumatic fever is generally gone after three weeks uninflated treatment and can and prolonged by alternate administration and withdrawal of salicylates, creating repeated "rebounds" that may be confusing.

Differential diagnosis also requires careful consideration of a large number of other conditions such as systemic lupus erythematosus, dermatomyositis, scleroderma, and polyarteritis. The authors' practice has suggested some other disorders commonly confused with rheumatoid arthritis and clues to their identification:

A. **Osteomyelitis or Septic Arthritis**, especially if treated with large doses of antibiotics for a brief period, may present as a chronic swelling and pain in a joint. Pain in such patients may be out of proportion to the visible signs of arthritis. X-ray evidence of osteomyelitis may not be seen for three months or more in such children. At the time of the original sepsis, the bone or joint complaint may not be noticed and a different diagnosis may be made; the local signs may disappear at first and then more gradually recur after treatment is withdrawn.

B. **Skeletal Pain** is common in the presentation of childhood leukemia, so much so that these children are commonly seen in arthritis consultation. Pain may seem out of proportion to the joint signs, and the child may refuse to stand. Muscle wasting may exceed that seen in juvenile rheumatoid arthritis. Tumors metastatic to bone may present in similar fashion. When the skeletal x-rays show lesions compatible with either juvenile rheumatoid arthritis or leukemia, a bone marrow examination is mandatory.

C. **Ulcerative Colitis** and regional enteritis may present without a history of diarrhea or with diarrhea hidden or neglected. In such children, inflammatory bowel disease may manifest itself by high fever, arthritis, and growth failure. Erythema nodosum, pyoderma gangrenosum, and mouth and genital ulcers may accompany the arthritis.

D. **Child Abuse** such as hitting the child across the fingers with a ruler may produce finger swelling suggestive of rheumatoid arthritis. Although periostitis may be seen with early juvenile rheumatoid arthritis, flakes of bone broken off from the phalanges are diagnostic of trauma, and involvement of fingers alone with persistent new bone formation is suspect. History of previous fractures, or fear of babysitters may be clues.

E. **Serum Sickness** and other allergic reactions including many drug allergies, and erythema nodosum may resemble arthritis. Cold urticaria may produce brawny erythema of the fingers and may be accompanied by cold fibrinogenemia or other cryoglobulinemia.

F.   Vitamin A Poisoning, a result of overdosage with vitamin A alone or with vitamin D, either by overzealous parents in young children or self-administered in teenagers, is being seen with increasing frequency. Signs of poisoning may include itching of great severity resulting in excoriations of the dry skin that resemble scabies infestation, frontal bossing, and papilledema accompanied by other signs of increased intracranial pressure. When associated with vitamin D, renal stones and hypercalcemia may also be present.

G.   Reactions to Rubella Vaccine, most frequently the "catcher's crouch" syndrome, in which children on arising assume this position and refuse to move, respond impressively to aspirin. On the next few mornings, however, pain may recur. We have seen repeated episodes beginning two weeks after injection and continuing over a 16 month period following rubella vaccination. Others report even longer periods of recurrent attacks. Brief attacks of polyarthritis may also accompany acute rubella, mumps, varicella, infectious mononucleosis, Chikungunya infections, and probably many other viral illnesses.

H.   Hysteria may present as joint and skeletal complaints without objective signs of arthritis and, characteristically, with more disability in terms of school absence or withdrawal from activities than is generally seen in children with proved rheumatoid arthritis with similar complaints. Rarely, a true rheumatoid will use the disease in similar fashion. The striking contrast between the remarkably active life of the well-managed rheumatoid arthritis patient and the constricted environment of these physically healthy-appearing youngsters makes the differential diagnosis inescapable to the alert physician.

I.   Infectious Hepatitis may present as hives and arthritis and, only much later, jaundice. Increasing numbers of cases are now being recognized. Serum complement may be decreased owing to binding of antigen antibody complexes involving Australia antigen. These studies and repeated measurement of serum transaminases have allowed diagnosis in acholic cases.

J.   Familial Arthritis.   Jacobs reported a unique familial arthritis, "E familial arthritis," characterized by onset of "trigger fingers" in the first three months of life followed by bland synovitis in major joints, which continues throughout life without associated signs of juvenile rheumatoid arthritis (Fig. 2–6).[19] Stickler has described a different familial arthritis associated with progressive myopathy and a familial syndrome of arthritis, osteolysis, and hypertension; and Shawarby and others have described a familial disorder called pachydermoperiostosis.[38, 43]

K.   Hypertrophic Osteoarthropathy may be familial or secondary to lung or liver disease. Periosteal new bone formation in infants and infantile cortical hyperostosis (Caffey's disease) may also be confused with juvenile rheumatoid arthritis.

L.   Hand-Foot Syndrome of sickle cell anemia in black infants.

M.   Osteoid Osteoma of the femur, causing hip pain.

N.   Gaucher's Disease causing hip pain with splenomegaly.

O.   Familial Mediterranean Fever (periodic disease) becomes evident if

Figure 2–6 Two of the affected "E" family showing trigger fingers, wrist effusions, and "synovial pouches."

one keeps an accurate diary of attacks when a family history is lacking.

P. Gonorrhea and Meningococcemia with arthritis are sometimes suggested by skin lesions, tenosynovitis, or "settling" in one large joint.

Q. Eosinophilic Granuloma causing cervical vertebral collapse and neck pain.

R. Craniopharyngioma causing recurrent episodes of neck pain.

S. Ganglioneuroma invading the spinal cord causing recurrent leg pains.

T. Anaphylactoid (Henoch-Schönlein) Purpura, usually with a distinctive rash.

U. Hemophilia and other coagulation defects.

V. Atrial Myxoma causing arthralgias, presumably secondary to mucopolysaccharide secretion by the tumor.

W. Acute Dysentery due to Salmonella, Shigella, or Yersinia.

X. Reiter's Syndrome with conjunctivitis, urethritis, and arthritis.

Y. Boeck's Sarcoid: usually a single tremendous boggy knee.

Z. Ankylosing Spondylitis in teenage boys, and agammaglobulinemia, sepsis, gout, Farber's disease, phosphate diabetes, villonodular synovitis, and the mucopolysaccharidoses.

No diagnostic criteria exist for juvenile rheumatoid arthritis that can satisfactorily identify most cases and exclude almost all who have something else, unless one systematically considers all these other entities and excludes them either on clinical grounds or with the help of laboratory and x-ray studies.

LABORATORY STUDIES

Anemia and elevated erythrocyte sedimentation rates commonly accompany severe disease. The anemia seems to result primarily from marrow inhibition and does not respond to iron, although elements of shortened red blood cell survival, increased gastrointestinal blood loss from medicines, and iron and folate deficiency from poor nutrition may be demonstrated. The albumin level is low in sick patients, and the gamma globulin high, except in isolated patients with specific defects in gamma globulin synthesis. Rheumatoid factor is present in only 10 per cent of patients, and these are usually those severely affected in whom a diagnosis is easily established. The majority of children referred to us because of the detection of rheumatoid factor do not have it when we retest them. In those in whom, on repeated testing, we do find rheumatoid factor, only two thirds have rheumatoid arthritis. Some youngsters have significant leukocytosis and occasionally significant eosinophilia. Hematuria and proteinuria (aside from amyloidosis) have recently been reported as frequent although rarely noted in our own patients.[5]

The early radiographic findings are joint effusions and juxtaarticular

Figure 2-7   A. C., age 13 years. Short stature, continuous effusions, deformities and chronic anemia (Hgb. 6 gm for many years) do not prevent this boy from playing softball.

demineralization. In young children with asymmetrical involvement, growth centers on the involved side become more advanced after months of disease, and eventually that extremity or a portion of it may become abnormally long. Signs of erosions and joint destruction are late. Unusual, but characteristic of juvenile rheumatoid arthritis, are changes leading toward fusion at the C2–C3 zygoapophyseal joints and growth disturbances at the temporomandibular joints.

Overall skeletal growth, however, is retarded by prolonged severe disease, resulting in short stature (Fig. 2–7). Since this is not due to growth hormone deficiency and is not responsive to exogenous growth hormone, it is presumably a disease-induced cellular defect.

In summary, diagnosis remains a clinical skill. Ancillary studies are needed, however, to exclude the many conditions that may be mistaken for juvenile rheumatoid arthritis.

COURSE

The early literature tended to suggest a poor prognosis, since interested clinics accumulated the most severely affected patients. It is now generally accepted that about two thirds of the children make a complete recovery and have no residual findings on examination after an average of two years of disease. About 5 per cent of affected children die of either complications of the disease or complications of therapy. These include amyloidosis, addisonian crises with stress following steroid withdrawal, overwhelming infections, rheumatoid cardiac nodules, and idiosyncratic reactions to drugs. Another 5 per cent become severely handicapped, either limited to a bed-chair existence or blind as a result of uveitis. The other 25 per cent include those with some residua of old but burnt-out disease and those whose disease remains intermittently active. On the whole, patients with severe systemic exacerbations followed by complete remissions do better than those with smoldering but continuously active disease.

MANAGEMENT

The most important factor in management is the optimistic attitude of a well-informed physician whose goal is to promote almost normal function of the child. As in all chronic disease, patients and their families become easily discouraged and, if depressed, maximize their disability and function poorly in all areas. Attention is paid to how the child is doing in life situations, including peer and family relationships and school. If there are additional handicaps beside arthritis, an effort is made to be certain that they also receive a maximum rehabilitative effort, including psychotherapy and, for teenagers, vocational guidance. While management thus requires a team approach, the pediatric rheumatologist, as coordinator of the team, has an opportunity to provide a kind of optimal comprehensive care.

Medication

Most children respond well to aspirin given in doses of 100 mg per kilogram per 24 hours divided between 6 A.M. and 11 P.M., if the children do not have high spiking fever, and at four hour intervals around the clock if they do. If the disease is adequately controlled by this regimen and no signs of salicylism appear, blood levels of salicylate are not assessed. If adequate control is not achieved after several weeks, blood levels are determined and dosage increased to the maximum tolerated amount. While we aim for a salicylate level around 24 mg per 100 ml, we have some children completely controlled with less and others requiring and tolerating prolonged levels as high as 48 mg per 100 ml, enough to be fatal in some other children. Parents and doctors must always be alert to signs of salicylism, including tachypnea (sometimes mistaken for "croup" in these children), vomiting (often called "gastroenteritis"), and depression with withdrawal to bed. (The psychiatrist was called while additional aspirin was given to one of our poisoned youngsters.) Educated parents are the best observers, and it is the physician's responsibility to teach them the signs of toxicity at the time of the initial visit.

Medication is continued in our clinic until six months after all signs and symptoms of disease have disappeared, as the aim of treatment is to enable the child to lead a normal or almost normal life, attending school regularly in a regular class. If aspirin alone does not achieve this goal, small doses of prednisone, 1 to 2.5 mg three times daily, may be added, starting with the lower dose. More recently, some of our more severely ill patients have received alternate day steroid therapy with 10 to 15 mg of prednisone every second morning as a single dose, plus their usual aspirin. Intraarticular injection of steroids is only rarely used and then only for a chronically extraordinarily swollen knee; this treatment is followed by procedures to encourage active mobilization.

The use of chloroquine has been discontinued because of possible retinitis, and phenylbutazone appears too toxic. The risks of azathioprine, methotrexate, and cyclophosphamide generally exceed any potential benefits.

Pericarditis, when present, is treated with large doses of systemic steroids for a few weeks, until it subsides. Uveitis is brought under control with steroid eye drops when possible, but if complete control is not achieved with local therapy systemic steroids in moderately large doses are used for several weeks, followed by an alternate day single dose regimen for maintenance so long as is necessary.

In our own clinic, we rarely use gold or indomethacin because of fatalities that have occurred when our patients received them elsewhere.

Maintenance of Function

The attitude of the physicians and allied health personnel must at all times exude confidence and commitment to the child's functioning. The child and the family will be buoyed by the example set for them. The specific program for each child is individualized, and the goal thoroughly explained to the family and to the child. The preservation of function is the ultimate goal but several steps are necessary to achieve that end. The analgesic and antiinflammatory effect of the medications are supplemented by physical measures to help relieve pain and to maintain and regain motion and strength. Children are generally awakened early in the morning and given their medication and then allowed to sleep for an hour. They then arise and take a hot bath or shower and go through a simple ritual of limbering-up exercises, then go to school. As the child grows older he may assume more responsibility for this program.

Later in the day, when both the child and the family are not pressed for time, the detailed therapy is continued. If pain is severe, heat in the form of hot baths or local application of hot towels or soaks may again be helpful. The maintenance of motion is achieved by putting every joint of the body, whether involved or uninvolved, through a full range of motion using positions that require as little resistance as possible. In those joints in which there is loss of motion special attention is required. At no time is passive motion or stretching ever allowed, as it will only cause more pain and reaction by the patient. Rather, the child is urged to move the joint in the direction of the limitation, and resistance, if any, is given against that motion. This procedure allows reciprocal relaxation of the antagonistic muscles and strengthening of the agonists.

Strength is frequently lost around the involved joints, and inactivity leads to generalized weakness. When joints are inflamed, heavy resistance usually aggravates the pain but simple isometric or tensing exercises that do not involve moving the joint can generally be tolerated and encouraged. In uninvolved areas and in joints in which inflammation is lessening, careful resistance exercises can be given. (Resistance applied by the patient's hand is the most reliable if he is instructed in the procedure.) As activity increases, the necessity for resistance exercise is less, but range of motion exercises are continued long after all evidence of disease disappears so that insidious recurrence of disease may be detected as early as possible.

Use of splints in the care of the rheumatoid child is controversial. We agree that complete immobilization is probably never indicated and can cause prolonged and even permanent loss of motion. Resting splints in optimum functional position, however, if their use is followed each day by regular range of motion exercise, can be helpful in minimizing pain and swelling and preventing or reducing deformity. They are applied when the child is at home and so do not adversely affect his range of motion or activities.

The most common and useful use of splints is for hands, wrists, and knees. They should be light, cheap, and easily made so that they can be adjusted and modified frequently as growth or reduction of deformity occurs. Families are to be instructed in the principles and purposes of the splints so that they can use them intelligently.

Another aspect of prevention of deformity and even correction involves positioning during periods of rest. Children sleep on firm beds, use no or low pillows and no support under the knees. Periods of lying face down with the hips in full extension and abduction are helpful in minimizing the common problem of hip flexion deformities. Such periods may be encouraged when the child watches television lying on the floor.

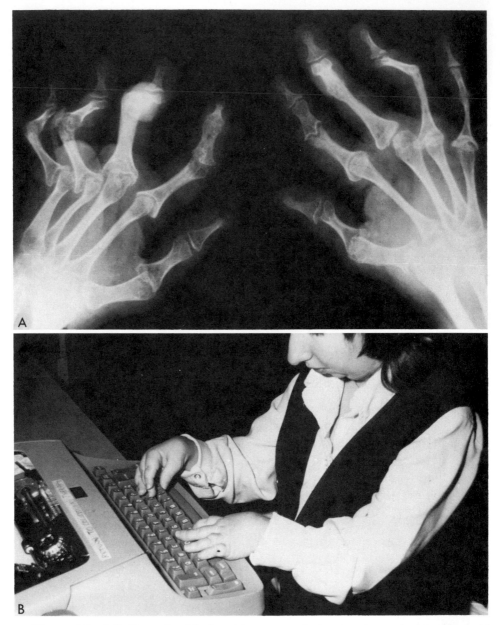

Figure 2–8 *A*. Radiographs of the hand show severe destructive changes in this college girl (J. N.) whose disease began at age three months. *B*. She is, nevertheless, an excellent typist (cosmetic surgery has improved somewhat the appearance of her fingers and did not interfere with her typing ability).

The careful education of the family in the concepts of management is essential, as they must assume responsibility for the child's total care. A good parent is better than any therapist! In addition to the physical maneuvers, the parent must encourage full independence in self-care by the child even at the cost of extra time in dressing and the like. In summary, the whole program is

Figure 2–9 At age 22 years, J. N. lives in her college dormitory.

simple, uses as little special equipment and personnel as possible, and is based at home and in the family rather than at the clinic.

None of our patients is allowed home instruction or attendance at special classes if we can avoid it (Figs. 2–8 and 2–9). When we have failed in this regard, it has always been as a result of psychological problems we could not resolve in the family or the attitudes of some school personnel (Fig. 2–10). Removing the child from a normal life setting is inevitably countertherapeutic. No exercise program can equal the activities of daily living.

Rest, except for what would be healthful for any child, is not a part of our therapy. If a child goes beyond what we might suggest, i.e., skiis on arthritic ankles, we compromise and keep our fears to ourselves, always remembering the importance of motor activities in the personality development of the child (Fig. 2–11). Preventing children from doing things for themselves, developing motor skills and thus achieving independence and autonomy, leads to feelings of helplessness and anger that are countertherapeutic.

"Prophylactic" Surgery

In recent years some clinics have embarked on a course of synovectomy aimed at preventing, rather than relieving, disability. Tried years ago in adult rheumatoid arthritis and abandoned, prophylactic synovectomy requires repeated hospitalizations and anesthesia, and leaves scars, both physical and psychic. Since two thirds of our patients get completely well, a very large multi-institutional study would be needed to document its value. To date, no such study has been performed.

Figure 2–10   *A.* After a year in an arthritis sanatorium insisted upon by her parents, D. M. returned to the main stream in her neighborhood high school. *B.* In music class and helping out in the book room she enjoys being with her peers despite severe deformities and almost total loss of vision, a result of chronic uveitis.

Figure 2–11   Hula hooping is not a prescribed or recommended exercise, but is tolerated since it's an admired special talent in A. M.'s neighborhood.

Corrective and Restorative Surgery

Soft tissue release operations, arthrodesis, debridement, and therapeutic synovectomy are useful in selected instances in juvenile rheumatoid arthritis. Epiphyseal stapling to correct valgus knee deformities and unequal leg length may also be useful. Total joint replacement has not been attempted in our children, but may some day be important. When a child has borderline function, the immobilization associated with surgery or with treatment of a traumatic fracture from a fall may be just enough to make the child a bed-chair invalid. Months or years of effort may be required to get him back to where he started. Where surgery is performed, it should be planned to allow rapid mobilization and return to school.

Long periods in hospitals or convalescent institutions are counterthera-peutic, leading to increased fear of returning to the normal life situation and increased anxiety and phobic avoidance when rehabilitation is attempted. Skeletal traction and circular plaster casts are contraindicated in our experience, causing increased deformity and decreased function.

Cosmetic surgery may sometimes be done, but function must not be sacrificed for appearance. For example, the youngster whose flexion contractures of the fingers from juvenile rheumatoid arthritis were the worst we have seen was her school typing champion. She was also a cheerleader, despite severe disease. A 15 year old boy with totally fused hips is the champion pitcher in his town Little League. Imprisonment for "therapy" does not lead to the feeling of control over one's disease or encourage maximum function.

Vocational Counseling

In the eleventh grade, it is desirable that all patients be given vocational testing and guidance by professional vocational counselors. The goal is to select the trade or profession best suited to the physical and intellectual prowess of the patient, so that he may become a useful member of society no matter what course his arthritis may take. College scholarships to obtain vocational training are often available to those who need them.

SUMMARY

The Power of Positive Thinking

Perhaps the greatest determinant of the extent of crippling in juvenile rheumatoid arthritis is the therapeutic goal of the physician and the health team. When this goal is to achieve normal or almost normal functioning in the child's life situation, this attitude is usually clearly projected onto the child and his family and provides hope, avoids depression, and instills confidence so that they can follow helpful suggestions.

If, instead, the physician emphasizes the amount of care needed and sets

Figure 2–12   C. J. A candidate for total hip replacement at some time in the future, this ninth grader is in the swing of things in her music class.

limitations of doubtful therapeutic value or suggests surgical procedures of questionable therapeutic value, the goals of therapy may become diffused and the child and family may lose sight of the importance of continuously rewarding participation in normal childhood activities. Play and school and the dynamics of family life are the "work" of the growing child; without them there is little chance that he will grow into a well-functioning adult. Maximum use of his capabilities and minimum handicaps from the disease are achieved by showing the family that he can function well in his society despite the disease. For this reason, home instruction and special classes for the handicapped are not used in our clinic. Also, almost without exception, residential rehabilitation efforts have failed in our patients.

While there are exceptions, it is most important to keep in sharp focus the prognosis for juvenile rheumatoid arthritis. In 70 per cent, remission occurs, leaving them in normal physical condition, without any therapy that is known to affect the long-term course of the disease. Therapeutic efforts that may aid the smaller number of more severely affected youngsters must be reserved for those who need them; their application to those in whom the disease itself will cause minimal problems may be harmful.

As the child develops a feeling of control over his disease, encouraged by learning how to use medications to allow maximum function and by developing new coping resources as his disease may require if he is to function in normal society, he develops ego strength that will be an asset in all parameters of his life. He's his own boss (Fig. 2–12).

References

1. Ahvonen, P., Sievers, K., and Aho, K.: Arthritis associated with Yersinia enterocolitica infection. Acta Rheumatol. Scand., 15:232, 1969.
2. Ansell, B. M.: Relationship of dosage and type of salicylate therapy to plasma levels in patients with juvenile rheumatoid arthritis. In Salicylates, An International Symposium. London, J. & A. Churchill, Ltd., 1963, p. 35.
3. Ansell, B. M., and Bywaters, E. G. L.: Still's disease. In Copeman, W. S. C. (ed.): Textbook of the Rheumatic Diseases. 4th Ed. Edinburgh, E & S. Livingstone, 1969.
4. Ansell, B. M., Arden, G. P., and McLennan, I.: Valgus knee deformities in children with juvenile chronic polyarthritis treated by epiphysial stapling. Arch. Dis. Child., 45:388, 1970.
5. Anttila, R.: Renal involvement in juvenile rheumatoid arthritis: A clinical and histopathological study. Acta Paediatr. Scand. (Suppl.), 227:1–73, 1972.
6. Brewer, E. J.: Juvenile Rheumatoid Arthritis. Philadelphia, W. B. Saunders Co., 1970.
7. Burrington, J. D.: "Pseudorheumatoid" nodules in children: Report of 10 cases. Pediatrics, 45:473, 1970.
8. Calabro, J. J.: Juvenile rheumatoid arthritis. CIBA Clin. Symposium, 23:2, 1971.
9. Calabro, J. J., Katz, R. M., and Maltz, B. A.: A critical reappraisal of juvenile rheumatoid arthritis. Clin. Orthop., 74:101, 1971.
10. Chaplin, D., Pulkki, T., Saarimaa, A., and Valtno, K.: Wrist and finger deformities in juvenile rheumatoid arthritis. Acta Rheumatol. Scand., 15:206, 1969.
11. Cleveland, S. E., Reitman, E. E., and Brewer, E. J.: Psychological factors in juvenile rheumatoid arthritis. Arthritis Rheum., 8:1152, 1965.
12. Ditkowsky, S. P., Goldman, A., Barnett, H., et al.: Normal periosteal reactions and associated soft-tissue findings. Clin. Pediatr., 9:515, 1970.
13. Ehrlich, G. E.: Arthritis in familial Mediterranean fever. Clin. Orthop., 57:51, 1968.
14. Fink, C. W.: Gonococcal arthritis in children. J.A.M.A., 194:237, 1965.
15. Fink, C. W., Windmiller, J., and Sartain, P.: Arthritis as the presenting feature of childhood leukemia. Arthritis Rheum., 15:347, 1972.
16. Greenwood, W. F.: Profile of atrial myxoma. Am. J. Cardiol., 21:367, 1968.
17. Grokoest, A. W., Snyder, A. I., and Schlaeger, R.: Juvenile Rheumatoid Arthritis. Boston, Little Brown and Co., 1962.
18. Grossman, B. J., Ozoa, N. F., and Arya, S. C.: Problems in juvenile rheumatoid arthritis. Med. Clin. North Am., 49:33, 1965.
19. Jacobs, J. C.: Familial arthritis. Presented at the Annual Meeting of the New York Rheumatism Assoc., New York, April 1965.
20. Jacobs, J. C.: "E" familial arthritis. Presented at the 11th Intnl. Congress on The Rheumatic Diseases, Mar del Plata, Argentina, December 1965.
21. Janeway, C. A., Gitlin, D., Craig, J. M., and Grice, D. J.: "Collagen disease" in patients with congenital agammaglobulinemia. Trans. Assoc. Am. Physicians, 69:93, 1956.
22. Jeremy, R., Schaller, J., Arkless, R., et al.: Juvenile rheumatoid arthritis persisting into adulthood. Am. J. Med., 45:419, 1968.
23. Jordan, J. D.: Cardiopulmonary manifestations of rheumatoid disease in childhood. South. Med. J., 57:1273, 1964.
24. Katz, J. F.: Recurrent avascular necrosis of the proximal femoral epiphysis of the same hip in Gaucher's disease. J. Bone Joint Surg. (Am.), 49:514, 1967.
25. Laaksonen, A. L.: Prognostic study of juvenile rheumatoid arthritis: Analysis of 544 cases. Acta Pediatr. Scand. (Suppl.), 166:1–168, 1966.
26. Ladd, J. R., Cassidy, J. T., and Martel, W.: Juvenile ankylosing spondylitis. Arthritis Rheum., 14:579, 1971.
27. Lietman, P. S., and Bywaters, E. G. L.: Pericarditis in juvenile rheumatoid arthritis. Pediatrics, 32:855, 1963.
28. Margileth, A. M.: Reiter's syndrome in children. Clin. Pediatr., 1:148, 1962.
29. Martel, W., Holt, J. F., and Cassidy, J. T.: Roentgenologic manifestations of juvenile rheumatoid arthritis. Am. J. Roentgenol., 88:400, 1962.
30. McDermott, J. F., and Akina, E.: Understanding and improving the personality development of children with physical handicaps. Clin. Pediatr., 11:130, 1972.
31. McEwen, C.: Arthritis accompanying ulcerative colitis. Clin. Orthop., 57:9, 1968.
32. McKusick, V. A.: Heritable Disorders of Connective Tissue. 3rd Ed. St. Louis, C. V. Mosby Co., 1966.
33. Mikkelsen, W. M. (ed.): Twentieth Rheumatism Review. New York, The Arthritis Foundation, 1973.
34. Nelson, J. D.: The bacterial etiology and antibiotic management of septic arthritis in infants and children. Pediatrics, 50:437, 1972.

35. North, A. F., Jr., Fink, C. W., Gibson, W. M., et al.: Sarcoid arthritis in children. Am. J. Med., *48*:449, 1970.
36. Rodnan, G. P.: Arthritis associated with disorders of hematopoiesis and blood coagulation. In Hollander, J. L. (ed.): *Arthritis and Allied Conditions.* Philadelphia, Lea & Febiger, 1966, p. 1095.
37. Scott, J. T.: Joint involvement in bone disease. In Dixon, A. St. J. (ed.): *Progress in Clinical Rheumatology.* Boston, Little Brown and Co., 1965, p. 305.
38. Shawarby, K., and Ibrahim, M. S.: Pachydermoperiostosis. Br. Med. J., *1*:763, 1962.
39. Smith, M. E., Ansell, B. M., and Bywaters, E. G.: Mortality and prognosis related to the amyloidosis of Still's disease. Ann. Rheum. Dis., *27*:137, 1968.
40. Spalter, H. F., and Jacobs, J. C.: Diagnosis, natural history and therapy of the ocular complications of juvenile rheumatoid arthritis. *Proceedings of Seventh International Congress of Ophthalmology,* Excerpta Med., Int. Congress No. 146, 338, 1966.
41. Spruance, S. L., et al.: Recurrent joint symptoms in children vaccinated with HPV-77-DK-12 rubella vaccine. J. Pediatr., *80*:413, 1972.
42. Stevens, D. P., et al.: Anicteric hepatitis presenting as polyarthritis. J.A.M.A., *220*:687, 1972.
43. Stickler, G. B., and Pugh, D. G.: Hereditary progressive arthro-ophthalmopathy II. Additional observations on vertebral abnormalities, a hearing defect, and a report of a similar case. Mayo Clinic Proc., *42*:495, 1967.
44. Still, G. F.: On a form of chronic joint disease in children. Proc. R. Med. Chir. Soc., *80*:47, 1897.
45. Sturge, R. A., Beardwell, C., Hartog, M., et al.: Cortisol and growth hormone secretion in relation to linear growth: Patients with Still's disease on different therapeutic regimens. Br. Med. J., *3*:547, 1970.
46. Sultz, H. A., et al.: *Long-Term Childhood Illness.* Contemporary Health Series. Pittsburgh, Pa., University of Pittsburgh Press, 1972.
47. Waldvogel, F. A., Medoff, G., and Swartz, M. N.: Osteomyelitis: A review of clinical features, therapeutic considerations and unusual aspects. New Engl. J. Med., *282*:198, 260, 316, 1970.
48. Zutshi, D. W., Friedman, M., and Ansell, B. M.: Corticotrophin therapy in juvenile chronic polyarthritis (Still's disease) and effect on growth. Arch. Dis. Child., *46*:584, 1971.

Chapter 3

Cystic Fibrosis of the Pancreas

by *Paul di Sant'Agnese, M.D.,*
and Robert C. Darling, M.D.

Cystic fibrosis (fibrocystic disease of the pancreas, mucoviscidosis) is a hereditary disease of children, adolescents, and young adults in which there is a generalized dysfunction of exocrine glands. Recent evidence, however, suggests that the abnormal gene is expressed in every single cell of the body. The syndrome is characterized clinically by the triad of chronic pulmonary disease, pancreatic deficiency, and abnormally high levels of sweat electrolytes. Total or partial sparing of organs or glandular systems usually affected in cystic fibrosis is frequently encountered and leads to many variations in the clinical picture of this truly protean disease.

In the United States, cystic fibrosis accounts for the great majority of cases of chronic (nontuberculous) progressive pulmonary disease in the younger age groups; for almost all cases of pancreatic deficiency; for most of the patients with severe malabsorption in the pediatric age span; for many of those with childhood hepatic cirrhosis, and for a significant proportion of intestinal atresia or obstruction in newborn infants.

HISTORY

The first investigator to recognize cystic fibrosis as a distinct clinical entity and to describe its association with chronic pulmonary disease was Fanconi in Switzerland in 1936.[14] Not until the extensive work of Andersen in New York in 1938, and of Blackfan and May in Boston and Harper in Australia in the same year, was cystic fibrosis firmly established as a separate disease.[1, 11] Prior to this time patients with this disorder succumbed most fre-

25

quently to bronchopneumonia or to malnutrition, usually in infancy. At times they were thought to have so-called "celiac disease," but the specific nature of the disorder was unrecognized. In recent years, owing to greater awareness of the entity, improved diagnostic techniques, and more effective treatment, the life span of patients has been greatly increased and the disorder has become recognized with increasing frequency.

Several distinct phases in the understanding of cystic fibrosis evolved:

1. The pathological changes in the pancreas at autopsy and the clinical effects of pancreatic deficiency attracted the attention of the early investigators and accounted for the name of the disease.

2. As long ago as 1945, it was pointed out that a widespread defect in mucous secretions could explain many symptoms of this disorder, and the name "mucoviscidosis" was suggested.[15]

3. With the demonstration in 1953 of consistent involvement of sweat and salivary glands in this disorder, it became evident that cystic fibrosis was a generalized disease.[5, 12]

4. Recent laboratory and clinical evidence suggests that every single cell of the body may be involved, and that cystic fibrosis may be a syndrome common to more than one genetic error.

It is important to realize, therefore, that despite its name, based on a pathological description of the disease, cystic fibrosis is not limited to the pancreas, but is rather a disorder in which this organ is frequently but not necessarily involved. The name traditionally given this generalized syndrome is a misnomer to be used only with the full realization of its limitations. In particular, it should be kept in mind that cystic fibrosis has nothing in common with any other cystic disease.

GENETICS

The basic defect in cystic fibrosis is not known, but there is general agreement that it is an inborn error of metabolism transmitted as a mendelian recessive trait.[7, 11, 27] Chromosomes are normal in cystic fibrosis; thus the defect must be at the genic level. Most authors believe that a single mutant allele causes the disease; however, the presence of multiple alleles at different loci cannot be excluded, especially as the question of heterogeneity has been raised recently. Homozygotes for the recessive gene present all or substantially all the manifestations of the syndrome; heterozygotes present no clinically recognizable symptoms. Although mean sweat sodium concentration in carriers is statistically significantly increased above the mean of control subjects, the overlap in values between the two groups is too great for these findings to be useful in the detection of heterozygotes.

The overall incidence of the disorder among siblings is one in four as would be expected from the hypothesis of recessive transmission. The finding of the disease in first cousins, the rarity of affected offspring following remarriage of parents, and the observation that all 11 children of 10 mothers with cystic fibrosis were phenotypically normal in the series reported by Grand et al. offer additional support for the thesis of recessive transmission.[16]

The age of the mother or the position of the index cases in families does not affect the frequency of the disease. No environmental factor has been demonstrated during pregnancy of the mothers of patients, and in most series both sexes are affected with equal frequency. According to some investigators there appears to be some similarity in the degree of organ involvement in the same family. This is certainly true of meconium ileus, which is frequently present in more than one member of a sibship.

Many estimates of the incidence of cystic fibrosis have been made, and the figures given have varied widely in the past. As originally computed from the percentage in various children's hospitals of patients found to have cystic fibrosis at autopsy, the figure was 2 to 4 per cent of necropsies. In recent years several studies reported from countries as far apart as Australia, Czechoslovakia, and the United States have been in general agreement on the incidence of this disease. A conservative and acceptable figure is 1 in 2000 live births in populations of Caucasian descent. It follows that about 5 per cent of these population groups must be carriers of the gene. All geneticists have been troubled by the unduly high mutation rate implied by these figures unless a heterozygote survival advantage or greater reproductive fitness can be demonstrated. Recent evidence from Switzerland and Australia that family size may be greater in cystic fibrosis families than in control ones, if substantiated, would suggest greater reproductive fitness as a possible answer.

As Steinberg pointed out, the figures for the incidence in percentage of live births and for carriers in the population make cystic fibrosis the most frequent substantially lethal genetic disease among white people.[11] The cystic fibrosis gene is five times more common in the total United States population than the gene for the next most common lethal hereditary disease in this country, sickle cell anemia (0.85 per cent of total population). Cystic fibrosis has, however, a striking racial distribution, and even in this country it is much more common in whites than in blacks; homozygotes are born in 1 in 10,000 to 12,000 black live births in the United States, although about 2 per cent of American blacks are carriers of the cystic fibrosis gene. Cystic fibrosis is rare in people of Mongolian descent and in African blacks. An excellent survey conducted by Wright and Morton of patients and autopsies in Hawaii over a 15 year period estimated the incidence in Mongolians as 1 in 90,000 versus 1 in 3800 in the white population.[45] He also clearly demonstrated that in individuals of mixed descent, the more Caucasian blood present, the higher the incidence of cystic fibrosis.

In some underdeveloped areas with poor medical and public health facilities (e.g., North Africa and India), although cystic fibrosis has been found, most persons with this disease probably do not survive long enough for the illness to be recognized.

PATHOLOGY

Non-mucus-producing glands, such as eccrine sweat glands or parotid glands, show no pathological or histological changes, although the chemical composition of their secretions may be abnormal. Little is known about the pathological changes in small salivary glands, which are thought to be of mixed type, mucous and serous, whose secretions are chemically abnormal.

In the mucus-producing glands the basic lesion throughout the body consists of accumulation of abnormally behaving secretions with consequent dilatation of the secretory gland itself. In some organs (e.g., pancreas and intrahepatic biliary ductules) the secretions precipitate or coagulate to form eosinophilic concretions in the glands and ducts, and obstruct the outflow of their secretions. Most of the pathological changes and consequent symptoms are thought to be secondary to this obstruction.

Pancreas

The most striking changes are observed in the pancreas in the more than 85 per cent of patients who have involvement of this organ. The pancreas grossly is smaller, thinner, and firmer than normal. Histologically, the findings include obstruction of pancreatic ducts by concretions, dilatation of secretory acini and ducts, and secondary degeneration of the exocrine parenchyma (Fig. 3–1). Pancreatic lesions are progressive; in the newborn infant most acini appear normal, although the lumina contain concretions with initial fibrosis and inflammatory changes. After several years the picture is one of pancreatic atrophy with extensive fibrosis and occasionally with replacement by fat. The process proceeds at variable speeds, and at a given age the pancreas of the patient may show different stages of its evolution. The islands of Langerhans are usually normal, although they tend to decrease in number and exhibit increasing disruption by fibrosis with advancing age. Hyalinization or vascular changes in the islets are generally not present even when glucose intolerance and glycosuria are present.

Among the more than 85 per cent of patients with pancreatic deficiency as a consequence of vitamin E deficiency, considerable deposition of ceroid pigment is found in the smooth muscle of the gastrointestinal tract in those who die after the age of three years. Lesions in the striate muscle due to deficiency of vitamin E, however, have never been demonstrated.

Liver

In the great majority of patients, even infants, at autopsy the liver shows localized foci of biliary obstruction, fibrosis, and neoproduction of bile canaliculi.[8] These changes become progressively more extensive and in a small percentage of patients may give rise to a distinctive type of multilobular biliary cirrhosis with large, irregular nodules, at times with clefts. The onset of hepatic lesions before birth or in early infancy and the different growth rates of scar tissue and liver parenchyma may account for some of the bizarre morphological findings. A trigger mechanism (cholangitis, viral hepatitis, nutritional injury, and others) is postulated to account for the spreading of localized lesions, as it is known that a basically abnormal liver responds abnormally to

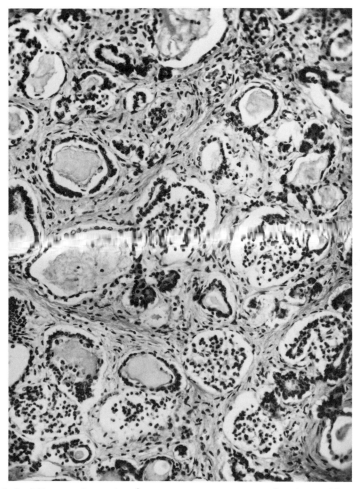

Figure 3–1 Microscopic section from pancreas at autopsy of patient with cystic fibrosis. Dilatation of ducts by eosinophilic concretions, fibrosis, almost complete disappearance of acini, and normal islands of Langerhans.

added insult or injury. The fatty infiltration of liver due to severe malnutrition described in earlier reports is uncommon now, although occasionally it may be seen even when nutrition appears to be adequate. Hepatic hemosiderosis was commonly found in the past in untreated patients, presumably as a consequence of the increased intestinal iron absorption secondary to pancreatic achylia per se. In patients who have continually received adequate pancreatic replacement therapy, however, this is rarely seen, as pancreatic extracts have been shown to decrease the iron absorption from the intestinal tract.

Lungs

The lungs appear normal in most patients who die of complications other than chronic lung disease in the first few weeks of life; the same is true of

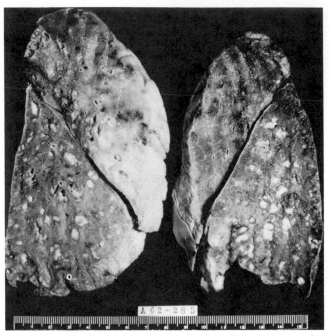

Figure 3–2   At autopsy, the lung of a patient with cystic fibrosis appears distended owing to the generalized obstructive emphysema, and most bronchi are filled with greenish mucopurulent secretions.

other patients who die before the onset of pulmonary involvement in early or late childhood from various complications. The initial lesion in the lung is bronchiolar obstruction; later the main bronchi are also plugged by muco-purulent material. Acute and chronic bronchitis, peribronchitis, patchy atelec-tasis, bronchiolectasis, and bronchiectasis are commonly found at autopsy in long-standing cases. Alveolar structure as such is relatively unimpaired and emphysema with destruction of alveolar walls is not commonly seen in pa-tients with cystic fibrosis; rather a diffuse obstruction with overinflation is usually prominent at necropsy. The gross appearance of the lung at autopsy is one of blockage by thick mucopurulent secretions of large, medium, and small bronchi and bronchioles (Fig. 3–2). Some changes may reflect only terminal events.

Heart

Right ventricular hypertrophy is the dominant adaptive cardiac change and is probably directly related to the obstructive bronchial disease and pul-monary hypertension. Significant thickening of the arteriolar wall may be present in pulmonary vessels. It tends to increase with age and is probably secondary to contraction of the arteriolar muscle induced by chronic hypoxia and acidosis. Occasional instances of perivascular myocardial fibrosis in scat-tered areas, predominantly of the left ventricle, have been reported; no expla-nation has been offered as to the etiology of these changes.

PATHOGENESIS

Present concepts of the pathogenesis of cystic fibrosis are summarized in Figure 3–3. The unknown basic defect gives rise to two main anomalies: the mucous secretion abnormality and the electrolyte defect, which is best expressed in secretions of the eccrine sweat glands but is also present in those of minor salivary glands.

Mucous Secretion Abnormality

Because of their abnormal physicochemical behavior these secretions develop precipitates and obstruct passages, resulting in virtually all the main clinical manifestations of cystic fibrosis—obstruction of pancreatic ducts and pancreatic achylia, obstruction of biliary ductules and cirrhosis of the liver, various forms of intestinal obstruction, and most importantly bronchial obstruction and chronic pulmonary disease.

For several years cystic fibrosis was considered an inborn error of glycoprotein metabolism. The evidence, however, is far from conclusive. In the first phase, attention was focused on the suggestion of Dische et al. that the primary alteration in glycoprotein fractions in cystic fibrosis might be an

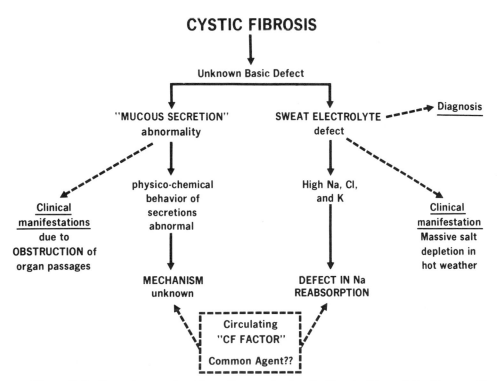

Figure 3–3 Present concepts of the pathogenesis of cystic fibrosis. (From di Sant'Agnese, P. A.: The pancreas. *In* Nelson, W., Vaughan, V. C., and McKay, R. J. (eds.): *Textbook of Pediatrics.* 10th Edition. Philadelphia, W. B. Saunders, in preparation.)

increase in methyl pentose fucose in the carbohydrate moiety and the consequent change in the ratios of fucose to sialic acid.[11] Some of the subsequent studies seemed to support these results, but detailed chemical analyses in general failed to support the evidence.

An intensive search has been conducted by immunochemical methods for a unique molecule that differs from its normal counterpart in antigenic determinant groups, but without success. Urinary macromolecules and especially the Tamm-Horsfall glycoprotein were studied extensively by two groups and were found not to differ in composition between patients with cystic fibrosis and normal individuals.

Recently Boat has been able to isolate in pure form a small phosphoglycoprotein of 11,000 molecular weight that appears in a separate band in acrylamide-gel electrophoresis of submaxillary saliva and has found it to be similar in the many chemical parameters studied in both patients with cystic fibrosis and normal controls.[3]

A different approach was made by Gugler, who studied the effect of abnormal ionic concentration in cystic fibrosis on the solubility of glycoproteins in this disease.[17] Chernick and Barbero had shown some years ago that in contrast to the clear transparent secretion from normal subjects, submaxillary saliva from patients with cystic fibrosis is turbid and its calcium content is increased to about twice the normal value.[11] To elucidate a possible interaction between the increased calcium and some of the organic constituents, Gugler et al. studied these reactions in vitro by acrylamide-gel electrophoresis and other chemical immunological methods. As shown in Figure 3–4, submaxillary saliva from normal subjects is different in gross appearance and in the polyacrylamide-gel electrophoretic pattern from the submaxillary saliva of patients with cystic fibrosis. When calcium levels in cystic saliva were reduced, some bands that had appeared weak or absent as compared to normal saliva reappeared. Conversely, the gross appearance and electrophoretic pattern of normal submaxillary saliva could be transformed to resemble those in cystic fibrosis by an increase in calcium concentration to levels comparable to those in such patients. Studies with specific antisera showed no immunological differences between the various bands or between fractions from patients with cystic fibrosis and normal persons. Gugler and his associates concluded that submaxillary saliva in both normal subjects and patients with cystic fibrosis contains as major constituents glycoproteins, probably identical, that combine or polymerize with calcium present in high concentration to form a reversible precipitate of high molecular weight (over a million) that cannot travel in the gel.

Since in cystic fibrosis widespread obstruction of organ passages gives rise to most of the pathological and clinical findings, such a reaction was postulated as one possible mechanism involved in various organs throughout the body. In support of this theory, in material from meconium ileus, feces, duodenal contents, and tracheobronchial secretions, calcium content was found to be increased in patients with cystic fibrosis. There is evidence that even in submaxillary saliva calcium levels are normal at first, but that as time passes and this gland is affected pathologically with increasing severity, calcium levels rise, and it is at this time that precipitation of calcium protein

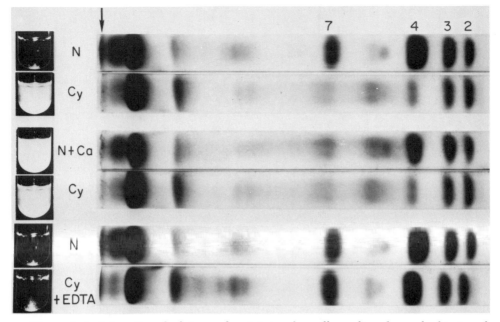

Figure 3-4   Interaction of calcium and protein in submaxillary saliva of normal subjects and patients with cystic fibrosis. *Left,* the appearance of submaxillary saliva in test tubes; *right,* the polyacrylamide gel electrophoresis of the samples. N, normal saliva; Cy, cystic saliva. (From Gugler, E., Pallavicini, J. C., Swerdlow, H., and di Sant'Agnese, P. A.: Role of calcium in submaxillary saliva of patients with cystic fibrosis. J. Pediatr., 71:585–588, 1967.)

complexes occurs. The sequence in other organs may be similar. In support of these observations, Horton found that the calcium transport ATPase in red blood cells of cystic fibrosis patients was depressed and a clear correlation existed between decrease in enzyme activity and severity of the disease.[22] This might well account for the rising calcium levels in some of their secretions.

In cystic fibrosis, however, there is no generalized disturbance of calcium metabolism, and in sweat and small salivary gland saliva as well as in serum, calcium concentration appears to be normal.

Electrolyte Defects

The sweat electrolyte abnormality is present from birth and throughout life, and is unrelated either to severity of the underlying disease or to whether other organs such as the pancreas or the lungs are involved. It leads, in patients with cystic fibrosis, to sweat chloride, sodium, and to a lesser extent potassium concentrations greatly increased as compared to the markedly hypotonic sweat levels found in normal individuals and patients with almost any other type of disease (Fig. 3–5). Main exceptions are renal diabetes insipidus and untreated adrenal insufficiency, both rare in the pediatric age group.

The only important clinical consequence is the massive salt depletion through sweating in hot weather, which may lead to serious and even fatal consequences through cardiovascular collapse.

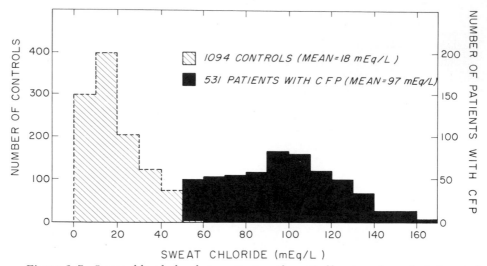

Figure 3–5   Sweat chloride levels in patients with cystic fibrosis and unselected controls (age range: one month to 20 years). (From di Sant'Agnese, P. A., and Powell, G. F.: Eccrine sweat defect in cystic fibrosis of pancreas [mucoviscidosis]. Ann. N.Y. Acad. Sci., 93:555–599, 1962.)

Various parameters of adrenal function in patients with cystic fibrosis have been found normal. Kidney retention of sodium is preserved even though sweat sodium levels are markedly increased. This is in marked contrast to untreated addisonians who cannot conserve salt via either the kidneys or the sweat glands. It is indeed this very striking dissociation between urinary and sweat electrolyte levels that is so characteristic of cystic fibrosis.

In contrast to the elevated concentration of sodium, chloride, and potassium, most other sweat solutes, the sweating rate, and other morphological (including electron microscopic), physiological, and chemical parameters of eccrine sweat glands studied so far are either normal or close to normal. This includes the calcium level as well as levels of lactic acid, urea, and amino acids. A number of different enzymes have been determined histochemically and chemically on frozen dried slices of sweat glands isolated by microdissection from skin biopsies of patients with cystic fibrosis; their activity is normal.

Grand et al. have shown in patients that significant decreases in sweat sodium or the potassium to sodium ratio can be achieved by the administration of exogenous aldosterone.[11] Therefore, it cannot be said that patients with cystic fibrosis do not "acclimate" to hot weather. The explanation for the "heat casualties" in this disease is that the sweat sodium and chloride levels are abnormally high even after the decrease.

A number of indirect studies have shown that sweat is isotonic to plasma in the sweat gland coil in normal subjects as well as in patients with cystic fibrosis. Schulz demonstrated, by direct approach with micropuncture of the coil, that the precursor solution of patients with cystic fibrosis is the same in osmolarity and sodium and chloride content as that of normal individuals.[35] A defect in the reabsorption of sodium and chloride in the sweat gland duct, therefore, was postulated. The findings of Mangos, confirmed by Kaiser, of the existence of a sodium inhibitory factor in the sweat of patients with cystic fibrosis gives a reasonable explanation of the increased sweat electrolyte levels.[23, 30]

The only other exocrine gland system that consistently manifests a sodium abnormality in cystic fibrosis is that of the small salivary glands found throughout the buccal mucosa.[44] While the sodium concentration in this type of saliva is markedly increased in patients with cystic fibrosis, those of all other ions determined, including potassium and calcium, are found to be within normal limits. In contrast, sodium, chloride, and potassium levels appear to be normal in submaxillary and parotid gland saliva as well as in the serum.

On the basis of studies of duodenal contents in patients with cystic fibrosis, but no pancreatic deficiency, Hadorn and others in 1968 suggested that failure in transport of electrolyte-containing fluid (bicarbonate as well as chloride and sodium) and consequent concentration of macromolecules in organs throughout the body might result in many of the pathological features of the disease.[20] So far, however, this hypothesis has not been proved.

Tissue Culture Abnormalities

In 1968 Danes and Bearn reported the presence of cytoplasmic metachromasia in tissue culture fibroblasts obtained from skin biopsies of patients with cystic fibrosis and their parents (obligatory heterozygotes).[4] This was soon followed by a report of Matalon and Dorfman demonstrating a variable, but at times marked, increase in total acid mucopolysaccharides in culture fibroblasts from homozygotic patients with cystic fibrosis, but with a normal percentage distribution of fractions.[31] Needless to say, these findings were startling, especially as there had been no previous morphological or chemical indications in the patients' tissues at biopsy or autopsy tending to incriminate the connective tissue in vivo or postmortem.

Unfortunately, subsequently a number of laboratories have experienced difficulty obtaining clear-cut and reproducible results with metachromasia of fibroblasts and have had differing results chemically, presumably due to slight but important differences in the methods of tissue culture. Thus, among other reported findings, there was a marked increase in glycogen content of fibroblasts and a deficiency of tRNA methylation. In an excellent study, however, Klagsbrun and Farrell found the tRNA methylation and all the methylases to be normal in cystic fibrosis fibroblasts.[25] Wiesmann and Neufeld, using turnover studies of sulfated mucopolysaccharide fibroblasts from a number of cystic fibrosis cell lines, showed that the accumulation of these compounds as well as the kinetics of their degradation was normal.[43] These results were quite different from those of patients with known mucopolysaccharidoses (e.g., Hurler's disease). Also, determinations of some 12 lysosomal hydrolases have shown them to be normal, and a normal excretion pattern of acid mucopolysaccharides was found in the urine of patients with cystic fibrosis, evidence that militates against a basic defect of acid mucopolysaccharide metabolism in cystic fibrosis. Possibly the varying results obtained by different investigators indicate that these findings are relatively nonspecific, but may reflect a metabolic or catabolic defect.

Despite these controversial findings tissue culture studies have had an important impact and should be pursued, as they represent the first experimental model outside the patients' bodies. They also point to the fact that all cells of the body and not just the exocrine glands may be involved in this disorder. Perhaps, most importantly, fibroblasts and lymphoid cells in culture appear to produce some of the cystic fibrosis factors that are discussed next.

"Cystic Fibrosis Factors"

In 1967 Spock showed that a factor exists in the serum of homozygotic patients and in the euglobulin fraction of heterozygotes that induces dyskinesia in the ciliary epithelium of rabbit tracheal explants.[38] Subsequently, many people have tried with limited success to develop simple assay systems by utilizing a variety of lower forms of life on the theory that cilia behave in a similar manner regardless of whether the organism is a mammal, a clam, an oyster, or another species. This factor appears to be heat labile, is nondialyzable, has a molecular weight of 150,000 to 200,000, and on Sephadex or DEAE columns is eluted with IgG.

Also in 1967 Mangos demonstrated by retrograde perfusion techniques the presence in mixed saliva and sweat from cystic fibrosis patients (homozygotes) of a factor that inhibits sodium reabsorption in experimental rat parotid systems.[30] This was confirmed by Kaiser in Switzerland in 1970 in the human sweat gland in situ, using comparable techniques.[23] This factor was characterized by Mangos as being a strongly basic macromolecule, heat labile, destroyed by freezing, and nondialyzable.[29] He also showed that other basic polyelectrolytes have similar action, probably by interacting electrostatically with the negatively charged surface of membranes, thus affecting their function. The addition of heparin, which is strongly negatively charged, eliminates the activity of sweat and mixed saliva from patients with cystic fibrosis. Kaiser felt the active sodium transport was probably normal, as it does not seem to be disturbed in other areas of the body and there is a normal response of cystic fibrosis sweat glands to aldosterone.[23] He thought that it was passive (leak) diffusion that presumably was affected. Various investigators also have tried to demonstrate an effect on sodium transport in the gut of animals with varying success and often conflicting results.

In the case of both ciliary and sodium reabsorption factors, the situation is rather similar. They both depend on technically difficult biological assay systems that are difficult to reproduce; this is what is holding up progress in this field at this time. It is possible that these are in reality one and the same factor, perhaps in association with diverse fractions in various biological fluids. This might explain the difference of behavior and of action in serum, sweat, and mixed saliva.

PATHOPHYSIOLOGY

Pulmonary Involvement

Bronchial and bronchiolar obstruction by abnormally viscous and tenacious secretions is the cardinal and primary manifestation of the pulmonary involvement in cystic fibrosis. The pulmonary dysfunction is characteristic of obstructive disease, and the increase in airway obstruction parallels the advance in clinical severity and improves in response to antibiotic and other treatment. The changes include an increase in residual lung volume and its ratio to total lung capacity, a decrease in ventilatory flow rate, and an uneven gas distribution throughout the body.

It has been shown by use of total body plethysmography that patients with cystic fibrosis have either a normal or markedly increased total lung volume depending on the severity of pulmonary involvement. With the conventional helium or nitrogen washout techniques, the total lung volume of such patients frequently appears to be decreased. The difference between the two measurements represents "trapped gas" and demonstrates that the former method is more accurate and reliable than the latter. There is an almost perfect correlation between clinical severity as determined by various clinical indices, and the ratio of residual to total lung volume as determined by body plethysmographic method. Almost all the patients with cystic fibrosis tested showed no significant changes in spirometric values after inhalation of bronchodilators. This is quite a different response from that seen in most other types of chronic obstructive pulmonary disease and has an important bearing on treatment.

Cardiac Involvement

Pulmonary Hypertension. Progressive obstructive pulmonary disease in cystic fibrosis frequently leads to pulmonary hypertension. Factors presumably involved include: pulmonary vascular compression, atelectasis, acidosis, hypercarbia, and hypoxia. Catheterization studies show that intrapulmonary arterial pressures are frequently increased and that they may decrease with administration of oxygen. The fact that the effects of bronchiolar and bronchial obstruction may be partly reversible is a strong argument for the use of all methods for evacuating mucopurulent secretions by physical and inhalational therapy, as well as for combating infection by the judicious use of antibiotics. Good results in decreasing pulmonary arterial pressure on catheterization were obtained by using a combination of tolazoline hydrochloride (Priscoline) and 100 per cent oxygen. The adverse effect of hypoxia due to altitude also has been emphasized and the recommendation made that patients with cystic fibrosis and chronic pulmonary disease should reside at or near sea level.

Cor Pulmonale. Cor pulmonale is a common complication resulting from the pulmonary hypertension, as shown by autopsy findings. Its recognition, however, in cystic fibrosis is difficult. Cardiac signs may be completely masked by the pulmonary manifestations; tachycardia may occur merely as a result of hypoxemia; the liver is frequently displaced downward by the obstructive emphysema. Overt edema occurs rarely and usually is a terminal feature. Bronchograms also can be misleading, as the relative size of the heart may be small because of the pulmonary emphysema and the increased posteroanterior diameter. Electrocardiograms and vectorcardiograms have not been reliable indicators of this complication, although a combination of various nonspecific abnormal findings such as hypertrophy of the right atrium or right ventricle or both, low voltage, or abnormally deep S waves in the left precordial leads appear to correlate quite well with the degree of involvement. Moss has proposed the three following criteria on the basis of which in his experience cor pulmonale is generally present: clinical evidence of severe disease with a Shwachman score of less than 40, a vital capacity of less than 60 per cent of the predicted normal, and inability to raise the arterial oxygen tension above 100 mm Hg after breathing 100 per cent oxygen for 10 minutes.[11]

Pancreatic Insufficiency and Malabsorption

Pancreatic achylia with the absence of all pancreatic enzymes, trypsin, carboxypeptidase, chymotrypsin, lipase, and amylase, occurs in 85 to 90 per cent of patients because of the complete destruction of the exocrine parenchyma of the pancreas.[9] Although the lesion is progressive and the histological findings are difficult to recognize at birth, absence of pancreatic enzymes secondary to obstruction of pancreatic ducts is present even at that time. Steatorrhea and creatorrhea are marked owing to intestinal malabsorption secondary to maldigestion due to the absence of pancreatic enzymes. In contrast to fats, proteins, though poorly absorbed, are well tolerated, making possible the attainment of positive nitrogen balance through increased dietary intake. Utilization of carbohydrates is less significantly impaired. Peroral intestinal biopsy specimens have usually shown no histological changes, but the disaccharidase activities, especially that of lactase, have been reduced, although usually not giving rise to clinical symptoms.

Because of the steatorrhea large amounts of liposoluble vitamins are lost in the stools. Vitamin D–deficiency rickets, however, has almost never been seen in cystic fibrosis, a fact that is unexplained. Vitamin K deficiency and prolongation of the prothrombin time due to intestinal malabsorption are seen occasionally. Vitamin E levels are low in serum and in liver as expected. Underwood and Denning, however, unexpectedly found in recent studies that while serum vitamin A levels were low even in patients receiving supplements, the vitamin A content of liver tissue at postmortem in the same patients was normal or increased.[42] This suggested to the investigators a defect in the transport of this vitamin. Smith et al. subsequently demonstrated that serum retinol-binding protein (needed for transport of unesterified vitamin A alcohol) indeed is decreased in many patients with cystic fibrosis, perhaps as a consequence of impaired liver function.[37]

There are important differences between pancreatogenous maldigestion such as that seen in cystic fibrosis and other diseases leading to pancreatic insufficiency (e.g., familial pancreatitis, alcoholic pancreatitis, pancreatic deficiency and bone marrow dysfunction and other types of steatorrhea secondary to failure of absorption (gluten-induced enteropathy, agammaglobulinemia, and the like). In addition to steatorrhea, azotorrhea is always present in pancreatic deficiency, but fecal nitrogen excretion is normal in most other types of malabsorption. In pancreatogenous steatorrhea there is a striking lack of correlation between levels of fecal fat and nitrogen and clinical symptoms; this does not obtain in most patients with steatorrhea secondary to impaired absorption states, who are apt to be very sick clinically with relatively small increases in fecal fat excretion. Finally, hypocalcemia has never to our knowledge been reported in patients with steatorrhea and maldigestion due to pancreatic deficiency. This is very different from many other types of malabsorption, such as gluten-induced enteropathy and agammaglobulinemia, in which hypocalcemia and its consequences frequently are seen in severe cases. This is probably due to the absence of splitting of neutral fats into fatty acids by pancreatic lipase in patients with pancreatic deficiency; as a result fats throughout the intestine are present as neutral fats, which do not form soaps with calcium as do fatty acids.

Immunology

Because of the frequency of chronic pulmonary infection the question arises whether patients with cystic fibrosis are more susceptible to infections than other individuals. Except for the respiratory tract, fibrocystic patients do not have greater liability to infections than normal subjects of comparable ages. This is exemplified by the almost complete absence of pleural complication as well as of blood stream infections despite the presence of chronic pulmonary infection in the great majority of patients.

Patients with cystic fibrosis have been shown to develop good levels of circulating antibodies to pathogenic bacteria and in response to immunization, and to have excellent immunoglobulin responses in serum to infection. The levels of IgG and IgA are either normal or increased in relation to the presence of respiratory infection and severity, while IgM levels are usually normal. IgE levels are also within normal limits. It has been shown that levels of IgA in saliva and in the gastrointestinal tract are either normal or increased and, by immunofluorescence, that the level of this immunoglobulin in bronchial cells is increased in patients with cystic fibrosis who have pulmonary infection. The rate of synthesis of intestinal IgA has recently been studied by Falchuk et al. by measuring labeled leucine incorporation in intestinal biopsies; it was found to be increased in fibrocystic patients, presumably because of greater local antigenic stimuli.[13]

The only immunological deficiency that has been shown in preliminary studies by Biggar et al. is a deficiency in phagocytosis of *Pseudomonas aeruginosa* by macrophages of the lungs in homozygotes with cystic fibrosis.[2] The phagocytosis rate of *Staphylococcus aureus* in the same subjects by the same cells is quite normal. This finding, however, was present in only six of nine patients and awaits confirmation.

It can be stated at the present time that patients with cystic fibrosis are immunologically competent, which makes their unusual susceptibility to respiratory infection difficult to explain. Bronchial obstruction preceding the pulmonary infection does not appear to be the whole answer. Close relationship between this disease and *Staphylococcus aureus* suggests a metabolic basis for this constant finding.

CLINICAL PICTURE

Chronic Pulmonary Disease

Chronic involvement of the respiratory tract dominates the clinical picture and determines the fate of the patient. It usually is severe and progressive, but the time of onset is variable. Weeks, months, or even years may pass before its onset, so that it may not be present when the patient is first seen. Eventually all patients have developed chronic pulmonary disease.

For some time the patient has a dry, nonproductive cough. Later, usually after an acute respiratory infection or following a viral infection of the bronchial tree (e.g., influenza), the signs of generalized bronchial or bronchiolar obstruction and secondary infection appear (Fig. 3–6). At this stage some degree of respiratory distress is present; at times it is severe and the patient is quite ill. After a variable but usually short period, the infection, until then mild and perhaps localized to the main division of the bronchi, becomes widespread and frequently severe. Respiratory distress is present; there may be marked anoxia, carbon dioxide retention, and air hunger. The patient is frequently quite ill, presenting the picture of severe generalized pulmonary infection.

At this stage in the past, spread of the infection to the blood stream and, frequently, massive lobar atelectasis often occurred.

The pulmonary involvement in cystic fibrosis is an intrabronchial disease due to precipitation of presumably abnormal secretions, and bronchial obstruction is its primary and cardinal manifestation. Prolonged and frequently severe secondary infection eventually causes permanent damage to the bronchial wall. The distressing picture of chronic pulmonary insufficiency with bronchiolectasis, bronchiectasis, and cor pulmonale develops and eventually leads to death within several years. Its course is punctuated by relapses in bronchial obstruction and secondary infection whenever intercurrent viral infections of the upper respiratory tract occur.

Numerous complications arise in the course of the severe pulmonary disease. Lobar atelectasis with collapse of one or more lobes, usually on the right side, occurs early in the course of the illness in 5 to 10 per cent of patients. Patchy lobular atelectasis throughout the pulmonary area is the rule. Lung abscesses were common before and early in the antibiotic era, but are seen rarely nowadays. Recurrent pneumothorax, often bilateral, has been a frequent problem especially in the older age group. Small hemoptysis is frequently seen especially in the older patients, and even in recent times,

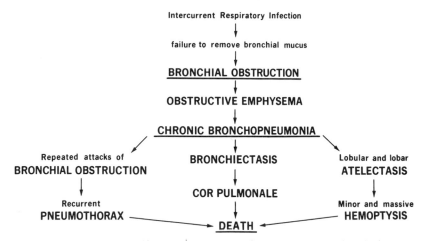

Intercurrent Respiratory Infection

failure to remove bronchial mucus

BRONCHIAL OBSTRUCTION

OBSTRUCTIVE EMPHYSEMA

CHRONIC BRONCHOPNEUMONIA

Repeated attacks of
BRONCHIAL OBSTRUCTION

BRONCHIECTASIS

Lobular and lobar
ATELECTASIS

COR PULMONALE

Recurrent
PNEUMOTHORAX

Minor and massive
HEMOPTYSIS

DEATH

Figure 2 C   Sequence of events in pulmonary involvement in cystic fibrosis. (From di Sant-Agnese, P. A.: Cystic fibrosis (mucoviscidosis). Am. Fam. Physician, 7:102–111, 1973.)

massive and at times exsanguinating hemoptysis has occurred. Acute cor pulmonale with dilatation of the heart may occur during attacks of sudden and severe bronchial obstruction. If the patient survives and responds to antibiotic treatment the heart may return to its normal size. Chronic cor pulmonale with clinical and roentgenographic evidence of enlargement of the heart and cardiac failure may be seen in cases of long-standing severe and progressive pulmonary disease.

Paranasal sinuses, as part of the respiratory tract, are almost invariably affected. Clouding of the sinuses is seen roentgenographically, and nasal polyps occur in about one third of the patients, especially the older ones. Three cases of mucocele with extensive bony destruction requiring surgical intervention have been reported.

The respiratory flora in patients with cystic fibrosis consists primarily of *Staphylococcus aureus* or *Pseudomonas aeruginosa* or both, the latter probably secondary to antibiotic treatment. *Haemophilus influenzae, Escherichia coli,* Proteus, and other organisms are isolated less frequently. Prior to and early in the antibiotic era *Staphylococcus aureus* was almost the only organism found in the respiratory tract of fibrocystic patients, even at autopsy. In recent years when Pseudomonas has become so prevalent in such patients, the clinical course and pathological findings have not changed significantly. Although there is some clinical improvement when anti-Pseudomonas antibiotics are used, the role of this organism and its importance in the pulmonary disease of cystic fibrosis is not clear.

Abdominal Involvement in Cystic Fibrosis

PANCREATIC DEFICIENCY AND MALABSORPTION

Pancreatic Achylia.   Achylia is present in 85 to 90 per cent of patients with cystic fibrosis. The results of untreated pancreatic insufficiency, especially among infants, lead to progressive malnutrition despite a ravenous appetite, abdominal distention, and abnormal stools that are increased in number, bulky, greasy, and foul. In the great majority of patients pancreatic achylia is present at birth, but in some children involvement of this gland may not be evident until later. In contrast to fats, proteins are well tolerated, making it possible to obtain positive nitrogen balance through increased dietary intake. It has been clearly shown by Fleisher et al. and Shahidi et al. that soybean protein is not used as effectively by infants with cystic fibrosis as the protein of cow's milk, and that hypoproteinemia may result.[11]

Liposoluble vitamins are lost through the stools, but vitamin A deficiency, a problem in the past, is rarely seen at present because of the supplements given orally. Vitamin K deficiency and hypoprothrombinemia are occasionally encountered. Vitamin D deficiency is not clinically apparent. Although some pathological changes due to vitamin E deficiency are found at autopsy, clinical manifestations due to deficiency of this vitamin never have been conclusively proved.

Lactosuria and Sucrosuria.   Lactosuria and sucrosuria are unexplained occurrences in a proportion of cystic fibrosis patients. Also difficult to explain is the reduced lactase activity in peroral intestinal specimens from some fibrocystic patients in the absence of clinical symptoms or histological changes. Occasionally, however, lactase deficiency may cause persistent diarrhea even after adequate measures have been taken to compensate for the effects of pancreatic deficiency.

Malabsorption.   In countries with adequate diets and good public health facilities cystic fibrosis is at present by far the commonest cause of severe malabsorption in the pediatric age group.[6, 9] Not usually recognized is the fact that cystic fibrosis in this country is by far the commonest cause of prolapse of the rectum in infancy and childhood. This complication occurs in as many as 15 to 20 per cent of patients with cystic fibrosis; it is more frequent in the younger patients, but occurs at times in older children. Its mechanism is obscure, although it is related in some ways to the effects of pancreatic deficiency, as symptomatic relief follows pancreatic replacement therapy.

In 10 to 15 per cent of patients pancreatic function ranges from normal to markedly decreased; even low levels of pancreatic enzymes, however, usually are sufficient to prevent the clinical manifestations of malabsorption and steatorrhea.

Malabsorption generally improves with age; while infants and young children are apt to need dietary restrictions and are quite dependent on pancreatic replacement therapy, symptoms appear to grow less and less with advancing age despite the absence of pancreatic function and the continued presence of marked steatorrhea and azotorrhea.

Pancreatitis.   Recurrent attacks of acute pancreatitis in patients with cystic fibrosis are very uncommon, but have been observed. Perhaps these patients may be the ones who have a late onset of pancreatic deficiency and spill enzymes in the surrounding tissues as a result of obstruction of the ducts. Pancreatic lithiasis also has been seen in rare instances in patients with cystic fibrosis.

Peptic Ulcer.   Peptic ulcer has been mentioned as a complication, but probably with no greater frequency than in the general population.

OBSTRUCTIVE INTESTINAL COMPLICATIONS

Regardless of age, all patients with cystic fibrosis are subject to intestinal obstructive complications because of the abnormal character of their intestinal contents.[33] Pancreatic achylia certainly plays a role in the intestinal obstructive syndromes, but it must be minor judging from the absence of these complications in other types of pancreatic deficiency (e.g., familial pancreatitis, pancreatic insufficiency and bone marrow dysfunction, alcoholic pancreatitis). The major factor in the etiology of the various types of intestinal obstruction in cystic fibrosis is undoubtedly the abnormal physicochemical character of intestinal secretions, which causes the intestinal contents to be solid or semisolid where the fecal stream is normally liquid, that is, in the terminal ileum and the ascending colon.

Meconium Ileus.   The best known and most common of these complications, meconium ileus, occurs in 5 to 10 per cent of newborn patients with this disease.[32, 34] Intestinal obstruction is present at birth; inspissated grayish rubbery meconium plugs the lumen of the small intestine, usually near the ileocecal valve. Proximal to it a large amount of tenacious viscid abnormal meconium accumulates and leads to distention of the intestinal loops, which, in one third of the cases, rotate upon themselves, giving rise to volvulus. If the surgeon is unaware of the possibility of the occurrence of this combination he may reduce the volvulus, but disregard the obstruction. Distal to the obstructed segment the colon is very small and apparently underdeveloped (microcolon) owing to disuse, but it returns to normal size within a few days after surgery.

Intestinal Atresia.   Intestinal atresia resulting from antenatal volvulus in patients with cystic fibrosis has not received as much attention as is warranted. Volvulus occurring early in fetal life, usually at high levels in the small intestine, probably is due to a mechanism similar to the one described for meconium ileus. Interference with the mesenteric blood supply and consequent perforation of the intestine result in aseptic healing and the production of atresia or stenosis and frequently of meconium peritonitis. According to many authorities cystic fibrosis is the cause of a significant proportion of all intestinal obstruction of the newborn seen in this country.[6]

Fecal Masses.   Palpable fecal masses are not uncommonly felt in the course of routine examination of cystic fibrosis patients. These masses are hard, 3 to 5 cm in diameter, usually mobile and nontender. When found in the cecal area, especially in the older patients, they may raise the suspicion of a tumor. Continuous antibiotic therapy may mask other indications of inflammatory disease (e.g., appendiceal abscess), and contrast x-ray studies may show merely a persistent filling defect. The realization that asymptomatic fecal masses are frequently found in fibrocystic patients suggests conservatism and continued temporary observation, since they almost always pass spontaneously over a period of days or weeks.

Obturation and Intussusception. Obturation (so-called meconium ileus equivalent) due to inspissated or impacted feces appears to be the commonest entity that gives rise to manifest abdominal symptoms in patients with cystic fibrosis. Intussusception is an occasional complication, even in children beyond the age of infancy. It is atypical, usually does not give rise to complete obstruction, and appears to be precipitated by adherent intestinal contents that cannot be propelled along the gut or through the ileocecal valve.

Adhesions. Adhesions from previous surgery coupled with the abnormality of the intestinal contents also increase the chance of later obstructive complications. As extensive intestinal manipulation at operation is often necessary because of the abnormal fecal contents, intestinal adhesions are quite frequent and may give rise to narrowed areas especially in the ascending colon where they may prevent progress of fecal masses.

Volvulus. Volvulus, as previously mentioned, is a frequent complication of neonatal meconium ileus, but it may occur also in older patients.

HEPATIC CIRRHOSIS

A fatty liver due to severe malnutrition, which was frequent in the earlier reports of untreated patients, is not seen as commonly nowadays. In 2 to 3 per cent of fibrocystic patients the destruction and consequent regeneration of the hepatic parenchyma from repeated attacks of biliary cirrhosis, alternating for years, leads to portal hypertension and its manifestations: ascites, hypersplenism, and gastrointestinal bleeding. This distinctive pathological process has been named multilobular biliary cirrhosis with concretions.[8] It is characterized by an absence or slight degree of icterus, and frequently liver function test results are normal, presumably because this type of cirrhosis is a focal process and large areas of normal hepatic parenchyma are usually preserved.

Other Complications

Hypoalbuminemia. Hypoalbuminemia is found in cystic fibrosis as an occasional complication. Several studies utilizing tagged albumin turnover studies as well as radioactive chromium tests for gastrointestinal protein leakage have been published. It is apparent that there are three causes for hypoalbuminemia in this disease of which by far the most common is hemodilution due to increased blood volume secondary to severe pulmonary disease and cor pulmonale. Hypoalbuminemia may, however, occur because of a decreased synthetic rate resulting from extensive hepatic cirrhosis. In infants with cystic fibrosis the use of soybean protein preparations, which are improperly utilized by these patients, has been shown to lead to low albumin levels. In severely ill patients a combination of two or three of these factors may contribute to the low serum albumin.

Glucose Intolerance. A progressive glucose intolerance may develop and lead eventually to glycosuria in some patients, but ketonuria, acidosis, and vascular changes are not present as they are in classic diabetes mellitus.[21] Dietary measures are usually sufficient for adequate control, although insulin may occasionally be needed. This inability to metabolize glucose adequately seems to be associated with increasing age and duration of the disease. When such patients are examined at autopsy, the islets seem to be disorganized by pancreatic fibrosis, which presumably interferes with their function. This type of glucose intolerance is thus different from familial diabetes mellitus, which can occur coincidentally in some patients with cystic fibrosis.

Massive Salt Loss. High atmospheric temperatures, especially sudden heat, cause profuse sweating. Since in patients with cystic fibrosis the concentration of sodium and chloride in sweat is comparable to that in serum, massive salt loss and hypoelectrolytemia may occur.[10] The accompanying dehydration is made worse by vomiting, which occurs regularly when the loss of electrolytes is sufficiently great. Reduction in extracellular fluid volume results and may lead to cardiovascular collapse, followed in fairly rapid succession by hyperthermia, coma, and death. Serum sodium, chloride, and carbon dioxide are decreased, but serum potassium is likely to be within normal limits if the sequence of events is rapid, as it usually is. This is because the extracellular fluid volume is primarily affected, while the intracellular fluid is involved only when the process has extended over a period of more than one day; serum potassium then is found to be decreased.

Hypertrophic Osteoarthropathy. As in other types of chronic pulmonary disease, pulmonary hypertrophic osteoarthropathy develops occasionally. This may give rise to arthritis and chronic periostitis; at times no symptoms are present, but periosteal new bone formation can be seen by x-ray in the lower extremities.

Ocular Lesions. Two types of ocular lesions occur and may coexist in children with severe pulmonary involvement. At times, with severe pulmonary disease, exudative retinopathy is present; the arteries and veins of the fundus are dilated, and hemorrhage and papilledema may be present. These changes parallel the extent of pulmonary involvement and do not appear to affect vision. Optic neuritis with a diminution of visual acuity has been observed in patients receiving prolonged therapy with chloramphenicol. Variable degrees of visual improvement have resulted when the drug was discontinued.

Aspermia. Aspermia occurs in more than 95 per cent of adult males with cystic fibrosis (see also Adolescents and Young Adults).[41]

DIAGNOSIS

The criteria required for a diagnosis of cystic fibrosis are listed in Figure 3–7. Frequently not all four criteria are present, especially the occurrence of siblings with cystic fibrosis. However, in addition to high concentration of sweat electrolytes, either chronic pulmonary disease or pancreatic insufficiency must be present.

DIAGNOSIS OF CYSTIC FIBROSIS OF THE PANCREAS

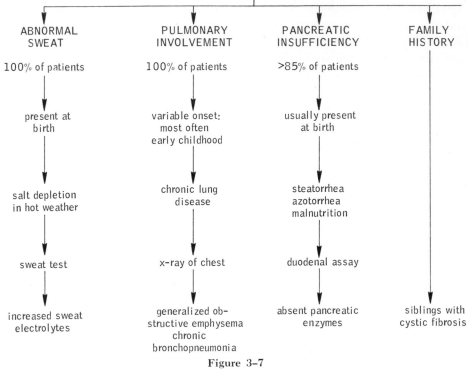

ABNORMAL SWEAT	PULMONARY INVOLVEMENT	PANCREATIC INSUFFICIENCY	FAMILY HISTORY
100% of patients	100% of patients	>85% of patients	
present at birth	variable onset: most often early childhood	usually present at birth	
salt depletion in hot weather	chronic lung disease	steatorrhea azotorrhea malnutrition	
sweat test	x-ray of chest	duodenal assay	
increased sweat electrolytes	generalized obstructive emphysema chronic bronchopneumonia	absent pancreatic enzymes	siblings with cystic fibrosis

Figure 3–7

Clinical Picture

In the great majority of instances the combination of symptoms of chronic pulmonary disease and of intestinal malabsorption suggests the diagnosis. Diagnosis of cystic fibrosis may present difficulties in patients in whom only malabsorption or only chronic pulmonary disease is present. Such ancillary manifestations as malnutrition despite ravenous appetite, history of rectal prolapse, nasal polyps, hepatic cirrhosis, heat prostration in summer, history of meconium ileus, or recurrent abdominal obstructive complications should also suggest the diagnostic possibility of cystic fibrosis. The sweat test will be positive in all instances. It follows that all children and adolescents with recurrent respiratory infections or malabsorption should have a sweat test as part of their diagnostic work-up.

Sweat Test

The sweat test is the simplest and most reliable laboratory method for the diagnosis of cystic fibrosis. Obtaining sweat by iontophoresis of pilocarpine, which utilizes a small electric current to carry this cholinergic drug into the skin and stimulate sweat glands locally, is safe, painless, and reliable for diagnostic purposes. Although differences of a few milliequivalents occur between the results of various laboratories, in our clinic up to the age of 20 years, a level of more than 60 mEq/L of sweat chloride is considered diagnostic of cystic fibrosis, and values between 50 and 60 mEq/L are highly suggestive of this disease. Concentration of sweat sodium is about 10 mEq/L higher than chloride. Potassium levels in sweat and sodium and chloride concentrations in saliva are not useful for diagnostic purposes because the overlap is too great. There are a few conditions other than cystic fibrosis in which sweat electrolyte levels may be elevated. Untreated adrenal insufficiency is the most important one; others in which occasional elevations have been observed are glucose-6-phosphatase deficiency, glycogen storage disease (Type I), Pitressin-resistant diabetes insipidus, and, in one family group, ectodermal dysplasia and sensory neural deafness. Sweat chloride values in adults rarely exceed 70 to 80 mEq/L. The effects of edema and malnutrition on sweat electrolytes are still in dispute, they have caused a transient increase in these ions that reverted later to normal values. Because of this and the fact that severely malnourished or dehydrated children may have transient pancreatic deficiency, it is best not to accept the results of either the sweat test or duodenal assay until a patient has passed the acute stage.

Reliable sweat tests are difficult to obtain in the first three to four weeks of life as the sweat glands do not yet function adequately. There has been considerable interest in developing a simple and reliable way of analyzing sweat or developing other screening procedures that could be applied to population surveys or to mass testing of newborns. None of the methods proposed so far has been satisfactory for screening purposes. In addition, there is no valid evidence that if cystic fibrosis is diagnosed in the first three or four weeks of life pulmonary complications are prevented in any significant number of patients. A high index of suspicion of this diagnosis is necessary, and any patient who is suspected of having this disease during the first few days of life must be treated as if he did until such time as a reliable sweat test can be obtained.

Diagnosis of cystic fibrosis also may be difficult in patients seen for the first time as adolescents or young adults, since they are not likely to present the classic textbook picture of the disease. For them the criteria for a definitive diagnosis should be more rigid than for children, especially in view of the moderately high concentrations of sweat electrolytes found after the age of 18 or 20 years in a few normal individuals (up to 60 to 70 mEq/L of chloride and sodium). As an aid to diagnosis in adult patients, the so-called "dynamic test" has been advocated. In this test the difference in response of sweat electrolytes to administration of salt-retaining steroids is assessed between normal subjects and fibrocystic patients. The finding of a variable but significant decrease in sweat sodium in cystic patients after exogenous administration of aldosterone, however, even though statistically somewhat less than in normal individuals, makes it impossible to use this test as a diagnostic aid.

Differential diagnosis should include other types of obstructive pulmonary disease (e.g., agammaglobulinemia, Kartagener's syndrome, Hamman-Rich disease, sarcoidosis, familial dysautonomia), all of which have been found to have normal sweat electrolyte levels, as well as other types of malabsorption. Although most children with pancreatic deficiency have cystic fibrosis, other causes of pancreatic achylia in this age group exist (e.g., aplasia of the exocrine pancreas, pancreatic insufficiency and bone marrow dysfunction [Shwachman-Diamond syndrome], familial pancreatitis). All such patients, however, have normal sweat test results and generally do not have chronic pulmonary disease.

Demonstration of characteristic pathological changes in specimens of rectal mucosa and of labial salivary glands obtained by biopsy has been advocated as a diagnostic aid. We have not found it necessary so far to use these methods.

Chemical and Other Investigations of Blood

Anemia is usually not a problem and serum iron and iron-binding capacity are generally normal. However, iron deficiency anemia with decreased serum iron and increased iron-binding capacity as well as the anemia due to chronic infection in which both iron and iron-binding capacity are decreased may occur. Leukocytosis and elevation of the erythrocyte sedimentation rate reflect pulmonary or other infectious processes. Serum electrolytes are within the normal range in patients with cystic fibrosis when they are reasonably well clinically. When there is severe pulmonary disease, the serum and electrolyte pattern may be that of uncompensated or more frequently of compensated respiratory acidosis. Hypoelectrolytemia occurs in patients with heat prostration and shock as a result of the massive outpouring of electrolytes in sweat. Serum potassium levels may remain within apparently normal limits under these circumstances if the process is rapid, but will decrease if the loss occurs over a longer period of time. Hypoelectrolytemia has also been observed in infants with cystic fibrosis during cold weather because of continued moderate salt losses through sweat combined with an inadequate intake of salt over a period of time. Such patients may erroneously be thought to have adrenal insufficiency.

The usual limited tests of liver function frequently do not reveal hepatic impairment. However, recent studies in 49 patients with cystic fibrosis, ages 3 to 41 years, revealed that about one third had serological evidence of hepatobiliary disease before clinical signs were evident.[24] The transaminases, γ-glutamyl-transpeptidase, and the liver isoenzyme of alkaline phosphatase appear to be the most reliable indicators of this complication.

Serum calcium and phosphorus levels are always within normal limits. Serum protein values are usually normal in patients in reasonably good clinical condition. Hypoalbuminemia may occur in the course of the disease and the various circumstances that have been previously discussed. The globulin moiety may be increased by a rise in IgG and IgA related to the respiratory involvement.

Pancreatic Insufficiency and Intestinal Malabsorption

Duodenal drainage is not generally necessary for diagnosis and not done routinely, but is of diagnostic assistance in patients without pulmonary symptoms who are thought to have cystic fibrosis. Determination of tryptic activity in duodenal contents is usually sufficient, but if determinations are made, all other enzymes are generally found to be absent. The fluid obtained in such patients is usually of small volume and its viscosity is frequently much greater than normal, although these findings are variable. In the 10 to 15 per cent of patients with cystic fibrosis, but no involvement of the pancreas, the pancreatic enzymes have normal activity.

In patients with pancreatic achylia, steatorrhea and azotorrhea are always present, although in variable amounts. At times the loss of fat and nitrogen through the stools is massive but compensated for by an excessive intake of food. This can be demonstrated on balance studies with stool collections performed for not less than three or four days. Single specimens of stools or even a 24 hour collection is too variable to give meaningful results.

Roentgenography

Persistent, generalized obstructive emphysema is not pathognomonic, but is highly suggestive of cystic fibrosis. Children with chronic lung disease, but without the signs of generalized emphysema, usually have other diseases. In moderately advanced and severe pulmonary lesions, there is a variety of additional roentgenographic changes that include bilateral disseminated infiltrative lesions of bronchopneumonia (Fig. 3–8), lobular and lobar atelectasis (Fig. 3–9), and widely disseminated miliary infiltrations often indistinguishable from those of tuberculosis. At times mucoid impaction of the bronchi are demonstrated as grapelike nodular densities. In older patients with long-standing pulmonary involvement peripheral cystlike blebs are frequently seen. The appearance of pneumothorax is no different from that in other patients with chronic pulmonary disease.

Changes in the x-ray motility patterns of the small intestine may be found in patients with pancreatic deficiency as in subjects with other malabsorptive disorders. It should be kept in mind that similar intestinal motility patterns may be seen in healthy infants and young children under various circumstances. In most patients with cystic fibrosis, abnormalities also have been seen in barium studies of the duodenum (Fig. 3–10).[39] These consist of markedly thickened folds, nodular filling defects, mucosal smudging, and dilatation. The etiology of these duodenal changes is obscure, but contractions of the muscle layer secondary to irritation from unbuffered gastric acid are the most likely explanation. It is important to recognize these abnormalities so that faulty diagnoses, especially of peptic ulcer, are not made. Roentgenograms of the skeleton occasionally show a moderate degree of osteoporosis.

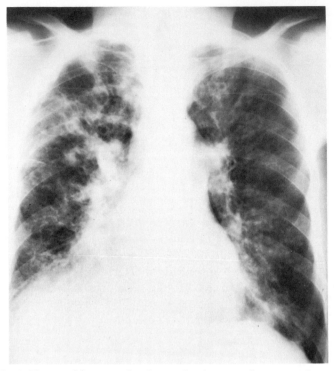

Figure 3–8   A 30 year old man with advanced pulmonary disease. Widespread changes in both lungs are more marked on the right side.

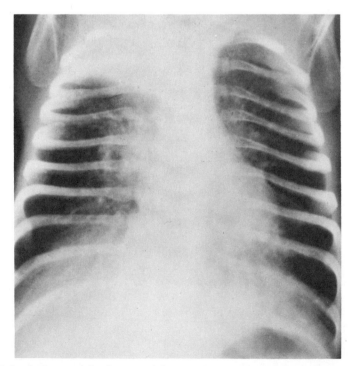

Figure 3–9   Atelectasis of right upper lobe in a one month old infant with cystic fibrosis during first episode of pulmonary involvement.

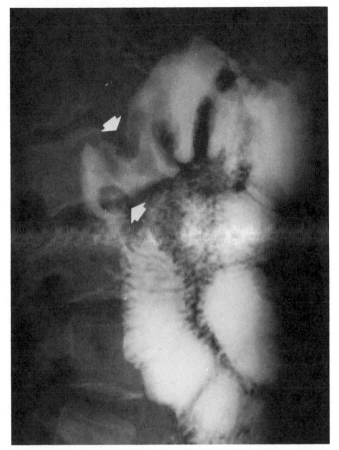

Figure 3–10 Multiple indentations in redundant duodenum *(arrows)* with coarse and irregular fold pattern in a 24 year old male with cystic fibrosis. (From Taussig, L. M., Saldino, R. M., and di Sant'Agnese, P. A.: Radiographic abnormalities of the duodenum and small bowel in cystic fibrosis of the pancreas [mucoviscidosis]. Radiology, *106*:369–376, 1973.)

PROGNOSIS

The pulmonary involvement usually dominates the clinical picture and determines the fate of the patient. The effects of pancreatic deficiency are less important to the ultimate outlook although proper attention should be paid to good nutrition and avoidance of vitamin deficiencies. Recent studies by Lapey et al. found no correlation between the degree of steatorrhea and creatorrhea secondary to pancreatic deficiency and growth, state of nutrition, or degree of pulmonary disease in 20 patients in the older age group.[26] Infants who survived the operation for meconium ileus have essentially the same outlook as do other patients with cystic fibrosis. Uncontrollable bleeding due to portal hypertension and massive loss of salt in hot weather are occasional hazards in this disease.

Although early diagnosis, early treatment, and aggressive therapy during serious pulmonary complications are effective in prolonging the life of the patient, the natural variation in the severity of cystic fibrosis is a very important factor in determining the outcome. Different penetration of an inherited disease or different genetic errors may account for some of these results.

It is essential for the patient's family and for the physician to know as accurately as possible the patient's current status and estimated prognosis. Previous scoring systems are outdated, as in the past few years the average age of patients has increased, the intestinal and other consequences of pancreatic insufficiency have become less important, while some of the pulmonary complications (massive hemoptysis, pneumothorax, and the like) have become more common. Therefore, Taussig et al. have devised a new, simple scoring system that permits objective assessment of a patient's past history, current status, and prognosis, and reflects the existing situation more precisely.[40] It is especially accurate after the age of five years.

Prognosis will improve further as diagnostic and therapeutic methods become more effective; although no precise figures are available on survival, a reasonable estimate is a mean survival rate of 15 to 20 years. Some patients with cystic fibrosis still die in infancy or early childhood, while an increasingly large number survive to the age of 20 or 30 years or longer. So-called cases of cystic fibrosis in which the patient is more than 30 years old must be regarded with suspicion unless all or substantially all criteria are met. The oldest patient meeting all these diagnostic criteria whom we are following at the present time is 42 years of age.

ADOLESCENTS AND YOUNG ADULTS

For adolescents and young adults with cystic fibrosis, rehabilitation and counseling are especially important. As a group, patients over the age of 15 to 20 years are doing better than average, perhaps because they have survived because of the relative mildness of respiratory involvement. Males have a slightly better outlook than females, a fact that is unexplained. Despite the handicap of chronic pulmonary disease, many of the older patients have been able to carry on a full-time occupation, and several are married.

The clinical picture in general is not dissimilar to that of children; the chronic pulmonary involvement is still the major problem. However, despite the lack of pancreatic enzymes and the persistence of steatorrhea and creatorrhea, patients appear to need fewer dietary restrictions with advancing age. Although retardation in growth traditionally has been considered an accompaniment of cystic fibrosis, the eventual height achieved is generally within the normal limits. In this respect it is interesting to note that growth hormone determinations have been reported as normal and there is little relation between height achieved and age at which the diagnosis was established and treatment was initiated. Certain complications are more common in the older age group than in younger children, such as abdominal obstructive complications, hemoptysis, spontaneous pneumothorax, sinusitis, and polyposis.

Both males and females have achieved the age of sexual maturation, although at times it is delayed in severely affected patients. The testicles are normally developed, all secondary sexual characteristics of both sexes are normal, and sexual function in males is normally preserved if they are not severely debilitated by their disease. The great majority of adult males with cystic fibrosis are infertile because of aspermia, but recently three cases of fertile males with cystic fibrosis have been reported as well as other cases of probable paternity.[41] It is imperative, therefore, to examine adequately all adult males with cystic fibrosis before counseling is given, and at a minimum a semen sperm count and assessment of the volume of the ejaculate should be performed. Females with cystic fibrosis are probably less fertile than normal; however, Grand et al. reported 11 pregnancies in 10 patients with cystic fibrosis resulting in normal children.[16] The normality of the offspring might be expected since the overall risk of having an affected child in the random mating of a woman with cystic fibrosis and a man of unknown genetic status is only 2.5 per cent. On the other hand, if the woman with cystic fibrosis mates with a male carrier, 50 per cent of the offspring will have the disease. As yet there is no practical method for positively identifying the heterozygotes in the population or performing an intrauterine diagnosis. Complications in the course of the mother with cystic fibrosis during pregnancy and delivery generally has paralleled the degree of pulmonary involvement. Therefore, pregnancy in cystic fibrosis is a potential hazard to the patient who has significant lung disease.

Adolescents and young adults with cystic fibrosis grow up with an unusual number of stresses related to their physical appearance, conflicts in their upbringing, and increased awareness of the future. Recent studies have shown that generally the father needs to be encouraged to become involved with the patient and that conversely the mother needs to be helped to allow the patient greater independence and to let him take more responsibility. Both parents and patients need to be aware of the benefits of an environment with free communication about cystic fibrosis.

The role of the physician is very important in helping the parents to allow the patient to develop normally emotionally, in listening to the patient's concerns, in leading group discussions of parents and at times of older patients themselves to offer practical and concrete ways to deal with daily concerns (e.g., handling separation, going to college, seeking employment, reorienting their goals more realistically). Patients (male and female) who get married need special counseling both before and after marriage to deal with common fears and frustrations. Specific concerns about sterility or adoption need to be discussed and then discussed again after the patient has had time to digest the facts. Finally, the physician should, if at all possible, encourage the patient to continue at school or work. Those who have had to stop, for whatever reason, have become lonely and depressed and have had low self-esteem.

TREATMENT

Almost all clinical complications of cystic fibrosis are secondary to obstruction of organ passages by abnormally behaving secretions. In addition, the potential threat posed in hot weather by the abnormally high sweat electrolyte levels should be appreciated. It must be realized, therefore, that until the basic defect in cystic fibrosis is uncovered, a rational, effective, and

truly lasting treatment cannot be devised. Present therapy is primarily palliative and aimed at combating, slowing, or preventing some of the secondary
complications of this disease.

Cystic fibrosis is not only a medical problem but a social one as well,
owing to the devastating effects of the emotional and financial stresses on the
family. There is need for a compassionate, helpful, understanding attitude on
the part of the physician. Every effort must be made to prevent the patient
from dominating the family emotionally and to allay the feeling of guilt and
the consequent overconcern or hostility of the parents, which are apt to develop in the case of an inherited, severe, and progressive disease. The support
of a medical social worker familiar with the problems of this disorder is desirable to allay the family's emotional response as well as to help them utilize to
the fullest the resources of the community.

A multidisciplinary approach to the manifold problems of the patient with
cystic fibrosis and his family is needed. The role of the physician should be
complemented by that of the social worker, the physical therapist, and if
needed the psychiatrist. The parents must clearly understand all the therapeutic measures to be carried out at home so that they can cooperate to the
fullest. The genetic aspects of this disease should be known by the family.

Every effort should be made to permit the child to lead as nearly normal a
life as possible. Depending on his age he should be encouraged to attend
school or work, if his condition permits; physicial activities should be restricted only as indicated by his tolerance. All routine immunizations should
be performed at appropriate ages. Because continued immunity against pertussis is desirable, booster injections are advised. Influenza vaccine and live
virus measles vaccine are recommended and should be administered to all
but the sickest patients, who may have untoward reactions.

Principles of treatment that should be kept in mind are as follows: (1) Active therapy of pulmonary involvement deserves the major emphasis. (2) Dietary measures are needed only when pancreatic deficiency is present and in
the younger age group. (3) Additional salt intake is required by all patients in
hot weather (unless contraindicated by cor pulmonale) regardless of the
pancreatic status. (4) Therapy should be individualized.[7, 18, 19, 36]

Control of Pulmonary Involvement

Since the pulmonary dysfunction is a result of both infection and the
mechanical effects of abnormally tenacious mucus that interferes with bronchial drainage, the measures to be taken are of necessity both mechanical and
antimicrobial. The two types of treatment are interdependent but can be discussed separately.

In the mechanical management are included both physical therapy to assist the patient in emptying the bronchi and aerosols that render the secretions more liquid and therefore easier to cough up. These measures should be
continued indefinitely in patients with even minimal pulmonary involvement, but have no proved merit for prophylaxis in patients with no clinical or
roentgenographic evidence of pulmonary involvement.

Physical Therapy. The physical therapy consists of the use of percussive or vibratory forces applied in the direction of the main bronchi to the affected part of the lungs. Since they are assistive to the normal cough, in older children they are accompanied by encouragement to cough vigorously. In infants the cough is favored by positioning that makes the loosened secretions stimulate reflex cough. Controlled measurement of daily sputum produced has clearly demonstrated the effectiveness of such physical therapy when applied by experienced physical therapists or specially trained nurses.[28]

Frequency, duration of treatment, and positions to be used should be individually prescribed on the basis of careful segmental auscultation of the chest and a review of the chest x-ray. Both the patient and the therapist should be comfortable during drainage. The patient's clothing should be loosened or removed, and there should be a supply of disposable tissues conveniently at hand along with a container for expectorated secretions. The patient is placed on a firm padded board or table that can be inclined to the proper angles for drainage of the middle lobe, the lingula, and the basal sections of both the lower lobes. Infants are best positioned on a pillow over the extended legs of the therapist.

After the patient is positioned, rhythmic clapping with the cupped hand is applied over the desired portion of the chest. After secretions are loosened, time is allowed for the patient to cough vigorously and raise as much sputum as possible. The procedure is repeated as long as secretions can be raised, then the patient's position is shifted appropriately and the process is repeated over other lung segments. Coughing may be assisted as necessary by thoracic squeezing and encouragement. Mechanical vibrators may be used although they are less effective than hand vibration; however, in the case of the young adult living away from home, or where assistance with physical therapy is not available, mechanical devices may be useful.

Inhalational Therapy. A distinction can be made between intermittent inhalational aerosol therapy, usually done in conjunction with bronchial drainage by physical therapy and more prolonged aerosol mist tent therapy. The object in both cases is similar: to hydrate bronchial secretions and to assist in their evacuation by physical therapy methods. To penetrate to the smaller bronchial subdivisions aerosol particles must be 0.5 to 5 μ in diameter; hand operated nebulizers do not deliver particles of small enough size. A small nebulizer such as those used in the treatment of asthma is sufficient for intermittent aerosol therapy, but for continuous nebulization in a mist tent a large-capacity nebulizer is needed. Compressed air can be used as a propellant if an appropriate pump is used. Ultrasonic nebulizers that produce a very thick mist with particles of small diameter are frequently used and are quiet to operate. Solutions generally contain 10 per cent propylene glycol in distilled water.

The schedule frequently recommended for intermittent aerosol therapy is as follows: Bronchial drainage is done for 5 to 10 minutes in the morning and evening and if needed in the middle of the day. This is followed by nebulization with the solution for 10 to 15 minutes; this sequence permits the moisture particles to penetrate farther along the bronchial tree. After nebulization the bronchial drainage is repeated for 10 to 20 minutes.

According to the severity of the condition, mist tent aerosol therapy can be given for the whole 24 hours or just for the night and naps. A large-capacity nebulizer with a compressor or an ultrasonic nebulizer should be used with the same solution mentioned earlier. Mist tent therapy is frequently used for patients who are hospitalized in acute relapse of their pulmonary disease — in conjunction, of course, with all other physical therapy and antibiotic treatments. Selected patients may use the tent at home during the sleeping hours. Since it may become quite hot inside the tent during summer, air conditioning is helpful. Prolonged mist tent therapy, unlike intermittent aerosol therapy, is not universally recommended; many physicians, especially in England, who do not use this mode of treatment have equally as good results as those who do. In addition, pulmonary function tests show only questionable improvement after the use of the mist tent, and in various studies utilizing labeled radioactive aerosolized solution, these have been found almost entirely deposited in the esophagus and stomach. Mist tent therapy has been advocated also as a prophylactic treatment to prevent the onset of pulmonary involvement, but has found limited acceptance.

Whether intermittent nebulization or mist tent therapy is used, clean equipment in good working order is essential to successful treatment and avoidance of complications. Daily or at least weekly thorough cleaning of inhalation therapy equipment decreases the chances of significant contamination, especially by *Pseudomonas aeruginosa*. Cultures of material from nebulizers should be made regularly.

Antibiotic Therapy.   Courses of intensive antibiotic therapy (usually for not less than one to three weeks) are indicated in an attempt to halt progressive deterioration during acute exacerbations of the pulmonary disease. It is important that these drugs be given for a long enough period of time and in a sufficient dosage to be effective.

The routes of administration selected depend on the severity and acuteness of the disease and on the type of antibiotic agent to be used. The choice of the antimicrobial drug should be based whenever possible on results of sputum or nasopharyngeal cultures and tests of the susceptibility to antibiotics of the bacterial pathogens isolated. The clinical situation is frequently so acute that a wait of one to three days for these reports is impossible; administration of a broad-spectrum antibiotic (frequently chloramphenicol) is then usually started, and if the presence of Pseudomonas is suspected from the greenish color of the sputum and previous culture results, gentamicin and carbenicillin may be used.

On the basis of the most frequent flora of the respiratory tract in patients with cystic fibrosis, as previously mentioned, an anti-Staphylococcus agent is usually selected to be used concomitantly with one or both of the anti-Pseudomonas drugs, gentamicin and carbenicillin.

If the child is less than eight years of age, one of the penicillins in combination with ampicillin can be used, especially as *Hemophilus influenzae* is a not infrequent inhabitant of the respiratory tract in this age group. If the patient is over eight years one of the tetracyclines usually is chosen. Chloramphenicol has been the most effective agent, but because of the risk of depression of the bone marrow and of optic neuritis its use should be avoided whenever equally efficacious antibiotics are available. If used, it should be given for only a short time (one to four weeks). Parents and patients should be forewarned to seek immediate medical advice if diminution of visual acuity appears; blood counts should be obtained at least once per week. The newer antibiotic agents mentioned have supplanted erythromycin, colistin, streptomycin, and kanamycin, which were widely used in the past, especially in view of the potential toxicity of the latter two.

Aerosol antibiotic therapy is to be regarded as a form of topical treatment and only as an adjunct to systemic administration during periods of intensive antibiotic therapy. Neomycin, polymyxin B, and colistin have not proved to be successful when administered in this manner. A variety of agents have been used by inhalation (e.g., penicillin G, nafcillin, ampicillin, gentamicin).

In most investigators' experience severe disease cannot be controlled effectively without continued antibiotic therapy for a period of months or even years. Upon admittedly, there is the risk of increasing resistance of strains of bacteria to antibiotics (especially *Staphylococcus aureus*) and as a result colonization with *Pseudomonas aeruginosa*. We favor the continued use when needed of an oral anti-Staphylococcus agent or one of the tetracyclines (if the child is older than eight years) in the smallest effective dose to prevent reappearance of symptoms. We do not favor rotation of antibiotics.

Surgical Treatment.   Because of the generalized nature of the involvement, pulmonary surgery is rarely indicated. However, a small number of patients have disease sufficiently localized so that a lobectomy or even total pneumonectomy can be performed with at least temporary success. Another indication for surgery may be repeated massive hemoptysis in which there is danger of exsanguination, provided localization of the bleeding is certain. Tracheostomy before surgery in order to permit adequate evacuation of secretions and, if necessary, assisted ventilation during the postoperative period is recommended. Seen with increasing frequency in recent years is pneumothorax, often repeated and at times bilateral. If it is unilateral and not more than 15 per cent, hospitalization and observation alone are indicated; if more than 15 per cent or bilateral, closed thoracotomy with tube insertion is performed. After two or three attacks of recurring pneumothorax, repeated instillation of a sclerosing agent is recommended (e.g., atabrine, appropriately diluted). Open thoracotomy with resection of blebs and pleural scarification or pleural stripping has been performed with some success. Vigorous physical therapy and deep tracheal suction are essential in the first few postoperative days.

Bronchoscopy, Lavage, and Aspiration.   Because of the risks involved, bronchoscopy for drainage should be attempted only in selected cases. A fiber optic bronchoscope may be of assistance in performing this procedure; however, there is not enough experience with the use of this instrument as yet. Pulmonary lavage with a total volume of saline of many liters should be performed only by an expert. It appears to be of limited use in patients with cystic fibrosis. Tracheobronchial lavage without complete filling of the lavaged lung is questionably effective; any possible benefit gained is outweighed by the risk of bronchoscopy. Deep tracheal aspiration should be used in severely ill patients, but of necessity must be limited to older individuals who cooperate with the procedure. Normal saline is a better solution for all types of lavage than acetylcysteine (Mucomyst), which may cause bronchial spasm and severe irritation of tracheobronchial mucosa.

Assisted Ventilation.   This has not been very effective and should be reserved for selected cases only. Intermittent positive pressure machines should be used only under supervision in the hospital. The experience generally has not been good with tracheostomy or nasotracheal intubation in very ill patients, as it has prolonged life for a very short period. Also, it has been found very difficult to wean the patient from the mechanical respirator.

Medication.   Expectorants are used frequently with some success; caution should be used to avoid excessive use of iodides. Antihistamines should be avoided because of their drying effect on secretions; bronchodilators are effective primarily if there is an associated allergic component. Mucolytics and enzyme preparations by inhalation and corticosteroid therapy have not been effective. Digitalis and diuretics are useful in the treatment of cor pulmonale, and oxygen therapy also may be needed. A climate change has not had strikingly beneficial effects.

Dietary Therapy

The consequences of pancreatic deficiency can be overcome readily by a diet of high protein, high caloric, and moderate fat content in conjunction with one of the pancreatic extracts. The patient's appetite should be a guide to the intake. Dietary measures are needed especially in infancy and early childhood when commercially available powdered high-protein milk preparations can be used to advantage; subsequently skim milk is advised until later childhood when homogenized milk can be given if the patient tolerates it. Soybean milk preparations should not be used. Medium chain triglyceride supplementation has been used with some success. Anabolic steroids are useful to increase appetite and promote weight gain, but only in short, repeated courses. There is no substantial evidence that they improve respiratory disease, as has been claimed. If lactase deficiency is present and symptomatic it may be necessary to limit the dietary lactose intake.

Dietary measures appear to become less necessary with advancing age, although individual variations are found. In general, the nutritional state is more closely correlated with the severity of the pulmonary infection than with pancreatic function.

Treatment of Abnormal Salt Loss.   Additional sodium chloride (2 to 4 gm per day) should be given to all patients in hot weather (regardless of pancreatic status), provided cor pulmonale does not contraindicate it. Massive salt depletion through sweating in hot weather may present a real medical emergency. As much as 10 ml per kilogram of isotonic saline solution intravenously in 15 minutes may be needed in patients whose extracellular fluid volume is severely depleted and who are in imminent danger of cardiovascular collapse. This should be followed by appropriate fluid replacement therapy.

Other Treatment

Intestinal Obstruction.   As previously mentioned, several intestinal obstructive complications occur at various ages. The most common is meconium ileus, which usually requires surgical intervention.[32, 34] Surgical procedures are described in detail in the appropriate texts, but the Mikulicz resection is the procedure of choice in many places. It is important to realize that in one third of the cases volvulus occurs because of the heavy intestinal loop filled with abnormal meconium proximal to the obstruction itself. In properly selected cases Gastrografin enemas have been successful in relieving the obstruction and thus avoiding surgery. Nutramigen, which contains a casein hydrolysate, or Portagen, in which medium chain triglycerides replace other fats, has been used successfully in the first few days or weeks postoperatively. Meconium ileus equivalent (intestinal obstruction in the older age group) and intussusception often result in incomplete obstruction and may respond to reduction by barium enema in the case of intussusception or to repeated high colonic enemas in the case of partial obstruction. Mucomyst orally has been used often with satisfactory results, and Gastrografin enemas also offer hope of success. In intussusception, time is of the essence in starting treatment, because if adhesions already have formed surgery will be inevitable. Fecal masses are usually passed spontaneously; constipation should be avoided by a moderate increase in dietary fat intake, a decrease in pancreatic enzyme therapy, and administration of an agent such as Colace (50 mg twice a day). Rectal prolapse responds well to medical and dietary treatment, and surgical intervention is rarely, if ever, needed.

Cirrhosis and Portal Hypertension.   In multilobular biliary cirrhosis and portal hypertension, melena and hematemesis may require the performance of surgical vein shunting procedures. If possible, it is preferable to wait until a child has full growth before these are attempted.

Polyposis.   Repeated polypectomies may be required for symptomatic nasal polyps. Mucoceles respond to surgical drainage. Associated allergic conditions should be treated as in other patients.

Glucose Intolerance and Diabetes.   In the occasional case of coincidental genetic diabetes mellitus, therapy should follow the same lines as in any other patient with this condition, keeping in mind the additional problems and dietary limitations of patients with cystic fibrosis. More common in this disease is severe glucose intolerance with glycosuria in which dietary measures and at times oral antidiabetic agents are usually sufficient, although some patients require the addition of insulin.

SUMMARY

Cystic fibrosis is a generalized hereditary disease of children, adolescents, and young adults. It is characterized clinically by the triad of chronic pulmonary disease, pancreatic deficiency, and abnormally high levels of sweat electrolytes. Cystic fibrosis is the most common semilethal genetic defect in Caucasian populations. It is transmitted as a recessive trait, and while its chief manifestations are in the exocrine glands, there is some evidence that all body cells have the unknown basic defect. It was thought at first to be a disorder of glycoprotein metabolism; this has not been substantiated as yet by chemical or immunological studies. Recently a number of different nonspecific defects have been found in fibroblasts in tissue culture obtained from biopsies from heterozygotes and homozygotes with this disease. Two circulating so-called "cystic fibrosis factors" have been found, one that is ciliotoxic and present in the serum of both heterozygotes and homozygotes, and another that inhibits sodium reabsorption and may give a reasonable explanation of the sweat electrolyte defect in these patients.

Most clinical manifestations of cystic fibrosis are secondary to obstruction of organ passages. The most serious involvement is in the lungs, leading in time to severe and eventually fatal obstructive pulmonary disease. Pancreatic achylia is present in 85 per cent of patients and is not difficult to manage by suitable replacement and dietary therapy. Intestinal obstructive complications (including meconium ileus) frequently necessitate surgical intervention. More difficult to treat is the occasional case of diffuse biliary cirrhosis, which frequently gives rise to the complications of portal hypertension.

The discovery of elevated sodium and chloride concentrations in the sweat in this disease has furnished the most convenient nearly specific objective test to establish the diagnosis, provided one or more of the clinical features of the disease are present. Various other chemical and roentgenographic tests are described.

Prognosis has improved in recent years because of early diagnosis, early treatment, and appropriate therapy. The natural variation in the severity of cystic fibrosis, however, is a very important factor in determining the outcome. Because so many patients are living into adolescence and young adult life, new problems are arising in the types of complications that are seen as well as in the counseling and psychological and psychiatric management of these older patients.

The pulmonary dysfunction in this disease remains the chief clinical problem. Therapy has progressed to better management and some slowing of the process, but it remains palliative. Treatment combines physical and inhalational methods of clearing obstructive bronchial secretions with the judicious use of antibiotics to combat infection.

As with many genetic defects, suitable tests to identify asymptomatic carriers of the disease and for antenatal diagnosis would be a major step toward understanding and some degree of control. Such a finding, along with other basic investigations, might also point the way toward more effective therapy.

References

1. Andersen, D. H.: Cystic fibrosis of pancreas and its relation to celiac disease; clinical and pathological study. Am. J. Dis. Child., 56:344–399, 1938.
2. Biggar, W. D., Holmes, B., and Good, R. A.: Opsonic defect in patients with cystic fibrosis of the pancreas. Proc. Natl. Acad. Sci., 68:1716–1719, 1971.
3. Boat, T. F.: Unpublished observations.
4. Danes, B. S., and Bearn, A. G.: Cystic fibrosis: Distribution of mucopolysaccharides in fibroblast cultures. Biochem. Biophys. Res. Commun., 36:919–924, 1969.

5. Darling, R. C., di Sant'Agnese, P. A., Perera, G. A., and Andersen, D. H.: Electrolyte abnormalities of the sweat in fibrocystic disease of the pancreas. Am. J. Med. Sci., 225:67–70, 1953.
6. di Sant'Agnese, P. A.: Cystic fibrosis (mucoviscidosis). Am. Fam. Physician, 7:102–111, 1973.
7. di Sant'Agnese, P. A.: The pancreas. In Nelson, W., Vaughan, V. C., and McKay, R. J. (eds.): *Textbook of Pediatrics.* 10th Ed. Philadelphia, W. B. Saunders Co., In preparation.
8. di Sant'Agnese, P. A., and Blanc, P. A.: Distinctive type of biliary cirrhosis of liver associated with cystic fibrosis of the pancreas: recognition through signs of portal hypertension. Pediatrics, 18:387–409, 1956.
9. di Sant'Agnese, P. A., and Lepore, M. J.: Involvement of abdominal organs in cystic fibrosis of the pancreas. Gastroenterology, 40:64–74, 1961.
10. di Sant'Agnese, P. A., and Powell, G. F.: Eccrine sweat defect in cystic fibrosis of pancreas (mucoviscidosis). Ann. N.Y. Acad. Sci., 93:555–599, 1962.
11. di Sant'Agnese, P. A., and Talamo, R. C.: Pathogenesis and physiopathology of cystic fibrosis of the pancreas. New Engl. J. Med., 277:1287–1295, 1343–1352, 1399–1408, 1967.
12. di Sant'Agnese, P. A., Darling, R. C., Perera, G. A., and Shea, E.: Abnormal electrolyte composition of sweat in cystic fibrosis of pancreas: Clinical significance and relationship to disease. Pediatrics, 12:549–563, 1953.
13. Falchuk, Z. M., and Taussig, L. M.: IgA synthesis by jejunal biopsies from patients with cystic fibrosis and hereditary pancreatitis. Pediatrics, 51:10–54, 1973.
14. Fanconi, G., Uehliner, E., and Knauer, C.: Das Coeliakiesyndrom bei angeborener zytischer Pankreasfibromatose und Bronchiektasien. Wien. Med. Wochenschr., 86:753–756, 1936.
15. Farber, S.: Some organic digestive disturbances in early life. J. Michigan Med. Soc., 44:587–594, 1945.
16. Grand, R. J., Talamo, R. C., di Sant'Agnese, P. A., and Schwartz, R. H.: Pregnancy in cystic fibrosis of pancreas. J.A.M.A., 195:993–1000, 1966.
17. Gugler, E., Pallavicini, J. C., Swerdlow, H., and di Sant'Agnese, P. A.: Role of calcium in submaxillary saliva of patients with cystic fibrosis. J. Pediatr., 71:585–588, 1967.
18. *Guide to Diagnosis and Management of Cystic Fibrosis.* National Cystic Fibrosis Research Foundation, Atlanta, 1971.
19. *Guide to Drug Therapy in Patients with Cystic Fibrosis.* Huang, N. N. (ed.). National Cystic Fibrosis Research Foundation, Atlanta, 1972.
20. Hadorn, B., Johnson, P. G., and Anderson, C. M.: Pancreozymin secretin test of exocrine pancreatic function in cystic fibrosis and the significance of the result for the pathogenesis of the disease. Can. Med. Assoc. J., 98:377–385, 1968.
21. Handwerger, S., Roth, J., Gorden, P., di Sant'Agnese, P. A., et al.: Glucose intolerance in cystic fibrosis. New Engl. J. Med., 281:451–461, 1969.
22. Horton, C. R., Cole, W. Q., and Bader, H.: Depressed (Ca^{++})-transport ATPase in cystic fibrosis erythrocytes. Biochem. Biophys. Res. Commun., 40:505–509, 1970.
23. Kaiser, D., Drack, E., and Rossi, E.: Inhibition of net sodium transport in single sweat glands by sweat of patients with cystic fibrosis of the pancreas. Pediatr. Res., 5:167–172, 1971.
24. Kattwinkel, J., Taussig, L. M., Statland, B. E., and Verter, J. I.: The effects of age on alkaline phosphatase and other serologic liver function tests in normal subjects and patients with cystic fibrosis. J. Pediatr., 82:234–242, 1973.
25. Klagsbrun, M., and Farrell, P. M.: Methylation of RNA by fibroblasts from normal humans and patients with cystic fibrosis. In Mangos, J. A., and Talamo, R. C. (eds.): *Fundamental Problems of Cystic Fibrosis and Related Diseases.* Miami, Symposia Specialists, 1973.
26. Lapey, A., Kattwinkel, J., di Sant'Agnese, P. A., and Laster, L.: Steatorrhea and azotorrhea and their relation to growth and nutrition in adolescents and young adults with cystic fibrosis. In preparation.
27. Lobeck, C. C.: Cystic fibrosis. In Stanbury, J. B., Wyngaarden, J. B., and Fredrickson, D. S. (eds.): *The Metabolic Basis of Inherited Disease.* 3rd Ed. New York, McGraw-Hill Book Co., 1972.
28. Lorin, M. I., and Denning, C. R.: Evaluation of postural drainage by measurement of sputum volume and consistency. Am. J. Phys. Med., 50:215–219, 1971.
29. Mangos, J. A., and McSherry, N. R.: Studies on the mechanism of inhibition of sodium transport in cystic fibrosis of the pancreas. Pediatr. Res., 2:378–384, 1968.
30. Mangos, J. A., McSherry, N. R., and Banke, P. J.: A sodium transport inhibitory factor in the saliva of patients with cystic fibrosis of the pancreas. Pediatr. Res., 1:436–442, 1967.
31. Matalon, R., and Dorfman, A.: Acid mucopolysaccharides in cultured fibroblasts of cystic fibrosis of the pancreas. Biochem. Biophys. Res. Commun., 33:954–958, 1968.
32. McPartlin, J. F., Dickson, J. A. S., and Swain, V. A. J.: Meconium ileus. Immediate and long-term survival. Arch. Dis. Child., 47:207–210, 1972.
33. Mullins, F., Talamo, R., and di Sant'Agnese, P. A.: Late intestinal complications of cystic fibrosis. J.A.M.A., 192:741–746, 1965.

34. Santulli, T. V.: Meconium ileus. In Mustard, W. T., Ravitch, M. M., Snyder, W. H., Jr., Welch, K. J., and Benson, C. D. (eds.): *Pediatric Surgery.* 2nd Ed. Chicago, Year Book Medical Publishers, 1969.
35. Schulz, I. J.: Micropuncture studies of the sweat formation in cystic fibrosis patients. J. Clin. Invest., *48*:1470–1477, 1969.
36. Shwachman, H., and Khaw, Kon-Taik: Cystic fibrosis. In Shirkey, H. C. (ed.): *Pediatric Therapy.* 4th Ed. St. Louis, C. V. Mosby Co., 1972.
37. Smith, F. R., Underwood, B. A., Denning, C. R., et al.: Depressed plasma retinol-binding protein levels in cystic fibrosis. J. Lab. Clin. Med., *80*:423–433, 1972.
38. Spock, A., Heick, H. M., Cress, H., et al.: Abnormal serum factor in patients with cystic fibrosis of the pancreas. Pediatr. Res., *1*:173–177, 1967.
39. Taussig, L. M., Saldino, R. M., and di Sant'Agnese, P. A.: Radiographic abnormalities of the duodenum and small bowel in cystic fibrosis of the pancreas (mucoviscidosis). Radiology, *106*:369–376, 1973.
40. Taussig, L. M., Kattwinkel, J., Friedewald, W. T., and di Sant'Agnese, P. A.: A new prognostic score and clinical evaluation system for cystic fibrosis. J. Pediatr., *82*:380–390, 1973.
41. Taussig, L. M., Lobeck, C. C., di Sant'Agnese, P. A., et al.: Fertility in males with cystic fibrosis. New Engl. J. Med., *287*:586–589, 1972.
42. Underwood, B. A., and Denning, C. R.: Blood and liver concentrations of vitamins A and E in children with cystic fibrosis. Pediatr. Res., *6*:26–31, 1972.
43. Wiesmann, U. N., and Neufeld, E. F.: Metabolism of sulfated mucopolysaccharides in cultured fibroblasts from cystic fibrosis patients. J. Pediatr., *77*:685–690, 1970.
44. Wiesmann, U. N., Boat, T. F., and di Sant'Agnese, P. A.: Flow rates and electrolytes in minor salivary gland saliva in normal subjects and patients with cystic fibrosis. Lancet, *2*:510–512, 1972.
45. Wright, S. W., and Morton, N. E.: Genetic studies on cystic fibrosis in Hawaii. Am. J. Hum. Genet., *20*:157–169, 1968.

Chapter 4

Hemoglobinopathies

by *James A. Wolff, M.D.*

The hemoglobinopathies comprise a number of genetic disorders, many of which are characterized by chronic anemia, life-long incapacity, and shortened longevity. Some of them are the result of genetic structural defects of hemoglobin, as found in sickle cell anemia, while others, the thalassemia syndromes, are caused by genetic defects in hemoglobin synthesis.

BIOCHEMICAL ABNORMALITIES AND PATHOPHYSIOLOGY

Sickle cell anemia was first described by Herrick in 1910, but it was not until 1949 that Pauling first demonstrated that the disease is due to an abnormality in the hemoglobin of affected individuals.[3] As a result of this observation, intense interest developed in the study of the chemical structure, biological activity, and genetic nature of this hemoglobin, which was named S hemoglobin. It was also shown at this time that the globin portion of normal hemoglobin in adults contains two pairs of polypeptide chains, labeled α and β, so that the structure of the globin of normal adult hemoglobin may be designated $\alpha_2 \beta_2$.[9] Ingram then demonstrated that the abnormal electrophoretic mobility of S hemoglobin is the result of a mutation that has produced a single amino acid substitution, valine for glutamic acid, at the sixth position of the β globin chain.[4] The designation for S hemoglobin is $\alpha_2\beta_2{}^S$.

Elucidation of the abnormality present in S hemoglobin led to the detection of a large number of other hemoglobins with amino acid alterations,

63

primarily in the α or β globin chains, which produce alteration in electrophoretic mobility and in some of them chronic anemia as well. Of these, C hemoglobin is next in importance and frequency to S hemoglobin. Much less common are structural defects of the globin chains that cause increased susceptibility of the hemoglobin to irreversible oxidation (hemoglobin Zürich, hemoglobin Köln), increased oxygen affinity (hemoglobin Chesapeake, hemoglobin Yakima), and increased oxidation of hemoglobin to methemoglobin (hemoglobin M).

Thalassemia was first described in 1925 by Cooley.[2] Following the discovery of the abnormality of the hemoglobin in sickle cell disease, it was postulated that thalassemia, another type of chronic hemolytic anemia, would prove also to be due to a mutation leading to alteration in the chemical structure of one of the globin chains. It is now known that this is not the case; rather, it is caused by a mutation affecting messenger RNA that suppresses β globin chain synthesis. The excess α chains form tetramers (α_4), which precipitate, producing inclusions in bone marrow nucleated red cells and reticulocytes. Hemolysis occurs as a result of these changes, with destruction of erythrocytes in the spleen. Mutation with suppression of α chain synthesis is found less frequently. In such individuals, tetramers of β chains (β_4) are formed, which are responsible for rapid electrophoretic mobility of the hemoglobin. This hemoglobin has been named hemoglobin H. Normal fetal hemoglobin has been shown to comprise two α chains identical to those in adult hemoglobin and two γ chains in place of two β chains. When a mutation involves the α chains of fetal hemoglobin, tetramers of γ chains (γ_4) are formed. This hemoglobin is known as Bart's hemoglobin.

In addition to A hemoglobin and a very small amount of F hemoglobin, normal hemoglobin, except in very young infants, contains another minor component known as A_2 hemoglobin, containing two α chains and two δ chains $(\alpha_2 \delta_2)$.[5] An increased percentage of A_2 hemoglobin is characteristic of individuals who are heterozygous for the β chain type of mutation in thalassemia.

SICKLE CELL DISEASE

Sickle cell disease (S-S disease) is characterized by chronic hemolytic anemia starting in early infancy and, at unpredictable intervals, by exacerbations of symptoms, known as crises. The individual with sickle cell disease is homozygous for the gene for S hemoglobin. S hemoglobin is found in approximately 10 per cent of black individuals in the United States and in a smaller percentage of the Spanish-speaking population of Puerto Rican extraction in this country. Homozygosity for S hemoglobin occurs in one out of 400 blacks. The disease is rarely found in Caucasians.

Symptoms

The crises of sickle cell disease are of three or, possibly, four types. The commonest is caused by vascular occlusion by sickled cells leading to infarction in various tissues. This is known as the symptomatic or thrombotic crisis. Thrombotic crises may be triggered by a number of stimuli, including complicating infections, dehydration, acidosis, or exposure to lowered oxygen tension. Many of them appear to have no demonstrable precipitating factor. Vascular occlusions may occur in any tissue or organ, but present most commonly as painful crises involving the extremities or abdomen. Fever, leukocytosis, and bone pain are frequent accompaniments of the painful symptomatic crisis. In infants and young children, infarction in the small bones of the hands and feet produce painful swollen hands and feet, the "hand-foot syndrome." Radiographic evidence of infarction can be found. With advancing age, fixed specific gravity of the urine occurs as a result of inability to concentrate the urine. Renal papillary necrosis caused by sickling in the kidney papillae may lead to necrosis and consequent hematuria. Thrombotic lesions occur in the cerebral vessels with resultant infarcts and in some instances subarachnoid hemorrhage. Sickling in the hepatic sinusoids may cause progressive liver damage, characterized by hepatomegaly, elevated direct and indirect bilirubin levels, and abnormal liver function tests. Infarctions in the spleen are extremely common, producing fibrosis and shrinkage of this organ, so that in older children the spleen is not often palpable.

Sequestration of sickled erythrocytes in the spleen, as a consequence of the rigidity of these cells as they pass through the splenic sinusoids, results in the second type of sickle cell crisis. The spleen may enlarge rapidly, with concomitant rapid lowering of the hemoglobin level. During this form of crisis, the reticulocyte count remains elevated. As described by Pearson, chronic sequestration and infarction in the spleen are responsible for the development of a functional defect, demonstrated by inability to visualize the spleen with labeled technetium.[8]

Sudden marrow aplasia is responsible for the third type of sickle cell crisis. This event may be precipitated by a viral infection, but frequently has no apparent cause. The spleen does not enlarge, and the reticulocyte count falls to extremely low levels, differentiating this type of crisis from acute splenic sequestration.

Hyperhemolysis has been described by some authors as a fourth cause of sickle cell crisis, but it is doubtful that a true hemolytic crisis occurs.

The chronic leg ulcers found in adult patients with S-S disease are rarely seen in childhood. Other manifestations of intravascular sickling and occlusion, however, such as dilatation and tortuosity of retinal vessels, are not uncommon. Many children develop cardiac murmurs, frequently difficult to differentiate from those of rheumatic fever, although rheumatic fever is uncommon in children with sickle cell anemia. Joint swelling, simulating both rheumatic fever and rheumatoid arthritis, also occurs. Bone infections, localized to areas of ischemic infarction, primarily with Salmonella or other gram-negative bacteria, occur with greater frequency than in the normal childhood population. Children with S-S disease, especially those in the younger age groups, are also more susceptible to pneumococcal pneumonia and septicemia. Increased incidence of Mycoplasma pneumonia has been described recently. Biliary stones secondary to chronic hemolysis occur and occasionally produce cholecystitis or cholangitis.

Laboratory Findings

These are variable. The majority of subjects with sickle cell disease have hemoglobin levels in the range of 6.5 to 8.5 gm per 100 ml, but levels as high as 10.0 to 11.0 gm per 100 ml may be encountered and some patients may have a persistent level of less than 6.5 gm per 100 ml. Sickled cells, although frequently absent, may be seen in the peripheral blood smears. The reticulocyte count is characteristically high, usually considerably above 10 per cent. Howell-Jolly bodies, small inclusion bodies in erythrocytes, occur as a result of functional failure of the spleen. Leukocytosis in the range of 15,000 to 20,000 with a predominance of granulocytes is the rule. The erythrocyte sedimentation rate is low even in the presence of infection, but occasionally may be somewhat elevated during the course of an infection or crisis.

The presence of S hemoglobin may be demonstrated by a number of laboratory techniques. A simple solubility test (Sickledex) has replaced the more cumbersome microscopic examination of red cells mixed with a reducing agent, such as sodium bisulfite, or by examination of a sealed coverslip preparation. Definitive identification, however, of S-S disease is possible only by electrophoresis. Electrophoresis of the hemolysate on cellulose acetate or on paper will show the presence of a single spot for a hemoglobin that migrates less rapidly than A hemoglobin. As each parent must be heterozygous for S hemoglobin, electrophoretic studies of each parent will show the presence of a larger amount of A hemoglobin and smaller quantity of S hemoglobin.

Roentgen Findings

Radiological changes result from both hyperplasia of the red cell precursors in the bone marrow and ischemic bone necrosis. Thinning of the cortices, widening of the medullary cavities, and accentuation of the trabeculae are produced by increased marrow activity, sometimes leading to the "hair-on-end" appearance of the skull bones. Bone infarction, on the other hand, is responsible for sclerotic and periosteal lesions.

Treatment

As of this writing, the management of sickle cell disease remains unsatisfactory. Until recently, efforts have been directed almost entirely toward the prevention and alleviation of sickle cell crises. Some degree of prevention may be obtained by avoidance of dehydration, acidosis, and exposure to lowered oxygen tension. Several reports of successful prophylaxis of recurrent crises by means of periodic exchange or simple transfusions have appeared. The value of this approach has not been well established and may be more than overbalanced by the hazards of viral hepatitis, transfusion reactions, and possible iron overloading.

Painful vasoocclusive crises, caused by intravascular sludging and increased viscosity, respond in varying degree to adequate hydration and avoidance of exposure to cold. Alkalinization with sodium bicarbonate or sodium citrate, administered intravenously or orally, have produced questionable results. Provision of high ambient oxygen concentrations has not been shown to be clearly beneficial. Plasma expanders, such as low molecular weight dextran, do not seem to be superior to simple hydration. As intravascular coagulation is not responsible for the initiation of the symptoms, the use of anticoagulants is not indicated. Administration of packed red cells as a simple transfusion or as part of a modified exchange transfusion, by lowering the percentage of cells containing S hemoglobin, has, in our experience, proved to be helpful in shortening the length of a severe and prolonged painful symptomatic crisis.

Aplastic crises are frequently life-threatening. Immediate transfusion of packed red cells should be given if the hemoglobin level has dropped rapidly in an aplastic crisis. Splenic sequestration crises also require transfusions and, if recurrent, should be treated by splenectomy.

Control of infection is extremely important. Antibacterial therapy, preferably with penicillin, should be started if pneumonia is suspected, even though the infiltrate may also resemble a pulmonary infarct. Exclusion of Mycoplasma infection, for which erythromycin is the drug of choice, must be carried out.

Extreme hematopoietic activity as a result of hemolysis may lead to folic acid deficiency. If the folate level is low, administration of folic acid is indicated.

In the last several years attempts to control the symptoms of S-S disease have centered on the reversal or inhibition of the sickling phenomenon.[1, 6] It has been proposed that urea, by disrupting hydrophobic bonds that form when deoxygenated S hemoglobin gels within the erythrocyte, should be beneficial to subjects with S-S disease. As urea is rapidly cleared by the kidneys, the high concentration necessary to disrupt hydrophobic bonds is difficult to attain and maintain in vivo. It has been shown that cyanate is in equilibrium with urea and forms covalent bonds with several functional groups of protein. In vivo studies have demonstrated that incubation of cells containing S hemoglobin with sodium or potassium cyanate inhibited sickling upon deoxygenation at 6 mm Hg of oxygen. This reaction, moreover, is irreversible. When administered, cyanate-treated cells from patients with S-S disease demonstrated a life span longer than that of untreated cells from the same subjects. Although it is not yet possible to define the therapeutic role of cyanate in S-S disease, this approach represents the first attempt to alter the genetic defect by modifying the abnormal protein.

SICKLE CELL TRAIT

The erythrocyte of the individual doubly heterozygous for S hemoglobin and A hemoglobin has 20 to 45 per cent S hemoglobin, with a normal level of F hemoglobin. The condition is known as sickle cell trait, ordinarily an asymptomatic state. Rarely infarction in the spleen, kidney, or brain may occur, especially when the affected individual is exposed to very low oxygen tension.

OTHER ELECTROPHORETICALLY ABNORMAL HEMOGLOBINS

A large number of hemoglobins, other than S hemoglobin, with electrophoretic abnormality have now been described. The most important of these is C hemoglobin, which is found in approximately 2 per cent of blacks in the United States. The abnormality is due to substitution of lysine for glutamic acid at the sixth position of the β globin chain. The blood smear of affected subjects shows an increased percentage of target cells. The patient who is heterozygous does not have clinical disease, while the homozygous condition is characterized by mild hemolytic anemia. Individuals doubly heterozygous for C hemoglobin and S hemoglobin (hemoglobin C-S disease) have a lesser degree of anemia than do those with S-S disease, but may be subject also to severe vasoocclusive crises. Aseptic necrosis of the femoral heads and osteomyelitis due to Salmonella have been reported to occur more often in C-S disease than in S-S disease. Other abnormal hemoglobins, all of which have a considerably lesser gene frequency than either S hemoglobin or C hemoglobin, may cause mild anemia because of an increased tendency to oxidation (hemoglobin Zürich, hemoglobin Köln) or produce methemoglobinemia (hemoglobin M).

CLASSIC THALASSEMIA MAJOR

Since the original description of thalassemia major (homozygous beta thalassemia) by Cooley and Lee in 1925, much has been learned about its pathogenesis, but considerably less advance has been made in its successful management.[2] The affected individual is homozygous for the gene for β thalassemia. The characteristic finding is a chronic hemolytic anemia occurring within the first year of life or occasionally slightly later. Unlike the anemia of sickle cell disease, there is almost no tendency for a state of equilibrium of blood production and destruction to become established. As a consequence, periodic blood transfusion is required to maintain life at even a suboptimal state of activity. Prior to the initiation of transfusions, as a rule, more than 50 per cent of hemoglobin is F hemoglobin, with levels as high as 80 per cent not unusual. A_2 hemoglobin is present in normal or decreased amount.

Symptoms

As the disease progresses, there is increasing enlargement of the spleen and liver. Splenomegaly becomes massive after a varying period of time but usually within the first few years of life. As a result of increased erythroid hyperplasia, expansion of the medullary cavity and thinning of the cortices takes place in the bones. This produces skeletal changes characterized by prominent cheek bones, prominence of the upper jaw, and widened intraocular space, the so-called "Cooley's facies." Thickening of the bones of the skull leads to frontal bossing and frequently a "hot cross bun" configuration of the skull. Older children, particularly those whose hemoglobin levels have not been well maintained by transfusions, are subject to fractures from minor trauma. Linear growth generally is adequate until the early teens when retardation in growth usually occurs. Pubertal development is severely retarded. Toward the end of the first or in the early part of the second decade, cardiovascular complications become prominent, characterized by episodes of arrhythmia, pericarditis, or congestive heart failure. The overwhelming majority of affected individuals in the past have died of cardiovascular disease by the age of 20.

Laboratory Findings

As mentioned earlier, the percentage of F hemoglobin is increased and the A_2 hemoglobin level is normal or decreased. The distribution of F hemoglobin in the erythrocytes is heterogeneous. Morphologically, marked red cell anisocytosis, poikilocytosis, and hypochromia are characteristic. Target cells, ovalocytes, and fragmented cells appear frequently. Basophilic stippling may be seen. The mean corpuscular volume and mean corpuscular hemoglobin are both greatly reduced.

Following splenectomy, large numbers of nucleated red cells and Howell-Jolly bodies appear in the circulation. The reticulocyte count is moderately elevated, averaging 5 to 6 per cent. Leukopenia and thrombocytopenia may occur as a result of overactivity of an enlarged spleen. The osmotic fragility of the erythrocytes in hypotonic saline solutions is reduced. The bilirubin level may be slightly elevated. The life span of the erythrocyte is moderately reduced both in the patient and in the circulation of normal recipients, indicating an intracorpuscular defect.

Roentgen Findings

The entire skeleton may be affected to some degree by the characteristic thinning of the cortices and widening and osteoporotic changes of the spongiosa. These abnormalities are seen especially in the small bones of the hands and in the femora. Widening of the diploic space of the skull bones is common and in some cases a "hair-on-end" appearance, due to the radial arrangement of the spongiosa, is seen. The paranasal sinuses may be encroached upon or obliterated as a result of bone marrow hyperplasia. All these changes increase with advancing age unless efforts are made to maintain a high hemoglobin level with blood transfusions. Late in the course of the disease there is a tendency for sclerotic changes to appear in some subjects.

Treatment

Prior to the last decade most children with classic thalassemia major were treated with blood transfusions at intervals necessary to maintain hemoglobin levels above 7.0 gm per 100 ml. Transfusion at levels considerably higher than 7.0 gm per 100 ml were avoided because of the fear of exaggeration of the iron overloading that these patients experience. Iron deposition in the heart as a consequence of periodic blood transfusions was considered to be solely responsible for the cardiovascular problems that were known to lead to death early in life. Increasing experience, however, has shown that some patients who have died of chronic congestive heart failure or other cardiac difficulties have had considerably less cardiac hemosiderosis than expected. This has led to the concept that cardiovascular complications may stem also from chronic tissue hypoxia, or more likely from a combination of both iron overload and hypoxia. Experimental evidence for the latter hypothesis has been advanced. For the past 10 years, in our clinic as well as in many others, treatment policy has provided blood transfusions as often as necessary to maintain the hemoglobin level persistently at 10.0 gm per 100 ml or more. Maintenance of these high levels necessitates transfusions at more frequent intervals, usually about every third week. It is apparent already that such "hypertransfusion" programs lead to lessening of the skeletal changes and organ enlargement that result from hyperactivity of the bone marrow and extramedullary hematopoiesis. Evidence is also accumulating that the decelerated linear growth noted in later childhood may be reversed.

The increased requirement for administration of blood transfusions necessary to maintain higher hemoglobin levels results in an increased degree of iron deposition in the tissues. In an attempt to minimize this potential toxicity, a number of iron-chelating agents have been investigated recently. Some of these have been discarded because of their ability to chelate and deplete the body of other ions, notably calcium and magnesium. Desferrioxamine (Desferal), however, has the unique capacity to bind iron only and to increase the urinary iron excretion of iron-overloaded subjects manyfold. Despite its hypothetical promise, experience has already shown that negative iron balances cannot be attained easily when frequent transfusions are also administered. Our experience, as well as that of others, has indicated that administration of desferrioxamine to patients already overloaded with iron has not been valuable. Whether the use of desferrioxamine in infancy, when transfusions are first begun, to minimize excessive iron deposition, may be of more value in preventing or postponing cardiac complications is now under investigation. The role of maintenance of high hemoglobin levels, without efforts to increase the urinary excretion of iron, in preventing early cardiac fatalities also cannot be evaluated at the present time.

With increasing splenomegaly, manifestations of hypersplenism develop. This is demonstrated most obviously by an increasing transfusion requirement. Numerous studies have shown a progressive decrease in donor red cell life span with increased erythrocyte destruction by the spleen. Leukopenia and thrombocytopenia may also occur. Splenectomy performed at this time will result in a definite decrease in blood transfusion requirement, because of a return to normal of the donor erythrocyte half life. Splenectomy may also be indicated in a minority of children prior to demonstrated increased splenic activity because of the incapacitating effects of a massively enlarged spleen. Because of the possible risk of overwhelming infection following splenectomy, penicillin prophylaxis for several years should be considered. The mortality rate from postsplenectomy infection in thalassemia has been much lower in our clinic than that reported by some others.

Marked erythroid hyperplasia in the bone marrow may result in overutilization of folic acid. Maintenance therapy with oral folic acid has been recommended by some investigators, but we have limited its use to children in whom it has been shown that serum folate levels are low.

THALASSEMIA MINOR OR TRAIT

The individual who possesses only one gene for thalassemia (heterozygous beta thalassemia) is rarely symptomatic. Frequently the condition is first detected when homozygous thalassemia has been diagnosed in an offspring. The characteristic finding is an elevation in the percentage of A_2 hemoglobin above the maximum normal level of 3.3 per cent. Subjects heterozygous for β thalassemia have higher levels than normal persons, in the range of 4.2 to 6.8 per cent. F hemoglobin levels are normal or only slightly increased, rarely over 5 per cent. Erythrocyte morphology is marked by hypochromia, microcytosis, anisocytosis, and poikilocytosis of varying degree but always less than that seen in the homozygous patient. Basophilic stippling is often prominent. The osmotic fragility of the erythrocytes in hypotonic saline solutions is decreased.

As most individuals have mild anemia or an excessively elevated red cell count despite a normal hemoglobin level, with red cell morphology suggestive of mild iron deficiency anemia, iron therapy is frequently prescribed. The importance of establishing the correct diagnosis is therefore particularly important, as frequent iron administration to these individuals may lead to iron overload. The importance of the lack of benefit from any form of therapy should be stressed.

OTHER THALASSEMIA SYNDROMES

Rate-limiting genetic defects of hemoglobin synthesis may involve globin chains other than the polypeptide chains. A defect involving the alpha chain is known as alpha thalassemia. Two such genes have been identified, α_1 and α_2. Heterozygosity for α_1 results in α thalassemia trait, whereas homozygosity leads to death in utero due to hydrops fetalis. The doubly heterozygous combination of α_1 and α_2 thalassemia produces the disease known as hemoglobin H thalassemia.

Either α thalassemia or β thalassemia may be found in a doubly heterozygous state with another abnormal hemoglobin such as S hemoglobin. The β thalassemia gene interacts with the gene for S hemoglobin, augmenting the amount of S hemoglobin found, whereas the α thalassemia gene does not produce such interaction. The individual doubly heterozygous for β thalassemia and S hemoglobin genes has the disease known as S thalassemia. This is a chronic hemolytic anemia resembling S-S disease but of less severity. Other combinations of double heterozygosity, which are less frequent, may be characterized by chronic anemia.

References

1. Cerami, A.: Cyanate as an inhibitor of red-cell sickling. N. Engl. J. Med., 287:807, 1972.
2. Cooley, T. B., and Lee, P.: A series of cases of splenomegaly in children with anemia and peculiar bone changes. Trans. Am. Ped. Soc., 37:29, 1925.
3. Herrick, J. B.: Peculiar elongated and sickle-shaped red blood corpuscles in a case of severe anemia. Arch. Intern. Med., 6:517, 1910.
4. Ingram, V. M.: Gene mutations in human hemoglobin; the chemical difference between normal and sickle cell hemoglobin. Nature, 180:326, 1957.
5. Kunkel, H. G., and Wallenius, G.: New hemoglobin in normal adult blood. Science, 122:288, 1955.
6. Nalbandian, R. M.: Molecular Aspects of Sickle Cell Hemoglobin: Clinical Applications. Springfield, Ill., Charles C Thomas, 1971.
7. Nathan, D. G.: Thalassemia. N. Engl. J. Med., 286:586, 1972.
8. Pearson, H. A., Cornelius, E. A., Schwartz, A. D., Zelson, J. H., Wolfson, S. L., and Spencer, R. P.: Transfusion-reversible functional asplenia in young children with sickle-cell anemia. N. Engl. J. Med., 283:334, 1970.
9. Rhinesmith, H. S., Schroeder, W. A., and Pauling, L.: A quantitative study of hydrolysis of human DNP-globin; the number and kind of polypeptide chains in hemoglobin A. J. Am. Chem. Soc., 79:4682, 1957.
10. Scott, R. B., Banks, L. O., Jenkins, M. E., and Crawford, R. P.: Studies in sickle cell anemia; clinical manifestations of sickle cell anemia in children. J. Pediatr., 39:460, 1951.
11. Weatherall, D. J.: The Thalassemia Syndromes. Oxford, Blackwell Scientific Publications, 1965.

Chapter 5

Rehabilitation of the Child with Chronic Asthma

by Armand V. Mascia, M.D.

Severe asthma usually has a complex etiology; it is often unresponsive to therapy and sometimes intractable. The rehabilitation of a child who suffers from this syndrome, therefore, requires the participation of specialists in several medical and paramedical disciplines. This team approach is often successful in helping an incapacitated patient to lead a happier and more productive life.

DEFINITIONS OF ASTHMA

The United States National Tuberculosis Association, in 1967, defined asthma as ". . . a disease characterized by an increased responsiveness of the trachea and bronchi to various stimuli, and made manifest by difficulty of breathing due to generalized narrowing of the airways. This narrowing is dynamic and changes in degree, either spontaneously or because of therapy. The basic defect appears to be an altered state of the host."

Chronic asthma may also be defined as a condition with unfavorable prognosis, with severe life-threatening attacks of wheezing, and with persistent and recurrent ventilatory defects often complicated by a hyperresponsive bronchial tree.

M. Murray Peshkin divides asthma into three stages: oppression, wheezing, and attack.[44] He defines asthma as a recurring dyspnea or labored breathing, usually more marked on expiration than inspiration and associated with wheezing. The first stage is that of respiratory oppression, or tightening of the chest, with difficulty in drawing a deep breath. This stage is seldom recognized or diagnosed. The second stage, the wheezing stage, follows repeated attacks of allergic rhinitis, inflammation of the nose, or bronchitis. The patient experiences an urgent need for air, which is called air hunger. Characteristic rales and rattles are heard in the chest on auscultation. The third stage is the attack stage. This is the peak of the asthmatic syndrome. The onset is acute and the attack may last from a few hours to a few days. When prolonged over a period of time, it is called intractable asthma. Subjectively, the patient feels a sense of suffocation, constriction or pressure in the chest, and an inability to draw enough air into the chest.

There are many different types and degrees of asthma. One classification groups patients with bronchial asthma into the "sensitive" type (who reacts specifically to antigens) and the "nonsensitive" type (who shows no evidence of positive skin reactions). Asthma has also been classified by Rackemann, in 1947, as "extrinsic" or "intrinsic."[45a] The condition is said to be extrinsic when the causative antigens can be demonstrated; when no causative allergen is found, the asthma is said to be intrinsic. Thus intrinsic asthma, in the clinical sense, is an exclusion diagnosis.

Many other classifications of asthma are used: atopic and nonatopic, allergic and nonallergic, immunological and nonimmunological, pollen asthma, perennial asthma, inhalant asthma, mold airborne asthma, infective asthma, and allergic spasmodic asthma of childhood. None of these is satisfactory.

A child with intractable asthma is defined by Peshkin as: (1) A child living in his own home environment who fails to respond to suitable conventional treatment that relieves about 90 per cent of asthmatic children or (2) a child requiring persistent, essentially uninterrupted administration of corticosteroids to prevent the appearance of intractability as defined under (1).

These children are often emotionally disturbed. Intractable asthma is considered a profound secondary emotional disturbance in children with asthma on an immunological basis. There are many cases of chronic asthma that are completely refractory to any treatment, including separation or residential treatment. These are often described as intractable intractables, completely crippled by disease.

More recently, some have classified asthma according to whether the bronchoconstriction is central or peripheral. The breathing of gases of different density has been used to determine where the site of obstruction is. Patients with central bronchoconstriction often show an increase in flow rates when breathing 80 per cent helium and 20 per cent oxygen, while those with peripheral constriction do not.

There is another group of children who have sudden onset of asthma around 11 years of age. They are beyond the age of infective asthma and are unresponsive to any medical approach. They often show aspirin intolerance and have negative skin tests. The family history is negative for allergies, they are subject to frequent respiratory infections, a fair number have nasal polyps, and they frequently need corticosteroids. Asthma of early onset, before three years of age, is reagin-mediated and is considered atopic.

DEMOGRAPHIC CHARACTERISTICS OF ASTHMA

To enhance public awareness of the potential severity of asthma without creating further misconceptions, certain demographic characteristics are helpful.

A national survey in 1959 revealed that there were some eight million asthmatics in the United States, of whom two million were under 15 years of age. Six per cent of children have some form of chronic respiratory disease, and of these about half have asthma. The remainder of the group includes those with chronic sinobronchial disease and cystic fibrosis.[37] Asthma and other allergies account for one third of all conditions reported for children under 17 years of age. Nearly one fourth of the days lost from school because of chronic conditions are due to asthma.[50] Childhood asthmatic deaths have increased throughout six sectors of the world in the last decade. The increased ease of management of asthma by aerosols, corticosteroids, intravenous fluids with medication, and blood gas monitoring has not resulted in a decrease in the mortality rate. In fact, in England and Wales, between 1960 and 1965, there was an eightfold increase in deaths from asthma, especially in the 10 to 14 year old group. Seven per cent of all deaths occurring in this group were due to asthma.[54]

Whether asthma is becoming more severe or a multitude of other factors account for, or at least in part account for, the rising morbidity and mortality rates is unclear. In some areas, a tenfold increase in asthma has developed over the past decade. A recent New Orleans asthma epidemic perhaps reflected the natural history of asthma as it affected the atopic population of a large urban community.[48] Some of these factors are mounting environmental stress, including atmospheric pollution, and iatrogenic problems such as those stemming from corticosteroid or aerosol therapy and improper use of medications. Large outbreaks of asthma have been correlated with increased particulate matter in the atmosphere and with local socioeconomic conditions that exist mainly among the indigent population who do not receive any continuity of care.[21]

Generally, the ratio of asthma in male to female is 3:2 or 2:1 prior to puberty. After puberty, the ratio seems to be 5:4 with females predominating. Although an increasing amount of asthma is being reported in non-whites, it still continues to be rather rare in Eskimos and American Indians. Financial status and social status apparently have little effect on the incidence of asthma. City dwellers, however, seem more prone to asthma than country dwellers.

Chronic asthma is a disease with social, economic, and emotional impact on both the patient and the family. The social and emotional aspects are extremely important in understanding chronic and frequently recurring asthma.

REHABILITATION OF THE CHRONIC ASTHMATIC

Goals and Scope

The goals of rehabilitation treatment of the chronically asthmatic child are to increase the usefulness of his life, to prepare him for extra physical demands by strengthening the chest muscles and teaching him to breathe properly, and to decrease the length and the severity of asthmatic attacks. The ultimate goal, of course, is independence and self-respect. It is important to give the chronic asthmatic relief as early as possible in the course of the disease. Total rehabilitation not only of the patient but also of his family may be necessary.

Rehabilitation is a great challenge, and there is great need for utilizing certain physiological techniques and proper psychological attitudes (including counseling, aiding emotional and physical problems, and developing independence from the family).

Following a comprehensive diagnostic assessment and planning for holistic management by integrating data from child, family, and environment, there should evolve a therapeutic regimen that is appropriate for each particular child. The responsibility for the care of the chronically ill asthmatic is not only that of the parents, but also of the institutions involved in their care, and the community.

Programs for specialized care include inpatient and outpatient facilities, some community facilities that have a nonmedical atmosphere, and some whole-day treatment programs. These programs need the support of many services: social, recreational, counseling, occupational, and vocational.

The asthmatic child with his incapacity, both physical and emotional, follows a plan that includes thorough evaluation, the institution of a regimen, and development of suitable programs. The regimen is instituted jointly by a medical and a psychological team (Fig. 5–1). The medical team includes the pediatrician, allergist, physiatrist, nurse, and dietitian; the psychological team includes the psychiatrist, psychologist, social worker, counselor, teacher, and recreation worker. In combination they attempt to develop motivation through education and to promote reassurance and independence, hoping eventually to return the patient to his community with the ability to live a nearly normal life.[37] The therapeutic measures include observation; treatment of allergies by avoidance, drugs, and guided and specific hyposensitization; physical therapy; inhalation therapy; psychotherapy; and recreation.

Assessment of Patients

Because of the many pitfalls in the management of the chronically asthmatic child, a complete work-up is necessary. The physician must recognize nonallergic causes of the problem. He must seek out possible hidden

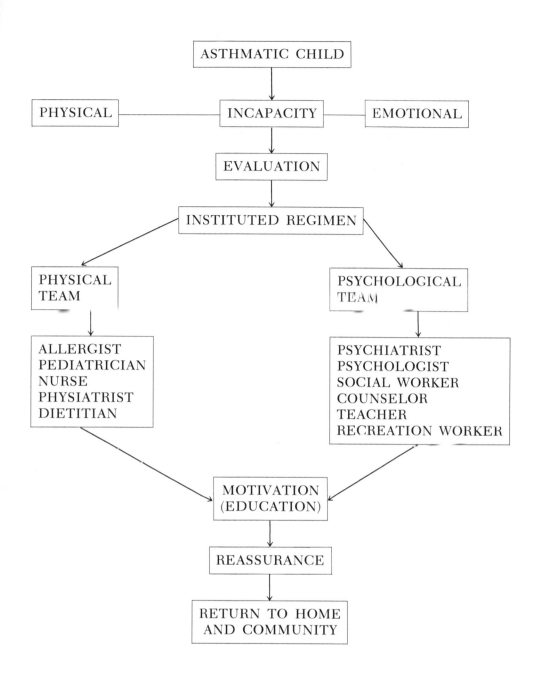

Figure 5-1 Flow chart of rehabilitation of the child with chronic asthma.

causes—infections, drugs, foods and food additives. An extensive series of studies may be necessary to evaluate and follow up the child with chronic asthma, including:

1. Complete and thorough history by interviews with parents, patients, and records from referring hospitals and physicians.
2. Complete physical examination with emphasis on the respiratory tract. Height and weight should be taken for careful follow-up. The majority are usually in the lower percentiles.

3. A hemogram, complete blood count and total circulating eosinophil count.
4. Immunoelectrophoresis, both qualitative and quantitative, to rule out immune deficiency diseases. Secretory IGA from parotid gland may be of some value.
5. Nasal and sputum smears for eosinophils.
6. Nasopharyngeal and sputum cultures.
7. Complete urinalysis.
8. X-ray studies including posteroanterior and lateral chest x-rays and sinus x-rays.
9. X-rays for bone age and bone growth.
10. Tuberculin test with intermediate PPD, monilial extract test 1:100.
11. Sweat test to rule out cystic fibrosis.
12. Pulmonary function tests, including peak flow rates, lung volumes, diffusion studies, and blood gas determinations. Flow volume curves are also extremely valuable in testing asthmatics. The frequency of such testing and a comparison of the results are most important.
13. Audiograms to evaluate hearing.
14. Serial electrocardiograms.
15. Ear, nose and throat evaluation.
16. Stool examination for ova and parasites.
17. Cortisol determinations in the plasma and urine.
18. Two hour postprandial blood sugar evaluation.
19. Serum alpha-1 antitrypsin determination.
20. Milk precipitants test.
21. NBT dye test.
22. Psychometric and psychological evaluation.
23. Psychiatric interview, when indicated.
24. Allergenic testing. Initial scratch testing (which correlates well with bronchial challenges) followed by intradermal testing if scratch tests are negative; conjunctival tests, and last, provocative challenges, either bronchial or nasal.

Medical Management

Medical care includes evaluation of general health and attention to nutrition. The management of the child with chronic asthma includes many additional modalities, such as environmental control, avoidance of noxious substances, electronic air cleaners, air conditioning, mold control, dietary restrictions, pharmacological control of bronchospasm, and immunological treatment or specific hyposensitization.

Children with persistent and continuous asthma should receive bronchodilators around the clock rather than only during attacks of wheezing since all have elements of bronchospasm, even when no wheezing is clinically evident.[27, 35] Medication requirements should be reviewed frequently. Bronchodilators, either singly or in mixtures, with or without expectorants, should be given with meals and at bedtime. When early morning wheezing is present, sustained-action bronchodilator drugs, e.g., aminophylline (Aminodur), theophylline (Tedral SA, Slo-phyllin) should be administered at bedtime. In the pharmacological approach, the physician must be well aware of proper dosage of medications given intravenously, orally, or rectally. Aminophylline products should be administered at a 3, 6, and 8 mg per kilogram ratio for intravenous, oral, and rectal use.

Expectorants are very often used. Iodides (50 mg per kilogram per day) are popular and apparently have a direct effect on lung resistance or surfactant. Up to 10 to 15 per cent of chronic asthmatics respond to them. They should not, however, be used for prolonged periods, as thyroid enlargement is not uncommon.

Cough suppressants are frequently used. Narcotics should be avoided, but phenobarbital in adequate dosage is often helpful. Codeine or Hycodan may be given to tolerance. The use of antihistamines in chronic asthma is illogical, since theoretically they have a drying effect, but if angioedema is present, antihistamines may be necessary.

The majority of severe asthmatics, or chronic asthmatics, are given corticosteroids, which may be life saving in acute severe status asthmaticus. For long-term use in chronic asthma, however, it is probably unwise to administer steroids, since they temporarily mask the chronicity and weaning the patients from them is often difficult. The use of corticosteroids on alternate days is valuable, as this allows for adequate bone growth, for recovery of adrenal homeostasis, and frequently for the loss of the cushingoid appearance.

The use of inhalation therapy (aerosol) with isoproterenol or nebulizers containing isoproterenol, or epinephrine-like products, may be good or bad, depending on the indications, age, and frequency of use. Recent reports indicate that overuse may cause chemical bronchitis or the "locked-lung" syndrome, and even deaths have been reported.[7] The combined effects of isoproterenol, epinephrine, and hypoxia may cause cardiac arrhythmias.

Children should be studied carefully before any elimination diets are prescribed. In some children, antiasthmatic diets may reduce the allergic load and make treatment more effective. Some feel that histamine products in certain foods should be avoided, especially in pollen seasons.

General measures are extremely important and environmental control is frequently a most important element in the management of the chronic asthmatic. A small room, emptied and thoroughly scrubbed and cleaned, with a bare wooden floor or a vinyl tiled floor, is recommended. Mattresses, box springs, and pillows should all be encased in nonallergenic zippered casings. Bedspreads and comforters should not be fuzzy. Stuffed animals and toys, especially those containing kapok, should be avoided. Blankets should be covered with broadcloth or sheeting, especially if they are made of wool. The room should be cleaned daily and given a complete cleaning at least once a week. If a central heating system of the forced-air type is present, electrostatic filters and humidification are very valuable, and layers of coarse cheesecloth over outlets are also helpful. The humidity of rooms should be at least 50 per cent. Drafts and chilling should be avoided. Smoke, sprays, and irritants should not be allowed in the patient's bedroom. Air-conditioning is always of value to the pollen sensitive patient, whose windows should be kept closed.

Nonspecific therapy, such as the administration of gamma globulin (.05 ml per kilogram per month) if the serum gamma globulin level is below 300 mg per milliliter is indicated, but there is no good evidence for the routine prophylactic use of gamma globulin.

Antibiotics in full therapeutic doses for acute bacterial infections are recommended. Prophylactic antibiotics have not been demonstrated as being of value and may cause emergence of resistant organisms, superinfection, and staining of teeth. Intrafamilial infections and family carriers must be searched for.

Specific therapy should be attempted in all cases of chronic asthma after a careful assessment by proper testing with allergenic protein and careful correlation of the history and past treatment. On the basis of responses to skin testing, the patient should receive a series of allergen injections of gradually increasing potency. Those who show positive scratch tests need large doses of up to 8000 to 10,000 protein nitrogen units (PNU). Those who show a negative scratch test but positive intradermal test may need larger doses of up to 20,000 PNU. Alum extracts permit the larger doses to be administered at longer intervals.

Bacterial vaccine therapy, with stock or autogenous vaccine, is still controversial. Whether its beneficial effects are due to desensitization to bacterial products, immunization, a nonspecific protein effect, or increase in antiviral factor is to be determined. An increase of interferon production has been demonstrated in a number of patients receiving bacterial vaccine. Mueller has shown the clinical efficacy of this form of therapy in infective asthma.[60]

A daily diary of the patient's medications and treatments may help the physician to evaluate him and also act as an excellent barometer of the effectiveness of treatment.

When status asthmaticus develops in any of these children with chronic asthma, immediate intensive care is necessary. Children in status asthmaticus should be admitted to a hospital where a team approach is practiced and intensive care is at hand. Proper monitoring equipment should be present, including that for estimating blood gases. Intermittent positive pressure breathing and a bronchodilator should be available.

Physical Therapy

Physical therapy is one of the standard adjuncts to the treatment of chronic asthma. Many of these children feel much better when involved in such programs as chest physical therapy, breathing exercises, physical training and inhalation therapy. There is some question whether the pulmonary function actually improves, but there is no doubt that general conditioning is good for all children with chronic diseases.

The goals of physical therapy are to produce physical and mental relaxation of the child, improve his posture, teach him diaphragmatic and lower costal breathing, strengthen his muscles in order to improve ventilation, and bring about more efficient patterns of breathing. Teaching a child proper coughing and drainage techniques is invaluable.

Before prescribing physical therapy, the general fitness of the patient should be evaluated—his muscular strength, his pulmonary function, his breathing patterns, his coughing mechanism, and his posture. Accompanying such evaluation, other aspects of the case should be considered, including the psychological and nutritional state of the child and, of course, the family relations.

Pressure changes within the chest as a result of forced inspiration and expiration in the chronic asthmatic, particularly in the child, tend to bring about the distortions that constitute the typical chest deformities seen in asthmatics of this age group.[29]

The asthmatic patient's chest deformities are usually produced early in childhood, before ossification of cartilaginous junctions occurs. When ossification takes place, the chest becomes fixed and, in the asthmatic, the rib cage becomes elevated. The thorax is distended, with a marked increase in costal angle, owing to the increased amount of residual air in the lungs. The posteroanterior diameter may become enlarged and even equal to the lateral diameter. There is a tendency for the shoulders to become elevated, and kyphosis of the spine may become exaggerated. Asymmetry of bone structure of the right and left sides of the thorax may develop as a result of an abnormally high intrathoracic negative pressure. Marked kyphosis of the spine may emphasize the tendency to thrust the head forward and to develop tight sternocleidomastoid and posterior neck muscles.

Chest physical therapy and bronchial drainage are valuable in clearing the mucus from the bronchial tree, especially in those with excessive secretions. Bronchial drainage and physical therapy often help stop prolonged attacks, and it has been shown that the peak expiratory flow rates improve 20 to 25 per cent after bronchial drainage. Segmental (postural) drainage of the bronchial tree aids pulmonary hygiene by improving patency and relieving obstruction due to accumulated secretions. Certain procedures will be helpful. They include clapping, tapotement or percussion, deep breathing, assisted coughing, and vibration. Tapotement and vibration help overcome inertia and increase the outward flow of secretions. Deep breathing may move secretions and encourage coughing.

Segmental drainage is important and effective in assisting the normal cleansing mechanism of the tracheobronchial tree. The patient is positioned to take maximum advantage of gravity, and drainage can be continued in each position anywhere from two to five minutes with percussion over each segment that is being drained. Duration, frequency, and positioning for drainage should be individually determined on the basis of auscultation and chest findings. Percussion loosens the secretions and causes increased ciliary action. The patient is encouraged to cough until the cough is no longer productive; supporting the sides of the lower part of the chest often decreases the strain. Drainage should be performed before meals to minimize vomiting, and night drainage may reduce nocturnal coughing spells. Use of aerosol medication prior to drainage may open up the airways and loosen the plugs. Bronchial drainage should be done at least one to four times a day.[59]

Breathing exercises and controlled breathing patterns may prove to be of some value if the child is motivated. It is not known whether breathing exercises abort attacks of asthma when employed at the onset. Improved patterns of breathing, however, are often valuable, since many chronic asthmatics often hyperinflate; if they are taught to breathe slowly and emphasize prolonging of expiration and breathing properly against pursed lips, this will tend to improve the strength of respiratory muscles, diaphragmatic excursion, and the efficiency of cough.

Stretching exercises may be of some value. The patient clasps his hands behind his head and lets the therapist or the parent pull back his elbows while stabilizing the trunk to stretch the pectoral muscles. Lateral bending is done to maintain increased flexibility of the ribs. Partial sit-ups and leg-raising can be incorporated into the program to increase the strength of the abdominal muscles and to aid expiration.[2, 19, 32]

Play techniques may be used for children: for instance, blowing against an object such as a ping-pong ball on a table, blowing a pinwheel, blowing a tissue against the wall and keeping it from falling to the ground, and blowing a balloon until it bursts. Doing breathing exercises to music may prevent boredom. The child should rest between exercises, and should do them at least three times a day. In summary, the important exercises are those that involve proper diaphragmatic breathing, side expansion breathing, shoulder stretching, forward bending, side bending and rotation, and that improve the mobility of the chest wall, particularly when the muscles of the chest have become fixed and shortened even with the chest expanded.

The value of physical training and sports has not been established. However, changing body positions, avoiding indoor confinement, and participation in sports are helpful in the total care and strengthening of the respiratory muscles. They improve diaphragmatic action, mobilize the thorax, and seem to play a significant role in general fitness.[2, 16, 17, 47, 49, 51] Exercise programs such as weight lifting and jogging may also be valuable and can build confidence. Recent surveys have shown that chronic asthmatics who swim feel better. It has also been shown that short periods of exercise (two minutes) very often improve peak expiratory flow rates.

Millman has shown that there are psychological benefits in good physical therapy—improvement in schoolwork and self-composure and less dependence on parents. His program consisted of 45 minutes of exercise three times a week, and included calisthenics; cardiorespiratory conditioning such as walking, skipping, running, sprinting, and vigorous exercises such as dodge-ball and soccer; and also some periods of less vigorous exercises.[40] Short bursts of activity, rather than prolonged sustained effort, seem to be more beneficial and minimize the possibility of provoking airway obstruction.

Itkin and Nacman attempted to increase the usefulness of the lives of asthmatics by physical conditioning in controlled exercises. The patients served as their own control over a three month period. None of the patients involved in this program was made worse. No changes in treatment were noted. Forty per cent showed improvement of forced expiratory volume at 1 second (FEV1). Two thirds improved in athletic ability and workload capacity. Three quarters showed an increased oxygen uptake.[30] Hyde and Swarts developed a program in perennial asthmatics with one hour of exercise per week, including physical fitness and breathing exercises. Their results noted that in a six to eight month period, 23.5 per cent improved, 26.5 per cent worsened in terms of pulmonary function studies, and 3.3 per cent showed moderate to marked obstruction.[27]

Inhalation Therapy

Inhalation therapy in chronic asthma includes several useful therapeutic measures: aerosolization of medications, intermittent positive pressure breathing, and mist therapy. The objectives of inhalation therapy are to provide more even ventilation of the lungs, to maintain normal humidification of the respiratory tree, to wet and thin the mucus, to increase oxygenation of the arterial blood and effectively eliminate carbon dioxide, and to deposit locally active medications on the mucous membranes. Medications include antiinflammatory substances such as corticosteroids, wetting agents or mucolytics to liquefy secretions, enzymes to digest DNA, antibiotics to combat infections, bronchodilators to relieve bronchospasm, and finally decongestants to shrink the swollen mucous membranes.

Water vapor in the inspired air has a beneficial effect on the airways and is a very important adjunct to the treatment of bronchial asthma. It may be supplied via the cold vaporizer or the fog tent. The aim of nebulization therapy is the deposition of particles of sufficient size of water or medication into the respiratory tract; the site of deposition depends on the particle size. The larger the particle, the higher it will be deposited in the respiratory tract. Ultrasonic nebulizers produce dense aerosols of small and more uniform particle size containing enough particles to provide adequately for humidification, with a significant amount left as particulate water for deposition in the periphery of the lungs. Normal pulmonary secretions are usually isotonic; in the asthmatic the added water restores isotonicity and eliminates most of the evidence of irritation.

Several factors determine the therapeutic effectiveness of nebulization. These include the density of the mist, the size of the respiratory tract, the rate and depth of breathing, and the route of administration. Very often in the bronchitic type of chronic bronchial asthma, in which infection plays a large role, the use of mist tent therapy is valuable. Mist tents in general should be operated with compressed air from oilless compressors, or air-pushed by fan. A small plastic tent or room air conditioner is necessary, or alternatively, a tent cooling unit.

Medicated aerosols may be used intermittently to shrink the edematous mucosa. Phenylephrine, 0.0125 per cent, and 0.05 to 0.5 ml of 1:100 solution of isoproterenol both in 2 ml of saline are used to reduce bronchospasm, and occasionally steroids and antibiotics are added.

Intermittent positive pressure breathing (IPPB) is a fancy technique for administering a bronchodilator, and should not be used if a simpler, less expensive method can achieve the same result. However, in certain cases of severe acute bronchospasm and in patients who have excessive secretions, IPPB can be most helpful.

It is essential that equipment be kept absolutely clean to decrease the chances of contamination with bacteria and fungus.

Mental and Emotional Therapy

The child with chronic asthma may develop severe psychological problems as a result of his disease. Asthma may interfere with the development of
normal social relationships, normal physical activities, and rapport with
others. Frequently, the parents believe that exercise precipitates attacks and
attempt to limit the physical activities of their children and overprotect them.
Many asthmatics are even confined to their homes and rooms; very often
home teachers are suggested by family physicians. Parents have many fears,
and the child is a constant worry to them.

A great deal of emphasis should be placed on the behavioral and emotional problems. Each patient must learn to accept and adapt to his chronic
asthma. Many have a poor self-image, are plagued with "self-devaluating" or
"worthless" feelings, and need psychological management to discover "Who
am I?," "What am I?," and "Where am I?" Learning to care for one's self is imperative. The child needs to be involved in major decisions regarding his own
management. Frequently the child's aggressive actions are interpreted as bad
behavior, and often a child interprets his asthma as punishment.[11] The
physician, family, and supporting team must be realistic, understanding, definite, honest, positive, and inventive. Disputes with parents must be avoided.

Comprehensive care is extremely important. The team needs to be constantly aware of the psychosocial status and the psychodynamics of the
parents and the child, the group dynamics of the medical team, and the proper
communication among the individuals caring for the child. Frequent airing of
attitudes toward the management of the child and periodic reviews are necessary.

Involvement with the parents of asthmatic children is essential. They
need help in mastering the adversity facing them and must be educated about
asthma before the child's total rehabilitation can take place. The family must
be able to handle the handicap if the child is to do so.

The psychodynamic factors in the family are many. Some of the processes
include denial of diagnosis, guilt feelings, ambivalent responses, rejection,
self-sacrificial devotion, depression, dependency, and projection of such
triggering factors as marital difficulties. The child and family must be handled
together. Frustration, anger, hostility, grief and guilt get in the way of treatment in chronic illness. Parents of chronically ill asthmatic children must be
made aware of the disorder; the demands of the illness; and where the fields
of battle lie between the child and the parent, parent and doctor, child and
doctor, and parent and neighbors. They must be aware that a secondary gain
may be attached to any chronic illness, i.e., the mother sleeping with the child
instead of with her husband. Because of such a mother's needs, the child
frequently retreats into illness because the ill child is rewarded.

The education of parents begins with the first interview with the physician, social worker, and nurse. Descriptive material should be easily available
for parents, including a treatise on the basic anatomy and physiology of the
respiratory system, the etiology of asthma, the names of drugs used in treatment, the doses, and the like. Instructions on how to free the bedroom of
allergens should be given and discussed carefully. Ongoing parent group

therapy is advisable, sibling support may have to be enlisted, referral of parents to family counseling services may be useful, and individual psychotherapy may be necessary for some parents.[18] In some instances removal of the child from the home and parents may be necessary.[41]

Group therapy is one of the vehicles for the management of the chronically asthmatic child, and may help uncover the patient's pattern of total dependence on his family and the medical personnel and help him to achieve a greater sense of independence, adequacy, and control of himself. Such therapy may provide the asthmatic with sufficient emotional insight and self-awareness to reduce his anxiety. Relief of feelings of frustration and guilt enhances the patient's self-concept, promotes a more self-assertive attitude, and decreases the need to utilize dependency channels for gratification.[38] Children with intractable asthma need intensive therapy in which parent figures and the fact that someone cares are beneficial.

NEED FOR COMPREHENSIVE CARE

Since asthma is such a frightening and debilitating disease, and the treatment is somewhat indefinite, a comprehensive approach to the management of this entity is most important.

Comprehensive care for the child with chronic asthma means completeness in the continuity of care. The treatment of the asthmatic child must be changed from crisis oriented care to a more compassionate approach, with proper therapy for the patient and the family, and with due regard to dignity. A system of delivery of that care in different geographic locations and for age defined groups must be developed. If the patient is to be spared the life of a respiratory cripple, comprehensive programs offering continuous care are necessary. The goals continue to be to maintain a happy, productive individual.

The delivery of care to the asthmatic must represent a full range of services. The system must develop a care plan following proper assessment and a study of the patient. The cycle of comprehensive care shows that the patient follows an individualized plan, depending on the assessment. This includes preventive, short-term, long-term, and residential programs. Careful follow-up and home care are part of the cycle. Emergency care is episodic and considered incidental to the cycle of comprehensive care — but is necessary. The system of comprehensive care must have proper organization, accountability, proper records, and communication. Such carefully designed programs also reduce the number of broken appointments. Summary conferences, parents' classes, home visits, all help decrease attrition of the delivery of proper medical care.[24]

CARE PROGRAMS AVAILABLE

A number of programs covering the different phases of management and control of asthma are being carried out. Both preventive and rehabilitative care are necessary, along with sick care. The supply of such services involves the private physician, hospital outpatient and inpatient services, extended care services, and general hospital day care and residential care. Institutions must learn what the needs are. "Shot clinics" do not deliver the kind of care that is necessary for chronic asthmatics. Extended care stay, six months to one year, should be reserved for severe asthmatics and should serve children with psychosocial problems or with inadequate, upset homes in ghetto areas. Freeing the child from severe asthma for a period of time is most helpful. Residential treatment centers serve the same purpose and are discussed later. Short-term care has been provided by some residential centers and some hospitals for chronic diseases, some extended care or self-care units in general hospitals, and some summer camp programs. Considering the magnitude of the problem, relatively few beds are now available for continuous treatment of asthmatics.[43]

A possible way of handling asthma in an urban area would be to establish day-care asthma centers. There, the asthmatic child would spend at least 8 to 12 hours per day in a facility five to six days a week. Patients would have access to a total rehabilitation program in which they could receive proper medication, proper schooling, group psychotherapy, and asthma education. Families would be incorporated into this program by parent groups and social service groups. In this way, the child with chronic asthma could receive proper management and control of his asthma. These asthma day care centers would be associated with a nearby general hospital for emergency care and hospital care.[1] A summer asthma camp program would serve in a similar capacity.

ROLE OF THE RESIDENTIAL TREATMENT CENTER

Since the majority of deaths from chronic asthma occur in children with intractable or chronic status asthmaticus, it is important to find ways to reduce the incidence of both these conditions. Temporary separation from an "asthma producing environment" is necessary for the proper rehabilitation of some of these children. Physicians find little to offer children with intractable asthma except corticosteroids. When corticosteroids are administered persistently, they tend to mask intractable asthma and the children become "hooked" on them, as some do on isoproterenol nebulizations. The steroid dependent child may develop, in addition to irreversible complications, an extremely poor response to further medication. The special therapy available in residential treatment centers, where the intractable is made tractable and from which the patient often returns home and remains well, is then unavailing. The philosophy of residential treatment centers has developed in response to this catastrophic problem. A multidisciplinary approach and an understanding of the complex medical, social, and psychological factors are extremely important.

The goals of management of the intractable asthmatic in these facilities include (1) the education of the child and parent in regard to the complexity of asthma; (2) the return of the child to his home to lead a normal life when he becomes amenable to therapy; (3) the weaning of the child from cortico-steroids and the reduction of other medications to a minimum; (4) the reduction of anxiety about his asthma; and (5) the education of the parents in ways to live with the asthmatic child and to avoid guilt.

The milieu of the residential center is most important. It takes the cooperation of the entire staff, and complete understanding of the chronically asthmatic child. The needs of these children must be met by professionals, and adequate time must be spent by staff members. Residential treatment centers can follow a more collaborative approach and work with a child who has been removed from his asthma producing environment. Good communication and frequent conferences among members of the team – the pediatric allergist, pediatrician, nurse, social worker, psychologist, psychiatrist, physical therapist, recreation workers, occupational therapist, teachers, speech and hearing therapists, and dietitians – must be organized.

There are some 18 such centers in the United States and Canada. The length of stay varies, depending on the philosophy of the individual institution. Most recognize that several years' separation may be indicated in a large percentage of cases. Some recommend a shorter period of institutionalization during the fall season – the time of greatest incidence of problems due to high exposure to ragweed, mold, infections, forced hot air heating, and tensions in school.[15, 22, 23, 36, 42, 55, 61]

FINANCIAL COST OF CARE

The cost of medical care to families of chronically asthmatic children is out of reach for most. A recent survey by Vance showed that the cost of this illness to a family ranged from $1644 per year to $17,000 per year in 1968.[62] The varying needs of the different social and economic groups, and the circumstances in different locations of this country, require some flexibility in the financing and delivery of medical care. Surely the best segments of private and public factors must be utilized, coordinated, and integrated. Resources now include Medicaid, Crippled Children's Services, Vocational Rehabilitation, Social Security, and Public Welfare.

NEED FOR POSTGRADUATE EDUCATION

Postgraduate education for physicians and ancillary personnel is urgently needed. All disciplines must be used to disseminate knowledge and experience to a large number of medical and paramedical people. Only in this way can the most recent advances in diagnosis and treatment be made available to the vast number of children with chronic asthma. There is need for special training in the comprehensive care outlined previously. A doctor cannot handle chronic asthma single-handedly; he must gain effectiveness and expertise with others and learn to work in concert with those in allied services. Workers in these other fields should have a broad clinical orientation and must be willing to work as a team in coordination with other programs. Each must be knowledgeable in comprehensive care, the socioeconomic impact of disease on the family, home care, extended care, residential care, and even day care programs. The physician should be involved in teaching paramedical personnel.

SUMMARY

The child with chronic asthma needs to be taught to live with his asthma. The aim of rehabilitation is to have him engage in normal activities with relative impunity. There is a need to change the self-image of the chronic asthmatic, who generally feels inferior, angry, resentful, and depressed. He must avoid feeling incapacitated and different. He needs motivation and reassurance to help him gain independence and self-respect.

The general management of the asthmatic child needs combined physical and psychological approaches. Therapy should be directed to all aspects of the disease: allergens, irritants, infections, and stress. A regimen must be evolved that is appropriate for each particular child. Optimal management cannot be achieved single-handedly and there is urgent need for a type of comprehensive care that is best provided by a multidisciplinary group. The medical approach is a holistic one, with a well-planned combination of drugs, elimination and avoidance of allergens, and hyposensitization. Inhalation therapy to help thin secretions and open bronchial tubes is also of benefit. Rehabilitative assistance includes therapeutic exercises with the object of restoring the chest to normal size and improving bronchial drainage.

The education of the child and the family concerning asthma is also part of the total approach. Group therapy and individual psychotherapy continue to be part of the treatment of these children. The rehabilitation of the family unit—utilizing group therapy and parent groups, both educational and psychotherapeutic—is important in aiding the emotional problems that so many of these children have and so many parents also have. There is a great need for vocational counseling to help these individuals to a better level of functioning. The support of social services is necessary to help them adjust to problems of family living and making contact for them with different parts of their rehabilitative assistance. Physician's assistants and counselors very often are beneficial in helping with schoolwork and recreation, and in being a "comforting shoulder" for these children. Facilities need to be developed so that care programs including inpatient and outpatient care, day care and residential treatment, and finally, postgraduate education for professionals who care for the child with chronic asthma are available.

It is necessary to look for new trends, ideas, concepts, and ways of delivering better medical care to these children. There is need to encourage new facilities in hospitals, new residential treatment centers in different parts of the country, and diagnostic medical centers with interdisciplinary teams equipped to give family oriented treatment. To rehabilitate children with chronic asthma must be the goal.

References

1. Allen, J. E., Landman, P. D., and Pryles, C. C.: Health delivery system for ghetto children. N.Y.C. J. Med., October 15, 1971, p. 2446.
2. Asthma Research Council, Kings College, London: *Physical Exercises for Asthma*. 6th Ed. Chicago Medical Book Co., 1946.
3. Bernstein, I. L., Allen, J. E., Kreindler, L., Ghory, J. E., and Wohl, T. H.: A community approach to juvenile intractable asthma. A new concept in treatment. Pediatrics, 26:586, 1960.
4. Blumenthal, M. N., and Peterson, E.: Physical conditioning program for asthmatic children. J. Assoc. Phys. Ment. Rehab., 21:4, 1967.
5. Bukantz, S. C., and Mascia, A. V.: Role of residential center in care of asthmatic children. N.Y.C. J. Med., 64:987, 1964.
6. Bikantz, S. C., and Peshkin, M. M.: Institutional treatment of asthmatic children. Pediatr. Clin. North Am., 6:755, 1959.
7. Caplin, I., and Haynes, J. T.: Complications of aerosol therapy in asthma. Ann. Allergy, 27:65, 1969.
8. Chai, H., Falliers, C., Dietiker, F., and Franz, B.: Long-term investigation into the effects of physical therapy in chronically ill asthmatic children. J. Allergy, 39:109, 1967.
9. Creak, M., and Stephen, J.: The psychological aspects of asthma in children. Pediatr. Clin. North Am., 6:755, 1959.
10. Dees, S. C.: Chronic allergy—crippler and killer of children. J. Chronic Dis., 12:326, 1960.
11. Dubo, S., McLean, J. A., Ching, A. Y., Wright, H. L., Kauffman, P. E., and Sheldon, J. M.: A study of relationships between family situation, bronchial asthma, and personal adjustment in children. J. Pediatr., 59:402, 1961.
12. Downes, J. J., Wood, D. W., Striker, T. W., et al.: Diagnosis and treatment: Advances in the management of status asthmaticus in children. Pediatrics, 38:286, 1966.
13. Epstein, N.: Rehabilitation of chronic asthmatic. Mod. Treat., 3:918, 1966.
14. Faillers, C. J.: Psychosomatic study and treatment of asthmatic children. Pediatr. Clin. North Am., 6:271, 1969.
15. Faillers, C. J.: Treatment of asthma in residential center: A fifteen year study. Ann. Allergy, 28:513, 1970.
16. Fein, B. T., and Cox, E. P.: Technique of respiratory and physical exercises in the treatment of bronchial asthma. Ann. Allergy, 13:377, 1955.
17. Fein, B. T., Cox, E. P., and Green, L. H.: Respiratory and physical exercise in treatment of bronchial asthma. Ann. Allergy, 11:275, 1953.
18. Fontana, V. J.: *Practical Management of Allergic Children*. New York, Appleton-Century-Crofts, 1969.
19. Fountain, F. P., and Goddard, R. S.: Breathing exercises for children with chronic respiratory disease. Lovelace Clin. Rev., 1:159, 1963.
20. Fuhs, V. R.: The growing demands of medical care. New Engl. J. Med., 279:190, 1968.
21. Girsh, L. S., et al.: A study on epidemiology of asthma in children in Philadelphia. J. Allergy, 39:347, 1967.
22. Goldman, M. D., et al.: Children's asthmatic rehabilitation program. Ann. Allergy, 24:345, 1964.
23. Green, M., and Allman, D. B.: A prototype of an asthmatic unit in a general pediatric convalescent home. Ann. Allergy, 18:1336, 1960.
24. Haggergy, R. J.: Symposium: Does comprehensive care make a difference? Am. J. Dis. Child., 19:122:467, 1971.
25. Harter, J. G., Reddy, W. J., and Thorn, G. W.: Studies on an intermittent corticosteroid dosage regimen. New Engl. J. Med., 269:591, 1963.
26. Haywood, T. J., and McGovern, J. P.: Holistic approach to management of bronchial asthma. Pediatr. Clin. North Am., 10:109, 1963.
27. Hyde, J. S., and Swarts, C. S.: Effects of an exercise program on perennially asthmatic child. Am. J. Dis. Child., 116:383, 1969.
28. Hyde, J. S., Swarts, C. L., Hannaway, P. J., et al.: Therapeutic strategy for children with chronic asthma. Ann. Allergy, 27:552, 1969.
29. Itkin, I. H.: Exercise for the asthmatic patient. J. Am. Phys. Ther. Assoc., 44:815, 1964.
30. Itkin, I. H., and Nacman, M.: The effect of exercise on the hospitalized asthmatic patient. J. Allergy, 37:253, 1966.
31. Jones, R. S., Wharton, M. J., and Buston, M. H.: The place of physical exercise and bronchodilator drugs in the assessment of the asthmatic child. Arch. Dis. Child., 38:539, 1963.
32. Livingstone, J. L., and Gillespie, M.: The value of breathing exercises in asthma. Lancet, 2:705, 1935.

33. Logan, J. B.: Asthma as a lethal disease. Am. J. Dis. Child., *110*:1, 1965.
34. Mascia, A. V.: The role of the residential treatment center in the care of the asthmatic child. Ann. Allergy, *22*:191, 1964.
35. Mascia, A. V.: Progress in the treatment of the asthmatic child in a convalescent setting. J. Asthma Res., *3*:239, 1966.
36. Mascia, A. V.: The goals and philosophy of residential treatment center for asthmatic children. J. Asthma Res., *2*:43, 1970.
37. Mascia, A. V.: Delivery of medical care to chronically asthmatic children. J. Asthma Res., *10*:171, 1973.
38. Mascia, A. V., and Reiter, S. R.: Group therapy in the rehabilitation of the severe chronic asthmatic child. J. Asthma Res., *9*:81, 1971.
39. McGovern, J. F., and Knight, J. A.: Allergy and human emotions. Springfield, Ill., Charles C Thomas, 1967.
40. Millman, M., Grundon, W. G., Kasch, F., et al.: Controlled exercise in asthmatic children. Ann. Allergy, *23*:220, 1965.
41. Peshkin, M. D.: Asthma in children: IX. Role of environment in treatment of selected group of cases: Plea for a home as a restorative measure. Am. J. Dis. Child., *39*:774, 1930.
42. Peshkin, M. M.: Management of the institutionalized child with intractable asthma. Ann. Allergy, *18*:75, 1960.
43. Peshkin, M. M.: Survey of convalescent institutions for asthmatic children in the United States and Canada. J. Asthma Res., *11*:181, 1965.
44. Peshkin, M. M., and Abramson, H. A.: The first national seminar of regional medical consultants. Ann. Allergy, *16*:473, 1958.
45. Peshkin, M. M., and Abramson, H. A.: Psychosomatic group therapy with parents of children having intractable asthma. Ann. Allergy, *17*:344, 1959. Part II, Adaptation mechanisms. Ann. Allergy, *18*:87, 1960.
45a. Rackemann, F. M.: A working classification of asthma. Am. J. Med., *3*:601, 1947.
46. Richards, W., and Patrick, J.: Death from asthma in children. Am. J. Dis. Child., *110*:4, 1965.
47. Rule, R. A.: Exercise for asthmatics, a pilot program. J. Phys. Educ., p. 66, January, 1961.
48. Salvaggio, J., Seabury, J., and Schoenhardt, F. A.: New Orleans asthma. V. Relationship between Charity Hospital asthma admission rates, semiquantitative pollen and fungal spore counts, and total particulate aerometric sampling data. J. Allergy Clin. Immunol., *48*:96, 1971.
49. Scherr, M. S., and Frankel, L.: Physical conditioning program for asthmatic children. J.A.M.A., *168*:1996, 1958.
50. Schieffer, C. G., and Hunt, E. T.: *Illness Among Children*. Children's Bureau Publication 405. U.S. Dept. of Health, Education and Welfare, 1963.
51. Sinclair, J. D.: Exercises in pulmonary disease. In Licht, S. (ed.): *Therapeutic Exercise*. Baltimore, Waverly Press, Inc., 1965.
52. Sly, M. R.: Exercise: Related changes in airway obstruction. Ann. Allergy, *28*:1, 1970.
53. Speer, F.: *The Allergic Child*. New York, Hoeber Medical Div., Harper & Row, 1963.
54. Spizer, F. E., and Doll, R.: A century of asthma deaths in young people. Br. Med. J., *3*:243, 1968.
55. Steen, W. B.: Rehabilitation of children with intractable asthma. Ann. Allergy, *17*:864, 1959.
56. Stewart, W. H.: The unmet needs of children. Pediatrics, *39*:157, 1967.
57. Stolley, P. D.: Asthma mortality. Am. Rev. Resp. Dis., *105*:883, 1972.
58. Strick, L.: Breathing and physical fitness exercises for asthmatic children. Pediatr. Clin. North Am., *16*:31, 1969.
59. Thacker, E. W.: *Postural Drainage in Respiratory Control*. London, Lloyd-Luke Medical Books, Ltd., 1965.
60. Tuft, L., and Mueller, H. W.: *Allergy in Children*. Philadelphia, W. B. Saunders Co., 1970.
61. Vance, V. J., and Taylor, W. F.: Status and trends in residential asthma homes in the United States. Ann. Allergy, *29*:428, 1971.
62. Vance, V. J., and Taylor, W. F.: The financial cost of chronic asthma. Ann. Allergy, *29*:455, 1971.
63. Vance, V. J., and Taylor, W. F.: Psychosocial problems in a pediatric allergy clinic. Ann. Allergy, *29*:582, 1971.
64. Wohl, T.: The group approach to the asthmatic child and family. J. Asthma Res., *4*:237, 1967.
65. Zausmer, E.: Bronchial drainage: Evidence supporting the procedures. Phys. Ther., *48*:586, 1968.

section two

Disorders
of the
Neuromuscular
System

Chapter 6

The Spinal Injury Patient

by *Stanley J. Myers, M.D.*

At first glance the human spinal cord seems impregnable: surrounded by a bony fortress, covered by tough membranes, bathed in shock absorbing fluids, and nourished by blood vessels that appear to arise from unlimited sources. With aging, however, the fortress may become vulnerable because of a decrease in tissue elasticity, narrowing of the spinal canal and foramina, osteoporosis, or structural fatigue of the bony elements. In children these factors usually do not play a great role, and although good statistical figures are not available, the child with a spinal cord lesion represents only a small fraction of the pediatric population seen either as inpatients or as outpatients. Nevertheless, the pediatric spinal injury patient is not uncommon at major medical centers or even in smaller communities and, owing to increased longevity following improved initial management, is likely to come to the attention of the pediatrician, urologist, neurologist, neurosurgeon, orthopedist, and physiatrist. Conversely, because a productive life is possible it behooves all concerned practitioners to familiarize themselves with proper management of the patient with spinal cord injury.

The principles of treatment, here primarily oriented toward spinal trauma, also pertain to all spinal lesions regardless of etiology.

ANATOMICAL REVIEW

For convenience of description the spinal anatomy can be artificially separated into three broad categories (Figs. 6–1 and 6–2).[38]

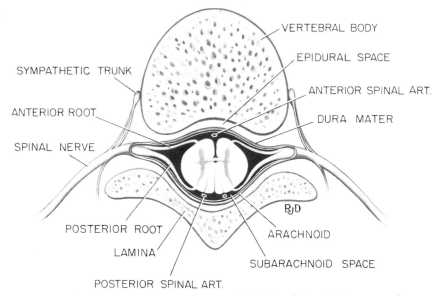

Figure 6–1   Cross section of the spinal cord at the T6 level showing bony, membranous, vascular, and neural elements.

The Vertebral Unit consists of the vertebral bony column together with associated ligaments and muscles. The mechanical stability and mobility of the body is affected by this unit with the exception of the first two cervical and the sacral vertebrae. All the spinal bony elements articulate by way of the intervertebral discs and posterolateral joints. The annulus fibrosus of the disc stabilizes the synarthrosis between the vertebral bodies, while the diarthrodial apophyseal joint is stabilized by its capsule together with the interspinous and supraspinous ligaments and ligamentum flavum. The thoracic spine is further supported by the rigidity of the rib cage.

The Cord Unit consists of the spinal cord together with its associated nerve roots and membranes. The spinal cord is the cylindrical extension of the brain stem and is suspended by means of its nerve roots and ligaments. It is in a fluid filled cavity and is confined by the dura mater, a relatively inelastic fibrous membrane, which is an extension of the inner layer of the cranial dura. The epidural space is the space between the spinal dura and the vertebral column, and contains numerous venous plexuses, fat, and ligaments. Entering and exiting nervous elements of the cord as well as vessels supplying the cord pass through this space. The spinal meninges consist of the dura and two additional membranes within the dural sack. The pia mater is applied to the external surface of the cord while the arachnoid layer is interposed between the dura proper and the pia. These membranes have a very close relationship to the nerve roots at the intervertebral foramina. The dentate ligaments are attached to the inner surface of the dura and the lateral surface of the cord, and anchor the cord to the dural surface. The paired spinal roots, which are divided anatomically into the anterior (motor) and posterior (sensory) roots, may also provide some mechanical fixation of the cord.

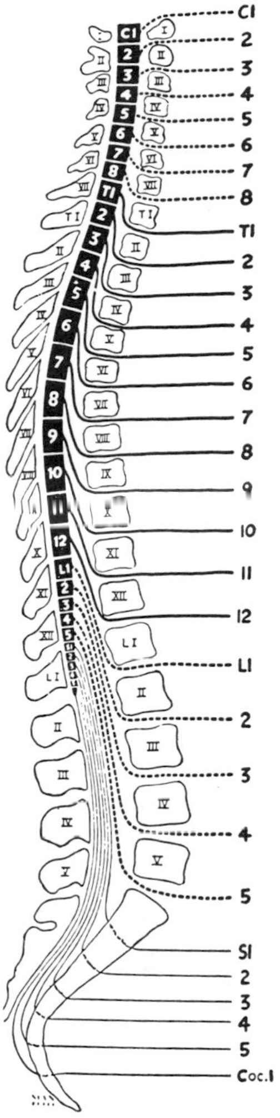

Figure 6-2 Relationship of spinal cord segments, intraspinal roots, and spinal nerves to the vertebral bodies, spines, and intervertebral spaces. The cervical nerves exit through intervertebral foramina above their respective vertebral bodies (seven cervical vertebrae, eight cervical nerves). The spinal cord ends at the L1 to L2 vertebral level, and lesions below this level involve the lower motor neuron. (From Mayo Clinic: *Clinical Examinations in Neurology.* Philadelphia, W. B. Saunders Co., 1971.)

The Spinal Vascular Unit. The blood supply to the cephalad part of the cord is mainly from the vertebral arteries. Before these vessels join inside the skull to form the basilar artery a branch is given off that fuses with one from the opposite side, forming the anterior spinal artery, which descends on the ventral surface of the cord. This artery mainly supplies the anterior two thirds of the spinal cord including the anterior and lateral columns. Small branches of the vertebral or posterior inferior cerebellar arteries continue caudally over the dorsal surface of the cord, usually as two small trunks, the posterior spinal arteries. Regional perfusion occurs by way of feeder or communicating branches arising from the thoracic and abdominal aorta, left vertebral, intercostal, and other vessels, and joining with the anterior spinal artery. While radicular arteries are present, entering at each side of the cord with the anterior and posterior roots, segmental distribution has not, in fact, been observed, as few vessels are of sufficient caliber to be effective. The cervical and lumbar segments of the cord have an ample blood supply; however, the mid thoracic area is usually supplied by one vessel, the artery of Adamkiewicz. In about 66 per cent of human subjects, it appears on the left side between T6 and L3, originating from an intercostal or upper lumbar vessel near the intervertebral foramen, and enters the anterior surface of the spinal cord. It then ascends as high as T5 or T6 and makes a hairpin turn to descend as the anterior spinal artery. A knowledge of the relatively poor feeder supply to the thoracic cord is important for understanding the risk inherent in operative interference and injuries at this level.

INCIDENCE AND ETIOLOGY OF PARAPLEGIA IN CHILDREN

Statistics about paraplegia in general and in children in particular are relatively rare on a national, state, or local level. Therefore, only isolated reports from medical centers can be used to give an overview of the nature of the problem. Melzak, citing figures from the National Spinal Injury Centre at Stoke-Mandeville Hospital in England, catalogs only 93 paraplegic children under age 14 who were admitted to the center between 1949 and 1969, and this is only a small fraction of the total number of patients admitted with spinal lesions.[28] Of these 93 children 31 per cent had lesions secondary to trauma, 20 per cent to spina bifida, 13 per cent to tumors, and 9 per cent of vascular etiology (Table 6–1). Except for spina bifida patients in whom cauda equina lesions were most common, the majority of the lesions were between T6 and T12. The numbers of boys and girls were approximately equal.

Birth injuries to the spinal cord are uncommon and are usually secondary to traction force during delivery of the head and shoulders in a breech presentation, the spinal column being stretched to the point of rupture of meninges and cord.[22] This usually occurs in the thoracic region, since the lumbar roots anchor the cord below as do the large cervical roots and medulla above, and the thoracic roots are relatively thin, providing little added support to the cord. There is rarely damage to the bony column with evidence of fracture or dislocation.

Automobile accidents are the most common cause of serious injuries in children.[15] In the decade from 1960 to 1969 approximately 10,000 American children under age four died in auto accidents. Fortunately, however, spinal cord trauma is uncommon before age 13. Burke studied seven children admitted to the Victoria Spinal Injury Center in the 15 months between April, 1968, and July, 1969.[4] Six were injured in auto accidents. Five of the younger patients had thoracic paraplegia but no evident vertebral injury. The two older children were injured by hyperflexion over a seat belt and had complete paraplegia below the upper lumbar segments with slight forward subluxation of L2 and L3. Similar reports concerning the lack of evidence of fracture-dislocation of the vertebrae have been published and this experience is not unlike that noted in adults.[15] In the automobile accidents, it is suggested, undue longitudinal traction possibly combined with angulation of the spine through a severe flexion-rotation force is the cause of the injuries.[4] The ver-

TABLE 6–1   ETIOLOGY OF PARAPLEGIA IN RELATION
TO LEVEL OF LESION*

Etiology	Number of Cases	Cervical		T1–T5		T1–T12		Cauda Equina
		Complete	Incomplete	Complete	Incomplete	Complete	Incomplete	
Trauma	29 (31.1%)	0	2	6	0	15	3	3
Spina bifida	19 (20.4%)	0	0	0	0	7	2	10
Tumors	12 (12.9%)	1	0	0	0	6	2	3
Vascular	8 (8.6%)	0	2	0	1	0	5	0
Transverse myelitis	6 (6.5%)	0	0	1	0	2	3	0
Cerebral palsy	5	0	5	0	0	0	0	0
Meningitis	5	0	0	1	1	2	1	0
Poliomyelitis	3	0	2	0	0	0	1	0
Epidural abscess	2	0	0	0	0	0	2	0

In children under age 14 admitted to the National Spinal Injuries Centre, Stoke Mandeville Hospital, 1948–1969. (From Melzak, J.. Paraplegia among children. Lancet, 2:45–48, 1969.)

tebral column composed of cartilaginous rings is capable of considerable elongation because of its elasticity and is thus less likely to show signs of injury while the spinal cord, its meninges, and its vascular supply are unable to withstand the same degree of traction. As with birth injuries, the predominance of upper thoracic lesions may be due to the anchoring effect on the cervical cord by the brachial plexus and on the lumbosacral cord by the cauda equina.

LIFE EXPECTANCY

There is little literature available about long-term survival of children with spinal cord lesions. Of the 93 patients studied by Melzak only two children died; both had spina bifida. One child with hydrocephalus succumbed to meningitis secondary to an infected Spitz-Holter valve at age 8 and the other to chronic pyelonephritis at age 12.[28] In general, one would expect that the life expectancy of children with low-level lesions and sterile urine would not be much affected. That of children with higher-level lesions would probably depend on the danger of aspiration and pulmonary and urinary tract infections.

INITIAL MANAGEMENT

The immediate management of the pediatric spinal injury patient does not differ from that of the adult. The patient should not be moved carelessly. The initial transport to an appropriate medical facility, preferably a spinal injury center, could be the most important aspect of the patient's care, as permanent damage can be done at this stage. The patient should be calmed and advised not to move. He should be lifted gently and without undue haste.

Usually a team of people coordinated by a leader is necessary to avoid twisting or bending the larger patient. If the child is conscious he should be placed in a supine position, preferably with a pillow under the small of the back. This in itself often tends to reduce any fracture or subluxation present. Casualties with suspected injuries to the spine who are unconscious should be placed in a lateral or semilateral position to avoid aspiration. Hard objects should be removed from the pockets in order to prevent development of pressure sores. While it is advisable to keep the patient covered, hot water bottles should not be used, as sensation may be impaired and burns produced. During transportation, pads of soft material (if available) should be placed between the knees and ankles to reduce pressure. The paraplegic should be transported on a rigid stretcher to prevent sagging and flexion of the spine. In general, it is not advisable to give morphine, especially to patients with cervical cord lesions who may have respiratory embarrassment. It is important, whenever possible, for medical personnel present at the scene of the accident to ascertain the level of the lesion and, in particular, the completeness of the motor and sensory paralysis so that later comparisons can be made.

Operative Versus Nonoperative Initial Treatment

In general hasty surgery should be avoided even when dealing with fracture-dislocation of the spine. The initial injury is often associated with damage of the vascular supply to the cord at the site of the trauma, and the associated concussion, laceration, or transection of the cord results in instantaneous clinical symptoms of complete or partial paralysis. Compression of the spinal cord from a vertebral fracture is very rarely the main cause of the paralysis; therefore, laminectomy or open reduction of the fractured vertebrae in an attempt to surgically decompress the cord may be ill advised. It is not uncommon to find an intact dura and spinal cord with permanent paralysis. The presence of a complete or partial subarachnoid block is not in itself prima facie evidence that this is the cause of the paraplegia.[18] Often, in spite of evidence of severe fracture-dislocation with compression of the spinal canal, clinical symptoms may be minimal or entirely absent, while on the other hand, complete spinal block can be due to temporary edema or subarachnoid bleeding that may ultimately resolve. It was found that in many patients at the Stoke-Mandeville Spinal Injury Centre considerable recovery of spinal cord function occurs in spite of persistent block and unreduced fracture-dislocation. Not only is there no proof that routine surgical intervention as an immediate therapeutic measure significantly enhances return of function, but, indeed, the converse may be true and further compromise of the vascular supply may result in prevention of return or an increase in the neurological deficit. The physician and neurosurgeon must resist the strong pressure placed upon them by the family to visualize the cord so that they can be definitely told whether the patient will have return of function. The concept that one has nothing to lose by laminectomy is not true.

There are some indications for early laminectomy. In the first few days following the spinal cord injury the lesion may ascend or descend one or two segments because of circulatory disturbances and edema around the damaged cord. Although this in itself is not an indication for laminectomy, progressively ascending symptoms over a large number of segments may be due to extramedullary hemorrhage or hematoma and may respond to surgical intervention. The most likely finding, however, will be spinal artery thrombosis or hematomyelia. The presence of foreign body fragments in the spinal cord, which could lead to inflammatory changes or infection, is indication for operative intervention. Motor or sensory symptoms in patients with incomplete cauda equina lesions that have progressed shortly after injury may recede spontaneously, and procrastination is not necessarily harmful.

New Concepts in Pathogenesis and Initial Treatment

Pathogenesis of Spinal Cord Trauma. Recent findings, mostly experimental, suggest the possibility of reversing the effects of spinal cord injury. The concept of immediate and permanent loss of spinal cord function following trauma appears to be fallacious in most cases. The trauma initiates a process of necrosis that eventually results in destruction of the cord, but there is a definite time interval before the destruction is complete. Wagner and Bucy and Dohrmann reviewed recent research on spinal cord injury.[10, 35] Morphologically the spinal cord appears relatively normal within minutes of experimentally induced injury. The earliest changes that take place in the damaged cord are a leakage of erythrocytes into the perivascular space surrounding thin walled vessels in the central gray matter followed by an extension into the parenchyma and the coalescence of these separate multiple hemorrhages within four hours. With these evolving hemorrhagic lesions, chromatolytic and ischemic changes are noted in the gray matter neurons. The surrounding white matter appears to be secondarily involved by the evolving changes in the central gray matter.[36] Tears in the muscular walls of venules are seen as early as 15 minutes after contusion and they rather than the capillaries appear to be the source of some of the early perivascular hemorrhages. While the capillary endothelium is swollen within four hours after injury, the walls remain intact. Fifteen to thirty minutes after contusion of the spinal cord in the monkey the white matter of the spinal cord begins to show changes. Selected myelinated fibers demonstrate enlarged periaxonal spaces. Changes are progressive, and by four hours after contusion one quarter of the fibers show breakage of the myelin sheaths, denuding of axons or marked attenuation of the myelin sheaths, greatly enlarged periaxonal spaces, and degeneration of the associated axons.[11] There is a reduction in perfusion of the central gray matter within one hour followed by involvement of the surrounding white matter within eight hours. By 24 hours the vascular pattern of the white matter returns toward normal, but the pattern in the gray matter remains markedly abnormal. Underlying the structural changes there are disturbances of tissue metabolites and alterations in the concentration of neurotransmitters during comparable intervals following trauma.

These findings have led to experimental evaluation of various treatments of lesions in which the cord has not been severed. These include regional hypothermia, corticosteroid administration, hyperbaric oxygenation, and the blocking of the synthesis of harmful neurotransmitter substances.

Regional Hypothermia.   Albin et al., using a controlled impact injury that would usually lead to irreversible paraplegia, produced a T10 cord lesion in 13 rhesus monkeys.[1] Localized cooling of the involved cord with a perfusion unit effecting selective reduction of cord temperature to 10° C with no change in cardiovascular dynamics or in brain and body core temperatures resulted in excellent return of function in 11 of the 13 monkeys within one month, but it was necessary to cool the cord within three to four hours postinjury. Hypothermic therapy initiated eight hours following contusion failed to prevent paraplegia. The protective effect of cooling was presumed to result from a reduction in spinal cord edema, a decreased metabolic demand, and better hemodynamic perfusion through a compromised area.

Corticosteroid Administration.   In an attempt to prevent the destructive edema resulting from concussion and contusion of the spinal cord Ducker and Hamit compared the effects of decompression (control), local cord hypothermia, intramuscular dexamethasone, and intrathecal depomethylprednisolone.[13] Each treatment started three hours after injury in four groups of dogs subjected to a standard experimental spinal cord trauma. Significant improvement and recovery of neurological function resulted from the use of the intramuscular dexamethasone and local hypothermia of the cord.

Blocking of Neurotransmitter Substances.   Spreading hemorrhagic necrosis of the central gray and later white matter is common to blunt trauma, deformation, or ischemia of the cord. Apparently there is an initial severe drop in oxygen content of the injured spinal cord tissue ultimately resulting in oxygen levels below tissue needs with ensuing central necrosis. On the basis of these observations Osterholm and Mathews studied naturally occurring spinal cord substances capable of producing intense vascular responses in microgram quantities, including norepinephrine, serotonin, and dopamine.[31] They found a doubling of concentration of norepinephrine in 30 minutes, quadrupling in one hour, and thereafter a slow decline approaching control values at four hours. The increases in norepinephrine were always associated with massive central hemorrhages and gray matter necrosis. Within two hours of injection of minute quantities of pure norepinephrine into the spinal gray matter of normal cats large central hemorrhages appeared that closely resembled the lesions associated with severe spinal injury. It was postulated that toxic quantities of tissue norepinephrine induced intense vasospasm, which impeded cord perfusion, resulting in neuronal necrosis, vascular rupture, and parenchymal self-destruction. These responses further act to depress or halt electrical activity of adjacent fibers and neurons producing the neuronal response of transient weakness or paralysis. Permanent loss of function ensues when the spinal cord tissue undergoes hemorrhagic autodestruction. Experiments were then designed to test the validity of the foregoing observations by assessing protection against traumatic hemorrhagic necrosis after specific norepinephrine synthesis blockade with alpha-methyltyrosine (AMT).[32] In cats, AMT administered 15 minutes after spinal cord injury decreased the norepinephrine accumulation, and there was much less hemorrhagic necrosis. Seventy per cent of the spinal cords from animals so treated were normal or had only minor gray matter changes while all untreated animals developed severely destructive lesions. Because of the toxic effect of this substance (renal disturbances in 40 per cent of the animals) use of AMT in humans is not yet recommended. Screening of other agents including reserpine, L-dopa, guanethidine, Dibenamine, and lidocaine showed that significant necrosis was prevented in most tissues of injured spinal cords. AMT provided nearly 97 per cent protection from hemorrhagic necrosis; however, reserpine had the next highest level of protection with 93 per cent normal tissue retention in injured cords.

Hyperbaric Oxygen. Kelly et al. demonstrated that tissue P_{O_2} in the normal spinal cord of dogs can be increased by ventilating the animals with 100 per cent oxygen or carbogen.[21] Following trauma to the cord, however, the tissue P_{O_2} responded only to hyperbaric oxygenation; at 2 ATA (atmospheres absolute at 14.7 lb per square inch) it was possible to raise the P_{O_2} of the traumatized spinal cord to well above the tissue P_{O_2} in the nontraumatized cord. A test group of animals rendered paraplegic and treated with hyperbaric oxygen recovered to a greater degree than those in the untreated control group.

Cortical Evoked Responses

It may be possible to use cerebrocortical evoked potentials as a means of ascertaining the presence of a block in transmission across the spinal cord and in determining whether this block is reversible. Using needle electrodes in anesthetized cats, Croft et al. recorded averaged potentials over the scalp following stimulation of a peripheral nerve.[8] Graded pressure on the spinal cord produced reversible blocking of these potentials. The block of motor transmission through the cord paralleled the block of sensory transmission, and these seem to be sensitive indicators of spinal cord function. This technique may be useful in prognosticating return of function in patients with spinal injury, in determining effectiveness of early prophylactic treatment, and as a monitoring agent in anesthetized patients undergoing spinal operations.

These experimental results are encouraging and clinical studies are being planned. Most major hospital centers do not receive the patient with spinal injury within four hours of the acute trauma and do not have a sufficient number of such cases to develop a trained spinal injury team with a set procedure. There is a great need for regional spinal injury centers in this country. It is possible that the pessimism attendant on prognosticating return of function in spinal injury patients may soon be replaced by a more optimistic outlook in that most acute paralysis will be partially or completely reversed following appropriate treatment at the correct time.

SPINE STABILIZATION

It is generally agreed by most physicians dealing with acute spinal cord trauma that there is little indication for early open reduction of fracture-dislocations of the spine followed by internal fixation using either plating or bone grafts. No proof is available that this promotes neurological recovery better than conservative methods, and it has been shown that morbidity might even be increased. In the vast majority of cases permanent stability of the spine can be achieved by postural reduction alone. During the period of time that this requires, usually from 6 to 12 weeks, the patient can be turned to prevent decubiti and can undergo bowel and bladder training as well as upper extremity strengthening to prepare him for later mobilization. The use of plaster casts or body jackets, in general, is to be avoided in most lesions above T12. It is only the rare severe fracture-dislocation that will require open reduction. Approximately 80 per cent of cervical injuries and almost 100 per cent of thoracolumbar injuries heal with only moderate displacement after careful conservative reduction. However, the battle as to the merits of early fusion for cervical spine injury, especially using the anterior approach, continues.[5, 30] There are some indications for this procedure, but they would seem to pertain only to a small percentage of cervical injury patients. If instability is present after an adequate period of conservative management, a stabilization procedure can then be done under optimal conditions.

CLINICAL PATTERNS OF TRAUMATIC INCOMPLETE LESIONS

Prognosticating return of function in a spinal injury patient soon after onset is unreliable. The chances for neurological recovery in initially complete lesions are usually poor if there is no return within 48 hours; however, it is safer to wait for three weeks in paraplegia and six weeks in quadriplegia.[29] It is imperative that in dealing with spinal cord injuries the absence of sensation in the perianal area be evaluated since patients with intact sacrally innervated sensation have a considerably better prognosis. In partial lesions it is wise to wait at least six months before dismissing chances for neurological recovery.

In new lesions a rise or fall of level by more than three segments within hours, days, or weeks of injury is seen in only a small percentage of cases while changes of one or two segments are not infrequent. Genuine recovery of power in a muscle completely paralyzed for up to two years after injury is occasionally seen in cauda equina lesions, and this type of lesion, which is predominantly lower motor neuron, is best considered separately from the more disabling higher level upper motor neuron lesions (see Fig. 6–2). A rise of neurological level several years after injury is infrequently seen. Severe permanent increase in spasticity occurring several years after injury without discoverable cause is seen as rarely as the opposite spontaneous gradual transformation from a spastic into a flaccid lesion.

Bosch et al. reviewed 60 cases of incomplete traumatic quadriplegia for purposes of aiding future prognosis.[3] Four syndromes were described: anterior spinal cord, central spinal cord, unilateral hemi-section (Brown-Séquard), and posterior spinal cord. The same classification could also apply to more distal upper motor neuron (non-cauda equina) lesions.

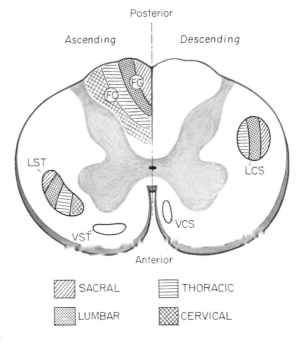

Posterior

Ascending | Descending

Figure 6–3 Cross section through the spinal cord at the C6 level showing major ascending and descending tracts. FG, fasciculus gracilis; FC, fasciculus cuneatus; LST, lateral spinothalamic tract; LCS, lateral corticospinal (pyramidal) tract; VCS, ventral (anterior) corticospinal tract; VST, ventral (anterior) spinothalamic tract.

Anterior

SACRAL   THORACIC

LUMBAR   CERVICAL

Figure 6–3 and Table 6–2 show some of the ascending and descending tracts of the spinal cord. There are the ascending pathways of the medial fasciculus gracilis and the lateral fasciculus cuneatus that carry sensory impulses mediating position sense, two-point discrimination, vibration, and occasionally deep touch and pressure from the sacral, lumbar, and lower thoracic areas of the body (gracilis) and from the higher thoracic and upper extremities (cuneatus). In the lateral compartments of the cord there are the crossed pyramidal tract (the descending corticospinal tract), which carries impulses for voluntary motion, and also the ascending lateral spinal thalamic tract, which transmits pain and temperature sensation from the opposite side of the body. The anterior columns contain the ascending ventral spinal thalamic tract, which carries the sense of light touch, and the direct pyramidal tract (descending uncrossed ventral cortical spinal tract), which normally extends to the upper thoracic cord innervating the muscles of the upper extremity and neck. The peripheral distribution of the sacral and lumbar fibers and the more medial placement of the cervical and thoracic ones on either the ascending or descending tracts should be noted.

During the 10 year period between January, 1956, and December, 1965, a total of 447 patients were admitted to Rancho Los Amigos Hospital with diagnosed spinal cord trauma.[3] Of this number, 213 had injuries at the level of the cervical segments (47.7 per cent). After incomplete records were discarded there were 60 (32.8 per cent) who had partial lesions. The sex distribution of these 60 was 14 females and 46 males. Ages at the time of injury ranged from 13 to 69 years, with a mean of 36 years. The most common level of injury was at C5–6. Forty-two of the sixty patients (70 per cent) were considered to have a central cord type of lesion. Symptoms compatible with anterior cord syn-

TABLE 6–2   IMPORTANT ASCENDING AND DESCENDING
SPINAL TRACTS

Tract	Function	Side Innervated
Ascending (Sensory)		
Fasciculus gracilis ⎫	Position sense and movement	Ipsilateral (fibers
	Vibration	cross in medulla)
Fasciculus cuneatus ⎭	Two-point discrimination	
	? deep touch and pressure	
Lateral spinothalamic	Pain and temperature	Contralateral (fibers cross in anterior commissures)
Ventral spinothalamic	Light touch	Contralateral (fibers cross in anterior commissures)
Descending (Motor)		
Lateral corticospinal (crossed pyramidal tract)	Voluntary motion	Ipsilateral (fibers cross in medulla)
Ventral corticospinal (direct pyramidal tract)	Voluntary motion (to muscles of upper extremity and neck)	Contralateral (fibers cross in anterior commissures) and ipsilateral

drome were found in 12 patients (20 per cent), and in 5 patients (8.3 per cent) findings were typical of hemisection lesions. Only one patient (1.6 per cent) of the 60 was thought to have suffered posterior cord damage.

The central cord syndrome is characterized by greater weakness of the arms than of the legs, varying degrees of decreased sensation, and a neurogenic bladder usually manifested as urinary retention. Since damage occurs centrally in the cord, the amount of recovery depends upon the degree of hematomyelia and cord destruction as opposed to edema. In adults the usual mechanism of injury appears to be severe hyperextension of an osteoarthritic cervical spine with or without bony destruction, although in experimental animals a similar lesion can be produced by blunt trauma or concussion. Of the 42 patients with a central cord type of lesion more than half were able to walk following a rehabilitation program. In general, involvement is the same in both hands though occasionally one side may be more affected than the other. Following a rehabilitation program 56 per cent had gained function while 44 per cent were classified as nonfunctional. Both ambulation and upper extremity function were significantly better after a rehabilitation program. Approximately half the patients had bladder and bowel control. The central cord type of lesion may occasionally be associated with later ascending symptoms such as increasing spasticity and pyramidal tract involvement.

The anterior spinal artery syndrome is characterized by immediate complete motor paralysis with hyperesthesia and hypalgesia below the level of the lesion associated with preservation of touch, motion, position, two-point discrimination, and vibration sense. This lesion is found with flexion injuries of the cervical spine, often producing a fracture-dislocation of the "tear drop" appearance. Two main factors are usually involved; direct damage to the anterior part of the cord by dislocated fragments of bone or herniated disc and vascular insufficiency secondary to occlusion of the anterior spinal artery, which deprives the anterolateral two thirds of the spinal cord of its blood supply, giving the typical picture in which only the posterior columns are unaffected. In the 12 patients with this lesion, none were ambulatory on follow-up. Hand function was present in two with low cervical lesions, but there was no functional return of lost power in these patients. Bladder and bowel control remained absent.

The clinical pattern in Brown-Séquard syndrome (hemisection of the spinal cord) includes loss of pain and temperature perception on the opposite half of the body below the level of the lesion with loss of motor, position sense, two-point discrimination, and vibration sense on the side of the lesion. This uncommon syndrome is not seen in closed injuries of the cervical spine, but usually follows open trauma. Of the five patients observed, all but one, who had multiple medical problems, were walking at follow-up. One patient did not have function in the involved upper extremity. Bladder control was initially present in all patients and was maintained.

The posterior cord syndrome is rare and is manifested by preservation of the anterior and lateral columns of the spinal cord with complete abolishment of epicritic sensation. There are few statistics about prognosis of this lesion.

REHABILITATION

Once the initial spinal cord insult has occurred and the acute period is over, the lesion is usually static and nonprogressive regardless of whether it is secondary to accidental trauma, congenital abnormalities, infection, treated tumor, or surgery. In treating patients with a spinal cord lesion, perhaps more so than in any other condition, a team approach becomes mandatory since the patient is likely to be followed by numerous physicians from different specialities, therapists, vocational counselors, psychologists, nurses, and others. One physician knowledgeable in the management of spinal cord lesions, regardless of particular specialty, should remain in charge, but frequent conferences with other members of the patient's team, the patient, and his family are necessary for continuity of care.

The early management of the spinal injury patient is mostly concerned with prevention of complications and maintenance of functions. During this early stage after the acute medical condition has stabilized, physical therapy and nursing play a major role. Decubiti, contractures, urinary tract infections, pulmonary emboli, respiratory infections, and other effects of inactivity are likely to occur at this time. These are usually preventable. Upper extremity strengthening is begun, and if this area is neurologically involved, muscle reeducation and manual dexterity training are instituted. When the patient is permitted more activity he is taught to use a wheelchair and given instructions in transfers and activities of daily living. During this time psychological adjustments are being made; this will continue. Later, social and vocational matters are emphasized and occur mostly outside the hospital. During all phases of rehabilitation, prevention of medical complications is essential. The earlier the patient and family understand and accept the nature of the disability, the easier will be later management. Friedland gives a detailed presentation of various aspects of management of the patient with spinal cord injury together with a comprehensive bibliography.[14]

Skin Care

The patient should initially be turned every two to three hours around the clock—by a specially trained team if maintenance of spinal traction is necessary. There are traction attachments for most contemporary turning-type hospital beds that permit changes of position while maintaining traction. Later the patient will learn to turn himself, and the frequency will depend on his skin tolerance and individual circumstances. The skin should be inspected for red areas at least once a day, and more often if indicated, so that pressure areas can be eliminated. It is much easier to prevent decubiti than to treat them. Decreased sensation, poor nutrition, low hemoglobin level, improper positioning, and spasticity all favor the development of skin lesions. The prominent bony areas are most prone to develop overlying skin breakdown; these will vary with position. Thus, the sacrum, scapuli, heels, and occiput are at risk when the patient is supine; when side lying, the trochanters and the lateral aspect of the heels and knees are pressure sites; and while sitting, ischial decubiti are most characteristic. Superficial sores most often seen in the bedbound malnourished individual are caused by shearing forces, but the most common type of pressure lesion begins in the deeper tissue and only later is visible at the skin surface. Therefore, what appears to be a minor red area on the surface may be indicative of a serious underlying necrotic area. The area should be felt for fluctuance, firmness, and heat, and the patient observed for other systemic manifestations of infection. The presence of decubiti hinders the patient's rehabilitation and later keeps him out of school and work. Even more serious are the complications of sepsis and osteomyelitis, occasionally leading to limb disarticulations and secondary amyloidosis. In addition to manual turning, other aids such as alternating air pressure mattresses, sheepskin coverings, foam pads over heels and other pressure areas, gelfoam cushions, rotating and rocking beds and water beds can be valuable. The use of these different devices depends upon availability, the patient's circumstances (i.e., spasticity, location of previously existing decubiti) and the prior experience of the patient's medical team. As long as body weight is adequately distributed so that prominent sites are not subjected to capillary occluding pressures, the patient's skin should remain clear. The importance of adequate cleansing and drying of the skin, especially in incontinent patients, cannot be overemphasized.

Exercises and Prevention of Contractures

Range of motion of the joints of the paralyzed extremities should be maintained. This is true even when the neurological deficit is permanent. Joint contractures can seriously hamper later function and contribute to complications by preventing free mobility, making dressing difficult or even impossible, and leading to the development of bony prominences favoring decubiti formation. Gentle range of motion exercises daily when joint motion is loose will be sufficient, but if tightness begins to occur, more frequent exercises are necessary. At times the use of various heating modalities may be of benefit in improving local circulation, relaxing muscular spasm, and perhaps altering the elasticitiy of certain connective tissue structures, but great care must be taken when using them over insensate areas. Diathermy, heating pads, or hot packs are contraindicated, while distant radiant heat where the skin can be carefully watched and ultrasound in which the dose can be controlled would be more suitable. Exercises must be gentle to avoid producing pathological fractures in bones that are depleted of calcium, and overstretching of joints should also be avoided to prevent loss of stability.

In most hospital beds the supine position predisposes towards flexion of hips and knees and equinus position of the ankles. Gatching of the bed should be avoided. A padded footboard or separate posterior splints to keep the ankles in a neutral position and relieve heel pressure together with periods of programmed prone lying is of considerable value.

Depending upon the degree of completeness of the lesion, passive, active assistive, active, or resistive exercises are provided. When paralysis is complete, passive exercises (i.e., done by the therapist) are given. Electrical stimulation may be of some benefit for muscle reeducation, but it does not practically prevent atrophy in denervated muscle. When mild spasticity is present exercises may aid in maintaining motion; when it is severe, however, contractures will usually develop and other means of dealing with the spasticity (discussed later) are necessary.

During the period of immobilization, as long as there are no medical contraindications, exercises should be directed toward maintaining and increasing strength of the patient's intact musculature. This helps to maintain metabolic balance as well as enhancing the patient's ability to care for himself as soon as possible. The importance of upper extremity strengthening in a paraplegic patient who will rely on these muscle groups for turning, transferring, dressing, and crutch walking is obvious. Specific techniques of the training program vary and are not discussed here, but the common factor is the placing of stress on the muscle groups to be strengthened. Resistive exercises, be they brief isometric or isokinetic with resistance movement, will tend to increase strength and muscle bulk while repetitive exercises to the point of fatigue, but not beyond, will tend to improve endurance and cardiopulmonary fitness. The older child can be given a bedside program of gradually increasing exercises that he can do himself when not involved in the more formal therapy program. A bedside overhead trapeze is helpful in enabling change of position and transfers in and out of bed, and it can also be used for exercising.

The very young patient has to be handled differently; his exercises can be structured in the form of play activities.

Metabolic and Cardiovascular Effects of Immobilization

Although most information about the effects of bed rest has been obtained from studies on adults, it can be assumed that similar findings apply to children. With bed rest there tends to be an initial pooling of blood in the thorax with a decrease in venous return to the heart and consequently a decrease in cardiac output. In adults this is the equivalent of a loss of 500 ml of plasma. In the presence of continued immobilization this loss is not made up. There is also a rapid shift to negative nitrogen and calcium balance with a decline in nutritional status and an increase in ectopic calcium deposition, urinary calculi, osteoporosis, and pathological fractures. Exercise and a high protein diet with adequate nutrients can reverse the negative nitrogen balance. The most important factor for maintenance of bone calcium appears to be the presence of active muscle contraction. In the presence of paralysis, however, maintenance of the upright posture can partially decrease the calcium loss. Adequate food intake, acidification of the urine, and prompt treatment of urinary tract infections will minimize calculi formation in the genitourinary tract.

Heterotopic Ossification. Ectopic or extraosseous bone formation has been reported in both incomplete and complete paraplegia appearing within the area of the neurological deficit. The hips are most often involved, followed by the knee, elbow, and shoulder areas. In a retrospective study of 447 quadriplegic and paraplegic patients there was x-ray evidence of heterotopic ossification in 20 per cent. Three per cent of the patients demonstrated ankylosis, which again was most frequently noted at the hip joint and was the most disabling because it forced a number of these patients to remain supine for the rest of their lives. Neither spasticity nor flaccidity appeared to be related to the development of heterotopic ossification, and the youngest patients were most prone to this complication. No beneficial effect from either diathermy or ultrasound was obtained. Although some maintain that vigorous range of motion exercise with soft tissue trauma is a causative factor in heterotopic ossification, this series did not bear this out. Because early lesions are vascular in nature and hyperemia is observed, the diagnosis is often initially confused with thrombophlebitis so that anticoagulants, and in some cases antibiotics, are prescribed to no avail. Surgical restoration of joint motion is usually not considered until ossification is complete, and so the patient may be forced to be nonfunctional for long periods of time. With the introduction of experimental calcium mobilizing drugs such as diphosphonates it may soon be possible to reverse or to minimize these complications.

Cardiovascular Deconditioning. In general, the higher the level of the lesion and the more complete the paralysis the greater the intolerance to the upright position. If a quadriplegic or even a low-level paraplegic patient who has been at bed rest for a long time is suddenly placed in the upright position,

syncope is likely to occur. This is secondary not only to immobilization causing deconditioning but also to the fact that vascular reflexes are not fully operative. When the patient who has already lost the equivalent of 500 ml of
plasma, secondary to bed rest, further pools an additional amount of fluid in
his lower extremities with little or no reflex vasoconstriction, decreased cardiac output, hypotension, and a decrease in cerebral blood flow causing
syncope follows. Fortunately, this intolerance to the upright position is
frequently reversible. The legs are wrapped with elastic bandages or stockings and at times an abdominal binder is used in order to decrease venous
pooling. In severe cases an Air Force type of antigravity suit may be beneficial, as may mineralocorticoids and peripheral sympathetic stimulating
agents. A program to gradually increase tilt table tolerance is followed
until the patient is able to remain at 70 degrees of upright tilt for over 20
minutes without significant change in pulse and blood pressure or subjective discomfort. The gravitational stresses in the upright position are
beneficial in reducing negative calcium balance, and therefore are of greater
value in patients with flaccid lesions in whom osteoporosis appears to be
more significant than in those patients with spasticity.

Pulmonary and Respiratory Complications. Respiratory difficulties can
occur in patients with midthoracic lesions in whom poor abdominal tone and
distention interfere with diaphragmatic movement and lead to dyspnea. If the
lesion is above T6 there is considerable interference with the accessory
muscles of respiration, and although tidal volume may be normal or only
slightly decreased, vital capacity begins to fall and exertional effort becomes
more difficult. Lesions above C4 involve the phrenic nerve, and assisted
ventilation is often necessary. Numerous devices for this purpose are available. At times, when awake, the patient can have enough control over his accessory muscles to provide adequate arterial oxygen saturation, but during
sleep it may be necessary for his ventilation to be assisted. Adequate respiratory toilet is important, and in any plegic patient confined to bed a good cough
and deep respiratory movements should be encouraged together with
frequent changes of position in order to decrease accumulation of secretions
and the likelihood of atelectasis. A rocking bed is of value in this situation not
only for mobilizing secretions but also for minimizing constant skin pressure
and aiding peripheral circulation.

Prevention of pulmonary emboli is another important consideration. Anti-
embolic stockings should be used, and wrapping of the lower extremities
from the metatarsal heads up to the gluteal folds should be carried out routinely. This also decreases peripheral edema and pooling in paraplegic patients and helps to reduce the severity of orthostatic intolerance. Consideration should be given to anticoagulation with oral agents, provided there are
no contraindications, since most recumbent patients are prone to stasis,
phlebothrombosis, and phlebitis. The problem occurs especially in the elderly
but also in young, otherwise healthy, paraplegic patients. Pulmonary embolism should be ruled out in any paraplegic patient who suddenly develops a
cough, respiratory symptoms, or fever. Periodic routine measurements of
lower extremity circumferences should be done. Once the patient is actively
mobilized and out of bed anticoagulation should be discontinued.

Temperature Regulation

In the intact subject both skin and central receptors play a role in maintaining body temperature. With a high spinal cord lesion above the T6 to T8 level the afferent impulses from most skin temperature receptors cannot be integrated and the patient is subject to the mercy of the environment and is poikilothermic, responding with a rise or fall in body temperature as the ambient temperature changes. Shivering will not occur below the level of a complete lesion; so heat production is decreased and body temperature falls with a fall in room temperature. It is important to see that high-level spinal injury patients are adequately covered. Conversely the rise in temperature associated with infection may not respond to salicylates since this drug exerts its effect through hypothalamic control of peripheral vasodilation of skin vessels resulting in sweating and evaporative loss of heat. These patients usually must have skin and central temperature lowered by exposure to a cooler environment either through removal of heavy covers or application of a cooling blanket to the insentient body.

It has been shown in patients with a sensory level below T10 that sentient skin cooling alone can initiate shivering (above the level of lesion) even when central temperature is kept constant at or near 37°C. In patients with lesions from T2 to L1 central cooling alone initiates shivering and increased metabolism even when the sentient skin is kept above 34° C. When the sentient skin is cool, shivering and increased metabolism begin at a higher central temperature than when the skin is warmer. Hand blood flow parallels these changes. Thus either central or sentient skin cooling alone will produce a decrease in hand blood flow and a rise in oxygen consumption. Combined central and skin cooling will cause an enhanced metabolic response greater than either stimulus alone.[12] Similar findings are observed for the effects of heat loss (sweating) as are seen for the effects of heat production (shivering). Thermoregulatory sweating is usually absent in areas below the level of the spinal cord transection with an overlap of several dermatomes above and below the somatic level due to overlap of autonomic dermatomes.

Bladder and Bowel

Bladder Physiology.   The bladder has both sensory and motor innervation. The sensory fibers from the skeletal muscle composing the external urinary sphincter pass to the first, second, and third sacral segments of the spinal cord via the pudendal nerves. (The somatic nerves also carry the efferent limb of a stretch or myotactic reflex that serves the external sphincter.) The sensory fibers from the bladder smooth muscle pass to the spinal cord via the pelvic nerves, and these serve as the afferent limb of the micturition reflex. The bladder sensory fibers traverse the dorsal root ganglia of S2, S3, and S4 and ultimately connect with preganglionic parasympathetic motor neurons in the intermediate gray matter of the sacral cord to complete the arc of the micturition reflex. Other sensory fibers terminate in the dorsal horn cells, contributing to sensations of pain and temperature. The motor innervation in the bladder wall is by both sympathetic and parasympathetic nerves. The preganglionic parasympathetic motor fibers arise in the lateral areas of the intermediate gray matter of the sacral cord and pass via the S2, S3, and S4 roots to the bladder through the pelvic nerves synapsing with postganglionic neurons in the bladder or vesical plexus. The sympathetic preganglionic fibers arise in nerve cells in the intermediolateral gray matter of the lower thoracic and upper lumbar cord and synapse in the inferior mesenteric ganglia or in the pelvic plexus. The postganglionic adrenergic fibers then pass via the hypogastric nerves to the bladder and pelvic organs. Adrenergic postganglionic sympathetic motor fibers appear to be mingled with postganglionic parasympathetic fibers supplying the bladder muscle. The parasympathetic nerves produce contraction of the bladder wall. The role of the sympathic innervation is still not clearly defined.

As the bladder fills, the detrusor muscle contracts and this is associated with an urge to void. Voiding is prevented by contractions of the pelvic floor musculature acting on the external urinary sphincter. When distention is mild these contractions are involuntary; however, with greater degrees of distention, a voluntary effort is required to prevent voiding. Voluntary voiding can be initiated by increasing intraabdominal, and thereby intravesical, pressure by means of a Valsalva maneuver. As intravesical pressure increases and the external urinary sphincter relaxes, the bladder muscle contracts and the bladder shape alters in such a fashion that the bladder neck opens, permitting voiding. The detrusor muscle of the bladder neck can function as an auxiliary sphincter but is not a distinct entity. With overdistention of the bladder the so-called internal sphincter remains open, contributing to incontinence.

If the bladder is denervated as in the acute phase of spinal shock or after lower motor neuron injury, the bladder wall is flaccid. It is important at this time to prevent overdistention since the bladder wall demonstrates a hysteresis effect in that each successive filling results in a decrease in passive pressure at any given volume. Thus, if the bladder is filled once, emptied and refilled a second time, there will be a decrease in pressure observed in comparison to the pressure noted following the first filling.

In an upper motor neuron lesion there is an increase in tone and contractions of the detrusor and abdominal muscles and also, at times, of the external urinary sphincter so that in spite of a hyperactive bladder, complete emptying is prevented and there may be residual urine. Reflux of urine from the bladder into the ureters is normally not seen because of ureteral peristaltic contractions, the antomical arrangement of the muscle fibers of the lower ureter whereby bladder contractions elongate and flatten the lower portion of the ureters, and the fact that the ureters pass through the bladder wall in a diagonal direction so that on contraction of the detrusor muscle that portion of the ureter in the bladder wall is compressed. A continuously elevated pressure in the bladder or distention of the bladder alters these arrangements, thereby promoting reflux.

Mason and Downey have adequately summarized basic urogenital physiology and discussed the complex neurological interrelationships.[27]

Urological Management.   Infection of the neurogenic bladder and resultant acute systemic and later renal complications are the most common and serious manifestations seen following traumatic paraplegia. Proper urological management is of great importance to both life expectancy and social acceptance. It is important that attention be directed to care of the neurogenic bladder as early as possible. Today there is little doubt that an indwelling catheter should be avoided whenever feasible. The method of intermittent catheterization popularized by Sir Ludwig Guttmann at Stoke-Mandeville Spinal Injury Centre in England is one that should be universally adopted, as it prevents many of the complications seen with an indwelling catheter and leads to bladder training whereby the patient can ultimately be completely catheter free. A study over an 11 year period on 476 traumatic paraplegics and quadriplegics revealed that of patients admitted within the first two weeks after injury, those who had indwelling catheters placed previously already had urinary tract infections. Intermittent catheterization proved highly effective in preventing infection of the paralyzed bladder. More than 62 per cent of the total number of patients had sterile urine on discharge from the hospital.[19]

An attempt should be made as early as possible, regardless of age, to keep the child relatively dry by regulating fluid intake and output and by initially trying manual expression of the bladder. This can be done regularly every two to four hours by hospital personnel or at home by the parents or a suitable attendant. At about age 10 the child can be trained to perform Credé manipulation himself. Should manual expression initially not prove successful, then intermittent catheterization can be tried, using sterile technique. Manual expression of as much urine as possible should be followed by catheterization and the residual volume should be measured. As the residual amount falls to appropriate levels, depending upon bladder capacity, the frequency of catheterization can be decreased. At times obstruction to outflow of urine, more common in adults, may make a transurethral resection or external sphincterotomy necessary. Both manual Credé expression and intermittent catheterization require considerable time and effort on the part of hospital personnel. It may be feasible to teach older patients to perform self-catheterization, and there are instances of patients who have gone for many years using this technique without complications.

The urine should be kept acid, since this decreases the likelihood of stone formation as well as inhibiting the growth of most bacteria. For this purpose ascorbic acid in doses of from 1 to 4 gm per day orally is usually more effective than the traditionally used cranberry juice. The urine pH should be tested with litmus paper each morning.

There are times when an indwelling catheter is necessary, and in these cases a Silastic type is more effective in preventing bladder irritation and the formation of stones around the catheter balloon. The catheter should be irrigated between two and four times a day, depending upon the amount of detritus present, usually with a dilute acetic acid or neomycin mixture. It may be wise to clamp the catheter for approximately 30 to 60 minutes at the end of the irrigation procedure after first instilling a neomycin solution. Continuous drip type of irrigation is not as effective, since only a small portion of the bladder is irrigated.

All spinal injury patients with neurogenic bladders should have intravenous pyelograms, cystometrograms, and triple voiding cystograms at least yearly, depending upon circumstances. It is also of value to check the residual urine volume periodically and to obtain hematocrit and blood urea nitrogen determinations as well as urinalysis and cultures. Attempts should be made to keep the urine sterile, especially in patients who are catheter free; it is more difficult in those with indwelling catheters. It is our policy to treat even asymptomatic bacteruria if a pathogen is cultured and concentration is greater than 10,000 colonies per cubic millimeter. If growth of the organism recurs, however, and the patient remains asymptomatic then he is carefully followed without using further antibiotics to avoid the development of resistant strains. Obviously, it is urgent that symptomatic urinary tract infections be treated as promptly and effectively as possible and that attempts be made to determine the cause of the infection and to remove this if possible. The use of urinary antiseptic agents such as methenamine mandelate is of value, and at times periodic prophylactic treatment with sulfonamides or other drugs is used.

The neurogenic bladder may present as a large capacity or small capacity organ, the former usually associated with a lower motor neuron lesion and the latter with an upper motor neuron lesion. The somatic physical status of the patient is also not always reflected by bladder physiology, and patients may manifest severe lower extremity spasticity and yet have a large capacity flaccid bladder and vice versa. This is often related to the initial management of the patient, the degree to which the bladder has been allowed to be distended, and the presence of chronic cystitis.

Although judicious Credé manipulation may keep the patient dry, not infrequently there are associated accidents and leaking in spastic patients, and therefore, in boys external drainage devices are of value. These can be taped or cemented to the penis, and if good hygienic precautions are taken, few complications are likely to develop. Unfortunately, there is no satisfactory external drainage device for girls, and it is necessary to use diapers and rubber undergarments. Unless the patient changes frequently she is likely to have an odor and be prone to skin breakdown and infection. Thus many female paraplegic patients, especially those with spastic-type bladders, eventually require a permanent indwelling catheter. Careful cleaning, frequent changes, and appropriate fluid restriction should be tried and good habits developed as early as possible to avoid this.

In the presence of vesicoureteral reflux, it is necessary to provide continuous bladder drainage, usually an indwelling catheter, either via the urethra or through a suprapubic cystotomy. There are some patients who develop a symbiotic relationship with the organisms grown in the bladder and remain free of difficulty; however, over the course of years, chronic cystitis and ascending infection are likely to occur. Cutaneous vesicostomy is felt by most urologists to offer little in the management of the neurogenic bladder. An ileal diversion procedure may be necessary should vesicoureteral reflux associated with continued bladder infection take place. This procedure consists of isolating a loop of ileum to form a receptacle, placing the opening of this isolated segment of gut to the skin in the abdominal area in the direction of peristaltic flow. The ureters are then implanted into this ileal loop. Not infrequently, the infected bladder is also removed. Major complications are those associated with closure of the ileostomy stoma, skin lesions at the stoma site, high residual urine in the ileal loop with associated infection, and unfortunately further ureteral reflux with hydronephrosis. Comarr reviewed conservative management of the urinary bladder among children six weeks to 35 years after spinal cord injury and found that more than 61 per cent of his patients had normal kidneys bilaterally and a very small percentage had a single kidney that was considered poor.[6] The statistics for conservative management of the urinary bladder in myelodysplasia were even better. Thus, although there are indications for the ileal bypass procedure, hasty decisions to operate are not indicated.

The use of electrical stimulators to improve bladder function is of interest. Implantation into the bladder wall of electrodes directly stimulating the bladder has been of limited clinical success, as the current spreads into adjacent regions of the pelvis and sphincter, causing inappropriate contractions and pain. The bladder wall may also be altered secondary to infection or distention with subsequent changes in reactivity to stimulation. Another approach is to place electrodes in the central gray matter (parasympathetic intermediolateral columns) of the sacral cord after the areas that result in most efficient bladder emptying have been determined.[17] Stimulation is provided approximately every four hours with a radiofrequency receiver. Three out of four patients have successfully been maintained in this fashion for over a year without complications.

Bowel Training.   It is easier to institute successful bowel training than bladder management. Problems in promoting the onset of defecation are usually few; rather one must control elimination until an appropriate time and location can be found. Sufficient roughage in the diet for adequate stool bulk and the insertion of a glycerin suppository, in either the morning or the evening at a convenient time is often all that is necessary to induce a bowel movement within 30 minutes to two hours. Once the patient is completely evacuated the likelihood of an accident in between is diminished. Stool softeners such as dioctyl sodium sulfosuccinate (Colace) are helpful. Occasionally the suppository is not needed and manual stimulation around the anal area may suffice to initiate evacuation, especially in the spastic patient. At other times the use of a more potent laxative such as bisacodyl, either by mouth or suppository or a combination of both, is necessary. Once an appropriate regimen has been determined, little variation from it is required. Regular bowel habits should be encouraged. Loose diarrheal movements can be indicative of underlying fecal retention, and disimpaction may be necessary.

Secondary Deformities

Deformities can result from immobilization, but muscle imbalance is their most common cause. The imbalance may be due to spasticity, prior surgery, or congenital anatomical deficits.

Vertebral Deformities.   Audic and Maury studied 60 paraplegic children aged up to 16 years.[2] Twenty-one of these had injuries (14 paraplegics, 7 quadriplegics), 19 had arachnoiditis or myelitis, 10 had tumors, 9 had malformations and congenital paraplegia, and there was 1 patient who did not fit into any of these groups. Of the 60 patients, 20 had no deformities. Scoliosis was the most frequent vertebral deformity noted in all groups although kyphosis appeared to be increased in the traumatic cases. Kyphosis, hyperlordosis, and kyphoscoliosis were frequently found in the same individual. The younger the patient at the time of paraplegia, the greater the chance of spinal deformity. The level of the cord lesion was also important. In paraplegia below T12 the abdominal, back, and paravertebral muscles were still mainly intact, preventing deformity. It should be noted that surgical procedures or radiotherapy on the spine can cause deformities. Laminectomy frequently results in kyphosis, whereas rib resections and spinal osteotomies often cause scoliosis.

The results of these deformities are alterations in sitting balance, limitation of independence, the development of pressure sores due to faulty positioning, and respiratory and cardiovascular deficiencies. Patients with spinal lesions should be carefully watched for the development of vertebral deformities, since early treatment and high quality nursing and physical therapy care can prevent serious complications. Exercises alone are rarely of value when constant muscle imbalance is present. Treatment may require limitation of sitting and standing together, with proper positioning until the child's vertebral growth ends. Although in certain instances spinal braces and corsets are used, extreme caution is advisable when lack of sensation and pressure over areas of bony prominences exist. In addition, spinal orthoses such as the Milwaukee brace are beneficial when the patient can actively oppose pressure forces, but this active power is usually lacking in the patient with spinal cord injury. The imposed restriction of activity can be detrimental to the child's future independence and emotional development, and this aspect should not be neglected. Surgical fusion of the spine to provide stability may be indicated, but can prove difficult in the patient with an osteoporotic spine, and again the patient must be watched very carefully in the postsurgical immobilization period.

Spasticity. Almost all patients with pure spinal cord lesions develop spasticity to some degree if there are no superimposed complications interfering with lower motor neurons. Proper positioning early in the course of the lesion tends to reduce the severity of the spasticity at a later date. Spasticity interferes with joint mobility and activities of daily living as well as promoting the formation of decubiti.

Almost any noxious stimulus passing to a spinal cord in which central inhibitory control is lacking will produce a spastic response. A distended bladder, urinary calculi, urinary tract infection, impacted feces, decubiti, or systemic infections will augment spasticity; therefore, predisposing factors should be looked for if a patient develops increasing or resistant spasticity. Local therapy such as the application of cold in various forms is usually not very effective, as benefits are very transient. Drug therapy appears to be of limited value although the degree of spasticity may be reduced. Chemotherapeutic agents such as diazepam and, more recently, dantrolene sodium are used with limited success. There are, to be sure, instances in which spasticity may be beneficial, aiding in standing, in maintaining trunk balance, and in bladder training, although more often than not it is detrimental. In cases of severe spasticity, range of motion exercises are probably not of much benefit in preventing contractures. There are numerous surgical procedures to reduce spasticity, ranging from tenotomies and neurectomies to dorsal or ventral rhizotomies. It is possible to produce chemical blocks by injecting neurolytic agents such as dilute phenol solutions into the muscle motor point, peripheral nerve, nerve roots, or intrathecally. Careful evaluation is necessary to insure that further function is not lost as a result of these procedures, since at times it is difficult to predict the new pattern of muscle imbalance that will result. Procedures that affect the sacral cord often produce a distal lower motor neuron lesion resulting in a flaccid bladder, decreased rectal tone, and loss of erections.

Autonomic Hyperreflexia

Patients with spinal cord lesions above T6 are extremely sensitive to both intrinsic and extrinsic stimuli that cause a generalized spread of sympathetic activity manifested by flushing of the face, sweating of the forehead, pupillary constriction, marked hypertension, and bradycardia. This can be a catastrophic event, and medical personnel should be alert to its occurrence in susceptible patients so that rapid therapeutic measures can be applied. The most usual cause of autonomic hyperreflexia is distention of the bladder or bowel, but decubiti, urinary tract infections, or even external stimuli such as irritating bedclothes can produce this syndrome. The higher the level of the lesion, the greater the extent of the sympathetic nervous system not under central inhibitory control. Irritating stimuli coming into one section of the spinal cord result in a mass reflex response with marked vasoconstriction below the level of the lesion and decreased blood flow to these areas. There is a concomitant rise in blood pressure due to the increased peripheral resistance and shift of splanchnic blood into the systemic circulation. Baroreceptors proximal to the level of the lesion then stimulate sympathetic cholinergic vasodilator nerves leaving the cord above the level of the transection so that there is vasodilation and increased perfusion above and beyond that caused by the increase in blood pressure. The skin of the face shows active vasodilation as blood pressure increases owing to both the intact carotid sinus mechanism and the parasympathetic innervation to that area. Since the sinoaortic pressure sensors are intact, the heart rate then decreases because of increased vagal tone. The end result is that there is no significant change in the cardiac output. In patients with lesions below T6 the extent of the vasodilation may be sufficient to prevent a significant rise in blood pressure although there will still be constriction of blood vessels in the lower extremities.

If removal of the causative agent alone is not adequate to control the syndrome, the emergency treatment of autonomic hyperreflexia consists of the intravenous administration of hexamethonium hydrochloride, 10 to 25 mg, and an oral maintenance dose of 125 to 250 mg every four to six hours. Mecamylamine (Inversine) 12.5 to 25 mg daily in four divided doses has also been recommended.

Wheelchair, Braces, and Other Appliances

The Wheelchair. The handicapped patient must utilize adaptive equipment so that he can function as efficiently as possible; such devices help him to increase his mobility, function, and endurance. The wheelchair is among the most valuable aids that a person with spinal injury can have, and attention should be given to its prescription. An improper wheelchair can negate many of the rehabilitative measures taught the patient. Consideration should be given to where the chair will be used most, be it in the house or outside. Door widths are important; if doorways are narrow the patient may be able to use a less wide chair. If the bathroom is not accessible a commode seat will be helpful. The family can bring in measurements and give medical personnel detailed information about the surrounding areas if a home visit is not practical. It is of benefit to have the therapist actually evaluate the patient in different types of wheelchairs. In our experience the patient sees the therapist first for a wheelchair evaluation and then the recommendations are reviewed by the physician with the therapist and family. The wheelchair should be neither too large nor too small, and there are chairs that adapt to the growing youngster. Detachable or rotating arm rests permit the patient to transfer without climbing over the arm and are usually necessary for most spinal injury patients. Detachable desk arms enable the chair to fit up to a sink or table (Fig. 6–4A) and can be reversed if forward support is needed to push up (Fig. 6–4B). The foot rests should also be detachable and should swing away to permit more efficient transfers (Fig. 6–4C). Patients with lower extremity edema benefit from elevating leg rests, as may patients prone to flexion contractures of the knees. A reclining back rest is helpful for patients with poor trunk balance, and here again elevating leg rests are helpful (Fig. 6–4D). Safety belts are valuable if trunk balance is poor, as are toe loops if there is considerable lower extremity spasticity. A proper wheelchair cushion should be provided. For patients with decreased sensation who will be sitting in the chair for many hours or those prone to skin breakdown, a Gelfoam-type cushion offers more protection than the standard 3 inch foam cushion. If there is weakness of the upper extremities, hand rim projections make propelling the chair easier, and brake lever extensions are also of value.

When the upper extremity disability is severe, various kinds of motorized wheelchairs can be used. Unless specifically indicated, however, motorized chairs are not advisable since they are more costly, the batteries add extra weight and need to be recharged, and the chairs are prone to mechanical breakdown. There are also limitations on speed and the degree of slope the chair can climb. Numerous control modifications for the severely handicapped quadriplegic patient such as mouth sticks or puff-type breath controls are available. The more complicated the control mechanism, the greater are the expense and time spent in repair shops. Simple devices such as a book holder or crutch holder attachment offer conveniences that can be quite important to those limited in mobility.

Lower Extremity Bracing. The main purpose of lower extremity bracing in the spinal injury patient is for ambulation. The role of orthoses in prevent-

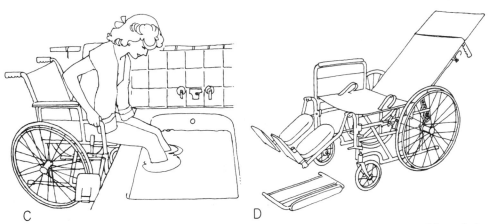

Figure 6–4   The wheelchair. *A.* Desk arms allow the patient to sit up against a table or desk. *B*, Detachable desk arms not only make transfers easy, but can be reversed to provide better leverage for getting up out of the wheelchair. *C.* Swingaway foot rests facilitate transfers and turning in crowded areas. *D.* Reclining back chair with elevating leg rests. (Courtesy of Everest and Jennings, Inc.)

ing or correcting deformities is limited because the development of skin lesions over an insensate area is a major hazard. The higher the level of the lesion, the greater the amount of support required, the greater the difficulty in donning the orthoses, and the greater the energy requirement in using it. Children are usually considerably more mobile than adults with similar lesions, yet it is rare for even a child with a complete upper thoracic lesion to ambulate with braces and crutches. The child who uses braces and crutches well will probably give them up as he enters adulthood since there is a corresponding increase in weight and energy cost and it is more convenient to get around in a wheelchair.

The patient with spinal injury below T9–T10 will require long leg braces with knee locks to prevent buckling and a rigid ankle for push-off. A hyperextended position (lumbar lordosis) usually provides enough hip stability so that a pelvic band with hip locks is not required. Low-level lesions are another story. Patients with cauda equina lesions may require only short leg braces with an appropriate ankle joint depending upon the degree of ankle function, or else posterior molded splints.

If gait training is to be carried out in a child who received his spinal injury before he normally would have begun walking, it is important that this start as soon as he is physiologically ready. In all cases care should be taken that shoes and braces are properly fitted and do not apply too much pressure to the skin. Since the gait pattern (especially in patients with high lesions) is likely to be uncontrolled, fractures and pressure sores on the feet may occur. Stair climbing is especially difficult, and very few patients with lesions above the lumbar level manage this. The latissimus dorsi is probably the only innervated muscle remaining attached to the pelvis that can provide some degree of hip hiking with the upper trunk and upper extremity stabilized. Properly fitted axillary crutches are usually required although some patients with lower level lesions can use forearm crutches. The difficulty in putting on the braces, taking up the crutches, and getting up from the bed or chair often so fatigues the patient that his functional ability is decreased before he even starts to walk. Hoffer et al. studied functional ambulation in patients with myelomeningocele.[20] As would be expected the factors important in achieving good walking included the level of the lesion, additional anomalies of the brain and kidney, intelligence, and home environment. In the follow-up group none of the patients with thoracic level lesions walked while all those with sacral level lesions did. Only half the patients with lumbar lesions were functional walkers with braces and crutches, and there did not seem to be a significant difference between a high and a low level. There are devices that permit the paraplegic patient to stand up and to move about without braces proper (e.g., Parapodium, Physico-Medical Systems Corporation, Montreal, Canada) and these may have psychological as well as physical applicability.

Appliances. There are numerous appliances available to aid the handicapped person in achieving maximal function and independence. Some are commercially available; others can be easily made or modified from existing equipment. Many are used as luxury items by normal persons and are not usually considered medical articles. Lowman and Klinger have compiled a volume entitled *Aids to Independent Living* that catalogs almost all the available self-help devices that can expand the range of activities and independence of the handicapped.[26]

Training in self-care should begin as soon as the patient is physically able and emotionally mature. From the use of transfer aids such as sliding boards and safety tub and shower rails to special grooming devices for the quadriparetic individual, the possibilities are limitless. The value of an activities of daily living (ADL) evaluation by the physical and occupational therapists cannot be overestimated. A home visit will provide an indication of the magnitude of the physical problems to be overcome as well as an understanding of the circumstances under which the patient must normally function and should enhance the accuracy of the prescriptions.

Energy Cost. One way of testing the efficiency of braces and appliances is to measure the energy cost of using them under controlled conditions. This has proved to be especially valuable in the design of braces. For example, a rigid ankle brace with a firm sole plate lowers the energy cost appreciably compared to one allowing free dorsiflexion. Paraplegics seem to select the gait pattern (four-point or swing through) that for them requires the least energy expenditure.[7] A paraplegic walking with crutches at the same speed as a normal person uses two to four times as much energy, and this energy cost increases rapidly with small increases in speed. Most normal subjects walk at approximately 2 to 3 miles per hour. The top speed for most paraplegic patients with braces and crutches is 1 to 2 miles per hour. The higher the level of the lesion, the greater the energy cost of ambulation for a given speed.

Wheelchair ambulation does not require any more energy than normal walking and permits the paraplegic patient to maintain the normal speed of other pedestrians on level ground; however, a slight incline requires a marked increase in energy. Wheelchair propulsion is predominantly upper extremity exercise, and although energy cost remains the same for a given speed, the heart rate is greater than when walking. Placing the large wheel in the rear gives greater steering accuracy, higher efficiency, lower energy expenditure, and smaller rise in heart rate.

Functional Significance of Spinal Cord Lesion Level

There is a correlation between the neurological level of the lesion and the functional potential of the injured patient. Obviously other factors such as age, environmental situation, and mental status are also important, as is the presence of decubiti, contractures, and bowel and bladder incontinence. The end functional result, given reasonable opportunities, is presented here, but it must be kept in mind that some patients will do better than others. Patients with incomplete motor lesions usually function better than those with complete lesions. The presence of intact sensation is also advantageous for proprioceptive input and for avoiding decubiti.

The following discussion has been modified from an older article by Long and his more recent chapter in *Handbook of Physical Medicine and Rehabilitation*.[24, 25] The lesions are taken to be complete and the levels listed are the lowest in which all musculature remains functional, i.e., there is no muscle power below the level of the lesion (Tables 6–3 and 6–4).

Fourth Cervical Level.   The quadriplegic patient with C4 intact has no voluntary function in his upper extremities, trunk, or lower extremities. The sternocleidomastoid, trapezius, and upper cervical paraspinal muscles are intact. While the phrenic nerve (diaphragm) is spared, there is little abdominal support, and respirations are often paradoxical. The patient usually shows no discomfort at rest, but vital capacity is decreased and there is poor tolerance for exertion or respiratory infection. Close care must be given to the respiratory toilet.

Upper extremity function requires the use of externally powered devices, and with these or head and mouth attachments the patient may operate an electric typewriter, turn pages, sometimes feed himself, and drive an electric

TABLE 6–3 CRITICAL LEVELS OF INNERVATION*

Cord Segment	Muscles	Action
C3, 4	Diaphragm	Inspiration (abdominal)
C5	Deltoid (C6)	Abduction, flexion and extension of arm
	Biceps (C6)	Flexion and supination of forearm
	also: Rotator cuff muscles of shoulder (C6)	
C6	Pectoralis major (C5, 7)	Adduction and medial rotation of arm
	Extensor carpi radialis (C7, 8)	Wrist extension
C7	Triceps (C0, 8)	Forearm extension at elbow
	Latissimus dorsi (C6, 8)	Adduction, extension, and medial rotation of arm (hip hike when arm is fixed)
	also: Wrist flexors, finger flexors and extensors (C6, 8)	
T1	Hand intrinsis (C8)	
T1–T6	Upper intercostals and back	Expansion of thorax
T6–T12	Abdominals and Thoracic extensors	
L2	Iliopsoas (L1–3)	Flexion of hip
L4	Quadriceps femoris (L2, 3)	Extension of knee
	Adductor magnus, longus, brevis (L2, 3, 5)	Adduction of thigh
L5	Tibialis anterior (L4, S1)	Ankle dorsiflexion
	Gluteus medius (L4, S1)	Abduction and medial rotation of thigh
S1–S2	Hamstrings (L4, 5)	Knee flexion, extension of thigh at hip
	Gastrocnemius-Soleus (L5)	Ankle plantar flexion
	Gluteus maximus (L5)	Extension and lateral rotation of hip

*Major innervation of muscles; other significant levels of innervation indicated in parentheses.

wheelchair. He is practically totally dependent for most activities of daily living and requires someone else to set up his equipment.

Fifth Cervical Level. With C5 intact the deltoid and biceps muscles as well as the major muscles of the rotator cuff are present to some degree. Thus, in addition to the ability to stabilize and rotate the neck and to elevate and ex-

TABLE 6–4   FUNCTIONAL SIGNIFICANCE OF SPINAL CORD
LESION LEVEL*

Activities	C5	C6	C7	T1	T6	T12	L4
Self-care: eating	±	±	+	+	+	+	+
dressing	−	−	±	+	+	+	+
toileting	−	±	±	+	+	+	+
Bed independence: rolling over, sitting up	−	±	+	+	+	+	+
Wheelchair independence (transfer to and from)	−	±	±	+	+	+	+
Functional Ambulation (including getting to standing position)	−	−	−	−	−	+	+
Attendant: lifting	+	+	±	−	−	−	−
assisting	+	+	+	±	−	−	−
Home-bound work with hands	−	−	±	+	+	+	+
Outside job	−	−	−	±	+	+	+
Private car	−	−	−	±	+	+	+
Public transportation (bus, subway)	−	−	−	−	−	±	+
Braces or devices	Hand	Hand	Hand		LLP ±S	LL	SLB

*Levels indicated are those at which innervation is intact. Abbreviations used: LL, long leg braces; P, pelvic band; S, spinal attachment; SLB, short leg braces. (Modified from Long, C., and Lawton, E. B.: Functional significance of spinal cord lesion level. Arch. Phys. Med. Rehabil., 36:249–255, 1955.)

ternally rotate the scapula, there is also scapula adduction, glenohumeral abduction, and internal and external rotation of the shoulder together with weak flexion and extension. Since the biceps and brachioradialis are partially innervated, elbow flexion is also possible. The wrist and hand lack muscular function. The patient is still unable to roll over or to come to a sitting position by himself in bed. It is usually not practical for him to manually propel a wheelchair, and a hydraulic lift is usually necessary to assist in moving him from bed to wheelchair, as is an adjustable height bed. Overhead shoulder sling suspension or balanced forearm orthoses (ball bearing feeders) provide support for the elbow and shoulder and these, together with appropriate hand splints or externally powered orthoses such as the McKibben muscle, permit the patient to feed himself if the food is first cut up, perform grooming activities, and use an electric typewriter.

Sixth Cervical Level.   The addition of just this one level provides a significant increase in function and demonstrates the importance of preserving as much neurological integrity as possible. The quadriplegic patient with a lesion below C6 has an intact rotator cuff as well as significant innervation of the serratus anterior, latissimus dorsi, and pectoralis major muscles. The nerve supply to the biceps and brachioradialis is complete, so there is good elbow flexion. There is partial innervation of the triceps muscle. A significant muscular addition is the extensor carpi radialis, which provides active wrist extension and with the use of a tenodesis splint makes finger flexor grasp possible. A universal cuff strapped to the hand permits use of implements such as toothbrushes and forks. These patients still have poor respiratory reserve but not only can perform all the activities of patients with higher lesions but can also assist in dressing and transfers. Some cases have been reported in which patients with C6 intact are completely independent in the latter two activities although this is not common. With the use of hand rim extensions, the wheelchair can be self-propelled.

Seventh Cervical Level. The major functional additions at this level are the triceps and finger flexors and extensors. The elbow can be stabilized in extension and the shoulder depressors, which are fully innervated, can act through the elbow to lift the body weight. Grasp and release is not yet powerful, and because the intrinsic muscles in the hands are not significantly innervated, dexterity is still lacking. Hand splints are often helpful. The patient is now almost completely independent at the wheelchair level although some assistance in transferring and lower extremity dressing may be required. These patients can roll over, can sit up in bed, and can eat independently. Respiratory reserve is still quite low. Outside employment usually is not feasible; however, home-bound work such as bookkeeping, telephone service, or typing is possible.

Thoracic Level (T1 to T10). The paraplegic patient in whom T1 has been spared has full innervation of the upper extremity muscles including the intrinsic musculature of the hand. Therefore, there is good strength and dexterity of the hand and fingers, and no upper extremity orthoses are required. Trunk balance is poor, even with lesions as low as T10, although this can be improved with training. This patient should be completely wheelchair independent. He can dress himself although, with involvement at the higher thoracic levels, it will be very difficult to lift the body while putting on lower extremity clothing. Grooming and transfers are possible as well as driving an automobile with hand controls. When the lesion is below T6 respiratory reserve and endurance are considerably improved. Functional walking is usually not feasible; the patient may, however, be braced for standing. As discussed previously, the energy cost of putting on long leg braces with pelvic band and spinal attachment is considerable. These patients, especially those with lower level lesions, may hold jobs away from home and may be able to get to work in their own automobiles but cannot manage public transportation such as buses and trains.

Low Thoracic – Upper Lumbar Level (T10 to L2). Patients with lesions at this level have full abdominal control, upper back control, and good respiratory reserve. While the patient with a lesion above L1 does not have primary hip hikers (quadratus lumborum and lower erector spinae) hip hiking can be accomplished by the secondary hip hikers including the internal and external obliques and latissimus dorsi. Ambulation with bilateral long braces is now possible, preferably without a pelvic band, utilizing a four-point or swing through gait. The patient can usually negotiate curbs although standard size steps without handrails are more difficult. The use of public transportation is still not feasible for most patients. Aside from the limits of architectural barriers and professional requirements, there are few vocational limitations in jobs not requiring much walking or standing.

Low Lumbar Level (Below L4).   The patient with sparing of the L4 segment has the addition of intact quadriceps muscles; however, because of severe weakness of the gluteus maximus and medius as well as flail ankles, gait is laborious and waddling. The lack of the gluteus maximus and hamstrings causes the patient to snap back sharply against the anterior hip ligaments after heel strike. Thus the knee must be maintained in tight extension, and the absence of significant hamstring function tends to produce genu recurvatum. There is also lumbar lordosis as well as floppy ankles. To make the gait more efficient, bilateral canes or Lofstrand crutches as well as short leg braces are used. These patients can have difficulty getting out of a chair but are otherwise essentially completely independent. Many patients never require a wheelchair, except for long-distance travel.

Psychosocial Rehabilitation

The patient with congenital or early acquired spinal cord injury often more readily accepts his disability than does the one in whom the paralysis appears after early childhood. In all instances not only must the patient's emotional responses be considered, but also the reactions of people likely to have most contact with him. A vigorous educational program is necessary so that the family understands the nature of the illness and can actively work with the patient to prevent deformities and medical complications as well as provide emotional support. The child should be treated as normally as possible. Standing and ambulation, if medically feasible, should be attempted at the age at which the nondisabled individual would have started to perform these activities. Goals must be realistic. The child must not be forced to attempt tasks that he is not yet physically and emotionally able to perform, but maximum independence must be encouraged. Follow-up medical and social review by the physician who is directly responsible for the patient and who also has a knowledge of spinal disorders and rehabilitation is essential, as are routine conferences of all personnel involved for coordination and future planning. Periodic psychological testing may be of benefit, with counseling by the social worker, psychologist, or psychiatrist as indicated.

Education and Vocational Planning.   Education should not be neglected, and if the child is able to attend a regular class, this should be encouraged and facilitated.

Vocational guidance and planning are necessary by the time the patient is in the first year of high school. If he is confined to his house, it may be necessary to make vocational plans earlier, although completion of a high school education should be advised. There are limited facilities whereby patients who are severely disabled can be trained for home-bound work while living in a supervised medical dormitory. Vocational planning should be realistic, depending upon the degree of disability and natural physical and mental assets as well as environmental factors. Intelligence and vocational testing play a role, and the social worker and rehabilitation counselor can assist the patient and his family. Most states or local municipalities have agencies such as the Crippled Children's Panel or Bureau of Handicapped Children that will provide counseling, testing, transportation and often considerable equipment (vocational and for activities of daily living) with the ultimate goal of achieving a degree of vocational independence.

Sexual Development. New problems are likely to arise as the patient with spinal injury reaches puberty, and the problems are likely to be intensified if the disability occurs during adolescence. Sexual development and awareness as well as changing perceptions of body image are prominent; loss in these areas deals a severe blow to the patient. It is perhaps at this point and in this sphere that psychiatric counseling can help. The physician must often take the initiative in discussing sexual function with the patient and his family. This counseling should not only be of a general nature, but as interest and understanding increase, specifics of physiology, prognosis, and sexual techniques should be taught.

While statistics are not available, there does not seem to be significant alteration in development of secondary sex characteristics. Given proper medical care and comprehensive rehabilitation, persons with spinal cord injuries can successfully participate in marital and family activities.[9] Most studies, however, deal with a well-motivated selected population that returns for follow-up care and may not be completely representative of the population as a whole.

The spinal injury patient is capable of sexually satisfying an appropriate partner be it male or female even if the use of the patient's "normal" sexual anatomy is impaired. The value of oral and manual stimulation can be pointed out, emphasizing that this is not abnormal and, indeed, its use is quite common. Although orgasm is lacking in the complete lesion, the benefits of seeing that one's partner is satisfied can be sufficient reward in a well-adjusted individual and can lead to further psychological and emotional security. The male patient with an upper motor neuron lesion may be capable of having reflex erections and with penile stimulation may maintain the erection for a sufficient time to produce a climax in his partner. Ejaculation however, depends upon intact somatic innervation at an S2, S3, S4 level and is usually not present, taking place in only about 7 per cent of patients. Electrical massage of the surface of the penis and the injection of intrathecal prostigmine are reported to increase the incidence of ejaculation. Erection is usually absent in patients with complete lower motor neuron lesions.

In males with complete spinal cord injuries only a very small percentage (1 to 5 per cent) have children because of the decreased incidence of successful coitus and loss of ejaculation. When present, ejaculation is often retrograde into the bladder, there may be scarring and blockage of the seminal passages as a result of infection, and spermatogenesis may be impaired.[34]

If the spinal lesion occurs in girls after the onset of menstruation there is likely to be a temporary halt and irregularity of menstrual flow. With time, however, the menses usually become regular so that ovulation and conception are possible. The patient must be educated and cautioned lest she indulge in sexual activities with the misconception that because she is lacking in sensation she cannot conceive. Labor and delivery usually proceed normally with the exception that in the absence of sensation, the patient may be unaware that she is in labor. Spasticity may be increased and in high thoracic or cervical lesions autonomic hyperreflexia may occur during labor. Most reviews of the literature indicate that the offspring will be normal providing the spinal cord injury did not occur during pregnancy, the onset of labor is recognized in time, and competent obstetrical care is given.[16, 33] X-ray examination of the mother's spinal column early in pregnancy should be avoided, since there have been instances of malformed babies born after such x-ray exposure. There have been no problems reported in breast feeding of babies by mothers with spinal injuries.

Architectural Barriers.   Architectural barriers are a major obstacle to successful rehabilitation. The home environment is crucial and attempts at improving this so that there is as much access and convenience as possible is important. A home visit by trained personnel who can advise the family as to the benefits and types of adaptive equipment will prove to be of considerable aid to them. Wheelchair ramps, transfer railings, adjustable beds, raised toilet seats, and ease of bathing all contribute to ultimate successful rehabilitation. Even assuming the spinal injury patient is able to leave the house by himself, there is often difficulty in crossing curbs, entering buildings, and fitting through narrow doorways. Enlightened city planners are now designing facilities to provide easy access to wheelchair-bound individuals, including ramps at curbs, a limited number of seats for wheelchair users at theaters, buses with provisions for conveniently picking up and transporting patients with wheelchairs, and public bathrooms that not only permit easy access but also have rails and supports to aid in transferring.

Most paraplegic patients are capable of independently transferring into an automobile and by using hand controls can drive safely.

Wheelchair Sports.   Recreational pursuits should be encouraged. These vary from the most sedentary such as reading and stamp collecting to active competitive wheelchair sports.

For the severely disabled individual the Library for the Blind and Physically Handicapped in Washington, D.C., offers a "Talking Book" service whereby audio tapes on many subjects and popular literature are distributed free of charge.

There are numerous regional wheelchair sports associations and events in which competition is reasonably equalized so that participants are matched according to relative levels of disability. Thus, even quadriplegics can compete in certain wheelchair races and swimming events. Competitive wheelchair sports provide the athlete with an opportunity for physical and psychological rehabilitation and personal adjustment (Figs. 6–5 and 6–6). There is an outlet for repressed energies through which many patients who are initially withdrawn and depressed improve their spirits and self image.[23] Wheelchair sports also bring a certain amount of publicity and subsequent public acceptance of handicapped people and appreciation of the disabled person's capabilities. It has been this author's fortunate experience to travel internationally with competing wheelchair athletes; the ability of these people to travel

Figure 6–5 Wheelchair sports: distance javelin. National Wheelchair Games. (Courtesy of National Wheelchair Athletic Association.)

under difficult circumstances for 8 to 12 hours without developing urinary or skin problems and to maintain esprit and camaraderie is remarkable. National and international competition includes such events as table tennis, weight lifting, various swimming and wheelchair heats and relay runs, wheelchair slalom, bowling, fencing, archery, discus and javelin throwing and shotput, not to mention the popular and exciting wheelchair basketball.

Figure 6–6 Wheelchair sports: Throwing the discus. XXI International "Paralympic" games, Heidelberg, Germany. (Courtesy of National Wheelchair Athletic Association.)

Of course, not all sporting events need be competitive. A weekly evening swim for example is not only fun but contributes to physical fitness and provides a period of time, although brief, when the patient's entire skin surface is free of uneven pressure points.

CONCLUSION

The spinal injury patient, in particular the child, requires vigorous and continuing care not only medically but for the achievement of potential and integration into society. It is not unusual for the hospitalized patient to respond well in a rehabilitation setting; however, the crux of true rehabilitation is how well he functions on the outside.

While many agencies are concerned with providing assistance to disabled people, there are several that are particularly valuable for the person with spinal injury and that will readily communicate with patients and their families. These agencies are: The National Paraplegia Foundation, Chicago, Illinois 60601; The Paralyzed Veterans of America, Washington, D.C. 20010 (Publishers of *Paraplegia News,* an excellent small magazine with information of interest to spinal injury patients and their families); The National Wheelchair Athletic Association, Woodside, New York 11377; and the National Association of the Physically Handicapped, Lincoln Park, Michigan 48146.

References

1. Albin, M. S., White, R. J., Acosta-Rua, G., and Yashon, D.: Study of functional recovery produced by delayed localized cooling after spinal cord injury in primates. J. Neurosurg., 29:113–120, 1968.
2. Audic, B., and Maury, M.: Secondary vertebral deformities in childhood and adolescence. Paraplegia, 7:10–16, 1969.
3. Bosch, A., Stauffer, E. S., and Nickel, V. L.: Incomplete traumatic quadriplegia. J.A.M.A., 216:473–478, 1971.
4. Burke, D. C.: Spinal cord trauma in children. Paraplegia, 9:1–12, 1971.
5. Clawson, D. K., Gunn, D. R., Fry, L. R., Garrick, J., Grainger, D. W., Hansen, S. T., Jr., and Mulholland, R. C.: Early anterior fusion for cervical spine injury. J.A.M.A., 215:2113, 1971.
6. Comarr, A. E.: Conservative management of the urinary bladder among children with spinal cord injury. Paraplegia, 10:232–241, 1971.
7. Corcoran, P. J.: Energy expenditure during ambulation. *In* Downey, J. A., and Darling, R. C. (eds.): *Physiological Basis of Rehabilitation Medicine.* Philadelphia, W. B. Saunders Co., 1971, pp. 185–198.
8. Croft, T. J., Brodkey, J. S., and Nulsen, F. E.: Reversible spinal cord trauma: A model for electrical monitoring of spinal cord function. J. Neurosurg., 36:402–406, 1972.
9. Deyoe, F. S.: Marriage and family patterns with long term spinal cord injury. Paraplegia, 110:219–224, 1972.
10. Dohrmann, G. J.: Experimental spinal cord trauma: A historical review. Arch. Neurol., 27:468–473, 1972.
11. Dohrmann, G. J., Wagner, F. C., and Bucy, P. C.: Transitory traumatic paraplegia: Electron microscopy of early alterations in myelinated nerve fibers. J. Neurosurg., 36:407–415, 1972.
12. Downey, J. A., Huckaba, C. E., Myers, S. J., and Darling, R. C.: Thermoregulation in the spinal man. J. Appl. Physiol., 34:790–794, 1973.
13. Ducker, T. B., and Hamit, H. F.: Experimental treatment of acute spinal cord injury. J. Neurosurg., 30:693–697, 1969.

14. Friedland, F.: Rehabilitation in spinal cord injuries. *In* Licht, S. (ed.): *Rehabilitation and Medicine.* New Haven, Conn., Elizabeth Licht, Publisher, 1968, pp. 460–535.
15. Glasauer, F. E., and Cares, H. L.: Traumatic paraplegia in infancy. J.A.M.A. *219*:38–41, 1972.
16. Göller, H., and Paeslack, V.: Pregnancy damage and birth complications in the children of paraplegic woman. Paraplegia, *10*:213–217, 1972.
17. Grimes, J. H., Nashold, B. S., and Currie, D. P.: Chronic electrical stimulation of the paraplegic bladder. J. Urol., *109*:242–245, 1973.
18. Guttmann, L.: Principles of initial treatment of traumatic paraplegics and tetraplegics. *In Aspects of Rehabilitation*, Hertfordshire, G. B., Garden City Press Ltd., 1966, pp. 18–28.
19. Guttmann, L., and Frankel, H.: The value of intermittent catheterisation in the early management of traumatic paraplegia and tetraplegia. Paraplegia, *4*:63–84, 1966.
20. Hoffer, M. M., Feiwell, E., Perry, R., Perry, J., and Bennett, C.: Functional ambulation in patients with myelomeningocoele. J. Bone Joint Surg., *55-A*:137–148, 1973.
21. Kelly, D. L., Jr., Lassiter, K. R. L., Vongsvivut, A., and Smith, J. M.: Effects of hyperbaric oxygenation and tissue oxygen studies in experimental paraplegia. J. Neurosurg., *36*:425–437, 1972.
22. Leventhal, H. R.: Birth injuries of the spinal cord. J. Pediatr., *56*:447–453, 1960.
23. Lipton, B. H.: The role of wheelchair sports in rehabilitation. Int. Rehabil. Rev., *21*:19–21, 1970.
24. Long, C.: Congenital and traumatic lesions of the spinal cord. *In* Krusen, F. H., Kotke, F. J., and Ellwood, P. M. (eds.): *Handbook of Physical Medicine and Rehabilitation*, Philadelphia, W. B. Saunders Co., 1971, pp. 566–578.
25. Long, C., and Lawton, E. B.: Functional significance of spinal cord lesion level. Arch. Phys. Med. Rehabil., *36*:249–255, 1955.
26. Lowman, E. W., and Klinger, J. L.: *Aids to Independent Living.* New York, McGraw-Hill Book Co., 1969.
27. Mason, R. C., and Downey, J. A.: Urogenital physiology. *In* Downey, J. A., and Darling, R. C. (eds.): *Physiological Basis of Rehabilitation Medicine.* Philadelphia, W. B. Saunders Co., 1971, pp. 245–263.
28. Melzak, J.: Paraplegia among children. Lancet, 2:45–48, 1969.
29. Michaelis, L. S.: International inquiry on neurological terminology and prognosis in paraplegia and tetraplegia. Paraplegia, 7:1–5, 1969.
30. Norrell, H., and Wilson, C. B.: Early anterior fusion for cervical spine injury. J.A.M.A., *215*:1114, 1971.
31. Osterholm, J. L., and Mathews, G. J.: Altered norepinephrine metabolism following experimental spinal cord injury. Part I: Relationship to hemorrhagic necrosis and post-wounding neurological deficits. J. Neurosurg., *36*:386–394, 1972.
32. Osterholm, J. L., and Mathews, G. J.: Altered norepinephrine metabolism following experimental spinal cord injury. Part II: Protection against traumatic spinal cord hemorrhagic necrosis by norepinephrine synthesis blockage with alpha methyl tyrosine. J. Neurosurg., *36*:395–401, 1972.
33. Robertson, D. N. S.: Pregnancy and labour in the paraplegic. Paraplegia, *10*:209–212, 1972.
34. Tarabulcy, E.: Sexual function in the normal and in paraplegia. Paraplegia, *10*:201–208, 1972.
35. Wagner, F. C., and Bucy, P. C.: Recent research on spinal cord injury. Arch. Neurol., *27*:465–467, 1972.
36. Wagner, F., Dohrmann, G., and Bucy, P.: Histopathology of transitory traumatic paraplegia in the monkey. J. Neurosurg., *35*:272–276, 1971.
37. Wharton, G. W., and Morgan, T. H.: Ankylosis in the paralyzed patient. J. Bone Joint Surg., *52A*:105–112, 1970.
38. White, R. J., and Albin, M. S.: Spine and spinal cord injury. *In* Gurdjian, E. S., et al.: *Impact Injury and Crash Protection.* Springfield, Ill., Charles C Thomas, 1970, pp. 63–85.

Chapter 7

Spina Bifida

by *Peter W. Carmel, M.D.*

Spina bifida is the second most important cause of chronically disabling motor lesions of congenital origin in childhood—second only to cerebral palsy.[74] Moreover, there is an apparent increase in the number of cases of spina bifida for which medical care is sought, due in part to improved prenatal obstetrical care given to mothers of these infants and postnatal care given to the infants themselves.[50] A generation ago relatively few of these severely afflicted children survived, but with the introduction of antibiotics to prevent neonatal meningitis, and with progressively efficient treatment of hydrocephalus, more of these children are surviving. The problem of their care and treatment, now of great magnitude, promises to increase in the future, and still more attention must be given to their *total* care so that their survival may be of useful quality.

DEFINITION OF TERMS

Spina bifida refers to a group of congenital defects. This term implies a failure of closure in the midline of neural, bony, or soft tissue. Clinical conditions covered by this definition may range from asymptomatic to severely disabled states. Two major categories may be outlined: spina bifida occulta and spina bifida cystica, the latter including meningocele and myelomeningocele (Fig. 7–1).

Spina Bifida Occulta. This term indicates a defect in closure of the vertebral laminae in which there is no exposure of meninges or neural tissue at

131

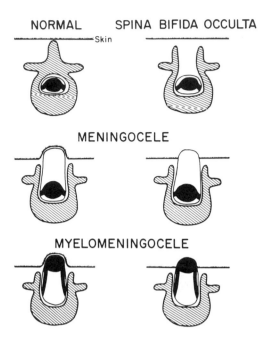

Figure 7–1 Schematic representation of normal and bifid spines seen in cross section. Spina bifida occulta lesions are always skin-covered, but meningoceles and myelomeningoceles may be covered (*left*) or present at the surface (*right*).

the skin surface. It does not define the clinical condition of the patient; these patients may or may not have neurological defects. There may or may not be an associated structural malformation of the spinal cord or nerve roots. Some of these patients may have external evidence of the underlying disorder; a hairy patch, pigmented nevus, small angioma, or dimple may cover the area of unfused vertebrae.

Spina Bifida Cystica.   In these malformations there is evidence on the surface of the back that there is underlying dysrhaphism. These cysts may or may not be covered by skin, or they may present as an ulcerating mass in the midline. It must be emphasized that this term covers a wide range of clinical conditions and pathological states that may further be subdivided into three convenient categories.

Meningocele refers to a cystic extension of the meninges that protrudes through the unfused vertebral arches. There is no evidence of myelodysplasia of the spinal cord, nor are there clinical signs of neural dysfunction. There may be sacral nerve roots adherent to the inner wall of the sac, but they appear to function normally. True meningoceles, devoid of nerve elements, and consisting solely of protrusion of the arachnoid and dura are rare.[40, 74]

Myelomeningocele indicates a fusion defect of the vertebral arches with cystic distention of both meninges and spinal cord through the defect. There is myelodysplasia of the spinal cord or cauda equina and there are accompanying neurological signs and symptoms.

Myeloschisis refers to presentation of dysplastic neural tissue at the surface of the sac. In this case the sac has not formed above the neural tissue. It is common among neurosurgeons to refer to this dysplastic neural tissue as the neural "placode" or "plaque."[6] (Embryologically, "placode" defines a thickened area of ectoderm intended for differentiation into a sensory organ. Its use to describe the dysplastic cord and nerve elements seems appropriate.) This form of anomaly is invariably associated with neurological deficits.

Although most spina bifida cystica may be divided into these three groups, there are some cases that are difficult to categorize. It is necessary to adapt both diagnosis and therapy to the individual patient under consideration.

SPINA BIFIDA OCCULTA

Failure of fusion of one or more of the vertebral arches is a common finding in normal children. Fawcitt described an 82 per cent incidence of unfused vertebral arches at one or more levels in radiological examination of 500 asymptomatic children.[19] In children under five years of age the incidence was 94 per cent. It is apparent that the vertebral arches continue to fuse into early adult years. Radiological examination of adults has shown spina bifida occulta in from 4.8 per cent to 36 per cent of patients.[21, 23]

All degrees of fusion failure may occur, ranging from a small notch in the spinous process to total absence of the vertebral arch and wide spreading of the pedicles. The most common sites for unfused vertebral arches are the fifth lumbar and the first sacral vertebrae and the axis. A summary of the level of the lesion and presenting clinical findings in 131 children reported by Matson is given in Table 7–1.[50] Radiological discovery of an unfused vertebral arch is in itself not clinically significant.

The great majority of children with occult spinal defects discovered in childhood reach adult life without showing evidence of either neurological or musculoskeletal dysfunction.[50] It is difficult to select in childhood that small

TABLE 7–1   LEVEL OF DEFECT AND PRESENTING SIGN
IN CHILDREN WITH SPINA BIFIDA OCCULTA*

	Number
Level of Defect	
Cervical	5
Thoracic	13
Thoracolumbar	12
Lumbar	38
Lumbosacral	38
Sacral	25
Presenting Sign	
Cutaneous abnormality	66
Lower extremity deficit	60
Sphincter disturbance	23
Total Number of Patients	131

*From Matson, D. D.: *Neurosurgery in Infancy and Childhood.* Springfield, Ill., Charles C Thomas, 1969. Reprinted with permission.

group in whom the central nervous system is involved by a spinal abnormality. There is seldom indication for a complete work-up of the child who presents with a cutaneous abnormality but without evidence of neurological deficit or orthopedic deformity. These cutaneous findings are, however, more significant when the child has a specific disorder involving the nervous sytem or the musculoskeletal system or has problems in micturition.

Children with orthopedic problems are usually referred for investigation at the time they are beginning to walk. At this time deformities of the feet, hips, or spine may first be noted. Muscle weakness that prevents proper gait or standing may also first come to the parent's attention. The most common symptom of late development of neurological deficit is a peculiarity of gait occurring at any age from 1 to 16 years.[32, 33] Children with gait or posture disturbances, deformities of the feet or ankles, or muscle weakness in the lower extremities should be carefully evaluated with x-ray examination for the possibility of spina bifida occulta.[7]

When spina bifida occulta is found on x-ray examination it is tempting to associate urinary incontinence or enuresis with the spinal defect. If enuresis occurs in a child after he has attained bowel training it may indicate a neurological deficit. The presence of dribbling urine or the easy expressibility of urine on abdominal palpation often indicates neurological loss. Neurogenic lesions of the bladder are constant, however; these children should not have periods of good control and periods of enuresis. The bladder is innervated by the second, third, and fourth sacral nerve roots, and one rarely fails to find other neurological abnormalities in the distribution of these nerves (such as a patulous anus or sensory loss in the perineum) in the child with true neurogenic incontinence, because these nerve roots also control the anal sphincters and supply the dermatomes of the perineum. Therefore, fecal continence and normal perineal pinprick sensation are strong indications against true neurogenic bladder.

The child with musculoskeletal disorder or with sphincter disturbance due to neurological deficit, who has radiological evidence of a spinal defect should have a further work-up. Iophendylate (Pantopaque) myelography is the most valuable examination. In children with spina bifida occulta causing neurological deficit there may be fibrous or fibrolipomatous masses, lipomas, bony spicules, and diastematomyelia. Lipomas may extend into the dural sac or be entirely intradural.[50] Traction lesions due to fibrous bands, dermal sinuses, or a tight filum termininale are found in most cases.[33] Dermoid cysts and other congenital anomalies such as intraspinal meningoceles have also been reported.[50] Most of these lesions will result in myelographic abnormalities.

Surgery for Spina Bifida Occulta

James and Lassman have laid down three criteria for selecting spina bifida occulta cases for laminectomy.[33] There must be: (1) progressive abnormality of gait associated with neurological deficit or neurogenic bladder; (2) radiological evidence of laminal deficits of levels other than S1; and (3)

TABLE 7–2 OPERATIVE FINDINGS IN 66 CHILDREN WITH
SPINA BIFIDA OCCULTA*

Lipoma	27
Fibrous stalk	20
Intraspinal meningocele	3
Dermoid cyst	3
No intraspinal abnormality	13
Total number of patients explored	66

*From Matson, D. D.: *Neurosurgery in Infancy and Childhood.* Springfield, Ill., Charles C Thomas, 1969. Reprinted with permission.

myelographic abnormality or evidence of low-placed conus medullaris. Matson stresses that operation for spina bifida occulta should be regarded as prophylactic rather than curative.[50] The purpose of the operation is to restore structural conditions to as near normal as possible to prevent an increase in neurological deficits as growth proceeds. An attempt is made to decompress the spinal cord and remove any extrinsic abnormalities that affect the cord or nerve roots. The operative findings as recorded by Matson are given in Table 7–2.[50]

Evaluation of the efficacy of surgery for spina bifida occulta is difficult, owing to the preventive nature of these procedures. Clearly, children who continue to have progressive neurological deficit represent failures, but it is difficult to assess the benefits of surgery. Results of operation for spina bifida occulta as described by James and Lassman are given in Table 7–3.[33]

SPINA BIFIDA CYSTICA

The syndrome of spina bifida cystica and its associated anomalies, including hydrocephalus, has been termed "the most important deformity syndrome in modern pediatrics."[18] The incidence of spina bifida cystica has been reported to be as low as 0.3 per 1000 live births in a study in Japan and as high

TABLE 7–3 RESULTS OF OPERATION IN CHILDREN
WITH SPINA BIFIDA OCCULTA*

Condition	Length of Follow-up (Years)				
	1–4	*5–6*	*7–9*	*10–13*	*Total*
Normal	2	5	8	2	17
Worse	0	0	1	1	2
Unchanged	2	21	10	5	38
Unchanged/Improved	1	1	7	0	9
Improved	3	11	12	8	34
Total	8	38	38	16	100

*From James, C. C. M., and Lassman, L. P.: *Spinal Dysraphism.* London, Butterworth & Co., Ltd., 1972. Reprinted with permission.

as 4.2 per 1000 births in Dublin.[10, 56] The average figure is approximately one infant in every 300 to 400 live births. There is a preponderance of females over males, with a ratio of about 1 to 1.25.[35a] As Smith has pointed out, at least one fourth of these children will survive to school age, most with serious neurological disability.[72]

Etiology

The cause of spina bifida cystica is not known. In the vast majority of patients there is no exogenous influence during gestation that could be held suspect. Doran and Guthkelch found no evidence of influence of maternal ill health during early pregnancy in mothers of these infants.[15] Coffey and Jessop, however, felt that there was indication that the incidence of spina bifida cystica was greater with malnourished mothers and in children whose mothers had viral influenza in the early stages of pregnancy.[10]

The familial incidence of spina bifida cystica is greater than that in the general population. Familial studies indicate that the incidence of recurrence in a family with one child with spina bifida cystica is likely to be four to eight times greater than normal.[39, 44] Carter felt that neural tube malformations are caused by a polygenetically inherited predisposition, which may be triggered by environmental mechanisms.[8] Families having a child with spina bifida cystica should be advised of the increased risk with subsequent pregnancies. Laurence points out, however, that if survival rates for this malformation are considered, the risk of having to bring up another seriously handicapped child is about 0.3 per cent—a risk that most parents can accept.[36a] There is also a greater incidence of congenital anomalies outside of the central nervous system in these children (Table 7–4).[74]

Renwick, using published epidemiological sources, found a correlation between the incidences of anencephaly and spina bifida cystica and severity of late blight in potatoes. He concluded that a specific, but unidentified substance in blighted potatoes has teratological properties.[59] It is not yet possible to assess this hypothesis, but studies have appeared that do not support Renwick's conclusion.[73]

The embryological cause of spina bifida cystica is not definitively known. In normal embryological development the neural plate first appears approximately 18 days after conception. The plate then forms a deep central groove, which deepens in a longitudinal fashion. The elevated groove edges, the neural crest, merge dorsally to enclose the neural tube. This closure starts in the midthoracic region and proceeds both rostrally and caudally. Closure of the neural tube is complete by the end of somite formation, which takes place approximately 28 to 30 days after conception. It is likely that the defect responsible for spina bifida cystica has usually occurred before the prospective mother knows she is pregnant.

A number of theories have been proposed for the basic pathophysiological process. Gardner has suggested that failure of the primitive rhombic roof to become permeable during fetal development results in dilatation of both the cephalic and spinal portions of the closed neural tube.[22] Barry et al. postulated that local overgrowth of a portion of the neural tube prevents its

TABLE 7–4 ASSOCIATED ANOMALIES IN 101 CHILDREN
WITH SPINA BIFIDA CYSTICA*

System Involved		Number
Vertebral	Sacral agenesis; hemisacra	18
	Hemivertebrae, transitional	
	vertebrae, fusion defects	18
Skeletal	Talipes	37
	Dislocation of hip	29
	Arthrogryposis	4
	Syndactyly	2
	Absent foot	1
	Absent fibula	1
Urinary	Dilated ureters, hydronephrosis	
	a) with vesicoureteral reflux	22
	b) without vesicoureteral reflux	4
	Double ureters and kidneys	3
	Hypospadias	2
	Horseshoe kidney	1
	Exstrophy of bladder	1
Alimentary	Imperforate rectum	5
	Cleft palate	1
	Tracheoesophageal fistula	1

*From Smith, E. D.; *Spina Bifida and the Total Care of the Spinal Myelomeningocele.* Springfield, Ill., Charles C Thomas, 1965. Reprinted with permission.

closure.[3] Other theories and experimental work have been reviewed by Källin.[34]

Matson has stressed the differential growth rate of neural and mesenchymal elements in producing neurological deficit.[50] In the three month embryo the spinal cord and spinal canal are approximately the same length. Owing to the greater growth rate of bony elements, however, the spinal cord is found at approximately the L3 vertebral level at the time of birth and at the L1 vertebral level by the time growth has ceased. Neural elements that may be fixed at the site of a lumbar or sacral spinal defect will be subjected to progressive traction stress.

Pathology

The defect of spina bifida cystica is usually discovered immediately at birth, although its appearance may vary considerably. Occasionally the defect is just a flat membrane covering the bony opening. This membrane may be thin and virtually transparent or may be fully epithelialized. A sac of varying size and distention is more usual. Some sacs may be pedunculated, with a narrow neck despite a sizable sac, while others are extremely broad based and sessile. If the sac is covered with a thin translucent membrane it may be possible to transilluminate it and visualize the neural contents. Although sacs of this type are especially prone to leakage and rupture, many will have moisture on the surface that is not due to leakage but is rather an exudate from the exposed surface. The sac may be partially or completely epithelialized at birth. This skin often has a bluish color, is thin, and may not be viable. Pigmentary or hemangiomatous lesions are common in skin over or surrounding the meningocele sac. Dysrhaphic cord and neural elements may be totally exposed at the surface of the sac and may present as a partially epithelialized, granulating, and ulcerating surface. In addition to the obvious dysplasia of the neural elements contained in the dome of the sac, the cord is frequently abnormal at spinal segments above sac level. Dysplasia includes degeneration of the cord, cyst formation and cavitation of the cord, and proliferation and overgrowth of neural elements.[74] Stark and Drummond have demonstrated by electrodiagnostic studies that paralysis in myelomeningocele is largely due to lesions of the upper motor neuron.[75] The upper motor neuron lesion may occur within the plaque itself or in the cord above the plaque, and was felt to be related to secondary changes occurring before, during, or shortly after birth.

Children in later infancy or in childhood have meningocele sacs of quite different appearance. The skin over the sac is usually thick, toughened, and multiply scarred. Scarring is due to the fact that these unrepaired sacs frequently ulcerate, become infected, and scar upon healing. There is occasionally leakage of spinal fluid from such unrepaired sacs, with risk of recurrent meningitis.

Cystic defects may occur at any point along the neuraxis. The greatest number occur in the lumbosacral region, which is the site of final invagination of the primary neural tube. The site of spina bifida cystica lesions in a large series is given in Table 7–5.[50]

Natural History

There are surprisingly few precise data on the clinical course of children with spina bifida cystica. Laurence analyzed 407 cases seen between 1947 and 1956.[35a] (This was a period when surgical therapy of myelomeningoceles was not aggressive by current standards.) Using actuarial techniques, it was

TABLE 7–5 SITE OF LESION IN SPINA BIFIDA CYSTICA

Level	Number of Patients
Cervical	51
Thoracic	103
Thoracolumbar	137
Lumbar	583
Lumbosacral	382
Sacral	119
Anterior	6
Thoracic (3)	
Pelvic (3)	
Undesignated	9
Total	1390

TABLE 7-6   HYDROCEPHALUS: 368 MYELOCELES*

Degree of Hydrocephalus	Alive	Dead	Total
1. Absent	97	3	100
2. Minimal (Cortex 3 cm)	21	12	33
3. Moderate (Cortex 1.5–3 cm)	32	48	80
4. Severe (Cortex 1.5 cm)	33	122	155

*From Laurence, K. M.: The natural history of spina bifida cystica. Detailed analysis of 407 cases. Arch. Dis. Child., 39:41–57, 1964. Reprinted with permission.

found that 35.4 per cent of infants with a cystic lesion could be expected to survive to age 12 years. For the 368 infants with myelomeningocele, the rate of expected survival to age 12 years was 29 per cent. These figures do not include infants who died before transfer to the referral center.

Laurence pointed out that the neurological condition of children with myelomeningoceles usually becomes worse soon after birth. This was attributed to biochemical changes, trauma, stretching, or infection of the neural plate. Despite this slight worsening, the pattern of paralysis was largely determined by the position and extent of the lesion.

Moderate or severe hydrocephalus was present or became apparent in 235 of 407 patients with spina bifida cystica (overriding this disorder) and was present at birth in at least 28 per cent of those who later developed hydrocephalus. The incidence of hydrocephalus was greatest with the dorsolumbar lesions (88 per cent) and smallest with the sacral myeloceles (37 per cent). Arrested hydrocephalus was most frequently noted between nine months and two years. In 53 of 235 cases spontaneous arrest took place, and approximately two thirds of children who developed hydrocephalus died during the course of the study. The outlook for children who did not develop hydrocephalus, or in whom hydrocephalus was spontaneously arrested, was considerably better than for those with progressive hydrocephalus, even if surgically treated. The influence of severity of hydrocephalus on survival in spina bifida cystica is shown in Table 7–6. Laurence regarded the development of progressive hydrocephalus as a "grave prognostic sign" in spina bifida cystica.

The Decision to Operate

There is considerable controversy as to which children with spina bifida cystica should be treated, and if indicated, when operation should be performed. Some feel that treatment should not be withheld from any affected infant, even if the infant is certain to have severe handicaps.[86] Others consider it wrong to treat those infants whose predictable quality of life would be poor.[49]

A great deal of data has been generated by the group at Sheffield, England.[46] Since 1959, a massive effort has been made by this group to offer total care to all patients born with spina bifida cystica. In this period more than 1200 infants have been treated. Criteria that were considered adverse to survival and function were: (1) paralysis of all muscles below the L1 level, (2) head circumference 2 cm greater than 90 per cent at birth, (3) kyphosis, and (4) associated gross congenital anomalies or major birth injuries. Results in 201 infants, seen on the first day of life during a two year period, and using the foregoing criteria, are shown in Table 7–7.

Lorber feels that it is possible to forecast at birth the *minimum* degree of future handicaps in the individual on purely clinical grounds. Since infants fulfilling the adverse criteria have little chance for useful life, it may be wiser to abandon the policy of immediate repair for all infants with spina bifida cystica, leaving the most severely affected children unrepaired.[48]

Hide et al. reported a series of children with myelomeningoceles in whom early surgery was not recommended.[29] Virtually all these children had complete or nearly complete paralysis of the lower limbs, and 71 per cent were considered clinically to have hydrocephalus. Of 99 children, 92 died before they reached their first birthday. These authors felt that if those infants whose quality of survival would be expected to be extremely poor were not operated on, it would be unlikely that large numbers of extremely handicapped people would survive. Similar results have been reported by Rickham and Mawdsley and by Laurence and Tew.[38, 61]

The physician undertaking care of an infant with myelomeningocele must consider the impact of this disease on the whole family. Social factors may well weigh in the decision whether to operate. For example, the chances of a handicapped illegitimate infant abandoned by its family are far worse than those of another infant cared for by his family.[46]

If operation is elected, it is usually performed as soon as possible after birth.[69, 71] Early repair has resulted in decreasing operative morbidity and death, largely by preventing secondary infections.[52] Closure also prevents damage of the plaque due to drying or mechanical or chemical trauma. Even if the sac is well epithelialized, traction from expansion of the sac walls may stretch and damage viable neural elements.

TABLE 7–7   RESULTS IN 201 INFANTS ADMITTED ON THE FIRST DAY OF LIFE*

Sequelae	No Major Adverse Criteria (n = 91)	Major Adverse Criteria (n = 110)
None	2%	—
Moderate	24%	—
Severe, normal IQ	37%	20%
Severe, retarded	7%	17%
Extreme	7%	13%
Dead	23%	50%

*From Lorber, J.: Results of treatment of myelomeningocele. Dev. Med. Child Neurol., *13*:279–303, 1971. Reprinted with permission.

Development of Hydrocephalus

Hydrocephalus is the most significant complicating factor in the course of an infant with myelomeningocele. Development of hydrocephalus increases the risk of death and decreases the prognosis for motor and intellectual function. The incidence of hydrocephalus with myelomeningocele has been studied by ventriculography and was demonstrable in 95 per cent of infants whose head circumference was above the ninetieth percentile in the first few weeks of life.[43] Hydrocephalus was detectable in 80 per cent of those studied in the first days or weeks of life, even if head circumference was not larger than normal, and even if other signs of increased intracranial pressure were not present.

Many neurosurgeons have noticed the clinical appearance of hydrocephalus immediately following closure of the myelomeningocele. Although Ingram and Matson felt that the closure precipitated a greater degree of obstruction in the cerebrospinal fluid pathways, Lorber found no evidence that repair of myelomeningocele in the early neonatal period increased the development of hydrocephalus as no infant who did not have it at first ventriculographic examination developed clinical or other evidence of it later.[30a, 43] Lorber maintains that in those cases in which hydrocephalus appears clinically for the first time following surgery, the hydrocephalus was already present at the time of the removal of the sac, and its appearance has just been accelerated.

Hydrocephalus associated with myelomeningocele will frequently undergo spontaneous arrest.[35a, 36, 37] Since shunting procedures run a fairly high risk of complication, it is important to identify those infants who might be spared unnecessary operation. Controlled experiments showed that children with cerebral mantles of less than 15 mm at the time of ventriculography, or in whom the resting cerebrospinal fluid pressure was 300 mm of mercury or more, did poorly if untreated.[43] Infants with cortical mantles of 35 mm or more, and without signs of increased intracranial pressure, did not develop hydrocephalus and did not require operation. Infants with cortical mantles of 16 to 34 mm, and no signs of pressure, had a variable course; 40 of 71 patients required no shunt and 35 of these children had normal intelligence four to eight years later. Hagberg and Naglo found similar results in 44 conservatively treated children.[25] If head growth was not rapid, lambdoidal sutures were not split, and psychomotor development was normal, operation could be avoided in almost one third of these infants. Stark points out that conservative management depends on careful follow-up so that progressive hydrocephalus can be recognized before irreparable brain damage or optic atrophy has occurred.[77]

Some clinics have advocated shunts for children with myelomeningocele in early infancy as a preliminary step before correction of the meningocele sac, but very few results are available from this sort of study. Shurtleff and Foltz noted that if hydrocephalus was treated first, they often achieved healing of the meningocele itself without direct repair.[72] They also noted that treatment of hydrocephalus by ventriculoatrial shunt often resulted in prompt clearing of meningocele infection. Lorber subjected the program of early shunting to a controlled clinical trial in which those infants selected for early treatment had a shunting procedure within the first week of life; he concluded that only a very small proportion of these infants benefited from early operation and suggested that only infants who had cerebral mantles less than 20 mm thick and who were free from infection should be operated on.[45] He stressed that shunting itself has many undesirable side effects and complications and should not be undertaken unless there were specific indications.

The large number of shunting operations that have been proposed, the proliferation of various types of valves and tubing available, and the divergent ways of handling complications attest to the lack of general acceptance of any single method. Attempts to divert the cerebrospinal fluid into the ureter, bladder, uterus, fallopian tube, and gallbladder have largely been abandoned. Diversion of cerebrospinal fluid through the jugular vein system into the right side of the heart, the ventriculoatrial (VA) shunt, is probably the most widely employed.[57a] Shunting into the peritoneal cavity was not notably successful before the introduction of medical grade silicone tubing, but the use of this inert material has greatly improved the useful life of ventriculoperitoneal (VP) shunts.[31] In a series comparing intervals between revisions of VA and VP shunts performed in a single clinic, the VP shunt survived almost twice as long (13 months) as the VA shunt (7.4 months).[42] For infants, the VP shunt has the additional advantages of shorter operative time and greater potential accommodation for growth.[81]

Infection is a serious complication of shunting procedures and can be difficult to treat. Ventriculoatrial shunt infections produce signs related to bacteremia, including spiking fever, malaise, and irritability, while those of ventriculoperitoneal shunts may lead to peritonitis. Ventriculitis may occur with either procedure and carries a grave prognosis. The organism most frequently found in cultures from VA shunt infections is *Staphylococcus albus,* which is not usually a pathogen. Most neurosurgeons find that these infections are difficult to eradicate with the shunt in place, even with massive doses of antibiotics.[50] McLaurin, however, has reported that vigorous antibiotic therapy has been successful.[53]

Other complications of ventriculoatrial shunts include thrombosis of jugular veins or vena cava, multiple pulmonary emboli, and erosion or infection of the scalp over tubes and valves.[5, 57] Most of these complications require prompt attention, and delay of correction is seldom indicated.

Urinary Tract Disorders and Spina Bifida Cystica

The major causes of morbidity and death among children with spina bifida cystica who survive beyond the first three years of life are pyelonephritis and renal failure.[63, 74] Renal tract abnormalities occur frequently in children born with myelomeningocele.[2, 64, 84a] Wilcock and Emery reviewed autopsy data on 4500 children and found that 29 per cent of infants with myelomeningocele showed such abnormalities, while only 5.3 per cent of those without myelomeningocele had a renal tract anomaly.[84]

Emery groups renal tract deformities into three categories:

Primary deformities apparently result from failure of the ureteric bud to develop and to form kidneys, resulting in total or partial absence of a kidney or in kidney fusion.

Dysplasias are developmental anomalies arising within the kidney.

Dilatation states are caused by inadequate elimination of urine due to any cause. His study indicates that about one third of these deformities in children were found in each category.[17]

While deformities due to agenesis or dysplasia are not amenable to therapy, deformities due to dilatation states require immediate attention. Defects of bladder innervation lead to chronic retention of urine and cause upper urinary tract damage early in life. This effect may be increased by intermittent recurrent infections. Several types of "neurogenic" bladder may occur. There may be total paralysis of all bladder musculature including the detrusor and striated sphincter muscles, usually associated with total bladder anesthesia. This type of paralysis may be due to lesions of the sacral spinal cord, the cauda equina, or more rarely, the nervi erigentes. There may be incomplete motor or sensory level lesions with a variable pattern of somatic or autonomic involvement. Upper motor neuron interruption may result in uninhibited reflex activity of the detrusor with preservation of sacral reflexes. This last type is much less common. Manifestations of renal disease and of urinary tract infections may begin as soon as the child is born.

Evaluation of urinary tract function of a neonate with myelomeningocele starts with observation of voiding. In infants with lower motor neuron defects there is intermittent dribbling of urine combined with a spurt of urinary flow when the child is crying or straining. The bladder can usually be emptied completely by Credé maneuver in these children. With partial motor or sensory loss, the voiding pattern is less predictable and is usually intermittent and spasmodic. Voiding may be initiated by bowel movement, rectal examination, Credé pressure, or any other activity that triggers detrusor contraction. These children are wet almost constantly, with no predictable voiding time.[24]

Cystometry may indicate the presence or absence of spontaneous detrussor activity and the degree of bladder sensation. This test is of greatest value in children with a total bladder denervation pattern but is less reliable in children with partial denervation.

Radiological evaluation of the renal tract in children with spina bifida cystica has recently been reviewed by Williams.[85] He recommends that all children admitted with spina bifida cystica undergo excretion urography (intravenous pyelography) and micturition cystourethrography before operation on the myelomeningocele. Micturition urethrography is repeated after the surgical repair. Sixteen per cent of infants with myelomeningocele examined within the first month of life had a demonstrable abnormality of the upper urinary tract. The most significant abnormality was hydronephrosis; however, small kidneys, pelvic kidneys, and single kidneys were also noted. Cystourethrography showed almost 80 per cent to have some abnormality, the most common being trabeculation and diverticulum formation. Almost one

third already showed clear indication of vesicoureteric reflux. Reflux incidence in myelomeningocele infants has been previously reported at 10 to 17
per cent.[9, 26, 80] These studies show that the incidence of reflux at one year was
approximately half that seen in the neonatal period.

Bacteriological examination is an indispensable part of continuing urological follow-up of these children. Urine may be obtained by suprapubic aspiration of the bladder, which eliminates specimen contamination, or by
catheter or bag collection. Harlowe et al. found infection in 53 per cent of the
newborn and 65 per cent of children who were two years of age; organisms
most frequently found were Proteus (47 per cent), Pseudomonas (21 per cent),
and Klebsiella (12 per cent).[11, 27] Management of urinary tract problems in
these children aims at preserving the upper renal tract, eliminating infection,
and if possible, providing continence.

In a child with a flaccid bladder and without evidence of vesicoureteric
reflux or outlet obstruction, the Credé maneuver may be used at two to four
hour intervals to provide continence. Devices for collection, such as catheterization or external bags have a limited use, but continuous catheter drainage
carries a high risk of infection. External bags may cause skin maceration or
chronic balanitis. No satisfactory collection apparatus for female children
exist. Penile clamps to provide urinary continence by urethral compression
are condemned by most authors because they cause pressure sores on the
penis.

The use of pharmacological agents to manage urinary problems in children with myelomeningocele has only limited application. Cholinergic
agents may be helpful in improving contractility in those with only partial
denervation of the detrusor muscle. Hypertonicity of the bladder and hyper-
irritability may be relaxed by parasympatholytic agents.

There are few studies of long-term conservative management of the
urinary tract in myelomeningocele. Bunch et al. reported results in 41 children treated by Credé manipulation and 7 children treated by urethral
catheterization. Urinary tract infection was present in 72 per cent of those
managed with Credé expression for an average of 72.3 months. Forty per cent
had ureteral reflux, and upper tract dilatation was found in 45 per cent.
Ninety-six per cent of the children of five years of age or older were incontinent. Almost 60 per cent of these children required surgery after the period
of the study. Culp et al. reported that 78 per cent of a small series of children
had good results with long-term conservative therapy with Credé expulsion;
however, Eckstein found that only 4 of 54 children were kept dry by use of the
Credé maneuver.[12, 16]

A number of surgical procedures can be useful in urological management
of children with spina bifida cystica. Transurethral resection of the bladder
neck, pudendal nerve block, and division of striated sphincters are procedures that facilitate bladder emptying. Urinary continence is lost, but improved emptying and absence of residual urine may significantly decrease the
chance of infection.

Urinary diversion, by-passing the bladder, may become necessary; the
most commonly used surgical procedure is cutaneous ileouretostomy (ileal
conduit) in which the ureters are transplanted into an isolated segment of

ileum.[1, 4, 28] Peristalsis of the ileal loop promotes continuous drainage of both kidneys so that urinary stasis is eliminated. The ileal loop is brought to an external stoma and fitted with an external collecting appliance. Indications for performing an ileal conduit procedure are urinary incontinence, persistent urinary tract infection, evidence of deterioration of the ureters or kidneys on x-ray examination, or evidence of deterioration of renal function.[62] The stoma of the isolated bowel is usually placed on the right side of the abdomen, but placement of the stoma will vary depending on the need for orthopedic devices, plastic surgery, and the like. The best time to perform ureteral ileostomy seems to be in the preschool years, as children of this age appear to become accustomed to the stoma and its appliances readily, and adaptation does not seem to be difficult. All authors agree that best results are obtained when diversion is performed before there is damage to the upper urinary tract. When the ureters have become grossly dilated and rigid and have lost peristalsis, there is poor drainage from the kidney that results in a higher complication rate.

Most children wear their appliance for four to five days between changes. Both the parents, and later the child, should be instructed in care of the stoma to prevent infection, ulceration, and possible stenosis. The most common complication of ileal conduit diversion, stomal stenosis due to erosion, ulceration, or infection, may necessitate revision in almost one third of the patients. Other complications include infection, intestinal obstruction, and urinary leakage. Most of the complications of operation can be handled without difficulty, provided they are treated in time and there is no progressive deterioration of the upper urinary tracts.[6] Data on changes in condition of upper urinary tract following construction of the ileal conduit are given in Table 7–8. While there is disparity between series on the number of improved and unchanged urograms, most authors agree that 10 to 25 per cent of these children undergo further deterioration of the upper urinary tract despite ileal conduit diversion.

Stimulation of micturition by electrical stimulation of the sacral spinal cord has been carried out in a limited number of patients.[55, 78] In these patients small electrodes are implanted in the sacral region of the spinal cord and linked to a small subcutaneous radiofrequency receiver. The patient then is able to stimulate the sacral cord by use of an external radiofrequency stimulator. Stimulus intensity may be varied and should be sufficient to cause bladder contraction but minimize other autonomic responses. All patients investigated to date have had isolated spinal segments, which were apparently morphologically intact. Whether this procedure is adaptable to children with lumbosacral myelomeningoceles is not yet known, but this line of investigation may be extremely fruitful in the future.

Rehabilitation Management in Myelomeningocele

The goals of orthopedic management in children with myelomeningocele include: (1) the maintenance of a stable and straight back, (2) stability and

TABLE 7–8 POSTOPERATIVE STATUS OF UPPER URINARY TRACT FOLLOWING INTESTINAL CONDUIT DIVERSION COMPARED TO PREOPERATIVE STATUS

Author[*]	Children with Myelomeningocele	Unchanged (Per Cent)	Improved (Per Cent)	Deteriorated (Per Cent)
Herzberg et al., 1969	31	46	37	17
Smith, 1965	115	80	5	15
Culp et al., 1970	47	23	51	26
Bunch et al., 1972	56	47	43	10

[*]Full bibliographic data are given in References.

alignment of lower extremities in weight bearing; and (3) the maintenance of plantigrade feet.[13] In addition, it is important that the hips be relatively mobile and that contracture at the hip and knees be prevented. If these goals are achieved the patient should be able to live alone, transfer to a wheelchair, drive a car (with special controls as necessary), and be as self-sufficient as his mental capacity will allow.[6] Most of these children can eventually bear weight and walk, even if this requires long leg braces and crutches. It is of interest, however, that many children who have been independently walking with braces and crutches voluntarily choose a wheelchair existence for mobility when they reach adult years because of the high energy cost of walking and difficulty with braces.

Bony deformities in children with spina bifida cystica may be due to congenital abnormalities with unequal growth potential, or may be secondary to muscle imbalance caused by motor paralysis. It is convenient to think of motor disabilities as related to a precise level of spinal lesion. It must, however, be stressed that in children with spina bifida cystica the neurological denervation may be irregular, with frequent "skip" lesions. Moreover, the neurological pattern may change as the child grows. Progressive motor changes may occur owing to stretching of the spinal cord with growth, ischemic changes within the spinal cord, or effects of anomalies in the neurospinal axis. Many of these children have both upper motor neuron and lower motor neuron denervation within the same limb, resulting in odd combinations of spasticity and flaccidity. A broad outline of motor deficiencies related to lesion level is shown in Table 7–9.

Joint mobility should be maintained and weight bearing begun as early as possible, in order to minimize muscle and bone atrophy.[13] Surgery should also be designed to reduce immobilization, restore circulatory flow in extremities, permit weight bearing as soon as possible, and avoid contracture through early joint motion. Sharrard outlined degrees of deformities that may be acceptable in view of the patient's paralysis.[65] He felt that flexion deformity of more than 25 degrees at the hip was unacceptable and that progressive limitation of abduction of the hip should be prevented. At the knee only a few degrees of fixed flexion were acceptable. The foot should be able to be dorsiflexed a little above a right angle at the ankle. Fixed equinus deformities should usually be corrected, and fixed varus deformities of the heel or forefoot

TABLE 7–9 DISABILITY RELATED TO SPINAL SEGMENTS
            IN MYELOMENINGOCELE PATIENTS*

Level of Spinal Lesion	Clinical State
Above L3	Total paraplegia
L4 and below	Hip extensors and knee flexors paralyzed Flail feet Bladder and rectal incontinence RETAIN use of knee extensors, hip flexors, and adductors
S1 and below	Hip extensors and knee flexors weak. Plantar flexors of feet paralyzed Weak inversion and eversion of feet Cannot spread toes or cup soles of feet Bladder and rectal incontinence RETAIN use of knee extensors, hip flexors and adductors, and dorsiflexors of feet; and some use of hip extensors and knee flexors
S3 and below	Bladder and rectal incontinence RETAIN normal lower limb use

*From Smith, E. D.: *Spina Bifida and the Total Care of the Spinal Myelo-meningocele.* Springfield, Ill., Charles C Thomas, 1965. Reprinted with permission.

arc seldom acceptable. Fusion procedures in lower extremities lacking sensation, however, frequently result in pseudarthrosis and Charcot changes.[47]

SPINAL DEFORMITY

At birth, more than 75 per cent of infants with spina bifida cystica show no abnormal lateral or anteroposterior spinal curvature. About 20 per cent have a kyphotic deformity in the region of the spina bifida, which is often of more than 90 degrees.[67] In 5 per cent there is congenital scoliosis; other spinal abnormalities found include failure of fusion (hemivertebrae formation), failure of segmentation, rib fusions adjacent to and continuous with vertebrae, diastematomyelia, and possibly hemimyelocele.

Several theories have been offered to explain the large number of kyphotic defects seen at birth in these infants. Sharrard points out that the U-shaped opening typical of the myelomeningocele vertebra (seen in cross section) may become so pronounced that laminae and spinous processes are turned outward and their normal posterior surfaces face anteriorly (Fig. 7–2).[67] The erector spinae and other posterior vertebral muscles are carried laterally. Weakness of dorsal musculature is probably the most important factor in the causation of kyphosis during uterine development. Because these kyphotic deformities are associated with a wide spina bifida and myelomeningocele, it is possible to overlook the kyphotic element at the initial evaluation, which should therefore always include lateral spine x-ray.[30]

Untreated congenital kyphosis is progressive. When the child starts to sit, compensatory thoracic or thoracolumbar lordosis develops above the level of

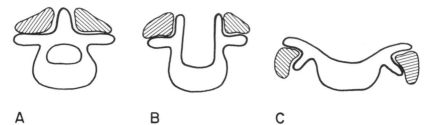

A   **B**   **C**

Figure 7–2 Schematic representation of normal *(A)*, spina bifida *(B)*, and spina bifida and kyphosis *(C)* seen in cross section. In most cases of spina bifida the longitudinal musculature *(cross hatched areas)* remains dorsal to the canal. When there is severe kyphosis these muscles move laterally away from the dorsal aspect of the canal.

kyphosis and becomes fixed. Because of their relatively anterior position, the erector spinae muscles function as flexors of the spine instead of extensors, adding an active deforming force. This deformity will hinder or prevent other aspects of rehabilitation, brace fitting, ambulation, and even wheelchair use. Because of the progressive nature of this deformity, Sharrard has recommended early removal of the atypical vertebral bodies, usually at the time of posterior defect closure.[66] Neonatal osteotomy—resection of the deformed portion of the spine—has been well tolerated.[67] Details of this procedure in older children have been given by Sharrard and Drenan.[68]

Several methods of treatment have been recommended for congenital scoliosis. One alternative is to remove the hemivertebra or unsegmented bars, but results of this procedure are occasionally quite unsatisfactory. Fusion of the convex side of the curve, or lateral epiphysiodesis may help in decreasing the rapid progression of curvature.

In children with developmental scoliosis the spine is straight at birth; scoliotic defects may not appear until four or five years of age. It is a common experience that scoliosis may develop very slowly over a period of years and suddenly accelerate and require surgery, often coincident with or just before the pubertal growth spurt. Progression of scoliotic tilt can often be delayed by external bracing, as with the Milwaukee brace, but great care must be exercised in employing this brace over iliac crests that are anesthetic. In many cases the presence of a large area of lumbar anesthesia will prohibit its use.

When spinal deformity reaches a period of acceleration, surgery may be required. This usually consists of some form of internal stabilization, either by Harrington rod or by spinal fusion. Before fusion is performed, a period of skeletal traction should be employed, generally using both cranial and femoral traction.[6, 67] A high degree of correction may be obtained by maintaining skeletal traction for a period of four to six weeks.

The choice of operation will depend upon the position of the scoliotic tilt, the severity of the scoliosis, and the presence or absence of lordosis. Fusion alone, Harrington rod insertion alone, or Harrington rod insertion combined with fusion may be the choice of the surgeon. Postoperative complications are frequent following spinal fusion in the meningocele child. Bunch et al. report an infection incidence of 20 per cent.[6] The presence of anesthetic skin prevents application of casts and makes wound healing and wound treatment much more difficult. Despite the difficulties encountered, Bunch et al. emphasize that because the paralytic curves of a myelomeningocele child will progress, a policy of waiting and watching is difficult to justify.[6]

HIP DEFORMITY

Deformity about the hip in children with myelomeningocele is usually secondary to dislocation or to muscle contraction. Congenital dislocation of the hip may be independent of the level of the neurological lesion. It is, however, most common in infants with total lesions below intact L3–L4 musculature. The functional iliopsoas, quadriceps, and abductors, unopposed by denervated hip abductors and extensors, cause unequal stress on the hip joint. It is necessary to reduce the hip dislocation and also to balance the motor power around the hip by transferring the iliopsoas tendon to the region of the greater trochanter. This procedure converts the iliopsoas, which is normally a flexor of the hip, into an abductor and extensor of the hip. Several techniques have been described for this procedure; the one most commonly in use is that described by Sharrard.[65] In some children not only is redislocation of the hip prevented, but antigravity power about the hip may be gained postoperatively.[14]

An important consequence of correction of hip dislocation is the minimizing of pelvic obliquity and the resulting developmental scoliosis. Raycroft and Curtis stress that pelvic obliquity was found in 51 per cent of children who had developmental scoliosis, and dislocated hip was implicated as a cause in 83 per cent of them.[58] Dislocation of the hips may not only prevent adequate standing and weight-bearing posture, but sitting may become impossible as well because of progressive scoliosis.

LOWER LIMB DEFORMITY

Many children with myelomeningocele are born with an equinovarus deformity of the feet that seems not to be related to the level of innervation present at birth. Smith has stressed the point that talipes equinovarus or calcaneovalgus in a newborn with myelomeningocele is usually an associated congenital deformity and not the result of paralysis.[74] Methods for correcting these deformities include use of casts and procedures for tendon lengthening, medial release, and transfer.[47] If the varus deformity is of the congenital type, casts and manipulative procedures may be of very little value. Correction of this deformity is often dependent on medial tendon release. If the deformity is due to an unopposed anterior tibial muscle crossing the ankle (L4 innervation) the ankle joint is usually more supple and may respond to serial casts, but these must be used cautiously because of the possibility of applying too much force to the anesthetic foot. Should the serial casts fail, transfer of the anterior tibial tendon to the lateral side of the foot may correct the deformity.[47]

While hard and fast rules for the timing of orthopedic correction of foot deformities cannot be made, these procedures are generally more difficult after the age of two or three years because of contractures and tendon shortening. In mild cases, however, conservative measures can often be effective and can avert or delay the need for operative intervention until later childhood.

THE FUTURE FOR THE CHILD WITH MYELOMENINGOCELE

Recent vigorous surgical treatment of infants with myelomeningocele has produced a dramatic increase in the number of surviving children. It has also led to development of "an almost unprecedented clustering."[82] Some of the problems this has created are now under investigation, but current assessment of the social and emotional trauma accompanying spina bifida must be regarded as tentative.

The impact of the birth of a deformed child first falls on the parents.[20,82] From the moment of birth they are subjected to a series of distressing and painful decisions. Families may find that the birth and care of a child with spina bifida causes strain on their marital relationship, tension in the home, and a sense of isolation from neighbors and community.[82] Mothers of these children are likely to be tired, worried, and depressed. There is interference with domestic routine and an adverse effect on siblings.[26] Finally, there are financial burdens imposed on the family for the care, training, and education of the child with spina bifida. Several national associations and a small number of research foundations have proved to be helpful to such families.

The quality of life for the child with spina bifida cystica will depend on his locomotion, his intelligence, and the condition of his renal tract. The last factor has already been discussed, but since most children can be provided with some method of continence, renal problems are more a threat to survival than an impairment of day-to-day life.

In a large series almost half the children who survived for 7 to 12 years after early repair were largely or entirely wheelchair bound.[46] Thirteen per cent walked with a limp or waddle but were not dependent on orthopedic aids. Finally, 18 per cent walked only with use of leg braces and crutches. Many paraplegics with lesions at spinal level L2 or above stop brace walking during the adolescent period, in part because of the greater amount of energy required to lift a larger body weight, and in part because of the greater speed and mobility many find with the wheelchair.[6] Continued walking, for at least short periods, is helpful in avoiding contracture, pressure ulcers, and osteoporosis.

Several studies have attempted to assess intelligence in children with spina bifida cystica with or without hydrocephalus.[35,54] These studies indicate that the major factor in determining intelligence of survivors is development of hydrocephalus. If hydrocephalus undergoes spontaneous arrest, there is a 75 per cent chance of the child's being educable and a 57 per cent chance of his attending a school for normal children.[35] Laurence also notes that children with myelomeningocele suffer from isolation because of restriction to home or institution, and have communication disabilities that result from reduced opportunities to interact with peers through play.[35] Formal education or training is impeded by frequent and prolonged hospitalizations.

Data on a large group of infants, operated on early in infancy, and indicating the effects of hydrocephalus are shown in Table 7–10. Lorber feels that 18 per cent of survivors have "quality of life not inconsistent with self-respect, earning capacity, happiness and even marriage," while 49 per cent are of nor-

TABLE 7-10 QUALITY OF SURVIVORS WITH SPINA BIFIDA CYSTICA*

Category	No Hydro-cephalus	Hydro-cephalus No Shunt	Shunt	Total	Per Cent of Survivors
No handicap	3	1	—	4	3
Moderate handicap	9	6	5	20	15
Severe handicap—IQ 80+	15	15	36	66	49
Severe handicap—IQ 61–79	2	5	21	28	21
Extreme handicap—IQ 60	2	1	13	16	12

*From Lorber, J.: Results of treatment of myelomeningocele. Dev. Med. Child Neurol., 13:279–303, 1971. Reprinted with permission.

mal intelligence but are severely handicapped.[46] They may be able to earn a living in sheltered employment, but their lives are full of illness and operations. Thirty-three per cent will always be totally dependent on others.

Additional emotional problems are certain to become prominent when the group of children vigorously treated in the past decade reach adolescence.[46] The problems of love, sex, and marriage are still to be encountered by this group. A small group of 27 adults has been studied, of whom several have married.[79] One man has fathered a normal child, and one woman has given birth to three normal children. Other information about sexual function in adult survivors is scanty.

Infants with spina bifida cystica will have problems that relate to many different medical and nomedical fields. Too often these children are shifted from one specialist to another, each dealing with one aspect of the child's handicap, and each with little idea of the therapeutic goals of his colleagues. Recently the use of a clinic of specialists that include pediatricians, orthopedic surgeons, urologists, physiatrists, neurosurgeons, social workers, and psychologists has received wide attention and increasing adoption.[6,28a] Several plans for management of multidisciplinary groups have been proposed; these will vary according to clinic population and facilities. In practice, the success of myelomeningocele teams is largely dependent on the interest of the professional staff and the energy of the coordinator. This coordinator is most likely to be a physiatrist or pediatrician; however, the choice should not be limited to these specialties. The team approach will fail if communication with the family physician and the community is not maintained.[6]

The team must remain mindful of the quality of life of these children. Lister asks, "What right have we to pay so little attention to the quality of life these people are being offered? Medical progress has made them survive. Social and educational progress must at least try to make them happy to survive."[41]

References

1. Albert, D. J., and Persky, L.: Conjoined end to end ureterointestinal anastomosis. J. Urol., 105:201–204, 1971.
2. Ashley, D. J. B., and Mostofi, F. K.: Renal agenesis and dysgenesis. J. Urol., 83:211–250, 1960.

3. Barry, A., Patten, B. M., and Stewart, B. H.: Possible factors in the development of the Arnold-Chiari malformation. J. Neurosurg., *14*:285–301, 1957.
4. Bricker, E. M.: Bladder substitution after pelvic evisceration. Surg. Clin. North Am., *30*:1511–1521, 1950.
5. Brisman, R., Stein, B. M., and Johnson, P. M.: Lung scan and shunted childhood hydrocephalus. Dev. Med. Child Neurol. (Suppl.), *22*:18–23, 1970.
6. Bunch, W. H., Cass. A. S., Bensman, A. S., and Long, D. M.: *Modern Management of Myelomeningocele*. St. Louis, Waren H. Green, Inc., 1972.
7. Carr, T. L.: Orthopedic aspects of 100 cases of spina bifida. Postgrad. Med. J., *32*:201–210, 1956.
8. Carter, C. O.: Polygenic inheritance and common disease. Lancet, *1*:1252–1254, 1969.
9. Chapman, W. H., Shurtleff, D. B., Eckert, D. W., and Ansell, J. S.: A prospective study of the urinary tract from birth in patients with myelomeningocele. J. Urol., *102*:363–366, 1969.
10. Coffey, V. P., and Jessop. W. S.: The incidence of spina bifida. Ir. J. Med. Sci., Jan. 30, 1955.
11. Cooper, D. G. W.: Urinary tract infection in children with myelomeningocele. Arch. Dis. Child., *42*:521–524, 1967.
12. Culp, D. A., Beckhrad, A., and Flocks, R. H.: Urological management of the myelomeningocele patient. J. A. M. A., *213*:753–758, 1970.
13. Curtis, B. H.: Principles of orthopaedic management in myelomeningocele. In *Symposium on Myelomeningocele*. Am. Acad. Orthop. Surg. Instructional Course Lectures. St. Louis, C. V. Mosby Co., 1972.
14. Donaldson, W. F.: Hip problems in the child with myelomeningocele. In *Symposium on Myelomeningocele*. Am. Acad. Orthop. Surg. Instructional Course Lectures. St. Louis, C. V. Mosby Co., 1972.
15. Doran, P. A., and Guthkelch, A. N.: Studies in spina bifida cystica. J. Neurol. Neurosurg. Psychiatry, *24*:331–345, 1961.
16. Eckstein, H. B.: Urinary control in children with myelomeningocele. Br. J. Urol., *40*:191–195, 1968.
17. Emery, J. L.: Pathology of the renal tract in neuro-spinal dysrhaphism. In *Symposium on Myelomeningocele*. Am. Acad. Orthop. Surg. Instructional Course Lectures. St. Louis, C. V. Mosby Co, 1972, pp. 115–122.
18. Emery, J. L., and Lendon, R. G.: Neurospinal dysrhaphism syndrome. In *Symposium on Myelomeningocele*. Am. Acad. Orthop. Surg. Instructional Course Lectures. St. Louis, C. V. Mosby Co., 1972, pp. 11–20.
19. Fawcitt, J.: Some aspects of congenital anomalies of the spine in childhood and infancy. Proc. R. Soc. Med., *52*:331–333, 1959.
20. Freeston, B. M.: An enquiry into the effect of a spina bifida child upon family life. Dev. Med. Child Neurol., *13*:456–461, 1971.
21. Friedman, M. M., Fischer, F. J., and VanDemark, R. E.: Lumbosacral roentgenograms of one hundred soldiers. Am. J. Roentgenol., *55*:292–298, 1946.
22. Gardner, W. J.: Anatomic features common to the Arnold-Chiari and the Dandy-Walker malformations suggest a common origin. Cleveland Clin. Q., *26*:206–222, 1959.
23. Gillespie, H. W.: Significance of congenital lumbosacral abnormalities. Br. J. Radiol., *22*:270–275, 1949.
24. Govan, D. E.: Functional evaluation of the urinary tract in children with myelomeningocele. In *Symposium on Myelomeningocele*. Am. Acad. Orthop. Surg. Instructional Course Lectures. St. Louis, C. V. Mosby Co., 1972.
25. Hagberg, B., and Naglo, A. S.: The conservative management of infantile hydrocephalus. Acta Paediatr. Scand., *61*:165–177, 1972.
26. Hare, E. H., Laurence, K. M., Payne, H., and Rawnsley, K.: Spina bifida cystica and family stress. Br. Med. J., *2*:757–761, 1966.
27. Harlowe, S. E., Merrill, R. E., Turman, A. E., Lee, E. M., and Trapp, J. D.: Clinical evaluation of the urinary tract in patients with meningomyelocele. J. Urol., *93*:411–413, 1965.
28. Herzberg, S. B., Persky, L., and Nulsen, F. E.: Fifteen years experience with urinary diversion in myelomeningocele patients. Am. J. Dis. Child., *118*:876–885, 1969.
28a. Hide, D. W., and Semple, C.: Co-ordinated care of the child with spina bifida. Lancet, *2*:603–604, 1970.
29. Hide, D. W., Parry, W. H., and Ellis, H. L.: The outlook for the child with myelomeningocele for whom early surgery was considered inadvisable. Dev. Med. Child. Neurol., *14*:304–307, 1972.
30. Hoppenfeld, S.: Congenital kyphosis in myelomeningocele. J. Bone Joint Surg., *49-B*:276–280, 1967.
30a. Ingraham, F. D., and Matson, D. D.: *Neurosurgery in Infancy and Childhood*. Springfield, Ill., Charles C Thomas, 1954.

31. Jackson, F. E., and Snodgrass, S. R.: Peritoneal shunts in the treatment of hydrocephalus and increased intracranial pressure. J. Neurosurg., *12*:216–222, 1955.
32. James, C. C. M., and Lassman, L. P.: Spinal dysraphism. An orthopedic syndrome in children accompanying occult forms. Arch. Dis Child., 35:315–327, 1960.
33. James, C. C. M., and Lassman, L. P.: *Spinal Dysraphism.* London, Butterworth & Co. Ltd., 1972.
34. Källén, B.: Early embryogenesis of the central nervous system with special reference to closure defects. Dev. Med. Child Neurol. (Suppl.), *16*:44, 1968.
35. Laurence, K. M.: Hydrocephalus and disability. Cerebral Palsy Bull., 2:170–179, 1960.
35a. Laurence, K. M.: The natural history of spina bifida cystica. Detailed analysis of 407 cases. Arch. Dis. Child., 39:41–57, 1964.
36. Laurence, K. M.: The survival of untreated spina bifida cystica. Dev. Med. Child Neurol. (Suppl.), *11*:10–17, 1966.
36a. Laurence, K. M.: The recurrence rate in spina bifida cystica and anencephaly. Dev. Med. Child. Neurol. (Suppl.), *20*:23–30, 1969.
37. Laurence, K. M., and Coates, S.: The natural history of hydrocephalus. Arch. Dis. Child., 37:345–362, 1962.
38. Laurence, K. M., and Tew, B. J.: Follow-up of 65 survivors from 425 cases of spina bifida born in South Wales between 1956 and 1962. Dev. Med. Child Neurol. (Suppl.), *12*:1–11, 1967.
39. Laurence, K. M., Carter, C. O., and David, P. A.: The major central nervous system malformations in South Wales. I. Incidence, local variations and geographical factors. Br. J. Prev. Soc. Med., *22*:146–160, 1968.
40. Lichtenstein, B. W.: Spinal dysraphism, spina bifida and myelodysplasia. Arch. Neurol. Psychiatry, *44*:792–810, 1940.
41. Lister, A. II.: Future for children with spina bifida. Lancet 2:982–983, 1970.
42. Little, J. R., Rhoton, A. J., Jr., and Mellinger, J. F.: Comparison of ventriculoperitoneal and ventriculoatrial shunts for hydrocephalus in children. Mayo Clin. Proc., *47*:396–407, 1972.
43. Lorber, J.: Systematic ventriculographic studies in infants born with meningomyelocele and encephalocele. The incidence and development of hydrocephalus. Arch. Dis. Child., 36:381–389, 1961.
44. Lorber, J.: The family history of spina bifida cystica. Pediatrics, 35:589–595, 1965.
45. Lorber, J.: Ventriculo-cardiac shunts in the first week of life. Dev. Med. Child Neurol. (Suppl.), *20*:13–22, 1969.
46. Lorber, J.: Results of treatment of myelomeningocele. Dev. Med. Child Neurol., *13*:279–303, 1971.
47. MacEwen, G. D., and Connally, T. F., Jr.: The lower extremity in myelomeningocele. In *Symposium on Myelomeningocele.* Am. Acad. Orthop. Surg. Instructional Course Lectures. St. Louis, C. V. Mosby Co., 1972.
48. MacKeith, R. C.: A new look at spina bifida aperta. Dev. Med. Child Neurol., *13*:277–278, 1971.
49. Matson, D. D.: Surgical treatment of myelomeningocele. Pediatrics, *42*:225–227, 1968.
50. Matson, D. D.: *Neurosurgery of Infancy and Childhood.* Springfield, Ill., Charles C Thomas, 1969.
51. Mawdsley, T., and Rickham, P. P.: Further follow-up study of early operation for open myelomeningocele. Dev. Med. Child Neurol. (Suppl.), *20*:8–12, 1969.
52. Mawdsley, T., and Rickham, P. P.: Improvement in the postoperative mortality following early operation for open myelomeningocele. Dev. Med. Child Neurol. (Suppl.), *25*:68–70, 1971.
53. McLaurin, R., and Dodson, D.: Infected ventriculoatrial shunts: Some principles of treatment. Dev. Med. Child Neurol. (Suppl.), *25*:71–76, 1971.
54. Merrill, R. E., Isom, J. B., Anslow, R. M., and Pinkerton, J. A.: Hydrocephalus and meningocele: The course of 100 patients. Pediatrics, *30*:809–814, 1962.
55. Nashold, B. S., Friedman, H., Glenn, J. F., Grimes, J. H., Barry, W. F., and Avery, R.: Electromicturition in paraplegia. Arch. Surg., *104*:195–202, 1972.
56. Neel, J. V.: A study of major congenital defects in Japanese infants. Am. J. Hum. Genet., *10*:398–408, 1958.
57. Nugent, G. R., Lucas, R., Judy, M., Bloor, B. M., and Warden, H.: Thromboembolic complications of ventriculo-atrial shunts. Angiocardiographic and pathologic correlations. J. Neurosurg., *24*:34–42, 1966.
57a. Pudenz, R. H., Russel, F. E., Hurd, A. H., and Sheldon, C. H.: Ventriculoauriculostomy. A technique for shunting cerebrospinal fluid into the right auricle. Preliminary report. J. Neurosurg., *14*:171–179, 1957.

58. Raycroft, J. F., and Curtis, B. H.: Spinal curvature in myelomeningocele: Natural history and etiology. In *Symposium on Myelomeningocele*. Am. Acad. Orthop. Surg. Instructional Course Lectures. St. Louis, C. V. Mosby Co., 1972.
59. Renwick, J. H.: Hypothesis: Anencephaly and spina bifida are usually preventable by avoidance of a specific but unidentified substance present in certain potato tubers. Br. J. Prev. Soc. Med. 26:67–88, 1972.
60. Retik, A. B., Perlmutter, A. D., and Gross, R. E.: Cutaneous ureteroileostomy in children. New Engl. J. Med., 277:217–222, 1967.
61. Rickham, P. P., and Mawdsley, T.: The effect of early operation on the survival of spina bifida cystica. Dev. Med. Child Neurol. (Suppl.), 11:20–26, 1966.
62. Ridlon, H. C., Berlin, B. B., and Cooke, R. N.: Myelomeningocele and the urinary tract. In *Symposium on Myelomeningocele*. Am. Acad. Orthop. Surg. Instructional Course Lectures. St. Louis, C. V. Mosby Co., 1972.
63. Roberts, J. B. M.: Spina bifida and the urinary tract. Ann. R. Coll. Surg. Engl., 31:68–69, 1962.
64. Rubenstein, M., Meyer, R., and Bernstein, J.: Congenital anomalies of the urinary system. 1. A postmortem survey of developmental anomalies and acquired congenital lesions in a children's hospital. J. Pediatr. 58:356–366, 1961.
65. Sharrard, W. J. W.: Posterior iliopsoas transplantation in the treatment of paralytic dislocation of the hip. J. Bone Joint Surg., 46-B:426–444, 1964.
66. Sharrard, W. J. W.: Spinal osteotomy for congenital kyphosis in myelomeningocele. J. Bone Joint Surg., 50-B:466–471, 1968.
67. Sharrard, W. J. W.: The kyphotic and lordotic spine in myelomeningocele. In *Symposium on Myelomeningocele*. Am. Acad. Orthop. Surg. Instructional Course Lectures. St. Louis, C. V. Mosby Co., 1972.
68. Sharrard, W. J. W.: Long-term follow-up of orthopedic management with special reference to posterior iliopsoas transplantation. In *Symposium on Myelomeningocele*. Am. Acad. Orthop. Surg. Instructional Course Lectures. St. Louis, C. V. Mosby Co., 1972.
69. Sharrard, W. J. W., and Drennan, J. C.: Osteotomy excision of the spine for lumbar kyphosis in older children with myelomeningocele. J. Bone Joint Surg., 54-B:50–57, 1972.
70. Sharrard, W. J. W., Zachary, R. B., Lorber, J., and Bruce, A. M.: A controlled trial of immediate and delayed closure of spina bifida cystica. Arch. Dis. Child., 38:18–22, 1963.
71. Shulman, K: Early neurosurgical consideration of the open myelomeningocele. In *Symposium on Myelomeningocele*. Am. Acad. Orthop. Surg. Instructional Course Lectures. St. Louis, C. V. Mosby Co., 1972, pp. 50–58.
72. Shurtleff, D. B., and Foltz, E. L.: Ten year follow-up of 267 patients with myelomeningocele. In *Symposium on Myelomeningocele*. Am. Acad. Orthop. Surg. Instructional Course Lectures. St. Louis, C. V. Mosby Co., 1972.
73. Smith, C., Watt, M., Boyd, A. E. W., and Holmes, J. C.: Anencephaly, spina bifida, and potato blight in the Edinburgh area. Lancet 1:269, 1973.
74. Smith, E. D.: *Spina Bifida and the Total Care of the Spinal Myelomeningocele*. Springfield, Ill. Charles C Thomas, 1965.
75. Stark, D. G., and Drummond, M.: The spinal cord lesion in myelomeningocele. Dev. Med. Child Neurol. (Suppl.), 25:1–14, 1971.
76. Stark, G.: Prediction of urinary continence in myelomeningocele. Dev. Med. Child Neurol., 13:388–389, 1971.
77. Stark, G.: Conservative treatment of hydrocephalus. Dev. Med. Child Neurol., 14:804–806, 1972.
78. Stenberg, C. C., Burnette, H. W. and Bunts, R. C.: Electrical stimulation of human neurogenic bladders: Experience with four patients. J. Urol., 97:79–84, 1967.
79. Swinyard, C. (ed.): Comprehensive care of the child with spina bifida manifesta. Rehabilitation Monograph 31. New York, Institute of Rehabilitation Medicine., 1966.
80. Thomas, M., and Hopkins, J. M.: A study of the renal tract from birth in children with myelomeningocele. Dev. Med. Child Neurol. 13:(Suppl.) 25:96–100, 1971.
81. Villani, R., Paolett, P., and Gaini, S. M.: Experience with ventriculo-peritoneal shunts. Dev. Med. Child Neurol. (Suppl.), 25:101–104, 1971.
82. Walker, J. H., Thomas, M., and Russell, I. T.: Spina bifida and the parents. Dev. Med. Child Neurol., 13:462–476, 1971.
83. Wallace, D. M.: Ureteric diversion using a conduit: A simplified technique. Br. J. Urol., 38:522–527, 1966.
84. Wilcock, A. R., and Emery, J. L.: Deformities of the renal tract in children with meningomyelocele and hydrocephalus, compared with those of children showing no such central nervous system deformities. Br. J. Urol., 42:152–157, 1970.
85. Williams, J. E.: The renal tract in spina bifida cystica. Br. Med. Bull., 28:250–254, 1972.
86. Zachary, R. B.: Ethical and social aspects of spina bifida. Lancet, 2:274–276, 1968.

Chapter 8

Cerebrovascular Disease in Children

by *Arnold P. Gold, M.D.,*
and *Yasoma B. Challenor, M.D.*

Childhood stroke is often misunderstood and misdiagnosed. Too many physicians envision only a hemiplegic youngster whose condition results from a thrombosed cerebral artery. On the contrary, children with strokes exhibit a variety of neurological disabilities that may require specialized rehabilitation programs. A comprehensive definition of stroke embraces all morbid processes that result from impairment or destruction of neural parenchyma due to alteration or interruption of arterial blood supply or venous drainage. Clinical conditions include: occlusive vascular disease caused by thrombus, embolus, or dissecting aneurysm; congenital anomalies including cerebral aneurysms or vascular malformations; entities that alter the permeability of the vascular wall; and the blood dyscrasias. Sequelae may include disorders of acuity, interpretation or integration of somatic sensory modalities or special senses; impaired volitional control, strength, coordination, or sequencing of motor function; and deficits in intellectual, motivational, and emotional growth and function.

Except in an acute and massive subarachnoid hemorrhage, which is usually the result of a ruptured intracranial aneurysm, children do not as a rule die from stroke, but live and often require life-long therapy. The fetus or newborn with impaired cerebral blood supply usually has impaired function that is nebulously labeled "congenital." The child with a stroke typically has a static neurological deficit that improves somewhat without therapy as more normal cerebral blood supply is reestablished, often through collateral channels, or by maturation of the central nervous system with increasing chronological age. Additional specific therapy can improve functional, although not neurological, outcome. Even the most intensive rehabilitative program, however, may not alter progressive conditions, which are most frequently second-ary to vascular malformations and typically result in increasing loss of func-tion. The rate of progression is crucial in determining the timing and nature of therapy. A rehabilitative goal is improvement of function beyond that as-sociated with increased chronological age alone, and it must aim to integrate that function into constructive family and school life.

Incidence, prevalence, and risk factors of vascular disease in children are difficult to delineate owing to the paucity of well-designed and implemented epidemiological studies. Little information is available about the number of children with strokes or the reason why some children become symptomatic and others do not. The condition, however, is not rare. Acute acquired hemiplegia in the otherwise healthy child may be observed only occasionally, but a large number of children with other nonhemiplegic deficits are seen in hospitals, clinics, or even in regular schools. Acknowledged specific risk fac-tors predisposing a child to a stroke include cardiac disease, trauma, infec-tions, hematological disorders, vasculitis, metabolic diseases, and drug abuse.

ETIOLOGY OF CHILDHOOD STROKE

Cardiac disease entities include congenital heart disease, most commonly cyanotic; rheumatic heart disease, usually with atrial fibrillation; other ar-rhythmias that may cause the formation of mural thrombi and resultant cere-bral emboli; acute or subacute bacterial endocarditis; and embolism arising from myxomas of the heart.

Infections that result in vascular disease may involve the central nervous system primarily or may arise from an extracranial site. Encephalitis of viral origin can occasionally present as, or be complicated by, hemiplegia. Postin-fectious and postvaccinal encephalitis causes perivascular demyelination and may result in a motor deficit, impaired speech, intellectual deficit, and seizures. Measles, and less commonly rubella, varicella, and mumps may be the responsible viral agents. Postvaccinal complications are observed follow-ing immunization against smallpox, rabies, and pertussis. Bacterial meningitis is occasionally complicated by vascular thromboses. Cerebral arteritis may be of obscure etiology or may be secondary to inflammatory disease arising from contiguous structures.

Infections of the ears, nose, throat, and paranasal sinuses are often as-sociated with enlarged lymph nodes, and by their proximity may involve the adventitia of the internal carotid artery with subsequent development of an intravascular thrombosis. Other causes of arteritis include mucormycosis in association with uncontrolled diabetes mellitus and the rare occurrence of childhood meningovascular syphilis and idiopathic granulomatous arteritis (Takayasu's disease). Chronic pulmonary infections, often with associated bronchiectasis, can give rise to septic emboli that may occlude a cerebral artery.

Trauma may cause a stroke. Brain contusion or laceration, as well as epidural, subdural, and intracerebral collections of blood, may complicate head injuries and result in neurological deficit. Less apparent are the injuries to the internal carotid artery resulting from blunt nonpenetrating trauma to the paratonsillar area. In these instances, a latent period of 3 to 24 hours elapses between the intraoral trauma and the onset of hemiplegia. Air embolism of the brain may occur during cardiac catheterization or cardiac, thoracic, and neck surgery. Fat embolism, usually after fracture of a long bone, is characteristically asymptomatic until 12 to 48 hours after the injury.

Vasculitis associated with collagen diseases can produce a variety of neurological deficits. Of the collagen disorders, lupus erythematosus, at times drug induced, and periarteritis nodosa are most commonly seen in children. The neurological deficits usually result from involvement of the small arteries.

Metabolic disorders rarely are associated with stroke in children. Homocystinuria has been associated with occlusive arterial disease and resultant, often alternating, hemiplegia. Diabetes mellitus may be associated with occlusion of small cerebral arteries, the so-called "branch occlusion."

Hematological disorders are commonly complicated by central nervous system hemorrhage. In leukemia, the most common of the blood dyscrasias, hemorrhage is most frequently observed in the white matter. Approximately 50 per cent of children with leukemia develop some evidence of intracranial bleeding, but only half have clinical symptoms attributable to these hemorrhages. Sickle cell disease presents as a stroke by either cerebral arterial occlusion or intracranial hemorrhage. Other blood dyscrasias including hemophilia, idiopathic or thrombotic thrombocytopenic purpura, hemolytic-uremic syndrome, and thrombocytosis are all high-risk conditions productive of hemiplegia and other deficits in neurological function.

A miscellaneous group of conditions has been associated with impaired cerebral blood supply or venous drainage. The neurocutaneous syndromes, notably, Sturge-Weber-Dimitri syndrome, neurofibromatosis, and tuberous sclerosis, have been associated with cerebral artery occlusion. Metastatic neoplasms, primarily neuroblastoma or rhabdomyosarcoma, can occlude dural sinuses, while primary brain tumors may encroach on vascular supply and cause occlusion and infarction. The carotid artery as it passes through the tonsillar fossa and carotid canal may be occluded by tumors of the base of the skull or disorders of bone, which include osteopetrosis and craniometaphyseal dysplasia.

CLINICAL DEVELOPMENT OF CHILDHOOD STROKE

The clinical picture, both acute and chronic, is primarily determined by the pathological vascular changes. Recognition of the manifestations at the time of onset and knowledge of the subsequent clinical course following cerebral arterial or venous thrombosis, embolus, and hemorrhage are essential in delineating a dynamic rehabilitation program.

Mode of Onset

Neurological manifestations vary according to the rapidity of development and the site and extent of damage. Cerebral embolism characteristically produces a rapidly evolving clinical picture, with maximum involvement within a few minutes. Hemorrhage also has an acute or even apoplectiform onset. In contrast, cerebral thrombosis is slower in development and may progress either intermittently or progressively during a period of hours or even days. Three forms of clinical onset are usually observed:

Apoplectiform Onset. The neurological deficit, most commonly hemiplegia, is usually associated with the abrupt development of seizures, fever of 101° to 103°F, and coma. Cerebral hemorrhage with subarachnoid involvement also has an apoplectiform onset and in addition shows "meningeal signs" including nuchal rigidity.

Acute Onset. The neurological deficit may occur rapidly during a period of minutes to hours without any seizure activity, fever, or alteration of the state of consciousness.

Intermittent or "Stuttering" Onset. Both transient and permanent episodes of neurological deficit are observed in some cases of cerebral artery thrombosis. Headaches, either focal or generalized and often associated with deviant behavioral patterns, may precede the onset of neurological signs by hours, days, or even months.

Clinical Manifestations

Clinical manifestations include abnormalities of motor function, sensation, vasomotor or cranial nerve function, speech, behavior, learning, and intellect, as well as the development of seizures.

Motor Dysfunction. Hemiparesis is a common and dramatic neurological deficit. When it occurs acutely, the extremities are initially flaccid and occasionally edematous, warm, and mildly erythematous. The upper extremity is usually more severely involved, both initially and residually. Hemiparesis may disappear rapidly, slowly regress for a period of several months, or persist indefinitely. Recovery of function in the lower extremity characteristically precedes and exceeds that in the upper extremity, probably owing to the more gross nature of the function required of it. Spasticity supervenes a few days to four weeks after the onset, and contractures may develop weeks or months later. Hemiatrophy (dwarfing of the involved limbs) is related primarily to parietal lobe involvement and is more likely to occur when hemiparesis occurs in a child under the age of five years.

Involuntary movements may further complicate motor function. Choreoathetotic movements imply basal ganglia involvement and usually become evident months or even years after the onset of the hemiparesis. Hand movements, such as grasping of objects, may be seriously impaired by athetosis, largely because of lack of proximal joint stability and control, and overflow of athetoid motions. Synkinetic or mirror movements also may complicate the hemiparesis. These are imitative involuntary movements involving the hemiparetic limbs when a purposeful movement is performed by the contralateral normal extremity. While early functional training may make use of this to facilitate movement in the involved limb, persistence of synkinesis hinders effective bimanual coordination of nonsymmetrical activities, such as those involved in manipulating utensils or dressing.

Deep tendon reflexes may be absent or hypoactive, and ipsilateral superficial abdominal reflexes silent during the flaccid stage. Hyperactive responses with an extensor response to plantar stimulation supervene during the spastic stage of the paralysis. Contractures or superimposed rigidity diminish the amplitude of the deep tendon reflexes.

Sensory Dysfunction. Sensory examination is most difficult in the pediatric age range, and may be limited to gross awareness of pain with a pinprick in infants. Sensory deficit most often is the result of impaired parietal lobe function. Superficial modalities for touch and pain are usually normal, but in the older child position sensation, stereognosis and two-point discrimination are often impaired and correlate with subsequent development of hemiatrophy. Rehabilitation is seriously complicated by parietal lobe involvement since the child may be unaware of or neglect the paretic limbs.

Abnormalities of Cranial Nerve Function. Eye abnormalities are common and include homonymous hemanopsia, strabismus, amblyopia, and myopia. Subtle disorders of conjugate or coordinate motion may also occur. Facial paresis of the upper motor neuron type is common, and is not necessarily related to the severity of the hemiparesis. Pseudobulbar palsy due to bilateral cerebrovascular disease is manifested by emotional lability and difficulty with chewing, swallowing, and speaking. In this condition the gag reflexes are usually intact, but there is disordered voluntary control of the normal appearing tongue. Strokes involving the vertebrobasilar arterial system characteristically exhibit cranial nerve palsies and cerebellar signs on the side of the infarction with contralateral hemiplegia.

Disorders of Speech. Speech defects are primarily dependent upon the age of the child at the onset of the stroke. The dysphasia encountered in older children and adults with dominant hemisphere lesions is rare in children before the age of five years. Unless associated with mental retardation, it is practically never observed with onset of stroke before two years of age. Mental retardation and bilateral cerebral lesions are the most probable explanations for the failure to develop speech. In contrast, dysarthria can occur with strokes at any age, and its development is independent of intellect.

Disorders of Behavior, Learning, and Intellect. Behavior and personality problems are common in children with strokes. When present, they adversely influence rehabilitation, school performance, and socialization. Occasionally the affected child is underactive, passive, and depressed, but more typically is hyperkinetic. The hyperkinesis, which may vary in degree, is manifested by uncontrolled motility, short attention span, low frustration threshold, temper outbursts, impulsiveness, distractibility, and aggressiveness. The child is often difficult to manage and may be overtly antagonistic or hostile to educators or therapists. Intellectual deficits and specific learning disabilities are common problems that, unless recognized and treated, may interfere with academic function and complicate rehabilitation.

Epilepsy. Children with stroke often have a seizure at the time of onset, and approximately 50 per cent will have subsequent epilepsy. All children with stroke must be considered seizure suspects for an indefinite period of time. Seizures may be either limited to one type or manifested as a mixed convulsive disorder. Seizure types include focal (motor or sensory), jacksonian, generalized, psychomotor, and minor motor. Focal motor and less commonly generalized major motor (grand mal) seizures may result in a transient or permanent increase in the motor deficit. Seizures associated with stroke may prove to be refractory to anticonvulsant medication, this seriously complicating all spheres of function. Hemispherectomy may be indicated in such children when there is coexisting hemiplegia.

Laboratory Findings

Blood count, urinalysis, and erythrocyte sedimentation rate may be normal; but strokes secondary to infectious diseases or intracranial hemorrhage frequently are accompanied by leukocytosis and an elevated sedimentation rate. The cerebrospinal fluid is usually normal in most cases of stroke, but may be bloody in those conditions associated with subarachnoid hemorrhage. Pleocytosis and increased protein content may be present during the acute phase, suggesting infection as an etiological factor, but these findings may be nonspecific after a few weeks.

Electroencephalograms often demonstrate a variety of electrical abnormalities. The amplitude of the background activity is usually reduced over the damaged hemisphere, but paroxysmal discharges, either focal or generalized, are more common.

Radiographs of the skull are characteristically normal in most acute stroke states. After a period of years, especially with an onset before three years of age, skull x-rays may show the features of cranial and cerebral hemiatrophy called the Dyke-Davidoff-Masson syndrome. Thickening of the cranial vault, overdevelopment of the frontal and ethmoid sinuses, and elevation of the petrous pyramid of the temporal bone ipsilateral to the cerebral hemiatrophy can be observed.

Echoencephalograms establish the position of the third ventricle and other midline structures. Cerebral infarction is often associated with cerebral edema, thus the tracing reveals a shift of the midline structures away from the involved hemisphere. After a period of months or years, however, cerebral hemiatrophy develops, and the midline trace becomes shifted toward the involved hemisphere.

Brain scans are usually normal except in the presence of arteriovenous malformations. Thermograms may visualize a "cold spot" of cerebral ischemia in children with cerebral occlusive vascular disease. Angiography is often the most important diagnostic tool. Retrograde femoral catheterization studies with selective visualization of all cerebral vessels should be considered in all children with stroke. Magnification and subtraction techniques enhance the diagnostic value of the study. Analgesia rather than anesthesia reduces the risks of cerebral angiography and is recommended.

THERAPY OF CHILDHOOD STROKE

Philosophy of Therapeutic Approach

The functional loss caused by cerebrovascular problems in children may require extensive therapy to stimulate development and function in perinatally acquired lesions (habilitation) or considerable retraining of function for lesions acquired later in childhood (rehabilitation). Evaluation of children for therapy must be in the context of the adaptive and maturational changes that are continuous, including development in the physical, emotional, social, and educational spheres.

The concept of developmental neurological assessment is essential in evaluating the nature of and priorities for various therapeutic modalities. Thus, the keynote of therapy for the pediatric stroke victim can be described as the appropriate application of functional training for a child in whom skeletal and neurophysiological changes are progressing, both adaptively and maturationally. In addition, the neural plasticity and general adaptability of children enhance the effects of the habilitation efforts, which aim to ensure productive growth and function for a future that most likely will last many decades.

While the child's disabilities and abilities in motor, mental, and emotional life may be the initial presenting problem, the social and family milieu, which has molded and will mold the child, must be included in assessments and therapeutic recommendations. It is clear that multiple talents are required for recommending and coordinating a therapeutic program that is optimal for the child and comprehensible and integrative for his family and school peer milieu. The interdisciplinary or team concept of therapy is the logical approach.

The specialization of training in medical and paramedical professions too often leads to fragmentation of therapy, conflicting priorities, or confusion in parental counseling. If the interdisciplinary approach is to be effective, the information from multidisciplinary assessments must be assembled into a picture of the child and his world, so that the nature of the necessary therapeutic influences on that world and the priorities for applying them will be global and cohesive. The integration of problems and therapeutic approaches is the role of the coordinator or conductor of the therapeutic ensemble.

The earlier the onset of central nervous system involvement, the more diffuse the potential personality alterations may be. The child's ability to adjust to the acquired deficits will depend on: (1) the nature and extent of physical limitation, (2) whether there is impairment of emotional control, (3) whether the problem is progressive or stationary, and (4) the child's original intellectual endowment and emotional background.

The physiatrist makes an initial assessment of the patient's joint flexibility, voluntary muscular control, somatic and special sensory function, ability to understand and communicate, and exercise tolerance. He then prescribes physical, occupational, and speech therapy, indicating areas for concentration in each, noting precautions for activity or position, and outlining short-term goals. As therapy progresses, the patient is reevaluated jointly and periodically by physiatrist, therapists, and others involved in the habilitative program. The various disciplines are thus encouraged to see all aspects of the individual child's style of learning and performance as long-range goals are planned.

Throughout the rehabilitation program, one aim is to set up a therapeutic milieu, rather than limiting therapy to fixed segments of the day. Similarly, for children treated as outpatients, therapeutic recommendations to be carried out by the parents are incorporated into the daily handling, eating patterns, and play activities in the home.

While tradition may apportion gross motor problems to the physical and fine motor function to the occupational therapist, there is and must be considerable overlap in actual treatment. For example, both types of motor function necessitate attention to axial alignment, which is particularly important when asymmetrical spasticity is the residue of stroke. Shoulder and thoracic alignment during hand activities as well as thoracolumbar and pelvic alignment during locomotion must be ensured to minimize the possibility of subsequent development of scoliosis.

Gross Motor Function

Documentation and maintenance of the range of joint motion, muscle strength, and endurance are as basic to evaluation and treatment, as are the encouragement of mobility in his environment and development of the child's abilities without overemphasis on his disability. Stimulation of motor activities vital to life, i.e., respiration, may have to precede the traditional basic approaches. In addition, the therapist must have considerable acuity in observing the child's performance, since there may be problems in the quality of performance, despite demonstrated ability to complete an activity. Often the largest portion of the therapy program may be devoted to observed problems rather than to specific joint and muscle limitations. Thus, possible joint malalignment caused by method of performance, cardiovascular efficiency of performance, and accentuation of abnormal muscle tone during performance each may need attention.

It should be apparent that strength is not synonymous with function. Spasticity, ataxia, athetosis, dystonia, or motor apraxia will influence the end to which available strength is applied. When the residue of childhood stroke involves disordered synergy and incomplete or incoordinate voluntary control, standard manual muscle testing often yields limited information regarding true functional capacity. The documentation resulting from detailed observation of joint, muscle, and function should provide a better indication of the child's style of moving within his environment. On the basis of observed variations from that which is considered normal, activities and positions are selected to stimulate movement within a new positional context and to discourage joint malalignment and involuntary motions.

Remedial activities for control and mobility are introduced in the prone, supine, sitting, kneeling, and standing positions.

In each of these positions, the aim is to encourage (1) head and trunk control, (2) postural symmetry, (3) ability to support weight, (4) ability to shift weight, (5) ability to rotate the trunk to initiate motion or as part of upper extremity reaching, (6) ability to change from one position to another, (7) ability to balance in kneeling and standing positions, and (8) ability to use the hands. Finally, if ambulation is possible and is eventually reached, the gait pattern is improved as far as possible. Sequenced training for body control in each of these positions constitutes a motor development program, aspects of which can be introduced even in infancy.

Considerable emphasis is placed on prevention of contractures from joint immobility and involuntary overflow of spasticity or dystonia into stereotyped postures, e.g., extensor thrust or head retraction. Although static positioning may be used for short periods during the day and during sleep to prevent contractures and maintain postural symmetry, greater emphasis is placed on controlled and coordinated mobility. The refinement of mobility training into performance skill is determined by the age, motivation, and functional needs of the child, within the limits imposed by nouromuscular deficit. Performance skill implies accuracy of performance in terms of precision and coordination, efficiency (to minimize energy expenditure and abnormal postures), speed of performance, and adaptability (e.g., ambulation over varied terrains or in both calm and hectic environments).

Fine Motor Function

Manipulatory skill is reflected in many self-care, school, recreational, and later vocational areas. The therapist may begin initial hand function evaluation in infants by observing spontaneous hand use, hand preference, positioning of wrist and digits during use, types of activities for which the infant chooses to use his hands, and influence of body position on hand function. The stabilizing ability of trunk and shoulder muscles is checked, as is symmetry of shoulders and back.

Evaluation of upper extremity somatic sensory acuity is more accurate after the child is five years of age. When certain sensory modalities are impaired but not absent, efforts are made to focus the child's awareness on the limb with impaired sensation so that the sensory residue is maximally used during functional activities. These measures can even be applied to infants, i.e., by tying a bell or bright ribbon to the less sensitive extremity. In general, functional use of such an extremity can be increased to some degree, particularly if the sensory deficit does not involve stereognosis.

Although therapy neither increases nor alters sensation, it can increase awareness of extremities. This is particularly true in those children whose sensory deficit is transient and leaves a habit of limb disuse. To a lesser extent, awareness can also increase when inattention or sensory extinction occur. The sensory feedback, once attended to, is an important part of motor learning. Partial or unattended sensation may also involve oral as well as extremity musculature. Thus, similar emphasis on concentrating attention on oral sensation may be an important part of a feeding or speech therapy program.

Having seated a child in a position of optimal balance and control, and having focused attention on the hands, the therapist introduces toys of varied sizes, weights, shapes, and textures, or other carefully selected activities. These activities can be for unimanual or bimanual use, depending on therapeutic goals. In the presence of visual field defects, activities are introduced on the intact side. The need for this is also communicated to the parents and the schoolteacher. The child should, however, be gradually taught to use head mobility to compensate for the field defect; initially auditory or moving visual stimuli can be used to attract attention and spur head turning to the involved side.

Even when visual fields are intact, lack of visual attentiveness may make it necessary to encourage attended motion from one visual quadrant to another without visually losing the object presented. Once visual attentiveness is established, activities for eye-hand coordination follow. This involves not only control precision, but control of the rate of eye-hand motion as well. Eye-hand coordination training is of primary benefit in children requiring compensation for impaired kinesthetic sensation, but has additional wider application in many areas of training for manual and finger dexterity.

The need to evaluate combined sensory and motor dysfunctions and to provide an appropriate therapeutic regimen necessitates close involvement of a knowledgeable pediatric neurologist or physiatrist in assessment and planning. The disorders of sensory interpretation and sensory motor integration that have been grouped under the terms "dyslexia," "perceptual problems," and "visuomotor disorders" are numerous and often difficult to delineate. Once documented, it may be difficult to pinpoint a causative relationship between the signs of dysfunction or test results and actual performance. Therapists should not be left to face this challenge unaided or unsupervised.

Activities of Daily Life

Self-care activities are introduced early in therapy, so that the child can derive satisfaction and, possibly, motivation from small increments in independence. When introducing age-commensurate self-support activities, the therapist keeps in mind the possible structural problems of the home in which these skills will be used. One or more home visits may be necessary to determine the most effective functional techniques for the child, and to suggest means of facilitating the parent's handling of the child in the home environment. In order to preserve independent function, specific types of clothing, garment fastenings, or adaptive devices may be suggested. During outpatient therapy, or prior to an inpatient's discharge, a school visit may help to minimize future functional problems.

Hearing, Language, and Speech

The importance of auditory acuity for sound reception and discrimination parallels the importance of visual or somatic sensory acuity. After demonstration of adequate hearing acuity by audiometrics or cortical audiometry, assessment of auditory perception must also consider ability to distinguish direction of sound, discrimination of individual phonemes, ability to separate foreground and background sounds, and general organization of received sound stimuli.

Language has been defined in many ways, but for the purposes of this discussion it may be thought of as the formulation of ideas into a meaningful sound or gesture system that is comprehensible and communicable to others. Sounds, words, or gestures are the symbols of the ideas and the expression of language. Even if language is not expressed, "inner language" can be assessed by observing the child's understanding of the use of common objects and toys, as well as his response to simple demonstrated tasks. Evaluation of this area is of particular importance when an impoverished environment or different cultural or language background is encountered. Comprehension may be indicated verbally, by selection of presented choices (using finger or eye pointing), or by response to verbal requests of increasing complexity.

Speech may be simply defined as the oral production of language, but encompasses the complex acts of respiratory control coordinated with lip, tongue, and pharyngeal mobility to control the escape of air and to contour the emitted sound. Impaired sucking may be the first clue to impaired oropharyngeal function in the infant with stroke. Later, feeding and chewing difficulties, and often drooling presage disorder in language function. The speech therapy for infants and children with stroke often begins with feeding: to obtain lip closure (related to future p, m, b sounds), tongue lateralization and mobility (the latter related directly to d, l, n, t sounds), and circumoral closure or puckering as in sucking through a straw (related to future w, f, v sounds). In both feeding and later articulation training, the stability of the head and trunk must also receive attention in order to facilitate the coordinate sequencing of the multiple muscles controlling and modifying the column of air that will emerge as speech sounds.

The complex series of neural circuits involved in hearing, comprehending, interpreting, formulating, and expressing ideas in speech or writing involves auditory and visual input and integration followed by motor output. Portions of these functional circuits can be tested. When deficits are found, appropriate therapy may be programmed.

When oropharyngeal dysfunction is severe enough to totally prohibit intelligible speech, an alphabet board, typewriter, or picture board may be necessary for communication. Because speech is one mode of self-expression in addition to idea expression, the limitations imposed by alphabet boards or other mechanical modes of communication may be frustrating to the child with intact intellectual ability. The older the child, the more this is likely to be true.

Whether the speech therapist is involved in simple developmental programming or in highly skilled diagnostic evaluations and complex therapy programs, the therapy activities must take place in the interdisciplinary context in order to meet all the patient's needs rather than solely those related to speech and language.

SUMMARY

In general, improvement following acquired neuromuscular deficit in childhood can be expected to continue during the first 18 to 24 months after onset. During the later months in that period, progress slows and reaches a plateau. Usually, the faster the recovery immediately after onset, the greater the functional ability eventually attained. Unlike treatment programs for older children and adults, one should not wait for the young child to reach a progress plateau before discharge from inpatient therapy. The younger the child, the more the stress placed on a home program of therapy administered by the parents with periodic supervision and adjustment of program by the therapist. The global goals of the therapy team are best served by focusing attention on the home and school as soon as the child's medical and functional status permit.

Because the child with stroke is continuing to grow and develop, periodic reevaluations should continue over many years, with the same cohesive rehabilitation team doing the planning when new or changing problems are encountered.

References

1. Aicardi, J., Amsili, J., Chevrie, J. J.: Acute hemiplegia in infancy and childhood. Dev. Med. Child. Neurol., *11*:62–173, 1969.
2. Banker, B. Q.: Cerebral vascular disease in infancy and childhood: I. Occlusive vascular diseases. J. Neuropathol. Exp. Neurol., *20*:127–173, 1961.
3. Bateman, B. D.: *Interpretation of the 1961 Illinois Test of Psycholinguistic Abilities.* Seattle, Wash., Special Child Publications, 1968.
4. Berry, M. F.: *Language Disorders of Children: The Bases and Diagnoses.* New York, Appleton-Century-Crofts (Educational Div. of Meredith Corp.), 1969.
5. Bobath, B.: The very early treatment of cerebral palsy. Dev. Med. Child Neurol., *9*:373–390, 1967.
6. Bobath, B., and Finnie, N. R.: Problems of communication between parents and staff in the treatment and management of children with cerebral palsy. Dev. Med. Child Neurol., *12*:629–635, 1970.
7. Brunnstrom, S.: Movement therapy in hemiplegia based on sequential recovery stages. J. Am. Phys. Ther. Assoc., *46*:357–375, 1966.
8. Byers, R. K., and McLean, W. T.: Etiology and course of certain hemiplegias with aphasia in childhood. Pediatrics, *29*:376–383, 1962.
9. Carter, S., and Gold, A. P.: Acute infantile hemiplegia. Pediatr. Clin. North Am., *14*:851–864, 1964.
9a. Challenor, Y. B.: Rehabilitation of childhood stroke. *In* Gold A. P. (ed.): Stroke in Children. Stroke, in press.
10. Chyatte, S. B., and Birdsong, J. H.: Assessment of motor performance in brain injury. Am. J. Phys. Med., *50*:17–30, 1971.
11. Dargassies, S. S.: Neurodevelopmental symptoms during the first year of life. Dev. Med. Child Neurol., *14*:235–246, 1972.
12. Eisenberg, L.: Behavioral manifestations of cerebral damage in childhood. In Birch, H. G. (ed.): *Brain Damage in Children.* Baltimore, Williams & Wilkins Co., 1964, pp. 61–73.
13. Ellis, E.: *The Physical Management of Developmental Disorders.* Clinics in Development Medicine, No. 26. Spastics International Medical Publications. Philadelphia, J. B. Lippincott Co., 1967.
14. Ellis, E.: Annotations: Very early treatment of cerebral palsy. Dev. Med. Child Neurol., *8*:206–207, 1966.
15. Fawcus, B.: Oropharyngeal function in relation to speech. Dev. Med. Child Neurol., *11*:556–560, 1969.
16. Fischer, E.: Factors affecting motor learning. Am. J. Phys. Med., *46*:511–519, 1967.
17. Gesell, A., and Amatruda, C. S.: *Developmental Diagnosis: Normal and Abnormal Child Development.* New York, Hoeber Medical Div., Harper & Row Publishers, 1967, p. 496.
18. Gesell, A., Ilg, F. L., and Bullis, G. E.: *Vision and Its Development in Infants and Children.* New York, Paul B. Hoeber, Inc. (Div. of Harper and Row), 1949, pp. 305–325.

19. Gillette, H. E.: *Systems of Therapy in Cerebral Palsy.* Springfield, Ill., Charles C Thomas, 1969, pp. 1–78.
20. Gold, A. P. (ed.): Stroke in children. To be published in Stroke and monograph by U.S. Government Printing Office.
21. Gold, A. P., and Yahr, M. D.: Childhood lupus erythematosus: A clinical and pathological study of the neurological manifestations. Trans. Am. Neurol. Assoc., 85:96, 1960.
22. Gold, A. P., Ransohoff, J., and Carter, S.: Arteriovenous malformation of the vein of Galen in children. Acta Neurol. Scand., 40(Suppl. 11):1, 1964.
23. Greer, M., and Schotland, D.: Abnormal hemoglobin as a cause of neurologic disease. Neurology, 12:114–123, 1962.
24. Groch, S. N., Sayre, G. P., and Heck, F. J.: Cerebral hemorrhage in leukemia. A.M.A. Arch. Neurol., 2:439–451, 1960.
25. Hatton, D. A.: The child with minimal cerebral dysfunction. Dev. Med. Child Neurol., 8:71–78, 1966.
26. Hilal, S. K., Solomon, G. E., Gold, A. P., and Carter, S.: Primary cerebral arterial occlusive disease in children, Part I: Acute aquired hemiplegia. Radiology, 99:71–86, 93–94, 1971. Ibid. Part II: Neurocutaneous syndromes. Radiology, 99:87–93, 94, 1971.
27. Huttenlocher, P. R., and Smith, D. B.: Acute infantile hemiplegia with thrombocytosis. Dev. Med. Child Neurol., 10:621–625, 1968.
28. Johnson, D. J., and Myklebust, H. R.: Learning Disabilities. New York, Grune & Stratton, Inc., 1967, p. 336.
29. Kelman, H. R.: The effect of a brain-damaged child on the family. In Birch, H. C. (ed.): *Brain Damage in Children.* Baltimore, Williams & Wilkins Co., 1967, pp. 77–99.
30. Kinal, M. E.: Traumatic thrombosis of dural venous sinuses in closed head injury. J. Neurosurg., 27:142–145, 1967.
31. Knobloch, H., and Pasamanick, B.: Predicting intellectual potential in infancy. Am. J. Dis. Child., 106:43–51, 1963.
32. Köng, E.: Very early treatment of cerebral palsy. Dev. Med. Child Neurol., 8:198–202, 1966.
33. Luria, A. R.: *Restoration of Function After Brain Injury.* Elmsford, N.Y., Pergamon Press, 1963.
34. Luria, A. R.: *Higher Cortical Functions in Man.* New York, Basic Books, Inc. Publ. Consultants Bureau, 1966.
35. Milani-Comparetti, A., and Gidoni, E. A.: A graphic method of recording normal and abnormal movement patterns. Dev. Med. Child Neurol., 10:633–636, 1968.
36. Pitner, S. E.: Carotid thrombosis due to intraoral trauma; An unusual complication of common childhood accident. New Engl. J. Med., 274:764–767, 1966.
37. Robson, P.: The prevalence of scoliosis in adolescents and young adults with cerebral palsy. Dev. Med. Child Neurol., 10:447–452, 1968.
38. Scrutton, D.: Prevention and management of incorrect spinal posture in cerebral palsy. Dev. Med. Child Neurol., 8:322–326, 1966.
39. Semans, S.: Specific tests and evaluation tools for the child with central nervous system deficit: A report of two symposiums. Washington, D.C., U.S. Department of Health, Education and Welfare, 1965, pp. 122–128.
40. Semans, S., Phillips, R., Romanoli, M., et al.: A cerebral palsy assessment chart. In The Child with Central Nervous System Deficit: A Report of Two Symposiums. Washington, D.C., U.S. Department of Health, Education and Welfare, 1965, pp. 129–135.
41. Shulman, S. T., and Grossman, B. J.: Fat embolism in childhood: Review with report of a fatal case related to physical therapy in a child with dermatomyositis. Am. J. Dis. Child., 120:480–484, 1970.
42. Solomon, G. E., Hilal, S. K., Gold, A. P., and Carter, S.: Natural history of acute hemiplegia of childhood. Brain, 93:107–120, 1970.
43. Treanor, W. J.: The role of physical medicine treatment in stroke rehabilitation. Clin. Orthop., 63:14–22, 1969.
44. Twitchell, T. E.: Variations and abnormalities of motor development. J. Am. Phys. Ther. Assoc., 45:424–430, 1965.
45. Tyler, H. R., and Clark, D. B., Incidents of neurological complications in congenital heart disease. A.M.A. Arch. Neurol. Psychiatry, 77:17–22, 1957. Ibid. Cerebrovascular accidents in patients with congenital heart disease. A.M.A. Arch Neurol. Psychiatry, 77:483–489, 1957.
46. Vulpe, S. G.: *Basic Skills Assessment.* National Institute on Mental Retardation of the Canadian Association for the Mentally Retarded, No. 43.
47. Wiscoff, H. S., and Rothballer, A. B.: Cerebral arterial thrombosis in children. Review of literature and addition of two cases in apparently healthy children. Arch. Neurol., 4:258–267, 1961.

Chapter 9

Cerebral Palsy

by *Niels L. Low, M.D.,* and *John A. Downey, M.D.*

Cerebral palsy is not a specific, well-delineated, clinical entity. It is a useful collective term to describe those nonprogressive encephalopathies that may have their beginning before or during delivery or in early childhood, and that have at least one motor impairment of cerebral origin as a major component. The etiology, clinical features, and course of cerebral palsy are variable. There are, however, good practical reasons to group these conditions together—with the understanding that when the diagnosis of cerebral palsy is made, it should be classified according to type and severity and probably also qualified by the listing of associated conditions. While the term "cerebral palsy" as a hospital discharge diagnosis tells us little, a sequential list such as: "cerebral palsy, spastic diplegia, moderate, with normal intelligence, without seizures, due to prematurity" becomes clear and useful.

ETIOLOGY

Cerebral palsy syndromes can be caused by anything that may interfere with cerebral physiology in prenatal and early postnatal life. Our knowledge of the causation of structural anomalies in the brain is limited, but it is known that such anomalies can manifest themselves clinically in various ways, including mental retardation, seizures, behavior disorders, auditory and visual handicaps and in impairment of motor function; which is cerebral palsy. Complications of childbirth, such as abruptio placentae, a prolapsed umbilical cord, complicated breech delivery, and other mechanisms that lead to tempo-

169

rary hypoxia or intracranial bleeding may cause nonprogressive motor impairment. It would be neither possible nor practical to list all the potential causes here, but further examples include toxins, metabolic diseases, hemorrhages, arterial and venous thrombi and emboli, encephalitis, meningitis and vasculitis, and especially also physical trauma. Blood group incompatibility with jaundice will cause cerebral palsy, but the syndrome occurs much less frequently now than in previous decades. In any group of patients with cerebral palsy, the most frequent single common denominator is low birth weight, whether this is due to prematurity, the "small-for-date-infant" syndrome, or multiple birth, as about 25 per cent of all children in most cerebral palsy clinics have a birth weight below 2500 gm. If one of twins is affected, it is usually the second-born. It appears that low birth weight predisposes to anoxia and hemorrhages, but it is also possible that a baby may be born prematurely because something is wrong with its brain. To reduce the incidence of these disabilities, progress must be made in the prevention of low birth weight.

PATHOLOGY

As cerebral palsy is not a single clinical entity, there are no characteristic pathological data that are applicable for cerebral palsy as a whole. Even within specific subgroups there are different causes and mechanisms, making it impossible to make many generalized statements on autopsy findings without writing a treatise based on a large number of cases, which would be beyond the scope of this chapter and book.

Most cerebral palsied children and adults do not die on hospital services for acute diseases where sophisticated neuropathological techniques and experts are available, and frequently no autopsy is performed because the next of kin are not convinced of the need for and benefit to themselves of postmortem examinations. The result is that much of our knowledge rests on single case reports and only a few more comprehensive texts.[1]

In about one third of the instances, the brain shows gross malformations. The changes in the other cases are primarily microscopic and mainly in cortical and subcortical layers. Included in the common cortical changes are laminar degeneration, loss of neurons, and cortical atrophy resulting in narrower gyri, wider sulci, and low brain weight. In subcortical areas one also finds evidence of atrophy, gliosis in the white matter, and sometimes cystic changes. Cortical changes are more commonly found in postnatally acquired cerebral palsy, while deeper findings are much more frequent in the prenatal cases and those with perinatal complications. In those patients who have exhibited athetosis, most changes are seen in the basal ganglia, especially the globus pallidus. But the pathological findings are not always limited to that area and may be found in the cortical gray matter and sometimes in the dentate and olivary nuclei.

Only little is known about the pathology of ataxic cerebral palsy. Degeneration or dysplasia in the cerebellum has been described in some cases, but in others the cerebellum was normal and other structures were affected.

CLINICAL CLASSIFICATION

There are three major types of cerebral palsy: the spastic, the dyskinetic, and the ataxic (Table 9–1). Combinations of any two or all three of these are also possible. The spastic group is further subdivided according to the site of the spasticity.

Spastic Cerebral Palsy

The characteristic physical signs of spasticity are increased stretch reflexes, increased muscle tone, and frequently weakness. Because cerebral palsy is a disease of the brain, we deal here with an upper motor neuron type of weakness.

Hemiparesis. The term "hemiparesis" signifies that one side of the body is affected; in most instances, the upper extremity is more involved than the lower. The paretic extremities are usually thinner than the healthy ones and may be shorter, with a smaller hand or foot. This diminished growth is believed to be related to parietal lobe impairment. In hemiparesis the facial muscles are often spared because of the bilateral, cortical representation of the upper face in the vast majority of people.

Parietal lobe damage leads not only to growth retardation but causes also impairment of sensory-cortical function. This can be diagnosed by absence or reduction of ability to recognize size, shape, and texture of objects held in the affected hand (astereognosis), and by impaired two-point discrimination.

Children with hemiparesis tend to have a characteristic pattern of spasticity. There is usually increased tone in the muscles of the calf, the hamstrings, and the hip adductors. These cause the child to tend to walk with the foot inverted and plantar flexed, the knee flexed, and the leg adducted. In the arm the increased tone tends to be in the shoulder adductors and internal rotators, the elbow flexors and pronators, and the wrist and finger flexors. This increased tone may be evident on casual examination, but in mild cases may only show up under stress or in association with running. For functional and therapeutic purposes it is essential to test all hemiparetics for the presence of homonymous hemianopsia, which is likely to occur in lesions of the posterior temporal and occipital areas.

TABLE 9–1   CLINICAL CLASSIFICATION OF CEREBRAL PALSY

I. Spastic	a) hemiparesis
	b) tetraparesis
	c) diplegia 1. hypertonic
	2. "atonic"
	d) paraparesis
	e) monoparesis and triparesis
II. Dyskinetic	a) athetoid
	b) other dyskinesias
III. Ataxic	
IV. Mixed Types	

Tetraparesis.   Tetraparesis implies spasticity of all four extremities to approximately the same degree; the lower and upper limbs are equally affected, but slight asymmetries may exist. The manifestations characteristic of hemiparesis are present bilaterally, but the lower extremities are more involved. This results in considerable tightness of the hip adductors and leads to difficulties in separating the legs and even causes crossover positions ("scissoring"), which tends to be a major obstacle to ambulation, in addition to the usual hip flexor and hamstring tightness. When in rare instances of tetraparesis the arms are more severely affected than the legs, the term "double hemiplegia" is sometimes used. In tetraparesis, both cerebral hemispheres are involved, and that may also manifest itself in supranuclear or pseudobulbar palsy. Speech is dysarthric, swallowing may be impaired, tongue protrusion is incomplete, and emotions are more labile with inappropriate laughing or crying.

Spastic Diplegia.   Children with spastic diplegia have involvement of all four extremities, though the affliction of the uppers is much milder than that of the lowers. The term is therefore not an accurate one but has remained in common usage since it was first coined by Sigmund Freud.[2] It is usually not difficult to recognize and separate this form from tetraplegia, but when the involvement of the arm is minimal it may be difficult to differentiate diplegia from paraplegia. True paraplegia based on cerebral involvement hardly ever occurs. In our experience spastic diplegia is the most common type of cerebral palsy, but there is some confusion in the literature because different classifications and definitions are used in different clinics, especially outside the United States and Canada. Although a prematurely born baby can suffer any type of cerebral palsy, the vast majority of low birth weight infants who have a motor deficit will show this type.

Atonic diplegia is a variant of this form of cerebral palsy. It is not clearly defined and the physiological basis is not clear either. This terminology is used in young children with general weakness, normal or hyperactive tendon reflexes, but muscle tone that is less than normal. One of the other characteristic findings is flexion at the hips when the child is suspended upright under the arms (Foerster's sign). Delay of all motor milestones and mental retardation accompany the other manifestations. Foerster's sign may also be present in other retarded children who do not meet the usual criteria of cerebral palsy. Atonic diplegia is not seen in older children because tone increases with age and a reclassification, therefore, becomes necessary. It is probably best to use this term sparingly.

Monoplegia, Triplegia, and Paraplegia.   Pure cerebral paraplegia, if and when it occurs, is characterized by tightness of the hip adductors, hamstrings, and calves, and increased reflexes in the lower extremities, but completely normal arms and hands.

Monoplegia and triplegia are rare conditions. When only one extremity is spared, it usually is an arm.

Dyskinetic Cerebral Palsy

Dyskinesia implies abnormal involuntary movements. The seat of origin of these movements is in the basal ganglia, especially the globus pallidus, and like all other abnormal basal ganglia movements, they disappear in sleep and are aggravated by stress. This type of cerebral palsy has been subclassified into many entities and special forms but this is neither necessary nor desirable because almost all these children have one major type in common, namely athetosis. The manifestations not only change gradually with time, but they are also variable from day to day or occasionally from hour to hour in some patients. Because of the accompanying anxiety, the children show the most active and violent movements when they are being examined by the physician, especially in a busy clinic setting. Athetosis is characterized by slow, wormlike, writhing movements that usually involve all extremities, the trunk, the neck, individual face muscles, and the tongue. The dyskinesia of the tongue and other pharyngeal, laryngeal, and oral muscles causes a dysarthria that can make it very difficult to understand the child. The continuous moving frequently causes hypertrophy of some muscle groups, especially around the shoulders and neck.

As the quality and speed of the movements tend to change with the course of time, certain choreiform and dystonic manifestations may be seen with athetosis. These two types of dyskinesia do not appear in pure form within the context of cerebral palsy.

Before the mechanism and sequelae of mother-child blood group incompatibility were recognized, about 50 per cent of athetoids had had kernicterus. Since the advent of early exchange transfusions, athetosis has become a much less frequent problem.

Ataxic Cerebral Palsy

Ataxic cerebral palsy is the least common type; it is characterized by nonprogressive ataxic phenomena from earliest childhood without any other apparent cause. Involved children have a wide-based gait and perform rapid repetitive movements poorly, and there is decomposition of movements of the upper extremities on reaching for objects. Other causes for ataxia have to be ruled out carefully and by repeated examination. Foot deformities and abnormal sensory findings would lead to different diagnoses. Because people can compensate for mild or moderate ataxia reasonably well, there is frequently a functional improvement with increasing age.

Mixed-Type Cerebral Palsy

The description of "mixed type of cerebral palsy" is used when spasticity and athetosis occur together in the same child. Although most spastics are "pure" spastics, the majority of athetoids have at least slight spasticity. Ataxia can also occur simultaneously with the spastic or dyskinetic forms. It can be difficult at times to separate the features of multiple involvement; the clinical manifestations in a child with mixed cerebral palsy are characteristically the summation of findings of each type.

The "dysequilibrium syndrome in cerebral palsy" described in Sweden apparently includes cases of what is known as the ataxic type plus other cases that are characterized by difficulties in achieving and maintaining an upright posture, especially during the first five to six years of life.[3] There is an overlap between this syndrome and the forms already described.

ASSOCIATED CONDITIONS

Children who suffer from cerebral motor deficits of a static nature (the definition of cerebral palsy) are very likely to have other central nervous system impairments. Their learning and reasoning power may be subnormal (mental retardation), their behavior and interpersonal relationships may be different from those of so-called normal children (minimal brain damage, MBD syndrome), there may be impairment of special senses, and seizures may occur. Any one of these associated conditions can be present in a cerebral palsied child, or any combination of two or more. Table 9–2 presents a simplified graphic concept of these interactions.

The incidence of mental retardation in cerebral palsy is difficult to assess as published data are usually based on skewed populations, such as a particular clinic, hospital, or school. The mildest cases may not attend a cerebral palsy clinic regularly, and a general pediatric clinic will see too few of these patients to be able to give statistical data. An inpatient service does not have all types of cerebral palsied children to an equal degree and will tend to discriminate against the mildest and the most severe cases; the same can be said about "cerebral palsy schools" and schools for the handicapped. Even when otherwise good information is available, it is still relatively meaningless to speak of the percentage of retardation as a whole; one has to qualify the figures according to the type of cerebral palsy. Figures given vary between 25 and 75 per cent. Hansen's report is probably the most reliable one because he surveyed the entire population of Denmark regardless of the place of medical care or education; the only cases that may have been omitted are those who had died in earliest childhood.[4] On the other hand, one does not know whether figures in Denmark are necessarily applicable in all other Western countries. Hansen found fewer retardates among the cerebral palsied than any other author. Spastic children are more likely to be retarded than the purely athetoid, and the ataxic have more chances to have normal intelligence than the others. Among the spastics, the tetraplegics have statistically a lower IQ than diplegics, hemiplegics, and monoplegics, in that order. The spastic with

TABLE 9–2   INTERRELATED SYNDROMES DUE TO BRAIN DAMAGE

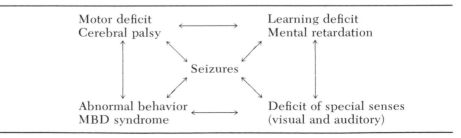

seizures is more likely to be retarded than one who never has had convulsions, and more severely so.

Seizures may have their beginning at any age from earliest infancy until adulthood. However, although the basic pathological process may be present from birth or even earlier, the peak incidence of the commencement of the associated seizures disorder occurs between two and six years of age. The most common seizure type is grand mal, with psychomotor and focal seizures next; petit mal practically never occurs in cerebral palsied children. Occasionally, in such infants infantile spasms may be seen. The electroencephalogram tends to vary with age; spikes may migrate not only on the same side but even from one side to the other in spite of the fact that one is dealing with fixed, static encephalopathy.

The minimal brain damage syndrome, MBD, is dealt with in another chapter, but it should be pointed out here that any or all characteristics of MBD may occur in patients with cerebral palsy. These children require the same management and education as other MBD children in addition to the usual cerebral palsy care. The chief presenting symptoms are poor attention span, marked distractibility, hyperactive behavior, and defects on various levels of integration that may interfere partially with reading, arithmetic, and speech, regardless of intelligence. Speech should be singled out here particularly because it may be impaired by various mechanisms. Not only does MBD affect speech, but so also do athetosis, ataxia, and marked spasticity, especially when bilateral. The type of dysarthria depends on which of the three major types of cerebral palsy is present.

Vision can be affected, owing to various mechanisms. The incidence of strabismus is much higher in spastics than in the so-called normal childhood population. Refractive errors have to be looked for routinely because their presence will increase the child's physical and educational handicap. When dealing with hemiparetics it is particularly important to test for hemianopsia and other field defects as early as meaningful estimates can be obtained. Other ophthalmological problems occur infrequently; however, in acquired cerebral palsy (such as postmeningitic and post-traumatic) optic atrophy has to be looked for.

Although reduced hearing (hypacusis) can be caused by numerous insults, in cerebral palsy it is usually a complication of kernicterus due to blood group incompatibility and may be associated with limited upward gaze. This is of importance because the athetoid child with deafness cannot hear his mother or the therapist's instructions; his hearing loss, being central, is primarily to high tones. Some cerebral palsied children may have no abnormalities in the inner or middle or outer ear, nor of the acoustic nerve, but may not respond well to the spoken word. They are believed to have defects in integration of auditory stimuli within the brain (dysacusis).

INCIDENCE

Just as reported data on the incidence of retardation in cerebral palsy are influenced by their source and the nature of the survey, so are published incidence statistics on cerebral palsy influenced by many extraneous factors. Among the most frequently quoted figures are those by Phelps of 7 in 100,000 population and by Hansen of 1.3 in 1000 births.[4, 5] Cerebral palsy is definitely on the increase in medically highly developed countries. If we remember that 25 per cent of children in cerebral palsy clinics were born with a weight of less than 2500 gm, it is easy to see that by saving the lives of more premature babies, one also saves more potentially handicapped children. Thirty years ago, almost all children with bacterial meningitis succumbed during the acute disease. While most of them survive now, some of them do so only with residua among which are cerebral palsy and mental retardation. Physical accidents are more common now and so are their sequelae. Saving of lives should continue, but every effort to reduce the incidence of prematurity and to lower the rate of accidents should be made, and meningitis should be diagnosed earlier to avoid permanent complications.

LABORATORY DIAGNOSIS

The common laboratory examinations of the blood and urine are rarely contributory in the diagnosis and differential analysis of the cerebral palsies. Individually selected examinations may reveal the cause in a minority of children, for instance, in the diagnosis of a hemoglobinopathy, homocystinuria, or blood group incompatibility. Newer techniques in radiology have shed more light on both the cause and the pathological changes in individual instances. Plain skull x-rays may reveal asymmetries of the vault of the cranium, and air studies may demonstrate localized or generalized atrophy, porencephaly, and other abnormalities. Angiography, especially when combined with magnification or subtraction techniques, has taught us much about vascular anomalies and occlusions in the causation of static motor deficits. These contrast studies should not be done routinely, but only on specific medical indication.

There are no electroencephalographic patterns that are diagnostic of cerebral palsy as a whole or of any particular type, but electroencephalograms are helpful in the management of cerebral palsied children, especially those with seizures. Seizure patterns are much more common than the clinical incidence of seizures; voltage and sleep spindle asymmetries are common in hemiparetics.

COURSE

Although cerebral palsy is a nonprogressive syndrome by definition, the clinical picture may change somewhat with age. Children with spasticity manifest a tendency to develop fixed deformities with time as they are kept in nonphysiological positions and substitute certain muscles or muscle groups for others. If proper prophylactic or therapeutic measures are not taken, they become functionally worse. Some ambulatory diplegics become nonwalkers at puberty because of increasing weight and energy requirements, although the disease process is static. Athetoids, on the other hand, may "improve." Their dyskinesia does not really diminish, but the physical and mental potential of young athetoids is often underestimated, and they therefore appear improved in the second decade. Justified depressions and frustrations may decrease the patients' motivation at times and will then make them functionally worse although the brain lesions are unchanged. There are adequate data to state that repeated severe convulsions lead to neuronal loss and increasing brain damage, and cerebral palsied children with inadequately controlled seizures may deteriorate secondarily owing to this associated complication.

TREATMENT

By definition, all forms of cerebral palsy are due to fixed and permanent pathological changes in the brain; therefore, treatment can never cure the condition or make the patient functionally normal. If therapy is not curative, other goals have to be set: (1) to prevent the handicap from increasing, (2) to increase or improve function, (3) to provide suitable education, (4) to enhance recreation, and (5) to ensure the best possible emotional life.

Some of these goals are discussed in better perspective and detail in other chapters, such as Orthoses for Children, Education for the Handicapped Child, and Psychiatric Complications of Chronic Illness in Children.

Preventing the Handicap from Increasing

In spastic children the affected extremities tend to be held in abnormal postures because of uneven action between agonists and antagonists. This phenomenon can be best illustrated by examples. With the elbow and wrist held in flexed positions all the time, contractures of the flexor muscles may occur and extension may become limited or impossible. To prevent shortening of muscle groups, the joints are put through passive range of motion exercises regularly by the mother or another member of the family. The key to effective treatment is the mother, who spends the most time with the child; the physician and therapist should teach her the proper techniques. The home program should be reinforced and modified by regular therapy sessions. Another common example would be gastrocnemius tightness leading to elevation of the heel and the impairment of gait if this posture becomes fixed. Prophylactic stretching of gastrocnemius muscle and heel cord can prevent, minimize, or delay the contracture.

Routine splints or braces or both are very valuable in supplementing the stretching program by insuring that the tight muscles and joints are kept in a functional position during the hours of rest. This is particularly true for the posterior calves (Perlstein braces), hamstrings (long leg braces), hip adductors (A-frames), and wrists and fingers (cock-up splints). These devices, as part of the total management, should be initiated early in the program and continued for months and even years, supplemented by the passive and active exercise program. The arrest of any incipient scoliosis by proper bracing should be particularly emphasized here (see Chapter 16).

Increasing and Improving Function

When evaluating a child with cerebral palsy, initial functional goals have to be set. The questions that must be asked are: Can sitting, standing, or walking be accomplished? Which activities of daily living appear to be realistic? Is it likely that he can ever feed himself, and if not, can it be made easier? Can he ever learn to dress himself partially or completely? Therapy should be directed toward tentative answers to these questions. The goals need to be reevaluated periodically because the first answer may have been too optimistic or too conservative.

The active therapy program via both the family and the physical therapist should be directed along the lines of stimulating the child to achieve his functional goals. Sitting balance and crawling are encouraged, and as soon as feasible, standing is attempted. If the balance or strength is poor, therapy must be directed toward improvement; it may, however, be supplemented by the use of braces, especially to control plantar flexion of the feet, and less often by longer braces to prevent knee flexion due to inadequate control of hip and knee extension and hamstring spasticity. If the child can stand only with extensive bracing, the beneficial effect of being upright may more easily be achieved in a standing table.

Walking, using reciprocal motion of the legs, should be attempted at the appropriate age even if it initially requires the use of braces and considerable help from the therapist. Later, progression to walking in parallel bars or using ambulatory aids should be encouraged as rapidly as possible.

The use of the hands for unimanual and bimanual activities should be initiated very early. Sensory deficits, particularly astereognosis, will limit the ultimate function, but that cannot be tested reliably until about four years of age. The child may need much help (and patience) in learning to feed and dress himself; many can do so if given the opportunity. As a child gets older, it is very important for his personal respect for himself to learn to care for all his personal needs without the help of a parent or nurse, if this is at all possible.

The question of surgery in cerebral palsy is often raised. If a child has deformities, one can usually find a surgeon who will attempt to change the posture into a normal one. The relevant question, however, is whether this surgical procedure will improve one or more specific functions. If, for instance, a tenotomy will enable the nonambulatory child with scissoring due to adductor spasticity to walk, the indication for surgery is clear. If surgical fusion of the wrist will improve the appearance or the use of a hand in a teenager, a specific goal has been accomplished and the patient is benefited. Conversely, when it is certain that a particular child never will be able to stand or walk, a heelcord lengthening procedure would only be cosmetic, not functional and often not justified.

The timing of surgery is important but not universally agreed upon. Generally, we favor surgical treatment only after conservative measures have been attempted, and then do the surgical procedure that is most specifically indicated to improve function. If, however, the spasticity causes progressive deformities, earlier operation may be desirable. Preoperative and postoperative therapy training toward functional goals are essential and integral parts of the total management.

Medications have a limited role in improving function in cerebral palsied children. Children with seizures should be managed with anticonvulsant medications even though the drugs do not modify the cerebral palsy directly. Overactive, distractible, and inattentive patients may perform better when receiving dextroamphetamine, methylphenidate, or phenothiazines.

Spasticity cannot be abolished by medications but can be modified beneficially in a limited number of children, especially in those cases complicated by major emotional factors and those with dystonic components. The most effective drugs in this context are diazepam (Valium) and its analogues. Local nerve blocks obtained with phenol or ethanol injections may reduce spasticity for a period of from weeks to months.

Sleep abolishes athetosis as it does all other involuntary movements. No sedative drug is effective in achieving this unless it is used in doses that lead the patient close to sleep. Levodopa has not been found to be helpful. There is a limited indication for antianxiety agents because tension and anxiety increase athetosis. When these factors perpetually reduce function, or on certain foreseeable occasions, it is reasonable to prescribe diazepam in dosages that do not cause side effects.

Ataxia is not reduced by medications, but certain agents such as alcohol and sedatives tend to increase it.

Education

One cannot generalize about the educational requirements of children with cerebral palsy. These have to be individualized after considering a particular child's needs and educational potential. This potential will depend on the severity of the disease and on the presence and degree of the associated conditions: learning impairment, abnormal actions and behavior, impaired visual and auditory functions, and seizures. Whenever possible, cerebral palsied children should go to regular classes in regular schools if their learning ability is estimated to be near normal. The physical structure of the school may make such a goal impossible or difficult, but one should aim at that goal. If the child is retarded, he should be with his retarded peers and benefit from the program for that group. The final outcome in a particular child can often be foreseen many years in advance, and the education should be geared to his *assets* more than to his handicaps.

Recreation

Cerebral palsied children have the same needs for recreation and non-school activities as other children. The boy who can't go out and play ball or the girl who can't participate in her peers' activities, needs another recreational outlet. They *can* compete in athletic and artistic activities; they often can play chess and cards. If it can't be done with "normal" children, programs with other handicapped children and teenagers have to be offered. Organized recreation is a form of therapy that stimulates the children's interest and curiosity, raises their ego, helps them to adjust to their handicaps, and improves their functional abilities.

Emotional Life

The emotions experienced by a child with cerebral palsy differ from those of normal children. The families of these children react differently than families without that experience. The physician who recognizes an infant or young child to be handicapped has a unique opportunity to practice preventive psychiatry. By presenting the facts and problems of the handicap to the parents of the patient in an understanding and compassionate way he can achieve a great deal in helping the family to have a healthy outlook on their difficulty and he can also indirectly influence the child's own perception of himself and his adjustment to the handicap.

All through childhood, the patient's self-image, his fears and doubts, his suspicions and frustrations, and his emotional strengths and confidence have to be taken into account. Decisions about the medical program, about education and vocational goals, about recreation and vacations should be partially influenced by his emotional assets and weaknesses, his needs and aspirations.

SUMMARY

Cerebral palsy is a collective term for certain nonprogressive motor handicaps that become apparent soon after birth or in early childhood. It has many causes and different types, and is often complicated by associated conditions that increase the disability. These children cannot be cured, but they can be helped by establishing realistic and specific goals of treatment. This help is most effective when all those who deliver care and treatment have the interest and potential of each child in their hearts and minds.

References

1. Christensen, E., and Melchior, J.: Cerebral palsy, a clinical and neuropathological study. Clin. Devel. Med., No. 25, London, 1967.
2. Freud, S.: *Infantile Cerebral Paralysis*. Transl. by L. A. Russin. Coral Gables, Fla., University of Miami Press, 1968.
3. Hagberg, B.: The dysequilibrium syndrome in cerebral palsy. Acta Paediatr. Scand. Suppl. 226, 1972.
4. Hansen, E.: Cerebral palsy in Denmark. Acta Neurol. Scand. Suppl. 146, 1960.
5. Phelps, W. M.: Etiology and diagnostic classification of cerebral palsy. In *Proceedings of the Cerebral Palsy Institute*. New York, N.Y. Association for Aid of Crippled Children, 1950.

Chapter 10

Lower Motor Neuron Diseases

by *Niels L. Low, M.D.,* and *John A. Downey, M.D.*

Lower motor neuron diseases are those pathological states that involve the anterior horn cells of the spinal cord and their efferent processes; the latter traverse the anterior roots of the cord and are carried via peripheral nerves to their final destinations. The cell bodies and axons of these anterior horn cells are collectively referred to as "the final common motor pathway." On the basis of embryological, functional, and clinical considerations, the motor cell units of cranial nerves III, IV, V, VI, VII, IX, X, XI, and XII also belong to this system.

Anatomically, an anterior horn is present in both the right and left halves of the spinal cord and is particularly prominent in the cervical and lumbar regions, the areas from which the nerves to the four extremities originate. From the root cells of the anterior horn column arise three types of fibers: larger (8 to 13 μ diameter) α fibers, which innervate striated muscles; smaller (3 to 8 μ diameter) γ fibers, which innervate the intrafusal fibers of muscle spindles; and very thinly myelinated fibers from the thoracic and lumbar and sacral ventral roots to sympathetic and parasympathetic autonomic ganglia, which originate in the lateral horns but pass through the anterior horns and leave the cord with the other fibers. Approximately 70 per cent of fibers in an anterior root are of the α type. Alpha fibers cause contractions of striated muscle fibers directly, while stimulation of γ fibers leads to contractions of muscle spindles only, which then send afferent messages back to α fibers in the ventral horns. This latter two-neuron reflex is called the γ loop.

181

CLINICAL EFFECTS OF LOWER MOTOR NEURON DISEASES

The basic clinical picture of lower motor neuron disease consists of weakness, reduction of muscle tone, decrease or absence of tendon reflexes, and eventually visible muscular atrophy. Because practically all skeletal muscles receive their impulses from several segmental levels in the cord, the degree of weakness in one particular muscle depends both on the severity and on the extent of the lesion. Usually, the anterior horn cells in at least three consecutive segments have to be interfered with to cause complete paralysis of one muscle.

To localize the site of disease or injury within the lower motor neuron, one must differentiate the clinical manifestations of anterior horn cell, root, and peripheral nerve disease from each other. At most levels, the destruction of anterior horn cells in a specified area causes the same pure motor results as destruction of ventral roots over the same levels, except that anterior horn cell disease alone does not cause those autonomic deficits that may be caused by root lesions in those parts that innervate autonomic ganglia. Lesions of mixed peripheral nerves cause weakness, hypotonia, and loss of tendon reflexes plus sensory loss with a dermatome distribution.

While weakness, hypotonia, and areflexia have a sudden onset in acute disease, the consequent muscle atrophy occurs only gradually over a period of one week to several months. Conversely, atrophy is not necessarily due to lower motor neuron lesions, but may also be caused by muscle disease or any other physiological or iatrogenic interference with muscle action, such as forced immobilization.

Fasciculations, which are irregularly occurring spontaneous contractions of groups of muscle fibers, may also occur in lower motor neuron disease, but they are rarely seen in children except in the muscles of the tongue, which are only covered by a relatively thin mucous membrane. Presence of fasciculations is normally interpreted as *active* nonacute disease of the twelfth nucleus or anterior horn cells. It is uncommon in peripheral nerve disease, but can occasionally be seen in normal people following extremely strenuous exercise of specific muscles.

ANTERIOR HORN CELL DISEASES

Poliomyelitis

Owing to the widespread success of immunization techniques against the three strains of poliomyelitis, this virus infection has become uncommon in the United States and Canada, but in many areas of the world it is still a frequently occurring acute disease that leaves chronic handicaps and long-lasting disabilities. The physiatrist and other physicians who deal with chronically handicapped children still see the after effects of poliomyelitis and will do so for many more years. Patients who develop poliomyelitis today will be requiring admission to children's hospitals for treatment of sequelae for another 16 to 18 years.

PATHOLOGY

Microscopic studies reveal the lesions primarily in the gray matter of the anterior horns of the spinal cord and the motor nuclei of the cranial nerves in the brain stem. The distribution is normally not symmetrical, but random; the cervical and lumbosacral enlargements are often more affected than other levels of the cord. The degree of involvement may vary from mild and potentially reversible chromatolysis to complete destruction and absence of motor cells. Meningeal involvement manifested by lymphocytic infiltrations is almost the rule; lesions in the cerebral cortex and cerebellum are rare except those that are secondary to anoxia rather than to the primary disease process.

CLINICAL TYPES

If we here limit the discussion to the paralytic types, because only they end in handicaps, we should differentiate between bulbar polio, spinal polio, and bulbospinal forms.

Bulbar Polio. One or more motor cranial nerve nuclei may be involved. The seventh nucleus is the most commonly affected one, and sometimes only the periorbital branch is weak or only one labial corner droops. Various degrees of sixth, third, and fourth nucleus palsy come next in frequency, but involvement of motor ninth and tenth nuclei is clinically the most important because of the potential serious consequences of dysphagia, dysphonia, and palate and vocal cord paresis. The motor nuclei of nerves V, XI, and XII are seldom diseased to a significant degree. Pure brain stem disease is the exception; the combined form, cranial nerve nucleus involvement plus spinal anterior horn disease, is much more frequent.

Spinal Polio. The distribution in the spinal paralytic forms is typically irregular and asymmetrical. Because there are more anterior horn cells in the cervical and lumbar enlargements than elsewhere, one can expect to, and does, find more involvement in the extremities than in the trunk. The lower extremities are more commonly, and often more severely, weakened than the upper extremities, and the proximal muscle groups seem to suffer more than the distal ones. There is one extraneous factor that seems to have an influence on the site and severity of paralysis. It has been a common observation and experience, which unfortunately cannot be easily documented objectively, that in a person who became acutely ill with poliomyelitis during strenuous exercise, those muscles that were most fatigued were the weakest ones. Reported examples are those of severe right arm paralysis in a tennis player and nearly total symmetrical leg involvement in football players.

If the intercostal muscles are paralyzed, breathing will be predominantly diaphragmatic. Diaphragmatic weakness, mainly C4, should always be looked for when extensive paresis of upper extremities is present. Paralysis of anal and urinary sphincters is rare.

Bulbospinal Polio. The combined forms are characterized by the summation of brain stem and spinal findings.

COURSE AND OUTCOME

The peak of paralysis is normally reached within one week of onset of weakness. Improvement or recovery will depend on the degree of motor cell disease. Cells that are destroyed in the acute stage are permanently lost, while those that are only swollen may become functional again. This recovery phase may start as early as the third week of illness, but spontaneous functional improvement may continue for as long as one year. The earlier and the faster some functions return, the better are the chances that the handicap may be mild. If fatal cases are excluded, manifestations of brain stem disease are much more likely to clear up completely than spinal paralysis. This is at least partly because the children with the most severe cranial nerve involvement run the greatest risk of dying during the acute disease. Permanent paralysis of bulbar muscles may occur, however.

Pain and muscle spasm occur early and are often severe, especially in the back and paraspinal muscles as well as in all the extremities, and also cause the patient to be reluctant to move. In addition the frequent asymmetry of the weakness enhances the tendency for a nonphysiological and fixed deformity to arise. This danger should be anticipated early in the disease so that preventive measures can be instituted long before contractures occur. Treatment will depend on the particular circumstances: which part of an extremity is involved, the degree of weakness, presence of pain, and other considerations. Heat in the form of hot packs or baths should be started as soon as the fever is down and should be followed with passive range of motion exercises, which may later have to include actual stretching. Temporary or intermittent splinting in fiberglass molds or other lightweight devices between treatment sessions will help keep the muscles in functional position and will further the same goals.

Well after the acute disease has ended and when spontaneous improvement has started, active exercises can be started with five potential goals in mind:

1. Maintenance of a normal range of motion of all joints;
2. Maintenance of strength of normally innervated muscles to prevent disuse atrophy;
3. Strengthening of muscle fibers that are partly atrophied because their neurons were temporarily not functioning but have survived;
4. Strengthening of parts of one muscle to take over for those fibers in the same muscle that are permanently atrophied owing to permanent destruction of individual anterior horn cell groups;
5. Strengthening and hypertrophy of muscles that are suitable substitutes for, or auxiliary muscles to, others that are permanently weakened.

After therapy programs of this kind have been carried out for a reasonable time and when a tentative degree of recovery can be estimated, various long-term orthotic devices have to be considered in order to achieve and maintain maximum function. Bracing can provide stability of a joint, prevent deformity, and protect or assist weakened muscles.

The question of surgery should not be entertained during the first 12 to 18 months. After that time, an indication for surgery exists when an operative procedure can be expected to overcome an obstacle to a specific function: for example, lengthening of a tendon to allow greater motion of a joint, transplantation of a tendon to substitute a normal muscle for an atrophied one, an arthrodesis to stabilize a joint.

Developing deformities along the long bones of extremities are relatively easy to see when one looks for them. Residual weakness and incipient contractures along the trunk and spinal axis are more difficult to recognize early, but require special attention. Asymmetrical trunk weakness is likely to lead to scoliosis; early recognition and treatment with a Milwaukee brace (see Chapter 16) or other suitable devices may prevent or minimize this complication and its sequelae. Scoliosis may also result from unequal leg length or pelvic deformity that is the aftermath of poliomyelitis.

Progressive Spinal Muscular Atrophy

There are several clinical pictures of chronic nature that are primarily caused by the idiopathic progressive degeneration of large anterior horn cells and partly, also, that of motor cranial nerve cells. Depending on the age of onset and on the rate of progression, various names are used such as Werdnig-Hoffmann disease, Kugelberg-Welander disease and juvenile muscular atrophy simulating muscular dystrophy.[9, 11, 17] There is no sharp dividing line between these diseases; it is probable that most of these syndromes represent a wide spectrum of the same disease. Another point in favor of such a holistic point of view is that one occasionally sees typical Werdnig-Hoffmann disease in one child and then the Kugelberg-Welander variety in a sibling. The usual mode of inheritance is autosomal recessive, but in rare families, an apparently dominant mode of heredity has been reported; although these cases provide an argument for the existence of at least two diseases, only the discovery of the real enzymatic or chromosomal cause will clarify the question. For the purposes of this chapter we assume that we are dealing with clinical varieties of one disease process.

PATHOLOGY

Examination of the spinal cord at autopsy reveals involvement selectively in the large anterior horn cells, mainly in the ventromedial group. All levels of the cord are affected including the diaphragm. The presence of changes at C4 has been documented in a few instances; earlier reports to the contrary stem from the experience that those children most commonly succumb to the disease or its complications before the diaphragm is weakened to a considerable degree. Chest fluoroscopy may show diaphragmatic paresis prior to death. The characteristic pathological finding is extensive loss of anterior horn cells with pyknosis of cell nuclei and neuronophagia in the still remaining cells. Little gliosis occurs. Although clinical findings are mainly confined to the twelfth cranial nucleus, involvement of other cranial nerve nuclei may be seen, especially the seventh, ninth, and tenth.

CLINICAL PICTURE

The disease very frequently has its onset in utero, with the result that abnormal clinical findings are apparent within the first few weeks of life or even at birth. These findings consist of a paucity of movements, obvious weakness, generalized flabbiness, and areflexia. Some mothers notice lack of movement even before birth. Occasional infants in this group have dislocated hips at birth (possibly due to lack of muscle tone) or some degree of arthrogryposis (presumably due to lack of motion in the involved joints). The earlier the onset of the symptoms, the more rapidly progressive the disease; most of these infants die within the first two or three years. Classically, the infant lies more or less immobile in the frog-leg position with the fists near the ears, shows very little rib excursion, but has predominantly diaphragmatic breathing. Because of poor ventilation, a small vital capacity, and an inadequate cough mechanism, these infants are prone to repeated pneumonia.

When the clinical manifestations appear after the first two months of life, the disease usually progresses more slowly. In these children there is usually more spontaneous movement, and the deep tendon reflexes may not completely disappear for some months. Fasciculations of the tongue are usually seen during the most active stages of the disease, but in infants it is sometimes difficult to differentiate them from normal movements. Fasciculations are rarely visible anywhere else, as the atrophic muscles are surrounded by fat and relatively thick skin, in contrast to the tongue muscles, which are covered only by stratified epithelium.

Longevity varies; these children may live for quite a few years, but often are not able to sit unsupported and rarely can walk. The course is variable enough, and occasionally the onset may be early but the progression so slow that walking may be achieved before being eventually lost again. In some families one or all the children may seem to be normal for one or two years. They then lose their reflexes and begin to show progressive proximal weakness, walk with a waddling gait for a number of years, and finally end up in a wheelchair.

Most of these were misdiagnosed as muscular dystrophy before Wohlfart's report, Kugelberg and Welander's paper, and the wider use of more sophisticated electrodiagnostic techniques. The oldest "child" whom the authors are currently following is 24 years old. The children who live for many years are plagued by a number of problems, among which are recurrent respiratory infections, osteoporosis, scoliosis, and the tendency to fixed contractures. Judiciously prescribed physical and occupational therapy can increase or prolong some of the activities of daily living, minimize crippling deformities, and retard the development of osteoporosis. Suitable corsets or braces may help control the degree of scoliosis. Such children, under proper care, will hardly ever require surgical procedures.

LABORATORY STUDIES

Laboratory studies should be used to make or to confirm the clinical diagnosis. The most valuable technique consists of the proper electrodiagnostic studies. The characteristic findings in active anterior horn cell disease are insertional fibrillations, increased duration and amplitude of action potentials, and normal nerve conduction velocity. In order to determine the normalcy of nerve conduction, the examiner has to be familiar with the norms during the various periods of early childhood. Slight delays in conduction do occur in the most severely advanced cases. The results of muscle biopsy can usually exclude primary muscle disease, but cannot necessarily differentiate anterior horn cell from peripheral nerve disease. Serum enzymes, including creatine phosphokinase, are either normal or only very slightly increased.

PERIPHERAL NERVE DISEASES

Acute Polyneuropathy

People of all ages may be subject to acute disease states affecting some, most, or all peripheral nerves and characterized by weakness, loss of deep tendon reflexes, and usually also some impairment of sensory functions. These illnesses have been described under many names; the authors prefer the term "neuropathy" because the word "polyneuritis" implies an infectious or inflammatory condition, which is not necessarily so. Other synonyms are polyradiculoneuropathy, infectious neuronitis, and Guillain-Barré syndrome. Because of the specificity of the clinical and laboratory picture that Barré described, it is not the most suitable and descriptive term.[6]

ETIOLOGY

The etiology of acute polyneuropathy is not apparent in most children, but the disease commonly follows an acute infection, either respiratory or gastrointestinal, and therefore, we often speak of acute postinfectious neuropathy. In some patients there is a very specific cause, either infectious or toxic. The acute infections include diphtheria, infectious mononucleosis, and Coxsackie virus infections. These are not common diseases in the United States in the 1970's, but the possibility of diphtheria must be included because of the very specific treatment required. One of the toxic agents that produces a very acute onset is tick paralysis, which also requires specific therapy. Children with rapidly developing symmetrical weakness who possibly could have been exposed to ticks should be inspected for one of these arthropods on the skin. Treatment consists of complete removal of the head of the tick. Although lead neuropathy is rare in this age group, the authors have become aware of several young children with this disease in New York during the last two years, and all of them also were heterozygotes for hemoglobin S (unpublished data). A connection between these two disorders is, however, not clear at this time. Arsenic and thallium poisoning can cause acute peripheral nerve disease. Children with thallium poisoning have coexistent acute alopecia. Children being treated with drugs derived from periwinkle (e.g., vincristine) and certain other medications for leukemia, neuroblastoma, and similar malignant diseases may develop toxic polyneuropathy as a complication of the medication.

PATHOLOGY

The early changes in the peripheral nerves consist of swelling and fragmentation of the myelin, sometimes with cellular infiltration around the nerve roots. As the process continues, more myelin is destroyed, and axis cylinders are interrupted. Cells in the anterior horn and in posterior root ganglia may become involved secondarily. In time, myelin globules are phagocytosed, regeneration occurs from the Schwann cells, and new axis cylinders that seem to be guided by the regenerating nerve sheaths grow at the rate of 1 to 2 mm per day.

CLINICAL COURSE

The mode of onset and the progression of the disease are variable, but the most common initial manifestation is symmetrical weakness in the distal portions of the lower extremities that tends to ascend over hours to days. In other cases, the involvement in all the extremities is virtually simultaneous. Paresthesia may precede or accompany the onset of weakness, but these symptoms are difficult to verify in young children. The degree of weakness varies but is usually quite significant. If intercostal nerves are involved, respiratory function may be impaired and, especially when associated with impairment of the ninth and tenth cranial nerves, may be life-threatening. Mortality rates, however, should be very low if appropriate respiratory measures including tracheostomy and assisted respiration are used early and well. In general, the distal muscles of the extremities are weaker than the more proximal ones. Atrophy of denervated muscles, especially in the hands, occurs early.

In children, there are fewer sensory findings than in adults. Position sense is the most frequently impaired sensory modality, with vibration, pain, and touch following in the order of frequency.

Deep tendon reflexes are abolished or considerably reduced in the affected parts. During recovery, the reflexes lag behind the return of strength.

Any of the motor cranial nerves may be impaired in the disease process either unilaterally or, more commonly, bilaterally. The most commonly affected nerve is the seventh, causing facial diplegia. Meningeal signs may be prominent during the first few days, causing confusion of acute polyneuropathy with acute poliomyelitis or acute leptomeningitis.

The peak of the acute disease is usually reached within 7 to 10 days, and about half the patients will show some clinical improvement by the end of the second week.[12] The beginning of the recovery phase can be delayed for several weeks and spontaneous improvement can be expected up to 12 months. In children, as contrasted to adults, full recovery is the most common outcome.

If the disease is severe and improvement is slow, marked atrophy occurs and contractures of the joints may occur owing to disuse, immobility, and chronic malpositioning.

LABORATORY STUDIES

Laboratory tests should be used to prove or to rule out infections and toxins that are known as possible causes for polyneuropathy. Routine blood counts, urinalysis, and determination of sedimentation rate will rarely be helpful. A spinal tap should be performed whenever this diagnosis is considered, partly to corroborate the clinical impression and also to rule out other diseases, especially acute meningitis. The classic spinal fluid picture, first reported by Guillain, Barré, and Strohl in 1916, is characterized by a high level of cerebrospinal fluid protein and a normal cell count (cytoalbuminous dissociation).[7] A slight cell increase, though, does not rule out the diagnosis, and the protein increase may be only slight or may reach several hundred milligrams per 100 ml. It is not uncommon for the protein value to be normal during the first few days of the disease and reach a peak after two to three weeks. The cerebrospinal fluid sugar is usually normal.

Electrodiagnostic techniques will confirm the presence of peripheral nerve disease. The most important finding, which differentiates neuropathy from anterior horn cell disease and muscle disease, is decreased motor or sensory conduction velocity of both in the peripheral nerves.

COURSE AND OUTCOME

As in all forms of lower motor neuron disease, rest is important and active exercise should be avoided in the early acute stages. General supportive measures such as adequate caloric and fluid intake should be emphasized. Careful attention to respiratory care can be life-saving when cranial and intercostal nerves are affected. Proper functional positioning of the body and the extremities, and early mechanical support of paralyzed limbs by molds, shells, or braces will prevent contractures and will shorten convalescence. Passive range of motion exercises soon after the most acute stage can facilitate rehabilitation and shorten this phase.

There is no good evidence that adrenocorticotropic hormones, oral steroids, or any other medication shortens or modifies the course of *acute,* nonrecurrent polyneuropathy. Salicylates, analgesics, and occasionally "relaxants" may give some symptomatic relief. When indicated, stool softeners or enemas should be used. Neurological involvement of the bladder is rare, and chronic indwelling bladder catheterization should be avoided, using instead intermittent catheterizations under absolutely sterile conditions and for only so long as absolutely necessary.

Starting during the early stages, proper functional positioning of the back and limbs in shells or splints can reduce discomfort and minimize contractures. Very early in the illness all the joints should be put through a full range of motion several times each day, with care to avoid overstretching of the joints. When transferring the patient as from bed to stretcher, flail joints, especially the hip and shoulder, need to be supported to avoid trauma and possible late complications. After the first few days a tentative record of muscle strength should be recorded and active exercise begun. The purpose of active exercise is to minimize disuse atrophy in innervated muscles and to take advantage of reinnervation of muscles as it occurs. The amount of exercise must be carefully graded to avoid local fatigue of the exercising muscles; this can only be decided after careful observation. Certainly a decrement in strength later in the day, or on the next day, is an indication that too much may have been allowed. Usually, the muscles are individually exercised through their full range against that resistance which can be overcome, for 6 to 10 repetitions.

The greatest difficulty comes in the use of muscles for which it is as difficult to limit the resistance as it is during functional activities such as using the hands — or standing and walking in patients with hip and trunk weakness. In peripheral weakness, muscles can be protected by braces and splints at rest or during activities. When this is not possible or feasible, e.g., around the hips, patients must be carefully guarded to prevent overuse and stretching of weak muscles that would cause added damage to the already weakened areas. Standing for short periods with support or walking in water may provide useful stages to strengthening and also give psychological support and evidence of progress. Overstrengthening or use of one group of muscles when their antagonists are weakened, however, may enhance the tendency to contractures and also retard return of strength in the weakened muscles.

In summary, muscle strengthening, to avoid disuse of unaffected areas or as reinnervation occurs, must be careful and supervised both as to quality and quantity. It requires the supervision of a staff acquainted with the management of lower motor neuron disease, who can instruct and supervise the patient in both his regular and bed program.

Chronic Polyneuropathy

In addition to acute polyneuropathy one also sees children (and adults) with recurrent and chronic peripheral nerve disease, and there is no sharp dividing line between the two conditions. Recurrent polyneuropathy is characterized by repeated episodes of acute disease over months or years, usually without full recovery of function between attacks. After each recurrence there is more residual loss of function.

CLINICAL CHARACTERISTICS

Chronic neuropathy may be a disease sui generis, a complication of a recognized systemic disease, an integral part of another illness; or it can be caused by drugs. Chronic polyneuritis of unknown origin may start any time from earliest infancy to the second decade. The chief manifestations are insidious onset of diffuse, usually distal, symmetrical weakness with atrophy and loss of deep tendon reflexes, with or without sensory loss. Over the course of a few weeks, the child is likely to be too weak to support his weight, and use of the hands may be severely curtailed. Just as in other lower motor neuron disease, there is a danger of contracture of muscles and tendons with subsequent limitation of motion around joints and deformities due to unsupported sitting or poor positioning. As mentioned before, the ultimate outcome in the untreated case may vary from recovery to progression and death. In general, children with onset of the disease during the first five years of life have a better outlook than those who suffer the initial signs and symptoms in later years.[15]

In addition to the "idiopathic" forms there is a syndrome of chronic progressive hypertrophic polyneuropathy with an autosomal recessive inheritance that was first described by Déjérine and Sottas, from whom it derived its frequently used eponym.[3] Without a family history this diagnosis would be difficult to make in the beginning, and even later, the hypertrophy is not diagnostic. Focal hypertrophy in various degrees is found in many forms of chronic neuropathy regardless of its cause.

As a complication of systemic disease, neuropathy can be found in diabetes mellitus, lupus erythematosus, polyarteritis, and porphyria. Porphyria is very rare in childhood, and diabetic neuropathy is also mainly an adult disease. Lupus should always be considered, looked for, and ruled out if possible. Clinical signs of neuropathy and evidence of decreased motor nerve conduction velocity have also been found in chronic renal failure.

A-beta-lipoproteinemia (Bassen-Kornzweig syndrome) presents itself in early childhood as a celiac syndrome but later primarily with chronic neuropathy, retinitis pigmentosa, thorny erythrocytes (acanthocytes), and reduced levels or absence of β lipoproteins in the blood.[1] Refsum's disease is a hereditary syndrome with chronic neuropathy, ataxia, ichthyosis, retinitis, and hearing loss. The diagnosis is based on the demonstration of phytanic acid, a hexadecanoic compound.[14] Chédiak-Higashi syndrome shows chronic weakness and atrophy due to deposition of the characteristic granules in Schwann cells; this is associated with abnormal pigment in the skin and pancytopenia.[8] Metachromatic leukodystrophy (arylsulfatase A deficiency) is primarily a disease affecting the brain, but also affects peripheral nerves, kidneys, and other organs. Clinical neuropathy may occasionally precede the other manifestations.

Charcot-Marie-Tooth disease (peroneal muscular atrophy) is caused by a dominantly inherited unidentified factor that involves spinal cord, peripheral nerves, and also muscles.[2, 16] The onset of the disease can usually be traced back to preschool age, but it may start much later. The nerves in the distal parts of the lower extremities are first and most affected, but the hands and fingers eventually become involved. Bilateral, but not necessarily symmetrical, foot drop is the outstanding manifestation, and the marked atrophy of the calves gives the characteristic "stork leg" appearance. The first signs in the upper extremities are flattening of the thenar and hypothenar eminences. Pes cavus always occurs, and this deformity is sometimes present in a parent or grandparent, with or without reflex loss, as the only manifestation of the disease.

Thiamine (vitamin B_1) deficiency is uncommon in North America but it presents itself primarily as chronic neuropathy. Spontaneous pyridoxine (B_6) deficiency with peripheral nerve disease is rarely seen but may occur secondarily to isoniazid therapy, although less frequently in children than in adults. Other common drugs that have been reported to cause neuropathy include sodium diphenylhydantoin (Dilantin), but only after regular administration for 10 years or more, and some of the newer approved and research drugs for the control of malignant disease.

LABORATORY STUDIES

Laboratory studies are primarily directed to proving or ruling out the aforementioned suspected clinical entities. While there is no known specific laboratory procedure for the diagnosis of Charcot-Marie-Tooth disease, diabetes or a-beta-lipoproteinemia can only be documented in the clinical laboratory. As in acute polyneuropathy, electrodiagnostic techniques can help differentiate chronic nerve disease from myopathy.

TREATMENT

The same general measures used to treat acute neuropathy are applicable here. The same attention to diet and fluid balance, the same careful observations for possible respiratory impairment, are needed. But because of the chronicity and duration of the chronic disease, more vigilance to prevent scoliosis or kyphosis, contractures, and other deformities, is necessary. Dealing with a potentially crippling process that lasts for months or years, one also has to use all treatment modalities that promote the performance of the activities of daily living to keep the nonambulatory child active, to have him in an educational setting, and to supply him and his family with the psychological supports to adjust to the disease. Braces may be necessary to prevent contractures and keep the spine straight. When sensory loss is significant, the hypesthetic parts have to be protected.

In cases of diabetic neuropathy, the specific prophylaxis and treatment is the best possible control of diabetes, but severe neuritis is not necessarily fully reversible. The same can be said about lupus neuropathy; lupus is usually treated with steroids. The neuropathy, however, may be cured, improved, or permanent, especially in cases of myeloradiculoneuropathy. The neurological complications of vitamin deficiencies are treated by giving the missing vitamins in sufficient doses.

Chronic and recurrent polyneuropathy of unknown origin usually responds to the administration of oral steroids such as prednisone. This medication usually modifies the disease favorably, but the degree of improvement is variable. It should always be used in an attempt to control the disease. The two common reasons for possible failure are inadequate doses and too brief trials. A good beginning dose for younger children is 2 mg per kilogram daily; somewhat less for children over 10 years. There still is controversy about whether daily or alternate day regimens are best; in some cases the latter form of therapy is adequate, but some other children definitely require daily doses. Because it is not known in advance when we can get by with every-other-day medication (with its other advantages), the daily regimen should be used in all cases initially in order to get better results without waste of time. Steroid therapy can produce four different kinds of results: a good response with early and marked improvement and mild side effects; slight benefit only; good improvement but with intolerable steroid side effects; and no benefit. In the first three cases one should not give up too soon, but should consider the addition of another immunosuppressive agent, azathioprine (Imuran), to the steroid. Three milligrams per kilogram of azathioprine may enhance the effect of prednisone or may have a prednisone-sparing effect, i.e., one can get by with much smaller doses and eventually without the steroid. On the other side, azathioprine has to be given for at least four to six weeks before any effect can be expected, and it also has potential side effects such as pancytopenia and increased danger of infection. Prednisone or azathioprine or both should be used as clinically needed as long as side effects are acceptable and reasonably safe.

Isolated reports and personal experience do not indicate that steroids are beneficial in Charcot-Marie-Tooth disease.

Specific Neuropathies

In addition to the acute and chronic syndromes already discussed, there are some selected neuropathic entities that are common and important enough in childhood to warrant some comments. Not all described conditions, but only those of greatest frequency, are mentioned here.

BRACHIAL PLEXUS INJURY

These paragraphs deal specifically with the injury (usually unilateral) that the brachial plexus can suffer as a complication of childbirth. These injuries occur most often in a difficult vertex presentation when either the head or, more commonly, the aftercoming shoulders are very large. Because of the difficulties of delivering the shoulder, associated clavicle fracture is common but clinically not very significant.

In the most severe cases a complete avulsion of the upper and lower trunk of the plexus occurs with resulting total paralysis of the upper extremity, including most shoulder muscles. Sometimes only the upper *or* lower trunk is injured, the greatest liability to injury occurring at the junction of C_5 and C_6 or C_8 and T_1 respectively. The characteristic presentation of upper plexus palsy is adduction of the humerus and internal rotation at the elbow with the wrist in flexion.[4, 5] One side of the diaphragmatic innervation (C_4) is occasionally involved. Lower trunk paralysis (Klumpke) manifests itself in forearm flexion, wrist and finger extension, and also in Horner's syndrome, if the sympathetic fibers of T_1 are interrupted.[10] Trophic changes of skin and nails may occur, and the affected arm and hand will grow more slowly than their mates. The weakness is apparent immediately following birth; the damage is done and cannot be reversed. There is no indication for myelography, if the diagnosis is certain, or for surgical intervention. There is either avulsion or hemorrhage in the plexus, and surgery may cause additional trouble and may further jeopardize spontaneous improvement. Because of the weakness and the already described positions it is important to place the limb in a position that reduces the danger of fixed deformity and contractures. Usually, the arm is placed in abduction at the shoulder with the elbow at a right angle. After the first week, the mother should be instructed in gentle range of motion exercises at all affected joints. Many years later, selected, appropriate surgical procedures may improve the function of either the shoulder or distal parts of the extremity.

SCIATIC NERVE INJURY

This nerve can be damaged in many ways but consideration is given here to neuropathy due to injection in its vicinity. Intramuscular injections in the buttocks should only be given in the upper outer quadrant well away from the course of the nerve. This is an adequate warning in well-nourished adults, but in infants and young and thin children, the distance of the sciatic nerve from the upper outer quadrant is insufficient to prevent possible injury to the nerve. Some drugs deposited in this area tend to be more neurotoxic than others, especially tetracycline and streptomycin. The diagnosis of this syndrome depends on the history of perisciatic injection and the characteristic findings. These findings depend on which fibers are affected, because the injury is usually incomplete. The fibers to the common peroneal nerve are most frequently involved, with resultant weakness of the peronei muscles (innervated by n. peroneus superficialis), the tibialis anterior, extensor digitorum longus, extensor hallucis longus, and extensor digitorum brevis. Injury of the tibial nerve affects the strength of the gastrocnemius, plantaris, soleus, popliteus, and posterior tibial muscles. The nerves to the hamstring are rarely involved. Because these are mixed nerves there is usually also sensory impairment: the superficial peroneal nerve has a sensory field on the anterior and lateral surfaces of the lower leg and the dorsum of the foot; the deep peroneal nerve conducts sensation from the web between the first and second toes and a small adjacent dorsal area. Sensation from the planta, the heel, and the dorsal aspect of the lower leg is mediated by the tibial nerve.

It is very important to test for hypalgesia and analgesia in order to be aware of it. Without knowledge of such defects the proper precautions against additional injuries cannot be taken. An example would be lack of pain or touch sensation over the back of the heel, which can lead to damage and necrosis due to friction from shoes or folds in socks. The most common motor deficit that is amenable to treatment is the drop foot from peroneal fiber damage. Short leg bracing or posterior ankle molds would markedly reduce such functional handicap, and passive and active heel cord stretching will avoid or postpone fixed shortening. Later foot inversion can be treated with tendon transplants, provided the posterior muscles are unaffected, or with arthrodeses in adolescence.

BELL'S PALSY

Facial nerve paresis in children may be due to a large number of causes including congenital paresis (Moebius syndrome),[14] damage from a forceps during birth, later trauma, brain stem glioma and other tumors, and other complications. The term "Bell's palsy" refers to an acute, presumably inflammatory, condition of the seventh cranial nerve that is poorly understood. The onset is very acute and in children the chance for full recovery within 4 to 12 weeks is much better than in adults. Two forms of treatment in the early stage have strong proponents, but the final answers are not yet in. The one is the surgical unroofing of the facial canal to relieve pressure from a swollen nerve, and the other is the use of large doses of oral steroids to counteract the swelling. Because there is incomplete lid closure on the affected side when the palpebral branch is affected, the cornea has to be protected against foreign bodies and injury. Other than prevention of contractures, due to overpull of the innervated side, and gentle passive stretching of the face, there is no physical treatment of demonstrable value. When recovery begins, active exercise of each muscle group of the face by the patient in front of a mirror can be helpful. In the early stages of recovery it can be useful for the patient to stabilize the normal side of the face with his hand to allow the weakened muscle to be isolated.

In those uncommon cases in which recovery does not occur or remains only partial, nerve anastomosis with the hypoglossal nerve or judicious use of cosmetic surgery may be helpful.

HEREDOFAMILIAL NEURITIS WITH BRACHIAL PREDILECTION

This is a rare, dominantly inherited syndrome characterized by recurring pain and weakness of shoulders and arms. No rational or effective treatment has been reported.

SUMMARY

Diseases of the anterior horn cells and of the peripheral nerves may be acute or chronic. Only for one of these, namely poliomyelitis, prophylactic treatment is currently available. No curative agent is known for any of the acute forms, but proper attention to respiratory management can save many children afflicted with these diseases, and their subsequent handicaps can be reduced with judiciously applied physical therapy techniques. The lives of patients with the chronic forms of lower motor neuron diseases can often be prolonged and maintained at a useful level by the application of the currently known principles of physiology in rehabilitation.

References

1. Bassen, F. A., and Kornzweig, A. L.: Malformation of erythrocytes in a case of atypical retinitis pigmentosa. Blood, 5:381, 1950.
2. Charcot, J. M., and Marie, P.: Sur une forme particulière d'atrophie musculaire progressive, souvent familiale, débutant par les pieds et les jambes, et atteignant plus tard les mains. Rev. Med., Paris, 6:97, 1886.
3. Déjérine, J., and Sottas, J.: Sur la névrite interstitielle, hypertrophique et progressive de l'enfance. C. R. Soc. Biol., 5:63, 1893.
4. Duchenne, G. B. A.: *De l'éléctrisation localisée et de son application à la pathologie et à la thérapeutique.* Paris, Ballière, 1855, p. 537.
5. Erb, W.: Über eine eigentümliche Lokalisation von Lähmung im Plexus brachialis. Verh. Naturhist. Med. Ver. Heidelberg, 2:130, 1874.
6. Guillain, G.: Radiculoneuritis with acellular hyperalbuminosis of the cerebrospinal fluid. Arch. Neurol. Psychiatry, 36:975, 1936.
7. Guillain, G., Barré, J. A., and Strohl, A.: Sur un syndrome de radiculonévrite avec hyperalbuminose du liquide céphalorachidien sans réaction cellulaire. Bull. Soc. Med. Hop. Paris, 40:1462, 1916.
8. Higashi, O.: Congenital gigantism of peroxidase granules. Tohoku J. Exp. Med., 59:315, 1954.
9. Hoffmann, J.: Über chronische spinale Muskelatrophie im Kindesalter, auf familiärer Basis. Dtsch. Z. Nervenheilkd., 3:427, 1893.
   Weiterer Beitrag zur Lehre von der hereditären progressiven spinalen Muskelatrophie im Kindesalter nebst Bemerkungen über den fortschreitenden Muskelschwand im Allgemeinen. Dtsch. Z. Nervenheilkd., 10:292, 1897.

Über die hereditäre progressive spinale Muskelatrophie im Kindesalter. Münch. Med. Wochenschr., *47*:1649, 1900.

10. Klumpke, A.: Contribution à l'étude des paralysies radiculaires du plexus brachial. Rev. Med., 5:591, 1885.

11. Kugelberg, E., and Welander, L.: Heredofamilial juvenile muscular atrophy simulating muscular dystrophy. Arch. Neurol. Psychiatry, *75*:500, 1956.

12. Low, N. L., Schneider, J., and Carter, S.: Polyneuritis in children. Pediatrics, *22*:972, 1958.

13. Moebius, P. J.: Über angeborene doppelseitige Abducens-Facialis Lähmung. Münch. Med. Wochenschr., *35*:91, 1888.

14. Richterich, R., van Mechelen, P., and Rossi, E.: Refsum's disease: an inborn error of lipid metabolism with storage of 3,7,11,15-tetramethyl hexadecanoic acid. Am. J. Med., *39*:230, 1965.

15. Tasker, W. G., and Chutorian, A. M.: Chronic polyneuritis of childhood. J. Pediatr., *74*:699, 1969.

16. Tooth, H. H.: *The Peroneal Type of Progressive Muscular Atrophy.* London, H. K. Lewis, 1886.

17. Werdnig, G.: Zwei frühinfantile hereditäre Fälle von progressiver Muskelatrophie unter dem Bilde der Dystrophy. Arch. Psychiatr. Nervenkr., *22*:437, 1891.
    Die frühinfantile progressive spinale Amyotrophie. Arch. Psychiatr. Nervenkr., *26*:706, 1894.

18. Wohlfart, G., Fex, J., and Eliason, S.: Heredofamilial juvenile muscular atrophy. A clinical entity simulating muscular dystrophy. Acta Psychiatr. Neurol. Scand., *30*:395, 1955.

Chapter 11

Diseases of Muscle

by *Abe M. Chutorian, M.D.,*
and *Stanley J. Myers, M.D.*

DIAGNOSTIC ASPECTS

The physician who suspects that a patient has a myopathy must first exclude those disorders that mimic myopathies. This calls for systematic analysis of the history and physical signs, and a selection of the most appropriate laboratory investigations in order to establish the diagnosis.

Weakness of skeletal muscle may reflect a pathological disorder at virtually any point in the neural pathway from the brain to the neuromuscular junction. The approach to the differential diagnosis of muscle disease must therefore involve the systematic elimination of disorders of those neural structures upon which muscle function depends for its proper stimulus. Figure 11–1 illustrates these pathways and indicates the distinction between the upper and lower motor neuron.

Identification of the anatomical compartment affected by disease is complicated in a few disorders by the coexistence of cerebral, spinal, and muscle abnormalities. In these instances it becomes important to recognize that, even though neural or myopathic features dominate the clinical picture, multiple systems are involved. These multiple-system disorders include Duchenne's muscular dystrophy, myotonic dystrophy, and certain of the glycogen storage diseases. In the first two disorders a significant incidence of associated cerebral dysfunction occurs; in the last the primary pathological process may involve both neurons and muscle fibers. There are also several disorders of a heredofamilial type in which central nervous system disease is associated with progressive polyneuropathy (e.g., spinocerebellar degeneration).

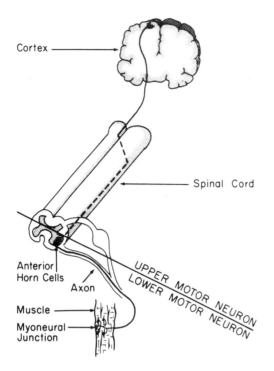

Figure 11-1 The upper motor neuron consists of the Betz cell in the cerebral cortex and its pyramidal fiber, which traverses the brain stem and spinal cord *(above diagonal line)* to terminate at its synapse with the anterior horn cell. The anterior horn cell, axon, and terminal nerve branches constitute the lower motor neuron. The motor unit consists of the lower motor neuron together with the myoneural junction and muscle fibers it supplies. (From Chutorian, A. M., and Koenigsberger, M. R.: Diseases of muscle. In *Brennemann's Practice of Pediatrics.* Vol. IV, Chap. 37, p. 2. Hagerstown, Md., Harper & Row, 1972. Reprinted with permission.)

In this section emphasis is placed on the clinical features shared by the various myopathies and the ways in which these features differ from those encountered when weakness of muscle is the result of recognized disorders of the brain, cranial nerve nuclei, long tracts, anterior horn cells, and peripheral nerves. The effects of lesions in these structures upon body posture and gait, muscle mass and tone, distribution of weakness, and the vigor and amplitude of deep tendon reflexes are described and compared with the findings encountered when the lesion primarily involves the muscle itself. Other signs commonly associated with the various nonmyopathic disorders are discussed as well as the results of laboratory investigations pertinent to the various anatomical lesions.

Physical Signs

In general, lesions of the upper motor neuron produce weakness associated with spasticity, increased deep tendon reflexes, and pathological superficial reflexes; lower motor neuron lesions produce weakness associated with flaccidity or hypotonia, diminished or absent deep tendon reflexes, and preservation of normal superficial reflexes. Extrapyramidal and cerebellar lesions do not as a rule produce muscle weakness, and thus do not belong in the differential diagnosis of the myopathies; however, hypotonia and diminished deep tendon reflexes can at times be prominent in cerebellar disorders. The associated ataxia may not entirely eliminate consideration of a lower motor neuron lesion, as some patients with polyneuropathy have significant ataxia, although patients with myopathy do not (Table 11-1).

TABLE 11-1 PHYSICAL SIGNS

Physical Signs	Pyramidal		Anterior Horn Cell	Peripheral Nerve	Myoneural Junction	Myopathy
	Spastic (hypertonic)	Flaccid (hypotonic)				
Posture	Flexion, of elbow and wrist; Extension, of knee; Plantar flexion, of ankle	Valgus knees and feet	Hyperlordotic; Frog position when supine	Foot drop; Wrist drop	Nonspecific	Hyperlordotic
Gait	Circumduction (unilateral); Scissoring (bilateral); Plantar (toe) stance	Valgus knees and feet	Waddling	Slapping	Nonspecific	Waddling
Tone	Hypertonic	Hypotonic	Hypotonic	Hypotonic	Hypotonic or N	Hypotonic
Distribution of weakness	D > P	Diffuse	P > D	D > P	P > D	P > D
Deep tendon reflexes	↑ to ↑↑ (sensitivity and amplitude)	↑	↓ to 0	↓ to 0	N	N early; ↓ late
Superficial reflexes	Abnormal (plantars, extensor; abdominals, depressed)	N	N	N	N	N
Sensation	N; Occasional ↓ cortical	Occasional ↓ cortical	N	Glove-stocking hypoesthesia	N	N

Symbols used: P, proximal   ↑, increased   ↓, decreased   N, normal
D, distal   ↑↑, greatly increased   0, absent   >, greater than

Symmetry of Weakness.   Pyramidal deficit often produces asymmetrical weakness, even with diffuse cerebral, brain stem, or spinal diseases. Acute transverse myelopathies represent an exception to this general rule, and an ascending myelopathy or a transverse myelopathy at a high cervical level may mimic a polyneuropathy. Disorders of the lower motor neuron, on the other hand, do tend to be symmetrical, with the exception of the mononeuritides and poliomyelitis.

Orthopedic Deformities.   Certain orthopedic deformities are due to flaccid muscle tone and paresis associated with lower motor neuron disorders. These may be detected at birth or in later infancy, and include congenital hip dislocations, multiple varus and valgus deformities of the joints, and arthrogryposis multiplex. Spinal muscular atrophy, chronic neuropathy, and infantile myopathy have all been implicated as the underlying disorder in such children.

Muscle Wasting.   Muscle wasting is characteristic of lower motor neuron disorders. Loss of muscle tissue can be prominent in upper motor neuron lesions that produce striking weakness and hence disuse of muscle due to paralysis, but as a rule, this diminution of muscle mass is slight. Wasting is more striking in the chronic polyneuritides and in spinal muscular atrophy, i.e., in the neurogenic lower motor neuron disorders, than in myopathies. This is particularly true early in the disease, as advanced progressive myopathies and certain specific congenital myopathies are characterized by impressive wasting of muscle. It must also be remembered that accumulation of fat can mask wasting of muscle, a phenomenon that is quite characteristic of infantile spinal muscular atrophy.

Muscle Fasciculations and Tremors.   Muscle fasciculations are not prominent in children with neurogenic lower motor neuron disorders; hence their absence cannot be considered to reflect a myopathic disorder. Conversely, the presence of fasciculations is suggestive of a motor neuron lesion. Tongue fasciculations are often seen in spinal muscular atrophy, but the quivering tongue of a normal infant may be mistaken for a fasciculating tongue even by the experienced physician.[14]

Irregular, fine, and often barely visible movements of a tremulous character, occurring chiefly in the fingers and enhanced by activity or emotional upset, are not uncommonly encountered in infants and children with spinal muscular atrophy. These movements have been termed "minipolymyoclonus." They do not tend to occur in myopathic disorders.

Muscle Tone.[6]   An acute pyramidal lesion may produce flaccid weakness with loss of deep tendon reflexes, but eventually spasticity follows, with exaggeration of these reflexes. Abnormal extensor plantar responses and diminished abdominal reflexes are also seen. A subacute or chronic pyramidal disorder is associated with these classic signs from the onset. As an important exception to this rule, however, infants and young children with bilateral diffuse cerebral dysfunction of varied etiology are sometimes hypotonic. At times the hypotonia is striking and may superficially mimic disorders of the lower motor neuron. This is particularly so in Down's syndrome, in which the other features of the disease eliminate any problem in differential diagnosis. If mental deficiency is impressive and the head circumference is small and suggestive of cerebral hypoplasia, or when earlier infantile reflexes of a more primitive character persist, the diagnosis of an upper motor neuron lesion is obvious. In those infants, however, who have diffuse encephalopathy as the result of nonspecific genetic, developmental, or perinatal insults, the differentiation may at times be difficult. Many of these infants have obvious mental deficiency and some have convulsions, but a significant minority have relative sparing of intellect and are subsequently proved to have only minimal brain dysfunction. In these instances, exaggeration of the deep tendon reflexes usually suggests an upper motor neuron lesion. The picture is further complicated in infants with impressive hypotonia, undocumented impairment of cerebral function with near normal intelligence, and normal or slightly diminished deep tendon reflexes. Such infants and children cannot easily be distinguished from those who have the various "congenital myopathies" or an early benign form of diffuse anterior horn cell degeneration (spinal muscular atrophy, early and late onset).[14] The diagnosis then depends upon ancillary studies, particularly electromyography and muscle biopsy. The cerebrospinal fluid and serum enzymes are usually normal in these disorders.

Experimental lesions of the cerebrum and of the medullary pyramids have resulted in persistent hypotonia with intact deep tendon reflexes, providing a firm pathophysiological basis for the association of cerebral dysfunction with flaccid skeletal muscles. Diminished muscle tone is typically encountered in all disorders of the lower motor neuron.

Gait and Posture.   Gait and posture are important aspects of the clinical evaluation. The infant with a pyramidal lesion may adduct the thumb and clench the fist (cortical fist), and either extend or flex the affected elbow and adduct at the shoulder (the "strap-hanger's" posture). Persistent posture of this type in an infant beyond the age of three months should arouse suspicion. In the supine position, the legs may be abducted at the hips and flexed at the knees; in vertical suspension the legs may compulsively flex at the hips (Förster's sign of pyramidal dysfunction) and either flex or extend at the knees. An alternate posture of the lower extremities in such infants is that of extension at the knees and plantar flexion at the ankles, with a tendency to scissoring of the lower extremities. This is the typical posture of the child with spastic diplegia.

In contrast, in the infant who is flaccid because of a lower motor neuron lesion, the lower extremities when suspended vertically hang limply. The normal infant moves the lower extremities vigorously and at random in this position.

The supine posture of an infant with a lower motor neuron disorder is one of limp relaxation of the upper extremities and abduction of the lower extremities. Persistent head lag (beyond the age of three months) may occur when the infant is lifted from the supine position, but this is also characteristic of the infant with a cerebral disorder. In the severely affected infant, the thoracic musculature is deficient and the ascent and descent of the diaphragm during expiration and inspiration may cause "abdominal respirations." This is often encountered in infantile spinal muscular atrophy and in cervical cord trauma. Myopathy of sufficient severity to cause this symptom complex is exceedingly rare in infancy, and occurs only preterminally in myopathies of older children.

Figure 11–2 Exaggerated lumbar lordosis in a child with Duchenne's dystrophy. Similar posture is seen in proximal weakness associated with lower motor neuron disorders. (From Chutorian, A. M., and Koenigsberger, M. R.: Diseases of muscle. In *Brennemann's Practice of Pediatrics*. Vol. IV, Chap. 37, p. 7. Hagerstown, Md., Harper & Row, 1972. Reprinted with permission.)

The ambulatory child who is hypotonic because of a cerebral disorder may also show some of the postural manifestations of the child with lower motor neuron disease, e.g., valgus deformity of the knees and ankles and genu recurvatum. Rarely, however, does the waddling gait of the child with a myopathy or with spinal muscular atrophy, or the slapping gait of the child with foot drop due to neuropathy, occur in a child with a central nervous system lesion. The ambulatory child who is spastic owing to a cerebral insult differs little in gait and posture from a similarly affected adult. He develops various postural deformities with flexion at the elbow, wrist, and fingers; extension at the knee; and plantar flexion and inversion at the ankle. Walking, he circumducts his leg to provide for clearance of the plantar flexed foot, or walks with the heel off the ground because of gastrocnemius spasticity. Children with muscular dystrophy and contractures of the calves may also walk on the toes of both feet; this fact should be borne in mind since this is the characteristic stance of the child with bilateral pyramidal lesions.

The various postural and gait abnormalities described result from the character of the distribution of weakness and altered muscle tone. Since patients with spinal muscular atrophy and the various myopathies are characteristically weaker proximally (i.e., in the shoulder and pelvic musculature) they display increased lumbar lordosis (Fig. 11–2), waddle, and have difficulty with tasks requiring the use of the large proximal muscles rather than the finer distal muscles of the extremities, e.g., climbing and rising from the supine or

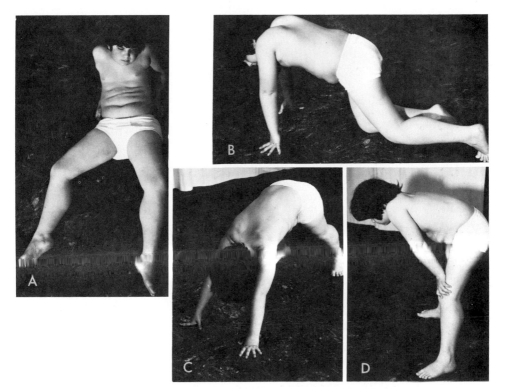

Figure 11-3 Gowers' sign is illustrated as the patient rises from the sitting position A, by placing both hands flat on the floor, B and C, and then supporting his trunk on his thighs to achieve the standing position, D. (From Chutorian, A. M., and Koenigsberger, M. R.: Diseases of muscle. In *Brennemann's Practice of Pediatrics.* Vol. IV, Chap. 37, p. 7. Hagerstown, Md., Harper & Row, 1972. Reprinted with permission.)

seated position. This is graphically demonstrated in Gowers' sign (Fig. 11-3). The supine child rolls to the prone position, places the palms on the surface of the floor, and brings each palm in turn to the surface of the thigh for added thrust to bring his trunk to the erect position.

The child with a neuropathy has weaker distal muscles and, therefore, shows the manifestations of wrist drop and foot drop.[40] Due to weakness of the anterior tibial and peroneal muscles, his gait is "slapping" as the forefoot drops to the floor without the normal restraint exerted by the anterior tibial and peroneal muscles, which dorsiflex and evert the foot. Early in the course of chronic polyneuropathy the gastrocnemius and posterior tibial muscles are relatively spared so that toe walking is possible while heel walking is impaired. As the disorder progresses, inversion and plantar flexion of the foot occur. In acute polyneuritis, which rarely poses a diagnostic problem, approximately 20 per cent of patients have preponderant proximal weakness. This does not occur in chronic neuropathies, which are more apt to enter into the differential diagnosis of myopathy.

Deep Tendon Reflexes. The deep tendon reflexes are brisk in patients with upper motor neuron lesions. Clonus and extensor plantar responses may be present. Occasionally the deep tendon reflexes are difficult to obtain in infants with "cerebral" hypotonia. It is helpful in such cases to reinforce the attempt to elicit the deep tendon jerks by simultaneously compressing the Achilles tendon or providing some other mild noxious stimulus. A brisk deep tendon reflex may be elicited in this fashion in children with disorders of the upper, but not of the lower, motor neuron. In older children, the Jendrassik maneuver may be employed; the child is asked to clasp the hands and squeeze them together as the tendon is tapped. By increasing afferent stimuli into the gamma system, facilitation of the response is effected.

The deep tendon reflexes are often preserved in the congenital myopathies and early stages of muscular dystrophies. As a myopathy progresses, the deep tendon reflexes diminish in magnitude, and in severe or late cases they disappear entirely. Absence of deep tendon reflexes early in the course of a disorder suggests a neural lesion (in the anterior horn cell or peripheral nerve).

Hypesthesia or anesthesia for any of the primary modalities of sensation, which is difficult to demonstrate in children who are under the age of five years, points to a peripheral nerve or a long sensory tract lesion and excludes myopathy and spinal muscular atrophy.

Laboratory Studies

The laboratory studies employed in the diagnosis of lower motor neuron disorders include assessment of serum enzyme and isoenzyme activity and creatine and creatinine metabolism, electromyographic and nerve conduction studies, cerebrospinal fluid examination, histological study of the sural nerve, and muscle biopsy. The general diagnostic features encountered in the various categories of disorder are summarized in Table 11–2.

Serum Enzymes.   Creatine phosphokinase (CPK), lactic dehydrogenase (LDH), aldolase, glutamic pyruvic transaminase (GPT), glutamic oxaloacetic transaminase (GOT) and phosphohexoisomerase activity have proved to be of diagnostic value in the myopathies. Those that have been most widely assayed for clinical purposes are CPK, aldolase, and GOT. The CPK determination is the most sensitive of these because of the virtual absence of that enzyme in significant quantity from tissues other than muscle.

The pathogenesis of increased serum enzyme levels is to some extent disputed, but is believed to involve malfunction of the sarcolemmal membrane of muscle. The more rapidly and extensively damaged membranes presumably permit greater egress of enzyme into the serum. Thus, while extensive muscle trauma can result in the release of large amounts of enzyme, even electromyography or intramuscular injections are known to cause significant elevation of serum enzymes. Recognition of this fact suggests the advisability of obtaining serum enzyme determinations prior to electromyography.

Striking increase of serum enzyme activity is encountered in Duchenne's muscular dystrophy, unless the disease is advanced and muscle wasting and paralysis are of long standing.[31] Moderately high CPK values are encountered in some patients with limb-girdle dystrophy. Usually the relatively static or slowly progressive myopathies have normal or only modestly elevated serum enzyme values. Moderate to marked elevations of serum enzyme activity (no-

TABLE 11-2 LABORATORY FINDINGS

Laboratory Findings	Pyramidal		Anterior Horn Cell	Peripheral Nerve	Myoneural Junction	Myopathy
	Spastic (hypertonic)	Flaccid (hypotonic)				
Serum (muscle) enzymes	N	N	N	N	N	N, ↑, or ↑↑
CSF protein	Nonspecific	Nonspecific	N	↑ to ↑↑	N	N
EMG	N (jerky firing)	N (occasional fibrillations and positive waves)	Denervation Fasciculations	Denervation	Decrement on repetitive contraction	Myopathic
Nerve conduction	N	N	N, occasional ↓	↓	N	N
Muscle biopsy	N	N	Grouped lesions	Grouped lesions	?Lymphorrhage	Myopathy (various types)

Symbols used: P, proximal   ↑, increased   ↓, decreased   N, normal
D, distal   ↑↑, greatly increased   0, absent

tably CPK) are seen in polymyositis. The neurogenic diseases including the anterior horn cell degenerations and neuropathies have normal or only slightly increased serum enzymes. The presence of moderately severe elevation (over tenfold) of serum enzyme activity thus implies a myopathic disorder of the dystrophic, myositic, or necrotic type.

Electrophoretic differentiation of various isoenzymes or subunits of specific enzymes has, to some extent, been useful in the study of muscle disease. To date, however, this kind of investigation has been of value primarily in indicating that certain types of muscle and muscle function are related to specific isoenzyme activity and that the presence of specific isoenzymes may characterize damage to a particular tissue. The normal absence from the brain of one of the three known isoenzymes of CPK and its presence in muscle further enhances the importance of this enzyme in the study and diagnosis of muscle disease.

Creatine and Creatinine. Creatinine content is proportionate to muscle mass. Reduction in muscle mass is, therefore, reflected in a diminished rate of excretion of creatinine, and accordingly, various disorders of the lower motor neuron that cause muscle atrophy may be associated with diminished rates of creatinine excretion. Creatine is synthesized in the kidney and liver, combines with phosphate in muscle, and is released during muscle activity. Creatine is then transformed into creatinine. When muscle bulk or activity or both diminish, therefore, serum creatine increases and creatine appears in larger quantity in the urine. (Creatinuria is normal in children but not in adults.) Thus, the normal creatine and creatinine coefficients (rate of excretion per unit weight), which are age dependent, can be compared with those of a given patient. However, creatine-creatinine ratios are nonspecific, which limits their diagnostic value.

Electrodiagnosis

Electrodiagnostic studies are important in differentiating lower motor neuron from myopathic disorders. These studies usually include measurements of nerve conduction and electromyography although in some instances electrical stimulation of muscle or motor points is carried out. Basic anatomical and physiological knowledge of nerve conduction can be applied in health and disease by recording the effects of nerve stimulation.[21, 23]

NERVE CONDUCTION

Motor Nerve Conduction. Motor conduction velocity is measured by stimulating a nerve at two points along its course and in each case recording the contraction of a peripheral muscle supplied by this nerve. In order to insure that all nerve fibers are appropriately excited, the intensity of stimulus should be supramaximal, i.e., 50 per cent above that sufficient to produce a maximum muscle response. For example, the median nerve is stimulated at the elbow and at the wrist, and the evoked potential from the thenar muscles is recorded (Fig. 11–4). The time for the impulse to reach the muscle (the la-

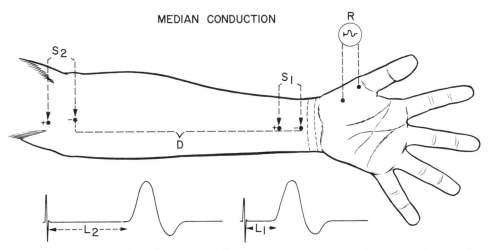

Figure 11–4   Procedure for motor conduction measurement in median nerve. S_1, stimulus distally (wrist); S_2, stimulus proximally (elbow); R, recording electrode over thenar muscle; L_1, distal latency (wrist to muscle); L_2, proximal latency (elbow to muscle); D, distance between stimulating electrodes S_1 and S_2.

$$\text{Conduction velocity} = \frac{D}{L_2 - L_1}$$

(From Lovelace, R. E., and Myers, S. J.: Nerve conduction and synaptic transmission. *In* Downey, J. A., and Darling, R. C.: *Physiological Basis of Rehabilitation Medicine*. Philadelphia, W. B. Saunders Co., 1971, p. 95.)

tency) is usually measured on a cathode ray oscilloscope from the stimulus artifact to the onset of the evoked potential. The shorter latency from the wrist stimulation is subtracted from the longer latency of the stimulation at the elbow to give the conduction time between the two points. The conduction velocity of the nerve from elbow to wrist is then calculated by dividing the difference of the latencies into the distance between the stimulation points. Each latency represents the time for the impulse to pass from the distal point of stimulation to the instant that the electrical reaction begins in the muscle. This, of course, also includes the time in the arborized axon and the time for neuromuscular transmission, which is eliminated in the foregoing calculation of conduction velocity. Other important parameters of the evoked muscle potential from nerve stimulation are the amplitude, duration, and complexity.

Sensory Nerve Conduction.   This can be measured by electrical stimulation of the fingers or toes using ring electrodes and recording the nerve action potentials directly over the nerves more proximally (orthodromic). Alternatively, the nerve can be stimulated more proximally with the recording ring electrode over the fingers or toes (antidromic); however, the sensory potential may be obscured or misinterpreted owing to interference by the evoked motor response. If the nerves are stimulated directly at the wrist and above, recordings from higher levels along the nerve will also include the motor fibers and should be regarded as mixed nerve potentials. When a single recording at the wrist from distal stimulation is obtained, a distal sensory latency will be recorded, but the amplitude of the sensory nerve action potential should also be measured. With standard techniques, this amplitude is important as a representation of the number of active fibers within the sensory nerve. If sensory or mixed nerve action potentials are also recorded at higher levels, conduction velocities can be computed. Low-amplitude potentials can more easily be

207

seen by superimposition of several traces. Averaging of low-amplitude nerve action potentials, particularly those below 5 μv, which is the noise level of most commercial equipment, has improved the recording of nerve action potentials.

Clinical Measurements and Application.   Normal values of nerve conduction velocity are usually in the range of 50 to 60 m per second in the distal segments of the nerves below the elbow, and between 60 and 80 m per second between the shoulder and the elbow. In the legs the normal values are usually between 40 and 50 m per second.

Nerve conduction in human infants at birth is about 40 per cent of the adult velocity, owing to the small size of the fibers and to the fact that a proportion of nerve fibers is incomplete in their myelination. Maturation occurs mainly over the first two years, and by the end of the third year most myelinated peripheral nerves are conducting in a normal range. The median nerve is an exception in that the full velocity may not be achieved until age five to seven. In the premature infant, there is a correlation between the post-conceptional age and the nerve conduction velocity, and this correlation may prove to be the optimal way to gauge prematurity.

Peripheral nerves reacting to destructive conditions, or undergoing degeneration, may be affected three ways:

1. A temporary disturbance of function, resulting from minor injury from which the nerve usually recovers completely in a period of less than two months is called neurapraxia and is not connected with any intrinsic morphological change. This produces a blockage of nerve conduction at the level of the lesion.

2. When the axon has been severely damaged, failure of conduction in the nerve distal to the lesion occurs and is called axonotmesis. Following the injury there is secondary or wallerian degeneration of the myelin sheath, which corresponds to the axonal disappearance. Nerve conduction returns only if a viable axon regenerates. The regenerating axon is thin at first, so conduction velocity is slow and becomes more rapid as the fiber diameter increases and as remyelination occurs.

3. When the primary damage is to the Schwann cell, whether by toxins or compression or anoxia, primary demyelination takes place. If the axon still remains intact, conduction is possible but at a much slower rate. With remyelination there may be great variation in the internodal distance, which also causes slow conduction velocity. Fibrosis around a peripheral nerve, which may be associated with this segmental demyelination, increases the threshold of stimulus needed to activate the nerve and also reduces conduction velocity relative to the degree of demyelination produced.

From the foregoing considerations, the clinical significance of conduction velocity and nerve stimulation is apparent. The contributions of motor and sensory nerve abnormalities to the various neuropathies can be measured and the type of nerve involvement can also be determined. The extent of regeneration and the degree of involvement of peripheral nerves can be assessed. The involvement may be diffuse as in peripheral neuropathy; in multiple individual nerves as in mononeuritis multiplex; or in local lesions of trunks, plexuses, or spinal segments. It is possible to localize the site of a lesion on a nerve by discovering evidence of blockage of conduction at a certain level or of localized slowing of conduction. Examples of this are the entrapment syndromes in the carpal or tarsal tunnels or in the deep palmar branch of the ulnar nerve; here one finds prolonged distal latencies, abnormal muscle evoked potentials, and impaired sensory distal conduction.

In disease of the anterior horn cell, in which muscle wasting may be associated with denervation in the affected muscles, nerve conduction may be relatively unaffected since the peripheral nerve is spared. Motor nerve conduction has occasionally been seen to be slow in patients with severe anterior horn cell disease, and this has been attributed to the effect of local cold on reducing conduction velocity as well as to degeneration of the faster nerve fibers. Sensory nerve conduction is normal in anterior horn cell disease.

In muscle disease, conduction velocity is normal, although the evoked potential may be of low amplitude and dispersed secondary to loss of muscle fibers.

ELECTROMYOGRAPHY

Electromyography is the recording of electrical changes occurring in muscle by electrodes either in contact with the skin over the muscle area or inserted into the muscle. Surface electrodes have been used to give a broad survey of action potentials from whole groups of fibers and can be of value in studying kinesiological patterns; however, because rapid, low-amplitude potentials are attenuated and fine detail of individual motor units cannot be routinely obtained, needle recording electrodes are used clinically.

The two principal types of recording needle electrodes are concentric (coaxial) and monopolar (unipolar). The needle electrode registers the average potential existing over its leading-off area, the recording surface being in direct contact with approximately eight muscle fibers of which only one or two belong to the same motor unit. The sharp spike of the potential recorded is primarily the result of the excitation of those few muscle fibers in close proximity to the recording electrode. However, the motor unit as a whole contributes to the total shape, amplitude, and duration of the recording potential.

Disease of the motor unit pathway at any point from the anterior horn cell to the muscle fiber itself can produce an abnormal pattern in the electromyogram. The higher nervous centers also influence the motor neuron apparatus so that upper motor neuron lesions may alter electromyographic findings. Since this is not intended as a clinical manual, the findings presented here are to illustrate pathophysiological changes that apply to groups of disorders as a whole.

The electrical activity produced by insertion of the needle, the spontaneous activity in the relaxed resting muscle, the interference pattern in full forceful contraction against resistance, and the character of the individual muscle action potentials during weak or submaximal contraction are all recorded (Fig. 11–5 and Table 11–3). The muscle is usually examined in several locations and it is often helpful to amplify the sound equivalent of the potentials, as the ear is quite sensitive to variations.

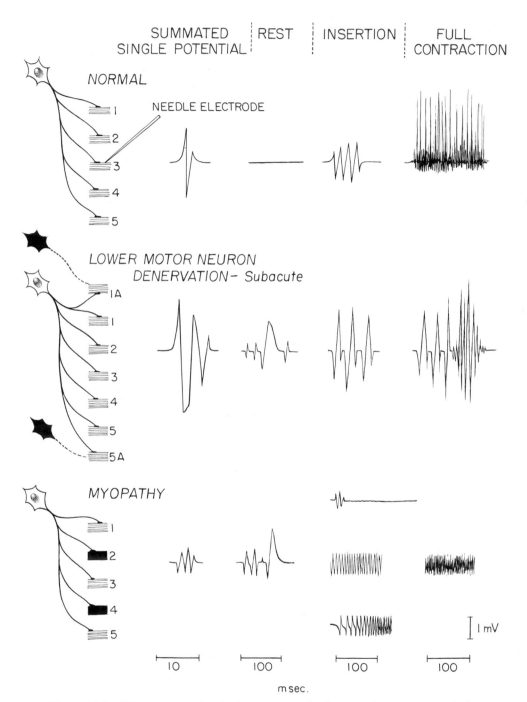

Figure 11–5 Electromyographic findings in normal subjects and in patients with denervation or myopathy (monopolar needle). See Table 11–3 for explanation.

TABLE 11–3 ELECTROMYOGRAPHIC FINDINGS IN NORMAL SUBJECTS AND IN PATIENTS WITH DENERVATION OR MYOPATHY (MONOPOLAR NEEDLE) *

	Summated Single Potential	Rest	Insertion	Full Contraction
Normal (Normal motor unit made up of single anterior horn cell that supplies many muscle fibers, here simplified as 5)	Muscle fiber (3) closest to electrode Excitation arrives first in fiber (1) and last in fiber (5) The summated potential differs from any component action potential	Silent at rest except for baseline "noise"	Short unsustained burst of activity usually lasting less than 50 msec	Full interference pattern with many units recruited Difficult to distinguish individual motor unit potentials Usual amplitude of pattern 3–6 mv
Lower motor neuron denervation (subacute)	Motor neuron degeneration with collateral growth from healthy axon to innervate muscle fibers (1A) and (5A) Both amplitude and duration of the summated potential are increased	Fibrillations and positive waves from denervated muscle fibers Fasciculations (not shown) may be present, especially in anterior horn cell disorders	Increased insertional activity with positive waves on insertion	Decreased number of motor units recruited Increase in complex polyphasic potentials, some of high amplitude (8–15 mv)
Myopathy	Loss of fibers (2) and (3) results in low-amplitude complex polyphasic potential (fragmented) Normal to decreased duration	May have fibrillations and positive waves (most marked in polymyositis)	(a) Decreased insertional activity with muscle atrophy and fibrous tissue replacement (b) Increased activity in inflammatory states (c) Myotonic discharge Waxing and waning runs (usually of positive waves	Firing rapid and number of recruited units normal or slightly reduced Amplitude of interference pattern low (usually 300–500 μv)

*See illustration in Figure 11–5.

Normally, muscle is silent at rest, i.e., with needle insertion no spontaneous activity such as fibrillations, positive waves, or fasciculations is noted. Fibrillations are spontaneous potentials of short duration (0.5 to 2.0 msec) and low amplitude (50 to 150 μv), although potentials of higher voltage have been recorded. They are usually diphasic and the initial deflection as seen on the oscilloscope screen is positive (downward), which differentiates them from potentials recorded in the area of the neuromuscular junction, which are of similar duration and amplitude but with an initial negative deflection. Fibrillations are caused by firing of single muscle fibers spontaneously. While felt to be indicative of denervation, they are also seen in muscle disease. Positive sharp waves are spontaneous potentials often seen in association with fibrillations, usually after denervation but also in myopathies. They are initiated by needle insertion and have an initial rapid positive (downward) sharp deflection that is followed by an exponential negative change that can continue into a prolonged low-voltage negative phase. Fasciculations are involuntary muscle twitchings that can often be seen on the surface of the skin. They are noted in many conditions, including benign myokymias, anterior horn cell disease, nerve root compression, ischemia, and various forms of muscle cramps. They are thought to arise mainly peripherally in the region of the myoneural junction, the impulse spreading antidromically to involve other branches of the axon, thereby accounting for the frequently observed polyphasic character and prolonged duration of the potentials. Fasciculations may also be caused by a central mechanism.

In our laboratory and using monopolar needles, activity produced by brief insertion of the needle electrode into the muscle has a duration of approximately 50 msec on the oscilloscope screen. Increased insertional activity is associated with irritability of the muscle membrane and can be seen in denervation as well as in primary muscle disease.

In normal subjects upon maximal contraction of a peripheral muscle there is a full interference pattern and it is difficult to distinguish individual muscle action potentials. Single motor unit potentials can be seen on submaximal contraction and are biphasic or triphasic with not more than four phases. The amplitude usually ranges from 500 μv to 3 mv, although normal values up to 8 mv can be seen. The duration is from 3 to 10 msec.

Lower Motor Neuron Disease. The electromyogram in lower motor neuron disease has certain general characteristics, which include fibrillation potentials and positive sharp waves, fasciculation potentials, increase in amplitude and decrease in the number of muscle action potentials observed during full effort, increase in average duration of muscle action potentials, and increased incidence of polyphasic potentials. Some of these changes also occur in myopathy, so a single criterion is insufficient to characterize the level of involvement along the motor unit pathway.

Anterior Horn Cell Disorders. The anterior horn cell is involved in disorders such as poliomyelitis, amyotrophic lateral sclerosis, the progressive spinal muscular atrophies, and hereditary degenerative conditions such as Charcot-Marie-Tooth disease. The characteristic features and clinical course vary according to the particular entity, but in general fibrillations and fasciculations are common. There is a decrease in total number of motor units, but an increase in the number of fibers making up each individual unit. Most muscle action potentials have a prolonged duration and increased amplitude that is more pronounced than is seen in muscles with impairment of peripheral nerves or roots. The motor unit territory may be increased by 80 to 140 per cent and the maximum voltage be five to eight times the normal value in severely involved muscles. There is extensive collateral regeneration, since the degenerating nerve fibers are scattered over wide areas and intact and degenerating nerve fibers often lie close together, giving rise to collateral branching from the surviving fibers. The action potentials are often polyphasic and of increased duration, again because of temporal dispersion of the enlarged unit.

Nerve Root and Plexus Injury. A nerve root or plexus lesion causes denervation corresponding to the segments involved, manifested by fibrillation potentials, occasional fasciculations, reduced numbers of muscle action potentials and complex polyphasic units often of increased duration. In the acute phase there may be electrical silence, with spontaneous activity appearing only as wallerian degeneration occurs. The peripheral nerve supply to individual muscles is composed of fibers from several spinal cord segments; as a result, normal and diseased motor units may be observed together. When atrophic changes occur in the muscle fibers, spontaneous activity disappears and evidence of chronic denervation is noted in the muscle supplied by the affected cord segments. Plexus lesions can be differentiated from nerve root lesions by examination of the paraspinal muscles, which are supplied by the posterior primary division of the ventral nerve root proximal to the plexus. In root lesions the paraspinal muscles innervated by the involved root manifest signs of denervation. On the other hand, the paraspinal muscles will be normal in the more distal plexus lesions.

Peripheral Nerve Lesions. A peripheral nerve damaged by disease or trauma may exhibit temporary loss of conductivity or varying degrees of degeneration. In physiological block (neurapraxia) continuity of the nerve sheath is maintained without wallerian degeneration and the condition is characterized by electrical silence at rest. There will be no voluntary action potentials if the block is complete, and a reduced number of normal potentials if it is partial. Immediately following severance of the nerve trunk no voluntary muscle action potentials are seen. The axon cylinder begins to fragment at about the third day, and at this time nerve conduction velocity distal to the site of injury rapidly decreases. Denervation potentials at rest begin approximately 10 days after the injury and occur in all areas of the muscle receiving their supply distal to the site of injury. Fibrillations last until the regenerating axon arrives at the surface of the muscle fiber and penetrates the end plate or until the muscle fibers atrophy. The voluntary motor potentials first seen on return of function are called nascent units and are of low amplitude, of variable duration, and polyphasic. They are due to early terminal reinnervation as well as to varying rates of distal conduction. As reinnervation progresses, the remaining motor units increase in area and number of fibers so that there is an increase in complex polyphasic units of prolonged duration and increased amplitude.

Motor End Plate Disturbances. A defect in transmission across the neuromuscular junction, as in myasthenia gravis, is characterized by a decrease in amplitude of the successively evoked potentials on repetitive stimulation. The amplitude of an individual single motor unit on voluntary contraction varies widely until, because of fatigue, the unit may fail to respond. The normal pattern may be restored by injection of neostigmine or edrophonium chloride.

A "myasthenic" syndrome is seen in adults with malignant intrathoracic tumors (and at times with nonmalignant diseases) in which signs suggestive of a neuromuscular transmission defect have been noted. Unlike myasthenia gravis, the initial response to a supramaximal stimulus is only a fraction of normal amplitude and as contraction continues there is a period of facilitation characterized by increasing responses.

Myopathy. Myopathies may exhibit one or more of the following electromyographic findings: (1) the presence of spontaneous activity at rest, i.e., fibrillations and positive waves; (2) myotonic discharges induced by voluntary contractile activity, by insertion of the needle, or by tapping the muscle near the needle; (3) a relatively normal interference pattern of muscle action potentials (in spite of muscle weakness and wasting); (4) a decrease in amplitude and average duration of the individual motor unit potentials; (5) an increase in the number of polyphasic potentials; and (6) diminished territory of the motor units with decreased fiber density within the motor unit.

Fibrillations have been noted in most myopathies. The mechanisms of the abnormal spontaneous muscle potentials are not clear. In progressive muscular dystrophy and hyperkalemic periodic paralysis the spontaneous discharges may be related to the increase in excitability resulting from low levels of intracellular potassium. It is also possible that the degenerating muscle fibers in the dystrophies may initially lose their terminal innervation. In the myositic disorders inflammatory involvement of the subterminal intramuscular nerve endings and end plate area has been demonstrated and could cause increased irritability. There is evidence of collateral reinnervation, and prolonged action potentials are occasionally noted, but since the sprouting is entirely peripheral, very large motor units and enlargement of motor unit territory are not found. Bizarre high-frequency potentials are often noted in myositis. These are high-frequency runs of identical appearing potentials, usually polyphasic, that start and stop abruptly. They are also observed in acute denervation.

In the myopathies most of the electromyographic changes are due to a reduction of the number of muscle fibers in the individual unit; however, the total number of motor unit potentials remains relatively unchanged until the very late stages. Muscle force and summated voltage are decreased, but the number of potentials is maintained by increased frequency of discharge. More electrical activity of action potential spikes is necessary to achieve the same amount of force as was attained prior to illness. Because of the random degeneration of muscle fibers, the smooth summated effect of the normal muscle action potential is lost and complex potentials of low amplitude are noted. The distalmost fibers from the recording electrode are likewise decreased in number, so there is a shortening of the duration of the recorded potentials.

Myotonia. Myotonia is an abnormally sustained contraction with difficulty in relaxation. The electromyogram shows runs of repetitive high-frequency waxing and waning discharges, usually of positive waves or biphasic potentials, the initial deflection being positive. Electrical myotonia may be seen in myotonic dystrophy, myotonia congenita, periodic paralysis (principally the hyperkalemic type), or with Pompe's disease. Myotonic-like phenomena may also be seen in inflammatory disease of muscle (dermatomyositis) although the discharges are not as pronounced and have less waxing and waning. They tend to begin abruptly and then to gradually taper off or suddenly stop. This has been called pseudomyotonia; in patients with pseudomyotonia, clinical myotonia is absent. In patients with myotonic dystrophy, the electromyogram may, on voluntary contraction, closely resemble that in a neuropathy in that high-voltage polyphasic potentials of prolonged duration may be mixed with more typical myopathic potentials, suggesting some primary involvement of the neuron.

Muscle Biopsy

Muscle biopsy may be helpful not only for the confirmation of a myopathic process but, using appropriate techniques in selected cases, for the identification of a specific myopathy (e.g., glycogen storage disease). Proper selection of the biopsy site, surgical technique, biochemical and histochemical studies, and histopathological interpretation must be combined optimally in order to justify muscle biopsy.

The muscle selected for biopsy should be clinically affected but should not be severely wasted; in the latter instance the characteristic architectural abnormality is often obliterated and may be replaced by fibrous tissue, fat, and distorted muscle fibers. The electromyogram can be helpful in selecting the optimal biopsy site if care is taken not to take the sample from the precise area of needle insertion.

The specific surgical procedures used in muscle biopsy and the methods of tissue fixation are beyond the scope of this text, but it is again emphasized that the ultimate diagnostic study that is contemplated predetermines the type of technique that must be used for handling the tissue. For example, frozen tissue is required for biochemical and histochemical studies, and the routine preparation used for light microscopy does not suffice when an electron microscopic study is contemplated. The normal histological structure of muscle is depicted in Figure 11–6A, for comparison with the pathological changes shown in B and C.

Myopathic changes include deposition of fat and increase in connective tissue relative to the amount of muscle present. Increase in the number of muscle nuclei and migration of the nuclei from a peripheral position to the center of the muscle fiber are seen. The nuclei may be enlarged and may contain prominent nucleoli. Granular or hyaline degeneration may be noted. Swollen muscle fibers lie intermingled with normal and necrotic fibers, so

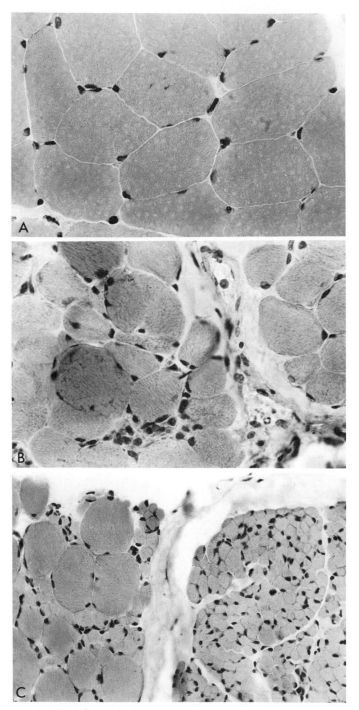

Figure 11–6 *A.* Normal muscle (human quadriceps). There is slight variation in muscle fiber size. Fibers are polygonal, and the nuclei are peripheral. Hematoxylin and eosin, × 125. *B.* Duchenne's muscular dystrophy. There is wide variation in muscle fiber size and an increase in endomysial connective tissue. Hematoxylin and eosin, × 125. *C.* Neurogenic atrophy (Werdnig-Hoffmann disease). There are large numbers of fibers of normal size adjacent to a large number of fibers of reduced size. Hematoxylin and eosin, × 80.

that variation in muscle fiber size is seen in random distribution throughout the section (Fig. 11–6B).

Neurogenic atrophy is characterized by "group lesions" rather than random variation in muscle fiber size, since a group of muscle fibers in a given area loses the innervation provided by specific anterior horn cells or nerve fibers. Connective tissue increase is not prominent, and few changes occur in myofibrillar or intracellular structure (Fig. 11–6C).

The histochemical study of muscle has advanced our knowledge of muscle structure and function considerably and has been of value in clinical diagnosis, notably in the glycogen storage diseases and certain of the congenital myopathies. Histochemical differentiation of type I and type II muscle fibers is based on the prominent staining for oxidative enzymes in the former, and for adenosine triphosphatase (ATPase) and phosphorylase in the latter. These fiber types vary in anatomical structure at various stages of development, are equal in number by the time of birth, and are differentially involved in various neurogenic and myopathic disorders.

THE MUSCULAR DYSTROPHIES

The muscular dystrophies show a strong heredofamilial disposition, but vary in age of onset, mode of transmission, rate of progression, and clinical and laboratory features. Their inclusion as a group is mainly traditional. As the biochemical error associated with each disorder is elucidated, its classification becomes more rational. Some of the more outstanding features that differentiate the muscular dystrophies are summarized in Table 11–4.

Duchenne's Muscular Dystrophy

Clinical Features.   Duchenne's muscular dystrophy (pseudohypertrophic muscular dystrophy) is inherited as a sex-linked recessive disorder. Only phenotypic females with the male genotype have manifested the disorder. The female carriers of the gene for muscular dystrophy of the Duchenne type may show increased values of serum creatine phosphokinase, but do not, except for occasional forme fruste features, manifest the clinical disease.[27] The disorder occurs in approximately 4 per 100,000 persons in the United States and has a world-wide distribution.

Symptoms may at times be dated retrospectively to the first or second year of life because of delay in motor development, particularly walking, but the presenting complaints usually appear in the third year of life.

The first difficulty is usually in running or climbing stairs. Later, abnormal gait on a level surface is noticed. The waddling gait gives rise to an impression of awkwardness or slowness. As a rule, only direct questioning elicits the complaint of difficulty in rising from the seated or supine position on the floor. Weakness of the upper extremities occurs later.

Since developmental gains may continue to outstrip the rate of progression of the disorder for the first few years of life, actual loss of function or defi-

TABLE 11–4　THE MUSCULAR DYSTROPHIES

	Duchenne	Limb-Girdle	Myotonic	Facioscapulo-humeral	Ocular and Oculopharyngeal
Inheritance	♂ R, (S)	r, D, S	D	D	r, D, S
Age at onset of symptoms	1–3 yrs.	>8 yrs.	Variable	>8 yrs.	>10 yrs.
Cerebral dysfunction	+	–	+	–	±
Distribution of weakness	Proximal	Proximal	Distal	Facial and proximal	Ocular, facial, and proximal
Progression	Rapid	Slow	Slow or ±	Slow or ±	Slow
Serum enzyme elevation	++	++	±	±	±
Myotonia	–	–	+	–	–

Symbols used:　♂ R, X-linked recessive　>, more than
　　　　　　　r, autosomal recessive　<, less than
　　　　　　　S, sporadic　　　　　　+, occurs
　　　　　　　D, autosomal dominant　++, elevated
　　　　　　　–, does not occur　　　±, may or may not occur

nite regression has not usually occurred when the patient is first seen by a physician. Occasionally an alert parent will notice the unusual prominence of the calves.

On examination the patient exhibits weakness more proximally than distally. There is exaggerated lumbar lordosis and a protuberant abdomen. The child walks with a waddle due to weakness of the pelvic girdle muscles. There is a distinct Gowers' sign (see Fig. 11–3). Pseudohypertrophy of the gastrocnemius muscles is seen in 80 per cent of the children (Fig. 11–7). The calves appear enlarged and rather muscular but feel unusually firm or woody on palpation. The deltoid and quadriceps muscles may also be affected by the pseudohypertrophic process. The deep tendon reflexes are preserved early in the disorder. As the disease progresses, the knee jerks disappear but the ankle jerks remain intact, reflecting the greater severity of involvement of the proximal muscles, with gradual distal progression. The facial, oropharyngeal, and respiratory muscles are spared until the terminal stages of the disease.

Mild mental retardation occurs in as many as 50 per cent of the patients.[46] In early childhood the awkwardness of a youngster with muscular dystrophy who also has cerebral dysfunction may be attributed to the cerebral process. The more severely affected dystrophic child is likely to have more intellectual deficit, but this is not an absolute rule.

Laboratory Features. In the first two years of life, serum creatine phosphokinase (CPK) values reach extremely high levels – 1000 to 2000 units. As the disease progresses the CPK values diminish but not to normal values until severe muscle wasting and incapacitation have occurred.[31]

Electromyographic changes include low-voltage sharp polyphasic potentials with a normal number of motor units (see Fig. 11–5). In the earlier, more

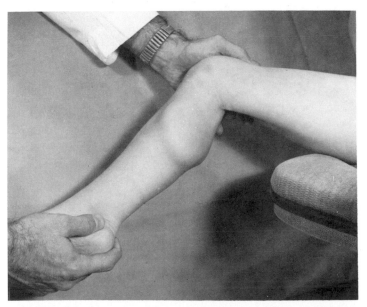

Figure 11–7 Pseudohypertrophy of the gastrocnemius muscle in a child with Duchenne's muscular dystrophy. (From Swaiman, K. F., and Wright, F. S.: *Neuromuscular Diseases of Infancy and Childhood.* Springfield, Ill., Charles C Thomas, 1970, p. 168.)

active stage of the disease, some fibrillations and positive waves may be seen, as in acute myopathies of the inflammatory type (polymyositis). In the late stage of the disease, insertional activity may be reduced and the number of motor units firing on voluntary contraction may be diminished as a result of replacement of muscle with fat and fibrous tissue.

Muscle biopsy reveals random distribution of fibers of varying size. The changes are those of a nonspecific myopathy (see Fig. 11–6).

The electrocardiogram may show prolongation of the P-R interval, slurring of the QRS complex, bundle branch block, and ST elevation or depression due to involvement of the cardiac muscle by the tenth year of life.

Course and Prognosis.   Early in the second decade of life, most patients with Duchenne's muscular dystrophy become wheelchair-bound. Death usually occurs between the ages of 15 and 25 years and is due to involvement of respiratory or cardiac musculature. Rarely, in less severe cases, they may survive to the fourth or fifth decade.

Differential Diagnosis.   In the typical two to seven year old male there is little difficulty with the diagnosis. Since patients with limb-girdle dystrophy may have pseudohypertrophic calf muscles and often have impressively elevated CPK values, the differential diagnosis is at times hard. Involvement in a female sibling, in the absence of aberrant genotypic features, suggests limb-girdle dystrophy.

Occasionally glycogen storage disease of muscle is encountered in young children and adolescents with pseudohypertrophy who have little or no obvious associated cardiomyopathy. This possibility requires serious consideration when the mode of inheritance is in doubt or clearly indicates autosomal recessive transmission. The need for histochemical or enzymatic analysis of muscle tissue with respect to glycogen content and the presence of α-glucosidase must be borne in mind.

Since striking increases in serum CPK values are encountered in polymyositis, this disorder must be considered in the differential diagnosis of muscular dystrophy. The acute or subacute onset, the skin rash in most cases, the muscle tenderness, the elevated sedimentation rate, and the typical electromyographic changes should permit differentiation.

Limb-Girdle Muscular Dystrophy

Clinical Features.   Limb-girdle dystrophy is usually inherited as an autosomal recessive trait. Except for a single family in which the disorder was limited to females, there has been no sex preponderance. A few patients appear to have inherited this myopathy by autosomal dominant transmission, and some sporadic cases have been reported. Since the disorder is not characterized by a specific biochemical lesion or clinical feature, this may not be a single clinical entity.

Clinical features appear most commonly late in the first decade or in the second decade of life. The initial manifestations may be weakness of either the shoulder or pelvic girdle, which then ascends or descends as the disorder progresses. When the first weakness is in the lower extremities, the symptoms are similar to those encountered in Duchenne's muscular dystrophy, i.e., gradually progressive difficulty in running or climbing stairs. If the initial weakness involves the shoulder girdle, such tasks as combing the hair become difficult before other manifestations appear.

On examination the findings are those of a nonspecific myopathy and are essentially the same as those described for Duchenne's muscular dystrophy with the exception that both males and females are affected. The degree of weakness at a comparable age will be typically milder, as the disorder has a later onset and slower progression. Gowers' sign can be present if the iliopsoas and gluteal muscles are severely involved at the onset. The anterior tibial and peroneal muscles are affected later. Pseudohypertrophy occurs in about one fifth of the patients, but the deltoid muscles are rarely affected in this manner. Marked scapular winging may occur since the rhomboids and serratus anterior muscles are frequently involved (Fig. 11–8). Typically, the biceps tendon reflexes disappear before the triceps reflexes, and the knee jerks are lost before the ankle jerks.

Laboratory Features. The creatine phosphokinase and other serum enzyme levels are elevated early in the disorder, but peak values rarely exceed half of that seen in Duchenne's muscular dystrophy.

The electromyogram and muscle biopsy specimens show nonspecific myopathic and dystrophic features similar to those in Duchenne's muscular dystrophy.

The disease begins insidiously and progresses more slowly than Duchenne's muscular dystrophy. Nevertheless, most patients are incapacitated within two decades of the clinical onset.

Differential Diagnosis. The differential diagnosis includes the disorders discussed under the diagnosis of Duchenne's muscular dystrophy. The later

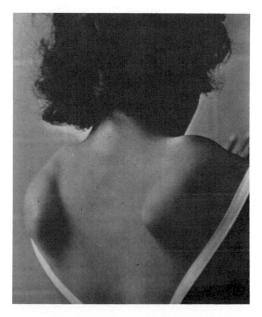

Figure 11–8 Scapular winging. This phenomenon occurs in many chronic neurogenic and myopathic disorders involving the serratus anterior and rhomboid muscles. (Courtesy of Dr. Bruce Berg, University of California, San Francisco Medical Center. From Chutorian, A. M., and Koenigsberger, M. R.: The muscular dystrophies. In *Brennemann's Practice of Pediatrics.* Vol. IV, Chap. 38, p. 6. Hagerstown, Md., Harper & Row, 1972. Reprinted with permission.)

onset, involvement of both sexes, usual absence of pseudohypertrophy, and slow progression serve to differentiate limb-girdle dystrophy from Duchenne's muscular dystrophy.

Facioscapulohumeral Dystrophy

Clinical Features. Facioscapulohumeral (Landouzy-Déjérine) dystrophy occurs in 2 per 100,000 in the general population. Inheritance occurs as an autosomal dominant trait. This form of dystrophy is rarely seen in the pediatric age group; however, the child of an affected adult may show facial weakness in the first decade of life.

Early complaints are not dissimilar to those encountered in limb-girdle dystrophy but are usually referred first to the shoulder rather than the pelvic girdle, although very occasionally a gait difficulty is the first disability to be noticed. The earliest sign in some patients is loss of normal facial contour (especially evident in a transverse smile), absence of frontal creasing, or difficulty with blowing and whistling and puckering the lips.

On examination the face and forehead appear smooth and unlined. Pursing of the lips and puffing of the cheeks are difficult. The shoulder girdle is wasted, and winging of the scapulae is evident. This is best demonstrated by having the patient extend the arms and push with both palms on an immobile structure (see Fig. 11–8). The weak and wasted scapular (serratus anterior and rhomboid) muscles, which normally fix the scapulae for this maneuver, permit them to "wing" outward unopposed.

The muscles of the lower extremities exhibit weakness commensurate with the stage of the disorder, with proximal preponderance. Weakness may be undetectable in the lower extremities for some years.

Laboratory Features. As might be anticipated, because of the extremely slow progression of facioscapulohumeral dystrophy, the serum enzymes are normal. Electromyography and muscle biopsy show changes similar to those seen in Duchenne's and limb-girdle dystrophy.

Course and Prognosis. The patient may worsen so slowly that progression is not appreciated. Many mildly affected and atypical cases occur. The life span is usually normal, without significant incapacitation.

Differential Diagnosis. Since prominent facial muscle weakness is more typical of neuropathy than myopathy, the proximal distribution of weakness in the extremities should direct attention to the myopathic character of the disorder, though a rare disorder has been described in which neurogenic atrophy occurs in a distribution simulating facioscapulohumeral dystrophy. The electromyogram, nerve conduction studies, and muscle biopsy thus assume importance in the differential diagnosis.

The question of myasthenia gravis may be raised by the presence of ptosis and can be settled by the absence of response to edrophonium bromide (Tensilon) and by the absence of decremental electromyographic change in response to repetitive stimulation. Facial diplegia is seen in myotonic dystrophy, in the ocular myopathies, and in some of the congenital myopathies.

Myotonic Dystrophy

Clinical Features.   Myotonia can be induced passively (i.e., by percussion) or by voluntary muscle contraction, following which the contraction persists for a time involuntarily. The phenomenon is potentiated by cold and may involve the skeletal, ocular, and tongue musculature. Clinical myotonia is encountered in myotonia congenita and hyperkalemic periodic paralysis as well as in myotonic dystrophy. The electromyographic concomitants of myotonia are also seen in glycogen storage disease of muscle and in exceptional patients with centronuclear myopathy.

Myotonic dystrophy is inherited as an autosomal dominant trait with variable penetrance and expressivity. The disorder may thus be mild in the parent and severe in the offspring. The forme fruste requires a search for electrical myotonia and slit lamp examination for cataract in other family members to identify the heredofamilial character of the disorder.

Manifestations may present in the neonatal period or they may be deferred to early or later childhood. In the newborn period facial diplegia, with sucking and swallowing difficulty, may occur and ptosis may be seen. More often hypotonia and delayed motor development are noted in later infancy and awkward gait is noted in the second year of life. When facial diplegia is prominent the various features of facial weakness described in the section on facioscapulohumeral dystrophy are characteristic.

The disease may escape detection in infancy, as some patients lack significant symptoms at this time and even in early childhood. They usually become symptomatic between the ages of 5 and 15 years. Ptosis, facial diplegia, and myotonia are the most characteristic signs in these patients (Figs. 11–9 and 11–10). Dyslalia and dysarthria are common, owing to the combination of facial weakness and glossopharyngeal myotonia.

There is a high frequency of borderline or frank mental deficiency, and impaired mentation is not infrequently the presenting symptom in the pediatric age group.

Myotonia can be elicited in a number of ways. Spasm of the superior recti causes the eyes to remain elevated briefly after forced closure. Percussion of the thenar and deltoid muscles, or of the tongue, results in a briefly sustained contraction. The thumb goes into adductor spasm for a few seconds following percussion of the thenar eminence. The area of the tongue that has been percussed is furrowed as the depression caused by the contracting fibers persists. The most characteristic feature is the inability of the patient to release a forced hand grip rapidly.

Cataracts occur but are usually not evident until the teens, although slit lamp examination may disclose a cataract earlier. The older child shows bitemporal muscle atrophy. In the teens, frontal baldness and gonadal atrophy develop, although the latter phenomenon may occur much later on in life.

Weakness of the extremities may appear to predominate in the hypotonic proximal muscles in infancy and early childhood, but distal muscle weakness and wasting are more characteristic of the child old enough to cooperate for evaluation of muscle strength and may progress to profound distal paresis. This relatively unusual phenomenon among the myopathies is shared with the

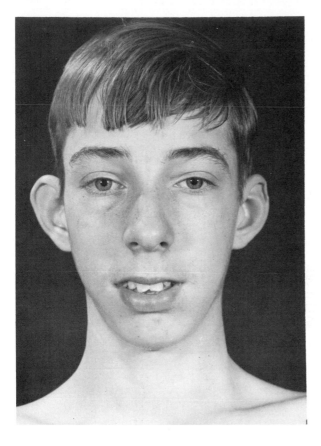

Figure 11–9 Myopathic facies in a patient with myotonic dystrophy. The laxity of facial muscles and ptosis are characteristic. (From Swaiman, K. F., and Wright, F. S.: *Neuromuscular Diseases of Infancy and Childhood.* Springfield, Ill., Charles C Thomas, 1970, p. 168.)

rare congenital distal myopathy in which the features of myotonic dystrophy are absent.[41] Congenital physical anomalies are encountered with a higher than expected incidence in myotonic dystrophy. These include clubfeet, cleft lip and palate, micrognathia, high-arched palate, and congenital heart disease.

Laboratory Features.   Needle electrode insertion on electromyographic examination elicits runs of high-frequency waxing and waning potentials resembling positive waves or with several phases, the initial positive, which produce a sound that is aptly compared with the acoustic effects of dive-bombing. These discharges are admixed with normal motor unit potentials and, in some patients, with nonspecific myopathic and neuropathic electromyographic features.

Myotonic discharges occur before clinical myotonia can be elicited. This phenomenon makes the electromyogram a valuable laboratory tool for confirming the diagnosis in atypical situations and for identifying asymptomatic relatives.

Serum enzyme values are rarely elevated. Levels of immunoglobulins G and M may be low. Isotope studies have indicated increased immunoglobulin degradation in patients with myotonic dystrophy.

For the most part, histological abnormalities shown by muscle biopsy are nonspecific. However, central nuclei arranged in chains and circular arrange-

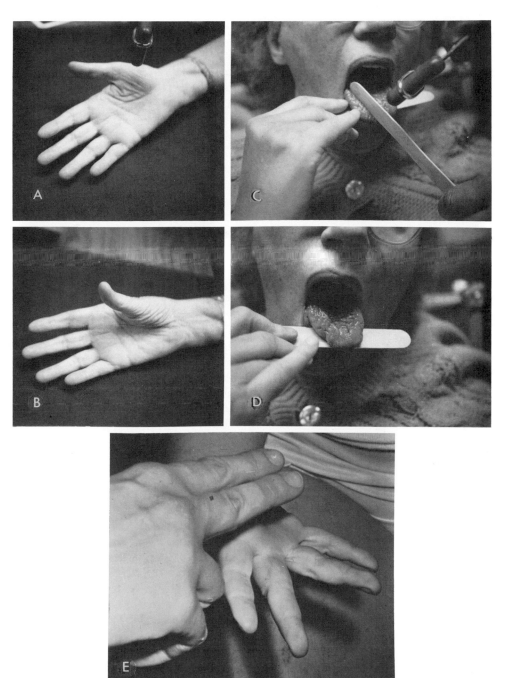

Figure 11-10 Myotonia. *A.* The hand of a patient with myotonic dystrophy at rest before percussion of the thenar eminence. *B.* After percussion of the thenar eminence. The thumb is maintained in involuntary adduction for a brief interval before relaxation. *C.* The method of tongue percussion employing the edge of a tongue depressor is demonstrated. *D.* After percussion, tongue myotonia is demonstrated by a briefly persistent furrow at the site of impact. *E.* Delayed release of hand grip. (Courtesy of Dr. Bruce Berg, University of California, San Francisco Medical Center. From Chutorian, A. M., and Koenigsberger, M. R.: The muscular dystrophies. In *Brennemann's Practice of Pediatrics.* Vol. IV, Chap. 38, p. 8. Hagerstown, Md., Harper & Row, 1972. Reprinted with permission.)

ment of myofibrils (ringbinden) tend to be particularly noted. Cytochemical abnormalities appear to involve type I fibers.

The electrocardiogram frequently becomes abnormal. Cerebral heterotopia and ventricular dilatation occur rarely and have been diagnosed by pneumoencephalography. Serial pneumoencephalography has in some instances demonstrated progressive cerebral atrophy.

Differential Diagnosis.   The differential diagnosis includes disorders in which sucking and swallowing difficulty occur in infancy, disorders in which the myotonic phenomenon is encountered, and in general, the myopathies in which ocular, facial, and bulbar muscles are affected.

The neonate or infant with myotonia who is hypotonic and has sucking and swallowing difficulty cannot easily be differentiated from the far more frequently encountered infant with cerebral dysfunction and pseudobulbar palsy, who has similar difficulty. In fact, the child with myotonia is more likely to be placed in the latter category. If facial diplegia is prominent, the differentiation is easier. Clinical and electromyographic evidence of myotonia should be sought in such patients before making the diagnosis.

Myasthenic infants are hypotonic and have feeding difficulty. These symptoms improve dramatically with neostigmine. This therapeutic cum diagnostic procedure should, therefore, be considered especially in dramatic or life-threatening cases, in addition to the other available diagnostic tools. The mothers of such infants usually have myasthenic symptoms, in which cases the disorder is transient, but the rare spontaneous case will be encountered. The older child with myasthenia has ptosis and shows facial weakness, but is easily recognized by the absence of myotonia.

Myotonia congenita, like myotonic dystrophy, may be associated with feeding difficulty.[15] Inheritance, as in myotonic dystrophy, is by autosomal dominant transmission, and symptoms may be deferred to later childhood or adolescence. However, unlike myotonic dystrophy, the disorder lessens in severity with maturation and there is no associated cerebral dysfunction. Muscular hypertrophy is prominent, but cataracts and testicular atrophy do not occur in myotonia congenita.

Disorders in which electrical myotonia occurs include hyperkalemic periodic paralysis and glycogen storage disease (acid maltase deficiency). The unique monomelic myopathy has been associated with myotonia, but cannot be confused with myotonic dystrophy.

In hyperkalemic periodic paralysis the paroxysmal character of the disorder overshadows the myotonia, and the serum potassium level is usually elevated during an attack. The attacks can be precipitated with a small dose of potassium chloride and terminated with a calcium gluconate infusion.

The infantile, late infantile, and juvenile forms of glycogen storage disease due to acid maltase deficiency are associated with the myotonic phenomenon chiefly on the electromyogram. In the infantile form, the severe rapidly progressive symptoms, with cardiac involvement, eliminate any considerations of myotonic dystrophy. The late infantile or older patients who show relative or total cardiac sparing strongly mimic those with Duchenne's muscular dystrophy, with proximal weakness and pseudohypertrophy, and do not resemble patients with myotonic dystrophy.

Centronuclear (myotubular) myopathy bears a resemblance to myotonic dystrophy by virtue of the facial diplegia and ptosis, the onset in infancy or early childhood, and the rare occurrence of electrical myotonia. Proximal preponderance of weakness is typical of centronuclear myopathy and is encountered in infancy in myotonic dystrophy, but the electrical myotonic phenomenon is exceptional in centronuclear myopathy. The diagnosis of centronuclear myopathy in such cases depends upon the significant impairment of extraocular muscle function and the characteristic histopathological changes shown by muscle biopsy.

Since myotonic dystrophy involves the facial muscles, the disorder may also mimic oculopharyngeal muscular dystrophy and facioscapulohumeral dystrophy. Clinical myotonia is, however, not encountered in these disorders.

Course, Prognosis, and Therapy. Progressive distal muscle weakness eventually leads to profound paresis. "Swan neck" develops as sternocleidomastoid wasting and weakness progress. Incapacitation has occurred in the majority within two decades of the clinical onset. Death may be caused by cardiac arrhythmia, but is more likely to result from respiratory insufficiency. Many patients with myotonic dystrophy remain mildly affected.

Drugs that have a stabilizing effect on the muscle membrane potential, including quinine, diphenylhydantoin, and procaine amide hydrochloride, have been shown to lessen the severity of the myotonic phenomenon, but they have no effect on the weakness.

Ocular Muscular Dystrophy

Clinical Features. This rare condition, also known as oculopharyngeal muscular dystrophy, which may progress to total extraocular muscle paralysis, is inherited as an autosomal dominant or recessive trait. A number of cases appear to develop sporadically. Although symptoms may begin in the teens, the condition is exceedingly uncommon in the pediatric age group.

The onset is characterized by ptosis, diplopia, or strabismus, and frequently by associated weakness of the facial muscles, especially the frontalis and orbicularis oculi. Twenty-five to fifty per cent of the patients develop dysphagia as a result of involvement of the pharyngeal musculature. Frequently the limb musculature is also involved. At times the preponderance of weakness in these patients is distal, but more frequently the shoulder girdle is affected. In some patients distal involvement is due to an associated polyneuropathy. Association with retinitis pigmentosa as well as with deafness, cerebellar ataxia, and varying degrees of mental deficiency has been recorded. Possibly some of these patients with "ophthalmoplegia plus" have neurogenic ocular signs.[5]

Laboratory Features. The serum creatine phosphokinase is normal, although modest increases occur when the limb musculature is significantly involved.

Electromyography discloses myopathic changes, particularly in the facial and neck musculature. Biopsy of the appropriate muscle exhibits only nonspecific myopathic changes.

Differential Diagnosis. The early and prominent involvement of the ocular muscles and, in some instances, of the pharynx and shoulder girdle, suggests a myasthenic process. The lack of relationship to fatigue, i.e., absence of relative remission on rising in the morning and exacerbation as the day progresses, and the failure of response to edrophonium chloride (Tensilon) or neostigmine enable differentiation of ocular muscular dystrophy from myasthenia gravis. However, since the ocular paralysis may be relatively refractory to edrophonium chloride or physostigmine in myasthenia, demonstration of decremental electromyographic fatigue or provocation with curare may be required.

Facioscapulohumeral dystrophy may be brought to mind by the not dissimilar facial features early in the course of the two disorders. The progressive paralysis of eye movements is not seen in facioscapulohumeral dystrophy.

Oculofacial involvement in the congenital myopathies, notably in centronuclear myopathy, may include progressive impairment of extraocular muscle movements. Generalized limb-girdle weakness is prominent in centronuclear myopathy, which begins at a much earlier age than ocular muscular dystrophy. Muscle biopsy settles the differential diagnosis, which may be difficult.

Course and Prognosis. The outlook for long survival is good, the limiting factor being dysphagia, which may lead to aspiration. This does not occur in childhood.

MYOSITIDES

Polymyositis and Dermatomyositis

These sporadic disorders are included in the group of collagen vascular diseases. Concurrent vasculitis and an increased incidence of polymyositis and dermatomyositis in patients with known collagen disease suggest this etiological association. The association with occult neoplasia that is seen in a significant minority of adults is rare in children.

At the present time there is no definitive evidence to indicate that childhood polymyositis without dermal lesions is fundamentally different from dermatomyositis. Both show generalized inflammatory changes in skeletal muscle, but in dermatomyositis these changes are accompanied by a widespread, patchy, reddish or violaceous skin eruption, typically involving the eyelids and the dorsal surfaces of bony prominences of the extremities, such as the periungual areas, interphalangeal joints, elbows, and knees. Occasionally, sclerodermatous features are prominent. Other points of clinical departure between polymyositis and dermatomyositis are overshadowed by their similarities, which, in brief, include the rapid evolution of the illness, its self-limited character, the occurrence of muscle pain and tenderness, and the frequent occurrence of dysphagia—a distinctly uncommon manifestation of myopathy. The differences may be summarized as follows: the incidence of polymyositis in childhood is considerably lower than that of dermatomyositis, a situation that is reversed in adult life; the morbidity and mortality rates of dermatomyositis are greater—a significant minority of children with dermatomyositis become nonambulatory and a similar number, perhaps 25 per cent, succumb to the disorder. Severe impairment of function or death from pure polymyositis is rare.

Signs and Symptoms. In both the presence and the absence of skin lesions, the myopathy at the onset manifests itself as a proximal weakness of the lower extremities, causing difficulty with running and climbing stairs and culminating in impairment of routine functions normally requiring minimal exertion. Proximal weakness of the upper extremities is noted soon afterward and is virtually always present by the time the patient is examined. The onset is acute or subacute and is only rarely sufficiently insidious to raise seriously the question of a dystrophic process. Symptoms become prominent in days to weeks.

Systemic manifestations may be severe and can include intermittent low-grade fever, lethargy and malaise, and pain in the extremities. Pain may be sufficiently prominent to overshadow weakness. Not uncommonly, dysphagia and even nasal regurgitation of fluids occur, indicating involvement of the muscles of the oropharynx and incompetent palatal closure.

On examination, Gowers' sign is typically present (see Fig. 11–3). While proximal weakness usually predominates, on occasion diffuse weakness is also striking and the major distribution of the weakness cannot easily be determined. The muscle bellies of the extremities are tender to palpation. Joint contractures may develop with surprising rapidity and are not uncommon after only a few weeks. These may be of a subtle degree and are particularly prone to occur in flexion at the elbows and knees, or to limit dorsiflexion of the ankles. The deep tendon reflexes may be normal or diminished, and in more severe or chronic cases may be lost. In rare instances, a vascular retinopathy occurs, suggesting a diffuse vasculitis. Deposits of calcium often occur subcutaneously, particularly in chronic cases. When widespread, the condition is termed calcinosis universalis.

Laboratory Studies. The erythrocyte sedimentation rate is frequently elevated and the serum protein electrophoretic pattern may be altered. Creatine phosphokinase and other enzyme levels are usually elevated, at times strikingly, although values comparable to the peak values seen in Duchenne's dystrophy are uncommon. The electromyogram is characteristic, although not pathognomonic. Insertional activity is increased and features usually seen in denervation such as fibrillations and spontaneous positive sharp waves and a myopathic pattern on contraction of low-amplitude fragmented units are admixed. Muscle biopsy shows a mononuclear, principally lymphocytic, perivascular infiltration, and vascular intimal hyperplasia is seen. These changes may also be noted on skin biopsy or pathological examination of other organs. Their occurrence in small nerves suggests the basis for the mild neuropathic changes that occur with the overriding myopathic changes on the electromyogram. Indeed, typical grouped lesions of neurogenic atrophy may occasionally be seen in muscle tissue (see Fig. 11–6). Discrete regions of muscle infarction, probably due to perimysial vascular occlusion, are encountered. In some instances, muscle biopsy tissue is unrewarding and shows little in the way of the changes described. Inflammatory cells may be absent in as many as one quarter of muscle biopsy specimens.

Clinical Course.[37]   The course of the disorder is unpredictable. Severe contractures and disability may occur in the more chronic cases, which can smolder or repeatedly remit and intensify over a number of years. Fulminant cases may progress rapidly, resulting in death within weeks, the fatal outcome occurring as the result of pharyngeal and respiratory paralysis or cardiac failure. Intercurrent infection is more common when the course is protracted, especially if steroid therapy has been employed on a long-term basis. Lasting remission without residual impairment ultimately occurs in approximately half the affected children. Survival may not be affected by steroid therapy, but there is evidence to suggest that symptoms may be alleviated, contractures delayed or prevented, and the duration of the disease shortened. The use of other immunosuppressive agents (e.g., azathioprine [Imuran], methotrexate) appears to be of more benefit in adults than in children. Oral aluminum hydroxide, which reduces intestinal absorption of phosphate and reverses ectopic calcification, is effective in the treatment of widespread subcutaneous calcinosis.

Other Myositides

Polymyositis may be associated with rheumatoid arthritis, Sjögren's syndrome, lupus erythematosus, or periarteritis nodosa. The specific collagen disorder dominates the symptomatology, although the symptoms of rheumatoid arthritis and polymyositis overlap and may be difficult to distinguish at times, particularly when joint contractures are present.

A number of specific infections and parasitic infestations may involve muscle in a focal or widespread manner. A prominent acute polymyositic syndrome occurs in trichinosis. The severity of the disorder depends on the number of organisms ingested that ultimately circulate to skeletal muscle and other organs. Fever, edema, and a generalized dermal maculopapular eruption may accompany widespread muscle pain, tenderness, and weakness. The diagnosis depends upon a history of ingestion of undercooked pork, a positive Trichinella intradermal test, and a muscle biopsy demonstrating the encysted organism.

Other parasitic infestations may involve muscle more or less dramatically; *Taenia solium* is implicated in multifocal deposition of calcium at the sites of encystment in skeletal muscle. Myopathy has been reported in association with Toxoplasma infections but is rarely clinically manifest in children.

MYOPATHIES AND SPECIFIC METABOLIC DISORDERS

Glycolytic and Glycosynthetic Disorders of Muscle

A variety of myopathic disorders are based on enzymatic deficiencies affecting the synthesis and breakdown of glycogen. These result in a greater or

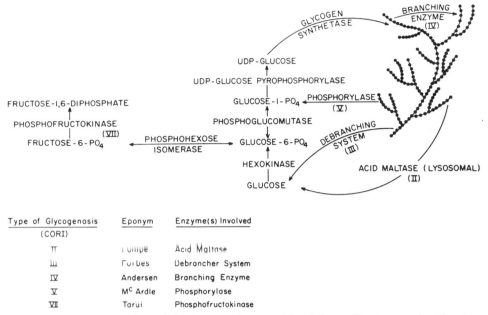

Type of Glycogenosis (CORI)	Eponym	Enzyme(s) Involved
II	Pompe	Acid Maltase
III	Forbes	Debrancher System
IV	Andersen	Branching Enzyme
V	M^C Ardle	Phosphorylase
VII	Tarui	Phosphofructokinase

Figure 11–11   Disorders of glycogen synthesis and breakdown affecting muscle. The sites of enzymatic deficiency are indicated in Roman numerals. Steps in glycosynthesis and glycolysis are indicated by arrows. (Courtesy of Dr. John F. Nicholson, Columbia University College of Physicians and Surgeons. From Chutorian, A. M., and Koenigsberger, M. R.: Myopathies associated with specific metabolic disorders. In *Brennemann's Practice of Pediatrics.* Vol. IV, Chap. 39B, p. 2. Hagerstown, Md., Harper & Row, 1972. Reprinted with permission.)

lesser accumulation of muscle glycogen, which may be normal or abnormal in structure (Fig. 11–11).

ACID MALTASE DEFICIENCY

Patients with acid maltase deficiency (Pompe's disease, Cori type II disease, alpha-1-4 glucosidase deficiency) vary greatly in age of onset, severity, and rate of progression of their disorder. Infantile, late infantile, juvenile, and adult patients have been identified with and without cardiac involvement and with rapidly fatal or slowly progressive courses. The patients with later onset disease tend to be less severely affected. This is especially evident in the adult, the accumulation of glycogen in muscle being relatively less marked. There is no apparent correlation between the severity of the disorder and the quantitative enzyme deficiency.

The best known type of acid maltase deficiency is the rapidly progressive infantile type associated with massive cardiomegaly. The disorder is inherited as an autosomal recessive trait. The infant may appear to develop normally for the first two to four months, but then develops impressive weakness and hypotonia, soon followed by respiratory distress and cardiac failure.

Examination discloses an inactive infant in the frog-leg position. Respiratory distress may be evident. A systolic murmur is usually heard, and percussion demonstrates cardiomegaly. The liver is enlarged, and incipient or overt cardiac failure is often present. The tongue is characteristically enlarged and may protrude. Bulbar difficulty is manifest as an impairment in swallowing with accumulation of pharyngeal secretions and a depressed gag reflex. Weakness and hypotonia are profound, and the deep tendon reflexes are depressed or absent.

The creatine phosphokinase level may be mildly elevated. Myopathic features are seen on the electromyogram, and myotonic potentials occur. These have also been recorded in the newborn siblings of affected patients. Fibrillations may occur. Chest x-ray confirms the cardiomegaly, and the electrocardiogram shows a characteristic high-amplitude QRS complex with depression of the ST segment and inversion of the T wave. Muscle biopsy shows glycogen accumulation in myofibrillar vacuoles (on light microscopy with the use of Best's carmine stain after fixing in absolute alcohol), and quantitative chemical analysis reveals abnormal accumulation of glycogen. Absence of alpha-1-4 glucosidase in muscle tissue can be demonstrated by appropriate assay.[18] Acid maltase may occasionally be present in the leukocytes while absent in muscle tissue.

The late infantile or early childhood form of acid maltase deficiency has not been sufficiently studied to give a composite clinical picture. Children have been encountered with and without cardiomegaly or visceromegaly and with and without pseudohypertrophy of muscle. Their weakness is similar to that of most other myopathies, being principally evident in the shoulder and pelvic girdles. Impaired anal sphincter tone, which has been described in this disorder, is not characteristically seen in other myopathies. Differentiation from Duchenne's muscular dystrophy on clinical grounds may not be possible. If present, cardiomegaly revealed by chest x-ray and cardiopathy by electrocardiogram are suggestive, as are myotonic discharges on the electromyogram and the muscle biopsy changes described. Enzyme assay establishes the diagnosis. The course may only be slowly progressive, indicating the prognostic importance of differentiating this disorder from Duchenne's muscular dystrophy and other myopathies.

DEBRANCHER ENZYME DEFICIENCY

This disorder (amylo-1,6-glucosidase deficiency, limit dextrinosis) is inherited in an autosomal recessive manner and is manifest in early infancy by hepatomegaly and failure to thrive. Hypotonia and proximal muscle weakness may occur and cause delay in motor development. Severe myopathy is rare. Muscle pain following exercise may occur without associated myoglobinuria.

The electromyogram reveals myopathic changes, and muscle tissue shows increased glycogen content of abnormal chemical structure, associated with amylo-1,6-glucosidase deficiency, which can be assayed from a preparation of leukocytes.

BRANCHER ENZYME DEFICIENCY

The hallmark of this disorder (amylo-1,4, → 1,6-transglucosidase deficiency) is progressive cirrhosis, heralded by growth failure and hepatosplenomegaly. Although hypotonia and delayed motor development occur, muscle disease per se has not clearly been established.

MYOPHOSPHORYLASE DEFICIENCY

Myophosphorylase deficiency (McArdle's disease) is inherited in an autosomal recessive fashion. The affected child fatigues easily and may have muscle cramps during exercise. However, persistent weakness may not develop and, in the asymptomatic state, no abnormality is observed on routine neurological examination. Repetitive muscle contraction under ischemic conditions (produced by a sphygmomanometer cuff placed over the upper arm and inflated to occlude arterial flow while the hand is forcibly and repeatedly clenched) causes a painful, sustained contracture of the forearm flexor muscles. This occurs within a minute of commencing the exercise and gradually disappears after deflation of the cuff and following a period of rest. If serial determinations of venous lactic acid are made, absence of the normal increase in lactic acid is evident, as the conversion of glycogen to glucose-1-phosphate is blocked by myophosphorylase deficiency.

Serum enzyme activity is normal at rest, but may increase with exercise. Nonspecific degeneration of muscle may be seen on routine light microscopy, and glycogen deposition is seen with appropriate stains. Electron microscopy indicates that the chief abnormality occurs in the region of the I-band; glycogen accumulates in the subsarcolemmal region and between the myofibrils. Definitive diagnosis requires assay of muscle tissue for myophosphorylase.

PHOSPHOFRUCTOKINASE DEFICIENCY

This disorder is inherited in autosomal recessive fashion. As in McArdle's disease, early fatigue occurs with exercise. Muscle cramps may occur, and myoglobinuria has been reported after severe exercise.

Developmental milestones are normal, and no abnormal findings are noted on routine neurological examination. Forearm muscle contracture can be induced by performing exercise under ischemic conditions in a manner similar to that described for the patient with McArdle's disease. The serum lactic acid concentration does not increase with ischemic exercise.

The serum creatine phosphokinase level may be elevated. Electromyography at rest may be normal, but repetitive stimulation has been shown to produce muscle action potentials of decreased amplitude. Muscle tissue obtained at biopsy shows increased glycogen content, the latter being normal in structure. Phosphofructokinase deficiency causes increase of glucose-6-phosphate and fructose-6-phosphate and decrease of pyruvate and lactate.

OTHER GLYCOLYTIC DISORDERS OF MUSCLE

Phosphoglucomutase deficiency results in a defect in anaerobic glycolysis that has been demonstrated in vitro. This disorder was observed in an infant who presented with paroxysmal tachycardia and required digitalization.

The child was otherwise normal until the age of two and a half years, when toe walking was first noted. Examination revealed some calf pseudohypertrophy, Achilles tendon contractures, and generalized mild weakness. Serum enzyme levels were elevated and the electromyogram revealed myopathic features. Deficient rise in lactic acid on ischemic exercise led to in vitro studies of anaerobic glycolysis, which revealed multiple defects in enzyme activity, particularly in phosphoglucomutase. Muscle biopsy showed increased amounts of glycogen having a normal chemical configuration.

Muscle pain and tenderness on exercise, beginning in childhood but unrecognized as a myopathy until adult life, has been ascribed, at least in one family, to phosphohexoisomerase deficiency. Lactic acid failed to increase on ischemic exercise, but in vitro glycolysis proceeded after the addition of fructose-6-phosphate. Possible inhibition of phosphohexoisomerase was suggested by the normal activity of the enzyme on assay. The clinical picture is not defined. The neurological examination and electromyogram are both unrevealing. Ischemic exercise produces only muscle tenderness and firmness, but no sustained contraction.

Periodic Paralysis

Paroxysmal weakness due to a muscle disorder is sufficiently uncommon to cause clinical confusion with epilepsy and hypoglycemia. A careful history will disclose the absence of involuntary movements and the absence of adrenergic responses such as pallor, tachycardia, and diaphoresis. This should prompt the suspicion of myogenic periodic weakness. As a rule, recovery from periodic paralysis is spontaneous and complete, and although weakness may at times be profound, life is rarely threatened.

FAMILIAL HYPOKALEMIC PERIODIC PARALYSIS

This disorder occurs more commonly in males than in females and is inherited in a dominant fashion. Typically, the disorder is first manifest in the second decade of life. However, it has been known to commence in infancy as well as in the young adult.

Excessive carbohydrate or salt ingestion may precipitate an attack; this typically occurs at rest, following exercise. The frequency of episodes is highly variable; they may be incapacitating, owing to daily occurrence, or relatively trivial with months of freedom from episodes punctuated by a transient attack. The attacks tend to occur at night or in the early morning, although they may occur at any time. Attacks have lasted from several hours to several days, but typically last less than a day.

In the interval between attacks the physical examination is normal, although in rare instances a persistent myopathy occurs. During an episode, flaccid weakness with striking diminution or absence of deep tendon reflexes is found. Myotonia of the eyelids may be elicited, while percussion myotonia of the tongue and thenar eminence are much more likely to occur in hyperkalemic paralysis.

The serum potassium usually ranges between 2 and 3 mEq/L. Normal values may be found during a mild attack. Electrocardiographic confirmation of hypokalemia may be helpful. The typical electrocardiographic changes seen in this condition consist of Q-T prolongation and T wave depression and inversion. The electromyogram shows an increase in polyphasic and short-duration units. A vacuolar myopathy with or without hyaline degeneration is at times demonstrated by muscle biopsy. The vacuoles, as revealed by electron microscopy, occur in the sarcoplasmic reticulum and probably consist of water, which does increase in the intracellular compartment during an attack. It should be noted that this vacuolar change is also seen in hyperkalemic and normokalemic myopathies. Intracellular potassium does not increase during an attack. The pathogenesis of the weakness is unknown. The contractile mechanism of electrically inexcitable fibers can be activated by calcium delivered directly to the myofilament spaces, suggesting that the defect is in the muscle membrane and that the abnormality probably affects the release of calcium from the sarcoplasmic reticulum.

When the clinical and laboratory features are atypical, especially if the serum potassium is normal or equivocal, provocative testing may be warranted. Under these conditions, an oral glucose load of 50 mg per square meter of body surface area may be administered over 15 minutes, together with insulin (10 units per square meter of body surface area). This should be preceded and followed by hourly serum sodium, potassium, and glucose determinations, frequent evaluations of muscle strength and reflexes, and electrocardiographic monitoring for hypokalemic changes. Although respiratory weakness is exceedingly rare, it should be anticipated and preparations made to assist respiration artificially.

Effective treatment is available for the acute episode in the form of potassium chloride, the serial administration of which should be monitored by repeated evaluation of muscle strength and deep tendon reflexes, serum potassium determinations, and electrocardiography. Attacks can be prevented by limitation of carbohydrates, salt, and strenuous exercise. Acetazolamide and spironolactone have proved effective as prophylactic drugs. Paradoxically, the former drug is also helpful for the prevention of attacks in hyperkalemic paralysis.

Persistent myopathy is uncommon; in fact there is often progressive waning of attacks after adolescence.

The differential diagnosis includes other forms of periodic paralysis that are discussed later. Renal disease should always be considered even when gross renal function is normal, remembering that either acidosis or alkalosis may accompany the hypokalemia of renal disease and that weakness may occur only periodically.

FAMILIAL HYPERKALEMIC PERIODIC PARALYSIS

This disorder (adynamia episodica hereditaria), which typically begins in the first decade, is also inherited in an autosomal dominant manner.

Attacks are generally more frequent but of shorter duration than the attacks of hypokalemic paralysis; multiple weekly episodes of less than two hours' duration are common. Daytime attacks are more characteristic of hyperkalemic paralysis, but nocturnal episodes also occur. As in hypokalemic paralysis, episodes tend to be precipitated during rest, following a period of exercise. Exposure to cold may precipitate or aggravate an attack, but ingestion of carbohydrate does not. The affected individual may complain of paresthesias of the extremities as an attack begins. As in hypokalemic paralysis, the weakness typically "ascends," the legs being affected first.

In the interictal period weakness is usually absent and the deep tendon reflexes are present. However, calf pseudohypertrophy may occur, and myotonia of the eyelids, tongue, and thenar eminence can often be demonstrated. Myotonia may be produced by the application of ice to the tongue or facial muscle.

During an attack, diffuse weakness occurs, with variable alteration of the deep tendon reflexes. These may, however, be preserved in the face of impressive weakness. Proximal preponderance of weakness is the rule.

Serum potassium is increased during an attack; levels of 5 to 6 mEq/L being suggestive of the diagnosis. A transient rise in the serum potassium level can be missed. Thus, normal potassium values should not be considered to rule out the disorder, but should prompt more frequent serial sampling in anticipation of and during a subsequent attack. Electrocardiographic confirmation of hyperkalemia may be obtained, the principal change consisting of a high peaked T wave.

Urinary excretion of potassium does not decrease during an attack, as it does when hyperkalemia occurs on the basis of renal disease. Renal function studies are, however, mandatory whenever hyperkalemia is present. In addition, normal serum sodium values should be documented to confirm the absence of hypoadrenalism.

Electromyography during an episode of weakness typically shows increased insertional activity, fibrillations, and myotonic discharges. Other myopathic features also occur. Muscle biopsy may reveal a vacuolar myopathy and degenerative changes as encountered in hypokalemic paralysis.

Provocative diagnostic testing should be considered if the typical clinical and laboratory features are absent, especially if the serum potassium value during an attack is normal or equivocal. In such cases, cautious administration of oral potassium is warranted. Beginning with a trial of 2 gm, subsequent attempts to provoke an attack may be made by increased increments of 1 gm until as high a dose as 10 gm per square meter of body surface area is administered in a single dose. In the rare event that a hyperkalemic crisis is precipitated in this manner, intravenous 10 per cent calcium gluconate can be used to abort the attack.

Intravenous sodium chlorothiazide can also be used to treat an induced or spontaneous hyperkalemic crisis, although the attacks terminate spontaneously for the most part. Acetazolamide and chlorothiazide have both been effective as prophylactic therapy. Avoidance of exposure to cold and warming during a mild attack may be helpful. Gentle exercise after exertion may ward off the attacks, which typically occur during complete rest after exercise.

Paramyotonia congenita is probably not a separate entity, inasmuch as the clinical features do not differ appreciably. Features that have been emphasized under this heading include myotonia induced by cooling and paradoxic myotonia, i.e., aggravation of myotonia with exercise, without impressive change in serum potassium values.

OTHER FORMS OF HYPOKALEMIC AND
HYPERKALEMIC ACUTE OR PERIODIC WEAKNESS

Hypokalemic attacks of muscle weakness may occur in children with primary aldosteronism, adrenal hyperplasia, licorice-induced hypokalemia, hypokalemic states associated with renal disease, gastroenteric disorders, iatrogenic disturbance of electrolyte and fluid balance, and thyrotoxicosis. In these conditions hypokalemia is the common disturbance, but the precipitating factors and clinical features in each disorder differ appreciably. Aldosteronism is characterized by hypertension, alkalosis, hypokalemia, and hypernatremia. These features also characterize licorice-induced hypokalemia, but although urine excretion is not increased.

Potassium wasting associated with renal disease is usually characterized by symptoms and signs of chronic illness, with persistent weakness in addition to more dramatic episodes of weakness that may occur. Laboratory investigation of renal function should permit the identification of renal disease.

In general, the disorders described present acutely or chronically rather than paroxysmally. The occurrence of flaccid muscle paresis may, however, be sufficiently dramatic to overshadow the features of the primary illness. Severe gastroenteric depletion of potassium has resulted in sufficient rhabdomyolysis to produce myoglobinuria.

Hypokalemic attacks of weakness occur in thyrotoxicosis. Extensive study of this disorder has revealed increased CPK in the attack-free interval, with further elevation of CPK values during an attack. Serum potassium is depressed, but sodium content is normal. The electromyogram shows myopathic features. Routine examination of muscle biopsy tissue is unrewarding, but electron microscopy shows vesicular changes in the I and Z bands and, at times, myofibrillar vacuolization. Paralytic attacks are alleviated by control of the thyrotoxic state.

FAMILIAL "NORMOKALEMIC" PERIODIC
PARALYSIS

It seems that this disorder is distinct in some respects from familial hypokalemic and hyperkalemic periodic paralysis. The distinguishing characteristics consist primarily of the normal serum potassium levels during an attack, the propensity for paralytic episodes to be alleviated by the ingestion of sodium chloride, and the prolonged duration of attacks. As has already been indicated, the serum potassium need not be depressed or elevated in the classic forms of periodic paralysis, which may require comprehensive investigation to establish the diagnosis.

The autosomal dominant inheritance and certain precipitating features are similar to both hypokalemic and hyperkalemic periodic paralysis. However, the unfavorable response to potassium and alleviation of the attacks by administration of sodium chloride in combination with prolonged infrequent episodes of early onset appears to be unique; provocation of an attack with potassium chloride is characteristic of hyperkalemic paralysis and early onset of prolonged infrequent episodes is more typical of hypokalemic paralysis. Moreover, the attacks may be impressively protracted, lasting several days to several weeks. There is no myotonia or pseudohypertrophy.

In the acute attack, paralysis may be complete or sufficiently mild to permit impaired activity. The severe phase lasts several days and typically is followed by several weeks of residual weakness. Examination reveals no abnormality between attacks. Early in the course of an attack, muscle stiffness occurs, but it gradually gives way to flaccid paralysis as the attack progresses. Weakness characteristically ascends, involving the legs first. The muscles of mastication may be involved, but bulbar and respiratory functions are not grossly affected.

Results of serum enzyme studies, electromyography, and muscle biopsy do not differ from those described for familial hypokalemic and hyperkalemic paralysis—with the exception of the absence of myotonic features and the presence of large motor units, which raises the question of an associated neurogenic component. This disorder is compatible with long survival and normal activity in the intervals between attacks. Attacks become fewer and less severe during young adult life in some patients.

The acute attack is not helped by calcium gluconate, is aggravated by potassium chloride, and is relieved by the administration of sodium chloride. Prophylaxis is effected by the administration of a high salt diet and 9-alpha-fluorohydrocortisone and acetazolamide.

DECREASED RELAXING FACTOR

This disorder is characterized by muscle stiffening on sudden rapid motion or vigorous exercise. The phenomenon is probably due to decreased ability of the sarcoplasmic reticulum to accumulate calcium ions. The disorder has been described in adults who were able to date the onset of symptoms to as early an age as five years. The stiffness disappears in these individuals after a few seconds of rest. It occurs more readily in cold weather and involves the facial as well as limb musculature.

The findings on examination at rest are normal. Only 10 to 15 seconds of repetitive muscle contraction with maximal effort produces brief paralysis of the muscle in its contracted state. Pain occurs only if effort to contract the shortened muscle is continued. This exercise intolerance is aggravated by lower temperature, but not by ischemic exercise.

Electromyography shows normal insertional activity during muscle shortening, followed by electrical silence. Tension myography shows progressive slowing of relaxation with continued exercise. Muscle biopsy tissue thus far has appeared normal. Muscle glycogen content and phosphorylase activity are normal. Microsomal uptake of labeled calcium has been shown to be diminished, and it is postulated that persistent aqueous calcium in high concentration prolongs myofibrillar shortening.

A form of "myokymia" usually beginning in the second decade of life, in which muscle stiffness and delayed relaxation occur, is distinguished from the disorder characterized by "decreased relaxing factor" on the basis of electrical studies. Electromyography in this form of myokymia shows prolonged involuntary bursts of repetitive units resembling motor unit action potentials. Occasional true myotonic discharges occur. Blockage of neuromuscular transmission abolishes the activity, suggesting that the defect in this form of myokymia is in the distal nerve fiber or motor end plate.

Endocrine Myopathies

MYOPATHIES ASSOCIATED WITH THYROID DYSFUNCTION

Thyrotoxic Myopathy. Chronic weakness in children with hyperthyroidism, although uncommon, is more recognized than the periodic weakness associated with hypokalemia in thyrotoxic states. There is a preponderance of female patients with hyperthyroidism, and the peak age incidence is adolescence, although the disorder does occur in infants and young children.

The usual symptoms and signs of hyperthyroidism dominate the picture and include tachycardia, excessive diaphoresis (especially nocturnal), tremulousness and emotional lability, eyelid retraction, wide pulse pressure, and enlargement of the thyroid gland associated with an audible and palpable thyroid bruit. Although myopathic signs and symptoms are obscured by this dramatic syndrome, at times weakness is sufficiently severe to interfere with such functions as rising from the supine or seated position and climbing stairs.

On examination, weakness is either maximal in or limited to the proximal muscles of the trunk and extremities, which may be wasted. The deep tendon reflexes are preserved. In mild cases, weakness may be absent or equivocal, although the electromyogram can show myopathic features.

Serum creatine phosphokinase (CPK) may be normal or modestly increased. Muscle biopsy tissue may be normal or may reveal subtle nonspecific changes. Electron microscopic data are sparse, but have shown mitochondrial changes and alterations of questionable significance involving the tubules and muscle fiber surface. Thyroid function studies establish the diagnosis.

The myopathy clears with restoration of the euthyroid state.

Hypothyroid Myopathy. Subtle changes of muscular function occur typically in hypothyroidism even when weakness is minimal or absent. These changes characteristically consist of hypotonia and delayed muscle contraction and relaxation ("hung-up" deep tendon reflexes).

The cretinous infant presents with a multitude of classic signs. These include inactivity, slow growth and development, constipation, dry skin, hoarse cry, sparse hair, and typical facies with depressed nasal bridge and flattened nares. On occasion, a striking muscular hypertrophy occurs (Debré-Semelaigne syndrome). The muscles are firm to palpation, but weakness and delayed contraction and relaxation are evident.

Serum enzyme activity is increased. The electromyogram is usually normal, but nerve conduction studies may reveal carpal or tarsal tunnel syndromes. Routine microscopic examination of muscle biopsy tissue has been disappointing, but a vacuolar myopathy has been seen in acquired hypothyroidism. Electron microscopic changes have included myofibrillar and mitochondrial alterations and reticular and lipopigmentary changes. The diagnosis is established by thyroid function studies.

Therapeutic restoration of the euthyroid state corrects the myopathy, with return of CPK levels to normal.

HYPERPARATHYROIDISM

Gait difficulty and generalized weakness with proximal preponderance may be encountered in hyperparathyroidism. In the usual situation, there is no impairment of deep tendon reflexes although signs of proximal muscle weakness are present.

While serum calcium is usually elevated and phosphorus decreased, impressive osteoporosis may preclude elevation of serum calcium and has resulted in delay in the search for a parathyroid adenoma. The CPK may be normal, but electromyography usually shows myopathic features. Muscle biopsy shows little alteration, but may reveal slight nonspecific myopathic changes.

Surgical excision of the parathyroid adenoma results in gradual remission of the myopathy.

HYPERADRENAL MYOPATHY

Myopathy occurs in Cushing's syndrome on the basis of endogenous hyperadrenal states as well as exogenous steroid excess. The latter has occurred with chronic steroid therapy for a variety of disorders.

Weakness is proximal for the most part and may be only mildly incapacitating, but can progress to total incapacitation. The deep tendon reflexes may be preserved, diminished, or absent.

Serum enzyme activity tends to be normal. Electromyography may or may not reveal myopathic abnormalities, and in similar fashion, nonspecific myopathic abnormalities are variable in muscle biopsy tissue. More impressive changes have been noted on electron microscopy, including abnormal sarcolemmal projections and vacuolated mitochrondria.

Treatment directed toward the specific cause of the hyperadrenal state results in gradual resolution of the myopathy.

MISCELLANEOUS DISORDERS OF MUSCLE

Myoglobinuria

Clinical Features.   Myoglobinuria occurs in a variety of myopathic states and is most likely to occur when the insult to muscle is acute. It is accompanied by pain, with weakness or contractures or both of the affected muscles. The urinary excretion of myoglobin gives the urine a dark brown color and occurs within several hours of the acute symptoms. Systemic symptoms may occur, e.g., chills, fever, and abdominal pain.

Examination during the symptomatic period shows muscle tenderness and weakness with or without hyporeflexia. Limitation of motion in a child with muscle pain and tenderness may create an impression of greater weakness than is actually present. With greater degrees of rhabdomyolysis, firm swelling may be appreciated.

Laboratory Features. Spectrophotometric analysis of the urine will distinguish myoglobin from hemoglobin and porphyrin; the latter is ruled out if the urine pigment is guaiac positive.

Serum creatine phosphokinase is increased shortly after an attack; the electromyogram shows myopathic changes. It is, however, contraindicated in the symptomatic state. Muscle biopsy may or may not reveal muscle necrosis.

Idiopathic Myoglobinuria. This designation implies a myoglobinuric disorder of muscle that has not been etiologically characterized. The number of such disorders has progressively diminished as the list of defined metabolic derangements of muscle grows. Sporadic cases of idiopathic myoglobinuria occur, and a familial form of paroxysmal myoglobinuria has been described in which the metabolic defect is not characteristic of any of the known enzymatic defects that have been discussed elsewhere in this chapter.[12]

Symptomatic Myoglobinuria. In addition to the disorders already described as being associated with myoglobinuria (glycolytic enzyme defects and hypokalemia due to licorice ingestion or gastroenteric disease), a number of pharmacological agents and toxins are capable of producing myoglobinuria (e.g., barbiturates, succinylcholine, amphotericin B, carbon monoxide, snake venom, and the toxin from eels). Rhabdomyolysis resulting from physical injury occurs in direct trauma, burns, and convulsive seizures. Ischemic necrosis of muscle due to vascular occlusion can also produce myoglobinuria.

Course and Prognosis. Recovery is spontaneous, but may take several weeks when the insult is severe and widespread. Massive myoglobinuria can in rare instances produce renal failure due to renal tubular necrosis or respiratory failure due to severe involvement of the respiratory muscles. In general, the prognosis is good; it depends upon the degree of involvement and the underlying cause of rhabdomyolysis.

Myotonia Congenita

Myotonia congenita (Thomsen's disease) is a benign disorder characterized by either dominant inheritance or sporadic occurrence of generalized muscular hypertrophy and myotonia. Approximately 50 per cent of cases are sporadic.

The muscular hypertrophy and myotonia may not be appreciated until the child is four or five years of age, but many cases can be retrospectively dated to the first or second year of life. The myotonia causes difficulty with rapid initiation of movements or release of objects; it improves with repeated exercise of the involved muscles, but is aggravated by cold. The difficulty with movements is often ascribed to clumsiness.

On examination, the muscular hypertrophy is usually apparent and may be rather striking. Percussion myotonia is best demonstrated by percussing the thenar eminence, tongue, or suprascapular muscles, and delayed relaxation of muscle is best appreciated by the delay in releasing a hand grip. Myotonia of the eyelids may be manifested by delay in opening of the eyes after forced eye closure, but this is the least reliable sign of myotonia, as it occurs in some normal individuals. There is little or no muscle weakness, and the deep tendon reflexes are normal.

Serum enzymes are normal. The electromyogram confirms the clinical myotonia. Muscle biopsy is of little importance, as only hypertrophied fibers and occasional central nuclei are seen, the specimen usually appearing normal.

The disorder may appear to worsen somewhat until after puberty and then lessens in severity. It never becomes incapacitating. Symptomatic relief is afforded by quinine therapy.

STRUCTURAL DEFECTS OF MUSCLE ("CONGENITAL" MYOPATHIES)

The "congenital" myopathies become manifest in infancy or very early childhood. This feature, however, is not unique, as a number of the so-called dystrophic myopathies and myasthenic and metabolic disorders share this feature with the "congenital" myopathies. Some of the disorders in this group are progressive while others are not. Some are compatible with long-term survival while others, even with apparently identical genetic and histopathological features, have led to early death. It is thus difficult to justify the inclusion of these disorders under a single category. This is done chiefly on the basis of common usage of terminology. Most of the conditions grouped under this heading are of relatively recent recognition, and it is only in the past 5 to 10 years that the mechanisms underlying them were comprehensively investigated.

Perhaps the most important characteristic that the congenital myopathies share in common is that they possess more or less characteristic histopathological features. Other common but less distinctive features include their heredofamilial nature and early onset. These myopathies are frequently named after their corresponding distinguishing histopathological features. Because of the relatively recent recognition of the disorders and the paucity of patients in each category, however, the true incidence, principal clinical features, and long-range prognosis in some instances remain indeterminate.

Central Core Myopathy

The "central core" in this disorder refers to the abnormal histological appearance of a core of tissue in the center of the muscle fiber. Inheritance occurs in an autosomal dominant manner. Patients with central core myopathy are hypotonic at birth or in early infancy. True weakness is suggested by the impressive delay in motor development, affecting all milestones except those of motor function that show a greater correlation with mental development, namely, ocular and manual functions. Ambulation may be delayed several years.

Weakness is manifest chiefly in the proximal limb musculature and primarily affects functions requiring fixation and power in the pelvic and proximal thigh muscles, i.e., rising from the lying or seated position and climbing. The degree of weakness may be severe, but does not prevent antigravity functions. Muscular atrophy is not prominent. The facial and ocular muscles are spared. The deep tendon reflexes are intact and may be of normal vigor and amplitude or diminished to some extent. Hip dislocation may be present.

Serum enzyme activity is normal. The changes characteristic of myopathy are seen on electromyography. Histological studies on the muscle show a central core of abnormally staining material, if care is taken to fix the tissue properly (saline and Bouin's fluid) (Fig. 11–12A). The central core tissue, evident with routine hematoxylin and eosin stain, is shown to better advantage with trichrome stain. In central core myopathy oxidative enzyme and phosphorylase activity is absent from this area when the tissue is studied histochemically. This has been correlated, by electron microscopic examination, with decrease in both sarcoplasmic reticulum and mitochondria in the core.

The outlook for long-term survival is good. In fact, there is no evidence that weakness is progressive. The occasional occurrence of scoliosis in later childhood or adult life probably reflects the unequal action of mature paraspinal muscles rather than progression of the disease.

The differential diagnosis is extensive; it includes those disorders that are manifest as hypotonia and weakness in infancy. The family history is helpful, but should not substitute for examination of the parents and siblings. Infants with spinal muscular atrophy rarely show intact deep tendon reflexes. Other congenital myopathies are identified in some instances by their clinical features but more specifically by the findings on muscle biopsy. The diagnosis is

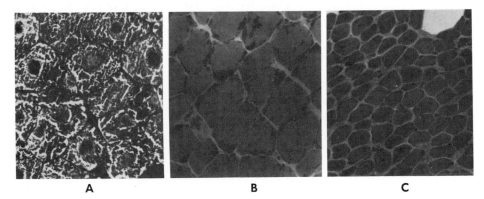

A   **B**   **C**

Figure 11–12   *A*. Central core disease. The muscle fibers contain a central core with altered staining characteristics. Trichrome, × 350. *B*. Rod myopathy. Rodlike structures are situated near the periphery of many muscle fibers. Trichrome, × 350. *C*. Centronuclear myopathy. Many muscle fibers contain central nuclei. Trichrome, ×350. (Courtesy of Dr. Donald Schotland, University of Pennsylvania. From Chutorian, A. M., and Koenigsberger, M. R.: In *Brennemann's Practice of Pediatrics.* Vol. IV, Chap. 39A, p. 2. Hagerstown, Md., Harper & Row, 1972. Reprinted with permission.)

suspected because of absence of progression of weakness or involvement of the facial and ocular muscles, but in the main depends on muscle biopsy.

Nemaline Myopathy

This myopathy derives its name from the nematoid (threadlike) appearance of structures seen within the muscle fiber on histological examination. The disorder is inherited as an autosomal dominant trait. The specificity of the disorder is in question to some extent inasmuch as coexistence of central core and nemaline material has been described and nemaline bodies have been seen in adult patients with myopathy of late onset. Nevertheless, there does appear to be a characteristic clinical profile.

Symptoms are manifest at birth or in early infancy by poor sucking and generalized hypotonia and weakness. Subsequent motor development is delayed, and diffuse weakness with the usual postural and gait abnormalities due to proximal preponderance of weakness are encountered. In addition, facial weakness and weakness of the sternocleidomastoid muscles are present. The deep tendon reflexes may be preserved, but more typically are diminished or absent. Generalized muscle wasting produces the illusion of slender elongation of trunk, limbs, and facies.

Short stature, high-arched palate and dental malocclusion, webbed neck, kyphoscoliosis, pectus excavatum, pes cavus, and simian palmar creases have all occurred with increased frequency in nemaline myopathy.

The severity of involvement is variable. Some patients appear to have a nonprogressive disorder, while others do not. Rare infantile deaths have occurred. For the most part, the disorder is static or slowly progressive.

Serum enzyme activity is normal. Myopathic changes are seen on the electromyogram. Muscle biopsy tissue on trichrome staining shows aggregates of reddish rods arranged randomly or in palisades, which on electron microscopy are found to correspond with Z band abnormality (Fig. 11–12B).

Centronuclear (Myotubular) Myopathy

This disorder derives its name from the central placement of the muscle nuclei and the associated absence of subsarcolemmal nuclei, which produce a perinuclear defect bearing resemblance to the normal myotubular stage of embryological muscle.

The disease is inherited in an autosomal recessive manner. It may become manifest either in infancy or in later childhood.

The striking involvement of the eyelids and extraocular muscles in most of the patients distinguishes this disorder from the other congenital myopathies and, indeed, from most other myopathies.[5] Generalized weakness and wasting occur. Facial weakness has been observed in approximately half the patients. The deep tendon reflexes are uniformly absent in infants and children with the disorder.

Convulsive seizures have been reported in a few patients in whom cerebral function and mentation was otherwise intact.

The disorder is progressive. In the infantile form, bulbar and respiratory weakness may cause recurrent cyanosis, pulmonary infection, and death. In the later childhood form a similar distribution of weakness, facial and ocular involvement, and absence of deep tendon reflexes are seen, and progression of weakness is observed in those children who have been followed for several years.

The serum creatine phosphokinase activity may be increased or normal. Clear-cut but modest increases occur (i.e., 50 to 300 units). Electromyography has failed, in some of the older children, to reveal significant abnormalities, but in one patient, myopathic discharges have been recorded in the absence of any clinical myotonic features.

Muscle biopsy tissue shows centrally located muscle nuclei with a clear surrounding area due to absence of sarcomere material (Fig. 11-14). Histochemical study has revealed the absence of myofibrils in the central region (negative adenosine triphosphatase reactions). Type I fiber hypotrophy has been described in association with central nuclei.[10]

Mitochondrial Myopathies

Mitochondral abnormalities require electron microscopic identification. Structural changes and alteration in the mitochondrial count have been noted. However, these are not unique histological findings, as they are also seen in several other disorders. The term "megaconial myopathy" was applied first to a congenital myopathic disorder in which large mitochondria were seen, and the term "pleoconial myopathy" was used to describe a child with periodic weakness whose muscle tissue showed increased numbers of enlarged mitochondria on electron microscopic examination.[30, 33]

The total number of patients that has been recorded to date is too small to justify a composite clinical picture, particularly since mitochondrial changes occur in neurogenic as well as various myopathic states.

Congenital Myopathy with Crystalline Intranuclear Inclusions

This disorder has been described in a flaccid areflexic neonate with respiratory difficulty and severe generalized weakness, who died of respiratory insufficiency at the age of eight weeks. There was no family history of neuromuscular disease.

Routine hematoxylin and eosin staining of skeletal muscles revealed crystalline nuclear inclusions, and sarcoplasmic crystals were seen with the use of special stains and electron microscopic examination. The sarcoplasmic rods had all the histochemical and ultrastructural characteristics of nemaline myopathy, and the nuclear inclusions were composed of material identical to that of the sarcoplasmic rods.

Other Structural Myopathies

A burgeoning number of myopathies are being reported, bearing titles that refer to their histological features. How specific these features will prove to be remains to be seen. These disorders include "reducing body myopathy" (so named because of abnormal bodies within muscle fibers, which are rich in sulfhydril groups and reduce some intermediate metabolites), "multicore disease" (a congenital myopathy characterized by multifocal degeneration of muscle fibers having mitochondrial abnormalities), lipid storage myopathy, congenital myopathy with fingerprint bodies, type I fiber hypotrophy, various fiber type disproportions, neuromuscular disorders associated with "ragged red fibers," and others. The disorders are thus far too few in number and insufficiently studied clinically to justify more than mention in this text.

MANAGEMENT

Drug Therapy

Unfortunately, specific treatment is not available for a number of the disorders described. However, the periodic paralyses, the endocrine myopathies, and the myopathies associated with electrolyte and toxic disturbances are amenable to specific therapy. These have been discussed where applicable in the appropriate sections.

Present concepts of the etiology and pathogenesis of Duchenne's muscular dystrophy are in a state of flux. There are preliminary indications that this disorder may not be a primary myopathy, but rather one in which the terminal nerve endings are involved, perhaps secondary to alterations in the microcirculation of muscle. There is some evidence to suggest that early and continuous treatment with a vasodilator substance, together with physical therapy aimed at improving peripheral blood flow and preventing stasis and microemboli, may be effective in slowing the development of the disability.

Exercise and Prevention of Contractures

The maintenance of function and the prevention of disability are the prime aims of all treatment. In the absence of effective specific chemotherapeutic agents, other means of achieving these goals become even more significant. These include range of motion exercises, surgery, bracing, maintenance of upper extremity function and performance of activities of daily living. Emphasis here is placed on the management of patients with Duchenne's muscular dystrophy in which the disability is severe, specific therapy unavailable, and life expectancy so shortened that it presents as a severe prototype of other chronic myopathies.

In the early phase of Duchenne's muscular dystrophy, weakness is the presenting sign and is responsible for alterations in posture and gait patterns. The program at this time is devoted to exercises designed to prevent contractures secondary to muscle imbalance and to strengthen weak muscle groups. It is during this early phase that physical therapeutic modalities are most likely to be effective in delaying the onset of severe disability. The program can be carried out at home as long as the family is responsible. An exercise regimen once or twice a day usually is sufficient, and the use of expensive devices or inordinately large amounts of time for this program is not warranted. It is important to document muscle strength and joint range of motion regularly. Functional tests such as timing the patient's ascent of several steps while recording the muscle patterns he employs are of practical value.

Active resistance exercises can usually maintain and possibly improve muscle strength, if the muscle is not severely involved, by causing hypertrophy of remaining intact muscle and decreasing disuse atrophy. Strength improves initially, but then usually reaches a plateau after about four months. Excessive fatigue should be avoided. The patient should be encouraged to keep active and the beneficial effects of normal play activities should not be neglected. Children with Duchenne's dystrophy should stand and walk for at least three hours a day to prevent disuse atrophy, to stretch contractures, and to preserve knee extension. During school months the child engages in less outdoor physical activity, and this associated with prolonged sitting may promote physical regression. It is especially important that a program designed to stretch the heel cords, hamstrings, and iliotibial band and hip flexors be emphasized (Figs. 11–13, 11–14, and 11–15).

Bracing

During the early phases of the disease the use of braces is usually not indicated and special shoes are, in most cases, of no value. As the disease

Figure 11–13   Passive stretching of heel cord. The knee is kept extended and the principal stretch is at the heel, minimizing the tendency for a "rocker bottom" foot. (From Vignos, P. J., Jr.: Progressive muscular dystrophy. *In* Licht, S.: *Rehabilitation and Medicine.* New Haven, Elizabeth Licht, Publisher, 1968, p. 609.)

Figure 11–14 Passive stretching of hamstrings. The contralateral side of the pelvis is stabilized to prevent lifting of the buttocks. (From Vignos, P. J., Jr.: Progressive muscular dystrophy. In Licht, S.: *Rehabilitation and Medicine.* New Haven, Elizabeth Licht, Publisher, 1968, p. 608.)

Figure 11–15 Passive stretching of the iliotibial band by pulling hip in toward examiner (adduction) while stabilizing the pelvis. Tight hip flexors are stretched by prone lying and by extending the hip as shown. (From Vignos, P. J., Jr.: Progressive muscular dystrophy. *In* Licht, S.: *Rehabilitation and Medicine.* New Haven, Elizabeth Licht, Publisher, 1968. p. 608.)

progresses the child eventually loses the ability to climb stairs. It is at this point that other means of support may be necessary, since ambulation is often lost within a year of this time. Strength is diminished, and the child may begin to fall. He becomes insecure about crossing large open areas and may walk holding on to walls or furniture for balance and support. Progressive postural changes are noted and characteristically include lordotic stance and equinus contractures of the feet secondary to a substitution pattern to compensate for weakening of the quadriceps and hip extensor muscles. Both the lumbar lordosis and the equinus position alter the center of gravity of the body so that it effectively falls in front of the knee, aiding extension and stability. Thus, these deformities constitute postural compensations for muscle weakness.[35] Attempts to correct the resultant contractures without substituting for the weak musculature are likely to prove disastrous, i.e., a heel cord release or lengthening may convert a patient who walks standing on his toes with an awkward gait into a nonwalker with normal range of heel motion unless suitable limitation be provided.

It is at this point in the more advanced stage of the disease, when the patient is having extreme difficulty in ambulating, that bracing may be of value. However, short leg braces per se usually have no effect in preventing heel cord contractures. Long leg braces may be more of a hindrance because of their added weight, the difficulty of donning them, and their failure to affect established hip and knee flexion contractures of more than a few degrees. Newer, lightweight, short leg orthoses such as posterior molded splints may be effective in improving the gait pattern or in delaying the onset of heel cord contractures, but will not correct fixed deformities. If the weakness is more distal a short leg brace may then be of considerable value in controlling foot drop and ankle instability. This is more commonly seen in adults than in children. Once a child is confined to a wheelchair the use of braces is rarely of any benefit.

Surgery

As implied in the foregoing discussion, it is usually only following surgery that bracing is effective in children with muscular dystrophy. By the age of 9 or 10 years most patients have contractures of sufficient severity to make them nonambulatory. After surgical correction of contractures, usually in conjunction with bracing postoperatively, ambulation can be maintained for about two or three years in a good number of patients. If surgery is performed the period of hospitalization should be kept to a minimum, and during this time physical deconditioning should be avoided as much as possible. Eyring et al. performed 54 therapeutic surgical operations on 17 patients. The procedures consisted of 14 percutaneous heel cord lengthenings, 17 iliotibial tract releases, and 23 posterior tibial tendon transfers.[11] The heel cord lengthening was performed on an outpatient basis but with the patient under general anesthesia in the operating room. Other procedures were performed during two-day hospital stays. The total hospital stays for all procedures averaged 1.5 days, and all patients began ambulation within 48 hours after surgery.[11]

If heel cord lengthening or tenotomy is performed when the quadriceps is weak, i.e., less than grade 3, long leg braces with knee locks will be required. Generalized weakness, as well as the necessity of locking the knees, prevents most patients from climbing stairs. It there is significant ankle varus deformity (turning in of the foot) a posterior tibial tendon transfer may be helpful. In this procedure the relatively strong posterior tibial muscle can be utilized by transferring the tendon through the interosseous membrane to the dorsum of the foot, thereby removing a major deforming force and possibly gaining active ankle dorsiflexion. In some patients who undergo this procedure bracing may not be required for a further period of time.

A tight tensor fascia lata (iliotibial band) contributes to the wide abducted gait, hip flexion contractures, and tight knee flexors. Tensor release, therefore, may result in a less abducted gait and reduce the severity of the hip flexion deformity. The literature is very sparse concerning the results of hip flexor releases although it has been reported that results are encouraging when combined with early ambulation. There appears in these cases to be some diminution of lordosis and improved postural stability and gait.

Surgery must always be followed up with a vigorous rehabilitation program of physical and occupational therapy. This may be done on an outpatient basis; however, transfer to a rehabilitation center may be advisable.

Wheelchair Use

In comparing the effect of "good" and "poor" care in Duchenne's muscular dystrophy, Demos showed that confinement to a wheelchair may be avoided until a mean age of 16 years in conjunction with a continuing good physical therapy program as opposed to a "poor" program in which patients enter the wheelchair at an average age of 9.5 years.[4] The use of a wheelchair in the early stages of the disease must be avoided as much as possible because it tends to accelerate deconditioning and promotes the development of hip flexion, knee flexion, and ankle equinovarus contractures. When the patient is incapable of extended walking, a wheelchair may be necessary so that he can participate in other activities and remain a part of the family. Of course, once the child becomes incapable of independent ambulation, a wheelchair is mandatory. Once placed in a wheelchair the patient tends to put on weight rapidly and this further interferes with his ability to function and makes it more difficult for others to help him. A proper diet, emphasizing adequate protein intake, is important.

The initial chair is often a lightweight folding chair; however, elevating leg rests enable the knees and ankles to be placed in a position other than flexion. A safety belt, desk arms, hand rim projections and brake lever extensions are of value (see Chapter 6, on spinal injury, for further details on wheelchair prescriptions). In addition to these attachments a wheelchair lap board will support the shoulders. A cushion may be necessary so that decubiti do not develop. Since shoulder strength is markedly diminished, balanced forearm orthoses (ball bearing feeders) can be tried by the occupational therapist. This will usually improve upper extremity function and with other appropriate appliances will permit the child to maintain a degree of independence in eating, grooming, school work, and the like. Once the disability is so severe that the child cannot propel his own wheelchair, an electric wheelchair may be of value although these are bulky and heavy, require frequent battery charging, and are prone to mechanical failure.

There are numerous other aids that facilitate independence and ease of management, and periodic evaluation is of benefit. Clothing adaptations, safety rails in the house, and lifts to assist in transferring the patient from the wheelchair to the bed or bath all tend to make life easier and bearable for the patient and his family.

Complications

Scoliosis. Scoliosis usually results from muscle imbalance, and the associated pelvic obliquity can result in an apparent leg length discrepancy that further interferes with walking in braces. Once the child is confined to a wheelchair, trunk musculature is quite weak and the scoliosis usually progresses. Rigid corseting makes mobilization extremely difficult, but in the advanced stage can enhance support. Care should be taken to see that respiration is not further compromised. Adequate rest periods in the recumbent position and proper support of posture in the wheelchair (at times with a reclining back) may at least reduce the rate of progression of deformity. Corrective surgery is rarely of benefit because the long period of immobilization required results in a greater deficit than the original deformity.

Cardiopulmonary Problems. The myocardium is usually involved in the degenerative process. There may be cardiomegaly and the electrocardiogram often shows a tachycardia and an abnormal QRS configuration with a tall right precordial R wave and lateral precordial Q waves. In spite of these findings the patient may be asymptomatic, although symptoms can appear relatively early in the course of the disease. Once heart failure appears the patient is treated in the usual way with cardiac glycosides, diuretics, and salt restriction. Death may be related to sudden arrhythmia.

Respiratory failure is another serious complication. As the condition progresses respiratory function deteriorates so that there is poor respiratory reserve. The vital capacity is usually markedly diminished. Breathing and coughing exercises should be encouraged, as pneumonia can be a serious complication.

Psychosocial Aspects

A number of these children may have mild or moderate mental retardation, but in addition to this serious emotional factors often play a role. The feelings of the child, as well as the parents, should be considered and their anxiety and depression controlled as much as possible. The family needs strong support, which it is the responsibility of those medical personnel dealing with the patient to provide. Psychiatric follow-up is often not feasible and the attending physician and social worker must assume this function. Intelligence tests aid in making realistic plans for the child's education. Attendance at local schools is advisable for as long as possible. When in school, activity should be encouraged to the extent of the patient's physical capacity. Later on, special schooling may be required. The Muscular Dystrophy Associations of America have many local chapters and may provide financial support for some medical care and adaptive equipment. They often have facilities for summer camps, workshops, and group family meetings.

Genetic counseling of the parents and their relatives must not be neglected. If there are other children they should be tested for the carrier trait by serum creatine phosphokinase determinations (it must be kept in mind that this will not pick up all carriers).

Other Myopathies

The later onset dystrophies and myopathies usually progress less rapidly than the Duchenne type and most patients will be ambulatory during the period of growth and public school education. The correct diagnosis is important for future vocational and social planning, as well as for genetic counseling. An exercise program designed to maintain strength is often initially of more importance than one emphasizing range of motion. In the inflammatory diseases of muscle, e.g., dermatomyositis, the muscles and joints may be very tender so that the patient does not permit joint motion. It is at this point that contractures are likely to develop. Protective splinting in a position of maximum function tends to minimize the severity of the pain and deformities. Gentle range of motion exercises, as tolerated, for a brief period daily will further decrease the likelihood of fixed deformities. Undue stressing of inflamed muscle is to be avoided; when the acute inflammatory stage is over a more vigorous program can be provided.

Adequate nutrition, the avoidance of overfatigue, and conversely avoidance of excessive inactivity should be stressed. Hamstring and heel cord tightness is common, and stretching exercises are of value. Weight control is important. Not only does increased weight impose greater stress on the cardiorespiratory system but also makes it more difficult for the patient with weakened musculature to function.

Thus it can be seen that the general principles involved in treating severe chronic myopathies are similar. Range of motion must be maintained, disuse atrophy prevented, bracing utilized when it will be advantageous, indiscriminate surgery avoided, and adaptive devices and appliances used to maintain function for as long as possible.

References

1. Adams, R., Denny-Brown, D., and Pearson, C.: *Diseases of Muscle. A Study in Pathology.* New York, Hoeber & Harper, 1962.

2. Bethlem, J., van Wijngaarden, G. K., Mumenthaler, M., and Meijer, A. E. F.: Centronuclear myopathy with type I fiber atrophy and myotubes. Arch. Neurol., 23:70, 1970.
3. Bradley, W. G., Price, D. L., and Watanabe, C. K.: Familial centronuclear myopathy. J. Neurol. Neurosurg. Psychiatry, 33:687, 1970.
4. Demos, J.: Early diagnosis and treatment of rapidly developing Duchenne de Boulogne type of myopathy. Am. J. Phys. Med., 50:271, 1971.
5. Drachman, D. A.: Ophthalmoplegia plus. Arch. Neurol., 18:654, 1968.
6. Dubowitz, V.: The floppy infant. Little Club Clinics Developmental Medicine, No. 31. London, National Spastics Society [J. B. Lippincott Co.], 1969.
7. Dyken, P. R., and Harper, P. S.: Congenital dystrophia myotonica. Neurology, 23:465, 1973.
8. Engel, A. G., Gomez, M. R., Seybold, M. T., and Lambert, E. H.: The spectrum and diagnosis of acid maltase deficiency. Neurology, 23:95, 1973.
9. Engel, W. K., and Brooke, M. H.: Muscle biopsy as a clinical diagnostic aid. In Fields, W. S. (ed.): Neurological Diagnostic Techniques. Springfield, Ill., Charles C Thomas, 1966.
10. Engel, W. K., Gold, G. N., and Karpati, G.: Type I fiber hypotrophy and central nuclei: A rare congenital anomaly with possible experimental model. Arch. Neurol., 18:435, 1968.
11. Eyring, E. J., Johnson, E. W., and Burnett, C.: Surgery in Muscular Dystrophy. J.A.M.A., 222:1056, 1972.
12. Favara, B. E., Vawter, G. F., Wagner, R., Kevy, S., and Porter, E. G.: Familial paroxysmal rhabdomyolysis in children. Am. J. Med. 42:196. 1967
13. Field, R. A.: Glycogen deposition diseases. In Stanbury, J. B., Wyngaarden, J. B., and Fredrickson, D. S. (eds.): The Metabolic Basis of Inherited Disease. 2nd Ed. New York, McGraw-Hill Book Co., 1966, p. 156.
14. Gamstorp, I.: Progressive spinal muscular atrophy with onset in infancy or early childhood. Acta Paediatr. Scand., 56:408, 1967.
15. Gilly, R., Jeune, M., Sabatini, R., Faronz, S., Raveau, R., and Grassant, A.: Thomsen's disease in the child. Pediatrics, 24:515, 1969.
16. Gonatas, N. K., Perez, M. C., and Shy, G. M.: Central "core" disease of skeletal muscle. Ultrastructural and cytochemical observations in 2 cases. Am. J. Pathol., 47:503, 1965.
17. Hefferman, L. P., Rewcastle, M. B., and Humphrey, J. G.: The spectrum of the rod myopathies. Arch. Neurol., 18:529, 1968.
18. Hers, H. G.: Alpha-glucosidase deficiency in generalized glycogen storage disease (Pompe's disease). Biochem. J., 86.11, 1963.
19. Jackson, C. E., and Strehler, D. A.: Limb-girdle muscular dystrophy. Clinical manifestations and detection of pre-clinical disease. Pediatrics, 41:495, 1968.
20. Jenis, E. H., Lindquist, R. R., and Lister, R. C.: New congenital myopathy with crystalline intranuclear inclusions. Arch. Neurol., 20:281, 1969.
21. Lovelace, R. E., and Myers, S. J.: Nerve conduction and synaptic transmission. In Downey, J. A., and Darling, R. C. (eds.): Physiological Basis of Rehabilitation Medicine. Philadelphia, W. B. Saunders Co., 1971, pp. 85–106.
22. Miller, J.: Management of muscular dystrophy. J. Bone Joint Surg., 49-A:1205, 1967.
23. Myers, S. J., and Lovelace, R. E.: The motor unit and muscle action potentials. In Downey, J. A., and Darling, R. C. (eds.): Physiological Basis of Rehabilitation Medicine. Philadelphia, W. B. Saunders Co., 1971, pp. 107–134.
24. Nihill, M. R., Wilson, D. S., and Hugh-Jones, K.: Generalized glycogenosis type II (Pompe's disease). Am. J. Dis. Child., 45:122, 1970.
25. Paine, R. S., and Oppé, E.: Neurological examination of children. Little Club Clinics Developmental Medicine, Nos. 20/21. London, National Spastics Society, 1966.
26. Peterson, D. I., and Munsat, T.: Clinical presentation of nemaline myopathy. Bull. Los Angeles Neurol. Soc., 34:39, 1969.
27. Radu, H., Migea, S., Török, Z., Bordlainu, L., and Radu, A.: Carrier detection in X-linked Duchenne type muscular dystrophy, a pleuridimensional investigation. J. Neurol. Sci., 6:289, 1968.
28. Rowland, L. P., and Layzer, R.: Muscular dystrophies, atrophies, and related diseases. In Baker, A. B. (ed.): Clinical Neurology. New York, Hoeber-Harper, 1971.
29. Rowland, L. P., Fahn, S., Hirschberg, E., and Harter, D. H.: Myoglobinuria. Arch. Neurol., 10:537, 1964.
30. Shafiq, S. A., Milhorat, A. T., and Gorycki, M. A.: Giant mitochondria in human muscle with inclusions. Arch. Neurol., 17:666, 1967.
31. Shaw, R. F., Pearson, C. M., Chowdhury, S. R., and Dreifuss, F. E.: Serum enzymes in sex-linked (Duchenne) muscular dystrophy. Arch. Neurol., 16:115, 1967.
32. Shy, G. M., and Magee, K. R.: A new congenital non-progressive myopathy. Brain, 79:610, 1956.
33. Shy, G. M., Gonatas, N. K., and Perez, M. C.: Two childhood myopathies with abnormal mitochondria. 1. Megaconial myopathy. 2. Pleoconial myopathy. Brain, 89:133, 1966.

34. Shy, G. M., Engel, W. K., Somers, J. E., and Wanko, T.: Nemaline myopathy, a new congenital myopathy. Brain, 86:793, 1963.
35. Siegel, I. M.: Pathomechanics of stance in Duchenne muscular dystrophy. Arch. Phys. Med. Rehabil., 53:403, 1972.
36. Spencer, G. E., Jr.: Orthopedic care of progressive muscular dystrophy. J. Bone Joint Surg., 49-A:201–204, 1967.
37. Sullivan, D. B., Cassidy, J. T., Petty, R. E., and Burt, A.: Prognosis in childhood dermatomyositis. J. Pediatr., 80:555, 1972.
38. Swaiman, K. F., and Wright, F. S.: *Neuromuscular Diseases of Infancy and Childhood.* Springfield, Ill., Charles C Thomas, 1970.
39. Swaiman, K. F., Kennedy, W. R., and Sauls, H. S.: Late infantile acid maltase deficiency. Arch. Neurol., 18:642, 1968.
40. Tasker, W., and Chutorian, A. M.: Chronic polyneuritis of childhood. J. Pediatr., 74:699, 1969.
41. van der Does de Willebois, A. E. M., Bethlem, J., Meyer, A. E. F. H., and Simons, A. J. R.: Distal myopathy with onset in early infancy. Neurology, 18:383, 1968.
42. Victor, M., Hayes, R., and Adams, R. D.: Oculopharyngeal muscular dystrophy. N. Engl. J. Med., 267:1267, 1962.
43. Vignos, P. J., Jr.: Rehabilitation in progressive muscular dystrophy. *In* Licht, S. (ed.): *Rehabilitation and Medicine.* New Haven, Conn., Elizabeth Licht, 1968, pp. 584–642.
44. Walton, J. N.: *Disorders of Voluntary Muscle.* Boston, Little, Brown, and Co., 1969.
45. Walton, J. N., and Natrass, F. J.: On the classification, natural history and treatment of the myopathies. Brain, 77:169, 1954.
46. Zellweger, H., and Hanson, J. W.: Psychometric studies in muscular dystrophy type III (Duchenne). Dev. Med. Child Neurol., 5:576, 1967.
47. Zundel, W. S., and Typer, F. H.: The muscular dystrophies. N. Engl. J. Med., 273:537, 1965.

Chapter 12

Minimal Brain Dysfunction

by Edward J. Hart, M.D., and Sidney Carter, M.D.

"Rehabilitation" in its original sense signified "restoration," and perhaps in no other area of rehabilitation medicine is this meaning more appropriate than in the rehabilitation of the child with minimal brain dysfunction (MBD). Not only does the "illness" extend throughout the entire span of childhood and beyond, but the manifestations permeate all aspects of the child's life — his relationships with parents and peers, his school performance, often his athletic abilities, his self-image. Thus the physician who would attempt to intervene and guide the restoration process must be prepared to involve himself wholeheartedly in the task of providing responsible guidance in many areas: He must consult with the school about educational programming and class placement, he must guide the parents through many difficult periods that might otherwise provoke frustration and guilt, and he must help the child develop a sense of self-worth despite his handicaps.

In recent years increasing attention has been turned to a group of children who, because of their atypical patterns of learning and behavior, have been a source of puzzlement and concern to their parents and teachers. Hyperactivity, distractibility, and poor impulse control are the hallmarks of the aberrant behavior, but academic achievement is often equally hampered by subtle dysfunction of central auditory and visual processes. Both kinds of difficulty have been ascribed to the same cause — minimal impairment of brain function. Estimates of the number of affected children vary considerably, but a conservative estimate of 3 per cent of the school-age population has been cited.[36] Boys outnumber girls by at least four to one.[34] It is obvious that an inability to modulate one's activity level or to focus one's attention leads to serious interference not only with academic learning but also with successful interpersonal relations. The critical years of growth and development are thus affected in many children by the consequences of presumed neurological dysfunction. If not dealt with appropriately, these handicaps can have far-reaching effects on the child's future educational, social, and psychological adjustment.

The concept of brain "damage" as the underlying mechanism of this dysfunction has justifiably been subjected to critical scrutiny. It should, nevertheless, be stressed that large numbers of children with very similar clusters of atypical behavior patterns do exist and that the means to help them significantly also exist. Within certain obvious limitations, the lack of a pure concept of the "syndrome" should not be an excuse to deny effective treatment to children and families desperately in need of it.

Two kinds of evidence have been offered in support of the theory that these behavioral and learning difficulties are the result of dysfunction of the nervous system. Numerous examples of the effects of known brain injuries on personality and learning abilities have been documented to show similarities with the atypical patterns of children with the so-called "minimal brain dysfunction syndrome." Parallel observations have been made of the behavior and learning characteristics of children who were born following difficult or complicated pregnancies, or who experienced trauma at the time of delivery, i.e., circumstances that might reasonably be expected to increase the likelihood of cerebral injury. Soon after the epidemic of influenzal encephalitis in 1918, it became apparent that many children who survived showed a catastrophic change in behavior. They became restless, distractible, irritable, unruly, and destructive.[23, 43] Observations soon followed on the effects of other kinds of cerebral insult on children's behavior and learning abilities. Byers and Lord studied the late effects of lead poisoning.[9] Bond and Appel further explored the behavioral effects of various kinds of viral encephalitides,[8] and others explored the sequelae of head injuries:

> The essential characteristic of the syndrome was a complete reversal of personality from that of a previously normal child to that of one who was asocial, unmanageable, and unyielding to any form of training. . . . Hyperkinesis was an outstanding symptom.[7]

The effect of brain damage on learning ability was a parallel concern of neurologists in this same period. Spurred by Goldstein's observations on soldiers with brain injuries after World War I, Strauss and Lehtinen noted similar defects in abstract and symbolic learning in children with brain injuries.[42] They again emphasized the by now well-confirmed characteristics of hyperactivity, distractibility, and short attention span. An intriguing phenomenon, well known to child neurologists and neurosurgeons, is the remarkable amelioration of abnormal behavior that often occurs following hemispherectomy. In this operation, done as a last resort for intractable seizures and hemiparesis originating in one damaged hemisphere only, the entire cortical mantle of the damaged side is removed. Quite consistently, in addition to improved or complete seizure control, a marked improvement in personality occurs, with diminishing of the short attention span and aggressiveness characteristic of the child's behavior prior to surgery. Certainly this, too, lends credence to the belief that aberrant behavior is often a result of brain dysfunction.

As an outgrowth of these observations studies have been made of children whose prenatal or birth histories were likely to predispose them to neurological injury. Many careful studies of children who were born prematurely or who suffered anoxia at birth have shown that such children run increased risk of developing hyperkinetic syndromes, often in association with perceptual deficits and other cognitive deficiencies.[16, 21, 53] The pioneering studies of Pasamanick and Knoblock demonstrated the relationship between prematurity, prenatal difficulties, and perinatal medical complications, and a variety of psychological, neurological, and behavioral disorders.[35] They advanced the concept of "a continuum of reproductive casualty," which provides a useful framework upon which to develop an understanding of the varieties of expression of neurological impairment. Since severe insults such as extreme prematurity or prolonged anoxia had both a high incidence and a great degree of brain injury manifested by marked retardation and spasticity, they postulated that mild, often unnoticed degrees of the same kinds of insult might produce very minor deviations in intelligence, behavior, and coordination.

Not all children who manifest signs consistent with the "MBD syndrome" are the products of difficult pregnancies or premature deliveries, or have suffered known head injuries, and it is often these children who present the most difficult problems in diagnosis. The common occurrence of similar problems in the parent (usually the father) lends support to the possibility of a genetic etiology. Two studies cited by Wender indicate that there is a rather large incidence of so-called "congenital stigmata" (high-arched palate, single palmar crease, microcephaly) in MBD children, which would suggest that effects of fetal maldevelopment can in some cases be manifested as the MBD syndrome.

MANIFESTATIONS OF THE MBD SYNDROME

It is a truism that when dealing with an organ as complex as the brain one can expect dysfunction to manifest itself in a variety of different patterns. Although certain well-defined patterns of motor, intellectual, and behavioral function often result from brain injury, yet the extent of disability in any or all of these spheres is remarkably variable from child to child.

Behavior Patterns

Unusual behavior patterns are of great concern to parents and teachers, and it is in this area that a child's dysfunction becomes most apparent. A typical child is described as being in almost constant motion, flitting from one object to another with apparent unconcern. At an early age this may manifest itself as continuous rocking in the crib, and a not uncommon historical tidbit is the complaint that a child was able to propel himself *and the crib* with this rocking. At the toddler stage, when attention span is normally short in all children, distinguishing the child whose hyperactivity is excessive is often difficult, but the "driven" quality becomes apparent after a period of observation, especially in a doctor's office. The child is unable to control his impulsive behavior, particularly when presented with a variety of shiny and distracting objects. At this age, too, visits to a supermarket provide an almost unbearable testing ground for the child and his mother, as the excitement and stimulation may prove to be too much for the youngster, leading to extreme displays of hyperactivity. At early school age, the hyperkinetic child may be tolerated in the relatively free atmosphere of a progressive "open-school" kindergarten, but when the demands of formal education are made in first or second grade, his restlessness will be readily apparent.

A concomitant symptom, closely associated with hyperkinesis, is the distractibility and short attention span quite often noted in MBD children. It is obvious that a child who is distracted by every rustled paper or dropped pencil is at a disadvantage in the learning situation, and that a child who cannot pay attention long enough to hear the teacher's instructions is similarly handicapped.

There are other symptoms commonly seen in children with the MBD syndrome, which by their very nature are often ascribed to purely psychological origins, whose frequency makes it likely that they are of organic origin as well. Frequent temper outbursts, inappropriate aggressiveness, impulsiveness, and lowered frustration tolerance are often noted. In general, especially in the older child, there is an inability to modulate emotional responses; their overexcitability often makes these children unappealing companions to their age-mates. In this area, more than in any other, the boundaries between psychiatry and neurology become blurred. It is almost impossible in most cases to sort out the various influences of family dynamics and school and social interactions in attempting to understand the reasons for a child's behavioral aberrations. A child who is innately difficult to deal with almost from the day of birth obviously arouses negative feelings in his parents, who then react in ways that perhaps exacerbate the unfavorable behavior. There is no doubt that the permissive rearing methods often resorted to out of exasperation and desperation tend to reinforce the wild, unfocused behavior that was the original source of concern. Yet well-meaning teachers, social workers, and psychologists who are too ready to ascribe any behavioral deviation in a child to the parent's failings often do a real disservice to parents who are struggling with an incredibly difficult problem. It is our observation that constructive programs of supportive counseling are often beneficial, whereas intervention based solely on assumed failings in the marital relationship or on psychological inadequacies of either parent often hinders the rehabilitation of the child.

Even as a parent's emotional reactions to his child are affected by the child's behavior, so too do a child's perceptions of himself contribute to his personality structure. Perhaps as an outgrowth of their sense of being different, a not uncommon pattern of "silly" behavior often emerges in certain MBD children in the 7 to 11 year old age range. They show a tendency to behave in ways that, if anything, overemphasize their difficulties in coordination, in learning, and in social behavior. It is as if they were saying that they act the buffoon or the class scapegoat or clown because they wish to, not because they have no other choice. A sense of identity based on these distorted feelings of self-worth is a poor basis from which to meet the approaching tasks of adolescence, and it is here that the need for sensitive psychotherapeutic counseling seems most indicated.

Not all children whose deviations from normal are thought to be based on minimal brain dysfunction are miniature "whirling dervishes"; it is of importance to stress that a significant minority of children so affected suffer from hypoactivity. These children may present a picture of social incompetence, gullibility, and sensitivity, behavior highly suggestive of a purely emotional etiology. Many of them, however, share some of the classic features of shortened attention span and learning difficulties that make the "organic" nature of the behavioral aberration more apparent.

Although some attempt to differentiate between emotional and organic or "innate" factors in the behavioral manifestations of minimal brain dysfunction seems appropriate, nevertheless it should be obvious that a multitude of factors affect a child's behavior and there is no pressing necessity for sorting out the exact proportions of each influence. These children need a great deal of help, and so do their families — and they need it from many different sources. Psychiatric help and counseling for a child and his family does not preclude the use of behavior-modifying medications or the need for special schooling. Similarly, a child who carries a label of "emotionally disturbed" from a child guidance clinic may deserve the individual attention and remedial tutoring given eagerly to the child who is considered to have the "hyperkinetic syndrome" with a "learning disability."

Disorders of Thinking Processes in MBD

Having postulated that the children under discussion have as the cause of their difficulties subtle brain dysfunction, one might expect that deviation in intellectual ability would be present as well. If one conceives of intelligence not as a single fixed attribute, but rather as a complex multifactorial collection of specific abilities, then the variations in learning ability become easier to understand. Depending on the site and extent of the presumed "brain damage," a continuum of deficiencies is theoretically possible, ranging from the extensive subtractive dysfunctions of true mental subnormality to the specific and circumscribed perceptual, intellectual, and memory deficits at the root of the so-called "specific learning disabilities."

The concept of "intelligence" has undergone numerous revisions over the last hundred years as we have progressed from the rather simplistic theories of the phrenologists who thought that each "faculty of mind" resided in a specific locale in the brain, to the search of early psychologists for an elusive single "number" to explain obvious differences in ability, to the more recent sophisticated neuropsychological mapping of the organization of the brain's higher functions.[48] Spearman, an early American psychologist, presented a "two-factor theory" to explain an individual's performance on an intellectual task; this concept, or variations of it, can still serve as a useful framework in understanding intelligence.[39] He felt that all operations have the same underlying ability or g factor in common, but that each has its own specific component also. This g factor relates to a general ability to grasp and apply principles, and is what is commonly accepted by most people as "intelligence." The specific factors, however, refer to such abilities as verbal comprehension and perception of spatial relationships, and deviations here can obviously account for quite marked variations in performance. Thurstone subsequently proposed a grouping of individual factors that in many ways resembles the various "subtests" on our more familiar "IQ tests" of today:

D,	deductive reasoning	P,	perceptual speed
I,	inductive reasoning	S,	spatial ability
M,	rote memory	V,	verbal comprehension
N,	number ability	W,	word fluency[45]

In addition to a general "ability" factor, which however elusive its measurement nevertheless attempts to measure an individual's reasoning ability, standardized tests have tended to subdivide intelligence into rather specific skills of both a verbal and a nonverbal nature.

A child who shows deficits in many areas of intellectual functioning with a rather uniform level of overall ability presents no major problem in classification, and his placement in school occasions no great controversy. Many MBD children, however, show atypical patterns of functioning and widely disparate abilities, presumably because brain damage or dysfunction is confined to specific areas. Thus a child with superior language ability and verbal functioning might have very inferior appreciation of spatial relations and defective visual perception, which in severe cases might present as almost complete inability to perform mathematical calculations.[28] Similarly, in extreme cases, a child may have such severe impairment of auditory and verbal abilities as to be in essence aphasic, and yet may have normal nonverbal abilities. It is these children, and those similarly but less severely affected, who present major problems in classification and educational placement.

Apart from these specific deficiencies, however, the thinking processes of brain damaged individuals are impaired in other more general ways. There is often a rigidity of mental processes that leads to perseveration: in ideas, in tasks, even in verbalizations. There may be a tendency to break down a complex task into its component parts (a loss of gestalt) and a consequent tendency to focus on inconsequential details rather than synthesizing or generalizing, a defect often resulting in poor ability to abstract or conceptualize. A parallel deficiency is inability to separate foreground and background details, in either the visual or the auditory sphere.

In the less severely affected child with MBD, these cognitive deficiencies may be responsible for selective difficulties with arithmetic, or reading, or spelling, in the presence of average or even superior performance in other school subjects. Quite obviously, a child with good intellectual function in at least some areas presents a puzzling challenge to both diagnosis and therapy. It is unfortunately true, however, that the overall intellectual level in most series of affected children is in the low normal or borderline range.[37]

One can group the specific cognitive deficits of these children (as opposed to the general factor as in Spearman's g factor) into two subgroups, the auditory-verbal and the visual-motor. Thus, deficits in the former sphere are manifested by auditory imperception (inability to blend sounds or to discriminate between similar sounding but different sounds) and diminished auditory memory; and in the latter by visual and spatial imperception, disordered orientation in space, or inability to reproduce copies of shapes, and by diminished visual memory. The integration of sensory information across these modalities has also been shown to be deficient in some cases, and it is this latter dysfunction especially that can often be implicated in reading failure.[15] Thus when reading, a visual symbol must be associated with a previously heard and remembered sound before it can be identified as part of a word. Similarly, in spelling, one must hear the word, analyze it into its sequential sounds (a task in and of itself often quite laborious for such children) and then recall a previously learned visual symbol for the specific sound. It is tasks such as these, which appear so simple to the individual who learn to read or spell with no particular difficulty, that a child with one or more deficits in cognitive skills will of necessity fail unless patiently and laboriously tutored.

Motor Accompaniments of the Syndrome

An aspect of the MBD syndrome that has received more than its rightful share of interest is the awkwardness and incoordination that so often are found in these children. Again if one conceives of a continuum of dysfunction, from the severe to the most mild, then the difficulties with fine and gross movement and coordination can be seen as the very mildest forms of spasticity, athetosis, and ataxia known in their extremes as "cerebral palsy." Organic pathological correlates to this dysfunction do exist, as amply demonstrated by Towbin in recent studies.[47] In studying over 600 neonatal brains he determined that two types of hypoxic damage occur: in the premature fetus and newborn, the deep cerebral structures (basal ganglia and periventricular regions) are primarily affected, whereas in the mature fetus and newborn the brunt of the damage is borne by the cerebral cortex. This differential susceptibility he ascribed to specific biological factors related to the developmental events at various stages of embryogenesis. During early gestation the deep cerebral structures are undergoing rapid development of their germinal matrix tissue and are hence more susceptible to the hypoxic insult that manifests itself as hemorrhagic infarction of the susceptible tissues. In the full-term infant, it is the rapidly maturing outer layers of the cortex that are most susceptible to similar hemorrhagic infarction.

The minimal hypoxic damage just described is extremely variable in its severity and to some extent in its locus, from case to case. If the frontal regions are primarily affected, then gross defects in mentation result; damage to the precentral portion of the cerebrum is commonly associated with spastic diplegia, and to the basal ganglia with choreoathetosis and dystonic phenomena. It is worth noting, however, that such variations in neuronal damage can, on theoretical grounds, account for the apparently contradictory lack of motor involvement in some children whose intelligence is severely affected and for the converse finding of "pure" syndromes of motor deficits in the absence of cognitive deficiencies.

In a syndrome whose manifestations may be interpreted variously as of primarily emotional versus primarily organic etiology, there has been an understandable desire to document and even to quantitate the deviant neurological abnormalities. It has been assumed, perhaps naively, that if clear-cut signs of neurological dysfunction can be documented in an individual case, then the diagnosis and, by inference, the therapy and prognosis will follow in a prescribed and orderly fashion. Although the latter conclusions are not wholly realistic, nevertheless, study of a child's motor coordination and neurological examination can be a useful adjunct to his evaluation.

Although in rare instances MBD children have normal or even superior motor abilities, more commonly there is a history of delay in achieving motor milestones and a persistent clumsiness in performing motor acts. Gross motor abilities, when affected, are often of concern to the child himself. Awkwardness in running, inability to hop or skip, fumbling attempts at catching and throwing, delay in learning to ride a two-wheel bicycle — these defects in functioning can be devastating to a child's self-image. Less noticeable to his peers, but still of significance to teachers (and pediatric neurologists) are the concomitant deficiencies in small muscle ("fine motor") coordination. At preschool age, this can be seen as excessive awkwardness in buttoning, in cutting with scissors, and in holding a pencil. As the child progresses in the early school years, tasks such as shoelace tying and handwriting become sources of concern.

Documentation of the motor accompaniments to the MBD syndrome requires a familiarity with the so-called "soft signs" of neurological dysfunction. Prechtl and others have noted an excess of choreiform-like movements of the outstretched fingers when the child attempts to hold the posture and similar minor asymmetries of posture, of reflexes, and of coordination in children with minor neurological impairment.[1, 10, 46] The standard or formal neurological examination is usually unrevealing, and thus emphasis should be placed on noting a child's hopping and running ability, muscle tone, and other more subjective indicators of motor function.

It is well to emphasize at this point that these phenomena are merely the motor accompaniments of varying degrees of presumed brain injury, and are not in and of themselves *responsible* for the associated difficulties in reading and the like that are often present. Much popular feeling has been attached of late to the notion that improvement in motor coordination will a priori result in improved reading or spelling skill; this has of course not proved true.

DIAGNOSIS

Once alerted to the characteristic features of the MBD syndrome as just discussed, the interested physician quite readily identifies those children with the typical clustering of motor incoordination, hyperactivity, and learning deficits. A sophisticated neurological examination often provides additional findings in support of the diagnostic impression. A far more challenging task awaits the physician when he is presented with a child whose only area of difficulty may be in behavior, or perhaps in learning ability. For here, as already indicated, the overlap with presumably purely "functional" disorders is great, and the often Solomon-like wisdom needed to unravel a complicated web of interrelated interpersonal, environmental, and innate factors is not readily available in these non-Biblical days. One must be prepared to admit in some cases that a specific diagnosis may not be immediately apparent; the rehabilitation of the child must then proceed along tentative empirical lines.

As with any other chronic medical condition of uncertain outcome, sufficient time must be taken with the family at the outset not only to be certain that one has obtained all the pertinent historical data, but also to begin laying the groundwork for a feeling of mutual trust without which any rehabilitation program is likely to fail. Parents of MBD children often carry an almost intolerable burden of guilt, both conscious and unconscious, and while seeking out possible contributing factors in the child's dysfunction, the physician should attempt to alleviate rather than to exacerbate these feelings.

A thorough inquiry into the history of the mother's health during the pregnancy, including ingestion of medications, vaginal bleeding, variations in blood pressure, and the like, must be made. Similarly, of obvious importance are facts such as the length of gestation and the circumstances surrounding the inception of labor (i.e., spontaneous or induced, and if induced, what the indications were). The delivery itself should be asked about, especially if the mother was awake. Even if no obvious problems were encountered to the best of her recollection, it is often revealing to request the birth records from the hospital, since resuscitation efforts may not have been discussed with her. Details of functioning in early infancy that are of special interest are the infant's sucking ability, his sleeping and waking cycle, and of course, undue irritability, overactivity, or "colic." It is by now well accepted that many excessively irritable babies later present as MBD children. It is not uncommon for a pattern of covert maternal rejection to begin at this early age when instead of tranquilly cooing and sighing, the infant continuously cries day and night. Undue reactions to immunization, serious febrile illnesses, and quite obviously, head trauma and intoxications must be inquired about in detail. Studies have shown transient abnormalities in electroencephalographic patterns during uncomplicated measles infection without evidence of true encephalitic symptoms; even if no clinical correlation with later school performance has been made, nevertheless such historical data is often helpful in an individual case.[18]

Although the timetable for reaching developmental milestones is notoriously variable in normal children, nevertheless certain delays in both motor and adaptive landmarks are often significant. Excessive falling at the toddler stage, with apparent lack of balance, may have been present despite the child's having learned to walk at the appropriate age. Language development is usually a more sensitive parameter of future dysfunction, and a delay in using words or phrases is often seen. Articulation defects are present as well, as another sign of minimal motor incoordination, but the failure to use complex sentences at an appropriate age is more significant. The child almost certainly will have belatedly begun to speak in full sentences by the early school years, but often these same children have the greatest difficulty in acquiring fundamental reading and spelling skills.

The actual school performance record, in an older child especially, is invaluable in assessing the child's actual levels of functioning, both academic and social. The teacher's classroom observations may give the clearest picture possible, and may be less biased than the parents'. A few minutes on the telephone will often clarify a confusing account of a child's behavior and will also open the lines of communication and enlist a teacher's cooperation in planning for the child's management.

The Neurological Examination

An outline of the neurological examination as adapted for the purpose of uncovering minor deviations in neurological functioning follows. Most of this has been adapted from several sources and it has proved to be a useful guide.[33, 46]

Physical signs
    Head circumference
    Abnormal facial characteristics
    Skin pigmentation patterns
    Palmar creases
    Skeletal anomalies

Neurological signs
    Right or left preference for handedness, footedness, eyedness
    Posture in sitting and standing (Look for asymmetry or instability, inability to maintain postures [motor impersistence].)
    Gait (Include tandem, heel, and toe walking. Look for wide base, unsteadiness, inability to make rapid turns smoothly, arm swing, circumduction, excessive associated movements of arms.)
        Tiptoe—by age three
        Heel walking—by age three (associated movements abnormal after age five.)
        Hopping—by age five (Most can hop 10 times on each leg.)
        Tandem—by age six
    Motor function (Judge bulk, tone, and power. Look for pronation or drift of outstretched arms.)
    Reflexes
        Deep tendon jerks (Look for abnormal intensities or asymmetries.)
        Plantar reflex (Extensor response abnormal after one year of age.)
        Palmomental reflex (Abnormal after age four.)
    Abnormal movements (Choreiform and athetoid movements observed at any time and especially of the outstretched fingers when the eyes are closed.)
    Coordination and cerebellar function
        Rapid wrist alternation—as if turning a doorknob (Look for associated movements and mirror movements [both minimal by seven or eight years of age].)

Finger to nose (Look for tremor.)

Finger opposition (Smooth transitions by age eight, minimal mirror movements by age 9 or 10.)

Observation of running, hopping, throwing (gross motor)

Observation of pencil-holding, manipulation of small objects (fine motor)

Sensation (Testing of primary modalities [e.g., pin, touch] unlikely to be fruitful.)

Stereognosis (Identify key, coin, and the like.)

Joint position sense, number-writing (age six or older)

Double simultaneous stimulation and "face-hand" test (Few errors over age six.)[4]

Cranial nerves

Visual and auditory acuity

Abnormalities of extraocular movements

Articulation defects

Tongue praxis

Choreiform movements of face

Physical Signs.   As indicated in the outline, the simple measurement of the head circumference with a steel tape measure can provide useful diagnostic clues. At the one extreme, head circumference of more than three standard deviations below the mean is known to be associated with mental subnormality, and children with such gross indications of cerebral hypoplasia may well present as school learning problems.[14] At the other extreme, an excessively large head should be an indication to evaluate the child more fully, since partially compensated hydrocephalus may present as minimal awkwardness and incoordination that has an appearance not dissimilar to minimal brain dysfunction from nonprogressive causes. Stigmata of congenital developmental defects often associated with neurological impairment should be searched for; these include hypertelorism, epicanthal folds, and high-arched palate as well as the characteristic skin pigmentations of neurofibromatosis and tuberous sclerosis.

Neurological Signs.   Although by tradition neurologists compulsively note the patient's hand preference, the value of these observations must be kept in perspective. For here too a tendency to oversimplify the significance of left-handedness and "mixed dominance" has led to fruitless attempts at "therapy" by the forcing of right-handedness or complete dominance. Although both cerebral hemispheres share sensory input and motor output tasks in a parallel and symmetrical manner, it is true that for certain functions, such as language, one hemisphere predominates or is "dominant."

Many studies have clearly shown that there is no significant correlation between good and bad readers and the incidence of such traits as their left-handedness, mixed laterality, or eye dominance differing from hand preference.[3, 38, 54] Similarly, there is no evidence that forcing hand preference will improve learning skills.[6] Useful data can be obtained, however, from observations regarding dominance. Since 93 per cent of the population is right-handed, the finding of a left-handed child amidst an otherwise right-handed family raises a suspicion of early damage or dysfunction of the left hemisphere leading to a shift of dominance to the opposite hemisphere.[5] There is some evidence that delays in language development are accompanied by delays in establishment of dominance, but this is more likely a reflection of coexisting neurological impairments rather than a cause and effect relationship.

> Dominance, laterality, and their disorders per se do not cause a disorder of language; rather they are concomitant symptoms, reflecting on a parallel level the basic deviation of brain function responsible for both the disorder of laterality and language.[44]

In addition to a general awkwardness, many neurologically impaired children show a tendency toward excessive "overflow" of movements, often across the midline. Although the exact mechanism for these so-called mirroring movements or synkinesia is not well understood, it has been commonly noted to an extreme degree in the paralyzed extremity of adult stroke patients when they are asked to perform rapid movements with the unaffected hand. Then, too, infants and young children are characteristically unable to isolate a specific fine motor act without bringing into play nearby muscle groups and corresponding muscle groups on the opposite side of the body. Whether this is a reflection of damage or immaturity, it is frequently observed that children with the minimal brain dysfunction syndrome are unable to perform repetitive motions such as finger to thumb oppositions without a good deal of overflow to the muscles of the wrist and elbow of the same side and similar "mirroring" movements of the opposite extremity.

Various disorders of eye movement have been implicated in the reading problems often associated with minimal brain dysfunction. Here again, it is true that strabismus and other defects of oculomotor function may be present, but more likely as a concomitant expression of neurological dysfunction rather than as the source of the cognitive disabilities. Several studies have shown that refractive errors and disorders of ocular motility are actually no more common in dyslexic children than in normal children.[17, 32] Additional information has come from the study of individual cases of extreme degrees of ocular motility disturbances. A child with complete congenital ophthalmoplegia was found to have reading, spelling, and arithmetic abilities at age level, as well as visual perception as tested by Frostig tests. His visuomotor abilities, e.g., reproduction of geometric forms or drawing diagonal lines, were markedly deviant, however.[25] Similarly, children with congenital oculomotor apraxia, a condition in which voluntary eye movements are severely impaired, show no difficulties in letter-sound association or other synthesizing skills necessary to read accurately, but only a slower than normal rate of reading because of the difficulty in moving the eyes across the page.[11]

Higher Cortical Function Examination

It is mandatory for the physician who cares for children with behavioral and school adjustment problems to become at least minimally aware of the ways in which a child's intellectual and educational functioning can be assessed. The degree to which he involves himself in this aspect of the evaluation of necessity depends upon such factors as his interest and training, the availability of skilled psychologists, and school resources. It should be stressed that the suggested outline of a suitable approach to such an examination is meant as a guide and as a way of allowing the interested physician to familiarize himself with the kinds of information to be obtained, rather than as a substitute for thorough psychological and educational testing. A qualified psychologist, experienced in evaluating children with MBD, can assess a child's patterns of functioning and can often suggest means of remedying or compensating for specific deficiencies.

Behavioral observations
  Hyperactivity
  Decreased attention span
  Distractibility
  Disinhibition
  Emotional lability
  Impulsiveness
  Hypoactivity
  Lack of spontaneity
  Low frustration tolerance
Fund of general knowledge and long-term memory
Tests of "intelligence" suitable for office use by physicians:
  Raven's Colored Progressive Matrices ([Psychological Corporation, New York, New York] nonverbal, visual perception, and integration)
  Ammon's Quick Test ([Psychological Test Specialists, Missoula, Montana] modified picture-vocabulary test, nonverbal)
Tests of reading, writing (spontaneously, copying, and to dictation), and arithmetic
Visual-motor abilities and spatial concepts (Copying geometric figures, choosing the "best one" of several, finding hidden figures, matching shapes, stick designs, and geometric puzzles)
Auditory-visual association and language use. (Tests of auditory discrimination, receptive and expressive language abilities [following commands, naming pictures, colors, shapes, letters, numbers, describing pictures, telling stories])
Short-term memory
  Visual (multiple choice recall of shapes, abstract figures, and the like)
  Auditory (sentence repetition, digit span, reproducing tapped rhythms)
  Digits (Six years: five forward, two or three backward. Ten years: six forward, four backward)
Orientation for right and left
  Six years—own body, single commands
  Nine years—double commands, own body
  Eleven years—single lateral identification, facing examiner
  Twelve years—crossed identification, facing examiner
Imitation of gestures, motor praxis

Finger agnosia (95 per cent of seven and a half year olds will give correct
response to six of eight trials.[26])
    Finger differentiation (one or two fingers stimulated by examiner's
    touch)
    Finger in between ("how many between the ones touched?")

In evaluating a child's higher functions, one is particularly concerned
with school-related skills. In talking with the child one attempts to gauge his
social poise, his fund of general information, and his ability to converse in logical, well-constructed sentences. Of course, comprehension, general information, and language use are different at every age, and one must have a knowledge of normal ranges for these attributes before one can make a judgment
about abnormal functioning. Although rote memory (both visual and auditory)
should be tested, tasks involving reasoning ability and conceptualizing skills
are often more highly correlated with school achievement and should be assessed in a manner appropriate to the child's age. Formal tests of intellectual
functioning, such as Ammon's and Raven's tests as suggested in the outline,
can be helpful when no other information about performance on standardized
tests is available, and can provide rough measures of language and performance abilities.

Asking a child to read a sample paragraph and to write words to dictation
are simple tests that often provide clues to the source of his failures. Many
show an almost total lack of phonetic skills and are unable to make even
simple letter-sound associations. This may in some cases be due to varying
degrees of auditory imperception, and thus simple tests of auditory discrimination should next be performed.[51] Others show good phonetic approximation
in spelling unknown words, such as "ondrstant" for "understand," an error
that might be indicative of an extremely poor visual memory or other visual
perceptual skills, but good auditory abilities. Testing such a child with multiple choice tests of recall of designs, for example, or asking him to reproduce
simple geometric figures often reveals significant areas of deficit.

Tests of calculation and simple mathematics appropriate to the age level
can similarly often give insight into the defective information processing
skills. Children with poor memories are obviously at a disadvantage in performing multiplication, and those with disordered spatial awareness may experience great difficulty in "carrying" digits from one column to another.

Ancillary Tests.   The electroencephalogram, because of the mystique associated with it, has been one of the most abused and overused of the diagnostic tools. The diagnostic impression of minimal brain dysfunction is arrived at
from a summation of results of evaluation and observations by professionals
from several disciplines; there is no single clinical or laboratory test that alone
can substantiate the diagnosis. Although various studies have tended to show
a greater than normal occurrence of abnormalities such as minimal degrees of
occipital slowing, the lack of true standardization in interpretation of electroencephalograms has made these findings tenuous.[24, 27, 41] There is by no
means a one-to-one concordance of such findings with other parameters of the
MBD syndrome, and in clinical practice an electroencephalogram is often of

little or no value in making a diagnosis. A recent suggestion by the National Institutes for Neurological Diseases and Blindness task force on MBD bears repeating:

> Indications for recording an electroencephalogram in patients with a history suggesting minimal brain dysfunction syndrome include the following:
> (a) paroxysmal behavior abnormalities,
> (b) history suggesting petit mal seizures as well as any obvious type of seizure,
> (c) history suggesting seizure equivalent states,
> (d) history and neurological examination suggesting progressive global or focal neurological dysfunction.[31]

The various specialized neurodiagnostic studies such as arteriography or pneumoencephalography are less frequently considered and have even less of a role in the diagnosis of minimal brain dysfunction syndromes. Similarly, despite excessive lay publicity, there is no evidence that deviations in vitamin or mineral metabolism play any role in the essentially static and unchanging encephalopathies that in their mildest forms account for the MBD syndrome.

PROGNOSIS

A crucial question that has yet to be truly satisfactorily answered is what is the ultimate outcome for children considered to have this syndrome? Some rather discouraging reports have appeared that largely through retrospective analyses have tended to show a rather high rate of incidence of psychiatric and adjustment problems in adolescents and young adults who probably had many of the features of the MBD syndrome as children.[20, 22, 29] Social awkwardness, inability to form meaningful personal relationships, and more serious sociopathic acting out have all been cited occasionally or even, in some series, frequently. It is difficult, though, to be certain of the criteria used to make the original diagnoses. It is only in recent years that the concept of minimal brain dysfunction has been broadened and expanded to include children who are in reality only mildly affected as compared with the more seriously impaired children for whom the label of "brain damaged" was formerly reserved. From personal observations, such pessimism seems unwarranted in most cases. It is a clinical observation that at least one aspect of the syndrome — the hyperactivity — tends to improve with age, so that by early adolescence it is rare to see marked degrees of distractibility or shortened attention span. Similarly, although severe reading handicaps may persist, the more obvious visuomotor difficulties seem less prominent as the child matures. Coordination also ceases to be an issue in most cases, although some degree of clumsiness may persist for a lifetime. If one were to attempt to isolate the single most predictive prognostic sign, it would probably again be the elusive quality of "intelligence." A child with better than average abilities in at least some cognitive spheres is better able to compensate for his impairments. Of obvious importance is the manner in which the child is handled during the crucial latency age when the manifestations of the syndrome are at their peak, since improper education or counseling may leave him with a poor self-image, negative family relationships, and a lack of academic achievement.

THERAPY

Helping MBD children and their families can be enormously satisfying. Many such families come to the doctor's office only as a last resort, at the suggestion perhaps of an interested schoolteacher, and with faint hope of any real solution to their problems. Years of confusion, of self-blame, and of constant discontent often have preceded the consultation. In a syndrome whose manifestations extend into all aspects of a child's life, it is the physician's responsibility to, at the very least, assume an explanatory and coordinative role. Explanation in unalarming terms of the possible sources of their child's dysfunction is in and of itself often therapeutic. The average parent in this Freudian-oriented society finds it hard to believe that a child could be born with a predisposition to hyperactivity and distractibility.

The degree to which an older child should be informed of the nature of his difficulties is a matter of controversy, some psychiatrists believing that a completely candid explanation is most advisable. Usually psychotherapeutic efforts with the child center not so much on the etiology of his behavior as on the day to day conflicts that it engenders. Environmental manipulations such as encouraging structure and consistency in parental handling are the most fruitful form of counseling, yet for some of the more seriously acting-out youngsters formal therapy, either individual or group, should be attempted. The cooperation of psychiatrists, psychologists, and social workers is obviously important in this aspect of the child's care, emphasizing the need for cross-discipline effort.

School placement is often the focus of the initial consultation with the pediatric neurologist. In some states, a child cannot be placed in specialized classes for children with minimal brain damage without the certification of a physician, which makes cooperation between the two disciplines more likely to take place. Although the decisions involving classroom placement are more clearly educational than medical, nevertheless the physician can provide the school authorities with some explanation and interpretation of the child's behavior. Whether a child should remain in a regular class with supplemental specialized tutoring or whether he should be placed in a special school or class with similar children is another question that has caused controversy. Clearly the individual circumstances should dictate this decision. It is to be hoped that the best interests of the child rather than the available school resources govern the final choice. Occasionally a child's behavior is so disruptive that he can no longer be readily contained even in a specialized day school, and residential treatment should be considered.

The curriculum content of special education programs involves both educational and medical decisions. Nevertheless, in our experience remedial programs based on ill-conceived notions of motor and perceptual-motor retraining have not led to the expected beneficial results — improved scholastic, and particularly reading, performance. As previously indicated, the deficits that account for an MBD child's reading problems are most often fundamental cognitive ones and are not based on abnormalities in motor or oculomotor coordination: "One reads with his brain and not with his eyes." Remediation along the lines proposed by Orton and Gillingham, which stresses a linguistic approach emphasizing phonics drilling and the like, has in our experience seemed to be more effective than other newer faddist techniques.

Medication

It is now well accepted that certain drugs, especially the amphetamine-like stimulants, can often quite dramatically ameliorate the atypical behavior of minimally brain damaged children.[13, 40] Paradoxically, such drugs as dextroamphetamine sulfate (Dexedrine) and methylphenidate hydrochloride (Ritalin) seem to calm a child, often enabling him to function in the home and school environment in a more normal manner. Studies have shown not only subjective clinical improvement in behavior, but psychological tests have also indicated some improvement in attention-related and perceptual-motor functions.[12] Theoretical considerations relating to the possible reasons for this have been offered recently.[2, 50] It is known that the amphetamines act at catecholamine-containing nerve terminals by enhancing transmission across synapses in several related ways. It has been postulated that stimulation of the ascending reticular formation of the brain stem and possibly also of a postulated "positive reward system" mediated by the median forebrain bundle may be responsible for the observed effects.

A trial of medication, especially of the stimulant drugs, is necessary when parental counseling and specialized classroom help do not modify the overactive, driven quality of a child's behavior. With beneficial results (to be expected in only about two thirds of cases) a child may become more accessible to the educational and counseling efforts made in his behalf. The range of effective dosages is quite wide, with a daily minimum of 5 mg of dextroamphetamine or 10 mg of methylphenidate to a maximum of 30 mg of dextroamphetamine or 60 mg of methylphenidate being found necessary in specific cases. Practical aspects of drug administration are important. Often the medication has been abandoned after a short or inadequate trial only to be found months later to be quite effective when adequate dosages are employed. The following information sheet for parents has been found helpful in initiating therapy, but repeated telephone calls and follow-up visits are often required to achieve an optimum regimen.

Instructions

1. The medication prescribed for your child has often been found helpful in improving attention span and ability to concentrate in certain children.

2. The dosage range is very wide and children vary in their reactions to the medication. It is impossible to predict in advance what the most effective dose for an individual child will be.

3. Beginning on a Saturday or Sunday, so that you can observe the child,

give a single tablet (or teaspoon) with breakfast. The effect usually begins within the hour and will last up to four to six hours before wearing off. If the child reacts in an adverse way (cranky, irritable, or unusual behavior) try a slightly smaller dose the next day. If this type of behavior is still noted, telephone your physician, since it is unlikely that the medication will prove to be effective.

4. If no observable effect is noted, or if there is a small but definite improvement in behavior, attention span, or the like, then increase the dose on the following day by another tablet or teaspoon. Every few days, increase in this way until either side effects become troublesome or improvement is no longer increasing with each increase in dose. Probably a maximum would be about 4 tablets or teaspoons, but this is variable. Try to enlist the teacher's cooperation in reporting on the effect of the medicine at various levels.

5. Once the morning dose has been adjusted for maximal benefit, give a second dose at lunchtime if it is noted that the beneficial effects wear off by the early afternoon. This should be adjusted in a manner similar to that used for the morning dose.

6. Side effects that are quite common are interference with appetite, and, if medication is given later than 3 or 4 o'clock in the afternoon, interference with sleep. These either will become less prominent with the passage of time, or if very troublesome, should be dealt with by decreasing the dose of medicine.

7. Some parents find that giving the medicine only on school days seems to work well, although many children take the medicine on a daily basis, including vacations. This is an individual decision and may be varied as circumstances change.

When the child's behavior is characterized by bizarre mannerisms, serious acting-out, or extreme negativism, the use of one of the major tranquilizers is indicated, either alone or in conjunction with a stimulant drug. Such phenothiazines as thioridazine (Mellaril) or chlorpromazine (Thorazine) are added to the regimen in small doses that are gradually increased depending on observed effects on behavior. These two phenothiazines are especially sedative, and in an attempt to modify this side effect, the major portion of a daily dose may be administered at bedtime with the expectation that the soporific effects will reach a peak during the night and the desired ataractic effects will persist into the next day. Trifluoperazine (Stelazine), which is more of a stimulant drug despite its phenothiazine structure, has been of some use in older adolescent patients. These more potent drugs are used in dosage ranges that, although seemingly excessive, have proved to be necessary to achieve a desired effect. Thus thioridazine in doses of between 50 and 100 mg a day for an eight or nine year old child is not unusual. Before prescribing these latter medications, the physician should be aware of the potential toxic reactions, which range from excessive appetite stimulation to severe liver toxicity, and should be prepared to monitor the blood count and serum chemistry as indicated. Medication of this magnitude must often be resorted to when the previously discussed available alternatives have been exhausted. In most cases the remote risks of drug toxicity are more acceptable to the family of a seriously disturbed child than is the alternative of residential placement.

Numerous other medications have been tried in an effort to alleviate the excessive motor restlessness of MBD children, often with only partial success. Large doses of antihistamines or the benzodiazapam derivatives, Librium and Valium, are advocated by some but in our experience have shown only minimal efficacy. The use of imipramine (Tofranil) has been suggested in those MBD children who suffer also from enuresis, a not uncommon association, in the hope that both needs will be met by a single drug.[52]

In general drug administration centers around the child's need for improved attention and control during school hours. Parents are encouraged to give drug-free "holidays" on weekends and school vacations. This practice, in addition to being physiologically sound, enables a parent to determine for himself whether medication is still indicated. Since there is a natural tendency for improvement with time, it is not uncommon for a parent to feel that medication is no longer indicated after a particularly successful summer.

It should be emphasized again that the effects of medication of MBD children can be so dramatically positive as to make a trial of methylphenidate or dextroamphetamine an almost essential part of the evaluation. Judiciously utilized, this is not a means of "drugging" a child or making him a docile robot, but rather may be a way to enable him to realize his maximum potential unhindered by excessive restlessness or stimulus-bound behavior. Parents often state that whereas they had previously only grudgingly tolerated their child, they now for the first time are able to see beyond the behavioral deviations and begin to derive some satisfaction from heretofore hidden attributes.

SUMMARY

From this discussion it is hoped that an appreciation has been gained of the possible organic or innate factors that influence a child's adjustment within the family and in school. The awareness of the existence of large numbers of children with behavior and learning difficulties presumably based on brain damage has resulted in the development of more refined techniques of diagnosis and therapy. A need for specialized programs for diagnosis and management in the community, and for educational remediation, seems pressing if the tremendous potential waste of human resources that these children represent is to be averted.

References

1. Anderson, W. W.: The hyperkinetic child: A neurological appraisal. Neurology, *14*:968, 1964.
2. Baldessarini, R. J.: Pharmacology of the amphetamines. Pediatrics, *49*:694, 1972.
3. Belmont, L., and Birch, H. G.: Lateral dominance and right-left awareness in normal children. Child dev., *34*:257–70, 1963.
4. Bender, M. B.: *Disorders in Perception.* Springfield, Ill., Charles C Thomas, 1952.
5. Benson, D. F., and Geschwind, N.: Cerebral dominance and its disturbances. Pediatr. Clin. North Am., *15*:759–769, 1968.
6. Birch, H.: Lateral dominance, lateral awareness, and reading disability. Child. Dev., *36*:57–71, 1965.

7. Blau, A.: Mental changes following head trauma in children. Arch. Neurol. Psychiatry, 35:723–769, 1936.
8. Bond, E., and Appell, K.: *The Treatment of Behavior Disorders Following Encephalitis.* New York, Commonwealth Fund, 1931.
9. Byers, K., and Lord, E.: Late effects of lead poisoning in children. Am. J. Dis. Child., 66:471, 1943.
10. Clements, S. D., and Peters, J. E.: Minimal brain dysfunctions in the school age child. Arch. Gen. Psychiatry, 6:185–197, 1962.
11. Cogan, D. G., and Wurster, J. B.: Normal and abnormal ocular movements. In *Early Experience and Visual Information Processing in Perceptual and Reading Disorders.* Washington, D.C., National Academy of Sciences, 1970. pp. 70–78.
12. Conners, C. K.: Psychological effects of stimulant drugs in children with minimal brain dysfunction. Pediatrics, 49:702, 1972.
13. Conners, C. K., Eisenberg, L., and Barcai, A.: Effect of dextroamphetamine in children. Arch. Gen. Psychiatry, 17:478, 1967.
14. Davies, H., and Kirman, B. H.: Microcephaly. Arch. Dis. Child., 37:623–627, 1962.
15. Diller, L., and Birch, H. G.: Psychological evaluation of children with cerebral damage. In Birch, H. G. (ed.): *Brain Damage in Children.* Baltimore, Williams & Wilkins Co., 1964.
16. Drillien, C. M.: *The Growth and Development of the Prematurely Born Infant.* Baltimore, Williams & Wilkins Co., 1964.
17. Flower, R. (ed.): *Reading Disorders.* Philadelphia, F. A. Davis Co., 1965.
18. Gibbs, F. A., Gibbs, E. L., Carpenter, P. R., and Spies, H. W.: Electroencephalographic abnormality in "uncomplicated" childhood diseases. J.A.M.A., 171:1050–1055, 1959.
19. Goldstein, K., and Scheerer, M.: *Abstract and Concrete Behavior.* Psychological Monographs, No. 239, 1941.
20. Hammar, S. L.: School underachievement in the adolescent: A review of 73 cases. Pediatrics, 40:373–281, 1967.
21. Harper, P. A., Fischer, L. K., and Ryder, R. V.: Neurological and intellectual status of prematures at three to five years of age. J. Pediatr., 55:679, 1959.
22. Hertzig, M. E., and Birch, H.: Neurological organization in psychiatrically disturbed adolescents. Arch. Gen. Psychiatry, 19:528, 1968.
23. Hohman, L. B.: Post-encephalitic behavior disorders in children. Bull. Johns Hopkins Hosp., 33:372–375, 1922.
24. Jasper, H. H., Solomon, P., and Bradley, C.: EEG analysis of behavior problem children. Am. J. Psychiatry, 95:641, 1938.
25. Kalverboer, A. F., Coultre, R. le, and Casaer, P.: Implications of congenital ophthalmoplegia for the development of visuo-motor function. Dev. Med. Child Neurol., 12:642, 1970.
26. Kinsbourne, M.: Developmental Gerstmann syndrome. Pediatr. Clin. North Am., 15:771, 1968.
27. Klinkerfuss, G. H., Lange, P. H., Weinberg, W. A., et al.: EEG abnormalities of children with hyperkinetic behavior. Neurology (Minneap.), 15:883, 1965.
28. McFie, J.: The diagnostic significance of disorders of higher nervous activity. In Vinken, P. J., and Bryn, G. W. (eds.): *Handbook of Clinical Neurology.* Vol. 3. New York, American Elsevier, 1969, p. 4.
29. Menkes, M. M., Rowe, J. S., and Menkes, J. H.: A twenty-five-year follow up study on the hyperkinetic child with minimal brain dysfunction. Pediatrics, 39:393, 1967.
30. Milman, D.: Organic behavior disorder. J. Dis. Child., 91:521–528, 1956.
31. *Minimal Brain Dysfunction in Children.* P.H.S. Publication No. 2015. Washington, D.C., U.S. Department of Health, Education and Welfare, 1969.
32. Nicholls, J. V. V.: The retarded reader. Postgrad. Med., 31:66–71, 1962.
33. Paine, R. S., and Oppe, T. E.: *Neurological Examination of Children.* Philadelphia, J. B. Lippincott Co., 1966.
34. Paine, R. S., Werry, J. S., and Quay, H. C.: A study of minimal cerebral dysfunction. Dev. Med. Child Neurol., 10:505–520, 1968.
35. Pasamanick, B., and Knobloch, H.: Syndrome of minimal cerebral damage. J.A.M.A., 170:1384, 1959.
36. *Report of the Conference on the Use of Stimulant Drugs in the Treatment of Behaviorally Disturbed Young School Children.* Washington, D.C., Office of Child Development, Department of Health, Education and Welfare, 1971.
37. Richardson, S. O., and Normanly, J.: Incidence of pseudoretardation in a clinic population. Am. J. Dis. Child, 109:432–435, 1965.
38. Rosenberger, P. B.: Visual matching and clinical findings among good and poor readers. Am. J. Dis. Child., 119:103–110, 1970.

39. Spearman, C.: *The Abilities of Man: Their Nature and Measurement*. London, Macmillan Co., 1927.
40. Sprague, R. L., Barnes, K. R., and Werry, J. S.: Methylphenidate and thioridazine: learning, reaction time, activity and classroom behavior in disturbed children. Am. J. Orthopsychiatry, *40*:615, 1970.
41. Stevens, J. R., Sachdev, K. K., and Milstein, V.: Behavior disorders of childhood and the electroencephalogram. Arch. Neurol., *18*:160, 1968.
42. Strauss, A. A., and Lehtinen, L. E.: *Psychopathology and Education of the Brain Injured Child*. New York, Grune & Stratton, 1947.
43. Strecker, E. A.: Behavior problems in encephalitis; clinical study of relationship between behavior and acute and chronic phenomena of encephalitis. Arch. Neurol. Psychiatry, *21*:137–144, 1929.
44. Subirana, A.: The relationship between handedness and the language function. Int. J. Neurol., *4*:215–234, 1964.
45. Thurstone, L. L.: *Primary Mental Abilities*. Chicago, University of Chicago Press, 1938.
46. Touwen, B. C. L., and Prechtl, H. F. R.: *The Neurological Examination of the Child with Minor Nervous Dysfunction*. Philadelphia, J. B. Lippincott Co., 1970.
47. Towbin, A.: Organic causes of minimal brain dysfunction. J.A.M.A., *217*:1207, 1971.
48. Vernon, P. E.: Analysis of cognitive ability. Br. Med. Bull., *27*:222, 1971.
49. Waldrop, M. F., Pedersen, F. A., and Bell, R. Q.: Minor physical anomalies and behavior in preschool children. Child Dev., *39*:391–400, 1968.
50. Wender, P. H.: *Minimal Brain Dysfunction in Children*. New York, John Wiley & Sons, Inc., 1971.
51. Wepman, J. M.: Auditory discrimination. Pediatr. Clin. North Am., *15*:721, 1968.
52. Whitsell, L. J.: Learning disorders as a school health problem. Calif. Med., *111*:433, 1969.
53. Wiener, G., Rider, R. V., Oppel, W. C., et al.: Correlates of low birth weight. Psychological status at eight to ten years of age. Pediatr. Res., *2*:110, 1968.
54. Zangwill, O. L.: *Cerebral Dominance and Its Relation to Psychological Function*. Edinburgh and London, Oliver & Boyd, Ltd., 1960.

Chapter 13

Language Disorders

by Martha B. Denckla, M.D.

RATIONALE FOR EARLY RECOGNITION OF SPEECH AND LANGUAGE DELAYS

The child whose speech is delayed or poor should be of concern to the physician. By 30 months (two and a half years), parental or medical observation can establish the existence of the problem, and evidence is mounting that the attitude expressed by the phrase "he'll outgrow it" is no longer justified. Admittedly, early concern about delayed or poor speech represents something of a change in attitude on the part of the physician, since this sign or symptom, in the vast majority of cases, does not indicate a progressive or life-threatening condition nor does it mean as much of a fixed handicap as is found in the static encephalopathies of cerebral palsy. In the traditional medical context of concern with dramatically abnormal, anatomically localized, or progressive or life-threatening disorders, therefore, the developmental disorders that present with poor or late talking are liable to be viewed as hardly physical at all, but rather closer to that ill-defined group of symptoms and signs that physicians may dismiss with the word "functional." It is something of a departure from tradition to exhort the physician to become concerned with dysfunction per se and to emphasize that dysfunction can be in itself, without regard to underlying cause, the generator of further dysfunctions.

Such is the case with the late or poor talker. Even when his underlying condition is as benign as the term "developmental" or "maturational" may imply, he is at risk for intellectual and emotional maladjustments in the present, and academic and social failures in the near future. As Ingram has pointed out, the problems of the child with speech and language disorders are likely to be uniquely related to that disorder, regardless of underlying cause or associated problems.[14] The inability to use spoken language effectively is in and of itself of crucial developmental importance, giving rise quite predictably to other problems, and is therefore worthy in and of itself of early detection and treatment. It appears that only the exceptional child, whose other abilities (behavioral, visual, and the like) are superior, manages to "outgrow" the consequences of a speech and language disorder fully, i.e., to compensate adequately for practical purposes. Even such an exceptional child may succeed only at great personal emotional expense.

The immediate detrimental effects of speech and language disorder in the preschool years appear as deficits in the areas of emotional control and cognitive functioning. As Luria has demonstrated, the use of language regulates motor behavior, influences the child's stabilization of perception even in the visual sphere, and has effects upon selective attention.[16] It takes only common sense to realize that the ability to understand instructions or explanations and the ability to comprehend and use words such as "later" or "after" are important mediators of behavior; postponement of gratification and control of impulse often depend upon the utterance and later the internalization of such words. The whole nature of the emotional interaction and the behavior of the child with the adults in his environment is altered by his possession of their words. It is important to realize that not only may failure to use language result from disturbed emotional relationships, but that the opposite cause-effect relationship may obtain. Intellectually the young child's exploration of the world is widened by the ability to use words—words to describe, words with which to ask questions, words with which to organize perceptions in time and space. As Vigotsky has demonstrated, language paves the way for abstract thinking.[25]

As there has been an increased appreciation of the enormous amount of learning that takes place in the preschool years, prior to any formal academic training, so there has been a proportionate increase in the appreciation of language acquisition in infancy. It is now felt that between the ages of 10 and 18 months there is an important spurt of receptive ability, so that the age at which a physician should become concerned about a baby is much earlier than was previously thought. It appears now that a male child who is not comprehending short commands by 18 months, not saying any words by the age of two years, or not speaking in phrases of two or more words by two and one half years of age should be considered a late or poor talker and something should be done about him. (The use of the male as an example is intentional, as the female reaches the language milestones somewhat earlier, perhaps as much as six months, and the incidence of speech and language disorders in males is several times that in females, the estimates running from between twice as frequent to five times as frequent, depending upon the reference).[14] If the child fails to comprehend simple one-stage commands by 18 months of age, there should be concern regardless of the rest of his functioning. Failure to meet comprehension milestones is more serious than output delays, for the language disorders with the receptive component are eventually more serious threats to the child's total future development. Disorders of comprehension or

production of the language, or both, should be regarded as symptoms in themselves deserving of treatment, with the diagnostic process proceeding parallel
to but not necessarily preceding the treatment. As is discussed later, the treatment program may consist of indirect treatment through the parent or family
group; the question, "what can you expect to do with a very young child?"
should not become a rhetorical expression of therapeutic nihilism with respect to the linguistically impaired toddler.

Once dedicated to early recognition of language impairment, the primary
physician or pediatrician must introduce into his repertoire of routine check-
up inquiries a set of definite questions to ask parents about their child's language level.[17] He should also attempt some sort of brief screening examination of this level, although this is not as likely to provide useful history in an
age group notorious for lack of cooperation, even under the best of circumstances. The following minimal criteria are expected:*

1½ years (18 months) Understands simple two word commands.
                      Points to at least one body part on self.
                      Points to at least five objects or pictures.
                      Uses minimum five words (usually nouns).

2 years (24 months)   Understands longer but still single-stage commands.
                      Points to at least four body parts on himself and
                        others.
                      Points to at least 10 objects or pictures thereof.
                      Uses a minimum 50 words, including own name.
                      Combines two words into phrases or questions
                        ("Where Daddy?", "Go car!")
                      Uses 25 per cent of consonants in his native language.
                      Intelligibility may be poor to strangers.

2½ years (30 months) Follows two out of three commands.
                      Understands at least two prepositions.
                      Uses minimum 100 words.
                      Makes noun-verb, pronoun-verb, and
                        preposition-noun phrase combinations.
                      Repeats two digits or syllables (if spoken to him
                        at a rate of one per second).

3 years   Understands four prepositions.
          Points to 25 objects or pictures.
          Uses minimum of 250 words.
          Uses 50 to 75 per cent of consonants in
            language.
          Intelligible to most strangers.
          Repeats three digits or syllables.

---

*Developmental minimal norms given are a composite of those stated in references 11, 17,
19, and 24 and the author's experience.

The parent who accompanies the child to the medical check-up visits should be asked specifically about the child's meeting of these criteria. The physician may attempt to elicit language performance in the course of the office examination—not so much expecting the toddler to perform as expecting the parent to grasp what the physician's inquiries mean. Although doting parents often exaggerate about the upper levels of their children's attainments, rarely will they conceal failure to meet minimal milestones.

If so young a child "fails" minimum speech and language requirements for his age, what is the physician to do? First the physician must depart somewhat from two tenets of the medical model: (1) that "abnormal" must be established, in which "abnormal" signifies "pathological," and (2) that diagnosis must precede treatment. The vast majority of children who fail to meet speech and language milestones do not, in the conventional sense, suffer from any pathological condition. (Of course, it is the mandate of the physician to search for the minority who do harbor disease, for in the words of Dr. Norman Geschwind, "doctors exist to diagnose rare diseases.") In most cases, the physician is justifiably loath to arouse the anxiety of parents whose children are indeed *not* "abnormal." The unmodified medical model forces the physician into an "either-or" position in which he either decides to pursue a diagnosis of disease or dismisses the dysfunction as "normal—he'll outgrow it." The middle position, in which the dysfunction is worthy of calm but definite recognition, implies that treatment may be needed even when there is no "diagnosis" beyond the "functional" level. Furthermore, treatment may have to begin before diagnosis is established. Even in the most obvious instance in which, once suspected, diagnosis is devoutly to be wished for (i.e., deafness), the treatment itself may be the route by which diagnosis is established. When dealing with an age group such as the one and a half to three year olds, the vagaries of any testing (audiometric, psychometric, neuropsychiatric) are such that repeated efforts at diagnosis may have to run concurrently with ongoing therapeutic efforts.

Serious errors in diagnosis (and certainly these justifiably arouse parental anxiety or distrust) and serious delays in therapy are likely to occur if the physician is unwilling to share with the parents his concern about present dysfunction and uncertainty about diagnosis. The physician learns "chronic" (unfolding) diagnosis in a new sense: "Call me again as he gets better," rather than "Call me again if he's any worse."

Why such urgency about therapy for speech and language delays or impairments? Why not "wait and see" whether the child's functioning falls so far behind that he is "clearly abnormal" at three and a half or four? Because functional disorders of the brain differ from functional disorders of, e.g., the heart (consider the functional heart murmur of childhood). The brain, as the organ of the mind, has to learn, and there is ample evidence that it learns certain things optimally at certain times—so-called "critical periods." Thus nurture complements or compensates for nature better sooner than later. For language, this means *before* the age at which the child may clearly qualify as "abnormal." As for arousing parental anxiety, most parents are already anxious about speech and language problems; although naturally gratified to be reassured that their child will probably eventually be normal, they also find "eventually" itself too open-ended to help in the here and now. Most parents find a program of specific action in itself anxiety-relieving. They understand and respond to the description of language disorder *as dysfunction,* which generates further secondary dysfunction, which generates further tertiary dysfunctions—the emotional and behavioral ones with which the parent already has to cope and the future academic problems that are discussed later in relation to learning disabilities.

The foregoing discussion of rationale leads to the following guidelines: (1) listen to parental complaints, take a speech and language history routinely, and attempt speech and language screening; (2) keep possible pathological abnormalities in mind, especially inadequate hearing, but do not dismiss as "normal" those who lack such diagnostic features; (3) be prepared to refer the patient for treatment of speech and language dysfunction before or during the course of diagnostic tests and studies.

CLINICAL SYNDROMES OF LANGUAGE DISORDER

Although major emphasis here is upon recognition and management of developmental language disorders, other possible causes of late or poor language development must be mentioned in passing. These are: (1) hearing impairment, alone or in combination with other causes; (2) primary psychiatric (affective) disorders (e.g., autism); (3) global mental retardation; (4) major neurological disorders including cerebral palsy syndromes and acquired aphasia with an illness or brain injury of known onset; (5) local structural defects of speech organs (e.g., cleft palate); (6) environmental deprivation; and (7) combinations of any of the foregoing. Discussions of these causes and useful charts on differential diagnosis by Paine and Oppé and Ingram are available.[14, 21]

In the experience of a neurologist known to be interested in developmental speech and language disorder, children suffering from cerebral palsy, dramatic brain injuries, local structural conditions, and severe hearing impairment are currently well-recognized and usually properly referred; seldom do such children reach developmental specialists for consultation. The "psychiatric-retarded-brain dysfunction" differential diagnosis is, however, an every-day situation in a language-oriented clinic and presents the greatest difficulties in the preschool child.

Case 1

A. O., white male, second of two children of middle class, college educated parents. Normal perinatal history and motor milestones. Parents concerned when boy, two and a half years old, had little speech or comprehension, wild behavior, and temper tantrums. Results of evaluation at a multidisciplinary hospital clinic were: skull x-ray normal; free field audiometry suggested normal; audiological and neurological examination allegedly impossible. Nevertheless, psychometrics were attempted and parents were told, "he is mildly retarded." Methylphenidate (Ritalin) led to worsening of behavior, and a private pediatrician declared that the boy was "schizophrenic."

Language therapy was started at age four, concomitant with attendance at a structured, kindly nursery school. Receptive vocabulary (Peabody Form A) rose from two years 11 months (at chronological age (CA) four years one month) to five years one month (at CA five years). He named more pictures than the average five year old. Behavior, including affectionate, improved dramatically when teachers and parents spoke slowly in short sentences. Despite continued hyperactivity, distractibility, and fine motor problems, he was able to attend a normal kindergarten although medication and a specially qualified teacher were necessary to maintain this placement.

Articulation troubles and stammering (stuttering) are the commonest speech defects in childhood, but 10 per cent of speech referrals are "in the nature of dysphasia"—i.e., are language disorders with associated speech production difficulties.

Table 13–1 summarizes one neurologist's experience with referrals for language disorders.[6]

It is important to note that a large number of these children have the hyperkinetic-distractible-impulsive disorder that is often considered *the* definition of minimal brain dysfunction. One may refer to such organically based hyperactive behavior as the dyscontrol subsyndrome of minimal brain dysfunction, as such behavior can occur without linguistic, perceptual, or obvious motoric syndromes or concomitantly with one or more of them. A speech or language disorder may be another subsyndrome within the MBD group, again existing solo or in combinations. Coexistence of behavioral dyscontrol and language disorder is common, and each subsyndrome modifies the prognosis of the other (Table 13–2).[4, 14]

As in case 1, young children with the combination of MBD dyscontrol and MBD language disorder are often pseudoretarded or pseudoschizophrenic. Interaction between poor learning of controls by reward and punishment and poor learning of language as a medium whereby one can control oneself and one's environment can produce a clinical picture of gross disorganization or

TABLE 13–1   GENERAL DIAGNOSES OF 50
PRESCHOOL AND KINDERGARTEN CHILDREN
REFERRED WITH CHIEF COMPLAINT OF
"LANGUAGE DELAY" (1970–1972)

Diagnosis	3 yr to 4 yr 11 mo	5 yr to 5 yr 11 mo	Total
Retardation	4	4	8
Classic autism	1	0	1
Brain damage ("schizophrenia-like")	1	3	4
MBD dyscontrol	7	10	17
Receptive-expressive disorder*	2*	3†	5
Articulation disorder (severe, unintelligible)	2	1	3
Expressive disorder	3	9	12
n =	20	30	50

*Only the two preschoolers had "central auditory imperception"; both were hyperlexic.

†One child had high frequency hearing loss.

TABLE 13–2 LANGUAGE PROBLEMS FOUND IN
17 PATIENTS WITH MINIMAL BRAIN
DYSFUNCTION (DYSCONTROL TYPE)

Disorder	Nursery School	Kindergarten	Total°
Receptive	2	1	3
Expressive	3	5	8
Repetitive (auditory, short-term memory)	4	7	11
Articulation	6	9	15
3 to 4 deficient areas	3	3	6

°Some individuals are represented by more than one entry.

withdrawal.[16, 27] Intervention via direct or indirect (parent as teacher) language therapy can provide consistent structure and the medium for self-structure (e.g., "I must run fast" uttered aloud by the child).

At present it appears best to avoid the use of the term "aphasia" in this context, even when called "developmental aphasia," and to reserve it for acquired language impairments of known time of onset after a period of normal language development has taken place.[7, 14] These are far less frequently encountered than are developmental language disorders. Such cases approximate adult aphasic syndromes in direct relation with age of onset. Young children, however, are not known to develop fluent aphasia, even with known acquired temporal lobe lesions such as result in the fluent paraphasic speech of Wernicke's aphasia. And although spoken language recovery is dramatically better than in adult cases, even young children who suffer acquired aphasia are impaired in verbal intelligence test and academic written language performance.[1]

Case 2

H. K., white female, second of three children of middle class, high school educated parents. Perinatal and developmental history were normal until acute viral encephalitis at age six years. After two weeks of coma and repeated convulsions, she was behaviorally uncontrollable, inattentive, and noncommunicative. After one year, motor and behavior control recovered spontaneously, but language remained severely impaired. Auditory-receptive and auditory-perceptual abilities were at most on a three and a half year old level (chronological age seven years seven months). Grammatical usage was telegraphic, on a two and a half year old level at most. Naming was at a six year old level but word finding in conversation was at a three year old level. Visual cues and stimuli produced H. K.'s most adequate performances (both language and nonlanguage, like Raven Colored Progressive Matrices), which were at a six year old (borderline retardation) level.

Her dysphasia did not conform to any of the adult acquired syndromes. Expressive (word finding and grammar) and audiophonetic receptive aspects were markedly impaired; articulation (speech sound production) and naming of visual items were relatively spared. To confound attempts at localization, the electroencephalogram was most focally abnormal in the right temporal region; but the child (and her mother) had always been ambidextrous before the illness.

Ingram provides a table of developmental language disorders based upon severity.[14] Figure 13–1, a modification of Ingram's diagram, based upon the

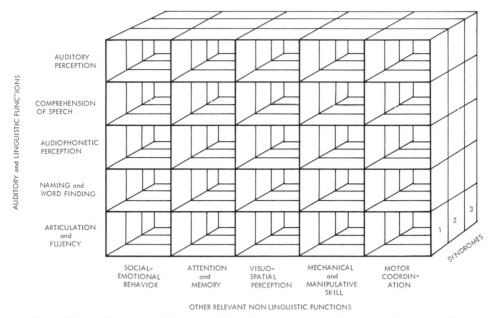

Figure 13–1   Diagram of language disorders in context of other dysfunctions. Number and degree of dark shaded surfaces define each "syndrome."

present author's experience in which both qualitative and quantitative factors are considered, is an attempt to diagram the way in which language disorder descriptions can be placed in context with respect to other language areas (vertical axis), and with respect to other nonlanguage areas of functioning (horizontal axis). The severity of a given child's problem can be visualized in terms of shading in the boxes, the number of boxes impaired and the intensity of shade (light gray to black) indicating the degree of impairment. For example, a globally mentally retarded child would have shading in every box; theoretically an "evenly" or "across-the-board" retarded child's chart would show the same shade of gray in each box. By contrast, the child with a "pure language disorder" might have shading only in "articulation" (light gray) and "expressive language" (dark gray) squares; this child, with no behavioral, attentional, limb-motoric, or visuospatial impairments, would be in total picture so "mild" that his diagram is not even shaded in three-dimensional boxes, only squares, yet the dark gray "expressive language" square indicates a significant area of difficulty. Thus may descriptions of consistent diagrammatic profiles constitute "syndromes" for the clinician. Such a diagram would have to be considerably more complex for the child over six years; but for preschoolers it is adequate.

The diagram allows the physician to clarify his own thinking about the relationship of specific developmental disorders (or minimal brain dysfunction) to mental retardation. The specific developmental disorder or minimal brain dysfunction *is* a retardation, i.e., a level of functioning below that expected for the child's chronological age. Had the child been younger, the test would have been considered "passed." With an increasing number of shaded-in areas indicating retardations, the continuum from "specific" or "minimal" to "global" retardation is visualized. Largely unanswered, however, is the important question of whether certain single "black-shaded" areas—language comprehension deficiency for example—are potentially malignant with respect to growth of other functions. Deafness, certainly, has been discussed in this way.[10, 12] And the organic disorders of behavior and attention can certainly be so pervasive as to impair virtually all the child's growth.[27] Other dysfunctions may be more susceptible to compensation or isolation; these, no matter how "black," might not be generators of further dysfunction.

With these theoretical considerations, and matters for future research in mind, the practical level of clinical syndrome description can be approached.

Receptive Language Disorder Syndromes

Central deafness, central auditory imperception (for very severe cases that include inconsistent failures to respond to nonlanguage sounds), central receptive aphasia, and central word deafness (for cases with demonstrable responses to nonlanguage sounds) are synonyms. Even more synonyms exist—e.g., auditory agnosia, by analogy with adult neurology—but do no more than further muddy the waters.

Although the names emphasize the most serious and distinctive element in the language disorder, all such cases include expressive language and articulatory impairment. There are no fluently speaking, expressively intact "receptive language disorders" in children, so the name is shorthand for the most global inclusive clinical picture (shown in the left-hand vertical column of Figure 13–1) within language syndromes.

There are variations in intensity of receptive disturbance. As just indicated, some cases respond so little to *any* sound that the differential diagnosis is that of peripheral sensory deafness. Repeated audiometry or combined electroencephalography and audiometry may be required to make the distinction.[2, 13] To further complicate the situation, severe central auditory unresponsiveness may occur in an illness already characterized by a high prevalence of deafness—congenital rubella.[2]

Most cases, however, show normal response or even hyperacusis to nonverbal auditory stimuli, and indeed, in the latter situation it has been suggested that painful levels of sound reception cause auditory "tuning out." This majority group of receptively "impaired" youngsters do not achieve language comprehension milestones on time; when seen at two and a half or three years they are still responding to single words only or to a few highly stereotyped familiar short commands. Their parents often describe such children as "not listening" rather than "not hearing," especially if hyperacusis is a complaint. Their speech is nominally sparse, agrammatic, and indistinct in articulation. They are frequently echolalic of fragments of others' speech. Since behavior is often wild (e.g., tantrums over sirens or fire engines) or withdrawn (no response to others' conversational approach), and motoric clumsiness is a frequent "neighborhood sign" of central nervous system dysfunction, such children look retarded or autistic or both unless one presents them with an opportunity to "show off" their islands of intact or superior functioning—their visuospatial or mechanical-manipulative abilities.

Many children with receptive language disorders become calm, attentive, and efficient when given visually guided "performance tasks" such as block designs, formboards, or puzzles. Not infrequently, such children name letters, numerals, and even "call" whole written words at an age when they name few common objects. Their indistinct articulation often improves to clear intelligibility when they "read" such visual symbols. Many are superficially hyperlexic, decoding long passages of newspaper, but giving no more evidence of comprehending the meaning of what they themselves speak-read aloud than what others speak to them. Such children gravitate toward familiar signs and symbols and seem to enjoy naming these; or they may smile and make eye contact or body-cuddle contact while absorbed in puzzle construction.

Case 3

J. S., white male, oldest son of middle class, high school graduates. Family history: father began to talk at three years, in kindergarten was still considered a "pantomimist." Mother had several miscarriages, a stillbirth, and another child with cerebral palsy; pregnancy with J. S. was complicated by frequent first-trimester hemorrhaging. Labor was induced with J. S. because of postmaturity, and delivery was complicated by hemorrhage.

J. S. sucked poorly and was allergic to milk. Early motor milestones were normal, and he allegedly obeyed some simple commands and said perhaps five words by 18 months. Between 18 and 30 months he had influenza with fever of 105° F (no convulsion) and many ear infections with high fevers. He was toilet trained at two and a half years and was not a behavior problem.

At three years, J. S. was referred to a speech and hearing clinic because his speech was still limited to single, poorly articulated words, e.g., "kuku" for cookie and "poo" for spoon. Free field audiometry revealed adequate hearing. He demonstrated comprehension of single words (Peabody Picture Vocabulary Test Form A), two and a half year level, at chronological age (CA) three years three months, if one pushed to hold his attention. He named single toys and pictures at appropriate language level, and demonstrated an eagerness to turn the Yellow Pages and "read" whole words—Esso, Mobil, Gulf, Texaco—and numerals. Articulation was best during such visually cued naming. His attention was often perseveratively riveted to visual materials. He could not perform action to single commands and neither responded to nor used "little words" of connected speech. He was affectionate and showed communicative intent.

After two years of combined direct and indirect (home program) language therapy plus nursery school, J. S. scored Peabody Receptive Vocabulary age of four years three months (CA five years four months). Articulation was immature but quite intelligible; his voice was louder than was appropriate. Both comprehension and use of grammatical structure remained deficient for age; naming pictures remained one of his better functions (four year nine month level); and more impressive, he was able to "read" aloud words he had never seen and did not understand. Motor and attentional deficiencies were clearer at five years, when more is normally expected. Leiter IQ was 97, after three sessions of training in what was required.

J. S. was placed in a small special communications disorder class; he could not follow directions in a regular kindergarten.

There is at present active controversy over whether "central deafness" or "central word-deafness" should be diagnosed and the patients treated any differently from those with peripheral deafness or the hard-of-hearing. Some authorities feel that most centrally impaired children reject amplification

TABLE 13–3 GENERAL DIAGNOSES OF 20
CHILDREN REFERRED WITH CHIEF
COMPLAINT OF RECEPTIVE DISORDER ("DOES
NOT UNDERSTAND LANGUAGE WELL")

Retardation	8
Brain damage ("schizophrenia-like")	4
Central auditory imperception	2
Mixed receptive-expressive disorder	3*
MBD dyscontrol	3

*One child had high frequency hearing loss.

and need and will benefit from auditory training—teaching "to the deficit."
Other schools of therapy argue for the helpfulness of amplification (hearing
aids) in most children who are unresponsive to normal or speech volume and
point to the hypervisual learning orientation shared by the peripherally and
centrally deaf. A critical appraisal of these positions on therapy will require
sorting out of the profiles of each group, as the "central" one is certainly not
entirely homogeneous; e.g., some are hyperactive and motorically impaired
and some are not, which modifies the approach just as much as hyperacusis,
as opposed to sound-ignoring behavior, does.

Severe receptive language disorders are comparatively uncommon, both
within the total group of children presenting with poor comprehension and
within the group with language disorders but normal intelligence (Table 13–
3).

Prognosis for normal adult functioning has been very poor in the receptively impaired group, many of whom slip from normal to "retarded" even in
visuospatial tests with increasing age.[8, 14] As with the deaf, thinking may initially be normal but fall behind for lack of language.[12, 13] Guarded optimism is
based on a few cases treated early and followed closely to prevent superven-
ing complications (such as transient conductive hearing loss with attacks of
otitis media or school placement in a noisy room with a fast-talking teacher).

There are, however, many patients in whom the semantic-receptive part
of the language disorder is relatively mild and shades over into the next category (see Fig. 13–1).

Audiophonetic Disorder

"Audiophonetic" is introduced here as a new compromise term for
audiophonic or auditory-perceptual disorder (British versus American terminology).

Such children do not appear deaf or unable to understand ordinary short
commands, although speech milestones are delayed. They may, however, appear "lost" when longer, faster strings of language come at them, may often
ask "what?" or appear dazed and inattentive. To emphasize this point
again—they are not expressively normal, but are often more distinct in speech
sound articulation than the more severely receptively or motorically impaired

discussed later. In these "middling" audiophonetic cases, repetition becomes a valuable diagnostic sign. Unlike the "receptive" who semiautomatically echoes but often falls mute when cajoled to repeat, these are youngsters to whom speech sounds convey meaning but cannot be efficiently processed (possibly a rate-dependent phenomenon). In repetition, their span or sequencing of speech sounds or both are below age expectation, but often they come closer to age level with meaningful sentences than with meaningless strings of digits or nonsense syllables. It is tempting to speculate—but not easy to prove—that their word finding and naming problems are more those of "medium" than "message" and that their tendency to misuse or misplace (rather than omit) arbitrary grammatical terms is another sign of "medium" difficulties that are nonmeaningful, i.e., not at the semantic level.

This is an extremely large group of children who frequently appear normal to parents until nursery school or kindergarten, when they are found to have difficulty in following multistage commands issued in the classroom. Because their speech sound production may be quite acceptable (although they tend to be laconic silent types), such children are often missed by "speech correctionists" in schools.

Case 4

P. G., white female, first of two children of a middle class, college educated family. Family history was equivocally positive—a paternal aunt said "what?" frequently and mumbled to herself, and an uncle was deaf-mute. P. G. had an unremarkable perinatal and early childhood history; all milestones, including speech and language, were reportedly normal, but short attention span was noted. Parents were surprised when P. G. at five years did poorly in kindergarten (the teacher called her "not with it") and was placed in a prereading transitional class rather than regular first grade. At age six, she scored poorly on a reading readiness test; WISC IQ was 93 (verbal 100, performance 86). The lower performance items and Bender Gestalt motor immaturity suggested neurological dysfunction but appeared contradicted by above-average visual-motor and visual-perceptual functioning on the Frostig test. A child psychiatrist ruled out significant psychogenic problems, but did not corroborate the psychologist's impression of organic impairment. Indeed, at six years nine months, classic neurological examination was within normal limits, but the child showed difficulty in following the commands of the examiner, especially if two-stage in length, and repeatedly asked "what?" or else repeated subvocally what had just been said to her. Auditory discrimination, repetition span, and sequencing were deficient (four and a half year level). Expressive word finding and naming were poor (e.g., "doctrist" for dentist, "target" for sling shot), but grammar and articulation were adequate. Single word comprehension (Peabody Form A) and short sentence comprehension (Illinois Test of Psycholinguistic Abilities) were just at age level for her six years and nine months. Audiological testing revealed normal hearing. (In fact, P. G. was gifted in music and rhyming words.)

After a year of auditory and language training, P. G. was reading at an early second grade level and had gone into a regular second grade. Slossen IQ was 112. Auditory span and sequencing had advanced dramatically (eight year old level). Subvocalization occurred only after she was presented with unfamiliar words (spoken or written). She was no longer considered inattentive and excelled in handwriting.

After two years of language therapy, at age nine years, P. G. was achieving at grade level in a regular classroom (although below the twentieth percentile by local standards). Auditory discrimination continued to be below the eighteenth percentile, and acquisition of new words remained slow. Otis group IQ was 115.

Both the beginning of speech and the rate of progress of speech are slower in the audiophonetic disorder group. Renfrew feels that "in cases of auditory perception disability there seems to be an innate weakness which cannot be completely overcome by . . . systematic training."[22] She goes on, however, to observe that such children improve with training more rapidly than do those with motor disability (articulatory dyspraxia). And a paradoxical situation exists in the relationship between audiophonetic disorder and reading: although the largest subgroup of "dyslexic" children are audiophonetically impaired, yet reading *once* mastered greatly helps the spoken language of such children by "capturing" sounds in visual form, which lasts longer than auditory.[6, 12, 22]

Audiophonetic difficulties are frequently present (and easily detected, if looked for) in cases of so-called "expressive language disorder"—children who have no everyday difficulty in comprehending or responding to ordinary requests or commands. Auditory discrimination, span, sequencing, and blending are of late receiving more attention from those concerned with treating poor expressors or articulators.[17, 18, 24, 26] In this regard, the physician must remain the advocate of repeated audiometry, as even the transient burden of intermittent hearing reductions from ear infections may further retard such a child's speech and language. Particularly between 16 and 36 months, even slight deficits in auditory sensitivity will interfere with comprehension or use or both. And the intelligent but partially hard-of-hearing will often fool the experts.

Case 5

B. G., third child (second daughter) of white middle class college educated parents. Family history on both sides was positive for speech and reading problems. Mother had "negative pregnancy tests" for first trimester of pregnancy with B. G. At term, B. G.'s heartbeat was inaudible and a fetal electrocardiogram was required to demonstrate it. Labor was induced "slowly," and delivery was "fast." Birth weight was 5 lb. A collapsed lung was present in which pneumonitis developed and was treated with penicillin and streptomycin. Weight gain neonatally was poor, as B. G. "couldn't keep food down." Three episodes of trauma (fall on the head, severe burn, and iron ingestion) occurred during B. G.'s first 18 months of life. Motor milestones were unremarkable. Single words were spoken at 15 months, short sentences at two years, and comprehension seemed excellent, but mother observed and pointed out "mushy indistinct speech." A home speech program, working on W for L substitutions, was given when B. G. was four years old. A speech therapist evaluated the child, and also an otolaryngologist removed wax from the ears. During kindergarten, speech correction continued, but there was no suspicion of hearing loss. Because of mother's persistent concern with the child's "mushy" speech and certain aspects of "stubborn" behavior, B. G. was referred to a major medical center audiology clinic when she was six years old. Audiogram there showed bilateral high frequency loss (starting at 1500 Hz), confirmed (and found to be slightly worse) three months later at recheck visit. Hearing aid and speech therapy including lip-reading were begun when B. G. was six and in first grade. The child herself expressed amazement at the sounds she was hearing for the first time.

Expressive Language Disorder

This term is used to refer to the problems of children who, although they may have detectable audiophonic and articulatory impairments, are brought to clinical attention because their language content is defective — i.e., "message" as well as "medium" is poor.

When there is severe articulatory impairment coexistent with expressive language content deficiency, the latter may not be detectable until the articulation becomes intelligible, often during speech therapy.

Curiously, most authors refer to immature grammatical production (e.g., "telegram speech") and do not refer to poverty of vocabulary in naming and word finding.[14, 21, 29] It is some authors' experience that incorrect or agrammatical expressive language is far less common than poor naming and word finding.[7, 8] Such anomic children, if they articulate intelligibly and are clever at circumlocution, may be thought of as "quite verbal," i.e., they talk a lot. As is the case with adult acquired anomic aphasia, such an expressive disorder is often described by the parent as "poor memory." Yet the parent may note that the child is a puzzle: for some things he has a photographic memory, he amazes the family, yet he asks for a cupcake by saying "the thing with paper around it and goo on top." Such a child is often a late talker whose disorder then seems of no consequence until kindergarten begins, when it is found that he cannot tell the teacher his last name, address, or birthday. And he, too, is at high risk for reading difficulties (Table 13–4).[7, 20]

Establishment of "naming norms" requires knowledge of cultural as well as age-specific vocabulary expectations. The factor of speed as well as correctness is at last being taken into account in recent research on naming.

TABLE 13–4 CHARACTERISTICS OF 20 CHILDREN WITH EXPRESSIVE LANGUAGE DISORDER

	Boys (11)	Girls (9)	Total (20)
Non-language characteristics			
Left hand, foot, eye dominance	0	2	2
Weak (ambiguous) handedness	2	1	3
Mixed hand, foot, eye dominance (RLR, RRL)	6	4	10
Hyperkinetic behavior	5	2	7
Gross motor deficit	2	3	5
Fine motor (includes graphomotor) deficit	10	7	17
Visuospatial deficit	1	2	3
Language deficits			
Articulation	6	4	10
Stutter (stammer)	1	1	2
Grammar	2	3	5
Naming (and word finding)	11	9	20
Repetition span (and sequencing)	11	8	19
Historical features			
Positive family history	7	3	10
Perinatal "high risk" history	4	5	9
Vision or strabismus problem	1	3	4
Hearing, ear infection problem	4	2	6
Late or poor speech (noticed by parents)	7	5	12

The expressive language disorder cases in which naming is the worst feature stand in direct contrast to those receptive disorder cases in which naming is the very best feature, a qualitative profile contrast that would not fit with Ingram's classification, which assumes only a hierarchical continuum of severity in children's language disorders.[14]

Case 6

S. B., white, female, third of three daughters of middle class college educated parents. Family history was positive for left-handedness, poor spelling, and one paternal uncle with some early reading trouble. Perinatal and milestone history was unremarkable, except that S. B. was later in forming sentences than were her older sisters.

At age four and a half, S. B. seemed to have "memory" problems with common words — e.g., saying that her father was "egg" instead of "big." She also transposed syllables in longer words and had immature articulation. Her kindergarten teacher noted speech and language expressive problems in this otherwise bright and lively girl who understood all directions promptly and well. The teacher wondered whether "some form of epilepsy" was interfering intermittently with S. B.'s expressive powers. The pediatrician, finding that the child could not whisper digits back to him correctly, ordered an audiogram, which was normal.

Parents felt that a "downhill turn" in language usage occurred at four and a half to five years — or at least that the deficiency became more apparent. S. B. could not answer, except by multiple choice, questions as to her address, town of residence, or birthday. She did poorly in first grade reading, often reading out an entirely different but associated in meaning word (e.g., "cookies" for cake). WISC IQ was 107, verbal 94 and performance 121. Bender-Gestalt drawings were above age expectation. Classic neurological examination, electroencephalogram, and x-rays were within normal limits.

Speech was intelligible and grammatical, and comprehension of three-stage commands was intact. Auditory discrimination was also normal for age. Word finding and naming were poor, with paraphrasic and circumlocutory responses ("lip-up" for "lipstick," self-corrected to "up-make," "keetot" for "teapot"). Articulatory errors were trivial, but phonemic substitutions and missequencing were marked.

Speech and language clinic evaluation confirmed the child's word finding and phonemic problems. On the Illinois test of Psycholinguistic Abilities, given at age six years and nine months, her Verbal Expression was that of a three and a half year old and Auditory Memory (Digit span) that of a two and a half year old. Receptive and Visual scores were, by contrast, superior.

Speech and language therapy was coupled with a sight-word approach to reading (no phonics), with which success in grades 1 through 3 followed. At eight and a half years, S. B. was discharged from therapy. She was doing excellent arithmetic, reading slowly but passably, and could spell familiar words (those in her sight vocabulary). She was unable to attack a new word phonetically to spell it from dictation. Her digit span was now on a seven year old level, as was sentence repetition (Binet). Auditory discrimination and articulation tests were passed at the eight year old "ceiling" of these tasks. Her parents still remarked upon her "poor memory for specific facts." S. B. is a good example of Boder's dysphonemic dyslexia, which is discussed in the section on prognosis in the school years.

Note: The main speech and language difference between S. B. and P. G. is S. B.'s lesser degree of audiophonetic difficulty. S. B. was also blessed with superior visuospatial ability, including an almost "photographic" visual memory, whereas P. G. was only average in this.

This author has seen cases in which naming ability is far worse than S. B.'s and phonetic ability far better. These cases are closer to the "pure" anomic (amnestic) aphasia seen in adults; but one difference is that auditory span (repetition auditory-vocal, short-term auditory memory) seems always to be somewhat subnormal in children with expressive anomia, whereas in adults it is not impaired (cf. discussion by Weiner[26]).

Articulatory Disorders

The centrally deaf, centrally word deaf, audiophonetically impaired, and expressive language impaired may all have articulatory deficiencies. Yet—to depart again from Ingram's hierarchy of severity—some persons with each of these types of language disorder have *no speech disorder*.[14] Conversely, there are children whose faulty speech sound production is their only impediment, the "medium" their only problem in communicating the "message." Simple "dyslalia," the persistently immature articulation of the so-called "lalling" phase of speech, is easy enough to notice and is often easily treated by school speech correctionists. These children are able to imitate the speech sounds of others but may continue for a time to mispronounce in their own spontaneous speech. Morley is of the opinion that treatment for the perfectly intelligible but infantile talker is far from urgent, in fact of low priority.[19] Treatment is of no urgency, but poor articulation may be a sign that indicates auditory perceptual problems or motoric immaturity (such as is often associated with minimal brain dysfunction) and hence merits some diagnostic attention as a "soft sign."[26]

Of greater concern is the severely unintelligible but comprehending child. Some may produce vowel sounds only—obviously a severely handicapping degree of speechlessness in and of itself. When such a child cannot imitate others' speech sounds, or perhaps cannot even, by watching them, imitate others' mouth positions, he is often described as suffering from "articulatory dyspraxia."[19] The use of the term "dyspraxia" in this situation is unfortunate, as there is no evidence that the problem of these children qualifies for its meaning—i.e., inability to perform a skilled act in the absence of sensory or motor deficit. The argument is advanced that it is justifiable to call this "dyspraxia" in contrast to the "paresis" of the child with cerebral palsy who has chewing, swallowing, and phonating weakness; but this may be countered by the observation that in many proved cases of motor system impairment, slowness and imprecision of movement without weakness is the motor manifestation. Ingram has observed slowness of tongue and lip positioning in children with delayed speech and motor impairment but free of spasticity or weakness. Furthermore, many poor articulators did indeed as infants have sucking, swallowing, and chewing deficiencies; these simpler, more automatic, highly practiced oral skills were mastered before speech, a far more rapid and varied oral motor performance. A massively impaired motor system, as in cerebral palsy victims, may not even allow simple oral acts; a less dramatically impaired motor system may allow the more automatic but not the complicated acts of speech. "Dyspraxia" should not be used as a synonym for mild motor impairment, but it is conceivable that true dyspraxia of speech may be demonstrable—if auditory perception, intraoral somesthesis and kinesthesis, and rapidity of buccoorolingual movement are all tested and found to be intact. Until such cases are reported, "severe articulatory disorder" would appear to be a safer and more accurate label for the cases commonly encountered.

Morley is quite guarded about the prognosis of severely unintelligible, nonimitating children; in fact, in terms of persistent severe communication handicap, she ranks them with the receptive-auditory-imperception group.[19]

Ingram estimates that if a child has said no intelligible words by the age of three years, he is unlikely to be intelligible until the age of eight years.[14] It is probable that finer attention to the audiophonetic and anomic problems would differentiate prognostic subgroups of articulatory disorder. And, as in case 5, hearing impairment must be treated.

Case 7

R. T., white male, fourth of five children of middle class college educated parents. Perinatal history was unremarkable, sucking and swallowing normal. Family history was possibly positive in that two siblings had poor fine motor coordination (e.g., pencil control) and one brother had cluttered, peculiarly articulated speech as a preschool child. R. T. had normal motor milestones but some difficulty in chewing solid food, and he often chewed his tongue until it was red and sore. Because of lack of intelligible speech at age 28 months, R. T. was seen by a neurologist who noted slow and laborious tongue and palatal movements; "facial apraxia" was suggested. R. T. started in speech and language therapy immediately. At three years of age, his receptive (Peabody Form A) vocabulary was four years. He was well-behaved and attentive, and appeared motivated for direct therapy. Although there were hints of auditory span and word finding problems, these were overshadowed by his extreme speech sound production difficulty. He had trouble making appropriate mouth molds for words heard (i.e., in imitation of the examiner's speech) and was totally unable to shift from one mouth mold to another or even repeat the same syllable, such as in "bye-bye" or "mama."

At four years his neurological examination revealed generalized motor clumsiness, i.e., he could not balance or hop upon either foot and used a crayon like a two year old. He could repeat single syllables, articulating clearly, but never produced two syllables. Behavior was remarkably cheerful and well-controlled. Intraoral sensation could not be tested by conventional methods, but stereognosis was intact as tested by an informal "matching" game involving differently shaped chocolate candies.

At four and a half years, after continued therapy utilizing visual imitation of pictures and the examiner's mouth, plus allowing direct placement of his mouth molds, he became intelligible at a three year level except for consonant blends. Grammar now emerged in infantile constructions ("Now me grow"). The word finding (anomic) difficulty previously suspected was corroborated by his use of associated function words or phrases for nouns, e.g., "call" for telephone or "dig" for shovel. Tongue chewing diminished but did not entirely disappear.

Stuttering (Stammering)

This most common of speech disorders (prevalence 1 per cent, incidence 3 to 4 per cent, according to Andrews and Harris[3]) is a dysrhythmia of the respiratory mechanism during speech. Prolongations, hesitations, and repetitions interfere with expression very commonly in the two and three year old, and it is in practice difficult to tell whether a given child will continue to stutter past the age of five years. Andrews and Harris report that 75 per cent or more of preschool children who stutter cease before age five or six.[3]

The situation is then similar to that in dyslalia—is therapy necessary for a usually self-limited speech disorder? The difference lies in the psychiatric penumbra that surrounds stuttering; certainly, whatever the cause and effect relationship may turn out to be (and there is a vast literature on this subject), there is a relationship between emotional tension and stuttering. Even a simple, nonpsychoanalytic view of stuttering brings out the vicious circle problem, the stuttering–anxiety–more stuttering pattern commonly seen.[3, 14] Thus most experts on stuttering have advised that at the very least, parents of preschool stutterers must be treated (or counseled) if perpetuation of stuttering is to be minimized. This is dealt with more fully in the section on therapy that follows.

There are two subgroups of preschool stutterers at high risk for persistent dysrhythmia: (1) those who talk late and poorly and have a family history of stuttering, and (2) those whose hesitations in speech are related to word finding difficulty—i.e., have expressive language disorder as well as speech dysrhythmia. Of course, some children may belong to both group 1 and group 2, and are therefore candidates for very close (but circumspect) follow-up, particularly if periods of emotional stress occur. In short, stuttering may persist if both genetic predisposition and anxiety-provoking emotional stress are allowed to interact to the detriment of the child's speech and language habits. Awareness of the genetic component may allow the professional to guide the susceptible individual away from the stressful environmental influences—e.g., discourage parental "correction" of the three year old's stutter.

Summary of Developmental Speech and Language Disorder Syndromes in Preschool Years

The most severe, in terms of immediate and potentially long-term interference with oral communication, are the disorders at either end of the process—those involving imperception (reception) and those involving articulation (unintelligibility). These must be recognized and appropriately treated as early as possible. The least severely affected are the simply dyslalic, immature articulators, although their poor articulation may be a "soft sign" of more generalized motor deficiencies that the physician should note for possible correlation with minimal brain dysfunction (see Table 13–4). Parents of preschool stutterers require "preventive guidance," especially if family history is positive; stuttering hesitations may be a clue to expressive language (anomic) deficiencies in the child. Patients with mild to moderate audiophonetic and expressive language disorders, if they comprehend and speak well enough (albeit later and less well than their peers) to get along in the "short run" of preschool life, deserve recognition because of the high risk of reading disability in the "long run."

THE PHYSICIAN'S ORIENTATION: DIAGNOSIS

Once aware of the existence of the primary specific disorders of speech and language, and having found a child who does not meet two to three year old milestones, what does the physician do?

First of all, refer the patient for audiometry. This should be a rule for every child who shows difficulty in communicating by speech, whether or not hearing loss is suspected.[10] Even transient conductive hearing loss, in itself insufficient to cause late or poor speech, may be "the straw that breaks the camel's back." The physician should acquire a veritable obsession for repeated hearing assessments, becoming acquainted with and using the services of a nearby audiologist or university clinic.*

Second (or perhaps concurrently with audiological referral, depending upon facilities available), a speech and language therapist should be brought into the picture to describe the child's status. (It is unfortunate that the prevailing professional title is "speech pathologist" rather than "therapist"; this runs counter to current practice in the speech and language field).

Early referral for early description (not diagnosis) and preventive treatment does not mean that the physician steps out of the picture. He has sought a detailed answer to the question, "what sort of speech defect does this child have?" It remains his function to be concerned about "what sort of child has this speech defect?"[22] The physician's ongoing concern is with the context, the other axis of Figure 13–1, for both parents and other professional persons will turn to him in this regard.

Tables 13–1 and 13–2 emphasize context. The classifications are based upon the history and neurological examination of children over three years.[8] The primary physician, however, will be confronting the problem of context in an age group in which examination is unrewarding except in picking up rather gross deviations in behavioral and motoric competence. Hence history will be of more importance in establishing context of speech and language disorders.

History

Milestones.   The physician will inquire about the age at which the child acquired skills in motor, social, and adaptive (i.e, performance with nonverbal items) tasks. Lists and charts of these criteria are to be found in many textbooks of pediatrics.[21] One brief and graphic form, intended as an examination, is the Denver Developmental Screening Test; it can be used to good advantage in history taking as well.[11]

One learns a great deal about the parents' attitudes and feelings during such history taking, so that data of a social-environmental nature come as a side benefit. The physician can formulate for himself a profile (as suggested in Figure 13–1) of where the child appears to be in the continuum from "specific" to "global" retardation.

Medical History.   Perinatal and childhood physical illnesses are of obvious concern and in some instances focus the physician's interest on the pursuit of known sequelae of certain conditions. The association of central auditory imperception, as well as deafness, with congenital rubella is one example.[2] Repeated ear infections, particularly between 15 and 36 months of age, may contribute to the speech problem. Prematurity, small size for date, low Apgar

---

*The physician may obtain the names of appropriate audiological and speech and language facilities, including both clinics and private practitioners, from the American Speech and Hearing Association, 9030 Old Georgetown Road, Washington, D.C. 20014.

score at birth, hyperbilirubinemia, hypoglycemia, early convulsions—all the conditions, in short, that define the "high risk for brain damage" child—should be inquired after and noted.

Family History.   There is growing evidence that genetic factors may be even more common antecedents of speech and language disorders than are medical events, congenital or acquired. Orton emphasized the familial connections of speech, reading, writing, and poorly defined or mixed lateral preference.[20] In practically all series of preschool speech and language disorders, male to female ratios run between 2:1 and 3:1. In school-age "dyslexics" the male to female ratios run between 5:1 and 9:1. In both groups there are more parents and siblings and aunts and uncles with histories of ill-defined lateralization (e.g., hand, foot), educational difficulties, stuttering, and slow or poor speech development than in the general population.[7, 14] The genetic patterns have not been worked out, but are receiving increased attention in recent years. Aside from theoretical interest, however, a specific child's family history may be of value in establishing context and prognosis for him, especially if he is a younger member of a large sibship of which all older members have followed a known course. The interested physician with access to a good laboratory might be on the alert to search for more biochemical causes of speech disorder occurring in family groups. Worster-Drought reports frequent family occurrence of congenital auditory imperception and has seen the condition in twins.[29]

History of Onset, Downhill Change, or Progression of Dysfunction. Whether a past static medical event or a genetic "event" has caused a language disorder is of little consequence insofar as future management is concerned. The physician must remember, however, that the rare brain tumor, subdural hematoma, or subacute encephalitis (e.g., subacute sclerosing panencephalitis) may be underlying a language disorder that is progressively deteriorating. Such a suspicion warrants referral to a pediatric neurologist. Psychiatric disorder is more often heralded by progressive or sudden mutism, but this again is a rare and difficult diagnostic situation requiring specialized consultation. For example, sudden mutism with bizarre behavior has occurred in a child with a temporal lobe abscess.[8]

Examination

The vagaries of developmental screening, plus the time involved, may deter most primary physicians or pediatricians from attempting standard test "batteries." For behavioral observation, however, the primary physician has an advantage over the consultant: contact with the child and his family on many occasions, both routine and crisis, over a period of time. The primary physician should note in his records how the child behaves in the waiting room, in routine examination, and in the office or at home when acutely ill. This constitutes the most difficult kind of examination—that of behavior under stress—and one to which the pediatrician brings appreciation of the norms from his experience. Paine and Oppé describe details of developmental examination.[21]

Special Tests and Studies

Except for the progressive type, which are carried out by consultants, the tests under consideration are of an outpatient nature. Electroencephalography with audiometry is most likely to be ordered by an audiologist in a medical center, as it is quite specialized.[13] Routine electroencephalograms are not useful for speech and language disorder management per se, but are of course indicated for coexisting convulsive or possible "equivalent" behavioral disorders.

Blood and urine screening for amino acid or lipid metabolic disorders is of interest if a family history suggests genetic predisposition and if suitable laboratories are available in distance and the expense is feasible. One might wish to defer such tests, however, if no practical decision is likely to be forthcoming and the upset to the child is a real consideration.

One sort of testing seems tempting but should be avoided — psychometrics. Even in "normal" children of preschool age, psychometric predictive power is limited since both underestimates and overestimates are frequent. Moreover, in a child whose main dysfunction lies in the area most depended upon in preschool psychometrics — language — the IQ numbers may echo rather than supplement knowledge about the child. Attempts to find good nonverbal intelligence measures have been frustrated because there is normally very little beside language development that can be expected before the age of five. If there is not much there to sample, one cannot be alarmed or reassured by the sampling. Of course it is nice if a child is superior (hence ahead of his chronological age) in drawing or puzzle construction, but this is probably going to be obvious from history or observation. In precisely those borderline cases in which one is haunted by the question, "Is he globally retarded?" the existing psychometric tests can be most misleading. If a child has a comprehension problem, then even so-called performance tasks may elude him, as he does not understand what he is expected to do with the materials. Still other expressively impaired children do poorly on a *silent* (assumed to be nonverbal) test because, although it does not require them to talk, it may require them to think of a name as a mediator of correct performance. For example, at the two year old level on the Leiter International Scale, a child must match four painted colored wooden blocks to a paper display panel painted with those "same" four colors. Yet the red painted on the block and the red on the paper are not the same hue, and the class name "red" may well be needed to mediate the allegedly "perceptual" matching. If a child speaks Spanish, this silent testing is fine, as he has the class name "rojo." But if he possesses *no* class name, the test has not circumvented his language disorder. In short, the physician must be vigilant for the meaningfulness of nonverbal intelligence testing of young children with language impairment. Unless he knows a psychologist who is unusually attuned to language disorders, he had best defer (and convince the anxious parents to defer) psychometric testing.

If he has already enlisted the audiologist and speech-language therapist in a treatment evaluation program, they can let him know something close to the heart of the IQ issue: how fast the child learns. Whether it be "catching on" to the audiological testing procedure or availing himself of language stimulation program cues, the child is demonstrating his learning curve and learning style. Until the school or some other institution demands a number, the learning-in-therapy estimate is good enough to detect the severely emotionally disturbed and the globally retarded.

THERAPY: WHAT GOES ON?

Since so much has been said about the role of therapy in diagnosis, some general description of speech and language therapy approaches is in order. For more detailed descriptions, the reader is referred to Bangs, to Berry, and to Wyatt.[4, 5, 30]

Because so much of therapy for the very young child must of necessity be indirect, parents are usually present at evaluation and training sessions. An essential function of the therapist is to teach the parents to be language teachers. Usually this means making parents conscious of the speed, complexity, and volume of their own speech. Parents of youngsters with receptive, audiophonetic, and articulatory deficiencies must be taught to speak slowly, in short phrases, and to focus the child's auditory attention by means other than loud voice. They must be taught to name objects and pictures as they are encountered throughout the day's routine; to spend definite short periods daily reading to the child from books with clear, uncluttered pictures; and to work with the child on scrapbooks of pictures, the names of which he has recently acquired. To a great extent this is simply making explicit and structured the sort of language teaching that most mothers do anyway. There is another side to the training of the mother, however, which emphasizes the use of positive reinforcement, encouragement rather than withholding (e.g., "I won't give it to you till you say it right" should be replaced by "I know you can say it better; try it again as I give it to you").

The language therapist, while didactic in terms of linguistic goals and behavior modifying approaches, also serves as an experienced and sympathetic supportive therapist for the mother. In the case of the young stutterer, the mother's anxieties must be ventilated somewhere other than in the direction of the stutterer, and a preventive approach is aimed almost entirely at the responders to the stuttering, rather than at the speech of the stutterer.[30] More elaborate methods of direct treatment of the older stutterer, involving manipulation of auditory feedback, pacing speech rhythm, and the like, are nearly as controversial as psychoanalytic approaches.[3, 14]

For the child over three years of age with speech and language disorder, more structured and task-oriented sessions with the professional therapist usually become profitable. Again, parents are often invited to stay and watch, so that "homework" sessions can be supervised. Auditory training exercises are combined with the use of visual cues for the patients with receptive and audiophonetic types of disorder. Motor training for the severely inarticulate child utilizes seeing the "mouth molds," the tongue and lip positions, in pictures and by watching the therapist and himself in a mirror. The goal is integration of visual cues with kinesthetic (feeling) and auditory cues.

Throughout the course of indirect and direct therapy the trained therapist remains vigilant for signs of hearing deficiency, local structural contributions to poor intelligibility, disorders of attention (absence attacks or hyperactivity) and psychogenic problems in the parent-child relationship. The physician should be able to count on the therapist to make periodic reports and raise questions as to further referrals.

Experience with indirect therapy for very young children has had the interesting side effect within the last 20 years of supporting such therapy for the mentally retarded. It has been found that language stimulation and direct language teaching can make it possible for the mildly retarded to tackle such subjects as arithmetic, previously regarded as impossible for retardates. Beside the practical application of the increase in skills and hence employability for the retarded, this experience has illustrated the necessity of language for simple reasoning.[22] Whenever possible, therefore, the young child with speech and language retardation, whether or not he shows normal nonverbal ability, should be given the benefit of indirect language stimulation programs.[22]

Such programs can be incorporated into good day nursery schools, and, indeed, for all language-deficient children a nursery school should be sought. Whenever possible it is preferable that most of the children in the class should be normal talkers, otherwise the environment is unlikely to give a full measure of language stimulation. Programs that emphasize silent, lone "discovery" methods of working with materials are not desirable for the child whose language is deficient. The physician who deals with children is well-advised to familiarize himself with the nursery schools available in his vicinity — their programs, attitudes toward minimally impaired children, and willingness to work with other professional persons.

Nursery school experience may also break the vicious circle of language deficiency leading to social isolation and immaturity leading to more language deficiency, a circle that often makes the older child with previously unrecognized language impairment appear to be primarily emotionally disturbed. Wergeland has had experience with autistic-appearing children who, after intensive residential treatment had "warmed them up," gave evidence of aphasialike language disorders that then were treated.[28]

WHAT TO TELL PARENTS

The most frequently raised objection to early recognition and referral of the language-delayed child is that undue anxiety may be aroused in the parent, leading in turn to anxiety in the child. But when the parent raises the question, "Is something wrong? He isn't talking well for his age," then the anxiety is manifestly present already. The parent of course welcomes reassurance that there is no dread disease causing the language deficiency. The parent also likes to have the physician point out areas of good functioning (when these are present), which calms fears about global retardation. However, even when the physician suspects mental retardation in a three year old, his evidence outside the language area is in fact so equivocal that it is just as well to focus upon language and say quite honestly, "Let's see how he does with a language program." It is submitted that much good and little harm to patient and parents (leaving aside the issue of utilization of facilities, which is another matter) can come of such an approach. Once parental anxiety is aroused, doing something that is in itself helpful — whatever the ultimate diagnosis — usually alleviates anxiety better than a simple "don't worry" or a premature closure with a diagnostic label.

If, on the other hand, the parent has noted nothing slow or unexpected about the child's language development, the physician may find himself in the delicate position of arousing concern for the first time. This can, of course, be handled with calm tact, perhaps combining the speech and language evaluation with the audiological testing, since focusing upon hearing, with speech and language incidental, may be less threatening or upsetting to parents. Emphasis upon precautions to prevent future "falling behind," rather than upon "look how far behind he is" may also be less anxiety-provoking.

With milder language disorders, such as audiophonetic, expressive, and articulatory, that do not interfere with the preschool child's adjustment so dramatically, the physician or speech and language consultant or both may make the decision that a therapy program is not warranted. In these cases, it is well to note down and discuss briefly (and cheerfully) with parents the possibility that the symptoms of language disorder may come to the clinical surface again as reading and spelling problems. Again, some may object that this sort of forewarning is too anxiety-provoking, but as such children are usually reassuringly normal in intelligence, the explanation and forewarning may serve to forearm parents and school against fruitless psychogenic interpretations of reading failure or long periods of waiting for investigation in the learning disability clinic. The physician's and speech consultant's notes about the child's preschool language status and the relevant family history should expedite prompt and proper reading therapy.

In short, although a few parents with problems of their own may overreact to early recognition of a child's language disorder, most parents find support and comfort in a "do-something" approach that emphasizes prevention.

SCHOOL PROGNOSIS

As already indicated, there is growing evidence that speech and language disorders are the most important correlates of reading disability.[9] After a period of emphasis upon visual-perceptual factors in reading, research at both basic and clinical levels has pointed in the other direction, toward reading as a linguistic process and dyslexia in the "aphasiological context."[7, 9, 15, 23] Some of this evidence, reviewed briefly, is as follows:

Ingram states that between a third and a half of "developmental dyslexic" children have a history of slow speech development, commonly with a similar family history.[14] Follow-up of speech clinic patients has revealed a high percentage with reading-spelling learning disability.[14] Critchley reports that in a series of 125 dyslexic children, 41 had been late in developing speech and some of these showed language immaturities in syntax and vocabulary.[7] Regardless of IQ, the risk of reading difficulties is as high as 75 per cent in children from middle class homes who at age four are 18 months retarded in speech development.[14] Boder notes that of dyslexics, the largest group, between 63 and 67 per cent, exhibit a "dysphonetic" reading-spelling pattern.[6] This "dysphonetic" group approximates the audiophonetic or auditory-perceptual group of other authors.[8, 14] In an analysis of 34 cases of "pure" reading-spelling disorder (ages 7 to 14 years), 41 per cent had a history of speech and language delay and 41 per cent and 53 per cent had clinically obvious persistent audiophonetic and expressive language deficiencies, respectively.[8]

By contrast, all the authors just cited have noted 12 to 18 per cent of poor readers with visual or visuospatial deficiencies; when present, these appear of more importance early in the course of learning to read and less important with increasing age.

The ample evidence for audiophonetic and linguistic factors in dyslexia, however, does not mean that early recognition and treatment of such deficiencies will in and of itself prevent reading difficulty from occurring. The same language learning "weakness" that led to speech delay is likely to lead to reading delay. The weakness appears to be "overcome" or compensated for, rather than "outgrown." Training in auditory attention, speech sound discrimination, comprehension, and articulation is probably useful in the prereading years for the language-deficient child, but there is no evidence that such training in the preschool period eliminates the need for reading and spelling therapy (although the duration of educational therapy may be lessened).

These comments apply to the group with mild to moderate language disorders. The severely orally handicapped group continues to need oral language training well into the school years. In fact, the hyperlexic (decoding) child with receptive spoken language deficit "reads" beautifully, but is far more educationally and socially handicapped than the audiophonetic-expressive-dyslexic one. The receptive and severe articulatory disorders do not allow a child to function in a normal or a learning disabilities classroom. Special "communications disorder" classes have been established for school-age children whose speech sound reception or production or both remain impaired. Reading may be helpful to the oral language of these children. Experience with receptive-hyperlexic children has been disappointing, however, as often they do not comprehend even what they so facilely decode, as though a connection from visual symbol to speech sound production has bypassed meaning (much as one reads aloud an unknown foreign language).

Prognosis of the language-deficient child in school may be determined as much by his other coexisting dysfunctions as by the language disorder itself. Hyperkinetic distractable behavior, poor hand coordination, and visuospatial dysfunction each adds to school handicap. Indeed, some of these children differ from the globally retarded only by virtue of small islands of normal learning ability, like sun shining through the clouds. Others, normal or superior in all areas but language, have a far more favorable prognosis in school and in social life.

SOME THEORETICAL CONSIDERATIONS

While Ingram voices the opinion that analogies from adult aphasia syndromes contribute little to the understanding of childhood language disorders, Critchley comments that the neurological concept of such specific disorders originated from familiarity with the adult forms of aphasia.[7, 14] In the absence of postmortem examinations of the brains of those with developmental language disorders, speculation on the neuroanatomy or physiology of these conditions is limited to analogies with adult cases and inferences drawn from the web of familial peculiarities. Pursuing the former course, Worster-Drought speculates that a defect (aplasia or agenesis) of temporal lobe cortex would best explain receptive (central auditory) imperception.[29] In favor of his view is the similarity between the hypervisual and hyperlexic receptive child and the recovering Wernicke's aphasic, who often names visually loaded items and "calls" whole written words at a time when he cannot converse meaningfully. Word finding difficulty, missequencing of syllables, shortened and distorted auditory-repetition span, difficulty reading aloud, and even adult-onset stuttering are seen in conduction aphasia; this syndrome involves the parietal area, including white matter.[8] Disturbed or delayed maturation of nerve cells and myelinated connections in and through the parietal area (supramarginal and angular gyri) is a possible anatomical basis for the audiophonetic-expressive-dyslexic constellation.[7, 8, 20]

Orton, working largely from the familial evidence, which includes peculiarities of lateralization of motor preferences, popularized the "incomplete cerebral dominance" theory.[20] This theory, advanced from the naive conception of the setting down of language and motor functions in one dominant hemisphere, is undergoing something of a revival in recent research inspired by "split brain" (interhemispheric commissurotomy) studies. Each hemisphere appears "dominant" in different tasks; the left still leads in language or tool use, and the right leads if visuospatial orientation is involved. "Dominance" for motor skills (hand, foot, eye) appears to be determined by two factors: task-specific controlling input and bias in the motor system itself. Thus observed motor preference is not related in a straightforward way to cerebral dominance. The best position at present is to acknowledge that mixed motor preferences, implying cerebral dominance, may be intriguing concomitants of language disorders but are not causes thereof.

Left-handedness is no more common in children with language disorders than in the general population, but poorly defined handedness and crossed or mixed hand-foot-eye combinations are observed more commonly, as is also the case in other children with "soft signs" of minor nervous system dysfunction.[7, 14]

Little consideration has been given in this chapter to causes and mechanisms of language disorders, because there is so little known. In the face of

Grateful acknowledgments are due to Dr. Beatrice Lieben, Mrs. Mary W. Masland, Dr. Richard Masland, and Mrs. Dorothy Unger for helpful suggestions about the manuscript; to Mr. Warren Wehmann for drawing the figure; and to Mrs. Diane Wolk for patience and perseverance in typing many revisions.

such ignorance, one cannot afford to throw away analogies between language dysfunctions that establish links between childhood developmental and adult acquired syndromes. At stake are the practical quest for effective therapeutic strategies and the intellectual quest for understanding of the human brain.

References

1. Alajouanine, T., and Lhermitte, F.: Acquired aphasia in children. Brain, 88:653–662, 1965.
2. Ames, M. D., Plotkin, S. A., Winchester, R. A., and Atkins, T. E.: Central auditory imperception: A significant factor in congenital rubella deafness. J.A.M.A., 213:419–421, 1970.
3. Andrews, G., and Harris, M.: The syndrome of stuttering. Little Club Clinics in Dev. Med. Child. Neurol., No. 17. London, The Spastics Society and Wm. Heinemann, Ltd., 1964.
4. Bangs, T.: *Language and Learning Disorders of the Pre-Academic Child.* New York, Appleton-Century-Crofts, 1968.
5. Berry, M.: *Language Disorders of Children.* New York, Appleton-Century-Crofts, 1969.
6. Boder, E.: Developmental dyslexia: Prevailing diagnostic concepts and a new diagnostic approach. Chapter XI. *In* Myklebust, H. R. (ed.); *Progress in Learning Disabilities.* Vol. II. New York and London, Grune & Stratton, 1971.
7. Critchley, M.: *The Dyslexic Child.* Springfield, Ill., Charles C Thomas, 1970.
8. Denckla, M. B.: Unpublished data and observations.
9. de Hirsch, K., Jansky, J., and Langford, W.: *Predicting Reading Failure: A Preliminary Study of Reading, Writing and Spelling Disabilities in Preschool Children.* New York, Harper & Row, 1966.
10. Fisch, L.: The contribution of audiology. *In* Renfrew, C., and Murphy, K. (eds.): *The Child Who Does Not Talk.* Little Club Clinics in Dev. Med. Child. Neurol., No. 13. London, The Spastics Society and Wm. Heinemann, Ltd., 1964.
11. Frankenburg, W. K., and Dodds, J. B.: The Denver Developmental Screening Test. J. Pediatr., 71:181–191, 1967.
12. Furth, H. G.: *Thinking Without Language: The Psychological Implications of Deafness.* New York, Free Press, 1966.
13. Gordon, N.: The concept of central deafness. *In* Renfrew, C., and Murphy, K. (eds.): *The Child Who Does Not Talk.* Little Club Clinics in Dev. Med. Child. Neurol., No. 13. London, The Spastics Society and Wm. Heinemann, Ltd., 1964.
14. Ingram, T. T. S.: Developmental disorders of speech. Chapter 21 *in* Vinken, P. J., and Bruyn, G. W. (eds.): *Handbook of Clinical Neurology*, Vol. 4, Disorders of Speech, Perception, and Symbolic Behavior. Amsterdam, North Holland Publishing Co., 1969.
15. Kolers, P. A.: Reading is only incidentally visual. *In* Goodman, K., and Fleming, J. (eds.): *Psycholinguistics and the Teaching of Reading.* Newark, Del., International Reading Association, 1969.
16. Luria, A. R.: *The Role of Speech in the Regulation of Normal and Abnormal Behavior.* London, Pergamon Press, 1961.
17. Masland, M. W.: Speech, language and hearing checklist. In *Learning to Talk.* Report of the Subcommittee on Human Communication and Its Disorders National Advisory Neurological Diseases and Stroke Council. Washington, D.C., U.S. Government Printing Office, 1969, pp. 22–24.
18. Monsees, E. K.: Temporal sequence and expressive language disorders. Except. Child., 35:141–147, 1968.
19. Morley, M. E.: *The Development and Disorders of Speech in Childhood.* 2nd Ed. Edinburgh, E. & S. Livingstone, Ltd., 1965.
20. Orton, S. T.: *Reading, Writing and Speech Problems in Children.* New York, W. W. Norton & Co., 1937.
21. Paine, R. S., and Oppé, T. E.: Speech. Chapter 6 in *Neurological Examination of Children.* Little Club Clinics in Dev. Med. Child. Neurol., double volume 20/21. London, The Spastics Society and Wm. Heinemann, Ltd., 1966.
22. Renfrew, C.: Spoken language in intellectually handicapped children. *In* Renfrew, C., and Murphy, K. (eds.): *The Child Who Does Not Talk.* Little Club Clinics in Dev. Med. Child. Neurol., No. 13. London, The Spastics Society and Wm. Heinemann, Ltd., 1964.
23. Ryan, E., and Sommel, M.: Reading as a constructive language process. Reading Res. Q., 5:59–83, 1969.
24. Templin, M. C.: *Certain Language Skills in Children: Their Development and Interrelationships.* Minneapolis, University of Minnesota Press, 1957.
25. Vygotsky, L. S.: *Thought and Language.* Cambridge, Mass., M.I.T. Press, 1962.

26. Weiner, P. S.: The perceptual level functioning of dysphasic children. Cortex, 5:440–457, 1969.
27. Wender, P.: *Minimal Brain Dysfunction*. New York, Wiley-Interscience, 1971.
28. Wergeland, H.: The autistic child. *In* Renfrew, C., and Murphy, K. (eds.): *The Child Who Does Not Talk*. Little Club Clinics in Dev. Med. Child. Neurol., No. 13. London, The Spastics Society and Wm. Heinemann, Ltd., 1964.
29. Worster-Drought, D.: Speech disorders in children. Dev. Med. Child. Neurol., 10:427–440, 1968.
30. Wyatt, G. L.: Speech and language disorders in preschool children: a preventive approach. Pediatrics, 36:637–647, 1965.

Disorders
of the
Musculoskeletal
System
and Injuries

Chapter 14

Childhood Orthopedic Syndromes

REPRESENTATION IN THREE DEVELOPMENTAL AGE PERIODS

by Jacob F. Katz, M.D.
and Yasoma B. Challenor, M.D.

Limping is one of the most compelling signs directing attention to many lower limb orthopedic impairments in childhood. The mechanism involved in their genesis varies with specific derangements and with specific anatomical sites. All may be associated with such nonspecific symptoms and signs as pain, tenderness, and restriction of motion. Historical data may be unreliable or considerably restricted because of the patient's immaturity.

In order to avoid an encyclopedic textbook listing of orthopedic disease and to highlight potentially long-term orthopedic disorders, three important orthopedic hip diseases have been selected for discussion. Each has an onset with predilection for a different portion of the childhood span of growth and development, i.e., infancy, early and mid childhood, and late childhood and early adolescence.

INFANCY—CONGENITAL HIP DISLOCATION

In past years hip dislocations in infants were purposely left untreated until two or more years of age. It was also commonly assumed that dislocations, though conditioned by prior acetabular anatomical defects, were provoked by weight bearing. Traditionally the approach to management of congenital hip dislocation in children had been to attempt salvage of overt long-standing displacement with forceful acute manipulative reduction.

Putti and Hilgenreiner are credited with effecting a change in attitude toward earlier treatment of congenital hip dislocation.[2, 6] This, in the early decades of the twentieth century, followed dissatisfaction with the results of treatment then in practice. Later Ortolani directed attention to the fact that the diagnosis of hip dislocation could be made early if a simple examination were performed on infants.[4] Gradually this led to performance of formal orthopedic evaluation in the nursery on newborns.

Etiology

Familial and geographic factors have long been recognized in the incidence of congenital hip dislocation. Northern Italy and Czechoslovakia, particularly, have had high concentrations of this disease.

Racial and cultural associations also exist. For example, congenital hip dislocation is virtually unknown in China, Japan, and other Far Eastern countries. It is common in the American Navajo Indian and Canadian Eskimo. It has a smaller incidence in American black infants. A common factor that may play a role here is the routine followed in caring for the infants. Among races with a large incidence of congenital hip dislocation, newly born infants are tightly wrapped in blankets, in other swaddling material, or on cradle boards; in races with a small incidence of congenital hip dislocation, mothers generally carry infants on their backs or hips in widely abducted straddle positions.

Hormonal derangement also has been considered a potential conditioning factor in congenital hip dislocation. Maternal pelvic laxity at termination of pregnancy is mediated by estrogens. Transplacental passage of these maternal hormones could produce similar changes in the fetal pelvic ligaments, thus leading to hip joint laxity. Postnatal hormonal influences are clearly seen in breast and uterine engorgements in neonatal infants. The greater incidence of congenital hip dislocation in female infants, five females to one male, may be explained by their greater reactivity to maternal estrogen. Although there is a report in the literature of increased urinary excretions of female sex hormones in infants with hip joint laxity and dislocatability, this has not been confirmed by subsequent investigators.

Other environmental factors, both intrauterine and extrauterine, also are involved in congenital hip dislocation. A reliable association between greater incidence of congenital hip dislocation in breech deliveries and cesarean sections does exist (the latter is often necessitated by an abnormal intrauterine position). Lower limb distortions in the prenatal period are believed to transmit stress to lax hip joints and contribute to dislocatability or dislocation.

Recently, a hip stabilizing mechanism involving physical forces related to surface cohesiveness and intraarticular pressure has been described. A clue to temporary iatrogenic joint instability was furnished by the appearance of an "air arthrogram" or the so-called "vacuum phenomenon" with forced abduction or traction on lower limbs in the course of routine hip radiography. Siffert et al. suggested that the presence of air introduced by forced motion in a susceptibly lax hip contributed to a break of the synovial fluid vacuum seal between the cartilaginous surfaces of femoral head and socket.[7] This could lead to "dislocatability," which is spontaneously corrected in the majority of infants but may persist in some as dislocation or dysplasia if untreated.

Classification

The common form of congenital hip dislocation appearing in the newborn infant is either a lax dislocatable hip or an established hip dislocation. The former is more frequent than the latter.

The atypical form of congenital hip dislocation in the newborn (also called teratological) is often associated with other anomalies and is almost always a complete dislocation. A frequent characteristic of this variety is its rigidity and failure to respond to customary therapy. Examples of such anomalous states are arthrogryposis, diastrophic dwarfism, Larsen's syndrome, and the chromosomal trisomies.

Clinical Identification

In the newborn, the usual abnormal hip appears as hip joint laxity rather than dislocation. These children have symmetrical lower limbs with full range of motion. Hip dislocatability is demonstrated by the Barlow maneuver (Fig. 14–1). This involves positioning the femur in adduction, pressing down

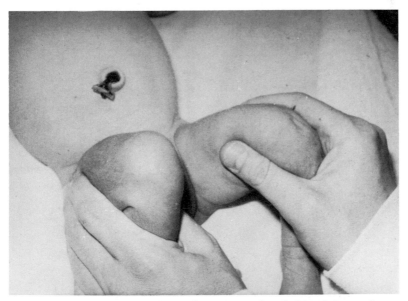

Figure 14–1 The Barlow manipulation demonstrates hip dislocatability in the presence of ligamentous and capsular laxity. This photograph illustrates the proper placement of the examiner's hands.

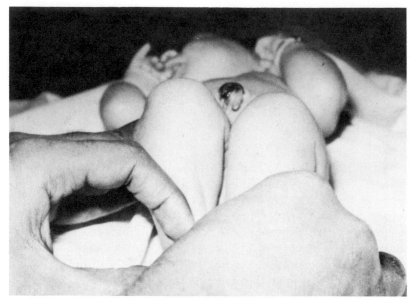

Figure 14–2 Femoral lengths are easily estimated by symmetrically aligning the flexed lower limbs and judging the level of the knees. Here with left femoral shortening, there is diminution in the height of the left knee.

axially, and pushing the proximal end of the femur outward. If the hip is dislocatable there is an accompanying snap and sense of movement of the femoral head.

The newborn infant with hip dislocation presents with shortening of the limb on the side of involvement, asymmetrical thigh and gluteal folds, broadening of the perineum, and restriction of abduction (Figs. 14–2, 14–3,

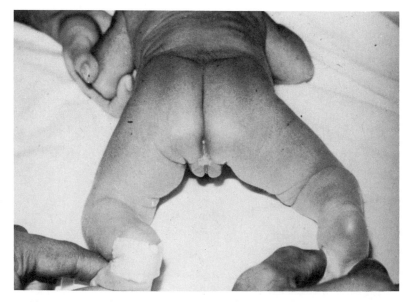

Figure 14–3 Lying in the prone position, this infant with left congenital hip dislocation exhibits an asymmetrical gluteal fold.

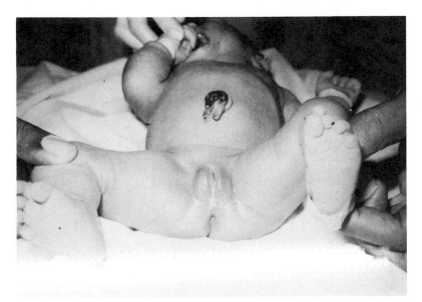

Figure 14-4   There is diminished abduction of the left thigh on the affected side.

and 14-4). The Ortolani test demonstrates relocation of the dislocated hip
(Fig. 14-5).[4] It is performed by abducting the thigh and applying traction on
the femur and inward pressure against the proximal femur. In the older infant
just starting to walk, the associated limp is difficult to detect until a stable gait
pattern has become established. In the older infant or child with acetabular
dysplasia, the only clinical clue may be restriction of thigh abduction. Radiographic examination is required for ultimate clarification.

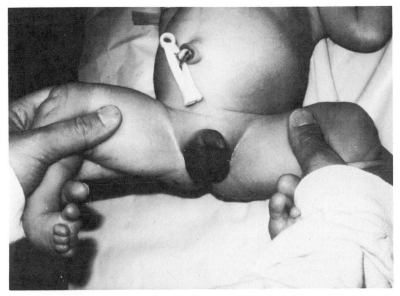

Figure 14-5   The Ortolani test of thigh abduction.

In the older child the signs of unilateral congenital hip dislocation are essentially those described for the walking infant. The dysplastic hip, similarly, may be silent symptomatically and cause only mild restriction of thigh abduction. Local discomfort and fatigability do not usually occur in childhood and tend to be reserved for later adolescence and adulthood.

With bilateral disease creating symmetrical deformity, shortening and joint motion restriction may be obscured. Broadening of the perineum, possible push-pull hip laxity (telescoping), and a waddling gait pattern are the clinical diagnostic elements.

Radiographic Changes

In older infants and children, radiographs are helpful in the diagnosis of congenital hip dislocation, in determining the adequacy of reduction, and in the follow-up of the developmental changes in the hip joints. They are less valuable in the newborn infant because of the difficulty in localizing wholly radiolucent cartilaginous capital epiphyses and the lack of positive roentgen features in hip laxity or dislocatability.

Lines of reference may be drawn on the film to help localize the proximal femur. (The Hilgenreiner Y line is drawn transversely, passing through the triradiate cartilage; Perkins' line is perpendicular, dropped from the superior margin of the acetabulum to the Y line; Shenton's line passes in a continuous arc from the inferior surface of the neck of the femur along the superior margin of the adjacent obturator foramen.)

Course

When complete dislocation exists in the newborn there is no promise of spontaneous recovery. Adaptive changes that produce elongation of the capsule and ligamentum teres and shortening of the hip flexors and adductors reinforce the tendency toward permanent displacement. Ultimately, anatomical impression of the pelvis at the level of the dislocated femoral head creates a false or secondary acetabulum.

When hip joint abnormality appears as laxity or dislocatability, spontaneous stability develops in 50 per cent of the infants within three weeks without treatment.

Management

Newborn. Treatment of the newborn infant offers the most favorable prognosis for restoration of normal bony architecture and function. When the problem presents as a dislocatable hip, simple abduction of the thighs usually suffices to create secure positioning until inherent stability is restored. This may take from days to weeks, and a protective device is worn for this interval. This abduction apparatus, which may be removed for bathing, may be a plas-

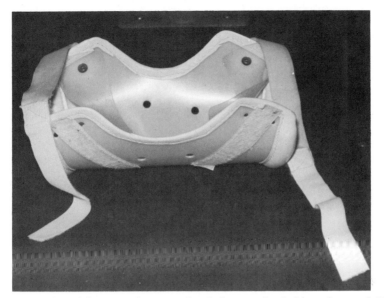

Figure 14–6 This abduction splint is made of plastic and is held in place with Velcro fasteners.

tic or a metal and leather brace prefabricated in various sizes (Figs. 14–6 and 14–7). Barlow noted and MacKenzie agreed that in from two days to three weeks, 50 per cent of infants with "abnormal" hips spontaneously regained stability.[1, 3]

Treatment for the dislocated hip in the newborn may also involve only the use of an abduction retention device, since the reduction is usually effort-

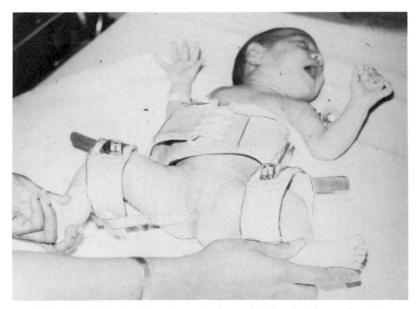

Figure 14–7 This abduction brace has a leather pelvic band with metal outriggers supporting thigh cuffs.

less. When there is difficulty in maintaining stable reduction a plaster hip spica is applied. This is reapplied at four to six week intervals to keep up with the child's growth. After three months there is sufficient stability to permit transfer to a removable abduction brace. Treatment is continued until radiographs show an ossified femoral capital epiphysis properly centered in an adequate acetabulum. This is customarily attained within the first year.

Older Infant and Young Child. The child with a dislocated hip exhibits shortening of the involved limb with contracture of the hip adductors and flexors. Gentle reduction is required to avoid damage to the femoral head. To permit this, preliminary traction is applied over a period of several weeks for gradual stretching of tight muscles (Fig. 14–8). When radiographs show that the dislocated femoral head has been pulled down to the proper acetabular level, reduction is usually possible with abduction. Plaster cast immobilization is used for maintenance. If reduction is not possible or if good central seating of the femoral head cannot be achieved, arthrography is indicated. An inverted limbus or other soft tissue obstruction may be at fault. When this has been confirmed, open reduction is performed and the obstruction is removed. Plaster spica immobilization is used postoperatively and, after four to six months, replaced with an abduction splint. Treatment is continued until radiographs show ossific centra in the femoral heads and the latter well centered in adequate acetabula.

Older Child. The problems of congenital hip dislocation in this age group are inherently more complex than in the preceding groups. More time in the dislocated state results in more extensive deformation of the primary acetabula and femoral heads, as well as in contractures of the capsule, ligaments, and muscles.

The requirements for successful stable reduction are: (1) freeing soft tissue contractures, (2) restoring the depth of the acetabulum, (3) removing intraarticular obstruction (limbus, ligamentum teres), and (4) modifying the torsion and neck shaft angle of the upper femur.

The alternatives for attaining these objectives are familiar in principle, i.e., traction, surgical section of tight muscles, surgical excision of fibrocartilaginous limbus or enlarged ligamentum teres, and osteotomy of the femur or pelvis. Arthrography preoperatively assists in defining the residual problem.

In a given situation, traction is always part of the management program; often, however, it fails to pull the femoral head to an adequate level and surgical release of the adductor and iliopsoas muscles must be added. Gentle closed reduction is attempted; if this is unsuccessful, arthrography will be helpful in evaluating the difficulty. An inverted limbus, hypertrophied and elongated ligamentum teres, hourglass capsular constriction, or other obstruction may be preventing a concentric reduction. Open reduction is performed and the defect preventing femoral head seating is corrected.

At this juncture, in either closed or open reduction, an assessment is made of the stability of the femoral head in the acetabulum. Secondary adaptive changes resulting from prolonged dislocation consist of shallow sloping acetabular contour and increased femoral anteversion, both leading to inadequate femoral head cover.

The approach to correct this deficiency may be either through (1) a pelvic

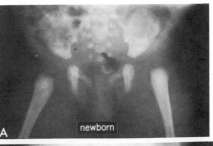

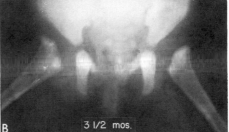

Figure 14–8 *A.* Examination in the newborn nursery disclosed dislocation of the left hip and dislocatabilty of the right hip. Bulky diaper splint for thigh abduction was recommended. *B.* At three and one half months of age on a clinic visit both hips were found to be dislocated. The mother had discontinued using the abduction device. *C.* Skeletal traction in place prior to closed reduction has restored femoral length and proper placement of the upper femora at acetabular level. *D.* Follow-up radiograph shows satisfactory reduction with proper femoral head centering in the hip joints.

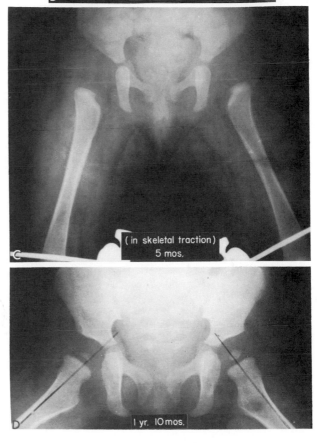

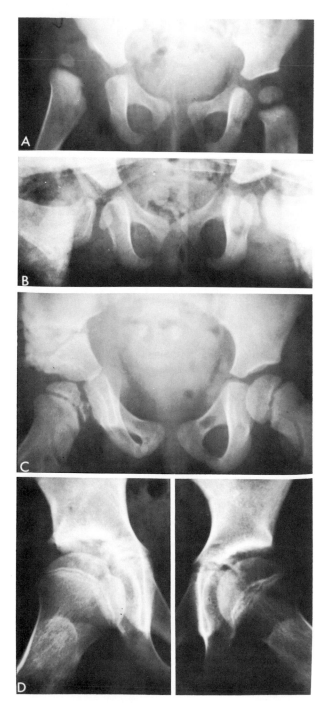

Figure 14–9 *A.* This child's right hip dislocation was diagnosed at one year of age. Note the upward displacement of the femoral head, smaller epiphyseal ossific nucleus, and sloping acetabulum. *B.* Two and a half months after traction and closed reduction. *C.* Because of residual acetabular shallowness, Salter innominate osteotomy was performed two years later. This radiograph illustrates the pelvic osteotomy two months postoperatively. Fragmentation of the posterior margin of the femoral epiphysis is evidence of residual avascular necrosis. *D.* Follow-up radiographs at 10½ years of age. Excellent clinical result with alteration in height and width of the proximal epiphysis is consistent with healed avascular necrosis.

osteotomy such as the Salter innominate osteotomy shown in Figure 14–9 or (2) the proximal femoral derotation and varus osteotomy recommended by Somerville.[9]

Postoperatively the limbs are maintained in corrective attitude in plaster casts for from 8 to 12 weeks (depending on the patient's age). Following cast removal there is a variable period in which weight bearing is prohibited but the hip and knee are mobilized by exercises. When range of motion and motor power have returned, progressively increasing weight bearing is permitted. Follow-up radiographs are taken at spaced intervals to follow modeling changes in the upper femur and acetabulum until epiphyseal closure.

Rehabilitation measures are most applicable to older patients with long-standing dislocation. Whether traction alone or traction and subsequent surgery are involved, the immobilization required in the earlier phases of treatment must be followed by remobilization of the hip and knee.

If surgery has included muscle lengthening or release around the hip, then often gait retraining must follow joint mobilization. Graduated muscle strengthening exercises are begun as soon as the surgeon permits, and these emphasize gluteus medius and maximus, and quadriceps strengthening. If the hip flexors have been lengthened or severed, then the rectus femoris is selectively strengthened as well. If there has been muscle substitution for hip flexion, retraining emphasizes rectus femoris contraction at the beginning of the swing phase of gait, when the knee is still flexed and the rectus femoris is still in a lengthened position mechanically favorable for a strong contraction.

If hip dislocation has been unilateral, asymmetry of gait may require attention postoperatively. A close watch is kept for possible development of postural deviation caused by habitually asymmetrical gait and stance or uncompensated leg length discrepancy.

Prognosis

There is general agreement that the earlier the hip dislocation is detected the better the prognosis. This relationship is very sensitive, and periods of delay as short as four to six weeks after birth may prolong the treatment required to restore the normal femoral contours. With long-standing dislocation, the anatomical distortion, as has been already suggested, involves acetabular shallowness, ovoid shape of the femoral head, and increased femoral anteversion. As normal pressure interrelationships are restored between the femoral head and its acetabulum, molding takes place, leading to congruity. Obviously if both components have been significantly distorted, normal spherical restoration of the femoral head cannot take place.

In addition to the anatomical alterations leading to subtle mechanical influences, there is the more serious complication of avascular necrosis (Fig. 14–10). The untreated hip never undergoes avascular change despite the severity of the dislocation. On the other hand, even simple therapy such as an abduction splint that forces wide abduction may produce ischemic necrosis. Forceful reduction maneuvers in hips with restricted range of motion almost certainly lead to avascular necrosis. Preliminary traction, surgical release of

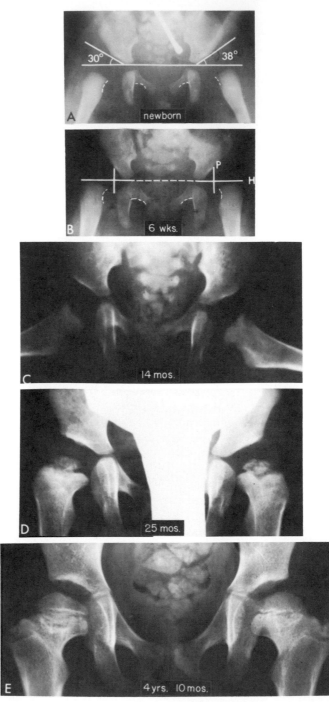

Figure 14–10 *A.* Radiographs of newborn infant showing bilateral dislocation. *B.* At age six weeks radiographs confirm earlier dislocation status. Treatment was inadvertently delayed until clinic visit at this time. Closed reduction was performed. *C.* Status at age 14 months when abduction treatment was discontinued. Acetabula appear shallow; no proximal femoral epiphyseal ossification is seen on either side. *D.* Both femoral epiphyses have fragmented appearance consistent with avascular necrosis at two years of age. *E.* The residuals of avascular necrosis seen at four years and 10 months are broadened shortened femoral necks, and femoral epiphyses of diminished height.

hip adductors and flexors when traction has been unsuccessful, and gentle reduction are necessary if one is to avoid vascular compromise.

Long-range studies such as Smith's have shown that "a perfect reduction must be achieved if one is to expect the long-range result to be a normal hip."[8] Prevention of vascular complications was found clearly to be an important factor in long-term good results.

Results

Results of therapy are best following early detection, worse in an older child, and poor in teratological or syndrome associated problems.

In congenital hip dislocation results of therapy can be stated only with important qualifications. Foremost of these are the youthfulness of the child and the absence of associated musculoskeletal disorders (arthrogryposis, chromosomal abnormalities, and genetically determined connective tissue disorders such as diastrophic dwarfism). The consensus is that 87 per cent of the newborn infants with hip joint laxity producing hip dislocatability that is promptly supported in an abduction device will continue with orderly development and be indistinguishable from normal by six weeks.[3]

Somerville found that end results deteriorated as the age at which treatment was started increased.[9] He analyzed 100 congenitally dislocated hips with follow-ups of 10 to 15 years after treatment. There was a drop-off from 93 per cent "normal or very good" results in children whose treatment started at one to one and one half years to 65 per cent in those started at two and a half to three years.

Ponseti's experience was similar. In a study of congenital hip dislocation with four to eight years' follow-up, good anatomical results were obtained in all patients treated before one year of age, in 78 per cent of children treated between one and two years of age, and 57 per cent of those treated at age two to four years.[5]

Smith's study with an average of 31 years' follow-up determined that a perfect reduction was the prerequisite of a normal long-term end result. Vascular complications associated with the reduction also exacted a toll of impaired end results. What was especially significant in his study was that symptoms, on the average, did not assume significant proportions until 22 years after treatment.[8] The obvious inadequacy of short follow-up evaluation needs no further comment.

CHILDHOOD – LEGG-CALVÉ-PERTHES DISEASE

Legg-Calvé-Perthes disease became a recognized entity with the original descriptions, in 1910, of the three investigators whose names are still eponymically associated with it.[11, 16, 20] The turn of the century had brought radiography for clarification of its clinical manifestations. This permitted documentation of the sequential alterations in the immature femoral head that lead to a form of recovery distinct from the relentless destructiveness of specific infections with which it had previously been confused.

The etiology of Legg-Calvé-Perthes disease is still not known though the mechanism is accepted to be an ischemic aseptic necrosis of the femoral capital epiphysis. The belief that it had an infectious origin was tenaciously held for a while, but no longer has any proponents. Its characteristic predilection for the male, four to one over females, suggested a genetically sex linked relationship, but this has not been supported by genetic analytical studies.

At Blythedale Children's Hospital, in a study of 350 children with Legg-Calvé-Perthes disease a 3 per cent incidence of familial association was found. Included were five pairs of siblings: two sisters, a brother and sister pair, and three pairs of brothers. None were twins and among these siblings, there was no parental or other familial history of the disease. Two female children had mothers with the disease and one male and one female youngster had affected fathers. One male youngster with Legg-Calvé-Perthes disease had an unaffected identical twin, and one female child (with an affected older sister) had an unaffected fraternal male twin. In the majority of instances, Legg-Calvé-Perthes disease appears to occur as isolated cases of a poorly understood hip disorder.

Clinical Characteristics

Children with this disease present with either a limp or pain referred to the hip in about 85 per cent of cases and with either a limp or pain referred to the knee in the remaining 15 per cent. Infrequently there is history of injury (15 per cent) leading to the symptoms and bringing the child to clinical attention and diagnosis. The injury is usually minor and of the sort that frequently occurs in ordinary play activities.

The disease is mainly unilateral, with each side equally susceptible. In a variable but small number of cases (9 to 15 per cent) the condition is bilateral. Usually one side is symptomatic, and bilaterality is discovered by radiographic evaluation. Occasionally second side involvement appears as a discrete new change either while the initial side is still under treatment or six to nine months after cessation of treatment for the first hip.

Similar clinical characteristics may be found in such specific conditions as sickle cell hemoglobinopathy or Gaucher's disease, following femoral neck fractures or congenital hip dislocations, after osteomyelitis of the proximal femur or hip sepsis (after control of infection), and in juvenile rheumatoid arthritis and nonspecific synovitis. The diagnosis of Legg-Calvé-Perthes disease is made by exclusion of competing diseases in which ischemic necrosis and synovitis of the hip play a role.

Roentgen Characteristics

The radiograph is indispensable in the diagnosis and progressive evaluation of the course of Legg-Calvé-Perthes disease. The earliest radiographic

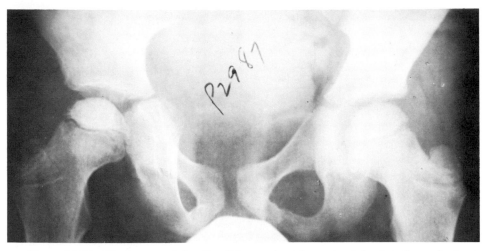

Figure 14–11 The increased density of the proximal femoral epiphysis is the earliest evidence of involvement with Legg-Calvé-Perthes disease in this six year old white boy whose symptoms started four months previously.

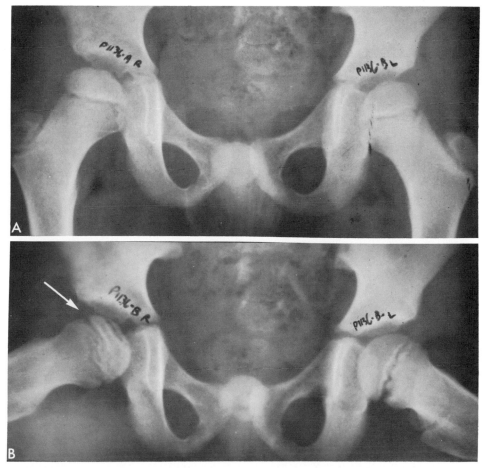

Figure 14–12 In this six and three fourths year old white boy, the initial radiographic finding is the subchondral lucency in the anterior half of the proximal femoral epiphysis seen only in the frog-leg lateral projection of the right hip. His symptoms dated back one month.

finding is an anatomically intact proximal femoral epiphysis with altered contrast between its apparent increased density and the porosis of the adjacent femoral metaphysis (Fig. 14–11).

This then continues on to some diminution in size of the ossific portion of the femoral capital epiphysis. In the lateral radiograph a strip of lucency in the subchondral region of the anterior portion of the epiphysis appears as a "crescent" phenomenon (Fig. 14–12). These changes when present signify that approximately six months have elapsed since onset of symptoms.

Progressively, further encroachment on the epiphysis by vascular resorption leads to increasing "fragmentation" (Fig. 14–13). This tends to reach its height at 12 to 18 months. At about this time or shortly prior to it, evidence of minimal peripheral new bone formation occurs. This marks the beginning of the "reparative" stage.

Continuing repair adds more new bone until larger amounts of the epiphysis are replaced. Since vascularization is restored peripherally in the

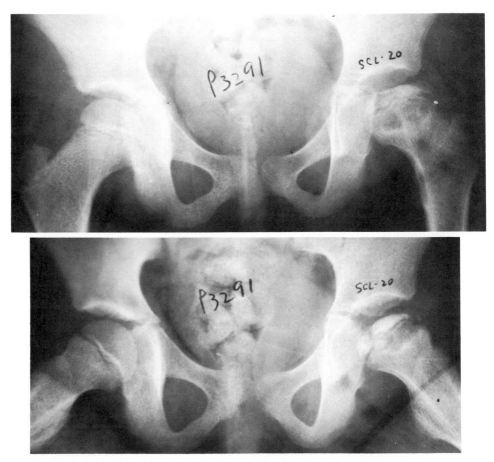

Figure 14–13   The early anteroposterior and lateral radiographs of this six year three month old white girl show fragmentation of the left femoral capital epiphysis with prominent diminution in height. Symptoms dated to seven months prior to admission. There is mild subluxation of the upper femur as well as prominent metaphyseal lucencies.

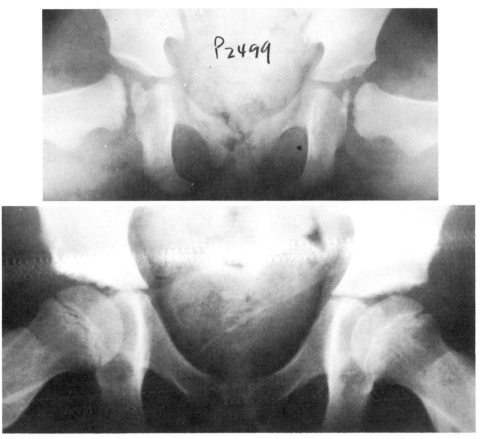

Figure 14–14 *A*. The earliest radiograph in this two year 11 month old white child shows prominent thinning and fragmentation of the left femoral capital epiphysis. *B*. On follow-up at age nine years the left femoral epiphysis appears slightly broader and lower than the unaffected right. There is full range of motion with normal function.

healing process, the most significant changes occur in the same sequence. The last area to be restored usually is a discrete central zone.

While these radiographic alterations of fragmentation and reparative restoration of the femoral epiphysis are proceeding, concomitant widening of the femoral epiphysis and metaphysis are also taking place. The usual final appearance shows some degree of enlargement of the femoral head and neck as well as some diminution in its height (Fig. 14–14).

One of the poorly understood facets of Legg-Calvé-Perthes disease is the variability of the stage of disease of the femoral capital epiphysis at the time the diagnosis is first made. To state this discrepancy statistically, the "initial" stage of disease (virtually intact epiphysis) was defined as 0 to 6 months after onset; "fragmentation" (vascular resorption of epiphysis) as 6 to 12 months; "reparative" (new bone formation) as over 12 months. In a recent review of the experiences at the Blythedale Children's Hospital, in 42 per cent of the children with Legg-Calvé-Perthes disease diagnosis was made in the "initial" stage, in 18 per cent in the "fragmentation" stage and in 40 per cent in the "reparative" stage.[15]

Treatment

In principle the traditional approach to treatment of this disease has been relief of weight bearing. The method of effecting this included such procedures as the use of crutches with or without a sling for the affected limb, wheelchair, plaster immobilization, bed rest with or without traction, weight-relieving ischial seat braces, and abduction braces in bed or improvised chair or stretcher (Fig. 14–15).

In the past decade, the consensus supported programs of hip abduction without weight bearing (Fig. 14–16). In recent years, several children's centers, including Blythedale, have been using programs that permit weight bearing with lower limb abduction maintained in braces (Figs. 14–17 and 14–18).[13]

To place this subject in perspective, it should be stated that concurrently with the larger programs using the conservative routines just described, smaller programs using surgical therapy also are going on. In these, two approaches have developed. One, recommended by Axer, consists of derotation varus osteotomy of the proximal femur; the second described by Salter, consists of innominate osteotomy.[10, 22] Both programs permit weight bearing after healing of the osteotomized areas, usually about three months. This mobilization is dependent upon satisfactory recovery of range of motion and muscle strength.

The common denominator in the surgical therapy programs and the weight bearing—in—abduction brace program is the improved cover of the femoral head within its acetabulum. Surgically this is created rapidly and permanently, conservatively it has to be maintained with braces throughout the

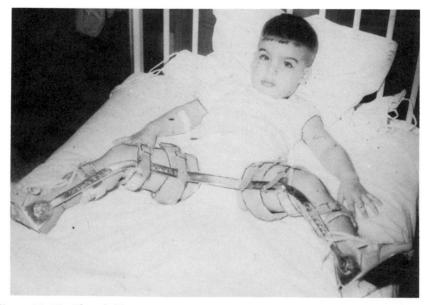

Figure 14–15 This child is wearing an abduction brace with foot plate attachment. At that time the program enforced non-weight bearing.

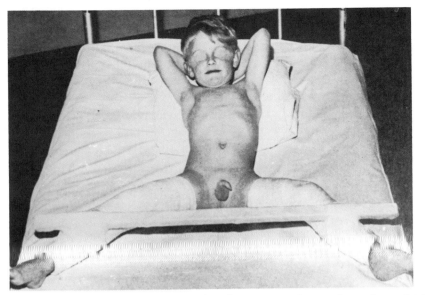

Figure 14–16 This child is wearing long leg plaster casts with a wood cross bar maintaining thigh abduction. (From Harrison, M. H. M., and Menon, M. P. A.: Legg-Calvé-Perthes disease. J. Bone Joint Surg., 48-A:1309, 1966. Reproduced with permission.

Figure 14–17 This child is wearing an abduction brace in the Newington Children's Hospital program.

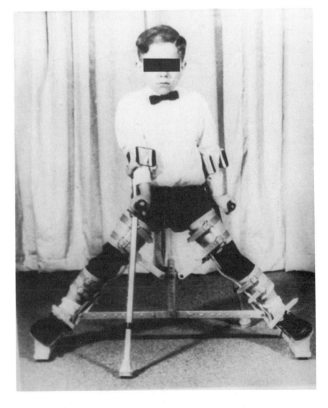

Figure 14–18 This child with Legg-Calvé-Perthes disease is wearing an abduction brace devised at the Blythedale Children's Hospital.

healing stage. The time consumed in the conservative therapy program for 50 per cent of the children was one and a half to two and a half years. Twenty-five per cent spent less than one and a half years, and an equal percentage spent more than two and a half years. If the ultimate experience should indicate equivalent end results with surgery, the alternative to the years now required in some form of restraint may prove attractive to parent, physician, and child.

Management

Throughout the period of femoral head restoration, the patient should be allowed out of the abduction appliance once daily for active exercises for range of hip, knee, and ankle motion. Isometric exercises to minimize muscle deconditioning are also well advised, particularly for glutei medius and maximus and quadriceps, i.e., those muscles that will later be maximally stressed on reambulation.

In the Blythedale Children's Hospital weight bearing–in–abduction brace program, it has been consistently noted that patients beginning to ambulate without braces after healing is complete have little if any gait disturbance. Earlier, patients maintained in abduction without weight bearing uniformly needed periods of gait retraining after healing to eliminate bizarre gait characteristics.

If surgical therapy has been used, then joint remobilization, muscle strengthening, and gait retraining follow cast removal. The aims of therapy are similar to those outlined for postoperative management of congenital hip dislocation.

Prognosis

Many evaluational analyses recorded in the literature have attempted to determine the elements influencing the prognosis either in the disease profile or in the methods of therapy. Two of these are especially significant: the age of the child at onset of disease and the type or severity of Legg-Calvé-Perthes disease affecting the child.

Age at Onset. There is an across the board agreement that the younger the child the better the prognosis. This accord has been unaffected by the particular kind of therapy or any other factor. In the Blythedale series, in children under six years of age the average number of poor results was half that for the

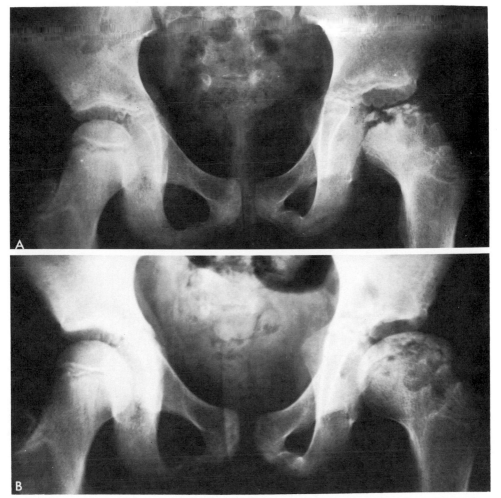

Figure 14–19 *A*. This is a nine and one half year old white boy with Legg-Calvé-Perthes disease of the left hip. The proximal femoral capital epiphysis is wholly involved. There are concomitant subluxation and also metaphyseal lucencies. *B*. Follow-up radiographs two and a half years later show broadening of the femoral head.

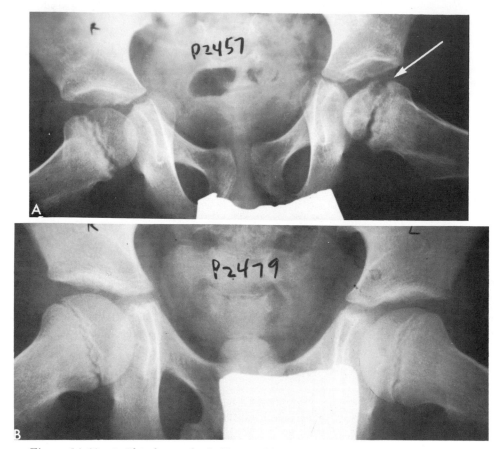

Figure 14–20 *A.* This four and a half year old white boy has partial involvement of the epiphysis in its anterior third. *B.* Follow-up five years later shows radiographic restitution closely resembling the unaffected side.

entire group. At age seven, the average number of poor results was greater than that for the whole study, and the trend continued as age increased.

Severity of Disease Process. As early as 1927, Legg had concluded that the prognosis of the disease of which he had been a pioneer investigator was dependent upon unknown factors present from the onset. He regarded the "mushroom" type to have a better outlook than the "cap" type despite the mode of therapy.[17] O'Garra helped to clarify the ingredient of the good prognosis form of Legg-Calvé-Perthes disease by his hypothesis of "segmental" or "partial head" involvement in some children versus "whole head" disease in others.[19] This has been affirmed by many subsequent investigators.[12, 21] In the Blythedale series about 28 per cent of the children had total head involvement and the remainder had varying degrees of segmental or partial involvement (Figs. 14–19 and 14–20). The totally involved femoral epiphysis was responsible for a higher percentage (29 per cent) of poor results and this is in agreement with the consensus in the literature.

Results

There is no single method of evaluating the results of therapy that has been generally accepted. Many extenuating circumstances can be cited for this deficiency. The method of measuring the end result in earlier years was a descriptive one, referring to the sphericity of the femoral head or its departure from it, i.e., ball, oval, or quadrangular. Because of the subjective element in such a system, mathematical analyses were devised. One of the first ones was the epiphyseal index (relation between the height and width of the epiphysis). This was followed by the epiphyseal quotient (relationship between the indices of the involved and uninvolved sides) and several other femoral and acetabular quotients leading to a comprehensive quotient. Subsequently another measurement was introduced to determine the sphericity of the femoral head accurately by using a template of concentric circles as an overlay. All these systems of measurement are described in the literature.[11, 16] For the sake of uniformity in the future, the consensus favors combination of the methods using the concentric circle template and the epiphyseal quotient. Using such a format, the Blythedale Children's Hospital end results were: good 39 per cent and satisfactory 39 per cent (acceptable 78 per cent), and poor 22 per cent.

Another important factor to consider in evaluating end results is the age of the children in the study. It has already been pointed out that younger children (under six) have a better prognosis despite the form of therapy. There is no doubt that the older children with less favorable prognosis offer the greater challenge to any therapy program.

It is also of value to know the type of disease present in a given child, i.e., partial or whole head involvement. If the prognosis is better in the partial head variety, the numbers of such children in any series would influence the distribution of good results.

Finally not only should there be a sufficient number of patients for statistical validity, but the follow-up should be long enough to obtain a functional rating in adulthood and maturity. Obviously the final picture is a conglomerate of many elements, each of which has to be identified.

ADOLESCENCE—SLIPPED EPIPHYSIS

Slipped femoral capital epiphysis refers to spontaneous displacement of the proximal femoral epiphysis in a posterior and inferior direction usually in children approaching adolescence.

In a recent survey of Connecticut residents Kelsey estimated its incidence to be 3.41 per 100,000 population under 25 years.[25]

Etiology

Although the precise etiology is unknown, there are empiricisms that offer interesting possibilities:

One of these is that the horizontal plane of the proximal femoral growth plate during childhood gradually is reoriented to a more oblique one in ado-

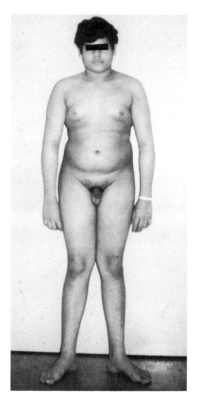

Figure 14–21 Fourteen year old adolescent boy with bilateral slipped femoral capital epiphysis. His body habitus is not strikingly abnormal; he is tall and mildly obese.

lescence. This in turn, makes the proximal epiphysis more subject to sheer stress. Alexander considered the slow slip to be a result of sitting stresses causing posterior growth migration of the head on the neck. Since this would add to sheer stress vulnerability of the head-neck junction, he viewed the erect position as sufficient to cause acute slipping by simple fracture through the growth plate cartilage.[23]

The other is that many of the affected children appear to have a particular type of body habitus: either the "Fröhlich" type on the one hand or the very tall thin type on the other (Fig. 14–21). This connotation of endocrine imbalance was especially emphasized by Harris, who showed experimentally that the resistance of the growth plate to sheer stress was decreased by growth hormone and increased by sex hormone.[24] These data suggested, as a corollary, that slipping of the epiphysis in the large obese child was related to a deficiency of the sex hormone and in the tall thin child to an excess of growth hormone.

The attraction of these concepts is that a mechanism is established for increased susceptibility, and then mechanical factors offer the triggering incident.

Clinical Characteristics

The ratio of males to females is about two and a half to one. The median ages at time of diagnosis are 13 years for males and 11 years for females. In unilateral cases, a higher rate of incidence on the left side than on the right has been occasionally reported. Bilaterality has varied from 16 to 28 per cent.

Onset is characterized by the gradual onset of pain or a limp or both. This may be continuous and progressive, or intermittent with periods of freedom from symptoms. Occasionally an injury may bring on acute initial discomfort or aggravate preexisting symptoms. Commonly there is no history of injury. The pain is referred to the groin or anteromedial aspect of the thigh or knee.

On physical examination, an early finding is restriction of internal rotation of the hip. As severity increases there is an adduction and external rotation deformity with complete loss of abduction and internal rotation.

Roentgen Features

The diagnosis of slipped femoral capital epiphysis requires radiographs in the anteroposterior and frog-leg lateral views. Early slipping of the epiphysis may be posterior initially, this would be visible only on the lateral film, and the anteroposterior view would reflect the displacement only as a slight apparent widening of the growth plate.

As the severity of the slipping increases, the displacement becomes both posterior and inferior (Fig. 14–22). A convenient arbitrary system of classifying severity is, according to Wilson, mild if it is less than one third of the epiphyseal diameter, moderate if less than one half, and severe if more than half. The degree of slipping is determined in the view showing maximum displacement.[29]

Course

Several varieties of clinical behavior have been noted: (1) An episode of trauma dramatically associated with significant impairment of a previously functional hip joint; (2) Gradual development of hip disability that continues and worsens; and (3) Intermittent bouts of disablement alternating with periods of well being, but showing signs of slipped epiphysis such as external rotation attitude in walking and concomitant restrictions in hip internal rotation and abduction.

In the first example, the likelihood is that an acute slip had taken place, and on radiographs the absence of adaptive changes at the epiphysis-metaphysis junction would be confirmatory. In the second example, a slow gradual slipping of variable (including minimal) severity is to be expected (Fig. 14–23). The hallmark of chronicity is the presence of adaptive change at the neck of the femur. In the third situation, chronicity is again implied, but the degree of slipping is presumed to be of greater severity.

Management

The treatment for slipped epiphysis varies with the degree of displacement and whether it occurs as a sudden acute change or as a slow chronic de-

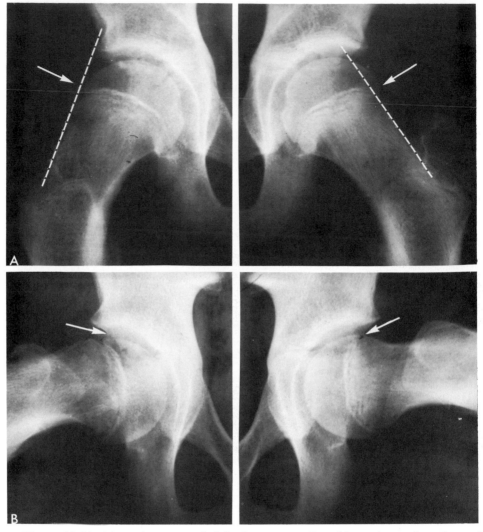

Figure 14–22 Minimal posteromedial displacement in slipped femoral capital epiphysis of the right hip. *A.* In the anteroposterior projection a line drawn along the superior margin of the neck normally will cut across a small overhanging peripheral portion of the femoral epiphysis. This is shown on the unaffected left side. On the involved right side the line fails to cross the margin of the epiphysis because of the medial displacement. *B.* In the frog-leg lateral view the continuous margin between the widening metaphysis and the margin of the adjacent epiphysis is shown on the unaffected left side. On the involved right side there is slight posterior migration of the margin of the epiphysis.

formation. The requirements to be satisfied by treatment include fixation of the proximal femoral epiphysis for stabilization and correction of deformity when its severity has become unacceptable.

In slipped epiphysis, either acute or chronic, when the deformity is mild the treatment of choice is simple pin fixation in situ (Fig. 14–24). The earlier single tri-flanged Smith-Petersen nail has now been replaced generally with multiple slender Knowles pins (Hague or Moore types are similar enough to

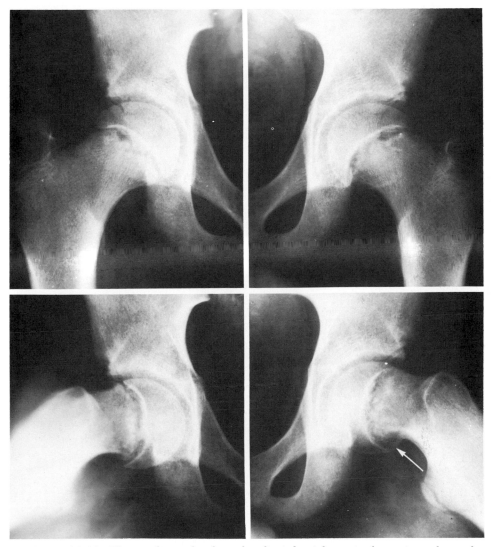

Figure 14-23 These radiographs show the slipped epiphyses in the patient whose photograph is shown in Figure 14-21. The displacements are mild and are seen most vividly in the frog-leg lateral radiographic projections. The adaptive bone proliferation along the inferior margin of the left femoral neck is characteristic of chronic gradual slipping.

be acceptable substitutes). This treatment for this stage of disease furnishes the best results. It eliminates the risk of further slipping, encourages epiphyseal closure, and permits rapid return to full activity before significant joint stiffness or muscle weakness occurs.

In chronic slipped epiphysis, in which the displacement occurs gradually and intermittently, if the severity remains moderate, the decision often is made to pin this in situ also. As already stated, chronic slips involve adaptive alterations that require osteotomy for correction, but the surgical risks and increased morbidity outweigh the advantage of improvement in external rotation attitude of the limb.

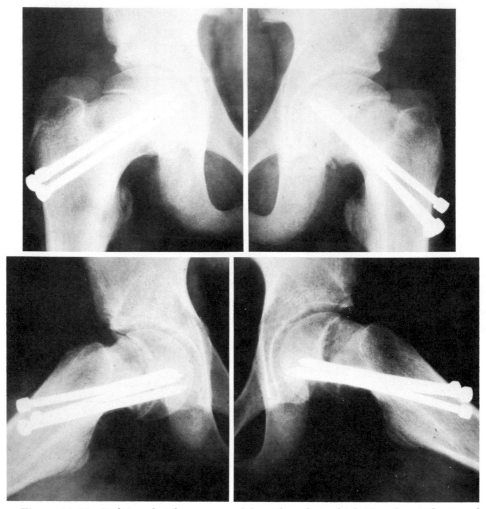

Figure 14–24   Radiographs taken one month later show the multiple Knowles pin fixation of the epiphyses shown in Figure 14–23.

In acute slipped epiphysis, with moderate or severe displacement, the principles of treatment include reduction and then pin fixation. Reduction is attainable because of the freshness of the displacement. It must be performed gently to avoid additional trauma and risk of vascular compromise. The reduction may be performed with gentle manipulation under anesthesia and immediately followed with pin fixation. Or the reduction may be obtained slowly with skeletal traction over a period of hours or days and then followed with pin fixation.

Active limb movement in bed is encouraged as soon as the operative wound is healed. The patient then progresses to crutch walking without weight bearing when adequate painless range of motion and muscle power are restored. If there are no identifiable complications, weight bearing is permitted as early as four to six weeks thereafter, continuing with collateral schedules of resistive exercises. This estimate may be optimistic for the

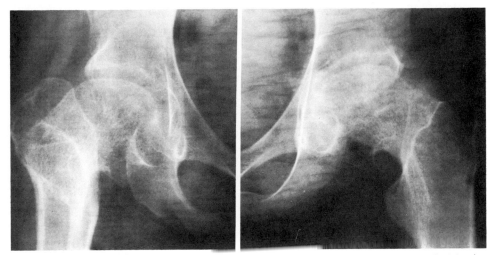

Figure 14–25 Thirteen year old black adolescent girl whose symptoms of right hip discomfort started at 11¼ years of age. One year later subtrochanteric osteotomy was performed because of severe deformity of the right hip. Subsequently she presented symptoms of joint pain with restriction of motion in both hips. Note narrowing of joint space and articular irregularity of left hip.

course of an acute severe epiphyseal displacement, even if well reduced and stabilized. Vascular impairment may occur at the time of the acute slip and lead ultimately to avascular necrosis, which may not be recognizable either from radiographic change or clinical symptoms for six to nine months after onset. Early mobilization neither precipitates nor adversely affects avascular necrosis in this preclinical prediagnosable stage.

In chronic slipped epiphysis with severe displacement there are no choices. The deformity must be corrected and the epiphysis stabilized against future slipping. The correction involves osteotomy of the proximal femur. Although the correction ideally should be made at the site of deformity in the femoral neck, extensive experience has shown this to be risky and frequently attended by vascular complication. The consensus is for compromise — performance of the osteotomy at a distance in the trochanteric or subtrochanteric areas (Fig. 14–25). The osteotomy usually is multiplanar, offering correction for flexion, adduction, and external rotation deformities. In the absence of complications, gradual progressive mobilization starts after osteotomy healing, which customarily takes three months.

Complications

Avascular necrosis of the proximal femoral epiphysis is a serious complication (Fig. 14–26). In Wilson's series it occurred in only five of three hundred hips.[29] It appears, however, as a significant risk in acute severely slipped epiphysis in which vascular damage may be part of the original displacement or be produced by injudicious techniques of reduction. In prior years osteotomy of the femoral neck for surgical correction led to high vascular com-

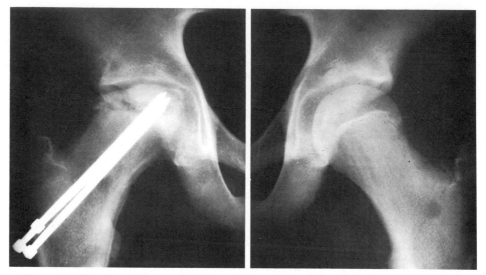

Figure 14–26 Fourteen year old white adolescent boy who sustained total displacement of the right proximal femoral epiphysis eight months previously. Closed reduction was performed immediately under general anesthesia. Knowles pinning was done several days later. The total disorganization of the epiphysis secondary to avascular necrosis is clearly shown.

plication rates. This has been modified by performing the osteotomy, when indicated, closer to the trochanteric area, thus causing a sharp decrease in the incidence of avascular necrosis.

Chondrolysis or cartilage necrosis is also a severe complication (Fig. 14–27). In Wilson's series there were twelve hips (six in black children) so affected out of three hundred.[29] In other series, Maurer reporting on Hawaiian, and Tillema and Golding on Jamaican children with slipped epiphysis, the incidence of cartilage necrosis was 28 per cent and 40 per cent respectively.[27, 28] Although the exact cause is not known, it has a greater incidence in black children; in children treated with open reduction, cast immobilization, or prolonged traction; and in patients with the most severe slips. The present consensus is that it is not associated with femoral head ischemia.

Most investigators entertain a dim view of the course of cartilage necrosis and find that its direction is toward ultimate ankylosis or progressive degenerative arthritis. It is suspected when there is persistent absence of motion in all planes ultimately confirmed by radiographic evidence of joint space narrowing. Usually it occurs within a year of the diagnosis of the primary condition.

In the face of permanent joint destruction, the timing of reconstructive orthopedic procedures is dependent upon the severity of the patient's pain and disability. Previously, hip arthrodesis represented the solution by creating a stable stiffened painless joint. The current practice is to offer cup arthroplasty, which aims to restore mobility.

Infrequently there is a reversal of the process with return of joint space suggesting articular cartilage restoration aided by appropriate rehabilitative therapy.[26]

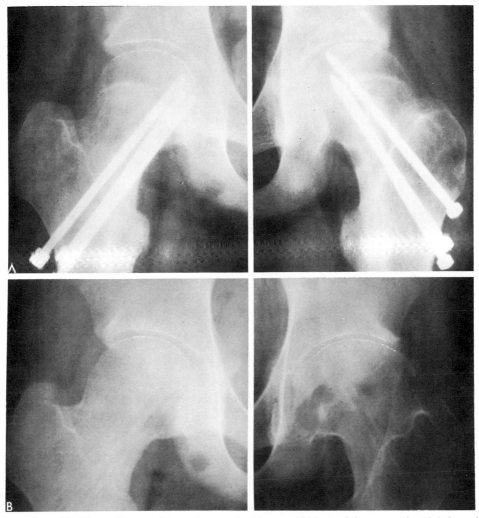

Figure 14-27   *A.* These radiographs are of a 13 year old black adolescent girl with bilateral slipped femoral capital epiphysis four months following Knowles pin insertions and three months after an accidental fracture of the shaft of the left femur. *B.* Clinically the patient had protracted pain and restriction in joint motion of the left hip. One and a half years later, the joint space narrowing of the left hip shown to be present in the earlier study is still present.

The process of functional retraining after surgical treatment follows that outlined for postoperative care of Legg-Calvé-Perthes disease. Where chondrolysis has occurred, however, range of hip motion exercises must be assiduously performed several times daily in order to minimize the eventual joint limitation. Often, the therapist must use hydrotherapy, analgesic hot packs, and reciprocal relaxation techniques in order to accomplish effective range of motion treatments, which should preferably be no more than active-assistive. Hip joint stretching by the therapist should only be done within the limit of pain.

Despite appropriate therapy several times a day, gains in range are usually slow. Some children may not actually gain motion, but in these children cessation of therapy is usually followed by steady loss of motion.

Because weight bearing on the hip with chondrolysis is restricted, the child may spend long periods in a sitting position. In order to minimize the tendency toward hip flexion contractures, it may be advisable for the child to spend an hour a day lying prone as well as sleeping in the prone position.

If chondrolysis and restricted weight bearing are unilateral, a high stool with a unilateral foot rest may be used to avoid long periods of sitting with the hip flexed at 90 degrees.

Because of the progressive loss of motion that may occur following chondrolysis, all the therapeutic measures mentioned are warranted even if the result is maintenance rather than increase in range. Aspirin has been used, on the basis of its reported ability to retard the cycle of chondrolysis in chondromalacia patellae, although to date without specific statistical confirmation in slipped epiphysis.

Prognosis

The important ingredients in the prognosis of slipped femoral capital epiphysis include the severity of slipping of the epiphysis, the presence of complicating avascular necrosis and cartilage necrosis, and the apparent greater risk in black children. Since minimal slips treated with prompt pinning lead to such excellent results, the important aim should be toward education and alertness for prompt diagnosis of early slips in the susceptible age and racial groups.

Once complications have developed the quality of the end results is affected. Special attention should be paid to early mobilization for its role in cartilage nutrition, muscle strengthening, and joint motion. Weight bearing is restricted only temporarily in minimal slips because of the usual prompt return of painless joint motion; it may have to be restricted longer when pain and stiffness persist in the more involved situations.

CONCLUSION

There is possible impact of each of these orthopedic conditions on the future development and function of the same major weight bearing joint.

Since there are different ages of predilection and susceptibility, the time of entry of these potential hazards varies. Each of the diseases has a spectrum of prognosis that ranges from perfect or nearly perfect to increasing degrees of impairment.

As is often true generally, in two of the problem areas the best results follow early recognition and treatment; this does not appear to apply to Legg-Calvé-Perthes disease with the same reliability, and here other uncontrollable prognostic ingredients appear, such as age at onset and type of involvement. The ultimate in disease control, namely prophylaxis, appears to have a role in congenital hip dislocation, in which identification of hip laxity and dislocatability may serve to eliminate the more serious hip dislocation and its sequelae.

References

CONGENITAL HIP DISLOCATION

1. Barlow, T. G.: Early diagnosis and treatment of congenital dislocation of the hip. J. Bone Joint Surg., *44-B*:292–301, 1962.
2. Hilgenreiner, H.: Zur Frühdiagnose und Frühbehandlung der angeborenen Hüftgelenkverrenkung. Med. Klin., *21*:1385–1388, 1425–1429, 1925.
3. MacKenzie, I. G.: Congenital dislocation of the hip. J. Bone Joint Surg., *54-B*:18–39, 1972.
4. Ortolani, M.: *La lussazione congenita dell'anca: Nuovi criteri diagnostici e profilattico-correttior.* Bologna, L. Cappelli, 1948.
5. Ponseti, I. V., and Frigerio, E. G.: Results in treatment of congenital dislocation of the hip. J. Bone Joint Surg., *41-A*:823–846, 1959.
6. Putti, I.: Early treatment of congenital dislocation of the hip. J. Bone Joint Surg., *15*:16–21, 1933.
7. Siffert, R. S., Ehrlich, M. G., and Katz, J. F.: Management of congenital dislocation of the hip. Clin. Orthop., *86*:28–33, 1972.
8. Smith, W. S., Badgley, C. E., Orwig, J. B., and Harper, J. M.: Correlation of postreduction roentgenograms and thirty-one-year follow-up in congenital dislocation of the hip. J. Bone Joint Surg., *50-A*:1081–1098, 1968.
9. Somerville, E. W.: Results of treatment of 100 congenitally dislocated hips. J. Bone Joint Surg., *49-B*:258–267, 1967.

LEGG-CALVÉ-PERTHES DISEASE

10. Axer, A.: Subtrochanteric osteotomy in the treatment of Perthes disease. J. Bone Joint Surg., *47-B*:489–499, 1965.
11. Calvé, J.: Sur une forme particulière de pseudo-coxalgie greffée. Sur des déformations caractéristiques de l'extremité supérieure du fémur. Rev. Chir., Paris, *42*:54–83, 1910.
12. Catterall, A.: The natural history of Perthes disease. J. Bone Joint Surg., *53-B*:37–53, 1971.
13. Cocchiarella, A., Challenor, Y., and Katz, J. F.: Orthosis for use in Legg-Calvé-Perthes disease. Arch. Phys. Med. Rehabil., *53*:286–288, 1972.
14. Heyman, C. H., and Herndon, C. H.: Legg-Perthes disease – a method for the measurement of the roentgenographic result. J. Bone Joint Surg., *32-B*:767–778, 1950.
15. Katz, J. F.: Conservative treatment of Legg-Calvé-Perthes disease. J. Bone Joint Surg., *49-A*:1043–1051, 1967.
16. Legg, A. T.: An obscure affection of the hip joint. Boston Med. Surg. J., *162*:202–204, 1910.
17. Legg, A. T.: The end results of coxa plana. J. Bone Joint Surg., *9*:26–36, 1927.
18. Mose, K.: *Legg-Calvé-Perthes Disease.* Copenhagen, Universitetsforlaget, 1964.
19. O'Garra, J. A.: Radiographic changes in Perthes' disease. J. Bone Joint Surg., *41-B*:465–476, 1959.
20. Perthes, G.: Über Arthritis Deformans Juvenilis. Dtsch. Z. Chir., *107*:111–159, 1910.
21. Ponseti, I. N., and Cotton, R. L.: Legg-Calvé-Perthes disease – pathogenesis and evolution. J. Bone Joint Surg., *43-A*:261–274, 1961.
22. Salter, R. B.: Surgical treatment of Legg-Perthes disease. In *Textbook of Disorders and Injuries of the Musculoskeletal System.* Baltimore, Williams & Wilkins Co., 1970, p. 277.

SLIPPED FEMORAL CAPITAL EPIPHYSIS

23. Alexander, C.: The etiology of femoral epiphysial slipping. J. Bone Joint Surg., *48-B*:299–311, 1966.
24. Harris, W. R.: The endocrine basis for slipping of the upper femoral epiphysis. J. Bone Joint Surg., *32-B*:5–11, 1950.
25. Kelsey, J. L., Keggi, K. J., and Southwick, W. O.: The incidence and distribution of slipped

capital femoral epiphysis in Connecticut and southwestern United States. J. Bone Joint Surg., 52-A:1203–1216, 1970.

26. Lowe, H. G.: Necrosis of articular cartilage after slipping of the capital femoral epiphysis. J. Bone Joint Surg., 52-B:108–118, 1970.
27. Maurer, R. C., and Larsen, I. J.: Acute necrosis of cartilage in slipped capital femoral epiphysis. J. Bone Joint Surg., 52-A:39–50, 1970.
28. Tillema, D. A., and Golding, J. S. R.: Chondrolysis following slipped capital femoral epiphysis in Jamaica. J. Bone Joint Surg., 53-A:1528–1540, 1971.
29. Wilson, P. D., Jacobs, B., and Schecter, L.: Slipped capital femoral epiphysis. J. Bone Joint Surg., 47-A:1128–1145, 1965.

Chapter 15

Limb Deficiency in
Infancy and Childhood

by *Yasoma B. Challenor, M.D.,*
and *Jacob F. Katz, M.D.*

The aspects of the habilitation of amputees that are of importance to those who treat infants and children and selected principles of biomechanics and prosthetics as they apply to the pediatric age group are considered here. Details of biomechanics and prosthetic fitting, alignment, fabrication, and check-out can be found in standard prosthetic texts and journals.

INCIDENCE AND ETIOLOGY

In recent surveys it has been estimated that 11 to 13 per cent of new amputees are under 21 years of age and that approximately 5 per cent are under age 11.[10, 19] If consideration is limited to amputees of age 15 or less, 50 to 60 per cent have congenital amputations, and an additional 10 per cent have anomalies treated as, or resulting in, amputation. Of the acquired amputations of children, over 30 per cent are related to disease or neoplasm, while nearly 70 per cent result from trauma.[22]

The relative frequency of trauma as a factor in childhood amputations is not surprising. Vehicular accidents and farm equipment mishaps each account for roughly 25 per cent of amputations, although car accidents may be more frequent in urban areas, and farm power tool injuries in rural communities. Explosions from firecrackers, homemade bombs, and chemical experiments,

341

and gunshot wounds from hunting accidents most frequently cause limb losses between 12 and 21 years, accounting for over 20 per cent of amputations. Railroad accidents, household mishaps, and thermal or electrical injuries account for approximately 13 per cent, 6 per cent, and 5 per cent respectively. The remaining small percentage is related to childhood recreational activities such as falls while climbing or injuries on playground equipment.[25]

CONGENITAL VERSUS ACQUIRED LOSSES

The multiplicity of congenital skeletal limb deficiencies has given rise to descriptive classifications, of which the revised Frantz and O'Rahilly system is the most comprehensive.[7, 17] Congenital amputations are divided into those involving complete absence of one or more limbs (amelia) and those involving partial absence (meromelia). These are subdivided into terminal and intercalary, each of which may have horizontal or longitudinal deficits (Fig. 15–1). Thus, complete radial aplasia with intact digits would be "meromelia, intercalary, longitudinal radial deficit." Standard abbreviations facilitate use of this classification. The common term "phocomelia," (i.e., rudimentary digits attached to shoulder or pelvic girdle with absence of intermediate segments), and other traditional terms do not appear in the Frantz and O'Rahilly terminology. Acquired amputations share the terminology used for adults; levels are described as being above or below a joint, or as being joint disarticulations. At present there is no internationally accepted uniform classification.

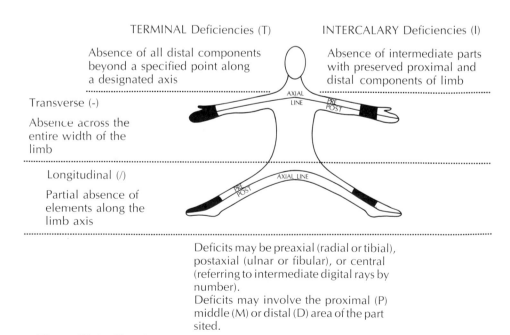

Figure 15–1   Classification of amelic or meromelic limb deficiencies. (Adapted from Burtch, R. L.: Nomenclature for congenital skeletal limb deficiencies. A revision of Frantz and O'Rahilly classification. Artif. Limbs, *10*:24–35, 1966.)

The necessity for preservation of stump length in children applies equally to congenital and acquired problems, but for different reasons. The primary aim in amputation surgery is preservation of epiphyses in order to allow maximal limb growth. Although this is true of congenital limb deficiency, an added and crucial factor is preservation of phocomelic digits for switch controls of externally powered prostheses in the upper extremities and for preservation of digital surfaces for tactile exploration and sensory feedback in both upper and lower extremities. The factors modifying this general principle are discussed subsequently.

The recent trend toward early fitting of prostheses for infants with limb deficiencies began in an attempt to match the apparent motor "readiness" of the infant. The goal of adherence to normal landmarks for motor and adaptive behavior is logical and favors natural progression of prosthetic use. Thus, an infant with an upper extremity deficiency is fitted with a purely passive prosthesis between three and six months of age, at a time when limb exploration is active, sitting is beginning, the extremities are needed for prop support, and bilateral hand activities are to be encouraged.[13, 26, 27] The prosthesis is then an extension of the infant's limb, which becomes incorporated into the developing body image. Just as handling, exploration, and use of toys are enrichments in the nonamputee child's development of sensory awareness and motor control, similar activities stimulate the child with a limb deficiency.

As research continues in the nature of neonatal learning processes, and as new prosthetic materials are developed, the fitting of upper extremity amputees prior to three months of age (currently estimated as occurring in 7.5 per cent of amputees[37]) should increase. According to current estimates, 20 per cent are fitted with prostheses before six months, and 65 per cent before one year of age.[37] In addition to the benefits already mentioned, early neonatal prosthetic fitting has been observed to: (1) encourage acceptance of prostheses by the family as well as by the child; (2) prevent habitual one-handed function; (3) prevent inefficient handling of objects in the axilla between humerus and chest; (4) improve balance and symmetry of posture and function while decreasing the tendency toward scoliosis; (5) facilitate development of much needed eye-prosthesis control and coordination; and (6) decrease hypotrophy of muscle and bone caused by disuse.

UPPER EXTREMITY DEFICIENCIES

Acquired or terminal transverse congenital amputations simulate the deficits encountered frequently in adults; tabulations of the residual functions and prosthetic substitutions available are ample.[23] Differences from adult problems begin with the appliance provided in infancy.

Functional Substitutions and Fitting Timetable

The initial prosthesis has in the past been a molded mitt, which provides length without function. Increasingly, the trend is toward provision of a passive, plastic-coated wafer, hook, or hand terminal device such as the Dorrance 12P hook or Variety Village 101 hand. This terminal device can be passively opened by the parents. Objects such as rattles or soft toys can be placed in it to encourage limb exploration and mobility. Active controls for the terminal device are introduced at 16 to 24 months, depending on the aptitude of the child. Elbow control, if needed, can be added subsequently (Table 15–1).

Bilateral amputees, particularly with severe limb deficiencies, are frequently fitted unilaterally. Although the second limb may add relatively little function, simultaneous bilateral fitting is desirable in order to maintain growth and postural symmetry, and to allow extremity preference to occur as a natural development rather than an imposition. Exceptions include the child: (1) in whom guides to laterality (eye, ear, foot preference) are lacking despite aptitude for an active terminal device; (2) for whom components for the requisite limb are fabricated for one side only; and (3) with asymmetrical deficiency whose longer extremity usually becomes the preferred limb, independent of other measures of lateral preference. Initially, the infant with bilateral amelia or phocomelia may be fitted with a harness for two prosthetic limbs whose terminal devices are passive wafer hooks. Later, active control of adduction for bilateral grasp between the wafers may be added. Still later, when age and aptitude permit, active control of one terminal device may be added on the side of lateral preference, if this is discernible, with a passive friction elbow. Last, elbow control may be added, either as simple elbow flexion and extension or as coordinated linked motion between elbow flexion and wrist rotation simulating forearm supination. The coordinated motions are most useful for feeding. Probably the greatest indication for early use of externally powered devices exists for infants with bilateral amelia or phocomelia.

At some point in prosthetic training, a cosmetic hand may be introduced. At present, this point is determined by the smallest size hands available, and the age at which they are congruous with general body parameters. Cosmetic and prehensile hands available for children include the APRL–Sierra No. 2 hand (five to seven years), the Dorrance No. 1 (five to seven years), Variety Village No. 105 electric hand (three to six years) or No. 108 (seven to nine years), Otto Bock 8K3 or 10A36 (five to eight years), and Northern Electric-Electrohydraulic Hand (8 to 12 years). (For hook sizes see Table 15–2 and Figures 15–2 and 15–3.)

It can be anticipated that growth will make a new prosthesis necessary every year until age 5, then every two years until age 12, and every three to four years thereafter.[26]

Preprosthetic Training

Preprosthetic training begins with stump hygiene and skin care. These natural extensions of infant and child care introduce the parents to a home program of therapy, which has the added benefit of encouraging the parents to feel that they are constructive participants in the infant's habilitation. Because

TABLE 15–1   UPPER EXTREMITY PROSTHESES

Amputation		Available Functional Substitutions		
		Active Control	Passive Positioning	Effects of Optional Passive Features
Wrist disarticulation	Hand	Prehension, voluntary opening or closing hook hand	Wide abduction of thumb	Permits grasp of larger objects
Below elbow	Wrist	Rotation with joint linkage or coordinated motion systems	Hook flexion-extension or rotation	Facilitates self-care and bimanual activities
Short below elbow	Forearm	Coordinated motion: pronation linked to elbow extension, supination to flexion	Pronation-supination simulated by wrist rotation unit	Adaptable for activities directed toward and away from body with less compensatory humeral and trunk motion
		Geared step-up of angle of flexion	Spring-lift elbow flexion assist	Gears augment flexion range for short stumps at expense of flexion power
Above elbow	Elbow	Flexion-extension	Friction elbow prior to age 2–3 years	
Shoulder disarticulation Phocomelia Forequarter amputation	Humerus		Humeral flexion and or abduction Rotation simulated by turntable just above elbow	Augments functional use of hook while minimizing sustained compensatory trunk posturing

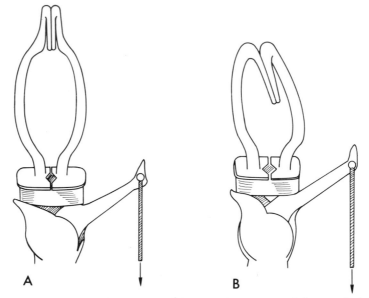

A   B

Figure 15–2 A. Diagram of a lyre-shaped hook with symmetrical digits, which facilitates lifting a glass or other large cylindrical object. B. Canted hook gives somewhat better view of small objects to be grasped. The canted hook is nonsymmetrical, and slightly angled toward the radial or "thumb" side. This may be of benefit if cervical motion is limited.

of diminished body surface area, the amputee's perspiration is copious, and heavy or restrictive clothing should be avoided.

Preserving range of motion is crucial, particularly in amputations following thermal or electrical burns, in which dense scar tissue potentiates the tendency to contracture. This same increased tendency, due to deeper structures, is present in both terminal and intercalary skeletal deficiencies such as radial or tibial aplasia: actual curvature of the limb may develop. In addition, contiguous hypoplastic muscle or fibrous bands or both may be present. In partial transverse intercalary deficiencies such as proximal focal femoral deficiency or radial meromelia, adjacent joints may also be dysplastic and show an accentuated tendency to develop contractures.

Selective muscle strengthening for prosthetic use should emphasize shoulder elevation and depression and scapular adduction and abduction. In bilateral amelia, strengthening of trunk muscles is emphasized, as well as trunk flexibility and rotation. Bilateral upper extremity amelia necessitates training of leg and toe use for self-care prior to donning prostheses, for functional independence if prostheses need repair, and for night activities after prostheses have been removed. Considerable hypermobility of hips and thoracolumbar spine is essential. Cervical mobility must also be encouraged, but only after clinical and radiological investigation of the cervical spine, since congenital amelia can be associated with cervical spine anomalies. Congenital cranial nerve palsy, particularly of the facial nerve, may also be associated with amelia.

Postural symmetry exercises have long-term benefit, in that avoiding significant scoliosis and subsequent fusion preserves the spinal mobility crucial

(Text continued on page 351)

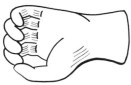

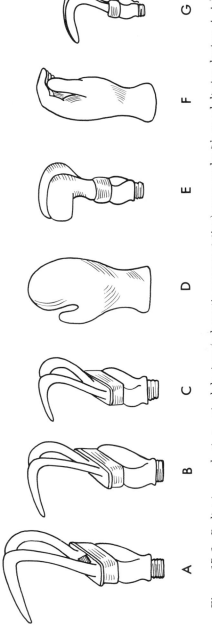

Figure 15–3 Pediatric prosthetic terminal devices (schematic representation) compared with an adult size device: A. Adult Dorrance 88 x (with neoprene lining). B and C. Pediatric 99 x and pediatric 10 x (both with neoprene lining). D. Passive molded mitt. E. Plastisol coated wafer. F. Variety Village 101 passive hand (objects can be placed between thumb and palm). G. Plastisol coated hook (smallest size available), 10P Dorrance. The appropriate ages according to device size are given in Table 15–2.

TABLE 15–2 PROSTHETIC TRAINING: UPPER AND LOWER EXTREMITY

Developmental Level	Goal	Limb Deficiency	Suggested Activities (partial list)°
2–4 mo	Head control	Meromelia (with and without prostheses)	Place on padded slant board with arms reaching forward to prop for support or for toys: prone and supine Increase angle of slant as control increases in prone position
		Amelia Without prostheses	Do not allow infant to remain supine. Encourage turning, which may be difficult to initiate Prop on sides alternately (padded slant board as above)
		With prostheses	Encourage use of prostheses for prop support when raising head and chest while prone
5–8 mo	Trunk control and Sitting balance	Meromelia	Position on sides, encourage rolling with upper arm in front and under arm stretched overhead Sit infant on lap or pillow, tilt slightly to encourage trunk balancing Increase tilt gradually to stimulate protective arm extension
		Amelia	Initiate rolling with gentle passive head turning, encourage shoulder and trunk rotation to follow Sit and tilt on pillow as for meromelia, continue even to marked increase in tilt (balance must be solely by trunk compensation)
	Reaching and bimanual grasp	Meromelia (first without, later with prostheses)	Suspend soft toys or noisemakers within reach Place rattle, bells, soft toys in terminal device Place cookie or bread in terminal device (i.e., Dorrance 12p hook)
		Amelia (with prostheses)	Encourage holding objects with both hands (large blocks or ball) Place string or handle of pull-toy in terminal device Encourage transfer of objects from hand to hand
		Phocomelia	Encourage active motion of appendage by tactile stimulation (place colorful ribbon or bell to attract attention and stimulate motion)
9–10 mo	Crawling and creeping	Meromelia or amelia (with prostheses)	Place prone on low pillow or low scooter, encourage reaching toward toys Encourage reciprocal leg motion for propulsion

Table 15–2 continued on opposite page.

TABLE 15-2 PROSTHETIC TRAINING: UPPER AND LOWER EXTREMITY
(*Continued*)

Developmental Level	Goal	Limb Deficiency	Suggested Activities (partial list)°
			Prop in creep position with prostheses, rock back and forth gently
	Reaching and using extremities	Meromelia or amelia (with prostheses)	Push-pull toys, vary size and shape Reach for, push, or catch balloons
		Phocomelia	Encourage active motion of appendages, exploration of various textured surfaces
10–11 mo	Standing	Meromelia or amelia (with prostheses)	Start in creep position, encourage rising to kneel by reaching overhead for toys
10–14 mo	Cruising	Meromelia or amelia (with prostheses)	Encourage rising to standing in crib or holding onto push-toy or chair Hold hips and shift balance from one leg to another For lower limb deficiency may be necessary to move legs reciprocally to encourage stepping Use infant walker or harness
12–18 mo	Walking	Meromelia or amelia (with prostheses)	Stand child with back supported by a wall After balancing encourage steps
	Self-care	Meromelia or amelia (with prostheses)	Feeding self a cookie Beginning use of spoon
18–24 mo	Maneuverability	Meromelia or amelia (lower extremity)	Accept infantile gait pattern, aim for stability and control of momentum Tricycling Walking up low stairs, getting up from sitting or squatting on the floor Later, climbing onto adult chair Pivoting, walking sideways and backward Climbing over obstacles
	Manipulation	Meromelia or amelia (upper extremity)	Building blocks, pegs into holes, pop-apart beads, snap-together blocks Vary humeral and elbow positions while terminal device is being operated Encourage manipulation with hands Vary size, shape, texture, weight of objects for combined foot and prosthesis handling and exploration (Suggested terminal device: Dorrance 10p hook or Otto Bock 10A25 hook)

Table 15-2 continued on following page.

TABLE 15–2 PROSTHETIC TRAINING: UPPER AND LOWER EXTREMITY
(Continued)

Developmental Level	Goal	Limb Deficiency	Suggested Activities (partial list)°
±1 yr	Manipulation	Meromelia or amelia (upper extremity)	Stacking cubes, retrieving ball, holding crayon and scribbling, hammering, stringing large beads (child should attempt same activities with feet or foot plus prosthesis)
	Self-care		Removing shoes and socks, drinking from cup, eating with spoon
±2 yr	Manipulation	Meromelia or amelia	Stringing 1 or ½ inch beads, manipulating zipper with prosthesis and/or feet
		Phocomelia	Manipulation of on-off switch with appendage
	Self-care	All	Washing and drying face, requesting and assisting with toileting Assisting with dressing and removing prosthesis
±3 yr	Manipulation	Meromelia or amelia	Copying circle, square, diamond, etc. as task becomes possible according to developmental level Opening and closing doors, drawers, latches, faucets
	Self-care	Meromelia or amelia	Manipulating garment fastenings, washing self, assisting dressing; donning and removing prosthesis (Suggested terminal device: Dorrance 10x hook or Variety Village 105 hand or Otto Bock 10A37 hook)
±4 yr	Balance and coordination	Meromelia or amelia	Running Stopping short Turning rapidly Balancing on one foot 4–10 sec (According to nature of amputation and type of prosthesis)
			Continue attention to sitting and standing postural symmetry (Suggested terminal devices: ages 6–8 yr, Dorrance 99x hook; 8–13 yr, Dorrance 8 or 88 hook; ages 13–adult, Dorrance 5x or 555 hook)

°For many more activities, depending on the aptitude of the child, see Blakeslee, B. (ed.); *The Limb Deficient Child* (Berkeley and Los Angeles, University of California Press, 1963); Gesell, A., and Amatruda, C. S.: *Developmental Diagnosis: Normal and Abnormal Child Development* (New York, Harper & Row, 1967); and Jentschura, G., Marquardt, E., and Rudel, E. M.: *Malformations and Amputations of the Upper Extremity* (New York, Grune & Stratton, Inc., 1967).

to compensatory foot use in severe meromelia or amelia. Shoulder alignment, symmetry of thoracic strength, leveling of the pelvis in sitting and standing positions, and attention to equal leg length and strength are part of both preprosthetic and prosthetic training.

Balance and coordination may be difficult for amelic or phocomelic children because of asymmetrical limb loss or absence of sufficient length of limbs for balance, compensating movements, and protective reactions if balance is upset. Truncal compensation for balance upset must be superior.

Breathing exercises for thoracic expansion may be of value for children with congenital cervicothoracic spinal anomalies or hypertrophic encircling scars from burns. Expansion of the chest must be adequate, particularly if extensive harnessing or thoracic extensions of prosthetic sockets are anticipated.

Self-defense training using the feet may be needed for carefully selected older children with severe upper limb loss. This training requires exceptional balance on one leg with varied truncal postures, and may be used as motivation for balance training—again for carefully selected patients.

Prosthetic Training

Prosthetic training also begins with the parents, since they must be taught to encourage the child to make age-commensurate adjustments to the environment. Too often, parents become overprotective and insist on fully adapting the environment to the child's disability. While some adaptations may be necessary, excesses will hinder the child's independence and possibly produce later maladjustments to school, and possibly vocational limitations.

Initially, the therapist's aim is to increase the length of time the prosthesis can be worn comfortably without skin problems. This is followed by training toward use of the terminal device. The earlier the child's intelligence and acceptance permit training for active terminal device control, the better the outlook for continued use of prostheses as the child grows older. The child should not be allowed to try spontaneous development of control, since poor habits of use may delay control and interfere with future function and training. Training progresses through feeding, play, toilet activities, and dressing. Pencil and paper activities follow, depending on the child's age (Table 15–2). Throughout training, use of the hook is emphasized because it is lightweight and usually offers more function than a hand (see Fig. 15–3). The hand is, however, provided as a cosmetic alternative for social use. It is to be expected that children will tend to use the terminal device for hammering, probing, prying, and other acts that may cause rapid deterioration or loss of cosmesis.

Complicating factors that may delay prosthetic training for traumatic proximal amputations include infections in the stump, conditions requiring revision or extensive skin grafting as in thermal or electrical burns, and concomitant injuries to other parts of the body. Unfortunately, prolonged fabrication or financing procedures may also delay prosthesis delivery. If delays do occur, limited intermediate goals may be writing or typing with simple devices utilizing the shoulder motions requisite for subsequent prosthetic control (Fig. 15–4). Complications more directly related to the cause of ampu-

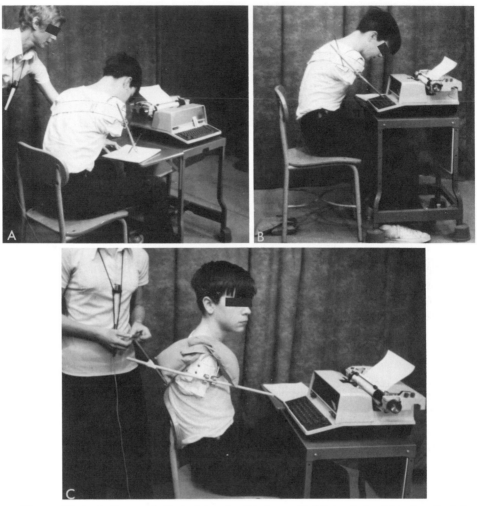

Figure 15-4   *A.* Preprosthetic training for this boy with bilateral shoulder disarticulation includes use of a harness and dowel to encourage shoulder protraction for writing. *B.* Typing is achieved by reversing the dowel and emphasizing scapular elevation and depression. *C.* Addition of weights strengthen the shoulder muscles later to be used for prosthetic control.

tation should not be overlooked, since their presence may alter training for or outcome of prosthetic use. Such complications could include peripheral neuropathy in thermal and electrical burns, and in the latter, possible myelopathy, delayed necrosis of bone, or lens opacity on the side of the injury.[31]

Current Developments

Upper extremity prosthetics have been developing in the direction of electrical or compressed carbon dioxide pneumatic control for proximal amputations, and myoelectric controls (amplified muscle action potentials) for control in distal amputations.[3, 32, 35, 36] The myoelectric principle of control has even been incorporated into prostheses fitted immediately after operation.[5, 8, 9, 29, 30, 34] Concurrently, new developments have also been related to conventional prostheses for proximal amputees, e.g., reduction of weight and surface coverage of the sockets and harnessing of above-elbow and shoulder disarticulation prostheses, and dual ring harnessing for facilitation of independent terminal device operation—both for bilateral amputees.[28, 33]

For over a decade it has been accepted that externally powered prostheses, including myoelectric prostheses, are still experimental, despite the fact that in Europe and Canada many multiple amputees rely on these devices and use them regularly and reliably.[26a] Certainly these prostheses can and will undergo extensive developments and improvements. One concept that is still truly experimental relates to the myoelectric arm being developed by researchers at the Krusen research center in Philadelphia. It has been observed that there is a certain reproducible distribution of shoulder girdle muscle contraction with every motion of the hand, wrist, forearm, elbow, and humerus. When multiple pickup electrodes are placed over the appropriate shoulder girdle muscles, the reproducible patterns of stabilizing contractions can be computerized, and the electrodes can be used to transmit myoelectric signals to activate a prosthesis. In effect, the amputee thinks of and attempts the distal motion he desires, and the computer reads the contractile pattern around the shoulder and interprets that pattern into the desired distal motion. Utilizing this principle, an above-elbow or shoulder disarticulation amputee can produce as he wishes: wrist flexion and extension, forearm supination and pronation (wrist rotation), elbow flexion and extension, and humeral internal and external rotation.[14, 15] Hook or hand opening and closing require separate myoelectric controls. The principle has been shown to be operable. It remains for the future, however, to minimize the weight of the prosthesis and the size and weight of the computer and power pack, and to make the electromechanical components reliable and easily repairable. Indeed, in the United States the technology and delivery of and maintenance facilities for even less sophisticated systems still await effective development.[26a]

LOWER EXTREMITY DEFICIENCIES

The desirability of developmental sequencing of stimulatory activities and prosthetic fitting for lower extremity limb deficiency parallels the upper extremity sequence (Table 15–2). A relatively cosmetic leg mold is applied at about five to eight months of age to aid in sitting balance, symmetry of limb activities, and incorporation of the new limb into the developing body scheme (Fig. 15–5). The limb should definitely be in place as creeping and standing begin. For proximal limb losses, the initial standing prosthesis does not incorporate knee motion; this can be added when standing, stair climbing, and pivoting are secure (two and a half to four years, depending on the aptitude of the toddler and the nature of the limb deficiency).

The current trend for management of lower limb congenital deficiencies is to allow maximal growth of the limb prior to any surgical revision or recon-

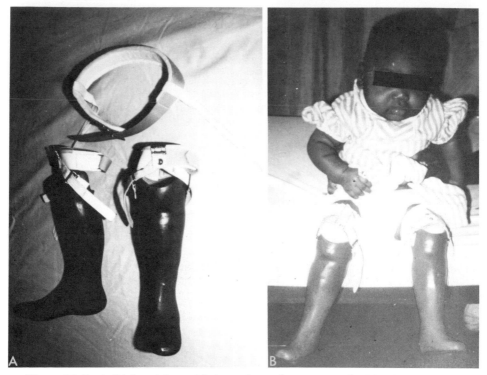

Figure 15–5 *A.* Lightweight molded prostheses for a six month old infant with bilateral below-knee deficiency. *B.* The infant moves the prosthetic limbs actively, explores them, and uses the added limb length to good advantage in achieving sitting balance.

struction. Adaptations of the prostheses accommodate the contour of the residual anatomical limb components. Surgery aimed at cosmesis or more efficient limb use may be introduced just before school age, or sooner if increasing deformity threatens to limit function. However, generalizations can be misleading. The multiplicity of possible deficiencies and deformities, compounded by the variables of the child's developmental and emotional and family status, make individualization of surgical and prosthetic planning mandatory.

The congenital amputee often has either dysplasia or instability of the joints or both in the involved limb or limbs. The stability of these joints may be an important determining factor in the nature and timing of surgery, and in the type of preoperative and postoperative prosthetic management (Fig. 15–6). In contrast, joint problems tend to be less severe in the child with acquired limb loss, for whom it is primarily asymmetry of epiphyseal growth or ligamentous stress that may make varus or valgus joint deviations of prosthetic importance. Genu valgum occurs frequently in below-knee amputees, and may require knee joints and a laced thigh cuff, rather than the more cosmetic patellar tendon bearing prosthetic variants (Fig. 15–7). Excessively short below-knee stumps may require similar fitting, with possible added adaptations to minimize the tendency for the stump to pull out of the socket during knee flexion (Fig. 15–8).

The most frequently prescribed components are solid ankle cushion heel

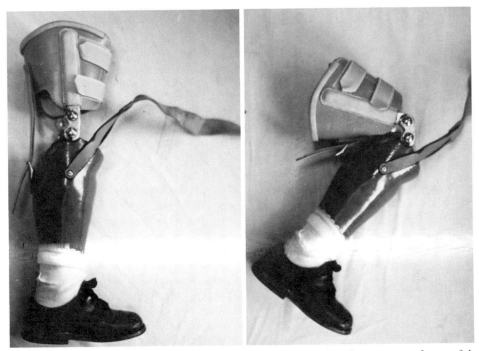

Figure 15–6   Knee joint incongruence or dysplasia may require close accommodation of the normal shift in the center of knee rotation as the knee flexes. A polycentric joint minimizes internal stress on the knee during flexion. Many more complex polycentric knee components have been incorporated into adult above-knee prostheses.

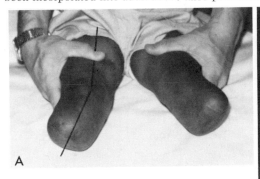

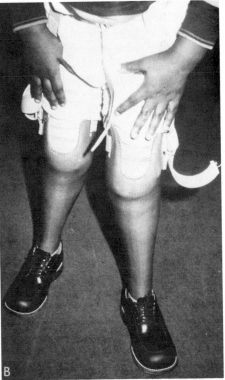

Figure 15–7   *A.* The tendency toward genu valgum persists in this six year old boy with bilateral below-knee amputations, despite high supracondylar supports on the patellar tendon bearing prosthesis. *B.* Addition of thigh corsets and knee joints was required. Future prostheses, however, might well emphasize insetting the foot during alignment for more adequate control of the genu valgum.

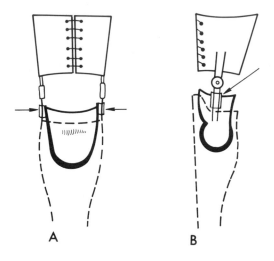

A   B

Figure 15–8 Modified patellar tendon bearing prosthesis with split socket, knee joints, and laced thigh corset for a very short below-knee stump. The solid line indicates the well molded inner socket. The discontinuous line indicates the outer cosmetic shell. *A.* Anterior view. *B.* Lateral view. On knee flexion, the inner socket remains in close contact with the stump, thus minimizing friction. The inner shell is attached to the lateral uprights by a channel which permits upward piston motion on knee flexion without allowing the short stump to pull out of the cosmetic shell.

feet, adjustable friction knees (with or without a lock), and for teenagers, a hydraulic knee unit to accommodate widely varying speeds of gait. For the most proximal limb losses, a Canadian-type socket and hip joint are used (i.e., for hip disarticulation or amelia).

Preprosthetic and Prosthetic Training

For both congenital and acquired amputations, preservation of joint range of motion and strength is necessary throughout training, with added and continuing importance in the presence of dysplastic joints, imbalance of muscle strength, or periarticular scar tissue. If prosthetic fitting does not immediately follow amputation or stump revision, then stump bandaging for shrinkage and conditioning parallels that for adult amputees.

The training sequence of activities progresses from basic balance and assumption of the standing position to ambulation and endurance training (Table 15–2). Maneuverability indoors is followed by training for independence outdoors and in school and playground situations if the extent of the amputation permits. The earlier before school age that independent function can be achieved, the better the potential for school and peer adjustment. The same applies to the provision of the most cosmetic prosthesis available for a given level and type of amputation. Thus, for toddlers and children, the training for voluntarily controlled motion of articulated cosmetic joints should be accomplished by four to five years of age. The perfection of fine points of maneuverability, it is hoped, comes with daily use of the prosthesis. Unfortunately, poor gait or posture habits may also develop. It is therefore necessary to check children every two to three months, not only for joint alignment, stump condition, posture and growth, but also to observe the nature of prosthetic use. It has been estimated that when prostheses are properly prescribed and fitted, child amputees followed to age 21 show 94 per cent all-day use for lower extremity prostheses, and 61 per cent all-day use for upper

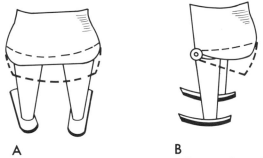

A   B

Figure 15–9 *A.* Posterior view of swivel or "rocker" type of prosthesis with footplates curved mediolaterally and anteroposteriorly. Rocking the trunk from side to side allows pivoting progression from one prosthetic limb to the other. The discontinuous lines indicate a plastic panel to prevent clothing being stuck under the sitting bucket. *B.* Lateral view of "rocker." The limbs can start at a low "stubby" height and increase as balance increases. The amelic infant gains confidence in this device prior to receiving prosthetic limbs. The footplate can be flat initially for added stability.

extremities.[26] With heavy use, the prosthetic replacements may be more frequent than the rates outlined for upper extremity prostheses.

Current Developments

The statement "replacement of lower extremity function is more efficacious than upper extremity functional replacement because of the simpler, less precise nature of leg function" constitutes a medical truism as well as a prosthetic fact. The bioengineering intricacies of myoelectric or external power sources have therefore not been applied to lower extremity prostheses. Instead, research and development have involved primarily (1) early postoperative prosthetic fitting and training; (2) use of hydraulic knee mechanisms for swing, and recently for both swing and stance phase control; (3) multiaxial ankle joints for adaptation to inclined or uneven surfaces; (4) modular interchangeable components for more rapid fitting and delivery; and (5) endoskeletal components with soft, molded cosmetic covers. While many of these new developments may be applicable to the adolescent and teenager, components of appropriate size are not yet available for the child. One development specific for the child with bilateral lower limb amelia or phocomelia is the platform preprosthetic device for standing balance and a form of progression that relies on trunk rocking (Fig. 15–9).[20] This design permits standing and locomotion for infants whose triple or quadruple limb deficiency limits crutch use.

SPECIAL CONSIDERATIONS

Proximal Focal Femoral Deficiency

This congenital deficiency is a femoral transverse partial meromelic dysplasia of the upper femur leading to lower limb distortions of varying magnitude. There are two major categories: I, those with a femoral head in an adequate acetabulum, and II, those with neither an identifiable femoral head nor a satisfactory acetabulum. There are subgroups in each of these classes: subgroup Ia, in which a fibrocartilage bridge usually is present between the femoral head and trochanteric segments with femoral neck varus inclination and mild shortening of the femur; Ib, in which there is failure of contact between the femoral head and neck with the upper shaft associated with more shortening of the femur than in Ia; IIa, in which there is absence of the femoral head and neck as well as a defective acetabulum and shortened femoral shaft fragment; and IIb, the same as IIa but with more shortening and less identifiable femoral shaft integrity.

It has been recognized that proximal focal femoral deficiency occurs unilaterally (86 per cent) much more frequently than bilaterally. It tends to be associated with other skeletal anomalies in about half the cases. The most common concomitant deformity is absence of the fibula in the same limb, although there may be deficiency in any limb. The characteristic clinical presentation is a shortened extremity held in flexion, abduction, and external rotation. Commonly the foot on the affected leg is at the level of the knee joint of the uninvolved limb.

The problems of deformity associated with proximal focal femoral deficiency include: lower limb shortening, instability, restriction of motion, and malrotation. It may be difficult to identify accurately the full impact of the anomaly until the child approaches the end of the first year. Femoral head ossification is usually delayed so that early separation into categories I or II may have to be postponed until such ossification occurs. Ultimately, roentgenograms show the presence of a femoral head and its relationship to the upper femur. In the most optimistic situation, subgroup Ia, there is coxa vara that can be corrected surgically with valgus subtrochanteric osteotomy (Fig. 15–10). In subgroup Ib the problem may be complicated by lack of contact between the femoral head and neck and a short overriding femoral shaft (Figs. 15–11 and 15–12). Surgery offers a means of stabilization by bone graft incorporation between the femoral head and shaft after sufficient growth of the femoral head and neck make it feasible. With successful establishment of continuity, leg length inquality remains the major consideration. Correction of the deficit is usually managed with extension through a suitable prosthesis. Associated deformities in the involved limb, such as absence of the fibula, aggravate the shortening. Without such complication the ultimate shortening has been shown to be milder in this variety (Ia and Ib) of proximal focal femoral deficiency (25 per cent growth inhibition of the femur) than in the IIa and IIb (50 to 75 per cent growth inhibition).[1]

In category II, all the aforementioned problems are aggravated. Hip instability is often severe because of the absence of the femoral head and acetabulum. Shortening is worse, and the shaft fragment may be so diminutive in IIb as to bring the femoral condyles into juxtaposition with the acetabulum.

The customary therapy in this situation is to utilize the existing structural elements for weight bearing in a specially constructed prosthesis. When the limb extends below the level of the opposite knee, a Syme type of ankle disarticulation is performed in order to preserve end weight bearing with a

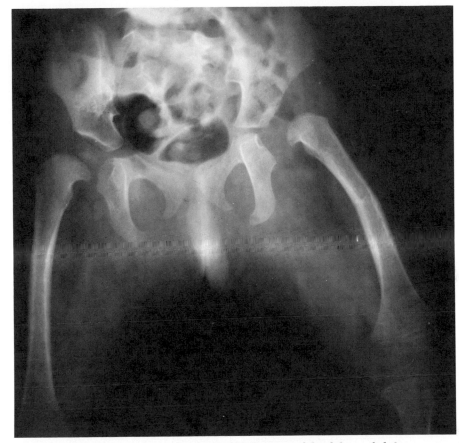

Figure 15–10 Mild deformity in unilateral left proximal focal femoral deficiency type Ia. Note coxa vara (the ossification center has not yet appeared, although that on the unaffected right side is present), the shortened left femur, and the mild medial angulation of the mid-shaft of the left femur.

prosthetic knee at the accustomed level. With bilateral involvement, the amputation revision is not recommended so that direct foot weight bearing remains for use in emergencies when the prosthesis happens not to be instantaneously available.

Congenital Fibular Meromelia

This anomaly is characterized primarily by partial or total absence of the fibula and has been reported to occur unilaterally three times as frequently as bilaterally. In our earlier discussion of proximal focal femoral deficiency it was pointed out that groups of limb malformations coexist and that absence of the fibula contributes to one of the likely mixtures. Kruger reported about a 10 per cent incidence of proximal focal femoral deficiency in the unilateral fibular meromelias and perhaps 35 per cent in bilateral involvement.[24] A suggested classification of the fibular meromelias is its presentation unilater-

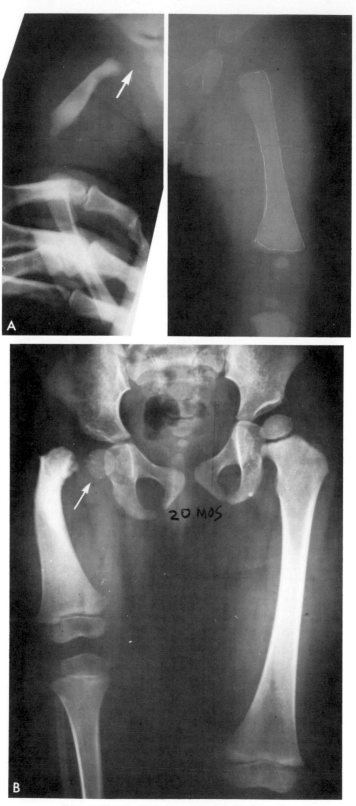

Figure 15–11 *See opposite page for legend.*

ally or bilaterally and the association of each of these with either a normal or a deficient femur.

The clinical appearance varies with the age of the child, since limb growth retardation is a prominent feature. Usually there is anterior bowing of the tibia, sometimes with skin dimpling over the apex of the angulation. The foot is usually deviated in an equinovalgus direction and often exhibits deformity due to absence of the fourth and fifth metatarsal rays (Fig. 15–13). Leg length discrepancy may reach as much as 3 inches by four years of age, and appears to be related inversely to the number of metatarsals present.

Treatment for this condition in the past was frustrating and demoralizing for both physician and patient. In the attempt to restore the limb to anatomical and functional status, multiple surgical procedures were required for realigning and stabilizing the foot and ankle – involving the morbidity associated with multiple hospitalizations and prolonged plaster cast fixation. Despite this, the result frequently failed its objective. Finally at this juncture, with a scarred shortened leg, the foot still not in weight-bearing alignment, amputation was performed.

To eliminate both this succession of operative failures and the detriment to the child's emotional and physical growth and development produced by the enforced invalidism, a striking and unusual plan of therapy has evolved. This is the prompt early amputation of the distorted unstable foot with a Syme amputation that permits end weight bearing. The child is then mobilized in a prosthesis of suitable length, allowing him to walk at the normal developmental age.

Congenital Tibial Meromelia

This is a significant anomaly that occurs less frequently than fibular meromelia. Like the latter, it also coexists with other anomalies. Tibial meromelia appears, however, to have a surprising relationship with congenital hip dislocation as well as upper limb phalangeal deformities. Bilateral incidence varies but has been reported to be as high as 50 per cent.[2, 6]

Clinically, the affected limb is identifiable at birth because of shortening, malrotation, knee joint instability, and varus deviation of the foot (Fig. 15–14A). The foot may have fewer than normal metatarsophalangeal rays in total longitudinal tibial meromelia, as shown in Figure 15–14B, or an intact though deviated foot in the intercalary or partial tibial meromelia.

Whenever possible, surgical realignment of the proximal end of the fibula into the center of the knee joint is performed before the infant reaches one year of age. This is intended to create a knee joint sufficiently functional to

(Text continued on page 365)

Figure 15–11 *A.* In neonatal proximal focal femoral deficiency there is no ossification of either proximal femoral epiphysis so that, despite marked femoral shortening, accurate classification is delayed. *B.* At age 20 months, classification into subgroup Ib is possible: a proximal femoral epiphysis is present with an acceptably contoured acetabulum, and there is failure of bony union between the head and trochanteric segments as well as moderate shortening.

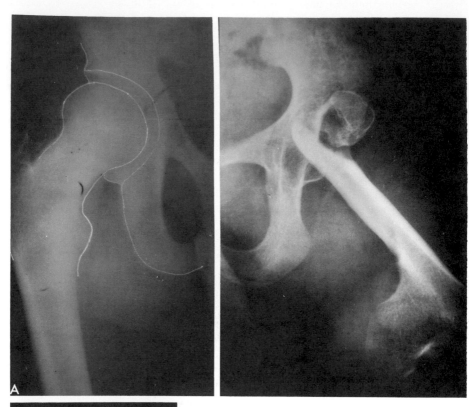

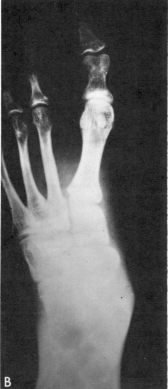

Figure 15–12 A. Radiograph of a severe left proximal focal femoral deficiency, subgroup Ib, in a 16 year old male adolescent. The elements of the deformity are a markedly shortened femur and the presence of a femoral head in a nonunion relationship to the femoral shaft. B. The foot on the affected side shows absence of the fifth ray, although the leg below the knee is normal.

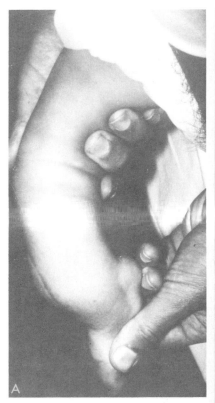

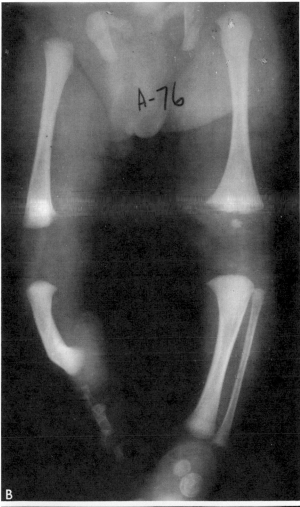

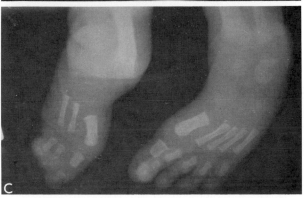

Figure 15–13 *A* and *B*. Tibial shortening with anterior bowing in congenital absence of the right fibula. The foot is held in an equinus position. *C*. Absence of the right fourth and fifth metatarsal rays is an associated anomaly. There is metatarsus adductus of the left foot without proximal abnormality on the left.

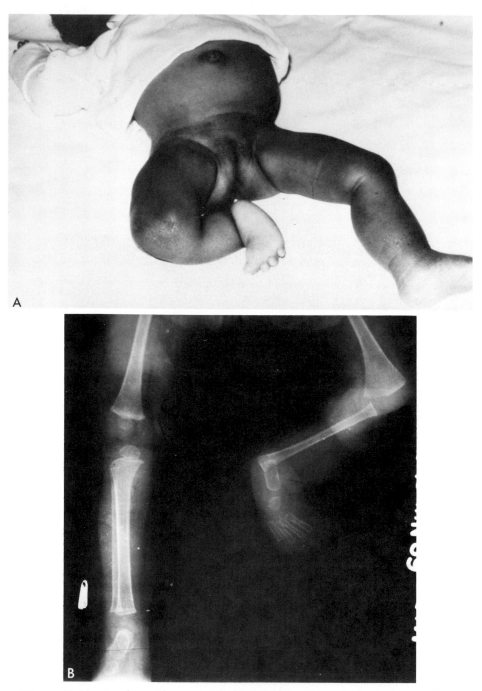

Figure 15–14 *A*. Infant with congenital absence of the tibia and prominent varus deviation of the right foot. *B*. This radiograph (reversed photographically, but representative of the limb involved in the infant in *A*) shows the fibular dislocation at the knee and ankle. There are four metatarsal rays in the foot.

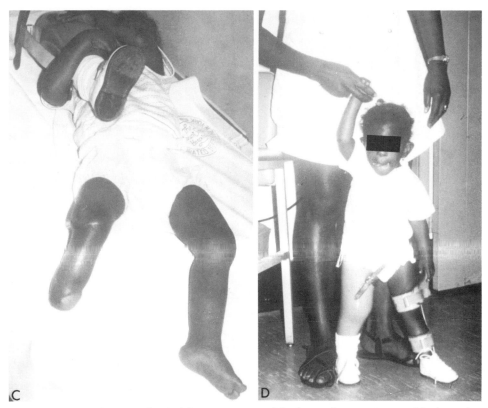

Figure 15–14 *Continued.   C*. After amputation of the foot and repositioning of the hypoplastic fibula under the femoral condyles, the knee was fused because of instability and absence of voluntary motion of the fibula. *D*. Prosthetic replacement incorporates the fused knee. At a certain point in growth, the distal stump end will be at a level allowing use of an above-knee prosthesis with a knee joint.

permit planning for a below-knee prosthesis. This is then rapidly followed with a Syme type of amputation of the unstable varus foot, converting the distal fibula to end weight bearing in the below-knee prosthesis (Fig. 15–14*C* and *D*).

Osseous Overgrowth in Amputation Stumps

Osseous overgrowth in amputation stumps is characteristically a complication of acquired childhood amputations without parallel in adult amputees. Its favorite sites are the humerus, fibula, tibia, and femur in descending order of frequency. It seems to occur without specific relationship to the surgical technique of amputation and presents clinically as a tapered extension of the distal bone end, gradually stretching the distal soft tissues until it leads to ulceration and perforation.

Roentgenography reveals tapering and mild angulation of the distal bone end with sclerosis and loss of the intramedullary space. Aitken reported plac-

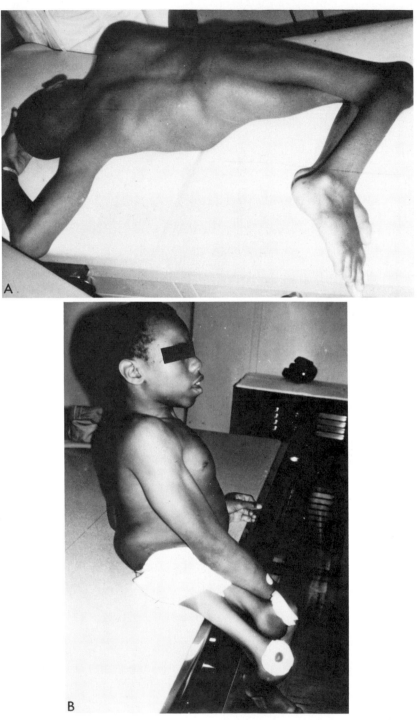

Figure 15–15 *A.* When seen, this eight year old boy with congenital absence of the sacrum had fixed hip and knee flexion contractures with prominent popliteal webs. *B.* Sitting on the hypoplastic pelvis was unstable and painful. Note the padding on the calloused knees; this boy tried to ambulate in a bizarre fashion by bearing weight on the knees.

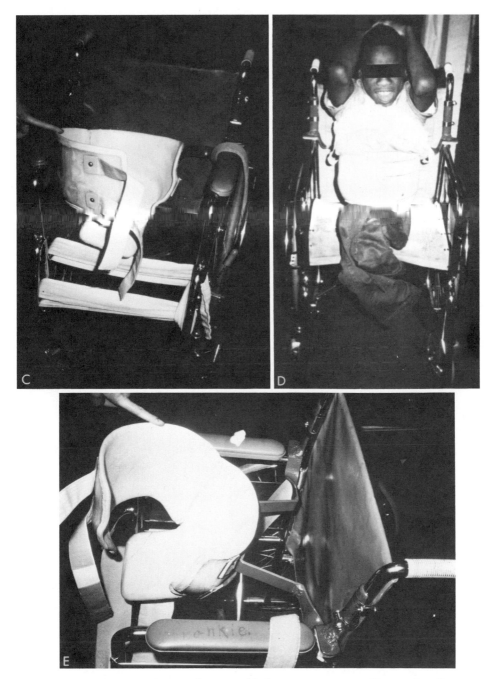

Figure 15–15 *Continued.   C* and *D*. A molded sitting support was fabricated to allow transfer of weight to the abdomen and lower thoracic areas. *E*. The sitting bucket was attached to a wheelchair; here it is viewed from above to show bracket attachments.

ing metal markers at the distal bone end during stump revisions and discovering later that growth of the bone stump occurred appositionally distal to the marker.[2]

Treatment for stump overgrowth is surgical revision prior to actual ulceration with its threat of infection and osteomyelitis. In dual-bone locations, such as radius and ulna or tibia and fibula, some success in controlling recurrent overgrowth by creating synostoses between the adjacent bone ends has been reported. As long as the epiphysis remains open, overgrowth of the bone stump is a potential hazard.

Unusual Prosthetic Applications

In addition to femoral, tibial, and fibular meromelic deficiencies, prosthetic principles have been used in the habilitation of children with sacral agenesis with or without absence of the lumbar vertebrae, and paralyzed or contracted lower limbs (Fig. 15–15A). If the child is seen before contractures occur, and sensation is found to be present in the limbs, bracing for ambulation may be tried. Contractures may, however, begin in utero, and in addition, sitting on the hypoplastic pelvic structures is both unstable and uncomfortable — with or without braces (Fig. 15–15B). If no limb sensation is present, particularly if there are contractures of the limbs, surgical ablation can be both cosmetic and contributory to eventual ambulation.[16]

The prostheses would allow weight bearing on the lower thoracic areas and partially on the abdomen and low back, with a socket contoured to avoid impeding respiration or excretory function (Fig. 15–15C, D, and E). The same weight distribution would occur in sitting and standing positions. Standing

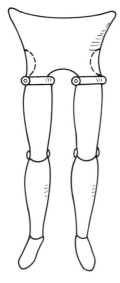

Figure 15–16 *A.* Diagram of the type of prosthesis used for children with sacral agenesis after limb amputation. The flared thoracic socket minimizes painful weight bearing on the hypoplastic pelvis. The discontinuous semicircular lines represent optional open areas, to allow redundant flesh to protrude. This aids suspension, which is primarily accomplished by shoulder straps. *B.* The alignment of the prosthesis is similar to that of a Canadian-type hip disarticulation prosthesis. The discontinuous straight lines represent a canvas strap to limit excessive knee rise during swing phase of gait.

A   B

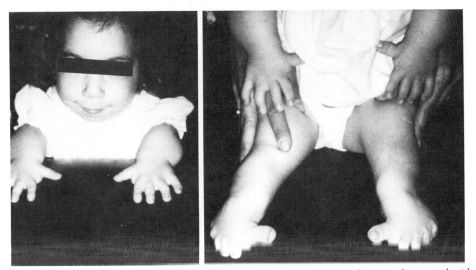

Figure 15-17 Hands and feet of a child with diastrophic dwarfism showing the typical wide abduction of the thumbs and great toes.

with the hip and knee joints locked would be followed by training in a swing-to or swing-through gait similar to that used by high-level paraplegics in locked braces (Fig. 15–16).

Another unusual application of prosthetic principles for ambulation occurs in the marked shortening and deformity of limbs in children with diastrophic dwarfism (Fig. 15–17). This complex of congenital deformities includes dysplastic hips and knees, hypoplastic long bones, and equinovarus ankle deformities that are notoriously resistant to surgical correction. Ambulation on the plantar-flexed feet is difficult and unstable, if it can be achieved at all. Supportive shoes may add surface area for standing, but do not contribute to stability of the dysplastic hips and knees (Fig. 15–18). In this condition, intelligence is usually normal, making prosthetic training feasible.

Adapted prostheses are designed to support the knees, to provide lateral hip stability with a pelvic band, and to conform to the contour of the malaligned joints (Fig. 15–19). Ambulation is then possible with a stiff-knee gait. The addition of height with the prostheses brings the child into the approximate size range of peers (Fig. 15–20). Although the upper limbs are also shortened, the length is usually adequate for self-care and beginning school activities. The growth lag is uniform for all body and limb components, so the upper limbs remain in relatively functional proportion to the head and trunk. Lack of total height becomes an increasing problem as chronological age increases; however, the addition of prosthetic length eventually has to cease in order to maintain overall proportionate size relationships of body parts.

Psychological Problems

The details and ramifications of the psychological problems related to limb deficiencies are complex enough to be beyond the scope of this chapter,

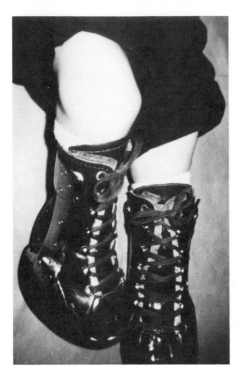

Figure 15–18   Metal reinforced shoes with which a child with diastrophic dwarfism had been fitted. The knees and hips are unsupported.

while being of sufficiently crucial import to prohibit their omission. Thus, only an indication of the types of problems encountered is possible.

Congenital deficiencies produce their initial impact on the parents, whose reaction of initial shock may be followed by feelings of guilt with perhaps anxiety, anger, and rejection of, or ambivalence toward the child as concomitants. Whatever the combination, the infant with limb deficiency will experience indirectly some of the parental emotional turmoil. The physician will probably be the first to help the parents to express and handle their emotions, with the continuing assistance of the knowledgeable social worker and psychologist or psychiatrist or both. The activities of the prosthetic team should be supportive in leading the parents to realize that the problem that the child represents will not be left to them to handle alone. At the same time, they must be made to feel an integral part of the planning and accomplishing of the child's habilitation. The weeks prior to the start of prosthetic training allow some time for emotional adjustment, although this may be an ongoing process over many years.[12]

The child with limb loss acquired after independent function had been established may perceive the loss as a catastrophic punishment for an unknown offense. Here, too, parental guilt may occur with fears of having protected the child inadequately. Both the child and parents must reexperience many functional and developmental learning activities during prosthetic training, a process that may prolong their grief at the limb loss. The therapists and team counselor (whether social worker or psychologist) must help the

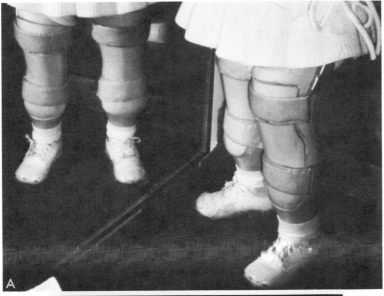

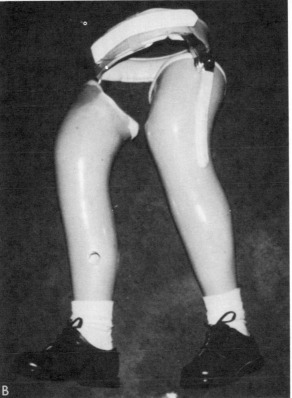

Figure 15–19   *A.* Initial prosthesis for patient in Figure 15–18 has an anterior flap to allow donning and positioning of the plantar-flexed feet and abducted halluces into the prosthetic socket. *B.* A subsequent prosthesis added length and accommodated limb growth. Cosmetic appearance was increased by use of a soft inner liner and a pull-through stocking as if for a suction socket. The hypoplastic pelvis prevents accurate location of the "pelvic band."

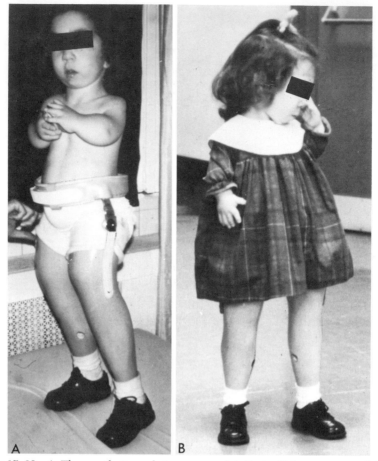

Figure 15–20 *A.* The prosthetic sockets accommodate limited hip extension, while the pelvic band prevents excessive abduction at the hips. *B.* Final appearance of the patient.

parents and child to see this relearning in terms of new levels of functional accomplishment of which all may be proud.

As the limb deficient child grows and learns, contact should be made with children of similar age and developmental level, both within and outside of the habilitation setting—both amputees and nonamputees. Whether the habilitation plan will lead to a normal nursery school will depend on the residual disability and on associated orthopedic or neurological problems. The earlier the child learns to relate well to peers, the greater the social-emotional contribution toward normal school placement. Another factor influencing the decision to recommend such placement would be the possibility of a parental sense of stigma attached to the child, which might lead to social isolation and overprotection of the child. This is a particular problem if there is a familial or hereditary pattern to the limb deficiency.

Once in school, it is hoped a school for normal children, the child should be able to work at activities without undue self-consciousness. This may be easier if there has been an opportunity to talk about the prosthesis with amputee and nonamputee peers during the play activities of preschool years. The child with acquired amputations has the advantage of being able to answer the expectable question: "what happened to you?" The school teacher may need preparation by the parents or prosthetic team in handling and channeling the natural curiosity of peers, should the amputee be unable to do so. In addition, the teacher should be aware of associated problems (i.e., the expressionless face of congenital facial palsy) and of the possibility of easy fatiguability from the constant need for concentration in performance of even routine activities. Adaptations for increasing the eye-to-paper distance to facilitate focusing when shortened upper extremities do not have prostheses may also be needed. Last, excessive head or body motion in sixth nerve palsy or cervical spine anomalies respectively must be explained as necessary compensations.[11]

The knowledgeable and coordinated prosthetic team may be able to anticipate and prepare the child and parents for many adjustment problems, although the child and parents themselves must work through to the actual adjustment. Similarly, the prosthetic team should be readily accessible to help with prosthetic, functional, emotional, and social questions or problems.

References

1. Aitken, G. T.: Surgical amputation in children. J. Bone Joint Surg., 45A:1735–1741, 1963.
2. Aitken, G. T.: Tibial hemimelia. In Aitken, G. T. (ed.): Selected Lower-Limb Anomalies. Washington, D.C., National Academy of Sciences, 1969, pp. 1–19.
3. Alderson, S. W.: The electric arm. In Klopoteg, P. E., and Wilson, P. D. (eds.): Human Limbs and Their Substitutes. New York, Hafner Publishing Co., 1968, pp. 359–408.
3a. Amstutz, H. C.: The morphology, natural history and treatment of proximal focal deficiencies. In Aitken, G. T. (ed.): Proximal Femoral Focal Deficiency. Washington, D.C., National Academy of Sciences, 1969, pp. 50–76.
4. Blakeslee, B. (ed.): The Limb Deficient Child. Berkeley and Los Angeles, University of California Press, 1963.
5. Bottomley, A.: The upper extremity prosthesis—control of external power. In Murdoch, G. (ed.): Prosthetic and Orthotic Practice. London, Edward Arnold Publ. Ltd., 1970, pp. 377–385.
6. Brown, F. W.: The Brown operation for total hemimelia tibia. In Aitken, G. T. (ed.): Selected Lower-Limb Anomalies. Washington, D. C., National Academy of Sciences, 1969, pp. 20–28.
7. Burtch, R. L.: Nomenclature for congenital skeletal limb deficiencies. A revision of the Frantz and O'Rahilly classification. Artif. Limbs, 10:24–35, 1966.
8. Childress, D. S., Hampton, F. L., Lambert, C. N., et. al.: Myoelectric immediate postsurgical procedure: A concept for fitting the upper-extremity amputee. Artif. Limbs, 13:55–60, 1969.
9. Committee on Prosthetics Research and Development: Report on the Sixth Workshop Panel on Upper Extremity Prosthetic Components of the Subcommittee on Design and Development. Orthot. Prosthet., 23:2:81–115, June 1969.
10. Davies, E. J., Friz, B. R., and Clippinger, F. W.: Amputees and their prostheses. Artif. Limbs, 14:19–48, 1970.
11. d'Avignon, M., Hellgren, K., Juhlin, I. M., and Atterback, B.: Diagnostic and habilitation problems of thalidomide-traumatized children with multiple handicaps. Dev. Med. Child Neurol., 9:707–712, 1967.
12. Dembo, T., Leviton, G. L., and Wright, B. A.: Adjustment to misfortune—a problem of social-psychological rehabilitation. Artif. Limbs, 3:4–62, 1956.
13. Edelstein, J.: News notes. Inter-Clinic Inform. Bull., 9:4:15–16, 1970.
14. Finley, F. R.: Pattern recognition of myoelectric signals in the control of an arm prosthesis. J. Can. Physiother. Assoc., 21:19–24, 1969.
15. Finley, F. R., Wirta, R. W., and Cody, K. A.: Muscle synergies in motor performance. Arch. Phys. Med. Rehabil., 49:655–60, 1968.
16. Frantz, C. H.: Complete absence of the lumbar spine and sacrum. In Aitken, G. T. (ed.):

Selected Lower-Limb Anomalies. Washington, D.C., National Academy of Sciences, 1969, pp. 29–48.

17. Frantz, C., and O'Rahilly, R.: Congenital skeletal limb deficiencies. J. Bone Joint Surg., 43-A:1202–1224, 1961.

18. Gesell, A., and Amatruda, C. S.: Developmental Diagnosis: Normal and Abnormal Child Development. New York, Hoeber Medical Division, Harper & Row, 1967.

19. Glatty, H. W.: A preliminary report on the amputee census. Artif. Limbs, 7:5–10, 1963.

20. Hölmgren, G.: Prostheses for the lower extremities after severe bone malformation. Prosthet. Int., 3:10:20–28, 1970.

21. Jentschura, G., Marquardt, E., and Rudel, E. M.: Malformations and Amputations of the Upper Extremity. New York, Grune & Stratton, Inc., 1967.

22. Kay, H. W., and Fishman, S.: 1018 children with skeletal limb deficiencies. Monograph of the New York University Post-Graduate Medical School of Prosthet. Orthot., p. 71, March 1967.

23. Klopsteg, P. E., and Wilson, P. D. (eds.): Human Limbs and Their Substitutes. New York, Hafner Publishing Co., 1968.

24. Kruger, L. M.: Fibular hemimelia. In Aitken, G. T. (ed.): Selected Lower Limb Anomalies. Washington, D.C., National Academy of Sciences, 1969, pp. 49–71.

25. Lambert, C. N.: Etiology of acquired amputation. In Aitken, G. T. (ed.): The Child with an Acquired Amputation. Washington, D.C., National Academy of Sciences, 1972, pp. 1–5.

26. Lambert, C. N., Hamilton, R. C., and Pellicore, R. J.: The juvenile amputee program: Its social and economic value—a followup study after the age of twenty-one. J. Bone Joint Surg., 51-A:1135–1138, 1969.

26a. Lyman, J.: Externally powered prosthetics/orthotics systems for children: present United States status. Inter-Clinic Inform. Bull., 12:11:7–15, 1973.

27. MacNaughton, A.: The role of the occupational therapist in the training of the child arm amputee. Physiotherapy, 52:201–203, 1966.

28. Maples, T. L.: Technical notes: A double-ring harness for the bilateral above elbow amputee. Bull. Int. Soc. Prosthet. Orthot., 3:4, July 1972.

29. Mongeau, M.: General principles in the rehabilitation of upper-limb amputees with conventional or externally powered prostheses. In Aitken, G. T. (ed.): The Child with an Acquired Amputation. Washington, D.C., National Academy of Sciences, 1972, pp. 132–138.

30. Montgomery, S. R.: External power systems for the upper extremity. In Murdoch, G. (ed.): Prosthetic and Orthotic Practice. London, Edward Arnold Publ. Ltd., 1970, pp. 387–397.

31. Panse, F.: Electrical lesions of the nervous system. In Vinken, P. J., and Bruyn, G. W. (eds.): Handbook of Clinical Neurology. Vol. 7. Diseases of Nerves. Part I. New York, American Elsevier Publishing Co., 1970, pp. 344–387.

32. Peizer, E.: External power in prosthetics, orthotics and orthopedic aids. Prosthet. Int., 4:1:4–60, 1971.

33. Ring, N. D.: A carbon-fibre body harness. Prosthet. Int., 4:2:29–33, 1972.

34. Schmidl, H.: The INAIL–CECA prostheses Orthot. Prosthet., 27:1:6–12, March 1973.

35. Scott, R. N.: Myoelectric control of prostheses and orthoses. Bull. Prosthet. Res., 10–7:93–114, Spring 1967.

36. Seamone, W., and Schmeisser, G.: Development and evaluation of externally powered upper limb prosthesis. Bull. Prosthet. Res., 10–16:169–176, Fall 1971.

37. Sypniewski, B. L.: The child with terminal transverse partial hemimelia: A review of the literature on prosthetic management. Artif. Limbs, 16:20–50, 1972.

Chapter 16

Scoliosis

by Jacob F. Katz, M.D.

Scoliosis is crookedness of the vertebral column. Specifically it has been defined as rotatory lateral curvature causing trunk deformity characterized by permanent deviation of one or more segments of the spinal column from the midline of the body.[6] The permanence of the deviation is caused by structural deformation of the vertebral elements interfering with spontaneous voluntary correctability. This deformity consists of wedging of vertebral bodies and rotatory distortions of spinous processes, transverse processes, and facet articulations as well as ligament and muscle contractures. Where ribs are in close proximity as in the thoracic region, they participate in the gross deformity with specific rotations (Fig. 16–1).

The Hippocratic treatises indicate an ancient awareness of scoliosis.[1] The statement that "there are many varieties of curvature of the spine even in persons who are in good health" is especially discerning. Idiopathic scoliosis in people of "good health" continues to furnish the greatest number of cases for treatment.

INCIDENCE

Cowell in a study of the familial incidence of idiopathic scoliosis found that 33 per cent of parents and siblings of patients with scoliosis had spinal curvatures greater than 10 degrees.[3] A companion control study revealed that in the general population the scoliosis incidence was 5.6 per cent. Filho and Thompson reported the incidence of idiopathic scoliosis to be 0.18 per cent, whereas in first degree affected relatives the incidence was 6.6 per cent.[4] Wynne-Davies found 5 per cent incidence in first degree relatives in comparison to 0.2 per cent in the general population.[13] She attributed the discrepancy

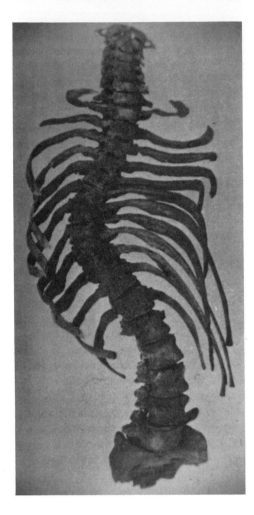

Figure 16-1 This skeleton of a young woman of the seventeenth or eighteenth century demonstrates the characteristics of a severe thoracic scoliosis with vertebral rotation and wedging as well as participating rib deformation. (From Wells, C.: Video recordings of paleopathology. Bull. N. Y. Acad. Med., 49:786–792, 1973.)

in the statistics to inclusion of "very minor curves" where the incidences were higher. Genetically, the findings were consistent either with dominant inheritance of reduced penetrance or with multifactorial inheritance.

DIAGNOSIS

The cosmetic deformity produced by scoliosis initially directs attention to it. Following that, it is confirmed by roentgenographic examination, which permits precise localization to specific areas of the vertebral column as well as exact angular measurements of the spinal curvature.

Measurement of Severity

The Cobb method of measurement is now generally accepted as the standard. The technique requires identification of the uppermost and lowermost vertebrae involved in the curve. Then a horizontal line is drawn parallel to the superior border of the vertebra at the top of the curve and a corresponding line parallel to the inferior border of the lowermost vertebra. Perpendiculars are constructed to each of these lines. The angle of intersection is the angle of the curvature (see Fig. 16–7).

Characteristics of flexibility or correctability of the curve can be inferred from roentgenograms of the patient lying, standing, and bending. The measurements from these separate films indicate the effect of relief of weight bearing as well as attempted correction by side bending. This is especially important in that it will identify the functional correctable curves that are usually present as compensatory curves above or below the structural curve.

In the ongoing management of the patient, subsequent study often can be limited to a single anteroposterior roentgenogram in the standing position.

Designation of Curvature

Since any segment or combination of or as of the vertebral column may be involved in deformity, the specific site has to be identified. If the curvature lies totally within the limits of one of the major spinal column sectors it is called cervical, dorsal, lumbar, or whichever is appropriate. If the deformity is not so precisely limited, but extends into portions of two regions, it then assumes a compound designation, for example, cervical-dorsal or dorsolumbar.

Additional information describing the direction of the curvature is also available from these roentgenograms. By general acceptance, the convexity of the curve is used to describe the direction of deviation. Thus for example, the curvature in the cervical, dorsal, or lumbar region or any overlapping combination of them has its convexity to the right or left side. The specific description includes this direction of convexity as in the following examples—right dorsal, left dorsal, right dorsolumbar, left dorsolumbar, or any other combinations of curvatures.

In idiopathic scoliosis, Ponseti found that most of the characteristics of a curve are present from the onset of the deformity.[8] Although the severity may increase, the direction of rotation, the apex, and the location of the curve remain the same.

CLASSIFICATION

Spontaneous
    Idiopathic (genetic)
        Infantile
        Juvenile
        Adolescent
Associated with other diseases or deformities
    Congenital
        Unilateral unsegmented bar
        Multiple hemivertebrae, etc.
    Muscular imbalance (paralytic)
        Cerebral palsy
        Myelomeningocele
        Poliomyelitis
        Muscular dystrophy

Thoracogenic
  Asthma
  Congenital heart disease
  Pulmonary complications, e.g., empyema, emphysema, chronic
    pleuritis
Miscellaneous
  Diastrophic dwarfism
  Marfan's syndrome
  Postirradiation of spinal or paraspinal tumorous conditions, e.g.,
    Wilms tumor, neuroblastoma

IDIOPATHIC (GENETIC) SCOLIOSIS

This variety of structural spinal deformity represents over 70 per cent of all scolioses. Its hallmark is the absence of associated etiological mechanisms. In recent years studies have shown genetic linkages that suggest that "idiopathic" may finally be redesignated "genetic."

Since idiopathic scoliosis may arise at any age in childhood, arbitrary division into subgroups—infantile (up to 3 years), juvenile (to 9 years), and adolescent (after 10 years)—has been devised. Those diagnosed in later childhood (adolescent) make up the largest group. For reasons not understood, the incidence of infantile scoliosis in Europe is decidedly higher (1.3 per 1000 infants under three years) than in the United States, where it is rare. The juvenile group is the smallest of the three.

Infantile Idiopathic Scoliosis. The characteristic curve is left thoracic. It is slightly more common in males. There may be associated anomalies such as congenital hip dislocation. Spontaneous resolution occurs in the majority of patients, but those curvatures that persist represent a serious problem because of potential progression throughout the long period of childhood growth.

Juvenile Idiopathic Scoliosis. Idiopathic scoliosis has its smallest incidence in this age category. It appears predominantly in girls, and the curvature is mainly right thoracic, resembling the adolescent variety. Mostly the course is progressive, the severity increasing as growth continues.

Adolescent Idiopathic Scoliosis. Any portion of the vertebral column may be affected; most curves, however, are middorsal, and the largest number present convexity to the right. These curves do not resolve spontaneously and most are progressive. This adolescent type of scoliosis is more common in females, approximately in the ratio of seven girls to one boy.

CONGENITAL SCOLIOSIS

A decade ago the general attitude toward congenital scoliosis was one of complacency. The consensus was that anomalous vertebrae, usually hemivertebrae, produced short acute apical curvatures that progressed slowly or not at all. There is currently better understanding and clarification of anomalous vertebral influences in the production of the scoliosis that makes up about 10 per cent of all cases.

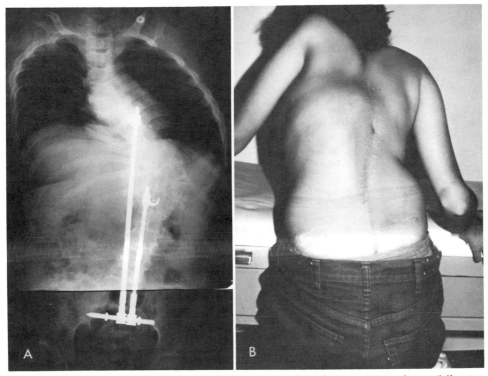

Figure 16–2 This adolescent male had severe trunk and extremity weakness following poliomyelitis in early childhood. *A.* The roentgenogram shows the postcorrection status of his paralytic scoliosis treated with Harrington rods and spine fusion. *B.* A photograph of the patient showing the operative area. Although he uses crutches and limb bracing for limited ambulation, most of his activities are wheelchair based. He has gained satisfactory trunk stability.

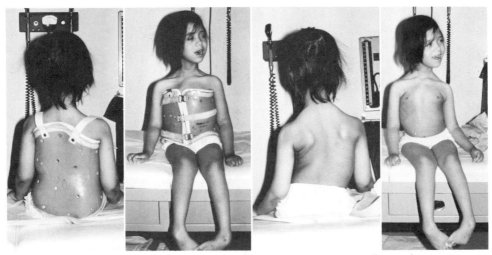

Figure 16–3 This child with severe generalized muscle weakness due to chronic anterior horn cell disease presented trunk imbalance associated with right dorsolumbar scoliosis. She is shown wearing a torso plastic jacket that furnished sufficient stability and control to permit neutral sitting.

The most serious bony abnormality in this type is the *unilateral unsegmented bar.* This is followed by steady progressive curvature throughout the extent of the growth period.

The next most pernicious anomaly is *multiple hemivertebrae* that lie near each other on the same side of the spine. There is prominent imbalance, which leads to inevitable curvature progression. The influence of an isolated hemivertebra is less certain, but it requires ongoing observation.

It must be stated for completeness that differential diagnosis requires distinguishing infantile idiopathic scoliosis from congenital scoliosis since both appear early in life.

PARALYTIC (MUSCULAR IMBALANCE) SCOLIOSIS

Prior to the advent of successful immunization, poliomyelitis contributed the largest portion to paralytic curvatures, which were estimated to represent 15 per cent of all scolioses (Fig. 16–2). At the present time cerebral palsy, myelomeningocele, and primary neurological and muscular affections are the principal causes of scoliosis in this subgroup. Almost all patients with Duchenne dystrophy develop scoliosis rapidly after they have lost the ability to stand and walk.[11] About 25 per cent of significantly involved spastic cerebral palsy patients develop scoliosis. Patients with myelomeningocele may have scoliosis as a congenital vertebral anomaly in the same manner as those who do not have myelomeningocele. Curtis found scoliosis in 62 per cent of 130 patients with myelomeningocele; both congenital and developmental types

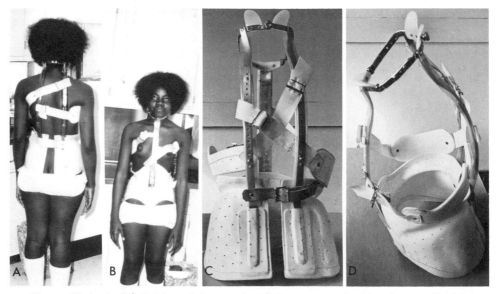

Figure 16–4 *A* and *B.* This adolescent female patient was found to have mild thoracic scoliosis while she was under observation and treatment for bronchial asthma. She is shown wearing a Milwaukee brace. *C* and *D.* The Milwaukee brace. The highlights of the brace construction are well illustrated. The pelvic support is meticulously contoured. (*C* and *D* by courtesy of Mrs. Marion Levy.)

were included. Twenty-seven children had vertebral body anomalies, and all of them developed scoliosis. Of the remaining 103 without vertebral anomalies other than spina bifida, 53 (52 per cent) developed curvatures, the majority appearing before age five and practically all before age 10 years.

Flaccid paralytic curvatures such as are shown in Figure 16–3 generally have long C curves with apparent collapse of the spine on weight bearing and, at early stages, retention of partial correctability on recumbency.

THORACOGENIC SCOLIOSIS

A large vector in the production of thoracogenic scoliosis disappeared with better control of pulmonary tuberculosis and the pneumococcal pneumonias. Thoracotomy and thoracoplasty were often necessary treatments for complications of these diseases. This resulted in interference with symmetrical pulmonary ventilation, which in turn led to thoracic scoliosis in susceptible children.

We have seen thoracic scoliosis in children with intractable asthma and varying degrees of chronic bronchitis and emphysema (Fig. 16–4A and B).

Roth studied 500 patients with congenital heart disease, noting an incidence of scoliosis with severity greater than 10 degrees in 12 per cent and greater than 20 degrees in 4.6 per cent.[10] Frequency of scoliosis increased with age and severity of the heart disease.

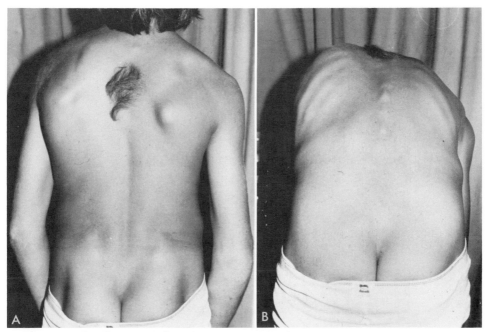

Figure 16–5 This patient demonstrates upper trunk asymmetry associated with left dorsal scoliosis. The patch of hair overlies a congenital defect. *A.* In the erect position there is evident elevation of the left shoulder. *B.* In the forward flexed position the posterior prominence of the upper ribs of the left side of the chest is seen.

MISCELLANEOUS CAUSES OF SCOLIOSIS

The heterogeneity of this group is implied in the heading. Some are developmental in mechanism and others may be associated with congenital vertebral anomalies (Fig. 16–5). Such syndromes as diastrophic dwarfism consistently are accompanied by scoliosis along with other musculoskeletal limb deformities (Fig. 16–6). In others such as the Marfan and Ehlers-Danlos syndromes, scoliosis occurs less constantly but with frequency in excess of that in the general population.

PROGNOSIS

The course and prognosis in idiopathic scoliosis vary from one pattern to another as well as with the age of onset. Thoracic curves tend to progress more rapidly, reach greater dimensions, and produce greater deformity than any

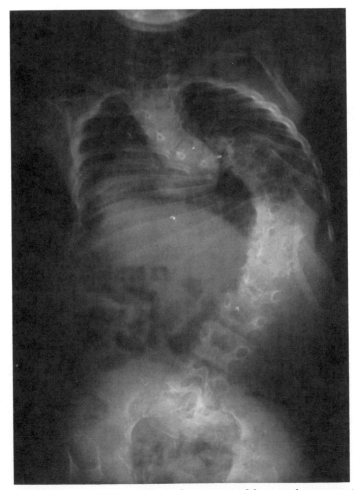

Figure 16–6   This roentgenogram reflects the severity of the spinal curvature in a child with diastrophic dwarfism. There were associated club feet and congenital hip dislocations.

other type. In comparison, thoracolumbar scoliosis has a better prognosis with better body alignment and balance if onset is after 10 years of age, but this advantage is lost when it starts earlier.

In congenital scoliosis, Winter notes that curves in the midthoracic area are most apt to progress.[12] This tendency toward increasing severity is customarily less in the cervicothoracic and lumbar regions of the spine.

Curtis finds spinal curvature in the myelomeningocele patient at an early age (majority before 5 years of age and most by 10 years) with highest frequency associated with upper and mid lumbar levels of paralysis and greatest progression in children with fixed pelvic obliquity.[9]

It was once believed that scoliotic curvatures did not progress after skeletal maturity. In a long-term analysis, Ponseti found an average increase of 15 degrees after termination of growth.[8] Others noted that the greatest increase takes place in curves measuring 60 degrees or more at the end of growth. Furthermore it is anticipated that an increase of 1 degree per year may occur in the unfused patient.

TREATMENT

In formulating a plan of therapy the first consideration is to identify the severity of the scoliosis, its etiology, the age of the patient, and the likelihood of progression of the curvature. The second consideration is to decide whether treatment is needed now and, if so, whether it should be conservative or surgical.

Moe states that in idiopathic scoliosis minimal curves of 20 degrees should receive prompt treatment if the curves are structural or progressive.[7] Curves of lesser severity, if flexible on supine voluntary lateral bending, may be observed with regular frequent roentgenograms.

Winter expresses his philosophy of treatment of congenital scoliosis by stressing the importance of determining whether the curvature is stationary or progressive.[12] He points out that if the curve is progressive then the specific nature of the anomaly is not critical and appropriate treatment must be rendered as in any other variety of scoliosis.

Conservative Treatment

The Milwaukee brace is generally accepted to be the core of adequate nonoperative management. Its uncontested value lies in the treatment of young children with progressive idiopathic, paralytic, or thoracogenic curves (Fig. 16–7). It may also be used in congenital scoliosis in which there is some curve flexibility and in which there is improvement on a trial of brace therapy. The response to Milwaukee brace treatment is usually *unsatisfactory* when the curves are short and rigid or are over 50 degrees. Although in many instances its use may be viewed as an alternative method of treatment, in congenital scoliosis the Milwaukee brace is usually regarded as an appliance to contain the curve until the optimal age has been reached for surgical stabilization.

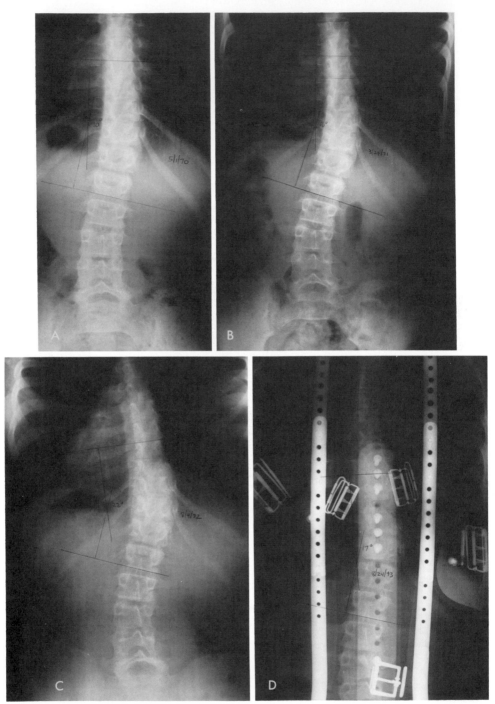

Figure 16–7 These are sequential roentgenograms of a child whose mild thoracolumbar scoliosis was discovered while she was under treatment for bronchial asthma. *A.* The initial film dated 5/1/70 exhibited a 10 degree curve measured by the Cobb method. *B.* On 3/24/71, almost a year later, the curve had progressed to 16 degrees. *C.* On 8/9/72 the curve had increased to 22 degrees. At this time Milwaukee brace treatment was started. *D.* One year later, 8/24/73, the curvature had been adequately held and its measurement was 17 degrees. As Ponseti had shown, the site and direction of curvature remained constant over the period of observation. The patient is now 12 years old and is still being treated.

384

Moe treated 169 patients with idiopathic scoliosis with the Milwaukee brace.[7] In that study no organized program of exercise was used, but this has changed subsequently so that exercise is now an important part of the brace treatment. He found that more correction was obtained when treatment was started before the appearance of the iliac apophysis and that it worked better for longer curves in all areas of the spine. The median total brace wearing time was 34.4 months. Surgical correction was necessary only in patients whose initial major curve was greater than 40 degrees.

Blount indicates that effectiveness of the Milwaukee brace cannot be taken for granted.[2] The results obtainable vary with the skill applied in fitting and adjusting the brace, the competence and cooperation of the patient in performing specific exercises on a regular basis, the age of the patient, and the flexibility of the spine. He recommends use of the Milwaukee brace for most adolescent patients with moderately severe idiopathic curves and for all young children whatever the cause of the scoliosis or the degree of deformity.

Exercise Program with Milwaukee Brace. Although Moe has demonstrated that some successful results may be obtained from the Milwaukee brace alone, he is now suggesting a companion exercise program.[7] This is the current consensus. One phase of the exercise program is general conditioning performed in and out of the brace.

The second phase includes specific exercises designed to attack the various components of deformity by assisting the brace in attaining correction. This includes manipulation of pelvic tilt by contraction and control of the gluteal and abdominal muscles. Initially this is performed out of the brace, lying supine on a firm surface. It is then practiced in the brace, lying and standing. When this has been mastered, the patient is taught deep breathing exercises with forceful rounding of the back attempting to make contact between the thoracic concavity and overlying bar of the brace. As this movement succeeds the posterior rib prominence comes against the thoracic pad on the contralateral side. The latter blocks its ultimate excursion, secondarily causing rotation of the spine and further contact of the concavity of the curve and the brace.

As the curve is progressively corrected the pads are brought into new position and the upright bars bent in on the convexity and out over the diminishing concavity.

In addition to the foregoing organized program, patients are advised to participate in non-contact game activities for supplemental muscle strength and tone.

Schedule of Milwaukee Brace Treatment. The brace is generally worn full time for about a year except for daily bath and skin care, which may consume one hour daily. X-rays taken at four to six month intervals permit identification of the response to treatment. If the curve has diminished and remains stable at the level of improvement during this year of therapy, one considers the feasibility of reducing the time the brace is worn. This is done exploringly by taking an x-ray of the spine in standing position, initially just out of the brace and then three hours out of the brace. If there is no loss of correction, the child may remain out of the brace for three hours daily. At several-month intervals repeat x-ray evaluations are made, and if the spine remains stable the weaning process can go on until the brace is worn only at night. It is not discarded entirely until after skeletal maturity is reached.

Surgical Treatment

In idiopathic scoliosis sound judgment is involved in making the decision when to operate. In some areas the zone of compromise is narrow and in others has considerable latitude. For example, in the management of idiopathic scoliosis, there is little disagreement in the choice of the Milwaukee brace for the *infantile* or *juvenile* varieties. Even if, at the attainment of skeletal maturity, the residual severity of the curve requires surgical correction, the containment of it during important years of childhood growth makes the whole thing worthwhile. There is more disagreement about conservative treatment versus surgical treatment in the *adolescent* group of patients. Blount includes adolescents with moderate curvatures as prime candidates for treatment with the Milwaukee brace. Much more frequently, however, such patients are advised to accept surgical therapy, and in most centers this would consist of correction with the Harrington rod technique, concurrent spine fusion, and a Risser-type plaster jacket.

For congenital scoliosis, Winter states that fundamental treatment is operative treatment.[12] He finds that because congenital spinal curvatures are progressive in 75 per cent of patients, and the Milwaukee brace is relatively ineffective for the majority, surgery remains the practical answer.

Modes of Surgical Approach. For the idiopathic scoliotic curve under 60 degrees, Goldstein finds Harrington rod instrumentation permissible without preliminary preoperative correction.[5] For curves between 60 degrees and 90 degrees, he advises correction by head halter and pelvic band traction for a week followed preoperatively by a localizer plaster jacket. This is then followed by Harrington rod insertion, spine fusion, and subsequent reapplication of a plaster jacket. For curves greater than 90 degrees he uses halo-femoral pin traction correction for two or three weeks before Harrington rod instrumentation and spine fusion (Fig. 16–8).

For congenital scoliosis there are a number of surgical alternatives that resemble those just described. These include spine fusion and localizer plaster cast application postoperatively. For more rigid curves, preoperative traction such as is obtainable with halo-femoral technique may be used. Sudden correction is avoided to protect against cord damage. If Harrington rods are used, no more correction is sought than has been obtained by the preoperative traction. In special situations with fixed pelvic obliquity or fixed lateral translation of the upper trunk relative to the pelvis not otherwise correctable, vertebral resection is performed. This is accompanied by spine fusion for stabilization.

After Care

The postoperative regimen for idiopathic scoliosis includes a period of bed rest for approximately three months. If there is stability of correction and maintenance of position of the Harrington rods as determined by x-ray at this time, meals out of bed and bathroom privileges are permitted as mobilizing activities. Gradually over the second three months, there is return to free out-

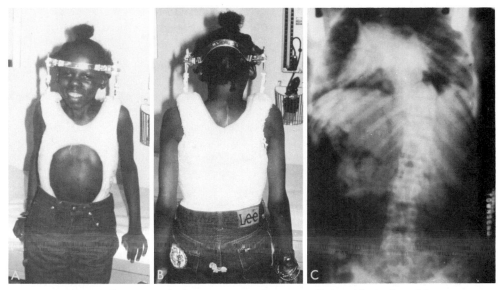

Figure 16–8 This patient had severe upper thoracic scoliosis with rigidity of the curvature. She was managed initially with halo-femoral traction, which was later modified as shown in *A* and *B* to include halo fixation to a plaster jacket. *C.* The roentgenogram taken through the plaster jacket indicates the residual of the upper thoracic scoliosis.

of-bed privileges at noncompetitive and nonstrenuous levels. The cast is changed at six months to a torso jacket for an additional three to six months depending on x-ray evaluation of the fusion mass.

The postoperative management of patients with congenital scoliosis is similar in pattern except the tempo is slower. Bed rest is usually continued for six months, after which walking is gradually permitted. A plaster jacket or Milwaukee brace may be used for an additional four to six months while the fusion mass is maturing and consolidating. In all instances pseudarthroses are considered when studying final x-rays.

In the postoperative period, physical therapy is used to maintain adequate tone of limb musculature, initially with isometric exercises. As the latter part of the initial three month period approaches, the exercises are changed to isotonic forms against mild graded resistance. This prepares the patient for the challenge of weight bearing when that is deemed appropriate. When full mobilization is attained, mild trunk strengthening exercises are added to the program even while the plaster support is still worn. At the stage of solid spine fusion and discontinuation of external support, the trunk mobilization exercise regimen is broadened to permit return to full activity.

CONCLUSIONS

It is generally agreed that most disasters in scoliosis that lead to crippling deviations of the spine are preventable. Early recognition of minimal curvatures, expert evaluation of their potential for progression, and a suitable program of prompt conservative management will go a long way toward eliminating the horrors of physical distortion.

Although technical competence has made great strides in coping with the serious vertebral rotations and angulations, the path toward diminution of morbidity in this complex problem lies in early diagnosis and early treatment with the conservative approach so ardently championed by Blount.

References

1. Bick, E. M.: *Source Book of Orthopaedics*. Baltimore, Williams & Wilkins Co., 1948.
2. Blount, W. P.: Nonoperative treatment of scoliosis. *In* Am. Acad. Orthop. Surg. *Symposium on the Spine*. St. Louis, C. V. Mosby Co., 1969.
3. Cowell, H. R., Hall, J. N., and MacEwen, G. D.: Genetic aspects of idiopathic scoliosis. Clin. Orthop., 86:121–131, 1972.
4. Filho, N. A., and Thompson, M. W.: Genetic studies in scoliosis. J. Bone Joint Surg., 53-A:199, 1971.
5. Goldstein, L. A.: The surgical treatment of idiopathic scoliosis. Clin. Orthop., 93:131–157, 1973.
6. Mercer, W.: *Orthopaedic Surgery*. Baltimore, Williams & Wilkins Co., 1943.
7. Moe, J. H., and Kettleson, D. N.: Idiopathic scoliosis — analysis of curve patterns and the preliminary results of Milwaukee brace treatment in one hundred sixty-nine patients. J. Bone Joint Surg., 52-A:1509–1533, 1970.
8. Ponseti, I. V., and Friedman, B.: Prognosis in idiopathic scoliosis. J. Bone Joint Surg., 32-A:381–395, 1950.
9. Raycroft, J. F., and Curtis, B. H.: Spinal curvature in myelomeningocele: Natural history and etiology. *In* Am. Acad. Orthop. Surg. *Symposium on Myelomeningocele*. St. Louis, C. V. Mosby Co., 1972.
10. Roth, A., Rosenthal, A., Hall, J. E., and Mizel, M.: Scoliosis and congenital heart disease. Clin. Orthop., 93:95–102, 1973.
11. Siegel, I. M.: Scoliosis in muscular dystrophy. Clin. Orthop., 93:235–238, 1973.
12. Winter, R. B., Moe, J. H., and Eilers, V. E.: Congenital scoliosis. J. Bone Joint Surg., 50-A:1–47, 1968.
13. Wynne-Davies, R.: *Heritable Disorders in Orthopaedic Practice*. Oxford, Blackwell Scientific Publications, 1973.

Chapter 17

Deformities of the Foot

by *Rosamond Kane, M.D.,* and *Wilfred Krom, M.D.*

Many people have foot problems, and nuisance though they may be to the individual, they seldom command the interest and attention devoted to his other medical problems. The common architectural aberrations — flatfoot, metatarsus adductus, and clubfoot — their characteristics, possible causes, and natural history; the goals and techniques of their treatment; and the more common neurological aberrations are discussed here.

FLATFOOT

Flatfeet are pandemic — so common that they appear to be "normal" for some ethnic groups. Why then do they merit attention at all and when do they require treatment? Because some feet do become symptomatic and modify the activities of their owners, we are challenged to cope with them. The problem is to identify these potentially troublesome feet.

Anatomically, flatfoot reflects a loss of the customary relationships between the bones of the hindfoot and secondary accommodations of the rest of the tarsal bones to that loss (Fig. 17–1). In essence the talus loses its secure seat upon the os calcis and droops medially and plantarward. The ptotic talar head is prominent medially, and the heel is valgoid. The anteromedially directed talar head exerts pressure upon the navicular and displaces it and its fellow midtarsal bones laterally. The distal tarsal bones follow, and the full-blown clinical picture of flatfoot ensues. In time further modifications may occur and a naviculocuneiform sag may develop. The problem lies in the reac-

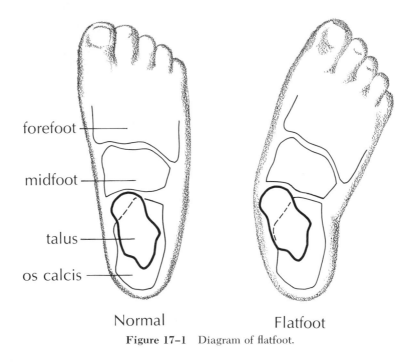

Normal   Flatfoot

Figure 17–1 Diagram of flatfoot.

tion of the tarsal bones and soft tissues to the accommodations they have been forced to make. At what degree of deviation from "normal" do symptoms appear and when does hypertrophic osteoarthritic spurring begin?

Etiology

A number of factors may operate concomitantly to produce flatfoot. The child may belong to an ethnic group in which flatfeet occur frequently or he may be the offspring of a flatfooted parent. His neonatal position may suggest an in utero calcaneovalgus position. In the presence of a normal amount of amniotic fluid and normal fetal activity, however, a fixed deformity is unlikely. The child's position of preference in his crib is much more influential. The child who perpetually sleeps prone with his legs in flexion and external rotation prepares himself for a Charlie Chaplin–like gait. After heel strike his weight is thrust down through the drooping talar head to the floor rather than from the heel to the heads of the first and fifth metatarsals. The forefoot remains abducted from his path of progression.

Paradoxically the child who perpetually sleeps prone with his legs internally rotated may also develop flatfeet. Persistent internal rotation appears to inhibit the natural resolution of the normal high femoral neck anteversion found in neonates. This child toes in when he walks, and tends to trip. Quite unconsciously he abducts his forefoot to avoid tripping, and his talus must bear the brunt of his weight. This child develops a compensatory flatfoot.

The child's build may also influence his feet. A short first metatarsal has been blamed for deranging the isosceles triangle–like pattern of normal weight bearing. The short metatarsal permits more weight to fall toward the medial side of the foot. Genu valgum (knock knees) also predisposes to flatfoot by permitting weight to be thrust through the talus. Finally, pelvic inclination may be increased and may produce internal rotation of the limbs, which will in turn lead to compensatory flatfoot.

Connective tissue laxity may be yet another factor. A significant number of basically normal youngsters are notably flexible. Their ligaments provide little initial stability, and in extreme cases their tarsal bones virtually collapse when they first attempt to stand. As muscular development progresses the posture of the feet improves during active walking and running although a variable amount of relaxation recurs when standing.

Tightness of the calf muscle, on the other hand, may also cause flatfeet. The gastrocnemius pulls the os calcis into equinus position and deprives the lateral support, allowing it to slide medially and anteriorly. In order to strike the floor with this equinus heel the child must now hyperextend his knee. He rolls his weight forward over his abducted forefoot and finally pushes off with the medial border of his foot (Fig. 17–2).

Finally flatfoot may be one component of a more serious disease. It may be a manifestation of neurological disease—occasionally very flat feet may be the presenting sign of cerebral palsy—or of a connective tissue disease such as Marfan's syndrome. They may also be seen with chronic severe illness—perhaps on a basis of diminished muscle tone.

Natural History

The great majority of youngsters fare well in adulthood, a few are overtly miserable, and an unknown number suffer minor restrictions of their activities—minor, but perhaps just enough to dull their joie de vivre.

In view of the natural history, our goal with respect to the management of flatfeet should be pain-free feet. It is unreasonable to expect to be able to convert a significantly flat foot into an architecturally normal foot. At best the course may be altered from one destined to be symptomatic to one that may be symptom free.

Treatment

Measures to ameliorate this condition may be instituted early in life. The child who perpetually sleeps prone may be spared the deforming force of his mattress by the use of a simple splint to maintain his limbs in neutral position. The Denis Browne splint and its many modifications provide convenient control. Prompt control may also permit significant resolution of anteversion to occur before the child walks and spare him from compensating with his feet. Control of excessive external rotation may abort future Chaplinesque gaits and spare the talus the brunt of weight thrust. Weight control should also be started early—before knees and feet sag beneath their burden.

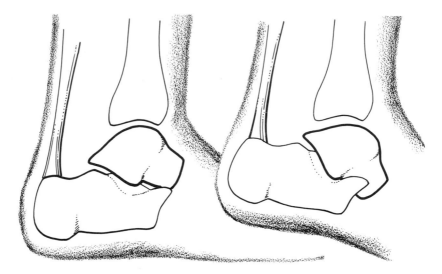

Normal Achilles Tendon   Tight Achilles Tendon

Figure 17–2   Diagram of tight calf.

Once the child is walking, an attempt can be made to help him bear weight in as nearly normal alignment as possible – in the hope that his bones will mold in a favorable fashion during the years of growth.

In the early years and in the absence of residual anteversion and previous metatarsus adductus, inflare shoes are helpful in shifting weight bearing away from the medial midfoot area. They may also bring about a marked improvement in an external rotation gait. In this instance the addition of a scaphoid pad seems to be of some value.

As youngsters increase in size sponge rubber and leather scaphoid pads have little, if any, effect. Wedges applied to the medial aspect of the heels and medial prolongations like Thomas heels may alter shoewear patterns sufficiently to suggest that there has been a change in weight bearing pattern (e.g., from wear at the medial aspect of the heel prior to treatment to wear at the lateral aspect of the heel with treatment).

When the rate of growth of the foot slows down and the weight of the child approaches 70 lb it becomes economically feasible to use molded arch supports. Whitman arches with lateral flanges are probably the most effective, but many children will not tolerate them. Arches without flanges are more likely to be used. Devices to maintain the hindfoot in alignment are advocated by some investigators and may prove to be of significant help.

There is a place for surgery in the management of flatfoot, but it must be reserved for that rare child who is symptomatic or has very severe deformity. Surgical efforts are directed at restoring the talocalcaneal relationship and sustaining it.

In the presence of a significantly tight calf muscle the Achilles tendon must be lengthened before the talus and os calcis can resume their normal relationship. From a relatively equinus position the os calcis must be allowed to assume its normal attitude. This will permit the talus that was squeezed forward out of the mortise to return to its proper seat upon the os calcis.

Procedures to maintain this restored relationship may then be carried out. An extraarticular arthrodesis as described by Grice will accomplish this end.

In the older child there has been some enthusiasm for restoring the naviculocuneiform relationship. A variety of procedures are available. Finally in the persistently unsatisfactory situation, triple arthrodesis may be offered near the completion of growth.

Control of adverse factors should be exercised in infancy, and judgment should be used in electing treatment for the walking child. Children rarely complain, and significant deformity must be the basis for deciding to treat most of them. It is pertinent to point out here that children with high residual femoral neck anteversion should not be treated for flatfeet despite deformity. Abduction of the feet is their obligatory mode of compensation for their hip problems. Children who avoid prolonged weight bearing, admit to fatigue, or complain of pain should be offered treatment.[*] The child with mild to moderate flatfeet requires few if any specific measures. If, however, he wears down the medial aspect of his shoes, these should be repaired promptly. His wear will in effect have created lateral heel wedges, and these will cause his weight to be borne through the medial midfoot.

Assessment of the long-range efficacy of treatment is almost impossible. Those few children who have overt symptoms may be relieved during the 5 to 15 years that they are followed, but follow-up into middle age is seldom achieved. Distressingly little knowledge of the long term is available to guide in the management of flatfoot.

METATARSUS ADDUCTUS

Metatarsus adductus is of nearly epidemic occurrence. It is a nuisance affliction, but one with a generally excellent outlook. It recurs readily if permitted the opportunity.

Forefoot adduction is the dominant feature. Although inconspicuous initially, valgus inclination of the heel is often found. Ankle motion is not affected and there should be no limitation of dorsiflexion. Internal tibial torsion frequently accompanies metatarsus adductus, and in the older child some persistence of femoral neck anteversion may often be found (Fig. 17–3).

Etiology and Natural History

The etiology of metatarsus adductus is unclear; often siblings have it, and frequently older members of the family suffer from bunions. This suggests that a genetic factor may be operating. The neonatal position of preference again may suggest in utero position as a contributing factor. Once more the bed may be incriminated as a deforming force. Infants observed to have no

---

[*]The child with pain may be offered medial heel and medial sole wedges initially. Although it puts him in the position of trudging along either side of the ridgepole of a roof, a situation not desirable for the long run, it will give him rapid relief.

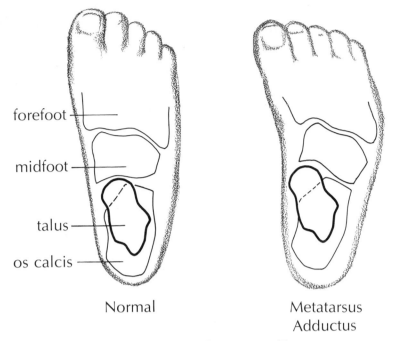

forefoot

midfoot

talus

os calcis

Normal

Metatarsus
Adductus

Figure 17–3 Diagram of metatarsus adductus.

significant foot problems at birth may be found to have metatarsus adductus at six to eight weeks of age.

If untreated the deformity may persist through life. In areas of the world where people do not confine their feet in shoes asymptomatic metatarsus adductus has been observed in almost a quarter of the adult population. Where shoes are worn the persistent deformity may cause discomfort and difficulty in fitting and tolerating shoes. It is tempting to think that the bunions we see in adulthood represent metatarsus adductus modified by shoes.

Treatment of metatarsus adductus produces generally satisfactory results. The forefoot deformity is usually well corrected, but the hindfoot flatfoot configuration usually persists in mild to moderate degree. It is important to identify this situation and discuss it with the parents at the beginning of treatment. They will then be prepared to accept the flatfoot that will be evident when the infant becomes a toddler. They will understand, too, the reluctance of the physician to use external rotation in the course of treatment.

Treatment

The earlier treatment is started, the more easily and rapidly correction can be achieved. When seen early the deformity may still be supple. There may not be a palpable convexity at the lateral border nor a palpable concavity medially, and the ligaments may permit passive correction beyond neutral position.

If passive correction is easily achieved and active eversion can be elicited, a simple splint to keep the child's feet off the bed will suffice. In an infant less than three months old, this can be accomplished with an inexpensive pair of soft infant shoes secured to tongue blades to make a light semimobile quadrilateral. Around three months of age the child becomes too strong for this splint and a Denis Browne splint or similar device becomes appropriate to prevent him from sleeping with his legs and feet in internal rotation. When passive overcorrection and active eversion cannot be elicited it is futile to use just a splint. Under these conditions serial plaster casts should be employed until correction has been achieved. The correction can then be maintained with the splint.

Theoretically it is possible to correct the deformities by manipulation. In practice, however, it is usually impractical. It is difficult for the physician to apply strapping that will adequately hold the heel in varus position while permitting the mother to carry out abduction manipulations of the forefoot, and it is truly hard for a mother to find sufficient exercise time to accomplish correction.

Although dynamic forms of treatment are generally more appealing, serial plaster casts provide a practical, convenient and satisfactory form of correction. The orthopedist can mold the heel in varus position and abduct the forefoot from the hindfoot to maintain proper alignment. The mother or baby sitter is relieved of the responsibility for frequent stretching exercises, and the correction proceeds uneventfully.

It is perhaps pertinent to mention here that the parents of the infant with newly applied casts should be prepared for their reception at home. Grandmothers respond with alarm and anxiety, but far more troublesome is the reaction of the toddler or preschool sibling. These children experience significantly increased feelings of jealousy toward the new intruder in the family, and there may be increased acting-out of rivalry. A twist of plaster applied to the sibling's favorite doll or teddy bear may relieve some of the jealousy. Whenever jealousy has been a problem, any stretching that is to be done in conjunction with the use of the maintenance splint should be done when the older child is asleep.

Once correction has been achieved the maintenance splint (Denis Browne or any of its modifications) should be worn nearly full time at first. If the correction is well maintained the splint time can be reduced gradually until it is used for nights and naps only. It should be continued until the child is an established walker. The feet may appear to be very well corrected at eight or nine months, and the parents may be very tempted to abandon the splint. When the child begins to walk, however, the abductor hallucis produces a varus deformity of the great toe. Soon the whole foot appears to turn in, and the parents become most distressed. If the child has been permitted to be free of his splint he will resent and resist efforts to reinstitute its use. It is preferable to wean the child from the night splint gradually and only after he has gained balance and can walk with ease.

Straight-last walking shoes should be obtained when the child pulls himself up and begins to walk with support. The shoes should be worn during all waking hours and they should be marked "left" and "right" to insure that the foot is in the same shoe each day and that the pattern of wear truly reflects the child's gait pattern. It may be necessary to continue the use of straight-last shoes for three or four years.

When anteversion has diminished to acceptable levels, internal tibial torsion has resolved, and the foot correction seems well maintained, then and then only may attention be directed to the residual flatfoot. Medial heel wedges may be added to the straight-last shoes at that time.

In the toddler, sleeping and sitting positions must continue to be monitored. Persistence in sleeping prone with legs and feet internally rotated is no longer suitably controlled by a Denis Browne splint. Indeed the feet may remain in neutral position on the splint but the femora may be internally rotated so that the patellae all but touch while the child sleeps. In this older child individual devices to limit internal rotation of each foot are preferable.*

Sitting cross legged "like an American Indian" or astride a make believe saddle on the arm of a chair or couch is to be encouraged. Sitting on the feet with the tibia and femur internally rotated must be prohibited.

A variation of metatarsus adductus is not infrequently seen in a child with "windswept" feet who sleeps prone with both feet turned to the right or to the left. This in effect results in one abducted foot and one adducted foot. The latter is more likely to require plaster correction than the former. Correction of this condition by a firm splint is in order.

Assessment of the treatment of metatarsus adductus is somewhat more satisfactory than that of flatfoot. Examination of the child at nursery school age will usually reveal resolution of his femoral neck anteversion to a level acceptable for his age, tibiae that now reflect adult torsional alignment, and feet that exhibit mild to moderate flatness but little or no residual of the flagrant early forefoot deformity.

CLUBFOOT

Clubfoot refers specifically to an equinovarus deformity. Such a deformity occurs between one and three times per thousand live births in most parts of the world. It may occur as an isolated aberration or as part of a complex of congenital anomalies. Overall, twice as many boys as girls are afflicted.

Physical findings are discussed in considerable detail to permit the nonorthopedist to familiarize himself with features more subtle than the glaring equinovarus deformity. It is hoped that this will enable him to reassure parents that these concomitant findings are "normal" in children with talipes equinovarus.

Foot. The familiar characteristics are the varus forefoot, varus heel, and fixed equinus position. Continued inspection will reveal a minimal to mild lag in development of the entire extremity—often manifested in the foot by a dis-

---

*Outgrown shoes with the toe boxes removed may be mounted on triangles of wood so that the lateral angles prevent internal rotation. Additional impediments to block plantar flexion may be necessary too to prevent the child from plantar flexing and then internally rotating his feet.

crepancy in size. In the neonate the hindfoot may be rather red and shiny, and there may be a relative paucity of soft tissue about the heel. The presence of a single deep transverse crease at the heel is almost pathognomonic of a deformity so severe that surgery will be required to release it (Fig. 17–4).

As correction progresses and the medial subluxation of the midfoot is reduced, the lateral protrusion of the talar head diminishes and a depression becomes evident just distal and slightly anterior to the lateral malleolus. This depression persists through life. Inspection of the lateral malleolus itself in the somewhat older child may reveal peroneal tendons riding right up against the posterolateral border of the malleolus rather than tucked in behind its posterior margin.

In children who have poor function of the peroneal muscles, especially the peroneus longus, the action of the anterior tibial is unopposed. The peroneus longus fails to depress the first metatarsal head and permits a supinating motion in the swing phase of gait. The head of the first metatarsal head tends to ride high and the metatarsophalangeal joint tends to flex. Around 10 to 12 years of age, a dorsal bunion may begin to develop. To date, in our foot clinic, only one older boy has complained about the flexion of his great toe and this bothered him only when barefoot. In the older child too, the interphalangeal joint of the great toe may be somewhat flexed, valgoid, and pronated. Anomalies of the other toes are quite common.

Ankle. The axis of motion through the ankle joint is altered to a greater or lesser degree and the foot may appear to dorsiflex rather obliquely. This may reflect tapering of the lateral aspect of the distal tibial epiphysis as well as ex-

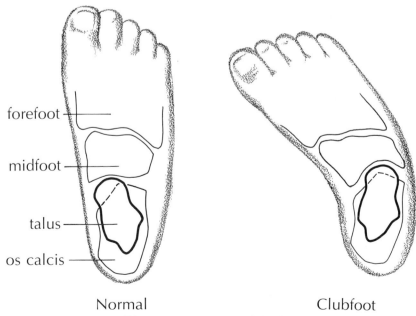

forefoot

midfoot

talus

os calcis

Normal   Clubfoot

Figure 17–4   Diagram of clubfoot.

ternal rotation of the hindfoot in the mortise. Characteristically in idiopathic clubfoot there is significant posterior displacement of the fibula suggesting, if anything, external tibial torsion.* In the clubfoot associated with a neurological defect this finding may not be present.

Lag in the development of the medial gastrocnemius is evident and persists throughout life. It is a finding frequently noticed by parents, who find the asymmetry of the calves quite distressing. Shortening of the tibia, if present, is minimal.

Knee.   At the knee three findings are encountered. Genu valgum may occur and the patella may be directed laterally. A varus position of the hindfoot seems to cause an apparent external rotation of the patella. The lateral position of the patella may complicate gait analysis and obscure femoral neck anteversion. Genu recurvatum may be present either as a compensatory mechanism for persistent equinus deformity or as a reflection of joint laxity.

Hip.   In many youngsters with clubfeet, especially those of idiopathic origin, the rate of resolution of femoral neck anteversion may lag. The residual anteversion may be responsible for a disappointing gait despite a satisfactory correction of the deformities of the foot itself.

Leg Length.   Leg length discrepancy reflects primarily loss in the height of the tarsus, some slight loss in the tibia, and even less in the femur. The customary measurement from anterior superior iliac spine to medial malleolus will not reflect this accurately but leveling of the iliac crests will.

Back.   The patient's back should be examined for the presence of scoliosis — compensatory or real. In the presence of one anomaly the possible occurrence of others must be entertained. The patient may have a leg length discrepancy or a vertebral anomaly or both.

Other Foot.   Frequently overlooked is the other foot. Of the youngsters with a unilateral clubfoot, rather a significant number have a flatfoot on the opposite side. This foot too may merit attention, and investigation should begin with an examination for residual femoral neck anteversion. Although less severe than on the affected side, it may be significantly higher than average and at least in some cases responsible for compensatory flatfoot.

Etiology

The etiology of talipes equinovarus is often unknown, but it is generally felt that probably multiple factors operate.

In any series of clubfoot patients a subgroup manifesting a genetic trend distinguishes itself. In our experience about 18 per cent of the families in the series (more than 100 cases) have had more than one affected member. Interestingly the sex ratio in this subgroup is one to one, a figure that agrees with Palmer's findings.[9]

---

*The best way to demonstrate this is to place the toddler or older child in a kneeling position at the end of the examining table with the feet extending beyond the edge of the table. With the tibial tubercles so fixed, the alignment of the malleoli can be determined.

The foot is largely formed in the second month of gestation. There may be a germ plasm defect that leads to malformation of the foot at this time. It is possible too that noxious factors in the milieu of the fetus at that time may inhibit proper growth and development of the foot.* Duraiswami has shown that clubfoot deformities can be produced electively in chickens by injecting insulin into the yolk sacs on the third day of gestation, and he reports that Bagg in 1918 was able to produce anomalies by subjecting experimental animals to x-ray, radium, and radioactive solutions.[2]

The foot deformity may be part of a more general disaster. It may be found in conjunction with hydrocephalus, myelomeningocele or diastematomyelia. It may be found in arthrogryposis multiplex congenita or in association with ligamentous relaxation. Wynne-Davies has noted a number of such cases in England, but it is an association that does not seem to be expressed frequently here.[11] Talipes equinovarus is also seen in diastrophic dwarfism and reported in a number of other syndromes.

Although the theory of intrauterine compression has been proposed it seems an inadequate explanation except when significant oligohydramnios is known to have occurred.

The talipes equinovarus deformity that is a manifestation of cerebral palsy, poliomyelitis, postnatal vascular accident, or peroneal nerve damage is discussed later in this chapter.

Natural History

The natural history of clubfoot is one of persistent deformity and progressive secondary changes in the associated structures. If untreated, the patient may walk almost on his lateral malleolus with his foot internally rotated and pointing posteriorly.

If it is treated we can usually look forward to a comfortable serviceable plantigrade foot. There need be no Philips of *Of Human Bondage*.[11] The psychosocial aspects are in fact quite favorable. Experience in our follow-up clinic reveals that we have no adult who holds a job dictated by the limitations of his feet. Only 2 of more than 100 patients manifest overt psychological difficulties. Both boys come from deeply disturbed home situations, and we feel that their psychiatric problems reflect their home situations more than their reactions to their foot problems.

It is of interest that many of our youngsters excel at sports. Several play on varsity football and lacrosse teams. One even majors in physical education.

In our initial contacts with the parents we feel it is very important to reassure them about the bright economic and social futures open to their children. At some time during the first year of treatment we also discuss the altered but still very favorable odds against a subsequent sibling being born with clubfeet. When the youngsters themselves reach their teens it is very important to

---

*Two of our mothers tried to abort the pregnancies, which led to the births of children with clubfeet. Neither had any family history of talipes equinovarus nor any other children with the deformity. One other child is known to have rubella syndrome.

review the genetic aspects of the deformity with them. Wynne-Davies states that the presence of talipes equinovarus in one child increases the risk of the same deformity in a sibling to 1:35.[11] Palmer feels the risk to a subsequent sibling is 1:10.[9] We have no figure to indicate risk to the progeny of individuals with talipes equinovarus. That there is some increased risk to their children does not, however, alarm these young people. The odds are in their favor and they have already experienced fully active lives themselves.

In summary, then, a clubfoot demands prompt, diligent, and sustained treatment. If these conditions are met the individuals will have serviceable feet and apparently comfortable ones too.

Treatment

In treating talipes equinovarus it is found that some feet respond readily, some only to prolonged vigorous and sustained efforts, and some, despite maximal effort, remain disappointing to the surgeon although not necessarily to the patient.

Non nocere should be our guideline. We wish to correct deformity and to inflict no further damage in the course of treatment. Salter has demonstrated that cartilage cells undergo necrosis if subjected to sustained pressures.[10] In treatment the integrity of the cartilage cells must be respected and only gentle gradual corrections undertaken in application of casts and the kicking splint. Surgical release is preferable to forced correction.

The overall plan is to correct the varus deformity of the forefoot and heel first. Only when the varus heel has been overcome is it appropriate to try to correct the equinus deformity. While varus heel persists the hindfoot cannot dorsiflex properly in the mortise. Attempts to dorsiflex the foot prematurely will result in a persistent equinus deformity of the hindfoot, and a spurious dorsiflexion through the midfoot. The result will be a "rocker bottom foot."

It is possible to use strapping of the foot as described by Sir Robert Jones. Strapping permits manipulation of the foot, but it sometimes results in excessive distraction of the forefoot from the hindfoot. Control of the hindfoot is then rendered very difficult.

Much as dynamic approaches are to be preferred, initial correction is perhaps most reliably achieved through the use of serial plaster casts. These should be instituted on the first day of life, if possible, and changed every 24 to 48 hours during the first 10 days.

As soon as a plantigrade foot has been achieved, use of a kicking splint may be initiated. It is critical that the foot and the heel in particular be firmly secured to the foot plate so that dorsiflexion will occur through the ankle and not through the midfoot. "Rockering" must be avoided.

To achieve correction the affected foot should be externally rotated only very gradually from 0 degrees to no more than 35 to 40 degrees. The bar too should be bent gradually away from the perineum. Each thrust of the contralateral limb then results in a calcaneovalgus thrust against the affected limb.*

---

*Compensation must be made in the angulation of the bar to spare an unaffected or perhaps even valgus contralateral foot from a calcaneovalgus thrust.

Once correction has been achieved, maintenance is of utmost importance, for neglect permits recurrence. During the waking hours the corrected foot must be used in the most satisfactory position possible. The child frequently has residual anteversion and poorly functional peroneals. These factors result in internal rotation of the leg and favor forefoot adduction. The child's gait will be aided by the use of outer sole wedges and his forefoot correction reinforced by the use of outflare shoes. Occasionally, braces are required to control marked internal rotation of the leg. Night splinting, as an overall policy, should be continued to the age of five or as long as a deforming habit persists.

Quite a few feet fail to reach an optimal degree of correction via nonoperative methods. Surgical correction should be undertaken and carried out early in life when soft tissue releases can achieve the most satisfactory corrections. As the child grows older soft tissues tighten and bony deformity progresses. Then only bone procedures can help and the results may be less gratifying.

Failure to achieve satisfactory dorsiflexion is the most common residual problem. Any discernible varus deformity of the heel must be corrected by medial release before an Achilles tendon lengthening and posterior capsulotomy can fully correct the equinus deformity. Our experience leads us to feel that a combined posteromedial release is not only the most gratifying approach when there is discernible residual heel varus deformity, but also well worth the effort if there is even the slightest question of its presence.

Varus deformity of the forefoot may also persist. When tissues are still supple it may be relieved by a tarsometatarsal and intermetatarsal release as described by Heyman, Herndon, and Strong.[7]

When bony deformity predominates, a second string of procedures may help to ameliorate the situation. A varus deformity of the os calcis may be reduced by a wedge osteotomy as described by Dwyer.[3, 4] Our experience has been limited to closing wedge osteotomies and, although the removal of the wedge further diminishes the height of the tarsus, the change in attitude of the hindfoot on heel strike seems to be of benefit to the patients. In our clinic the shortening is compensated for by a heel and sole lift if it is 1/4 inch or more.

The opening wedge osteotomy described by Dwyer in 1963 has the advantage of increasing the height of the tarsus as well as correcting the varus deformity.[4] We have, however, been reluctant to challenge our soft tissue closures with the additional stress of that increased height.

Mention must be made at this point of the consequences of infection in clubfoot surgery. Any inflammatory process elicits tremendous fibrosis, and the resulting contractures may be catastrophic to the correction of the foot. For this reason the greatest care must be taken to ensure tension-free skin closures. This may make it necessary to accept less than full correction at operation and subsequently to manipulate the foot to the desired position. The child should be suitably sedated and the position improved gradually by manipulations and cast changes beginning on the fifth postoperative day and repeated every 48 hours until satisfactory position has been achieved.

Attempts to correct residual fixed forefoot deformity should be preceded by careful evaluation of the heel. It is imperative that any residual varus inclination of the heel be corrected prior to correction of the forefoot. A variety of tarsal and metatarsal osteotomies may be employed to correct the forefoot. The rather extensive work required to reduce the deformity and realign the forefoot may provoke a fair amount of fibrosis and stiffening of the foot. Should the heel correction subsequently be found unsatisfactory, it might be very difficult to align a stiffened forefoot with a newly oriented heel.

A shortened medial column of the foot is a relatively uncommon problem in our population but does occur. To cope with this problem Evans offers the child of about six years a medial release supplemented by wedge excision of the calcaneocuboid joint.[5] With this bilateral approach he has been able to reduce the subluxation of the midfoot and balance the medial and lateral columns of the foot and in so doing relieve the varus heel as well.

If correction is still inadequate as maturity approaches, a triple arthrodesis may be necessary. Before that procedure is elected, however, a careful evaluation of the tibiotalar and subtalar ranges of motion should be carried out according to Heywood's method.[8] If significant tibiotalar incongruity and limitation of motion are found, then consideration should be given to the possibility of correction through the tibiotalar joint instead, as recommended by Heywood and Commerell.[1]

Pantalar arthrodesis remains as a final resort for the obstinate foot. With the institution of early and vigorous treatment only the most incorrigible of feet should remain so unsatisfactory that the sacrifice of all motion is warranted to achieve a tolerable alignment.

The patients who have reached adulthood seem to have few problems. In our own series only a handful of patients beyond the third decade of life continue to attend the follow-up clinic. Most of the patients between 20 and 30 years of age are free of pain and disability. Those aged 10 to 20 years impress us with their activity and enthusiasm for sports. We have no adults with symptomatic clubfeet in the active treatment clinic. What few complaints we have been able to elicit have concerned knees rather than feet. These symptoms have been related to genu valgum and genu recurvatum, and we hope we have learned to forestall those caused by genu recurvatum.*

CEREBRAL PALSY

Fixed foot deformities are most commonly seen in the spastic type of cerebral palsy; in fact, equinus deformity may be one of the earliest signs of spastic diplegia that can be elicited in an infant. The most commonly seen foot deformities in the palsied child are equinus deformity, spastic equinovarus deformity, and calcaneus deformity.

---

*We have learned to modify our approach to equinus deformity. If there is tibiotalar incongruity or some other reason for its persistence, we accept the equinus inclination in order to spare the knee. In these cases we recommend a heel of sufficient height to give the ankle enough plantar flexion to prevent the knee from going into recurvation.

Equinus Deformity

This refers to a position of relatively fixed plantar flexion at the ankle joint. It is most often associated with spasticity of the triceps surae muscle or motor imbalance at the ankle. The motor imbalance in cerebral palsy differs from that seen either in myelomeningocele or following poliomyelitis in that there is rarely any actual paresis of the antagonistic muscles because one deals with upper motor neuron lesions. Because of associated spasticity of the muscles controlling the joints proximal to the ankle, however, the function of these antagonistic muscles may be increased or decreased. For example, it has been found that the recurrence rate following heel cord lengthening in a patient who has an inordinately spastic quadriceps muscle is high. Such a child is unable to initiate dorsiflexion at the ankle joint using the anterior tibial muscle and the toe dorsiflexors owing to the fact that the knee remains stiff in extension during the swing phase because the quadriceps fails to relax; i.e., no synkinetic pattern of gait can be achieved at the ankle during swing phase.

An important variant of the equinus deformity is the equinovalgus deformity that is best described by the term "valgus-ex-equino." The underlying pathogenesis of this deformity is primarily that of a tight heel cord with some intoeing either at the hip or at or below the knee. The tight heel cord acts as a tether attached to the heel so that when the stance phase is initiated and in association with an internal rotation thrust, the forefoot migrates laterally into abduction in relation to the hindfoot at the midtarsal joint. The force continues into the hindfoot at the subtalar joint, and the os calcis is subluxated laterally on the overlying talus. This achieves a mechanical improvement in the foot in that the child has a more stable base on which to walk because the foot becomes much more plantigrade. This pseudocorrection, however, occurs at the expense of a total subluxation of the entire foot around the talus (see Fig. 17–1). This stretched out valgus-ex-equino position becomes apparent soon after the child begins to bear weight; the foot becomes increasingly stiffened in the deformed position as the child grows and continues to ambulate. Factors that make this deformity even greater are internal rotation of the femur or tibial torsion, increasing weight gain by the child, and severe tightness of the heel cord.

Ambulatory kinesiological electromyography has shown that the majority of patients who have spastic pes equinus show greater spasticity of the gastrocnemius than of the soleus muscles; in fact, the soleus may not show a spastic pattern at all. The Silfverskiold or confusion test in which the knee is flexed and the child asked to dorsiflex the foot against resisted hip flexion may show that the equinus inclination disappears once the knee has been allowed to flex. The test can be used to show that the gastrocnemius is spastic and the soleus not; however, it is felt that this may actually reflect a synkinetic inhibition of the triceps surae and a reciprocal activation of the dorsiflexors in relation to the flexed position of the foot, knee, and hip.

The best treatment for spastic equinus deformities that do not respond to conservative procedures including stretching and day or night bracing or both is surgical elongation of the triceps surae either in part or as a whole. Because of the fact that the gastrocnemius appears to be spastic in most cases, recession or elongation of this muscle alone has given some lasting results in terms of elimination of equinus deformity. Experience has shown, however, that in the presence of a spastic quadriceps muscle, the recurrence rate is high. In such cases, release of the rectus femoris muscle in addition to the triceps lengthening permits a more normal pattern of knee flexion during the swing phase.

Treatment of the valgus-ex-equino problem is considerably more difficult because of the fact that a secondary deformity has arisen as a result of the primary equinus deformity. The former occurs at the forefoot as well as the hindfoot and ankle joint. Attempts to brace such a foot in order to correct both the equinus and the valgus deformities have never been very successful because in so doing one is trying to correct three deformities with a single brace. In the older child this deformity sometimes remains fixed and cannot be corrected with an orthosis. Therefore, if a decision is made to correct the foot deformity, it should be based on certain criteria:

1. The equinus deformity should be corrected by a heel cord lengthening or gastrocnemius recession.

2. The internal rotation thrust occurring above the ankle joint should be corrected either by soft tissue hip surgery such as an iliopsoas recession associated with a varus derotation osteotomy of the femur or merely a soft tissue iliopsoas recession alone.

3. If the hips remain normal and internal rotation is due to internal tibial torsion, this should be corrected either before or after the heel cord and foot surgery.

After the internal rotation thrust and the heel cord have been corrected, a decision must be made whether the valgus deformity can be held with an orthosis or whether supplemental surgery is required in the form of a Grice-Green procedure. In an older child, a triple arthrodesis may be necessary to maintain the stability of the foot so that once again its medial border becomes straight and the os calcis is no longer subluxated into valgus position. If this is not achieved, recurrence in the form of a valgus-ex-equino deformity will occur.

Spastic Equinovarus Deformity

In these children, the heel cord may be tight, but the main problem appears to be that of a spastic posterior tibial muscle that causes a varus heel at the subtalar joint and forefoot adduction and supination at the midtarsal joint. The mechanical disadvantage of a varus foot other than the ungainly gait produced by intoeing is due to the fact that the talus cannot engage properly within the mortise of the ankle joint because it is held in a viselike grip on its medial aspect. This prevents normal pronation at the subtalar and ankle joints during phases of dorsiflexion of the foot. Surgical release of the posterior tibial muscle will allow this to be achieved and the heel cord tightness may not appear to be as severe once this has been done. In terms of orthosis, it is virtually impossible to splint or brace an exceedingly tight posterior tibial muscle, and this is best treated surgically. A word of warning should, however, be given with regard to this procedure; if an internal rotation thrust above the ankle joint occurs or continues to occur after release of the posterior tibial muscle, the opposite deformity, i.e., valgus-ex-equino, may be precipitated. It is therefore important to be certain that no proximal rotatory stresses are being applied to a foot in which a posterior tibial release is contemplated. In some rare instances of spastic pes equinovarus the ankle dorsiflexors do not appear to be functioning synkinetically with the confusion test and, in these cases, anterior transfer of the posterior tibial muscle through the interosseous membrane should be considered in order to mobilize the ankle dorsiflexors and obviate recurrent equinus deformity or foot drop postoperatively.

Calcaneus Deformity

This is almost always an iatrogenic deformity caused by injudicious lengthening of heel cords at the time of surgery for equinus or valgus-ex-equino deformities. It may be quite disabling and has all the characteristics of the calcaneus deformity seen following poliomyelitis or in myelomeningocele. The gait of an afflicted child is that of a "stamper" or "plodder" with no push-off during stance phase. Calcaneus deformity is most commonly seen in children who are nonambulatory and on whom heel cord lengthenings have been performed in order to allow normal footwear to be used. These children assume a sitting position for most of their waking hours, and this creates a flexion pattern whereby continuous bombardment of impulses to the ankle dorsiflexors occur with inhibition of the lengthened triceps surae. This leads to a synkinetic imbalance in which the dorsiflexors achieve the upper hand and the opposite deformity to the original develops.

MYELOMENINGOCELE

The child with foot involvement related to spina bifida must contend with two serious problems, the first being the deformities, which are due to either muscle imbalance or muscle fibrosis, and the second, which is the varying degree of anesthesia of the foot. Six varieties of deformity predominate in myelomeningocele: equinus, equinovarus, equinovalgus, calcaneus, calcaneovarus, and cavus deformity with clawing of the toes. The explanation for the pathogenesis of foot deformities appears to be reasonably simple on the basis of the neurological lesion in each individual case, but in practice this is often not so. Secondary deformity may arise as a result of delay in ambulation (equinus) or because of weight bearing (valgus). It is also difficult to predict motor function in an infant; if repeated observation and examination fail to determine whether a muscle or group of muscles has contractility, information can be obtained from electrodiagnostic tests. Often, a deforming force may be a fibrotic remnant of a muscle similar to the type seen in a child with arthrogryposis. For these reasons, surgical correction is best deferred until the child is about 18 months old, but should not be delayed too long in order to prevent fixed bony deformity from occurring.

Objective of Treatment of Foot Deformities

Many children born with myelomeningocele can be taught to walk provided they retain proprioception at the hip level and the joint deformity can be corrected or prevented by a combination of surgery and bracing.

Adequate hip function is necessary for ambulation, but established foot deformities may preclude the use of braces or footwear and so delay the habilitation program. Therefore, the major objective in the treatment of these foot deformities is to create a plantigrade foot that will fit into a shoe or brace. The other goals are to produce a foot that will require as little external support as possible and one that will not be subjected to uneven areas of pressure during weight bearing and thus reduce the unit load on pressure sensitive or anesthetic skin.

Conservative methods of treatment such as those used in the conventional treatment of congenital clubfoot have little place in the treatment of these feet, primarily because of the problem of anesthesia of the skin. Daily passive stretching by a therapist combined with passive range of motion exercise and care of the skin plays an important role in preventing the establishment of static deformities. The use of devices such as plaster casts to correct established deformities should be avoided.

Surgery, therefore, paradoxically offers the least traumatizing and surest method of correcting an established deformity and preventing its recurrence. The basic principle of surgical treatment is the division of tendons of the deforming muscles, if these muscles are without innervation. The release or excision of restraining structures such as ligaments, joint capsules, or the actual bones themselves, and the transfer of active muscles into new position both to remove a deforming force and to establish a new corrective force that will, it is hoped, prevent a recurrence of the original deformity are procedures that are also employed.

Methods of Correction

The following methods of surgical correction are used to treat the common deformities that are encountered:

Equinus Deformity. Heel cord lengthening to allow the heel to reach the floor combined with operative bracing and passive stretching to prevent recurrence is recommended if this deformity alone exists. It usually occurs in an anesthetic flail foot.

Equinovarus Deformity. This is the commonest type of foot problem seen in children with myelomeningocele. Correction of this deformity requires heel cord lengthening as well as lengthening of the large toe flexors, posteromedial release of the foot, and possible transfer of the anterior tibial or posterior tibial tendons (if preoperative evaluation has shown these muscles to be functional).

Despite liberal releasing of soft tissues in such feet, the foot may not be satisfactorily correctible. In these instances, talectomy will allow correction of all three deformities of this neurological "clubfoot."

Calcaneus Deformity. To obtain correction in such feet, release or elongation of the tight anterior structures such as the toe and foot dorsiflexors and anterior joint capsule combined with transfer of the anterior tibial and peroneus tertius (if functional) into the tendo Achilles will be required. Tenodesis of the cut distal end of the tendo Achilles into the back of the tibial shaft may also give a satisfactory result.

Equinovalgus Deformity. Surgical correction of this deformity is particularly difficult and rarely results in full correction.

The effect of tendon transfers in the feet of children with myelomeningocele is less predictable than in patients who have suffered from poliomyelitis because the feet never had normal innervation.

References

1. Commerell, J. J.: A new approach to the untreated or relapsed club foot in adults. J. Bone Joint Surg., 45-B:430, 1963.
2. Duraiswami, P. K.: Experimental causation of congenital defects. J. Bone Joint Surg., 32-B:742, 1950.
3. Dwyer, F. C.: Osteotomy of the calcaneum for pes cavus. J. Bone Joint Surg., 41-B:80–86, 1959.
4. Dwyer, F. C.: The treatment of relapsed clubfoot by the insertion of a wedge into the calcaneum. J. Bone Joint Surg., 45-B:67–75, 1963.
5. Evans, D.: Relapsed clubfoot. J. Bone Joint Surg., 43 B:722–733, 1961.
6. Grice, S. D.: An extra-articular arthrodesis of the subastragalar joint for correction of paralytic flat feet in children. J. Bone Joint Surg., 34-A:927–940, 1952.
7. Heyman, C. H., Herndon, C. H., and Strong, J. M.: Mobilization of the tarsometatarsal and intermetatarsal joints for correction of resistant adduction of the fore part of the foot in congenital clubfoot or congenital metatarsus varus. J. Bone Joint Surg., 40-A:299–310, 1958.
8. Heywood, A. W.: The mechanics of the hindfoot in club foot as demonstrated radiographically. J. Bone Joint Surg., 46-B:102–107, 1964.
9. Palmer, R. M.: The genetics of talipes equinovarus. J. Bone Joint Surg., 46-A:542–556, 1964.
10. Salter, R. A., and Field, P.: The effects of continuous compression on living articular cartilage. J. Bone Joint Surg., 42-A:31–49, 1960.
11. Wynne-Davies, R.: Family studies and the cause of congenital club foot. J. Bone Joint Surg., 46-B:445–463, 1964.

Chapter 18

Orthoses for Children

by *Yasoma B. Challenor, M.D.*

The greatest need in prescribing orthotic devices for children is a clear analysis of the anatomical problem requiring a device. Then the appropriate components are selected to meet the child's needs. Implicit in this simple statement are: (1) the abandonment of prescription by fixed tradition in favor of reliance on observation of the pathomechanics of dysfunction combined with *current* orthotic knowledge, (2) consideration of the energy and endurance of the child and selection of materials and extent of orthoses accordingly, and (3) realization that the child's growth makes accuracy of fit crucial to prevent distortion of anatomical structure or alignment by the prolonged use of an inappropriate or poorly fitted orthotic device.

Orthotic goals may include:

1. Aid or substitution for weak muscles. During childhood this goal is encountered more often in upper extremity problems. The weak lower limb more often requires item 2.

2. Stabilization of joints for weight bearing.

3. Alignment control and maintenance.

4. Prevention and occasionally correction of contractures.

5. Immobilization of painful joints.

6. Relief of weight bearing.

7. Training for function, i.e., preoperative evaluation and training, or postoperative retraining.

8. Positioning the proximal part of a limb for functional use of the hand or foot.

Each of these orthotic goals ultimately aims at improving function, and the orthotic aim must be understood by the child or the parent as well as by the therapist who works with the child. A negative attitude, confusion, or frus-

409

tration in the parent or therapist may directly influence the child's acceptance of a device. The appearance, weight, and simplicity of design contribute to the acceptance of an appliance, as does comfort. The accuracy of orthotic contour is crucial when devices are applied to insensitive, easily traumatized, or easily inflamed structures, and pressure must be distributed over as wide an area as possible. Inevitably, the availability of components and the skill of the orthotist influence our success in providing an optimal orthosis.

It is beyond the scope of this selective discussion to include all the clinical conditions encountered in an orthotic clinic, to describe details of basic biomechanics, or to list all available devices and components since standard sources cover these areas at length.[13, 29, 30, 36, 43] Instead, an overview of those areas of the orthotic aspects peculiar to infants and children is presented. Throughout the discussion it should be remembered that an orthotic device is an inseparable although sometimes minimal part of a total therapeutic program, which may also include judicious selection and timing of surgical procedures.

UPPER EXTREMITY

Neuromuscular Imbalance

Spasticity.   Spastic muscle imbalance in the upper extremity influences orthotic goals according to the severity and distribution of the increased muscle tone. Here we consider typical childhood problems progressing from distal to proximal joints.

The adducted and flexed thumb of the child with cerebral palsy ("cortical thumb") may be a key to increasing function if spasticity is mild or moderate. Often passive abduction or extension of the thumb facilitates voluntary extension of other digits. Maintenance of the thumb in the widely abducted or opposed position would increase hand function for such a child, and would prevent web-space contracture. Spasticity of the adductors of the thumb may be severe enough to prevent extension of the metacarpophalangeal (MP) joint, despite fair voluntary extension of the interphalangeal (IP) joints of the thumb and other digits (Fig. 18–1A). On repeated attempts to grasp an object, the constant pull of the long thumb extensor against the spastic adductor may eventually cause laxity and hyperextension of the metacarpophalangeal joint. This joint may become painful—initially from ligamentous stretching and later because of degenerative arthritis secondary to prolonged use of the joint in the malaligned position. A simple molded opponens orthosis should prevent the malalignment and secondary problems, as long as it is applied before web space contracture has occurred (Fig. 18–1B).

Imbalance of digital flexor and extensor spasticity may allow voluntary extension at the metacarpophalangeal joint, with concomitant interphalangeal and wrist joint flexion (Fig. 18–2). The hook-type grasp that results may be quite useful for the child. If excessive wrist flexion causes pain or interferes with the strength of interphalangeal flexion, a wrist support may be desirable.

The goal for the orthosis is to protect the wrist while preserving function. It is, however, essential to select the wrist position with care: too much wrist extension may place enough tension on the spastic finger flexors to prevent voluntary interphalangeal extension. Trials of wrist positions are necessary to find where there is maximal function, and this may even be with the wrist in mod-

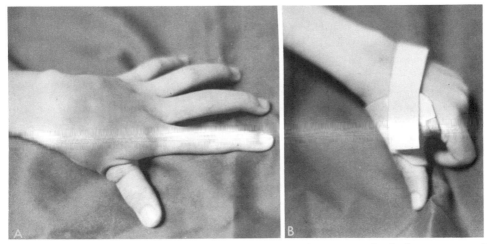

Figure 18-1   A. Spastic adductors of the thumb cannot be overcome by the long extensor of the thumb. Hyperextensibility of the metacarpophalangeal joint results, with pain and instability. Overall spasticity is moderate; it is imbalance of spasticity that causes the problem. B. A molded short opponens splint supports the joint and maintains the web space.

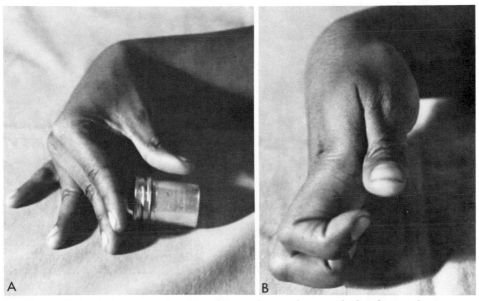

Figure 18-2   A. Spasticity of wrist and finger flexors, despite which voluntary finger extension is present. B. A hook-type grasp is feasible. Excessive wrist extension by an orthotic device may prevent the finger extension required to place digits for a useful hook grasp.

erate flexion. Hook grasp is thus allowed, as is donning of sleeved garments unimpeded by an excessively flexed wrist.

For some children, a total predominance of flexor tone may cause flexion of the wrist and all digital joints without voluntary extension. If epicritic sensation (stereognosis, position sense, two-point discrimination) are reasonably intact, a trial of night splinting is warranted (Fig. 18–3). The empiric rationale for the positioning is the maintenance of the muscles and tendons in a comfortably stretched position, which is beyond the point where a stretch reflex is elicited for each joint.[22] Each joint should be splinted in maximal comfortable extension, even if it is quite unlike the anatomical functional position (Fig. 18–4). Because this extended position is maintained only at night, there is no danger of extension contractures. Often, maintenance of such a position for several hours is followed by relaxation sufficient to allow some voluntary control of digital motion, which can be elicited both in therapy and in daily activities. Even when no function of the extremely spastic hand is expected, splinting may supplement therapy in preventing loss of range of joint motion so that hand washing, finger-nail care, and donning of sleeved garments are possible.

When severe constant spasticity is present at the finger or wrist joints or both, a platform orthotic design may be optimal (Fig. 18–5A). The design of this device allows the fingers to be inserted first while the wrist is flexed, after which the splint itself is used to extend the wrist slowly (Fig. 18–5B). With the exception of this specific indication for a dorsal orthosis, selection of a volar or dorsal device is optional. The rationale for dorsal devices stresses the facilitation to extension provided by the contact of the orthosis with the dorsum of the hand and forearm. However, because nerves adapt rapidly to a sustained, unchanging pressure, that facilitation, even if initially present, is lost after the

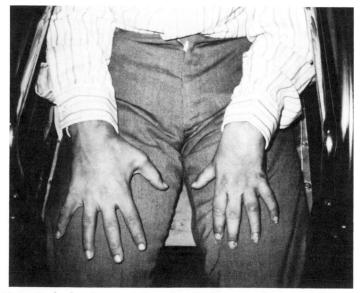

Figure 18–3 Underdevelopment of one hand with parietal lob (epicritic) sensory deficit. Pressure and pain sensation are preserved, but rapid accommodation to pressure makes safe control of spasticity difficult, since sustained excessive pressure may not be perceived.

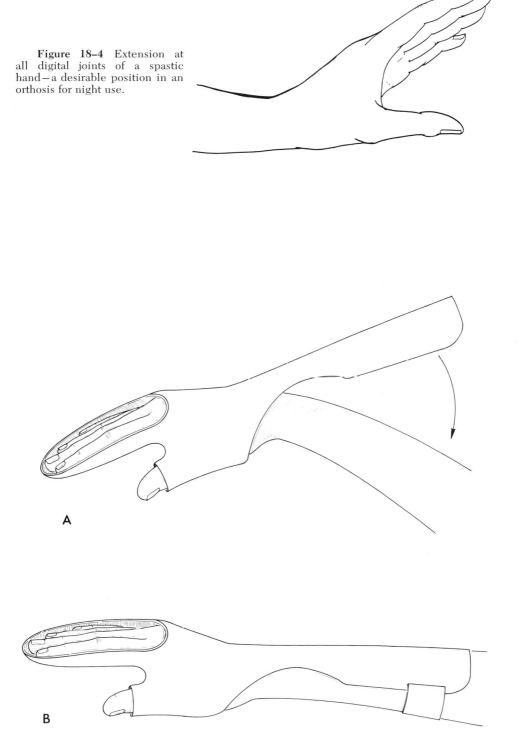

Figure 18–4 Extension at all digital joints of a spastic hand—a desirable position in an orthosis for night use.

A

B

Figure 18–5 *A.* The spastic digits are placed on the platform. *B.* The splint is then used as a lever to slowly extend the spastic wrist.

orthosis has been in place for a short time. Moreover, the volar surface is left uncovered and exposed to changing, incoming stimuli that may facilitate flexion. Similarly, a volar device should rapidly cease to facilitate flexion, after its sustained contact no longer excites sensory afferent impulses, i.e., after these nerves have accommodated to the unchanging contact.

Spasticity of forearm pronators may not be of concern, since most hand activities away from the body involve pronation, although activities directed toward the midline of the body usually include a combined flexion-supination synergy. The small but significant number of activities requiring the forearm to be in midposition or supination may, however, be a problem. Because an orthosis that controls or assists forearm rotation adequately must cross, and therefore restrict motion at, the elbow, such orthoses are not used for daily function, but may occasionally be used at night. The maintenance of forearm rotatory range and control is appropriate to therapy rather than to orthotic application. Similarly, elbow range and control are fostered by therapy, with occasional supplementary night splinting. Therapy aims for control of motions other than those limited types imposed by the synergies of spasticity – a goal beyond orthotic applications for the upper extremity.

Spasticity of hemiparetic shoulder muscles often induces adduction and internal rotation of the humerus. The arm should be placed to discourage this position when the patient is seated. Quadriparetic or diplegic children often hold the arm in abduction with external rotation of the humerus and scapular retraction during many activities. A handle or dowel on the table or lapboard that may be grasped by the patient will help to prevent this nonfunctional position.

Flaccidity. Flaccid neuromuscular imbalance, in direct contrast with spastic imbalance, may require dynamic assistance for function or positioning. In addition, functional positioning of the chronically denervated hand must be maintained, although for some problems of hand spasticity it may be set aside (Fig. 18–6A).

Functional positioning aims to align each digital joint in the position opposite to that in which joint and ligamentous structures would most tend to produce contractures. Thus, for the metacarpophalangeal joint, the tendency is for contracture in extension or hyperextension, so the position of function would be 50 degrees of flexion.[5, 12] The interphalangeal joints, which are more often predisposed to flexion contractures, should be nearly at neutral position (maximum of 15 to 20 degrees of flexion). The thumb should be in wide opposition, i.e., fully rotated so that the finger pulp is opposite the index and long fingers. The contour of the system of palmar arches is important, with the eccentric distal transverse (metacarpal) palmar arch requiring most careful preservation (Fig. 18–6B).[5, 12]

In children, flaccid distal muscle weakness is usually difficult to correct with commercially available orthotic components, because of the limited range of available sizes, and custom molded devices are required for optimal contouring and alignment. For distal ulnar nerve lesions (roughly equivalent to a T_1 level motor loss) a molded thumb support would incorporate a metacarpophalangeal joint extensor stop (lumbrical bar), which allows the long extensors to extend the interphalangeal joints of the ring and little fingers while

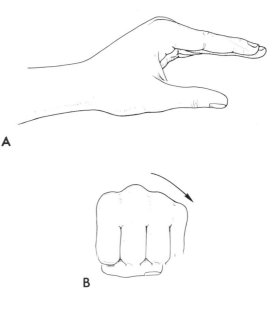

Figure 18–6 *A.* Position of function overcoming the tendency to contracture determined by the particular joint contour and ligamentous structure. *B.* The distal transverse palmar arch is eccentric in that it is formed primarily by descent of the fourth and fifth metacarpal heads.

preventing a "clawhand" position (Fig. 18–7A). A distal median nerve lesion is roughly equivalent to a lesion isolating the C_8 segment, and requires a molded opponens orthosis. A distal combined median and ulnar nerve lesion, corresponding to the loss of hand function of C_8 level quadriparesis, would still be manageable with a short orthosis, as would a C_7 level weakness. For the latter, a short finger-driven prehension orthosis assists finger flexion (Fig. 18–7B). A similar device could be used for a proximal combined median and ulnar nerve lesion, which corresponds to the hand weakness of C_7 quadriparesis.

Wrist control is necessary for C_6 level lesions, for which a reciprocal prehension orthosis is applicable: active wrist extension is harnessed to provide prehension (Fig. 18–8).[10, 23] If wrist extension is too weak to permit use of this device, a harness and cable suspension, similar to a prosthetic suspension, can be used so that humeral flexion produces prehension via the cable. With C_5 level lesions, weak shoulder muscles can still produce distal hand placement (although without manipulation or prehension) by using one of the balanced forearm orthoses, of which the Michigan mobile arm support is most adaptable.[41, 42] The weight of the arm is supported on a forearm trough connected to a series of ball-bearing linkages. Minimal shoulder motion can set the frictionless linkages in motion for hand placement. The wrist and fingers must be supported.

The fact that many cervical lesions result in spasticity in distal hand muscles has led to attempts to stimulate the intact lower motor neurons to produce function.[33, 47] The long-term feasibility of such stimulation has not yet been proved. More conventional sources of external power (pneumatic or electrical) may, however, be indicated for the child with permanent paralysis from a partial brachial plexus lesion, in whom tendon transfers are not feasible.[8] The successful use of external power depends on the age, intelligence, and motivation of the disabled child.

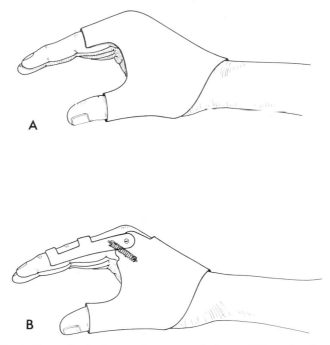

Figure 18–7 *A.* The orthosis for an ulnar nerve lesion stabilizes the thumb metacarpophalangeal joint and prevents hyperextension of the digital metacarpophalangeal joints, particularly the fourth and fifth. *B.* A finger-driven prehension orthosis provides passive flexion via a spring ventral to the center of metacarpophalangeal motion. The fingers must be capable of active extension.

Another difficult management problem relates to birth trauma to the brachial plexus. Traditionally, injury to the upper components of the plexus affecting primarily shoulder muscles has led to positioning the infant's arm in humeral abduction and external rotation to avoid stretching. This limits neonatal exploratory use of the extremity, and has on occasion led to contractures in this nonfunctional position.[48] Maintenance of joint mobility and protection of the shoulder are more appropriate to therapeutic goals than orthoses. The parent should be taught protective measures to avoid stretching the plexus, and range of joint motion exercises to be done several times daily (i.e., whenever the diapers are changed). Similarly, injury to the lower plexus components, af-

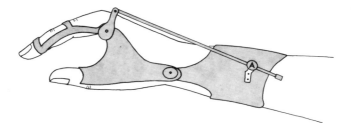

Figure 18–8 Wrist-driven prehension orthosis links active wrist extension to prehension. Adjustment at point A varies amount of wrist extension needed to produce pinch.

fecting the hand and wrist primarily, are problems initially for therapy. At about six months, when exploratory use of the hands is considerable, appropriate functional orthoses determined by assessment of a given infant's deficit may be used.

Joint Inflammation

In juvenile rheumatoid arthritis, exacerbating joint inflammation may call for devices to place the joints at rest during episodes of inflammation. Such orthoses should be easily removable so that active motion of the joint may be allowed several times during the day. Dynamic assistive devices are contraindicated for inflammatory problems because they may add further stresses to already injured tissue. On the other hand, static night splinting to preserve joint range is certainly warranted, even between periods of inflammation

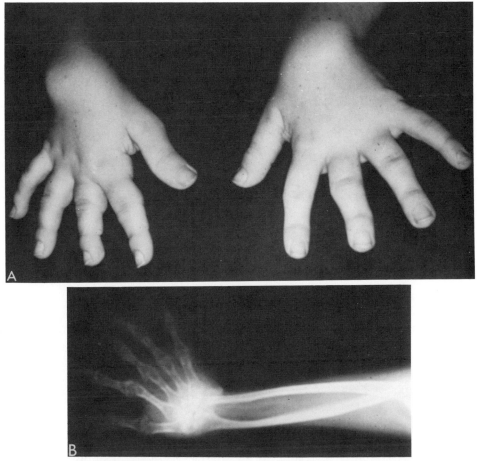

Figure 18–9 A. This 14 year old boy has had rheumatoid arthritis since childhood. There is volar subluxation of the carpus, ulnar deviation at the wrist, and fusiform swelling of the interphalangeal joints. B. X-rays show loss of carpal architecture and subluxation.

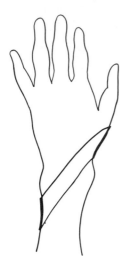

Figure 18 10 Diagonal placement of a strap for retaining the rheumatoid hand and wrist on a resting orthosis. There is no pressure on the radial or ulnar styloid processes.

Care must be taken to apply corrective forces accurately when progressively adjusting position to accommodate increasing range of joint motion. The status of joints to be splinted must be known radiographically so that subluxation is not mistaken for contracture (Fig. 18–9). Retaining straps must be placed to deliver appropriate retaining force in the three-point pressure system, while avoiding locations susceptible to trauma from pressure or friction (Fig. 18–10). If early signs of digital volar subluxation at the metacarpophalangeal joints or intrinsic muscle shortening are observed, the metacarpophalangeal flexion described earlier in the functional position definition should be decreased. If the tendency toward digital ulnar deviation at the metacarpophalangeal joint can be detected early, the mediolateral wrist position should be selected with care, to lessen the tendency of this deviation to progress.[35] The pathomechanics of wrist positional influence on distal deformity has only recently been clarified, and is of considerable significance in orthotic applications in rheumatoid arthritis.[35]

Thermal Burns

Orthotic devices can and should be used for optimal hand position and joint alignment before, during, and after any necessary skin grafting procedures.[9] The functional position of the hand in the orthosis involves one change from that previously outlined in that the metacarpophalangeal joints should be flexed as close to 90 degrees as feasible so that the collateral ligaments are at maximal length. This ensures some retained prehension, no matter how severe the tissue destruction (Fig. 18–11A). Incorporation of traction into the orthoses for circumferential burns prevents loss of optimal position caused by the hand slipping on the orthosis. Traction can be accomplished without skeletal pins, and the orthosis can be easily removed from dressing the hand and for therapy several times daily (Fig. 18–11B). For less extensive

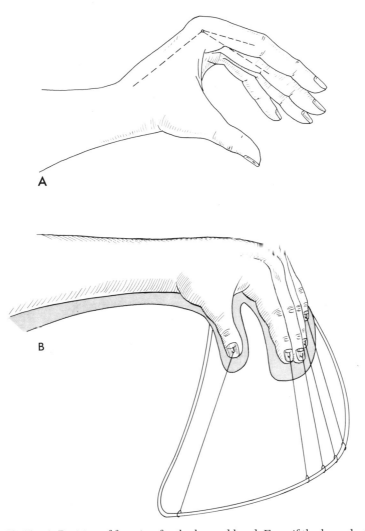

Figure 18–11   A. Position of function for the burned hand. Even if the burn destroys extensor tendons, prehension is preserved. This would not be true if the metacarpophalangeal joints were positioned or contracted into extension. B. The traction orthosis for burns: (1) maintains functional position, (2) is easily removable to allow exercise, and (3) is washable so that ointments used in burn treatment can be removed; and (4) the frame keeps the hand elevated to minimize edema. The traction is applied via rubber bands attached to dress hooks, which are glued onto the nails with epoxy or acrylic adhesive. This idea was developed at the Brooke Army Medical Center. The index finger is flexed as close to 90° as possible, and each successive digit 5–10° more.

burns, functional position may be achieved without traction by using molded orthoses. Those thermoplastic materials with some resilience, i.e., Plastozote and Stalite, seem to be most comfortable for the burned hand.

Scarring subsequent to burns can cause insidious loss of range of joint motion, even months after healing is complete. A static night splint should be used for up to nine months after healing to minimize this tendency, particularly if the child tends to form hypertrophic scars or keloids. The hypertrophic scarring itself can be minimized and even reversed to a startling degree by use of elastic bandaging at night to keep the orthotic device in place.

Axillary burns, with or without skin grafting, may contract slowly so that humeral abduction range decreases. It has been shown that orthotic positioning may have to be maintained long after the convalescent period, since rest, comfort, and natural usage all tend to keep the humerus adducted. Night use of orthoses to keep the humerus abducted, combined with specific therapy, should prevent loss of the initially obtained range after healing or surgery. In selected cases, maintenance of abduction during the day can be achieved with comfort and minimal functional limitation by a balanced forearm orthosis for ambulatory use (see Fig. 18–15E, F, and G). Whenever the humerus is immobilized in abduction beyond 90 degrees, care must be taken to allow 15 to 30 degrees of humeral forward flexion to prevent any vascular or neurocompressive problems.[44]

Thermal burns of the neck, if adequate positioning is not attended to over an extended postconvalescent period, may produce considerable secondary facial disfigurement, either from soft tissue pull as scar tissue contracts or from actual secondary osseous facial asymmetry if scarring is asymmetrical. The pull of scar tissue on the jaw may also lead to malocclusion. Semiresilient thermoplastic materials are recommended for cervical molds, as is an inflatable lining for the cervical orthosis.[49] These measures ensure maximum comfort by conforming to irregular or sensitive scarred areas, and distributing pressure over wide rather than concentrated areas. Because cervical position is maintained in comfort, it is less likely that the child will discard the orthosis before medical recommendation to discontinue its use. Night use for from six to nine months may be needed.

Congenital Dysplasias

Some congenital malformations of the hand and arm may be amenable to orthotic application either prior to prosthetic management, or in conjunction with surgical procedures. Transverse amelia at the transcarpal or metacarpophalangeal levels can be fitted with a simple volar mold, so that wrist extension and flexion allow grasp of objects between the "palm" and the orthosis (Fig. 18–12). Absence of the central digital rays (bifid hand) may not require an orthotic device since prehension is usually good (Fig. 18–13A and B). Later cosmetic demands may, however, require orthoses. Both the bifid and transverse metacarpophalangeal amelic hand can be fitted with a modified wrist-driven prehension orthosis, which incorporates molded digital replacements rather than the usual finger loops (Fig. 18–13C).[6, 39]

Congenital radial dysplasia, when severe, is a complex problem usually requiring staged surgical procedures with interim use of casts or orthoses. Except for maintenance of position after joint fusion, orthoses are preferable to casts for hygienic reasons and because they are lighter in weight. Also, removal of the devices during short periods of the day encourages tactile exploration, which usually is not possible when casts are applied. If resilient fibrous bands are present in the elbow or forearm areas, or if muscle shorten-

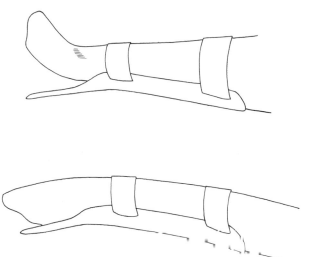

Figure 18–12 An opposition post allows grasp and release by wrist flexion and extension. This device is optimal for transverse terminal deficits near the metacarpophalangeal level.

ing is likely, turnbuckle splints can be applied to maintain or increase extension (Fig. 18–14A and B). If dislocation of the hand on the ulna is occurring, or if excessive pronation or supination is present, dually adjustable orthoses are needed (Fig. 18–14C, D, and E). Congenital ulnar dysplasia may also be treated similarly.

One of the mildest forms of radial dysplasia, which is often overlooked, involves minimal shortening of the radius, and variable hypoplasia of the thumb, often with associated thenar muscle hypoplasia or aplasia. An opponens orthosis may be useful for training substitute patterns of muscle use for opposition. If the thumb hypoplasia is severe, a molded thumb post may be used to stabilize the thumb for prehension. If sensation is present in the deficient thumb, exposure of a portion of the volar area is recommended to allow greater sensory feedback. As the child grows, a more cosmetic prosthetic thumb can be supplied.

Recent Developments

A difficult management problem for adults and children is isolated proximal weakness of the arm with intact distal function. The hand and wrist may have normal strength, and yet cannot be placed in useful positions because of shoulder weakness. The glenohumeral joint may subluxate because of insufficient deltoid strength, predisposing to brachial plexus traction, and possibly additional weakness. Causes of such isolated proximal weakness include poliomyelitis and traction or other trauma to the upper components of the brachial plexus.

In the past, management of this problem has included use of an arm sling to support the glenohumeral joint, or a padded scapular harness or plastic mold to stablize the scapula, or both. These measures are protective, but do not allow full use of the hand and wrist in varied positions; indeed the sling

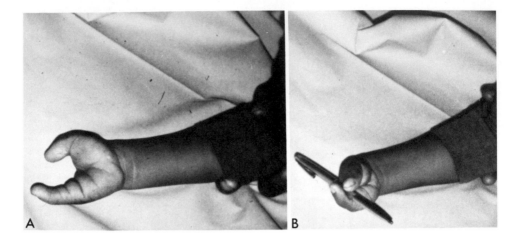

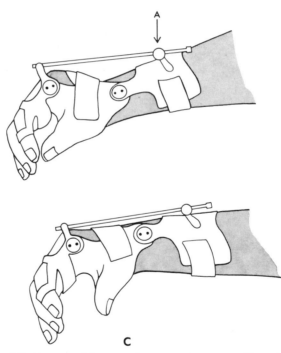

Figure 18–13 *A* and *B*. Absence of the central rays may be compatible with pseudo prehension of the first and fifth digits. *C*. A wrist-driven prehension orthosis may improve cosmesis while allowing sensory feedback from intact digits. It can be used for amputations across the metacarpophalangeal joint area. Plastic finger molds are incorporated into the prehension device. Adjustment at point A controls the amount of wrist extension needed to produce opposed pinch.

tends to discourage hand use. Asymmetry of shoulder girdle musculature, particularly if sling support is not frequently and optimally adjusted throughout the day, predisposes the child to cervicothoracic scoliosis. An optimal device for this problem would support the glenohumeral joint, level the shoulders by

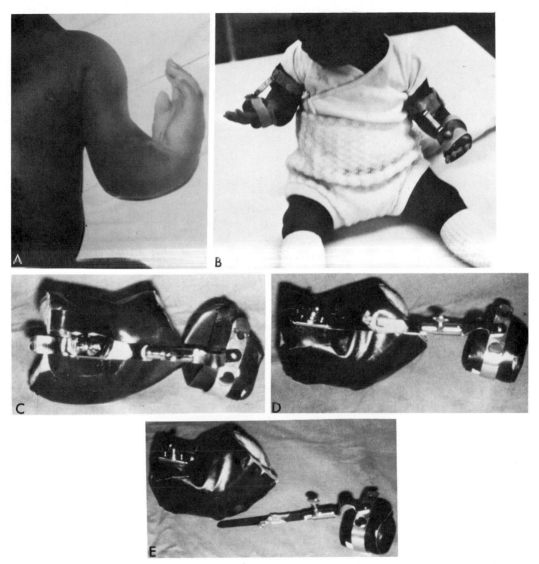

Figure 18–14 *A.* Bilateral radial dysplasia (severe) with radial subluxation of the hand at the distorted wrist articulation, curvature of the ulna, and flexion contracture at the elbow. One forearm is pronated and the other supinated. *B.* The turnbuckle allows positioning of the hand and wrist while elbow extension is increasing. *C.* When the infant is older, the limbs are large enough to accommodate a device, which, in addition to elbow extension, has adjustable pronation and supination. *D.* Limit of adjustability for elbow or forearm stretch. *E.* Detached components to show dual adjustability. (Orthosis by courtesy of Mrs. Sue Polansky, O.T.R.)

eliminating the need to elevate the shoulder or tilt the trunk to assist in supporting the weight of the arm, and allow whatever minimal shoulder function is still present to place the intact hand in a wide range of useful locations.

One suggested device that accommodates these requirements is a balanced forearm orthosis for ambulatory use (Fig. 18–15). When the child is introduced to this orthosis, emphasis is placed on the temporary nature of its use

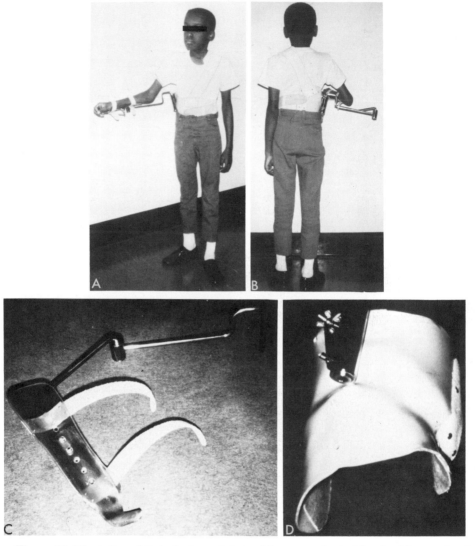

Figure 18–15 *A, B,* and *C.* Ambulatory balanced forearm orthosis. The shoulders are level. The poor shoulder muscles can place the hand in a wide functional range while the glenohumeral joint is supported. *D.* The support for the orthosis is molded at the waist with a flare over the iliac crest to prevent pressure, and relief over the lower rib to prevent pressure on deep inspiration.

(Figure 18–15 continued on opposite page.)

(while awaiting reinnervation, hypertrophy of existing residual shoulder muscles, or tendon transfers with or without surgical shoulder stabilization). If the child understands the function of the device, its mechanical appearance is tolerated and it may become a conversation piece rather than a curiosity. Certainly the lessened shoulder fatigue and increased hand function are apparent to the child during use of the orthosis.

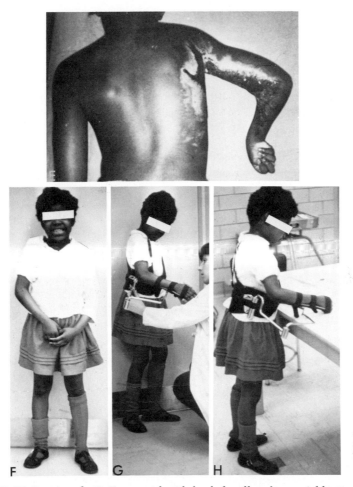

Figure 18–15 *Continued* *E.* Young girl with healed axillary burns. Adduction contracture causes shoulder elevation and spinal curvature when active abduction is attempted. *F.* Habitual posture maintains the same deformity. *G* and *H.* Balanced forearm orthosis levels the shoulders, eliminates the need for compensatory spinal curve, and maintains humeral abduction while allowing active motion. (Orthosis by courtesy of Mrs. Sue Polansky, O.T.R.)

LOWER EXTREMITY

Neuromuscular Imbalance

Flaccidity. In flaccid paralysis of the lower extremity, orthotic goals differ according to the degree of muscle weakness and imbalance. Positioning in standard orthoses is usually satisfactory, although adaptations for cosmesis or accuracy of control may be desirable. If distal weakness and imbalance are of so minimal a degree that only metatarsal or subtalar joint alignment is required, a shoe insert or "heel seat" may suffice (Fig. 18–16).[18] When muscle imbalance requires more forceful or extensive control at the ankle and

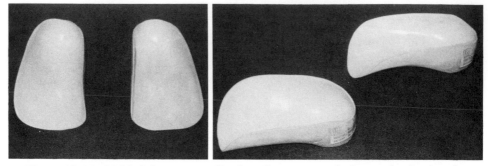

Figure 18–16 Molded shoe insert or "heel seat" can support the longitudinal arch and position the subtalar joint.

subtalar joint, a dual-axis orthosis such as the University of California Biomechanics Laboratory design may be tried.[25] While this device allows adjustable control of the two joints, it is less cosmetic than some alternate devices. An insert orthosis similar to the New York University design can be worn with any pair of shoes, as can a solid molded foot-ankle orthosis (Figs. 18–17 and 18–18).

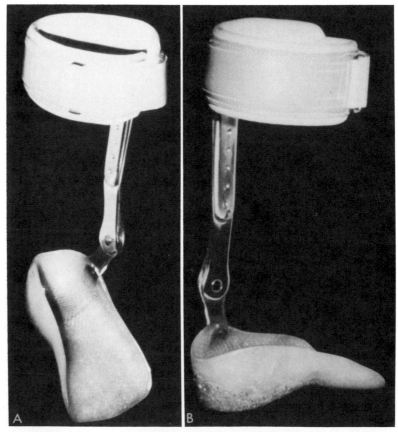

Figure 18–17 Molded insert orthosis, which can be inserted into any shoe.

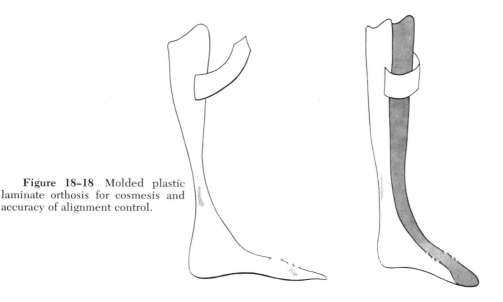

Figure 18–18 Molded plastic laminate orthosis for cosmesis and accuracy of alignment control.

When metal orthotic ankle joints are used to assist or limit motion, those joints with dual (plantar and dorsiflexion) adjustability, such as the Pope or Becker joints, allow trials of assists and limits prior to final positioning, as well as finer control of limits and assists for motion. At present, these joints are available in sizes appropriate to children and teenagers, but are too large for orthoses for toddlers and smaller children.

In addition to dorsiflexion and plantar flexion control, attention must be directed to rotatory alignment in the transverse plane; as long as any amount of ankle motion is allowed, existing tibial torsion must be accommodated. If tibial torsion is not accommodated, then continued use of the orthosis as the child grows will cause changes in anatomical structures to adjust to the malaligned mechanical components.[26, 31] When flaccid weakness exists, it is most often muscle imbalance that produces torsional disturbance. Excessive internal or external tibial torsion may, however, result from prolonged lying or sitting rotational position—with or without muscle weakness, e.g., sitting on the heels or in the tailor or yoga position for long periods. In the presence of weakness, the orthosis is applied for support and alignment and perhaps for dynamic assistance for a muscle group; and tibial torsion is evaluated and accommodated. If positioning alone produces tibial torsion, an orthosis may be applied to supplement a home program of therapy to control or correct the torsion, depending on the age of the infant or child, and on the severity of the torsion (Fig. 18–19).[24]

The orthotic control of flaccid muscle imbalance around the ankle and subtalar joints deserves a long trial before consideration of any surgical procedure that restricts subtalar motion (e.g., extraarticular arthrodesis), since the plasticity of the growing ankle may favor development, instead of an ankle mortise, of a "ball and socket" ankle joint, which has increased rotary motion to compensate for the lost subtalar motion (Fig. 18–20).[19] This type of ankle joint is structurally unstable and may be predisposed to early degenerative arthritis.

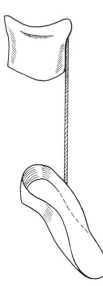

Figure 18–19 A tibial torsion orthosis with plastic proximal tibial and foot molds. A cable twister forms the lateral upright and can be adjusted for direction and strength of corrective rotatory force. A more inclusive foot mold can be used if the orthosis is meant to be used at night without the retaining effect of a shoe.

Control of the flaccid knee in the sagittal plane may be achieved in many ways: (1) by using a conventional above-knee orthosis with a knee lock; (2) fitting a below-knee orthosis with the ankle in slight equinus position to produce an extensor movement at the knee during stance phase (this may, in the child, predispose to genu valgum that develops slowly if the hamstrings are strong, and rapidly if they are weak); (3) using a posteriorly offset knee joint so that at mid-stance the weight bearing line is anterior to the knee center of rotation; (4) using a hydropneumatic knee-ankle orthosis; and (5) incorporating a spring assist to knee extension into the knee joint.[27, 45] Control of the knee in the coronal plane (mediolateral control) may involve using corrective straps or molded plastic components. The corrective straps may cause discomfort when sitting, while the plastic molded knee controls may require change to accommodate growth at a rate that makes the expense excessive.

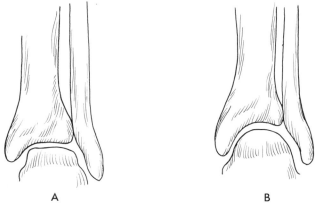

A   B

Figure 18–20 A. The talotibial articulation normally forms a stable ankle mortise. B. The rounded contour of the talotibial joint, which may follow subtalar joint fusion during the growth period, allows mediolateral motion as well as dorsiflexion and plantar flexion.

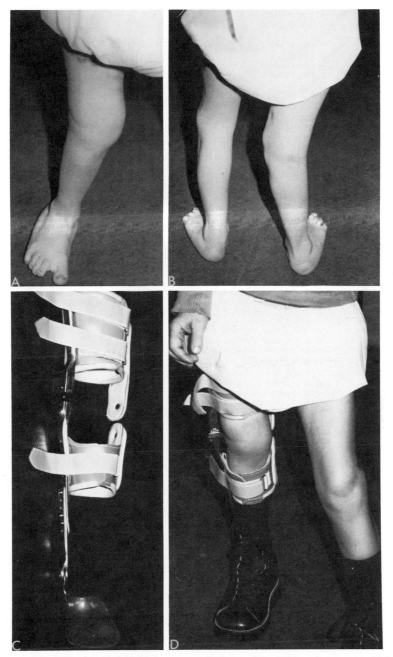

Figure 18–21 *A* and *B*. Marked ligamentous laxity in this child with congenital hip dislocation allows severe pronation of the subtalar joint and genu valgum. *C* and *D*. A molded fiberglass footplate aligns the foot and subtalar joint, while specially contoured thigh and calf cuffs control knee alignment.

The plastic device may also be beyond the range of available orthotic expertise in fabrication. Mediolateral control without straps or plastic, however, can often be achieved with judicious contour and placement of conventional thigh and calf cuffs (Fig. 18–21).

Hip control in all planes of motion can originate from a contoured conventional pelvic band. When a young child needs only rotational control at the hip, cable twisters may be applied (Fig. 18–22). These twisters are usually less effective for older, larger children, and are totally ineffective for heavier teenagers.

Total control of hip, knee, and ankle usually involves extensive and weighty orthoses. Weight can be considerably minimized, however, while using standard components, depending on the height, weight, body habitus, and mobility of the child (Fig. 18–23).

Flaccid paralysis resulting from myelomeningocele deserves special attention to the thoracic or lumbosacral areas for protection of possibly insensitive surgical scars. Avoidance of pressure on surgically covered spinal defects can be achieved by contouring spinal upright bars or pelvic bands away from the defect, preferably with an inner soft leather apron to prevent the metal from contacting the back (Fig. 18–24).

It is well known that myelomeningocele with secondary flaccid paralysis and muscle imbalance frequently is associated with hip dislocation as a tertiary problem, with the tendency to dislocation being directly related to the

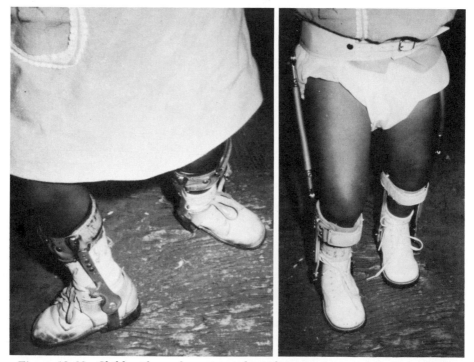

Figure 18–22 Child with myelomeningocele with an asymmetrical L_4–L_5 neurosensory level. Severe external hip rotation is uncontrolled by below-knee orthoses alone. Cable twisters from a pelvic band attached to the orthoses control hip rotation.

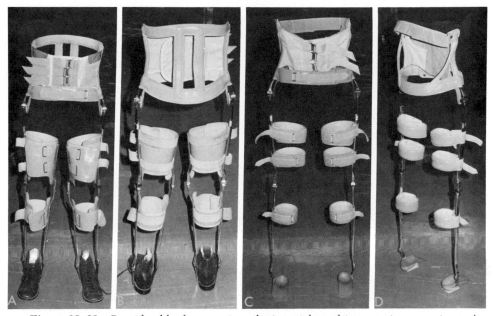

Figure 18–23 Considerable decrease in orthotic weight and increase in cosmesis can be achieved using standard components. *A.* and *B.* Standard ankle, knee, and hip control orthosis. *C* and *D.* Single upright ankle, knee, and hip control orthosis. The footplate can be inserted into any shoe. This orthosis is fully 3 lb *less* in weight than the standard device in *A* and *B.* The ankle joints on both devices have limited dorsiflexion, providing sufficient stability for the devices to stand alone; in addition, the improved standing balance for the patients lessens stress through weight transmission on the upper extermities (cf. Fig. 18–26).

level of neuromuscular loss. Weight gain is sometimes a problem related to decreased mobility, which tends to decrease still further with increasing age and size. Experience, however, with both low and significantly high levels of paralysis from myelomeningocele and other acquired parapareses (above T₈) shows that ambulation may be functional for many childhood years (Figs. 18–25 and 18–26). In view of the prevalence of architectural barriers to wheelchair use, even limited amounts of ambulation can add considerably to functional independence.

Every child with the intelligence to benefit from ambulation training (and intelligence need not be very great for this) should be given the opportunity for ambulation, no matter what the thoracic neuromuscular level. The development of the "Parapodium" standing device for early training should facilitate early trials of therapy for ambulation for patients with thoracic lesions.[34]

Spasticity.   Spasticity with weakness or disordered voluntary control of the legs is frequently an indication for orthoses. For this problem, however, traditionally prescribed devices may not be optimal. One standard orthosis for ankle control in the presence of spastic gastrocnemius-soleus muscles is a below-knee orthosis with a caliper attachment to a shoe, and one of a variety of types of plantar flexion stops. The center of mechanical ankle motion for this device is at the heel, rather than at the anatomical level of motion (Fig. 18–27). This mechanical-anatomical incongruence results in considerable

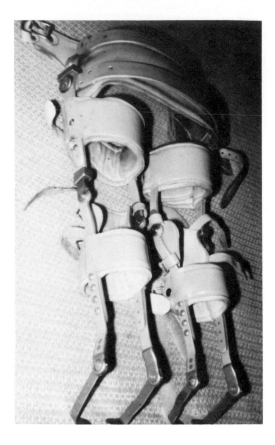

Figure 18–24 Orthosis for myelomeningocele. The soft leather apron of the posterior pelvic area is not in contact with the metal supports so that spinal defects may be protected.

joint and soft tissue stress on dorsiflexion. Another standard device does place the ankle joint correctly, but masks undesirable compensatory tarsometatarsal and intertarsal motions (Fig. 18–28). The orthosis and shoe may be aligned well with regard to one another, but the calcaneus to tibia angle still may be in plantar flexion. The compensation for the continued plantar flexion involves hyperextension at the intertarsal and tarsometatarsal areas, subtalar pronation with medial displacement of the head of the talus, and often abduction of the forefoot.[1] The pronation may be accentuated by a spastic peroneus longus (Fig. 18–29). A shoe with an inner lacing such as the Benesch inner-lace, window-heel brace-boot gives only slightly better control of alignment. Full control of metatarsal, subtalar, and ankle alignment can, however, be achieved by using a shoe insert molded below-knee orthosis (see Fig. 18–18).

The successful use of a molded below-knee orthosis depends on several factors. The patients selected to use this device should be those who have only mild or moderate spasticity of the ankle plantar flexors and evertors (gastrocnemius-soleus and peroneal muscles) *in the standing position.* Often it can be observed that control of spasticity and alignment of the involved joints seem to be good in the lying or sitting positions, but much less satisfactory when the child stands and walks. If spasticity of the gastrocnemius-soleus and peroneus longus is severe during standing, it is often revealing to have the child rotate the pelvis fully toward the weight bearing side, the external pel-

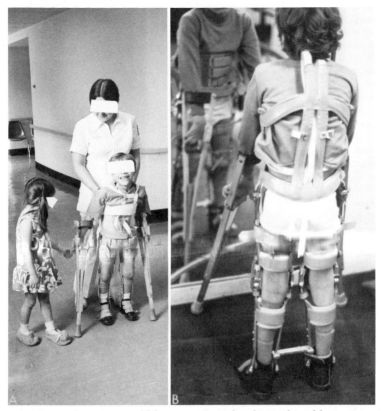

Figure 18–25 *A.* This 10 year old boy as a C_8–T_1 level spinal cord lesion acquired in the neonatal period. He is ambulatory with a drag-to gait for moderate distances in and out of doors. *B.* A spreader bar is placed between the medial uprights because of significant adductor spasticity.

vic and femoral rotation being transmitted to the tibia. Normally this rotation causes elevation of the medial longitudinal arch and allows a good assessment of the correctability of foot alignment in the standing position. If spasticity is so severe that no correction is possible, then the molded orthosis would have to accommodate the standing alignment. The goal for use of the mold is to correct alignment when possible, and to prevent further deformity if correction is not possible. For the child whose spasticity is so severe that standing deformity is not correctable, heel cord lengthening or peroneus longus release or transfer, or both, should be considered.

Accuracy of molding and fitting are essential for comfortable use of the orthosis.[20] This molded orthosis can be fabricated with laminated plastic or fiberglass. Our orthotist currently finds the fiberglass easier to work with. The strength of the device is adequate for exuberant childhood usage, and currently the below-knee molded orthosis is less expensive than standard metal devices.

The combination of hip and knee flexion with ankle plantar flexion is so common that often the hasty examiner fails to observe that ankle dorsiflexion may be found in leg spasticity, with or without previous tendo Achilles

Figure 18–26 *A.* This teenager has flaccid paraplegia below T_6 and ambulates with a swing-through gait. The single-bar above-knee orthoses are attached to molded footplates (fiberglass), which can be inserted into any shoe. The orthoses are worn over the slacks for demonstration only. *B.* Diagonal supports from the pelvic band to the lateral uprights of the trunk support minimize bulk under dresses and blouses, as does the canvas upper cross strap of the trunk support (cf. Fig. 18–23).

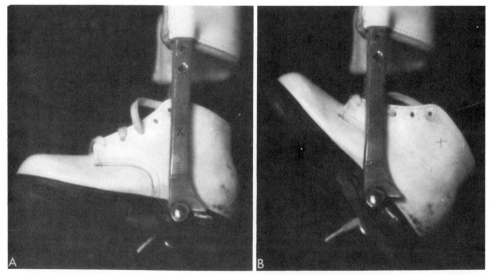

Figure 18–27 *A.* Caliper attachment of a below-knee orthosis. The "x" marks the level of the ankle joint. The center of rotation is at the heel, i.e., there is considerable incongruence of the anatomical and orthotic centers of rotation. *B.* On dorsiflexion the incongruence becomes more apparent. Considerable stress is exerted on soft tissue and joints.

434

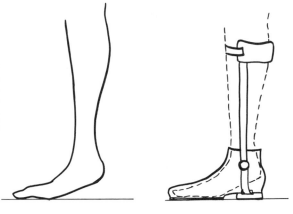

Figure 18–28 The spastic gastrocnemius prevents the heel from touching the floor. This tendency is masked, but not corrected, by a traditional ankle control orthosis. Hyperextension of the intertarsal and tarsometatarsal joints can still occur.

surgery (Fig. 18–30). An equally hasty decision is made to use a plantar flexion stop on an orthosis, without significant resultant change in ambulation posture (Fig. 18–31). For this problem a dorsiflexion stop at the ankle is indicated. In addition to careful observation of the distribution of spasticity in weight bearing and non–weight bearing positions, thorough assessment of gait should prevent this common misprescription. Electromyographic kinesiology during gait can clarify the predominating distribution of muscle activity during different portions of the gait cycle. This record may have physical therapeutic, orthotic, and surgical significance.[7]

Spasticity of the knee muscles most often causes flexion because of excessive hamstring muscle activity, or because of a poorly controlled or weak quadriceps. Standard orthoses can control the knees by locking them in extension. In many children with spasticity associated with cerebral palsy, a surprising amount of quadriceps spasticity may be masked by the greater hamstring activity, but can be seen by electromyographic kinesiology studies. Surgery aimed at removing or decreasing hamstring activity in the hope of discarding orthotic knee controls may, for such a child, produce genu recurvatum during stance because the spastic muscle imbalance has been shifted in favor of the quadriceps. The result may be persistent need for orthotic knee controls to prevent the deformity. This type of problem, which has counterparts at the hip and ankle, may be illuminated preoperatively by appropriate electromyographic studies, and by local anesthetic motor point blocks of muscles thought to be producing the greater problem. These measures also allow a more accurate prediction of the results of surgery and the need for orthoses postoperatively.

If knee flexion contractures exist, they can be accommodated by dial or fan locks, which are adjustable to match the knee extension increase achieved by therapy or surgery. Spasticity of the quadriceps in some paraparetic children (particularly after transverse myelitis) may be strong enough in the standing position to support body weight during ambulation without orthotic knee controls. It is rare, however, to find such a child who does not need alignment control for the ankle or subtalar joint or both.

Spasticity of hip muscles in infants and children can produce secondary

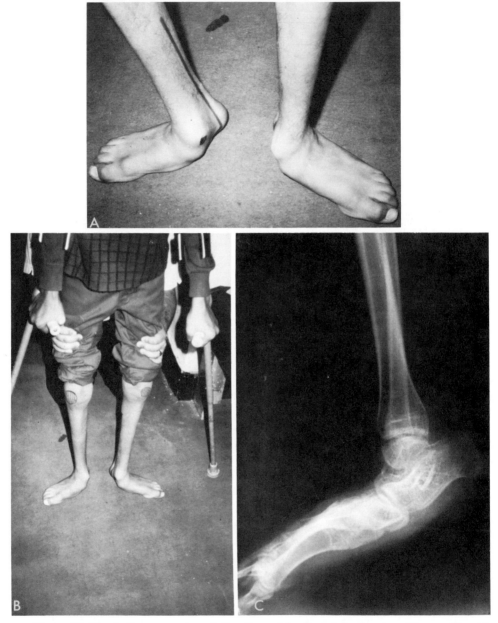

Figure 18–29 *A.* Severe equinus deformity and forefoot abduction in a 12 year old with spastic diplegia. The heelcord is subluxated laterally, and the head of the talus is medially displaced. *B.* The patellae and medial malleoli are marked. *C.* X-ray of left foot shows plantar flexion and medial displacement of the talus. The longitudinal arch is markedly depressed.

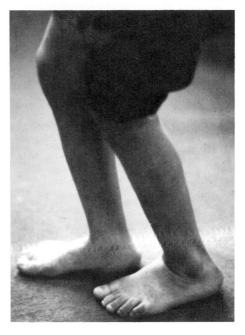

Figure 18–30   The flexed hip and knee of a child with spastic diplegia. Increased tone in the tibialis anterior causes dorsiflexion at the ankle.

Figure 18–31   Excessive ankle dorsiflexion uncontrolled by traditional plantar flexion stop. The knees and hips must flex in order to keep the center of gravity over the feet.

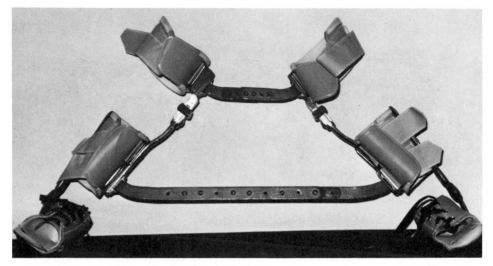

Figure 18–32 Static abduction frame for night use. The cross bars are detachable to allow use of the knee orthoses individually.

proximal femoral deformity and hip subluxation as the child grows.[2] Hip alignment prior to the development of deformity or instability may be achieved by static abduction orthoses for night use, with the hips positioned just beyond the point at which the adductor stretch reflex is elicited. The rationale for this position is the same as that mentioned earlier for the spastic hand. Knee and ankle controls can be incorporated into the same night orthosis (Fig. 18–32). A less restrictive hip abduction orthosis can also be used (Fig. 18–33).[16] For children old enough and able to benefit from ambulation training, an adjustable hip control orthosis is often useful during training (Fig. 18–34).[15] This device encourages more normal alignment of the hips in the coronal (mediolateral) and transverse (rotatory) planes, while allowing free sagittal plane motion (flexion and extension). The improved alignment favors use and strengthening of the relatively less active hip abductors, and secondarily improves alignment at the knees and ankles (Fig. 18–35). This hip control orthosis can be incorporated into a motor development program for reciprocal hip motion in the quadrupedal and kneeling positions as well.

Hip adduction spasticity acquired when the child is older is less likely to produce hip deformity, but still may need control in order to achieve a wide enough base of support for ambulation. Spreader bars between the medial uprights of above-knee orthoses are quite effective as controls of adductor spasticity, and may be static or mobile, allowing reciprocal gait (Figs. 18–36 and 18–37).

Asymmetrical spasticity affecting abdominal and paraspinal muscles can predispose to scoliosis; therefore, control of postural symmetry is an important aim of physical therapy. In addition, careful attention to the size and design of seats and tables at home and particularly in school is essential for optimal spinal alignment. For those spastic children whose scoliosis is progressive, however, and for whom spinal fusion either is not contemplated or

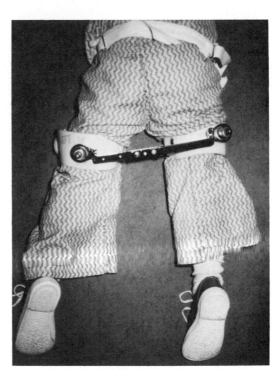

Figure 18-33 Hip abduction orthosis — Ilfeld type.

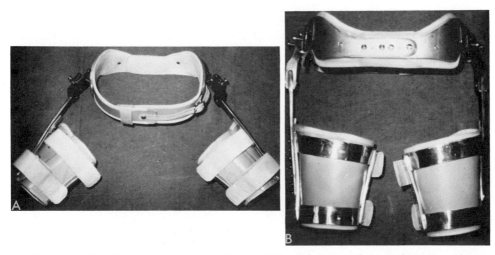

Figure 18-34 Hip control orthosis with adjustable abduction and external rotation. Flexion and extension are unlimited, as is abduction. Adduction is adjustably limited, as is internal rotation. *A.* Anterior view: maximal abduction and external rotation. *B.* Posterior view: minimal abduction and external rotation; the pelvic band is adjustable for growth.

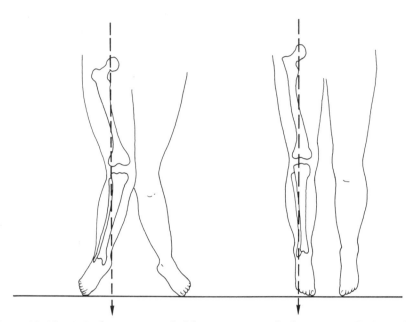

Figure 18–35 *A.* In the presence of adductor spasticity the knees are pulled together. The child may develop a genu valgum tendency as a result of efforts to get the feet apart for an adequate base of support. The weight bearing line is displaced in a direction that increases genu valgum and pes valgus. *B.* By positioning the femora in neutral alignment with a hip control orthosis, the knee and ankle positions can also be controlled.

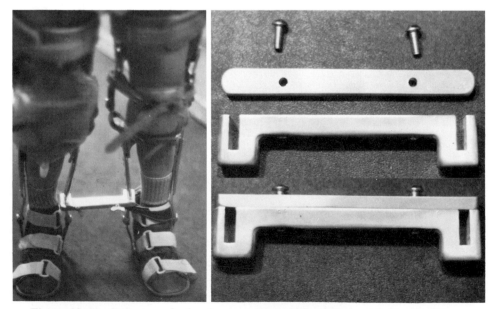

Figure 18–36 Static spreader bar for prevention of hip adduction (cf. Fig. 18–25).

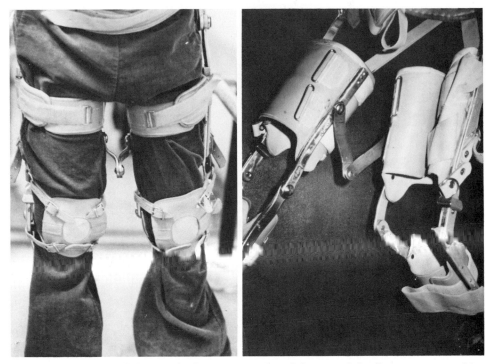

Figure 18–37 Mobile spreader bar maintains hip abduction while allowing reciprocal leg motion.

has not controlled scoliotic progression, a sitting support may be warranted (Fig. 18–38).

Athetosis. Athetosis is rarely an indication for lower extremity orthoses. If an athetoid child has concomitant spasticity and is thought to have ambulation potential, orthoses may be used with goals aimed at control of the spasticity alone. The medieval method of full control braces to lock a child in the sitting position, in addition to being uncomfortable, may also produce overflow of more uncontrolled athetoid movements in the unrestricted upper extremities. One other possible indication for orthotic application is the presence of uncontrollable abrasive motion of one body part on another. Locally, protective orthoses may be applied to the so involved upper or lower extremity. Optimal positioning for control of athetosis may often be achieved by using adapted seats or standing devices.[7]

Joint Inflammation

Inflammation of joints may occur as a result of juvenile rheumatoid arthritis or hemarthrosis secondary to hemophilia. For both disorders, there may be periodic indications for resting orthoses to position the knee in extension and the ankle in neutral position. If ambulatory orthoses are prescribed, ana-

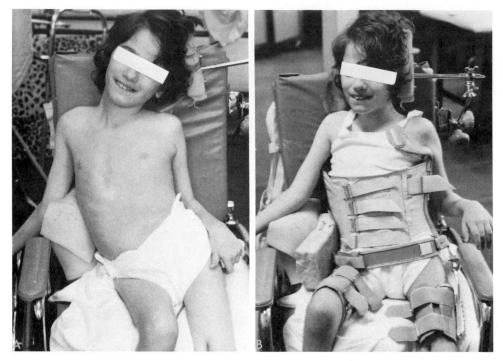

Figure 18–38 *A.* Severe asymmetrical spasticity has caused pelvic obliquity with flexion contractures of the hip and knee on one side, extension of the hip and knee on the other side, and adduction of both hips. The thoracolumbar and cervical spine areas are curved, and the left shoulder is protracted. Sitting is unstable and fatiguing. *B.* A sitting orthosis aims to correct alignment of the spine and of each joint as much as the contractures will allow. Sitting is stable and further joint deformity is prevented.

tomical-mechanical joint congruence is essential. In addition to the ankle and tibial torsion alignment necessities previously described, orthoses for inflammatory disorders should incorporate a polycentric knee joint to accommodate the translational movement of the knee center of rotation during flexion and extension (Fig. 18–39).[14, 43] It is appropriate to mention here that a similar strict obligation to achieve congruent joint fitting when joint motion in the orthosis is allowed exists for children with osteogenesis imperfecta as well as those with arthritis and hemophilia.

Congenital Lesions

Congenital lesions involving the lower extremities may be amenable to orthotic applications for preprosthetic ambulation training, particularly when joint instability or leg length discrepancy are severe (Fig. 18–40). Those congenital lesions involving angular deformity without shortening or joint dysfunction (e.g., pseudarthrosis of the tibia) may be slowly corrected in the neonatal period by using a molded orthosis. The mold can be fabricated from a thermoplastic material that allows easy progressive adjustment, and can be of

(Text continued on page 447)

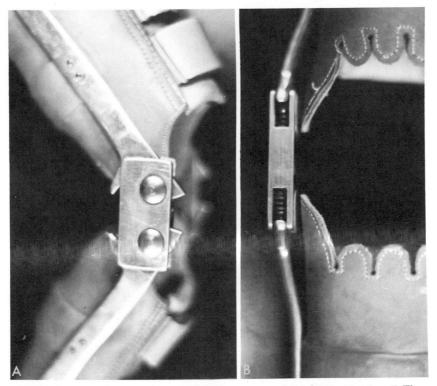

Figure 18–39 *A.* Polycentric knee joint with a spring assist to knee extension. *B.* The spring is visible posteriorly.

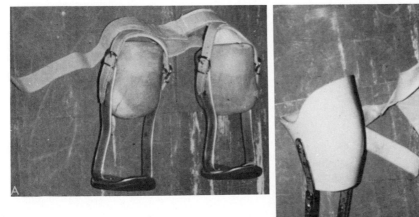

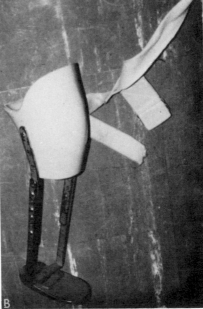

Figure 18–40 *A.* Orthotic uprights and patten for short-term use for a bilateral below-knee amputee. *B.* A similar device may allow some rotary motion at the patten to minimize torque forces transmitted through the limb.

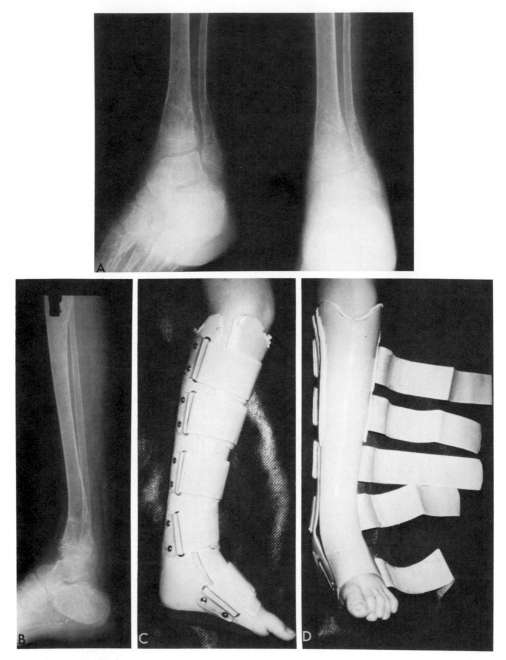

Figure 18–41 *A* and *B*. This 11 year old boy with thalassemia has bone marrow hyperplasia with thinning of the cortex of the long bones resulting in repeated multiple fractures. There was repeated swelling and effusion of the left knee following supracondylar femoral fracture, and delayed union of a distal tibial fracture with residual posterior and lateral angulation. *C* and *D*. A closely molded plastic laminate orthosis was used to support the leg and ankle during ambulation training. The total contact, rather than patellar tendon bearing, orthosis was selected because weight bearing was to be encouraged with support to the angulated fracture site.

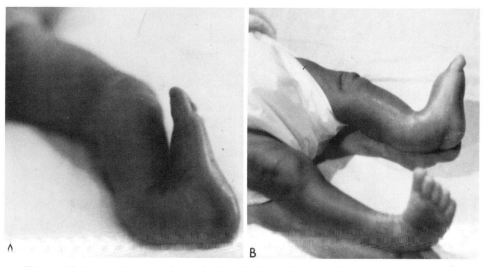

Figure 18–42 *A*. Congenital pseudarthrosis of the tibia and fibula in a neonate. A molded orthosis similar to that in Figure 18–41 and of suitable size can be used to increase extension progressively at the site of deformity. *B*. After six weeks of orthotic use with weekly adjustments, improvement is considerable. Use of a device that is removable for short periods allows skin inspection, stimulates limb use, minimizes disuse atrophy of muscle, and encourages sensory awareness of the limb.

Figure 18–43 Orthosis for a teen-ager with osteogenesis imperfecta. The posterior handle on the spinal attachment initially was used for transfers (the boy was lifted by his parents) and later for guarding during ambulation training. A heel with limited swivel range minimizes transmission of torque through the limbs during ambulation.

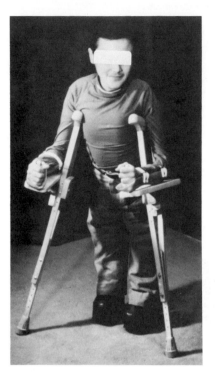

Figure 18–44 This teenager with osteogenesis imperfecta ambulates with standard ankle, knee, and hip orthoses for maximal skeletal support. The height of the shoes was increased at the patient's request. Molded forearm supports for the crutches minimize stress along the curved radius and ulna, and make the discrepant length of the arms relative to overall height less apparent.

Figure 18–45 *A, B*, and *C*. A stationary prone board can be used in therapy or school to allow erect position and use of trunk muscles. This device is adjustable according to the height of the child.

Figure 18–45 continued on opposite page.

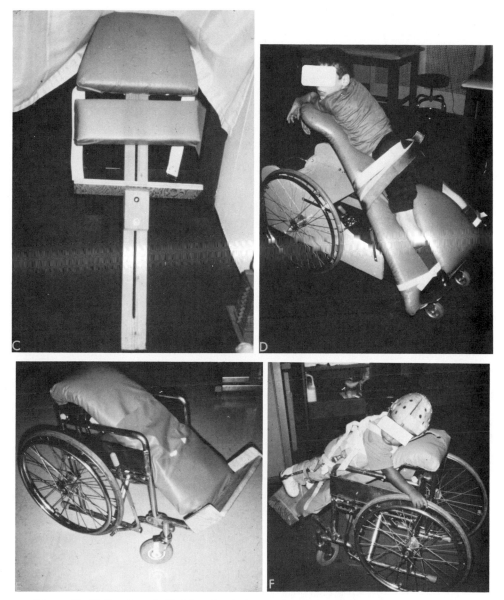

Figure 18–45 *Continued* D. The wheeled prone board serves the same purpose as the static appliance, and in addition maintains hip abduction and allows self-propulsion. *E* and *F*. Similar device for a toddler with thoracic myelomeningocele. Standing balance is just beginning; the erect position can be assumed via adjustable slant for significant portions of the day.

a design similar to devices used for protection of delayed fracture union sites (Figs. 18–41 and 18–42).

One of the hereditary connective tissue disorders that challenges orthotic use is osteogenesis imperfecta. Orthotic devices may be applied early for protection of the brittle bones, as well as for lifting and transferring the child.

Later in the course of the disease, when the tendency to fracture decreases (usually around puberty), orthotic supports for ambulation may be supplied (Fig. 18–43). If surgical intervention has not prevented or corrected bony deformities, the orthoses must accommodate the deformities. Placement of mechanical joints must be as congruent to the anatomical joints as possible. Children with osteogenesis imperfecta have a shortening of stature that is often in direct proportion to the number and severity of previous fractures of the extremities, ribs, and vertebrae. Frequently, the upper extremities appear less affected, so that growth is less impaired. This may cause an uncosmetic disproportion of arm length to total height that is apparent in the standing position. While orthoses cannot fully mask disproportions in stature or angular limb deformities, some compensations are possible (Fig. 18–44). Use of platform crutches may deemphasize arm length. A few inches in height may be added with shoe lifts, depending on the size, balance, and needs of the teenager. Swivel discs, which allow a few degrees of rotary motion, may be incorporated into the heels to minimize transmission of torque through the legs, as well as to facilitate limb advancement.

The general hypomobility imposed by fear of fractures may, as in the case of generalized weakness from other causes, predispose to excessive weight gain. The child with osteogenesis may require a diet regimen for weight loss in order to achieve comfortable orthotic fitting and functional orthotic use. Such dieting may not be feasible or acceptable to the child until surgical stabilization or the start of standing or both provide motivation toward a goal with sufficient immediacy to be meaningful.

Recent Developments

Recent developments in lower extremity orthotics have involved a more systematic approach to patient analysis for orthotic prescription that is very much needed and as yet too infrequently applied.[32] The growing use of plastics for accurate orthotic fit, alignment, and control has benefited adults primarily, as well as some teenagers. As material expense decreases and the orthotist's expertise and the physiatrist's knowledge expand, similar plastic materials and related designs should be used for children as well. The benefits of many other new nonplastic design concepts can, however, even now be incorporated into currently available orthotic components: rubber torsion disc ankle joints to allow more selective control of triplanar ankle and subtalar motion as well as to absorb shock and torque stresses; hydropneumatic knee-ankle control systems to stabilize the weak knee without locking it; and ankle rotation units to accommodate subtalar motion without loss of mediolateral control.[28, 38]

SPINAL ORTHOSES

The single most important area in which orthotic components for children's spinal supports differ radically from those used for adults is in bracing

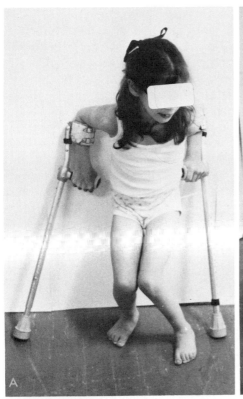

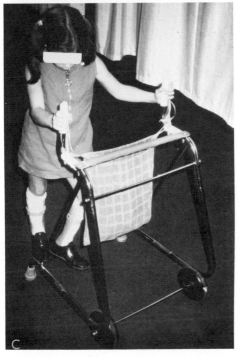

Figure 18–46   Minor adaptations for commercial walking devices encourage external humeral rotation. *A.* For this girl with spastic diplegia, ambulation with crutches facilitates humeral rotation and forearm pronation and generalized increase in flexor tone. *B.* External rotation of the humerus and forearm supination are reflected in less flexor spasticity at other joints; general alignment is considerably improved. *C.* Support of the ankle and subtalar joint further improve alignment. Ambulation is independent in and out of doors.

for scoliosis. The principles of scoliosis orthoses are described in a separate chapter. Two ideas, however, deserve emphasis in this discussion. The current use of a small supracricoid anterior mold rather than a mandibular platform in the Milwaukee orthosis has eliminated complications relating to dental malocclusion from prolonged orthotic use. Secondarily, this small design change has improved orthotic cosmesis and acceptance. In addition, the use of the Milwaukee brace is an example of the need for therapy to accompany orthotic use. The results of either therapy or orthoses alone are poor, and yet the combined corrective effect of both measures is considerable.

A childhood spinal problem that often tends to be overlooked is the scoliosis that accompanies asymmetrical neuromuscular dysfunction in cerebral palsy.[37] Because there is impaired control of voluntary isolated motions, the exercise program integral to successful Milwaukee brace use may not be feasible. The earlier in infancy and childhood the asymmetry is detected, the better the opportunity to prevent fixed deformity by positioning and by encouraging symmetrical postures in all motor activities. The use of a slant board initially for prone or side lying facilitates symmetry as well as encouraging paraspinal muscle use.[40] Similar devices can be used for more erect activities as well (Fig. 18–45). A wide variety of postural control devices for sitting and standing are also available for children.[4, 17, 21]

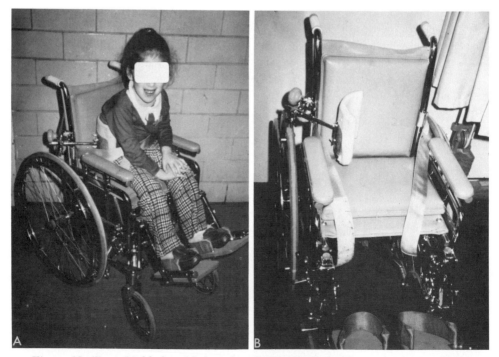

Figure 18–47 *A*. Molded, padded trunk support with adjustable attachment to wheelchair. *B*. For this child with lack of trunk control, the trunk support prevents the torso from collapsing over the arm of the chair.

MISCELLANEOUS AIDS TO REHABILITATION

Pediatric therapy is increasingly being accepted as a subspecialty with a wide area of expertise in terms of training and treatment. Similarly, the use of special assistive devices suitable for positioning, training and function for the activities of infancy and childhood are being developed. The special nature of childhood problems may lead to major or minor adaptations for existing equipment as illustrated in Figures 18–46 and 18–47, or development of totally new devices.[7, 46]

Throughout the course of rehabilitation, the problems encountered in encouraging the child's understanding of and cooperation with the goals of therapy are also encountered in relation to the acceptance of orthotic or assistive devices. It is difficult indeed to convince a child that even a mild temporary current inconvenience or change in appearance may lead to a functional goal at some future time. The effort to foster this understanding is well spent, and its success is usually in direct proportion both to the age of the child and to the eventual degree of acceptance reached. The same proportional relation to successful orthotic use applies to detailed patient assessment, accurate outlining of orthotic goals, and prescription of appropriate devices. This combination of factors can best be applied according to accurate and current knowledge, rather than relying on habits or traditions of prescription.

References

1. Baker, L. D., and Hill, L. M.: Foot alignment in the cerebral palsy patient. J. Bone Joint Surg., 46A:1–15, 1964.
2. Baker, L. D., Dodelin, R., and Bassett, F. H. III: Pathological changes in the hip in cerebral palsy. J. Bone Joint Surg., 44A:1331–1342, 1962.
3. Beard, J. E., and Long, C.: Followup study of usage of externally-powered orthoses. Orthot. Prosthet., 24:2:35–42, 1970.
4. Blockey, N. J.: Aids for crippled children. Dev. Med. Child Neurol., 13:216–227, 1971.
5. Brody, G. S.: Immobilization of tiny hands. Hand, 3:97–100, 1971.
6. Bunnell, S.: The management of the non-functional hand—reconstruction vs. prosthesis. In Selected Articles from Artificial Limbs. Huntington, New York, Robert E. Krieger Publ. Co. Inc., 1970, pp. 177–203.
7. Challenor, Y.: Rehabilitation of children with stroke. In Gold, A. (ed.): Strokes in Children (Monograph). U.S. Gov't. Printing Office (in press).
8. Collins, D. W.: The modular concept in orthotics. In Murdock, G. (ed.): Prosthetic and Orthotic Practice. London, Edward Arnold, Ltd., 1970, pp. 495–498.
9. Dobbs, E. R., and Curreri, P. W.: Burns: Analysis of results of physical therapy in 681 patients. J. Trauma, 12:3:242–248, 1972.
10. Engen, T. J.: A "modification" of a reciprocal wrist extension—finger flexion orthosis. Orthop. Prosth. Appl. J., 14: 1 March 1960.
11. Engen, T. J.: Development of Upper Extremity Orthotics. Orthot. Prosthet., 24:2:1–31, 1970.
12. Flatt, A. E.: The Care of the Rheumatoid Hand. 2nd Ed. St. Louis, C. V. Mosby Co., 1968.
13. Frankel, V. H., and Burnstein, A. H.: Orthopaedic Biomechanics. Philadelphia, Lea & Febiger, 1970.
14. Gardner, H. F., and Clippinger, F. W.: A method for location of prosthetic and orthotic knee joints. Artif. Limbs, 13:2:31–35, 1969.
15. Garrett, A., Lister, M., and Bresnan, G.: New concepts in bracing for cerebral palsy. J. Am. Phys. Ther. Assoc., 46:728–733, 1966.
16. Ilfeld, F. W.: Management of congenital dislocation and dysplasia of the hip by means of a special splint. J. Bone Joint Surg., 39A:99–109, 1957.
17. Information Center on Technical Aids: Technical Aids for Physically Handicapped Children. Bromma, Sweden, 1972.

18. Inman, V. T.: UC-BL dual axis ankle-control system and UC-BL shoe insert. Bull. Prosth. Res. BPR *10–11*:130–145, Spring 1969.
19. Inman, V. T.: The influence of the foot-ankle complex on the proximal skeletal structures. Artif. Limbs, *13*:59–65, 1969.
20. Jebsen, R. H., Simons, B. C., and Corcoran, P. J.: Experimental plastic short leg brace. Arch. Phys. Med. Rehabil., *49*:108–109, 1968.
21. Kamenetz, H. L.: *The Wheelchair Book.* Springfield, Ill., Charles C Thomas, 1969.
22. Kaplan, N.: Effect of splinting on reflex inhibition and sensorimotor stimulation in treatment of spasticity. Arch. Phys. Med. Rehabil., *43*:565–569, 1962.
23. Kay, H. W.: Clinical evaluation of the Engen plastic hand orthosis. Artif. Limbs, *13*:1:13–26, 1969.
24. Kite, H. J.: Torsion of the legs in young children. Clin. Orthop., *16*:152–163, 1960.
25. LeBlanc, M. A.: A clinical evaluation of four lower-limb orthoses. Orthot. Prosthet., *26*:27–47, 1972.
26. Lehneis, H. R.: Orthotics measurement board for tibial torsion and toe-out. Orthop. Prosthet. Appl. J., *19*:211–213, Sept., 1965.
27. Lehneis, H. R.: New developments in lower-limb orthotics through bioengineering. Arch. Phys. Med. Rehabil., *53*:303–310, 1972.
28. Lehneis, H. R.: New developments in lower-limb orthotics through bioengineering. Arch. Phys. Med. Rehabil., *53*:303–310, 1972.
29. Licht, S. (ed.): *Orthotics Etcetera.* Baltimore, Md., Waverly Press, Inc., 1966.
30. Lipskin, R.: Materials in orthotics. Bull. Prosth. Res. BPR *10–15*:107–122, Spring 1971.
31. Lusskin, R.: The influence of errors in bracing upon deformity of the lower extremity. Arch Phys. Med. Rehabil., *47*:520–525, 1966.
32. McCollough, N. C., Fryer, C. M., and Glancy, J.: A new approach to patient analysis for orthotic prescription—Part I: The lower extremity. Artif. Limbs, *14*:2:68–80, 1970.
33. Mortimer, J. T., and Peckham, P. H.: Electrical excitation of the paralyzed muscle in the upper limb. In *Functional Neuromuscular Stimulation.* Washington, D.C., National Academy of Science, 1972, pp. 39–46.
34. Motloch, W.: The Parapodium: An orthotic device for neuromuscular disorders. Artif. Limbs, *15*:2:36–47, 1971.
35. Pahle, J. A., and Raunio, P.: The influence of wrist position on finger deviation in the rheumatoid hand. J. Bone Joint Surg., *51B*:664, 1969.
36. Perry, J., and Hislop, H. J.: *Principles of Lower-Extremity Bracing.* Washington, D.C., American Physical Therapy Association, 1967.
37. Robson, P.: The prevalence of scoliosis in adolescents and young adults with cerebral palsy. Dev. Med. Child Neurol., *10*:447–452, 1968.
38. Rubin, G.: Tibial rotation. Bull. Prosth. Res. BPR *10–15*:95–101, Spring 1971.
39. Rubin, G., Danisi, M., and Lamberty, E.: A wrist-driven hand prosthesis. Interclinic Bull., *12*:6:13–17, March 1973.
40. Scrutton, D.: A ramp-shaped cushion for prone lying. Dev. Med. Child Neurol., *13*:228–230, 1971.
41. Smith, E. M., and Juvinall, R. C.: Theory of "feeder" mechanisms. Am. J. Phys. Med., *12*:3:113–139, 1963.
42. Smith, E. M., and Juvinall, R. C.: Design refinement of the linkage feeder. Arch. Phys. Med. Rehabil., *44*:609–615, 1963.
43. Staros, A.: Joint designs for orthotics and prosthetics. Prosthet. Int., *3*:10:1–19, 1970.
44. Steinbrocker, O.: The painful shoulder. In Hollander, J. L. (ed.): *Arthritis and Allied Conditions.* 7th Ed. Philadelphia, Lea & Febiger, 1966, pp. 1233–1287.
45. Strohm, B. R., Bray, J., and Colachis, S. C., Jr.: The UCLA functional long leg brace: Biomechanics and fabrication. J. Am. Phys. Ther. Assoc., *43*:713, 1963.
46. Sumida, C., Setoguchi, Y., and Shaperman, J.: The C.A.P.P. electric cart: Recent developments. Artif. Limbs, *15*:2:11–15, 1971.
47. Vodovnik, L., Kralj, A., and Jeglic, A.: Some recent orthotic systems using functional electrical stimulation. In *Functional Neuromuscular Stimulation: Report of a Workshop.* Washington, D.C., National Academy of Science, 1972, pp. 21–28.
48. Wickstrom, J.: Birth injuries of the brachial plexus. Clin. Orthop., *23*:187–192, 1962.
49. Yeakel, M. H., and Ousterhout, D. K.: Fabrication technic for inflatable splints. Orthot. Prosthet., *23*:3:119–130, 1969.

Chapter 19

The Burned Child

by *Bard Cosman, M.D.*

Few accidents can match a major burn in the speed with which the unlimited possibilities of youth are shriveled and handicap replaces promise. The surviving burned child may have a variety of functional, cosmetic, and psychiatric disabilities. The more common of these problems are presented here with emphasis placed on the rehabilitation measures that may be undertaken after successful initial resuscitation. Restoration of the burn victim takes many years, and the effort may have to continue even beyond the time of completion of the child's growth. Seen in this light, the burn injury takes its place among the other chronic disabling illnesses of childhood.

INCIDENCE

Each year in the United States an estimated 2,000,000 people are treated for burns and about 7000 to 8000 die of their injuries.[16, 31] Approximately half of all burn victims are below the age of 20. In one study of 1819 patients, 2 per cent were infants under one year of age, 20 per cent of the burns occurred in children five years of age or under, and 36 per cent occurred in children 10 years of age or under.[26] Such exact statistics relative to burn injury are not available for the country at large, although a National Burn Information Exchange has begun collecting and comparing experience in a uniform, standard, computerized form.[12] It is, nevertheless, clear that children form a disproportionately large part of the burn population and their needs require special consideration.

453

CAUSES

The majority of childhood burns occur as a result of the interaction of a poorly supervised child with a poorly supervised environment. There is often an element of real, as well as imagined, guilt in the thoughts of both children and parents following a burn accident. The child who is burned playing with matches he should not have been able to get hold of is a prime example. Most children are burned at home. Hot water scalds are more frequently a cause of serious burns in very young children than they are in older children or in adults. One type of electrical burn—that involving the lips and mouth—is specifically restricted to young children who suck and chew on electrical outlets. Burning is also a significant way in which child abuse is manifested.[37] Many burns are compounded by the flammability of the child's clothing. Nearly 70 per cent of burn victims in one study were exposed to the hazard of clothing ignition; the highest rate of risk was in the 5 to 14 year age group.[2] While laws are slowly beginning to prescribe minimum standards of fabric flammability, much yet remains to be done to establish and enforce reasonable degrees of fabric flame resistance.[18] On the basis of experience in other countries, there is no reason to doubt the efficacy of such measures in reducing the severity of children's burns.[23]

BURN TIME LINE

The burned child's course may be divided conveniently into an initial brief period of burn shock and resuscitation, a subsequent longer interval of wound debridement and coverage, followed by a last period of still longer duration that may be termed skin restoration and reconstruction (Fig. 19–1). The first two to four days are a battle by patient, physician, and staff to meet the acute physiological challenges posed by the burn wound. The next three to six weeks are spent in the disposal of the gutted tissue remnants and the coverage of the nakedness that remains. Merging with this period is that of skin restoration and reconstruction. Depending on the point in time in the child's life when the burn was suffered, this latter period may extend for many years as growth and development impose new requirements for function and appearance.

BURN SHOCK AND RESUSCITATION

The prime physiological alteration of an acute burn consists of a plasma leak through the walls of the damaged capillary network underlying and surrounding the burned skin, and the failure of these vessels to reabsorb this fluid. The wound may be thought of as a pool of plasma sequestered from the circulation—a "third space"—separate from the normal intravascular and extravascular fluid compartments. Circulating plasma volume is decreased and shock ensues; if the plasma volume is not replenished the burn victim may suffer the further consequences of renal shutdown and acute tubular necrosis.

In addition, there are several other results of the burn wound that play a

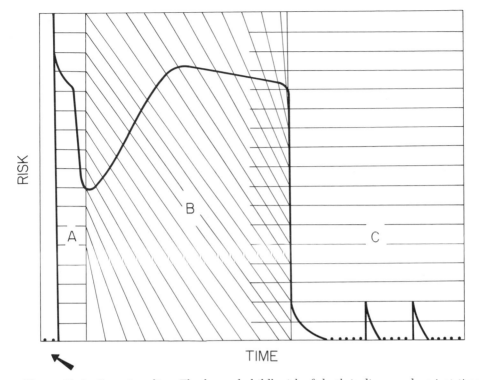

Figure 19–1 Burn time line. The burned child's risk of death is diagramed against time from injury. Risk is highest at the time of burn *(arrow)*. Risk decreases but remains high during the period of burn shock and resuscitation A, which lasts two to four days and is ended with diuresis. Entering the period of wound debridement and coverage B, risk—primarily from sepsis—increases, then slowly decreases and abruptly falls toward normal as coverage is completed. Approximately six weeks are involved in this period, but longer times may be associated with greater burns. The period of skin restoration and reconstruction C merges with that of B. Several years may be involved punctuated by reconstructive operative procedures represented by the brief rises in risk depicted.

part in the development of burn shock. The death of the stratum corneum and the alteration of its lipid content robs the patient of his normal water evaporation barrier, and large water losses may occur. Blood destruction may occur in the burned area. Significant blood loss is rare, but may be seen in burns of more than 50 per cent of full thickness and may in such cases amount to more than 30 per cent of circulating red cells in 40 hours.[40] A last consequence of a burn wound is a hypothetical one—the formation of a "burn toxin" from the heat altered skin proteins. While denigrated as a factor in human burn shock, the lethal effects of burn blister fluid can be demonstrated in some small animal preparations. For practical purposes, however, burn shock is a low circulatory flow state caused by plasma leakage into and out of the burn wound.

Assessment of Burn Severity

The severity of burn shock is directly related to the size of the burn area more than to its depth, since both second and third degree burns have equivalent fluid losses, the former sometimes exceeding the latter. Assessment of burn area is facilitated by use of the "Rule of Nines" (Fig. 19–2). There are differences between children and adults in the percentage constituted by body regions. An aid to remembering these variations is to be found in substituting the "Rule of Fives" for the "Rule of Nines."[26]

Burn depth is of importance in overall prognosis, however. The definitions of first degree, second degree, and third degree burns are well known, but their clinical appearance may vary widely (Fig. 19–3). The first degree burn erythema is of no practical significance. Second degree burns may be "superficial" or "deep." The former can heal from epithelial remnants; the latter have so few remnants left that for practical purposes they should be considered with the third degree injuries, which by definition lack residual epithelial remnants. Blistering is typical of the superficial second degree inju-

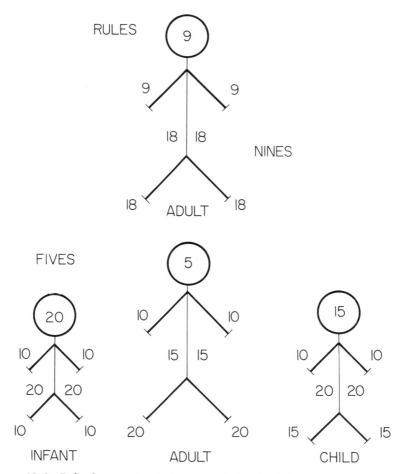

Figure 19–2 Rules for assessing body areas. The "Rule of Nines" is most widely employed for adults and is a remarkably accurate expression of actual body areas. As seen in the "Rule of Fives," however, in infants under the age of five the head constitutes a markedly greater percentage of body area and the lower extremities a correspondingly lower percentage than in the adult. From 5 to 15 the child exhibits a similar but lesser degree of head and limb difference from the adult.

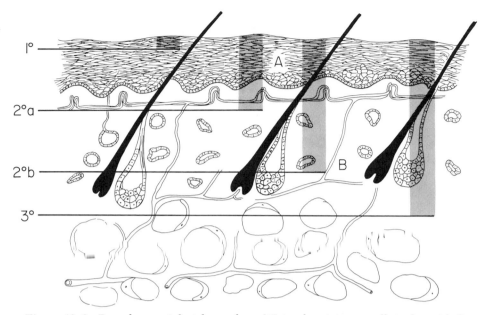

Figure 19-3 Burn degree. A first degree burn (1°) involves injury to cells in the epithelium *A* as represented by the stippled area. Erythema of the dermal capillaries just beneath the epithelium is the only clinical response. A superficial second degree burn (2°a) kills the epithelium and some dermis *B* at a level that leaves many accessory skin structures (sweat glands, sebaceous glands, and hair follicles) behind from which regeneration of the epithelium can take place. A deep second degree burn (2°b) leaves only a few such remnants. Clinically such a burn may behave like a third degree burn (3°), which kills tissue extending into the subcutaneous fat *C*, leaves no epithelial sources behind, and if a wide area is involved, requires a skin graft for recoverage.

ry, may or may not be present in deep second degree burns, and is usually absent in the third degree injury. Because of the depth of injury the third degree burn is often hypesthetic initially, but this distinction is hard to make in a terrified child immediately after injury.

Although in a young adult burns of less than 30 per cent of body area are unlikely to require intravenous fluid administration and consequently are not considered "serious," the greater metabolic lability of children reduces this figure to 10 per cent. Failure to appreciate this narrower tolerance may lead to fatal neglect of a child's burn, and even smaller burns may be "serious" if vital functional areas like the lungs, the perioral region, the hands, or the perineal region are involved.

Fluid Therapy

Many different fluids and fluid regimens have been advocated. A review of the most commonly used formulas is given in Table 19-1. Suffice it to say that experience in the use of any one approach can permit the achievement of a successful resuscitation rate of more than 90 per cent; burn shock in most patients is successfully treated. The most common difficulty in the resuscitation

TABLE 19–1 FLUID THERAPY FORMULA STATEMENTS

Evans Formula
  A. Colloid = 1 ml (blood or plasma) × body weight (kg) × per cent body area burned
  B. Electrolyte = 1 ml (N NaCl) × body weight (kg) × per cent body area burned
  C. Water = 2000 ml 5 per cent dextrose in water
  For first 24 hours: ½ of A and of B plus all of C for second 24 hours

---

Brooke Army Formula
  A. Colloid = 0.5 ml (blood, plasma, or dextran) × body weight (kg) × per cent body area burned
  B. Electrolyte = 1.5 ml (Ringer's lactate) × body weight (kg) × per cent body area burned
  C. Water = 2000 ml 5 per cent dextrose in water
  For first 24 hours: ½ of A and of B plus all of C for second 24 hours

---

Brigham Burn Budget
  A. Colloid (plasma, plasmanate, albumin, or dextran) = 10 per cent body weight (½ first 12 hours, ¼ second 12 hours, ¼ second day)
  B. Renal needs (½ N NaCl) = 2400 ml per 48 hr, i.e., 1200 ml per 24 hr
  C. Lung losses (5 per cent dextrose in water) = 3000 to 10,000 ml per 48 hr, i.e., 1500 to 5000 ml per 24 hr; to include 1000 ml 10 per cent mannitol per 24 hr
  D. Skin losses (Ringer's lactate) = 2000 to 8000 ml per 48 hr, i.e., 1000 to 4000 ml per 24 hr

---

of children is inappropriate fluid replacement. Overestimation or underestimation of burn areas consequent on failure to appreciate the true body area percentages is one factor in this; another is failure to consider the child's special free water needs (Table 19–2).[3] In most cases, however, burn shock is avoided or reversed, and within two to four days the damaged capillaries recover their ability to hold and to resorb plasma. Diuresis begins and with it the next period of burn care.

Surgical Therapy

Three major interventions may be necessary in this period. The first is the performance of a tracheostomy. If facial burns and neck edema are present and if evidence of pulmonary involvement becomes clear, tracheostomy may become vital. On the other hand, the tracheostomy wound is a significant complication to deal with, and the fluid losses via the tracheostomized bronchial tree are much greater than through normal respiration. To these facts must be added the greater difficulty of performing tracheostomy in a child than in an adult. Temporary assurance of an airway can be achieved by passage of an endotracheal tube, and this may obviate the need to suffer the long-term consequences of a tracheostomy.

Development of edema beneath a constricting circumferential burn may

TABLE 19–2 WATER REQUIREMENTS IN CHILDREN

Given as 5 per cent dextrose in water	
0–1 year	80 ml/kg
1–5 year	60 ml/kg
5–8 year	40 ml/kg
Thereafter approximately 2000 ml per day	

lead to the necessity for releasing incisions — another major surgical procedure of this period. Observation of extremity pulses and temperature may
reveal significant vascular occlusion in an incipient state. Incision down to
and through the deep fascia will permit tissue expansion and release of pressure on the blood vessels. Similar chest wall incisions may be needed to ease
the work of rib expansion beneath a rigid burn eschar shell.

The third early intervention may be the performance of lid adhesions to
prevent corneal exposure in periorbital and eyelid burns. The development of
protective scleral lenses has relieved the emergency nature of this procedure.[6]

WOUND DEBRIDEMENT AND COVERAGE

The resuscitated child now faces the challenge of life without a complete
skin. When more than 60 per cent of the body area has been burned fewer
than half the patients will survive even with the best of present supportive
measures. Even with smaller serious burns the mortality rate may be as high
as 20 to 30 per cent.[30] These deaths and, indeed, the ultimate handicaps of the
surviving burned child are a direct consequence of skin loss.

The longer the wound surface lacks a skin cover, the longer the risk of in-
vasive sepsis lasts. Fluid loss through the uncovered wound persists and contributes to the hypermetabolic state of the burn patient and the enormous
stress of that state. The longer the wound is open the greater the volume of
scar tissue that will be laid down within it and the greater the extent of its contraction, with subsequent deformation and functional limitation. For these
reasons speedy skin coverage is the fundamental goal of this period. The
speed of skin coverage is determined by the time needed to remove the burn-
damaged tissues, the time necessary to prepare the viable surface to receive a
skin graft, the availability of a skin donor site, and the method of application of
the skin graft itself.

Debridement and Burn Eschar Separation

The necrotic mass of heat denatured skin and subcutaneous tissue proteins — the eschar — remains bound to the viable surface beneath it by collagen

fibers. At the interface of viable and dead tissue, leukocytes break down releasing enzymes (cathepsins) that aid in severing these bonds. The body is, however, slow to achieve the dissolution of these collagen attachments; three or more weeks are usually required, and during this time bacteria are proliferating in and beneath the eschar and periodically invading the body beneath. Attempt to excise the eschar has always seemed reasonable to the surgical mind.[38] Unfortunately, the loss of possible viable tissue to the surgeon's enthusiasm and, above all, the increased mortality rate for massive early eschar excisions have thus far defeated this approach.

The amelioration of sepsis by local use of substances capable of penetrating the eschar and battling the bacteria where they live has been much more successful and is the proudest recent accomplishment in burn therapy. Antiseptics like 0.5 per cent silver nitrate and antibiotics like mafenide (Sulfamylon) and gentamycin have proved effective.[3] Nothing is achieved without a price, however. Counted in the cost are occasional complications such as acid-base and electrolyte disturbances and the rarer problems of methemoglobinemia and agranulocytosis.[29, 39, 42] Another more frequent cost is the delay in eschar separation with an increase in the period prior to the possibility of skin coverage. The proper timing in the application of these substances to achieve sepsis control but prevent retardation of eschar separation has yet to be worked out. In the offing now, however, are certain enzymes (sutilains) whose application to the eschar may achieve a rapid separation even while local antibiotics are preventing sepsis.

Wound Surface Preparation

Hydrotherapy. At the present time the most significant measures in the preparation of the burn wound surface for the reception of a skin graft involve surgery, hydrotherapy, and dressing changes. Surgical debridement sets the stage for the development of granulation tissue but must be supplemented by frequent cleansing and further nontraumatic debridement. This is best achieved by hydrotherapy, which macerates and helps separate small necrotic remnants, mechanically reduces bacterial surface contamination, and stimulates capillary ingrowth. Accordingly, most present regimens of burn wound care prescribe daily whirlpool baths. The bath is also used to facilitate dressing changes and to remove the spent antibiotic ointments and reapply them.

The nature of the hydrotherapy solution has been debated often. The granulating wound surface is a capillary bed capable of considerable absorption. Complications in the use of hexachlorophene solutions have been reported although this substance in dilute form has been used for many years without known ill effects. Absolute sterility of the solution and equipment has been advocated, but this is simply not practical; use of a disposable plastic liner for the tank can, however, achieve the cleanliness and ease of preparation that is desirable. Use of isotonic solution is also to be preferred so that it will neither dehydrate the granulating surface nor leach body electrolytes from it.[13] A physiological bath solution can be prepared by adding 9.6 kg of salt (0.85 gm sodium chloride per liter) and 34 gm of potassium chloride (0.03

gm per liter) to 300 gallons of water.[19] Temperatures of 35 to 37° C are well tolerated for periods of 15 to 30 minutes. Agitation of the water in the bath is useful in debridement, but jet stream debridement seems unreasonably painful and frightening, especially for the child patient. Because temperature lability in the burn patient is a real problem, to avoid chilling, the room temperature should be close to bath temperature. Drying under heat lamps and using the lamps for added warmth during dressing applications will make the burned child much more comfortable. Ultraviolet light as a drying and bacteriostatic agent has less merit in burn therapy now than in the past since the local antibiotics are more effective in the latter problem and the hazards of further burning can be avoided.

Temporary Skin Graft Application. In addition to these mechanical means of surface preparation, another technique of great value is that of homograft skin therapy.[15, 35] The wound is dressed with homograft skin, thus exploiting the little understood phenomenon whereby such grafting is associated with a decrease in bacteria count beneath and around the grafted surface. Stripping off the homografts two to four days later leaves the surface cleaner and seemingly better able to accept a definitive autogenous skin graft. The method depends on the availability of homograft skin. The technique works in similar fashion but less well when freeze dried skin or even heterograft skin is used. Further, the plan presupposes the availability of autografts to replace the homografts or heterograft skin. If these are not replaced early, the rejection syndrome will ensue in about three weeks and the wound surface will not be suitable for quick autografting. While some heterografts like porcine skin may not evoke a classic rejection phenomenon, the partial incorporation of graft fibers at the wound surface will similarly impede final skin coverage.

Skin Application

Fresh autogenous split thickness skin graft is the definitive coverage for the burn wound. However, the graft donor site is in essence another second degree burn. Coverage of a broad burn area with a sheet of skin would impose a new burn of magnitude comparable to that being covered—even assuming that such an ample donor site were available. Accordingly, a number of donor site conserving techniques are used. Most routine is the cutting of the graft skin into "postage stamp" sized pieces, placing them several millimeters apart from each other, and relying on the epithelial outgrowth from each to effect a junction with its neighbors. Striking increases in the effective area coverage based on the same principle can be achieved by use of a "meshed" graft in which multiple perforations permit stretching like an accordian.[27] Use of thin skin grafts also permits rapid healing of the donor site, and recropping of the same area is possible in three to four weeks under favorable circumstances. Use of autogenous epithelial cell explant cultures poured onto the wound surface can achieve coverage, but in the absence of dermis the wound contraction is excessive and the stability of the "skin" so formed is very poor.

Skin Availability and Substitutes

While autogenous skin is the ultimate replacement for skin loss, in the absence of donor areas the benefits of skin coverage can be achieved temporarily for the seriously ill child by use of homologous and heterologous skin.[15, 32] The use of fresh cadaver homografts has had extensive trial. Such grafts appear to "take," making capillary connections like an autograft, only to undergo infarction when the homograft rejection response ensues. The most available heterograft — porcine skin — does not seem to establish such vascular connections, but otherwise is similar in behavior.[36] Freeze dried homograft and heterograft skin can also be effective in reducing surface bacterial counts and fluid losses through the wound surface. The use of collagen fiber membrane impregnated with the water-holding lipid of the stratum corneum is also being explored.[17] Much interest has been shown in developing "artificial skins" using various plastics in several physical configurations, but none of these membranes has performed as favorably as the natural substances mentioned.[5, 21] Despite all, the burned child must ultimately be given his own skin again if he is to live.

THE CHILD BENEATH THE BURN

In a very literal sense, as diuresis begins on the second to fourth day, the swollen edematous child begins to resume his preburn appearance. With this return, pain becomes a prominent complaint. There is no escaping the fact that a major burn is one of the most severe traumas that the body can survive and one of the most painful it can endure. Adding to the reality of pain is the child's increasing perception of the extent of his injury. Apprehensions expressed and repressed add to the emotional toll.[24] Unavoidably, too, the necessary treatment measures involving isolation and around-the-clock interruptions tend to depersonalize and confuse the patient. Helpless, the child usually begins to show regressive behavioral tendencies. Whining and screaming are distressing to those who must care for him. The tendency of the staff is to cover their own pain in contact with the "flayed" child by treating him as an object rather than as a person. Their own anger at having to give pain may lead them to a kind of insulated withdrawal from the patient.

The child's agonies, mental and physical, impinge on his preburn personality, which may have had many weaknesses. There is much suggestive evidence that many severely burned children prior to their injury had shown self-destructive tendencies.[4, 25] Previous accidents are common in their histories. Loss of a parent or grandparent is said to be a more frequent finding than can be accounted for by chance alone.[33] Involved in this stressful period is the guilt felt by most children — their assessment of injury and pain as proof of their own intrinsic evil. Imagined guilt of this sort is combined with the real guilt involved in many instances.

Psychosomatic Stress Manifestations

Bizarre reactions such as amnesia, catatonia, opisthotonus, seizures, and hypertensive episodes have been noted. While occasionally clearly a part of a specific encephalopathy, these responses may be uncorrelated with ongoing fever or sepsis, and may occur without apparent physical cause. Recovery from these manifestations seems the rule. Stress ulcerations, especially in the duodenum and stomach (Curling's ulcers) are the most important of these stress induced reactions. Bleeding or perforation may require operation through burned surfaces. Only occasional children suffering such complications are salvaged.[1] An antiulcer regimen must be a part of the routine management of the burn patient, adult or child.

Psychiatric Help for the Burned Child

In the face of a child's pain, apprehension, depression, aggression, and withdrawal there is temptation for the physician to resort to psychiatric polypharmacy. Pain medication, sleep medication, this for depression, and that for agitation add up, in the child, to further hallucinations and greater depersonalization. Firm reassurance based on real knowledge of the measures to be used in dressing, operation, and management is more helpful in calming the child. The surgical and nursing staff in most intimate contact with the child are the best sources of this reassurance and direction. Maintenance of the same staff throughout the treatment of a burn is very desirable. Many children view a change in staff as indicative of their own unworthiness, and their own misdeeds as having driven away the people who were to help. The job of reassurance cannot be delegated to the child psychiatrist, important as his long-term contribution may be in the occasional seriously disturbed child. The psychiatrist cannot know the precise time the child will have a tub bath or a dressing change, and it is against these everyday facts that the child tests the truthfulness of the adults who are treating him. Awareness of the psychiatric implications of the burn injury and its care are more important than the official unraveling of the complex mechanisms involved in an individual patient.

TEMPERING CARE TO THE SHORN LAMB

The establishment of a routine of treatment does much to reduce the child's anxiety. It gives a frame for the day's pain. Wound management must be arranged to minimize this necessary pain; the simplest dressing technique involving the least manipulation is best, and the most practical means is to center dressing changes and local antibiotic applications on the time of hydrotherapy. Dressing removal is easier in the water. Dressing change can then be made a part of physical therapy. This last is of great value in convincing the child of continued physical ability. Range of motion exercises are best carried out in the water, at least at first, although when at all possible, ambulation should be insisted upon as soon as resuscitation is completed.

Operation Timing

Operative intervention should be adjusted to the needs of the child instead of being bound by administrative constraints. Where a burn unit is equipped to operate when it wishes this is of less note than in a general or special surgical service where burn cases must follow the regular elective cases and where operating days are rigidly set. In such instances multiple debridements and skin grafts become one long series of anxious anticipations for the child. They also are prolonged periods of semistarvation, since the child is allowed nothing to eat in anticipation of the forthcoming anesthesia. Scheduling the operation at night has merit in this situation.[7] The child can eat during the day and is put to sleep at the time of usual sleep; when he wakens the next morning the routine of care is resumed.

Especially in children, major debridement is difficult to accomplish during hydrotherapy, and persistent attempts lead to fears that make ongoing care very difficult. Carrying out such procedures under anesthesia or hypnoanalgesia is better. The availability of new intravenous agents has made this a practical as well as a kind approach. Proper operative timing is vital in order to permit such frequent intervention.

Decubitus Ulcers and Ectopic Calcification

Untended, the pain racked burned child will do little turning or moving. Decubiti of the occiput, sacrum, and heels are to be seen in such neglected children. These are avoidable complications. The circle electric bed is an ad-

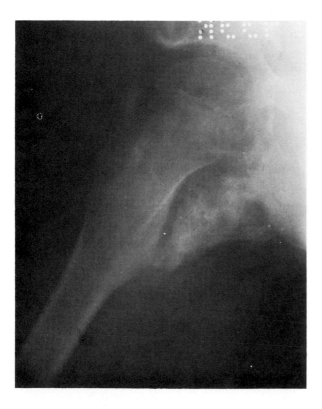

Figure 19–4 Ectopic calcification. Periarticular right hip calcification in an eight year old girl with 40 per cent burn no part of which involved the hip. Immobilization, however, had been required for more than four months prior to successful skin coverage and mobilization.

vance over the Striker frame for turning the massively injured. Air mattresses are of less use. Water beds make performance of nursing care difficult and are themselves bulky and too conducive to the child's adoption of a fetal position prone to flexion contracture. The use of an "air cushion" hover-craft type of patient suspension has been advocated, but many difficulties in temperature control as well as other technical details remain to be worked out. Continuous immersion in a silicone bath is another experimental approach with no present clinical application.[41]

The motionless septic child undergoes significant bone decalcification. Some degree of decalcification is an inevitable consequence of bed rest alone. In a small number of children generalized decalcification is accompanied by local periarticular calcification (Fig. 19–4).[9, 14] Periosteal irritation from an adjacent area of sepsis is responsible in some instances, but in others the location does not suggest this mechanism and the cause remains unclear. Prolonged immobilization is the only common denominator. Fortunately, this complication seems to be decreasing in frequency as more rapid mobilization, hydrotherapy, and physical therapy become routine parts of burn patient care.

Skin Grafting and the Routine of Wound Care

When the burn wound debridement is completed and a granulating surface is ready, autogenous skin grafting can begin. The routine of hydrotherapy and dressing change is altered following each grafting procedure to allow the immobility that is required for graft "take." Skeletal traction is of special use in allowing the posterior surfaces of extremities to be immobilized to avoid shearing off of grafts and yet permit open wound inspection (Fig. 19–5). In

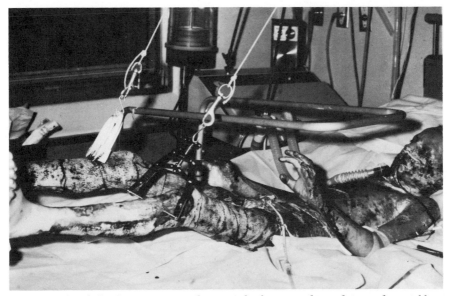

Figure 19–5 Skeletal traction. Use of traction facilitates grafting of circumferential burns of the lower extremities in a critically ill 14 year old boy.

general, however, the most accessible parts should be grafted first to allow the least lengthy interruption of routine and assure the greatest chance of successful use of autogenous skin. Resumption of hydrotherapy is often possible within the first week after a graft and should be resumed as rapidly as possible.

Burn Contractures

As survival begins to seem assured, the desire to prevent burn scar contractures becomes a valid one. The term "contracture" should be understood clearly. All body wounds close in part by contraction and the formation of the special reparative tissue known as scar. The rate of contraction for a wound of a given shape is a species specific constant. The exact mechanism of the motion is unknown, but the driving force seems to reside in the tissue beneath the wound margins rather than that located centrally or at a distance. Contraction and scar formation continue as long as the wound remains open. A successful skin graft is able to reduce contraction and scar formation in the wound it covers to an extent related to the thickness of the graft; the more nearly full thickness it is, the more nearly complete the reduction.

When wound contraction produces deformity of surrounding parts or when it limits function, it is said that a "contracture" is present (Fig. 19–6). As may be seen, then, "contraction" is normal and "contracture" is pejorative. "Contracture bands" may form, especially on flexion surfaces. This use of the term refers to an elevated bowstring-like band of scar tissue (Fig. 19–7). Such a band is believed to form as a result of microtrauma to the scar tissue along the line of flexion leading to microhematomas, organization, and the laying down of more scar tissue. The term "contracture" also is used as a description of the stiffness of a joint mechanism consequent on the tightness and shortening of unused periarticular ligaments.

Prevention of all deforming contractures in burn healing is an impossible goal. However, prophylactic amelioration is desirable. Joints can be splinted in positions of function or of extension so that even disused ligaments will be kept at functional length.[10] Such splinting can be external or internal. Attention to active and passive motions of such joints may, where feasible, keep mobility without the need for splinting.[20] Such measures are directed against only one of the "contractures" mentioned. The others are not affected favorably, and, indeed, motion may tend to stimulate contracture band formation. Skin surface coverage is the means whereby wound contraction itself can be reduced. In certain areas it may be feasible to use an "outlay" technique for grafting—applying an excess of skin so that even though some contraction occurs the remaining skin surface will be ample and loose. Skeletal traction has been advocated as a force to counter wound contraction. The wound shortening usually becomes only too apparent, however, when traction is finally stopped. Pressure on the grafted skin surface has been enthusiastically advocated as an effective means of contracture prevention or alleviation.[11] When technically feasible the method has some value but, again, is difficult to apply in the patient with a major burn in that early stage when the patient's life itself is in the balance. The consensus is clear, however, that the most efficacious step in ameliorating contracture is the achievement of complete skin coverage and the resumption of normal activities that that permits.

It must also be apparent that survival, not contracture avoidance, is the major goal of early burn therapy. It is often impossible to afford the skin necessary to cover functional areas like the hand with the complete thick skin graft that would minimize their contraction, but revision of contractures is possible for the living patient. Present survival must, of course, temper thoughts of future reconstruction. Even when autogenous skin is abundant, however, it is often wise to leave one or two prime donor sites like the buttocks unused if it is already clear that good quality skin will be needed for revision of important areas of contracture like the hand and neck.

SKIN RESTORATION AND RECONSTRUCTION

With the completion of skin coverage the burn patient is no longer at risk of death. Rapidly the skin grafts coalesce and the resumption of activity becomes a real possibility. Enthusiasm for mobilization must not proceed too far too fast; the patient with lower extremity grafts must not be permitted to have his limbs dependent immediately or microhemorrhages beneath the grafts will lead to local skin breakdown. The healing skin must be accustomed to the full hydrostatic pressure of the erect position over a period of about two weeks with increasing periods of dependency and with protection and support by elastic bandages.

Late Healing Areas

Tiny unhealed areas often remain scattered over the body. Not large enough to require another skin graft, they nevertheless heal with exasperating slowness. The possibility exists that specific deficiencies consequent on long dietary impoverishment may be present to explain this phenomenon.[22] Small areas of breakdown occur with minor trauma, especially in the thin-skinned scar area at which adjacent grafts join. Patching these areas with small pieces of petrolatum gauze rather than using large dressings is the best approach. Daily washes, air drying for one half to one hour, and occasional touching of central granulations with silver nitrate will serve to heal these residual openings, albeit more slowly than would at first be believed.

Itching

At this time in the healing of the burned child, itching becomes a serious problem. Small factitial ulcers may be opened by the child's scratching. There is no easy remedy for this symptom. Antipruritic medication is usually ineffective or too sedative. The size of the areas involved precludes use of superficial x-ray therapy. Application of corticoid creams has not helped much. Lubricat-

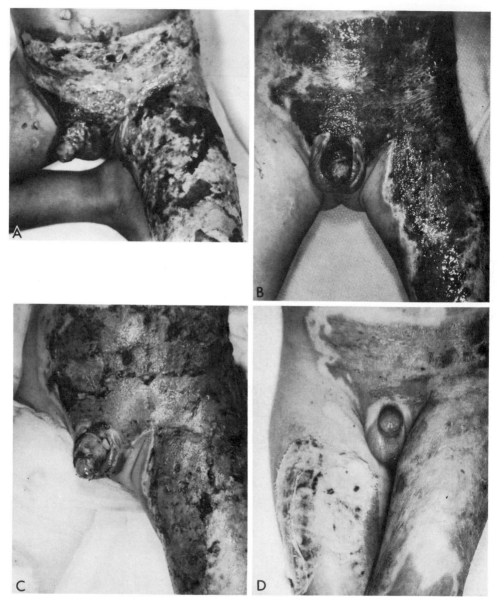

Figure 19–6 Natural history of a burn wound. A five year old boy set his pajamas on fire while playing with matches. *A.* The wound on the tenth day just prior to surgical debridement. *B.* The appearance of the granulating wound at 21 days. *C.* Large "stamp" grafts of autogenous skin have been applied. *D.* They had coalesced and appeared well healed at 30 days.

Figure 19–6 continued on opposite page.

ing the skin with cold cream, lanolin, A and D ointment, or cocoa butter is beneficial but not completely so. When specific areas can be outlined the local application of ice can be very effective although relief is of only short duration. The discomfort is greatest at night at bedtime when the child's attention is undistracted by surrounding day events. Cutting the fingernails short, use of light gloves, and actual restraint may be necessary, especially in the young

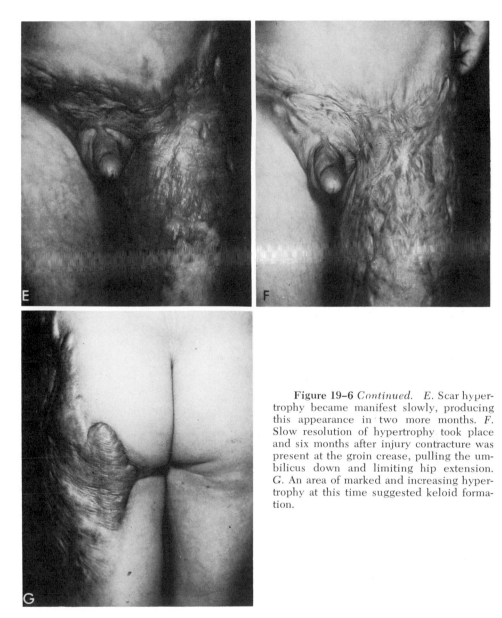

Figure 19-6 *Continued. E.* Scar hypertrophy became manifest slowly, producing this appearance in two more months. *F.* Slow resolution of hypertrophy took place and six months after injury contracture was present at the groin crease, pulling the umbilicus down and limiting hip extension. *G.* An area of marked and increasing hypertrophy at this time suggested keloid formation.

child. Duration of this itching period is variable and depends greatly on the character of the child's scar. If it is hypertrophic, the itching will continue a long time; if more normal, itching may last only a month or two.

Scar Hypertrophy

In preparing parents for the home care of their child mention must be made of scar hypertrophy. Especially in children, some degree of hypertrophy

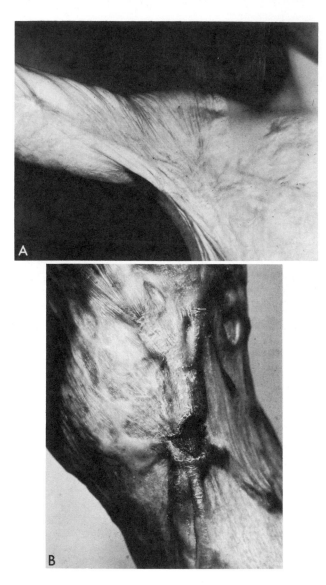

Figure 19–7 Contracture. *A.* Axillary contracture band one year following burn and skin grafting. *B.* Popliteal contracture with chronic ulceration along line of stress associated with repeated healing and subsequent breakdown.

is normal. Hypertrophy occurs weeks to months after initial healing, and areas once flat become raised, red, and angry in appearance (see Fig. 19–6). If unprepared, the family will be shocked by this change. After several months, resolution occurs if keloid formation does not. It may take one to two years, however, for this scar resolution to be completed in children, as opposed to a faster course in adults. Although some scar resolution is desirable prior to reconstruction, certain residua such as neck contracture deserve quick action. Emphasis on early reconstruction for such visible deformities is desirable and enables the parents and the child to accept the changes in appearance that have occurred.

LEAVING THE HOSPITAL AND FAMILY REENTRY

Leaving the hospital is a major hurdle for the burned child. The reestablishment of family discipline is a vital point upon which parents should be advised. Some children exploit the family's real or imagined guilt and emphasize their own disability to escape from normal discipline at home. The catering to their desires that they experienced while ill is a pattern they reestablish at home. On the simplest level, we have seen a number of such children who have become massively obese in the first year after their recovery; on a different level it has been observed that usual sibling rivalries are too often decided by reference to the past injury rather than upon present merit. Parents must be encouraged to reintegrate the burned child into the family with love, firmness, and justice.

Success in the reestablishment of the family is usually associated with successful adjustment in the broader social sense. The child soon comes into contact with others whose reaction to his appearance is not sympathetic. Family and physician support is necessary at this point to avoid a withdrawal in defeat. Reconstruction may in fact be able to alleviate some of these deformities and should be emphasized. On the other hand, some residua will be permanent, and unrealistic expectations cannot be encouraged. A balance of emphasis on acceptance and eventual improvement must be struck. Fortunately, despite the many psychopathological manifestations noted during the acute burn stress, the majority of studies have indicated generally satisfactory late adjustment for most burned children. The occasional child with permanent obvious psychiatric difficulties related to the burn stands out in memory, but is in fact unusual. What hidden residua exist have yet to be studied.

PHYSIOLOGICAL BURN RESIDUA

Neither scar tissue nor skin grafts are true replacements for normal tissue. Both are simplified substitutes. Scarred skin lacks the elastic fibers of normal skin and tends to break down more easily (see Fig. 19–7). Accessory skin structures are few in both scar and graft, so skin surface healing is slower. Such repeated breakdowns and slow rehealings may set the stage 20 to 30 years later for a Marjolin's ulcer, a squamous cell carcinoma of a burn scar. There is also a deficiency of sebum and a decreased ability to sweat concomitant with this deficiency of accessory skin organs. The grafted areas tend to be dry and flaky because of sebum lack. The sweating deficiency may be so severe as to limit heat tolerance under stress, but ordinarily is compensated for by "excessive" sweating from remaining areas of normal skin.[43] Skin nerve endings are also in short supply in scar and skin graft, and fine two-point discrimination is not usually present although protective sensation is to be expected. In addition, scar and skin grafts do not grow at the same rate as the rest of the child. This lag becomes clinically apparent during the childhood growth spurts. Intermittent skin additions are usually necessary to permit appropriate growth of hands, chest, abdomen, and breasts. Parents must be made aware of this need for skin supplements. The requirement for repeated restorative and reconstructive surgery must be foreseen if such surgery is to be accomplished appropriately.

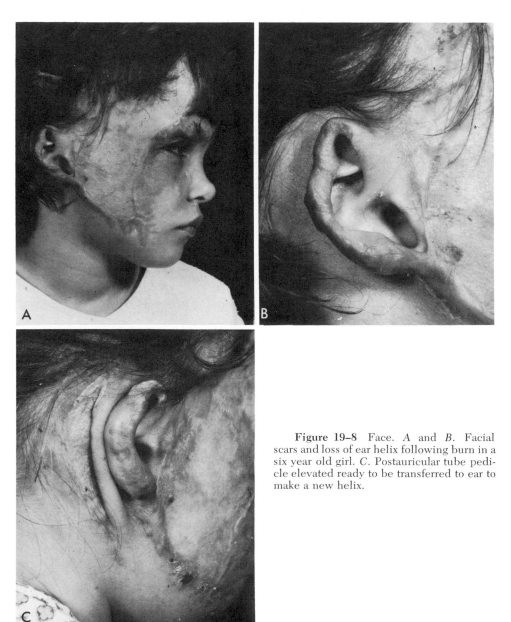

Figure 19-8 Face. *A* and *B*. Facial scars and loss of ear helix following burn in a six year old girl. *C*. Postauricular tube pedicle elevated ready to be transferred to ear to make a new helix.

Figure 19-8 continued on opposite page.

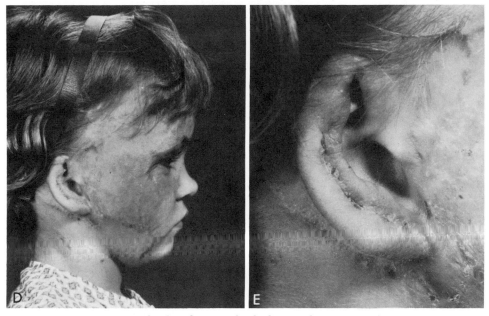

Figure 19–8 *Continued.* *D* and *E*. Result of tube transfer, excision of scar, and upward advancement of neck and cheek skin.

Specific Area Coverage and Reconstructive Considerations

FACE

Facial deformity constitutes one of the most severe of postburn disabilities. Hair follicles and skin rete pegs are deeply situated on the face, and many burns heal spontaneously that would elsewhere be third degree; unfortunately, however, this is less true of the child than of the adult. Where feasible, necessary skin grafts should be made to correspond to facial "cosmetic units," i.e., junction lines should simulate natural folds and expression lines. Donor sites should be chosen for similarity to facial skin. All of this, however, cannot always be accomplished in the skin coverage period, and residual defects are many.

These deficits can be thought of as involving line, contour, color, and substance in varying combinations (Fig. 19–8). Scar lines may give the appearance of a fixed grimace. The scars may be elevated, depressed, red, or pigmented. Grafted areas may be hyperpigmented, depigmented, wrinkled, or depressed. Areas of secondary healing are often hypopigmented. And there may be actual substance loss as in an ear crumpled by postburn chondritis, or a missing nostril. Substance losses may be masked by the contracture that is present, as in the ectropion of the lip or eyelid whose release requires a surprising amount of skin.

Line and contour defects may be ameliorated by scar revision and alteration of scar direction by Z-plasty one to two years postburn when the most acute scar activity has resolved. Small areas of color difference can be excised and closed directly. Broad areas can be dermabraded in the hope of lightening the abraded surface. The result, however, is unpredictable and often uneven. Overgrafting by abrading the surface and using a cosmetically more closely allied body area as the new skin source is also an unpredictable method.[34] For substance defects of the nose and nostrils, composite grafts are useful. Classic techniques of tube pedicle and flap transfer may be involved in the repair of large losses. There is no magic, however, in any of these measures, and by no

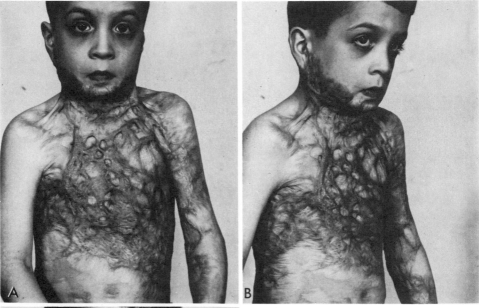

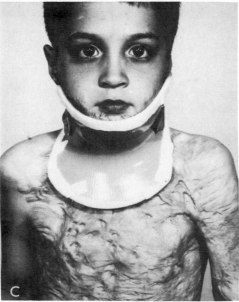

Figure 19-9   Neck. *A* and *B*. Neck contracture following flame burn. *C*. Fiberglass moulded splint worn for six months following release of contracture and split thickness skin graft.

Figure 19-9 continued on opposite page.

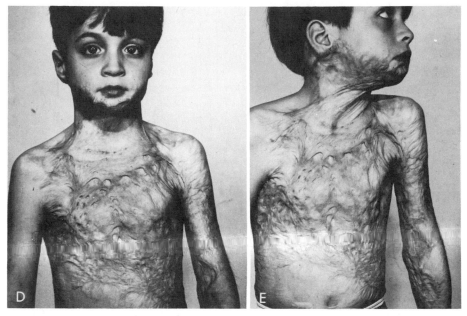

Figure 19–9 *Continued.* *D* and *E*. Satisfactory results 11 months after neck release and five months after cessation of splinting.

stretch of technique or imagination can the preburn appearance of the child be completely recaptured.

NECK

The anterior surface of the neck is a frequent site of burn scar contracture. As the flames rise from a child's clothing the extended neck and chin are burned. It is rare that the large sheets of skin required to resurface this area are available during the skin coverage phase of care. Positioning the neck in extension and preventing motion with laterally placed sandbags has been tried in an effort to avoid contracture. The difficulty in maintaining the position and its impracticality so far as the more important goal of maintaining the patient's motion is concerned fault this approach. Use of neck braces and splints is also difficult, since shoulders and chest are usually also burned and the seating of such apparatus is thus impossible. Some of the earliest American plastic surgical procedures were done for the burn scar neck contractures of children. Tissue from a distance was thought to be required, since skin grafts contracted so badly on the anterior neck surface. At present, however, it has been clearly demonstrated that six months of precise splinting, pressure, and partial immobilization will overcome this tendency and make very satisfactory results possible (Fig. 19–9).[42] The use of ketamine for initial anesthesia for the division of the neck contracture has markedly eased the hazards of revisional surgery in the patient whose neck initially cannot be extended and in whom one wishes to avoid a tracheostomy.

HAND

For many years it has been recommended that burned hands be immobilized in the position of function, grafted quickly, and maintained in the position of function until healing was complete. However, in the presence of a major burn, quick grafting for the hands is more often a preaching than a practice. The tendency of the burned hand to flatten its palmar arch and to go into hyperextension at the metacarpal phalangeal joints and flexion at the proximal and distal interphalangeal joints was very difficult to control (Fig. 19–10). This was especially true in the child's hand in which small size precluded effective positional dressing and splinting. In addition, most hand burns are on the dorsal surface and involve loss of the thin skin of the phalangeal area. Acute flexion at the proximal interphalangeal joint tended to bare the central tendon

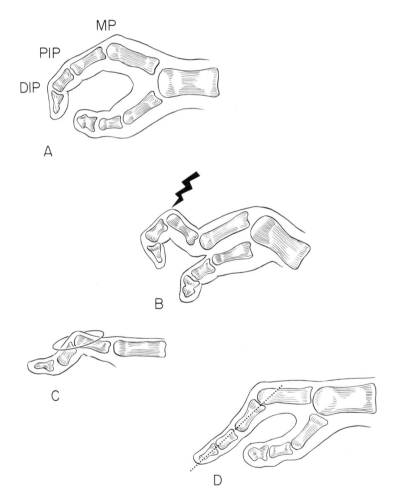

Figure 19–10 Hand attitudes in burn injury. *A.* Position of function with flexion at metacarpophalangeal joint (MP), proximal interphalangeal joint (PIP), and distal interphalangeal joint (DIP). *B.* Contracture of dorsal burns tends to reverse the dorsal as well as transverse arch of the palm and leads to acute flexion of the DIP and PIP joints together with hyperextension of the MP joints. The PIP joints are especially at risk, and tendon exposure and loss *(jagged line)* is frequent. Loss of central slip permits inferior subluxation of the lateral bands, which become fixed below the axis of the PIP joint, producing acute flexion there and extension at the DIP joint. This constitutes the boutonnière deformity, *C. D.* Fixation of the finger in flexion at the MP joint and extension at the DIP and PIP joints by means of K wire (position of "intrinsic plus").

slip. Subsequent loss of the tendon produced a boutonnière deformity.[28] In addition, stiffness in the shortened periarticular ligaments of the clawed fingers was especially hard to overcome.

More recently better results have been obtained by initial K-wire fixation of fingers in the "intrinsic plus" position shown in Figure 19–10. This attitude relaxes the tension on the central tendon slip. The position also favors adequate skin grafts for the dorsum of the hand itself, since, bent at the wrist, the dorsal skin is then stretched out to the limit of its need. Ligaments in the finger joints are kept at more appropriate stretch. Epiphyses are not damaged by judicious use of small-gauge wires. Reconstruction of burned hands involves appropriately placed Z-plasties, resurfacing skin grafts, tendon transfers, and joint capsulectomies. Arthrodesis involving destruction of epiphyseal plates is to be avoided in the growing child although a useful measure in the adult. Severe deformities may benefit by "simplification," that is, amputation to allow greater function for the remaining fingers. Such simplification can be effectively combined with phalangization of adjacent metacarpals when digits have been lost. Volar surface burns pose a special problem in the growing child. Repeated additions of skin are needed to keep up with size increase and to avoid functional limitation. A child with a palmar burn at age two will probably require another skin graft every two to four years until the age of 10 or 12.

FEET

The basic reconstructive need after a foot burn is the provision of a stable skin surface capable of sustaining weight on the plantar surface and shoe wear on the dorsal surface. A subsidiary consideration is the elimination of projecting surfaces that make shoe fitting difficult. Most foot burns involve the dorsal surface. Contracture usually leads to hyperextension at the metatarsal phalangeal joint. Revision involves internal fixation of the toes straight out and an ample dorsal skin graft. Single persistently deformed toes may be arthrodesed or excised without significant loss. Plantar surface burns are fortunately rare. In the heel area spontaneous healing usually produces a better result than grafting. In general, hairless skin grafts are better on the plantar surface than fat hairy flaps. Most scars on the plantar surface show secondary hyperkeratosis, which may require the attention of a podiatrist on a routine basis.

AXILLA AND GROIN

Burns of these areas are difficult to deal with primarily and usually come to secondary release and skin graft reconstruction. However, adjacent skin usually stretches sufficiently so that, unlike palmar surfaces, these areas usually do not need repeated skin grafts after one effective release. Unrelieved axillary contractures can significantly affect the growth and development of the shoulder. Like the neck, both these areas are susceptible to early postburn release; one to two years need not pass before they are reconstructed.

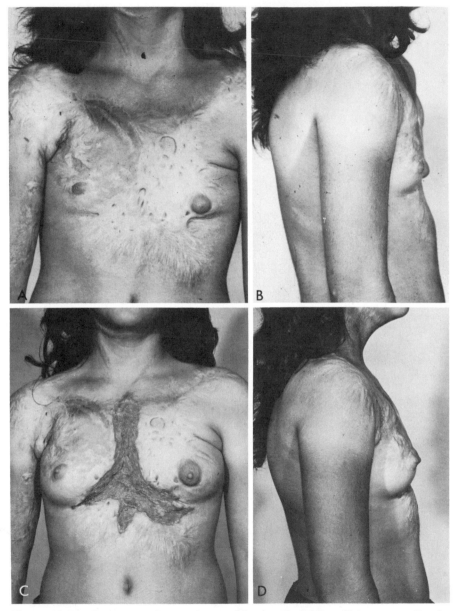

Figure 19–11   Breast. *A* and *B*. A 12 year old girl with skin insufficiency retarding breast development. Child was burned at age three. Note transverse chest contracture, forward positioning of shoulders, and restricted breast development. *C* and *D*. Three weeks following autogenous split thickness skin graft that simultaneously allowed chest to expand transversely and breasts to rise superiorly.

BREASTS

If nipples remain after a chest burn, breast development will most likely occur. Even when nipples appear to be gone, deposition of fat in the breast area is usually seen. In either case, however, it is common to find that at age 12 to 13 semilunar skin grafts beneath each breast and an elliptical graft vertically in the midline are required to allow breast development to proceed (Fig. 19–11). Even in the event of failure of breast development, the use of a prosthetic augmentation is feasible. This too may require skin graft release of the chest in order to be most efficacious.

SUMMARY

Burns are among the leading causes of accidental death in childhood and the survivors have major disturbances of appearance and function. The steps involved in resuscitation, in wound debridement and coverage, and in skin restoration and reconstruction have been considered. The rehabilitation of the burned child begins as part of the program for eschar removal and continues as survival becomes assured. The physiological residua of the burn wound, the contractures produced, and the cosmetic impairment involved may require intermittent intervention throughout the period of the child's growth and development. The child surviving a major burn is, therefore, in many ways like the sufferer from a chronic illness. Amelioration is possible, but complete cure does not occur: the best of reconstructive efforts cannot erase the marks of this severest of traumas.

References

1. Abramson, D. J.: Curling's ulcer in childhood: Review of the literature and report of 5 cases. Surgery, 55:321, 1964.
2. Barancik, J. I., and Shapiro, M. A.: Pittsburgh Burn Study, Pittsburgh and Allegheny County, Pennsylvania. Pittsburgh, Pa., University of Pittsburgh Press, 1972.
3. Bruck, H. M., Asch, M. J., and Pruitt, B. A., Jr.: Burns in children: A 10 year experience with 412 patients. J. Trauma, 10:658, 1970.
4. Candle, P. R. K., and Potter, J.: Characteristics of burned children and the after effects of the injury. Br. J. Plast. Surg., 23:63, 1970.
5. Chardock, W. M., Martin, M. M., Jewett, T. C., and Boyer, B. E.: Synthetic substitutes for skin: Clinical experience with their use in the treatment of burns. Plast. Reconstr. Surg., 30:554, 1962.
6. Constable, J. D., and Caroll, J. M.: Emergency treatment of the exposed cornea in thermal burns. Plast. Reconstr. Surg., 46:309, 1970.
7. Cosman, B., and Crikelair, G. F.: Night operations on burned patients. Plast. Reconstr. Surg., 43:266, 1969.
8. Cronin, T. D.: The use of a molded splint to prevent contracture after split skin grafting on the neck. Plast. Reconstr. Surg., 27:7, 1961.
9. Evans, E. B., and Smith, J. R.: Bone and joint change following burns. J. Bone Joint Surg., 41-A:785, 1959.
10. Evans, E. B., Larson, D. L., and Yates, S.: Preservation and restoration of joint function in patients with severe burns. J.A.M.A., 204:91, 1968.
11. Evans, E. B., Larson, D. L., Abston, S., and Willis, B.: Prevention and correction of deformity after severe burns. Surg. Clin. North Am., 50:1361, 1970.
12. Feller, I., and Crane, K. H.: National burn information exchange. Surg. Clin. North Am., 50:1425, 1970.
13. Gotshall, R. A.: Sodium depletion related to hydrotherapy for burn injury. J.A.M.A., 203:984, 1968.

14. Griswald, M. L., Jr.: Extra-articular bone formation as a burn complication. Plast. Reconstr. Surg., *32*:544, 1963.
15. Haynes, B. W., Jr.: Skin homografts – a life saving measure in severely burned children. J. Trauma, *3*:217, 1963.
16. Iskrant, A. P.: Statistics and epidemiology of burns. Bull. N. Y. Acad. Med., *43*:636, 1967.
17. Jelenko, C., III: Purification of the water-holding lipid of intact skin and burn eschar. Am. Surg., *35*:864, 1969.
18. Joliet, P. V.: Conference on burns and flame-retardant fabrics. Bull. N. Y. Acad. Med., *43*:615, 1967.
19. Koepke, G. H.: The role of physical medicine in the treatment of burns. Surg. Clin. North Am., *50*:1385, 1970.
20. Koepke, G. H., and Feller, I.: Physical measures for the prevention and treatment of deformities following burns. J.A.M.A., *199*:127, 1967.
21. Lamke, L-O: The influence of different "skin grafts" on the evaporative water loss from burns. Scand. J. Plast. Reconstr. Surg., *5*:82, 1971.
22. Larson, D. L., Maxwell, R., Abston, S., and Dobrkovsky, M.: Zinc deficiency in burned children. Plast. Reconstr. Surg., *46*:13, 1970.
23. Lehr, E. L.: Controlling the clothing fire problem: Observation on the British experience. Bull. N. Y. Acad. Med., *43*:711, 1967.
24. Lewis, S. R., Goolishian, J. A., Wolf, C. W., Lynch, J. B., and Blocker, T. G., Jr.: Psychological studies in burn patients. Plast. Reconstr. Surg., *31*:323, 1963.
25. Loy, R. T., and Cope, O.: Emotional problems of burned children. N. Engl. J. Med., *264*:1121, 1961.
26. Lynch, J. B.: Thermal burns. *In* Grabb, W. C., and Smith, J. W. (eds.): *Plastic Surgery*. Boston, Little, Brown, and Co., 1968.
27. MacMillan, B. G.: The use of mesh grafting in treating burns. Surg. Clin. North Am., *50*:1347, 1970.
28. Maisels, D. O.: The middle slip or boutonnière deformity in burned hands. Brit. J. Plast. Surg., *18*:117, 1965.
29. Maurer, L. H., Andrews, P., Rueckert, F., and McIntyre, O. R.: Lymphocyte transformation observed in Sulfamylon agranulocytosis. Plast. Reconstr. Surg., *46*:458, 1970.
30. Nelson, G. D., and Paletta, F. X.: Burns in children. Surg. Gynecol. Obstet., *128*:518, 1969.
31. Ollstein, R. N., Symonds, F. C., and Crikelair, G. F.: Current concepts of burn injury. N. Y. State J. Med., *68*:1278, 1968.
32. Rappaport, I., Pepino, A. T., and Dietrick, W.: Early use of xenografts as biologic dressing in burn trauma. Am. J. Surg., *120*:144, 1970.
33. Seligman, R., Carroll, S., and MacMillan, B. G.: Emotional responses of burned children in a pediatric intensive care unit. Psychiatry in Medicine, *3*:59, 1972.
34. Serafini, G.: Treatment of burn scars of the face by dermabrasion and skin grafts. Br. J. Plast. Surg., *15*:308, 1962.
35. Shuck, J. M.: Use of homografts in burn therapy. Surg. Clin. North Am., *50*:1325, 1970.
36. Song, I. C., Bromberg, B. E., Malm, M. P., and Koehnlein, E.: Heterografts as biological dressings for large skin wounds. Surgery, *59*:576, 1966.
37. Stone, N. H., Rinaldo, L., Humphrey, C. R., and Brown, R. H.: Child abuse by burning. Surg. Clin. North Am., *50*:1419, 1970.
38. Switzer, W. E., Jones, J. W., and Moncrief, J. A.: Evaluation of early excision of burns in children. J. Trauma, *5*:540, 1965.
39. Ternberg, J. L., and Luce, E.: Methemoglobinemia: Complication of silver nitrate treatment of burns. Surgery, *63*:328, 1968.
40. Topley, E., Jackson, D. MacG., Cason, J. S., and Davies, J. W. L.: Assessment of red cell loss in the first two days after severe burns. Ann. Surg., *155*:581, 1962.
41. Weeder, R. S., Brooks, H. W., and Boyer, A. S.: Silicone immersion in the care of burns. Plast. Reconstr. Surg., *39*:256, 1967.
42. White, M. G., and Asch, M. J.: Acid-base effects of topical mafenide acetate in the burned patient. N. Engl. J. Med., *284*:1281, 1971.
43. Wilson, R. D., Knapp, C., Priano, L. L., and Troper, D. L.: Thermoregulatory failure of the burn scar. J. Trauma, *11*:518, 1971.

Chapter 20

Cosmetic Surgery for the Disabled Child

by Bard Cosman, M.D.

It is appropriate to include cosmetic considerations in the rehabilitation program of the handicapped child. On the one hand, the appearance of the defect itself may be a part of the disabled child's disability. The appearance may, in fact, *be* the handicap. On the other hand, if there is no possibility of altering the child's basic disability, improvement of some parts of the defect or of general appearance per se may prove significant in total rehabilitation.

COSMETIC SURGERY CASE CATEGORIES

Four categories of cases merit discussion. First, there are those instances in which the handicap is fundamentally cosmetic and can be cured by cosmetic surgery. Second, in other patients, the defect is cosmetic and surgery cannot cure it but can substitute a more acceptable iatrogenic defect for the original one. Third, and perhaps most important, many cases exist in which the basic defect is not within the scope of surgery at all, but some manifestations of the handicap can be improved by cosmetic surgery. Last, there are patients in whom neither the specific defect nor any of its manifestations are amenable to cosmetic surgical improvement but in whom general appearance can be improved and adjustment to a fixed handicap thereby improved.

Definitive Surgery for Basically Cosmetic Handicaps

The decision to offer surgery is easy when the disability is primarily cosmetic and amenable to essentially complete surgical repair. Two problems do

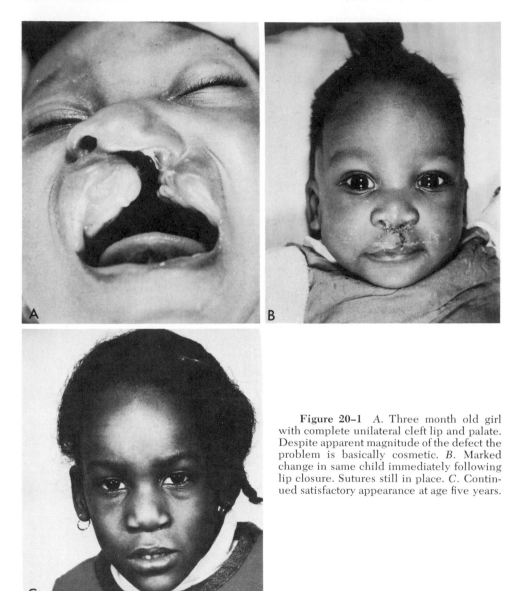

Figure 20-1 *A.* Three month old girl with complete unilateral cleft lip and palate. Despite apparent magnitude of the defect the problem is basically cosmetic. *B.* Marked change in same child immediately following lip closure. Sutures still in place. *C.* Continued satisfactory appearance at age five years.

arise in this category, however: the cosmetic nature of the defect must be recognized so as to avoid the rough and ready methods appropriate to emergency surgery; and it must be appreciated that some cosmetic defects are significant general handicaps and deserving of treatment. A cleft lip is an example of a handicap whose basically cosmetic nature is often unrealized (Fig. 20–1).[2] Depending on the width of the cleft there may be some difficulty for the infant sucking, but good nutrition is possible with careful feeding. Breathing is no problem. Later on, speaking is perfectly possible with an open lip cleft. In short, life can go on with an unrepaired cleft lip. The repair of the lip

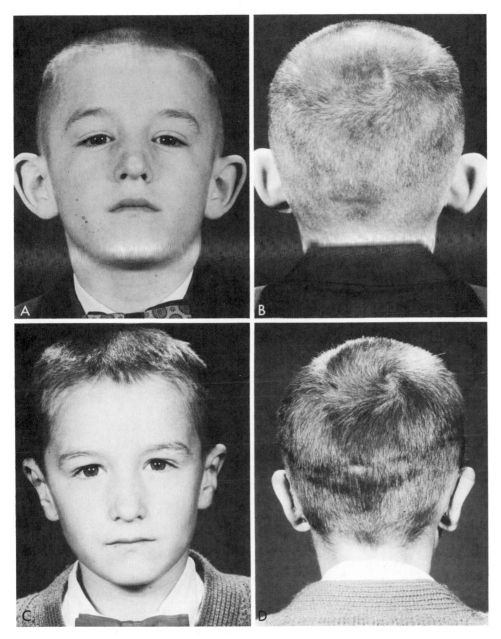

Figure 20–2   *A* and *B.* Anterior and posterior views of belligerent young man who had suffered several years of teasing directed at his prominent ears. *C* and *D.* Appearance after otoplasty carried out via hidden postauricular incision. To achieve such an improved appearance without leaving evidence of surgical intervention is the goal of cosmetic surgery. Operation was carried out after age of four when external ear had essentially completed its growth.

is cosmetic surgery; as an elective procedure it should be performed with due deliberation and not treated as a postnatal surgical emergency. An example of a defect whose handicap is often unrecognized is the prominent ear (Fig. 20–2). Counterproductive aggressive behavior and other difficulties may result

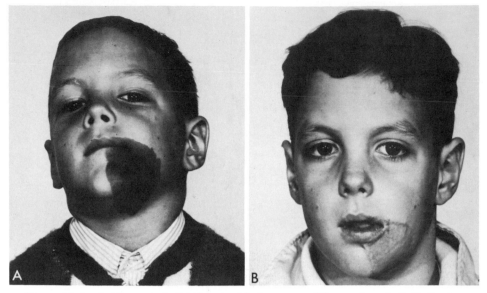

Figure 20–3 *A.* Pigmented slightly raised hairy nevus of face and neck. *B.* Following excision at level deep enough to remove hair follicles and adjacent melanocytes. Split thickness skin grafting was performed. The surgical substitute appearance has been well accepted in a follow-up of five years.

from this deformity and handicap the child. Complete cosmetic surgical cure is possible.

Substitutive Surgery for Cosmetic Handicap

The second category includes those patients whose defects are not amenable to complete surgical repair but for whom surgery can substitute a socially more acceptable defect. An example may be seen in this child with a large pigmented hairy nevus of the face (Fig. 20–3). There was no doubt that this lesion constituted a profound handicap. Nearly complete breakdown in the child's social functioning led to consultation. Excision and skin grafting left a very visible mark also, but as a surgical residuum it was easier to explain than the congenital "dirty spot" the child had been born with. Experience shows that such "surgical substitutions" are frequently viewed as significant improvements by children and their families even when the caliber of the result is less than completely gratifying to the surgeon. This principle should not be taken as carte blanche for every surgical attack. The ill-advised efforts to improve hearing in this child with unilateral microtia with first and second branchial arch syndrome (a fundamentally cosmetic handicap) produced an open, fish-gilled appearance that the minimal hearing increase achieved could not begin to justify (Fig. 20–4). Much extra effort was required to overcome the surgical handicap that had been added to, rather than substituted for, the original congenital defect.

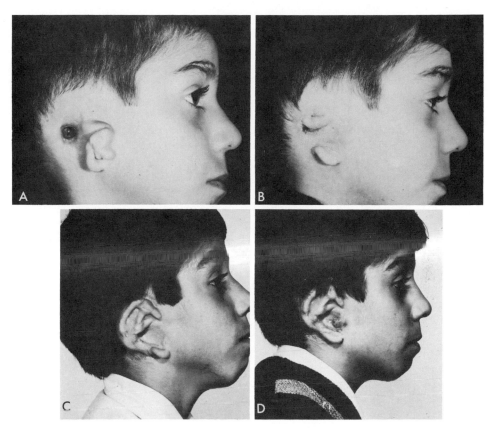

Figure 20–4   *A.* Child with unilateral first and second branchial arch syndrome. Hearing was excellent on normal side. Mastoid fenestration opening added little to hearing but did produce marked peculiarity of appearance. Opening lay in area of proposed autogenous cartilage graft reconstruction of external ear. *B.* Rotation of ear remnant tissue to partially close fenestration opening. *C.* After insertion and elevation of autogenous cartilage graft. Hypoplasia of mandible may be noted on the affected side. *D.* Following autogenous rib onlay graft to mandible via intraoral incision.

Cosmetic Surgery for Manifestations of a Non-Cosmetic Handicap

There can be little controversy about offering cosmetic surgery for cosmetic handicaps. Much more uncertainty exists in the third category, that of patients whose handicap is not surgically treatable but in whom some peripheral manifestations of the basic defect can be improved upon by cosmetic surgery. Many unrealized opportunities for surgery exist in this group. Properly chosen patients can be truly helped. Inappropriately performed cosmetic surgery, however, is meddlesome or worse.

The decision to offer surgery must be arrived at by balancing technical possibilities and ethical imperatives. Technical aspects are easier to assess; the ethical considerations are more subtle. For the patient, medical tradition prescribes the application of our best efforts, within the limits of hazard to life. For the child's family the situation is, on one level, the same: the most extensive efforts are desirable. On another level, however, the results should justify the emotional and economic costs involved for the family. Closure of a cleft lip in a child with 13–15 trisomy and limited life expectancy can only be a technical success, not a meaningful one. One cannot encourage the spending of family resources in this way. As regards society, concentration on the handicapped is open to these same objections. Resources are limited, and it is difficult to defend neglect of others more likely to be productive than the handicapped child, especially in regard to cosmetic surgical expense. Beyond the socioeconomic implications are those of genetic import. Certain genetic defects may be thought of as being promoted and their deleterious genes given an improved chance of passage by effective individual cosmetic rehabilitation. A repair of a facial deformity following radiotherapy for retinoblastoma could conceivably make a blind teenager more marriageable, and so promote the transmission of this dominant trait to new offspring.

Maximizing the Minimal. The principles of surgical intervention when undertaken in this third group of cases are designed to meet these negative considerations. Dealing with the multiply handicapped individual, one must seek to maximize the minimal even when the basic handicap cannot be directly affected. An example is seen in this young man with spastic cerebral palsy who had velopharyngeal insufficiency after cleft palate repair plus articulatory problems relative to the palsy (Fig. 20–5). A "cosmetic" pharyngeal flap helped reduce the nasality of the voice; other improvement was not anticipated and did not ensue. It would be wise to suggest otoplasty in a retarded child if by that means outstanding ears that emphasized a moderate microcephaly could be set back and the head size made to seem more normal. Alteration toward normal of the medial slanting "almond" eyes of this retarded girl proved an emotionally significant improvement although clearly not altering

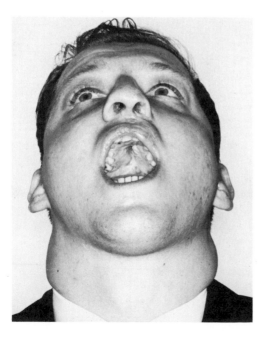

Figure 20–5 Sixteen year old boy with spastic cerebral palsy and voice nasality after cleft lip and palate closure. Many articulatory problems were present. Nasal escape of air was partially blocked by pharyngeal flap, and "cosmetic" improvement in speech quality was achieved.

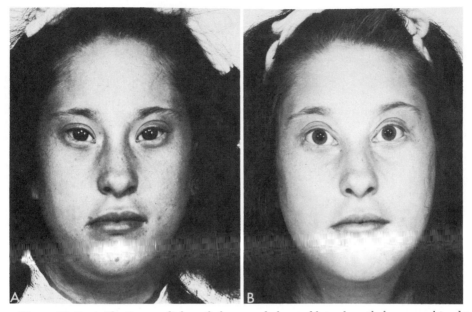

Figure 20–6   *A*. Slanting medial canthal area and elevated lateral canthal area combined to produce a mongoloid appearance of eyes in this retarded girl. *B*. Alteration of canthal positions was satisfactorily achieved with resultant improvement in appearance and marked satisfaction to child and parents.

her basic brain damaged condition (Fig. 20–6). The child was gratified. Her self-awareness like that of many of the handicapped was quite acute even if imperfectly expressed.[1] The family found its burden less heavy when less obvious. Even if institutionalization is anticipated, the child's life within the institution can be made easier if its appearance is less aberrant. Removal of bulging glial masses from the face of the retarded, epileptic, and disturbed child shown in Figure 20–7 was undertaken with this understanding.

   Minimizing the Interventions.   Another principle applicable to the multiply handicapped child in whom cosmetic surgery is decided upon is to minimize the number of such interventions. The smallest number of procedures is the best. Combinations of surgical procedures should be sought and several surgical teams used so that operating time and hospital time can be reduced and cosmetic rehabilitation achieved as quickly as possible. This is more valid emotionally and less stressful for the child as well as answering some of the family and societal objections noted. This sort of combination of procedures to reduce operative stages and hospital time is demonstrated in Figure 20–8.

Cosmetic Surgery Unrelated to the Handicap

   The fourth category of cases is that in which neither the defect nor its manifestations are the object of the cosmetic surgery. Rather such surgery is

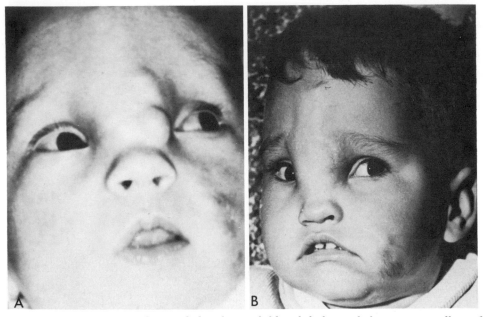

Figure 20–7 *A.* Severely retarded epileptic child with bulging glial masses in midline of face and in cheek. *B.* Excisions were carried out to improve situation to be anticipated in projected institutionalization.

undertaken just as in the normal child—to achieve a general cosmetic improvement (Fig. 20–9). The rhinoplasty undertaken for this surviving teenage fibrocystic high school girl was performed for quite normal and usual reasons prior to her entry into college. The rhinoplasty request was weighed on its own merits without regard to the guarded prognosis so far as longevity was concerned. In addition, however, the principle of maximizing the minimal lent a little greater impetus toward satisfying her wish. Certainly the desire of the handicapped for the kind of improvement sought by the normal should not be denied on the basis of the handicap if the surgery itself will not pose a threat to life or function.

TIMING OF COSMETIC SURGERY IN THE HANDICAPPED

The desirability of rapidity in cosmetic rehabilitation brings up the question of surgical timing. Two considerations are operative. One may be termed the psychological constraint, and the other the growth constraint.

The concept of body image is well known. A child establishes such an image very early in life. If it is possible to achieve favorable body alterations before this time, the better rather than the poorer image will be incorporated. In this regard, the desirability of removing portions of anomalous tissue early may be mentioned. If it is possible to decide that digit nubbins, for instance, are to play no part in reconstruction, then early removal is advisable before

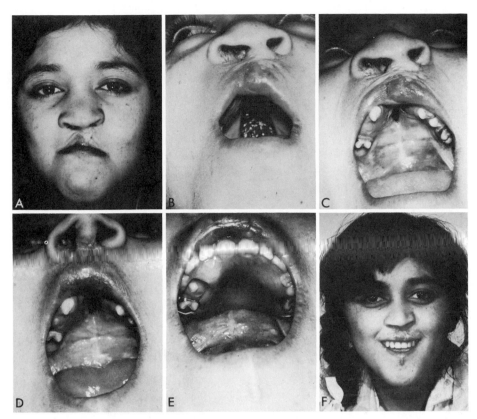

Figure 20–8 *A and B.* Retarded child after bilateral cleft lip closure with unrepaired cleft palate and severe residual lip distortion. Child had been kept out of school by parents because of facial appearance. *C.* In first operation palate was closed and in addition a pharyngeal flap attached to improve speech. *D.* In second operation center of upper lip was used to rebuild columella, nostrils were rotated inward, lower lip segment was used to replace center of upper lip, and bone graft was employed to rebuild flattened nose. *E.* Postoperatively a dental prosthesis was fitted over the remaining palate defect and over the residual teeth. *F.* Result two months after these two operative procedures. Marked change in appearance has been achieved. Moderate hypertrophy of scars is beginning to resolve.

these objects become a part of the image (Fig. 20–10). Attempts to remove them later during definitive reconstruction will be treated as attempts to amputate real fingers. Such anomalous tissue becomes the subject of morbid interest if it is allowed to persist. Rapidity of repair is also good for the child vis à vis the family. As appearance improves, acceptance by the parents is likely to improve. The family response is a part of the general social response and is reinforced by the latter as well.

Generally against early repair, however, is the constraint of growth. To a large extent the earlier the surgery the more difficult it is to predict the result as growth occurs. Actual growth interference may be caused by the surgery. While it is good to achieve satisfactory appearance early on, it is clearly inadvisable to foreclose the future in favor of the present. This is especially true in the first two case categories in which the handicap itself is cosmetic. The interference in facial growth caused by early maxillary bone grafts in cleft lip

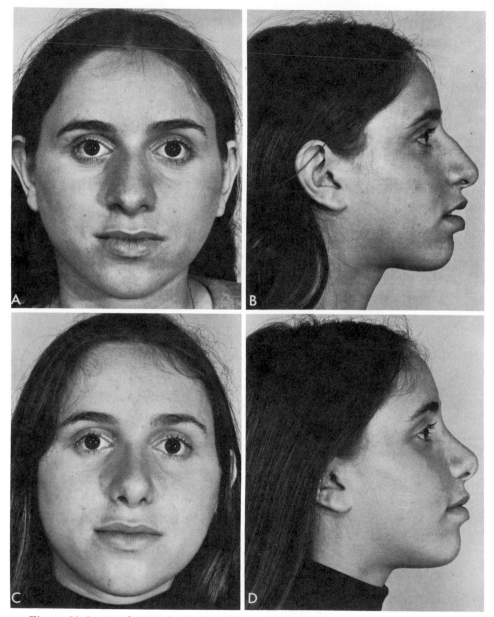

Figure 20–9 *A* and *B*. High school graduate with fibrocystic disease who requested rhinoplasty. Operative procedure has nothing to do with the defect or its manifestations; the operation was undertaken for general cosmetic reason. *C* and *D*. Appearance postrhinoplasty—an example of cosmetic surgery unrelated to specific handicap.

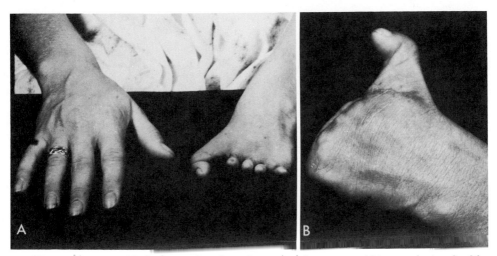

Figure 20-10 A. Marked ectrodactyly with residual finger tip nubbins producing footlike appearance in deformed hand. B. Excision of nubbins removed objects of morbid curiosity and attention without reducing function. Appearance now suggests a traumatic defect instead of a difficult to explain congenital deformity.

patients is a prime example of cosmetic surgery now proved to have been performed too early.[4] The decision as to the timing of surgery represents a compromise between these two constraints.

"CHRONIC COSMETIC SURGERY"

Certain hamartomatous lesions may be so extensive and involve normal tissue so intimately as to preclude total excision. Periodic removal of tissue must be the accepted course.[3] Among these lesions the plexiform neurofibroma and lipohemangiolymphangioma must be included (Fig. 20–11). The impetus for these excisions is cosmetic. As growth of the lesion keeps pace with the growth of the child, so surgery must keep equal pace with both. This state of "chronic cosmetic surgery" in the handicapped child leads to very distinct requirements in patient-physician relations. Nonadherent dressings and dissolving suture techniques should be chosen if at all possible, and painful procedures minimized so that the child does not come to fear the continuing surgical intervention that will be necessary.

CONCLUSION

Even without stretching the meaning of the term "cosmetic," it remains true that surgery undertaken to improve appearance plays an important part in the rehabilitation of the handicapped child. In some instances the handicap itself is a cosmetic one. The definitive treatment or an acceptable substitute appearance may be achieved by surgery. Perhaps the most neglected group of

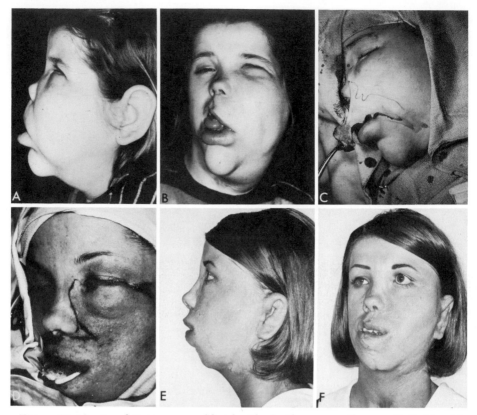

Figure 20–11 *A* and *B*. Four year old girl with plexiform neurofibroma of left side of face with macroglossia, macrocheilia, and macrotia. Lesion extends into maxillary bones. *C*. Through and through removal of section of face. All removed tissue was said to be plexiform neurofibroma. Macroglossia was reduced and macrotia resected. *D*. Seventeen years later after 19 operations, continued growth of area beneath left eye and cheek led to reexcision and partial maxillectomy. *E* and *F*. Status after 23 operations at age 24. The lesion has gradually occluded left lacrimal apparatus, and patient has most recently had four more operative procedures for formation of lacrimal tube and subsequent insertion of prosthetic device for tear drainage. Further operative procedures for reduction of tumor growth must be anticipated.

patients are those whose handicap is not amenable to surgery but who do have manifestations of the basic defect that can benefit from cosmetic surgery if the latter's possibilities are realized. Cosmetic surgery should not be denied to the handicapped; if anything, it should be encouraged so as to achieve the most complete rehabilitation possible.

References

1. Aufricht, G.: Philosophy of cosmetic surgery. Plast. Reconstr. Surg., *20*:397, 1957.
2. Crikelair, G. F.: Why repair a cleft lip? Cleft palate J., 6:93, 1969.
3. Crikelair, G. F., and Cosman, B.: Histologically benign, clinically malignant lesions of the head and neck. Plast. Reconstr. Surg., *42*:343, 1968.
4. Jolleys, A., and Robertson, N. R. E.: A study of the effects of early bone-grafting in complete clefts of the lip and palate — 5 year study. Br. J. Plast. Surg., 25:229, 1972.

section four

Dentistry

Chapter 21

Dental Care for the Handicapped

by *Solomon N. Rosenstein, D.D.S.*

Dental care for handicapped children is frequently neglected. Some children may require lengthy hospitalization followed by long convalescent periods, and the need to limit movement of these patients plus the burden of medical and feeding requirements may relegate the measures to promote good oral health to a lower priority. Other patients may not require hospitalization, but taking them out of their homes may be difficult because of neuromotor or other disability. Home therapy exercises and daily body care may take precedence over other services, and there may be no consideration or provision for regular dental treatment and advice.

In families with handicapped children the first recognition of need for dental care frequently follows the unexpected onset of acute pulpitis or dental abscess formation during the night or upon eating. The intense pain and, if untreated, resulting infection are conditions the handicapped should not have to bear and should have been prevented.

There are several good reasons to plan for and prescribe oral health care for every handicapped child besides the advantages of preventing these emergency situations. The awareness of a healthy clean refreshed mouth helps the child to feel better. Clean teeth and firm looking gums contribute to an attractive smile and improvement in morale, so important to any child whether in the hospital or at home. Equally important is the elimination of the burden of extensive remedial dental treatment, made possible by a preventive program of regular dental and home care procedures.

Regular dental examination and care should be started as early as possible. The dental team can make an assessment of the child's oral conditions, their relation to background factors, and the potential for motivation and cooperation in the preventive and corrective procedures that are indicated.

495

GENERAL CONSIDERATIONS

While special considerations are involved in the care of children with specific conditions, there are basic guidelines that apply to the entire group of children with handicaps.

An understanding of the handicapping conditions and a knowledge of the child's illness are essential for intelligent management by the dentist, who can then develop an approach to the child as an individual to develop the necessary rapport and cooperation. It is important, therefore, that the patient's history be available before treatment. On the basis of the medical and paramedical background the dentist can assess the child's potential for cooperation, indications or contraindications for premedication, and need for other precautions. The author has found, during operation of a large dental program for handicapped children, that dental treatment provided on this basis with repeated visits under normal conditions promotes interpersonal reactions and contributes to the social and emotional development of these children. It also provides repeated opportunities for follow-up review of home care and oral hygiene procedures.

Complete dental care rather than palliative care should be planned and provided. The child's total needs can then be fulfilled and further breakdown of untreated teeth prevented. The concept of complete dental care includes the principles and procedures for preventive dentistry, which are important because prevention of new lesions and inflammation means that only minimal treatment will be required in the future.

PREVENTIVE DENTISTRY

Noninstitutionalized Patients

The child's first visit to the dentist is a very important occasion. The necessary history taking, examination, and diagnosis are accomplished, and in addition, the dental prophylaxis followed by topical application of a fluoride compound contributes significantly to lowering the incidence of dental decay. This visit is also an opportunity for instruction and demonstration of the home care procedures that should be instituted, including proper tooth brushing, flossing, and rinsing. It is important that the parent be present for this instruction, as the parent must supervise and, at times, perform the procedures.

Toothbrushing instruction should include recommendation for brushing after meals (and before going to sleep if food is eaten between dinnertime and bedtime) with a child-size brush with soft nylon rounded-end bristles. A dentifrice containing fluoride may be used. The brushing after eating removes acid-producing food residues and microorganisms and prevents plaque formation on the teeth. These procedures contribute to prevention of decay; they contribute as well to improvement in gingival health and the prevention of gingivitis and subsequent periodontal disease.

Other important factors in lessening the potential for dental and gingival disease are eating habits and choices of foods. In many of the handicapping conditions, such as the head and neck neuromotor disability of cerebral palsy, intake frequently consists of soft carbohydrate foods and mixtures that require little or no chewing. Under such conditions pasty residues are left about the teeth for long periods of time. Repeated daily, this contributes to dental disease and soft tissue inflammation. The recommended dietary regimen is three regular mealtimes each day with more favorable food choices. Firm and crisp foods should be chosen as much as possible and pasty-type foods should be limited. With regular mealtime eating there is less need for between-meal snacks. Also, the mealtime foods are usually the protective foods that furnish the factors required for the child's growth and development. The meals can include all foods, even desserts for the later major meals; fruit dessert is better than the pasty carbohydrate dessert. In any case, the meal should be followed by brushing. If a midafternoon snack is required, carbohydrate foods, such as candy or cookies, should be avoided and instead, fruits that require firm chewing, such as oranges or crisp apples, or cheese on toasted bread or muffin should be given. Milk may be given alone and should be followed by two or three swishings with water that is then swallowed. The regularity of meals that occurs in hospitals and day centers is also recommended for the handicapped child at home.

Other oral hygiene recommendations and instruction may be given to children at day centers by the staff members. There are dental organizations interested in dental health for the handicapped, and many dentists have been trained to provide necessary dental care. These dentists can also provide in-service training for day center personnel to train them to instruct and supervise their patients in daily oral hygiene procedures.

Institutionalized Patients

All children should be scheduled for prophylaxis and fluoride application, even in areas where the water is fluoridated. These procedures can be performed by the dental hygienist, and followed by an initial screening for carious involvement.

For many of these patients instruction in daily oral hygiene procedures can be provided by the dental staff; subsequent regular supervision and follow-up can be carried on by ancillary personnel at bedside or sink. For other patients who cannot make the necessary movements, ward personnel and aides must assist in the cleansing procedures. If usual rinsing movements cannot be accomplished the desired cleansing can be done so that the water either flows into a kidney basin or is evacuated by suction apparatus. A digestible dentifrice has been developed for patients who cannot be moved.

RESTORATIVE PROCEDURES

Not all handicapped children require restorative dentistry. For any particular population, a survey should be conducted early by the dentist or dentists to determine individual needs. This can be accomplished readily at the inpatient facility or day care center and permits scheduling of immediate treatment for those who require immediate care and later regular care for the others.

Restorative requirements for young patients usually consist of fillings, but occasionally pulp management procedures and full crown coverage are required. If dental decay is widespread some teeth may require extraction, and premature tooth loss may lead to the need for space management appliances to prevent malocclusion.

Older children who have had the benefit of continuing surveillance and preventive care should require only continuation of these procedures with repeated instruction in eating habits and food choices, as eating habits frequently change during the early teenage period.

Not infrequently, however, one sees handicapped children in the middle and late teenage periods whose mouths show evidence of long neglect, often as a result of preoccupation with therapies or inability to obtain dental care easily. These older children may require extractions, treatments for gingival inflammation, and fairly extensive oral prosthetic restorations. Such oral rehabilitation is usually expensive and, where the families cannot afford the costs, the hospital or other municipal or health agency may be called upon to defray costs.

In addition to the technical aspects of treatment planning for restorative dentistry, measures for pain control during operative procedures must also be considered. Most handicapped children are amenable to, and benefit from, dental treatment under normal conditions, and local anesthesia usually suffices for pain control. For some handicapped children who are very apprehensive or hyperactive and resistive, preoperative sedation is helpful to calm them sufficiently to permit more ready acceptance of dental procedures. Relative analgesia with nitrous oxide and oxygen is also helpful in promoting cooperation during dental procedures. For a small minority of severely and multiply handicapped children who cannot understand the significance of the treatment situation and cannot cooperate, complete dental care under general anesthesia with nitrous oxide and oxygen may be indicated.

SPECIAL CONSIDERATIONS FOR SPECIFIC CONDITIONS

Cardiovascular Disorders

Because of the circulatory deficiencies found in children with cardiovascular disorders it is essential that preventive procedures be applied early and include indoctrination of parents. Oral health must be maintained to prevent gingival inflammation, as the tissues lack the usual normal resistance factors supplied via normal circulation. Dental caries, if present, should be treated early to prevent pulp involvement because the lowered resistance of the pulpal tissue militates against prevention of pulpal degeneration and infection.

In normal children pulp involvement can be treated by suitable pulp management procedures; in children with circulatory disorders, these procedures are contraindicated because of the decreased ability of the pulp tissue to heal.

Most of the procedures indicated for complete dental care for these children require antibiotic coverage. Periods of such coverage should be arranged to permit a series of two or three dental visits in daily succession with periods of rest between series.

Early preventive care and treatment for caries are necessary for these children in order to prevent bacteremia. Bacteremia occurs in children following dental extractions and gingival and periodontal treatments and may be serious in children with rheumatic heart disease. Therefore these treatments should be covered by preoperative and postoperative antibiotics.

Psychological management of these children for dentistry is often made difficult because of background factors in their history. Because of prolonged sheltering they are apprehensive to a much greater degree than are normal children; they may cry and resist treatment and become highly excited. After corrective surgery has been accomplished and circulatory deficiencies have been eliminated these fears and stresses may be managed as with normal children.

Starting regular dental care early for these children helps to orient them to acceptance of dentistry at a time when the treatment required may be comparatively uncomplicated. It also permits training in the habits of oral hygiene at a young age. Cooperation of parents is essential for effective home care and preventive dentistry.

Cerebral Palsy

Dentistry for children with cerebral palsy may be more difficult than for the normal child for several reasons. The lack of muscle control gives rise to dyskinesias and excessive movements that may result in instability of the child in the dental chair. Cerebral palsy is frequently accompanied by speech and hearing disability, which may limit communication, and if severe retardation is present, understanding of the dental procedure is also lacking. Many patients with head and neck involvement also have impairment of oral functions with aberrant oral muscle action. These factors frequently create difficult problems involving malocclusion, attrition of the posterior teeth, and disorders of the gingival tissues.

Oral hygiene is frequently poor because if the hands are involved in the neuromotor disorder the toothbrush cannot be held and manipulated properly. Reshaping the brush handle to fit his abnormal hand position permits the child with cerebral palsy to hold the brush securely for brushing his teeth. Occasionally the parent can supervise and assist in this procedure at home. The automatic action toothbrush can sometimes be used effectively when the manual brush cannot.

Gingival and occlusal disorders are found more frequently in children with cerebral palsy than in the normal population. The gingival disorders usually arise from difficulty or inability to maintain good oral hygiene and home care. The major disorders of occlusion or malocclusion usually arise from aberrant oral muscle function, most frequently, incorrect tongue positioning and abnormal swallowing. Extensive caries may be present in some mouths, but on the average total susceptibility to decay is no greater than in a comparable group of normal children. Programs for early dental care for these children are essential in order to prevent early loss of teeth, and to intercept developing gingival disease and malocclusion.

Many of these children can be treated successfully in the same way normal children are when the dentist understands their conditions and extends an attitude of personal interest and friendliness. They can cooperate with the dentist and they benefit from the dental care and the interpersonal relationship. Simple aids are available for use by dentists: some help to keep patients' mouths open during intraoral procedures; others help to maintain stability in the dental chair.

For a comparatively small number of these children, in whom marked apprehension and dyskinesia may be present, the dentist may prefer to use a combination of drugs for preoperative sedation in order to calm the patient but still maintain the conscious state necessary to develop cooperation. It is important that the dentist be informed of any medication the patient has been taking so that compatible drugs in properly adjusted dosages may be administered.

The dentist serves in another role for the child with severe cerebral palsy who is quadriplegic and needs an oral prosthetic appliance to assist in holding, grasping, and manipulating objects. Usually these patients have severe athetosis or mixed athetosis with spasticity and there is inability to control hand movements. While head and neck involvement is usually present, lips, teeth, and tongue can be used to pick up small objects when the patient is supported adequately, as during sitting. An oral appliance can be constructed to fit over the upper and lower teeth with an opening at the middle of the anterior portion for, or with, plastic extensions.

Where an opening is used a sipper can be inserted to permit taking of liquid nourishment, or a pusher, pencil, or holder appliance can be inserted to permit the patient to push a lever, or write, or press keys on a typewriter. Tweezer type of extensions may also be used to enable the patient to grasp and pick up small objects.

Cleft Lip and Palate

While these conditions may occur alone, they frequently occur as signs of several chromosomal aberrations and other syndromes. Severe sequelae may occur in infants with cleft palate with Pierre Robin syndrome in which the complications of abnormal sucking and swallowing movements become compounded by the posterior action of the tongue in the constricted mandibular space. Temporary palatal appliances can be helpful, with other measures, in developing proper feeding habits and leading to normal oral function and its contribution to growth of the oral structures.

The improvements in corrective surgical procedures during the past two decades have brought concomitant improvement in the oral conditions of many children with cleft lip or palate or both. These include improved feeding and eating habits, lowered prevalence of decay and loss of teeth. Early restorative and orthodontic care has also contributed to improvement in facial appearance.

Dental care should be begun as early as possible and maintained at regular intervals for two reasons. First, to develop habits of good oral hygiene early, and second, to prevent loss of teeth. If the palatal cleft involves the premaxilla, dental development in the region of the incisor teeth may be disturbed. In some children supernumerary teeth may be present; in others lateral incisors may be absent. Careful planning is required for corrective procedures for both types of case, and the dentist should be in frequent consultation with the pediatrician and the surgeon.

An abnormal intermaxillary relationship indicates the need for orthodontic treatment. In older patients who have lost several upper teeth a proper prosthetic appliance, at times with speech bulb extension, must be designed and constructed.

The need for good speech, good appearance, and adequate function usually involves a multidisciplinary effort in which dentistry's role becomes very important; the cleft palate team should include a pedodontist, an orthodontist, and a prosthodontist.

Cleidocranial Dysostosis

The bizarre dental developmental phenomena that frequently accompany this condition require regular surveillance by the dentist. X-rays may disclose many supernumerary teeth in the upper and lower jaws, and the upper permanent lateral incisors may be missing. There is usually also a retardation of the dental developmental processes such as eruption of primary molars, root resorption of primary teeth, and eruption of the permanent teeth.

Long-range treatment planning must be based upon evaluation of the findings in each individual child because of the variation in number and distribution of the supernumerary teeth.

Cystic Fibrosis

Generally dental treatment can be performed in a routine manner for these children. Oral conditions are not unusual, except that salivary output is usually increased. Early care is recommended to promote good oral habits, maintain good oral health, and prevent infection.

Occasionally rampant caries is seen in these children. This can be related to unfavorable eating habits, such as prolonged use of the nursing bottle, with the bottle kept in the mouth through the night, and this habit continued well past the age at which use of a bottle should be discontinued. This unfavorable habit is noted frequently with normal children, but the dental sequelae are managed more easily in normal children than in those with cystic fibrosis.

Frequently these children have a history of repeated need for antibiotic administration. If the tetracyclines have been used early during the periods of formation of the teeth, there will be staining with more or less marked darkening of the teeth depending upon length of administration. Should front teeth be involved and aesthetics become an important consideration requiring corrective procedures early, the teeth can be prepared to receive temporary plastic tooth forms.

Diabetes

Contact between physician and dentist is essential so that the dentist becomes sufficiently aware of the extent of the child's condition, response to medication, time of medication, and other conditions.

Without control of the diabetic condition there may be severe deterioration of the oral soft tissues. The gingivae lose their integrity, become puffy, and bleed easily. Blind subgingival abscesses may develop, and dental supporting structures deteriorate. Local oral treatment is not adequate until the diabetic condition has been brought under control. Gingival and periodontal treatment should be repeated at intervals of about three to four months, and radiographs should be taken at suitable intervals to check on the condition of alveolar bone.

Timing of appointments for dental treatment should be related to the patient's usual routine for insulin administration and eating, to avoid a possible insulin reaction. Usually morning appointments are recommended so that dental treatment can be performed some time after the medication has been administered and food has been ingested.

As a rule dental treatment for the diabetic can be performed in the routine manner with provision for the precautions just mentioned. Should procedures be indicated that require general anesthesia, it is recommended that the patient be hospitalized and treated as an inpatient.

Dysautonomia

The disturbance of autonomic function in familial dysautonomia is reflected in the oral cavity by such signs as abnormal chewing and swallowing, drooling, and a marked tendency to excessive grinding of the teeth. Usually these children are on a daily regimen of tranquilizing agents such as thorazine, and salivation is reduced.

Where excessive grinding is present premature loosening of primary teeth is likely to occur. A removable oral appliance (bite plate) can be made to be worn over the teeth of the mandibular arch, which will prevent or lessen the tendency toward loosening of the teeth.

Epilepsy

For children with this disorder who are to receive diphenylhydantoin sodium (Dilantin) therapy to control seizures, thorough instruction in intensive home care procedures for good oral hygiene is essential. This should consist of demonstration and instruction, with the patient (and parent when necessary) participating in a thorough tooth brushing procedure. Thorough brushing should be done four or five times daily and followed by vigorous rinsing. Further stimulation of circulation and maintenance of gingival tone will be derived from eating crisp fruits and vegetables that require hard chewing. The automatic action toothbrush may also be effective.

Where good circulation can be maintained the fibrous enlargement of the gingival tissues associated with diphenylhydantoin therapy can be prevented or greatly limited. Since the reported cases of hypertrophy appear to be related to poor oral hygiene, the prevalence of this gingival hypertrophy and distortion can be lessened appreciably by emphatic attention to good oral hygiene at the beginning of treatment.

In many instances in which hypertrophy has occurred it can be reduced by conservative gingival treatment and good home care. Not infrequently the firm fibrous enlargement becomes complicated by additional shiny, reddened, putty signs of superimposed inflammatory changes of gingivitis that may be associated also with the poor oral hygiene.

Dental treatment consists of subgingival curettage and cleaning, and instruction in thorough brushing, rinsing, and sometimes, massage. Regular follow-up visits at short intervals are recommended. Such conservative treatment usually causes improvement, but the patient and the parents must be impressed with the need to continue this home care regimen along with regular dental visits.

Occasionally the hypertrophy is more severe and the affected tissues may cover the teeth on the lingual, buccal, and labial aspects. If intensive curettage and massage do not reduce such hypertrophy sufficiently, surgical removal (gingivectomy) is indicated. Following gingivectomy there must be instruction again in intensive home care procedures to prevent recurrence.

Hemophilia and Other Blood Disorders

Dental evaluation and care should be instituted early. If care is delayed or avoided dental and gingival disease may progress to a point at which procedures may be required that represent a further threat to the health of the patient. Early evaluation detects small lesions; simple corrective care can be instituted readily, and a sound preventive regime can be instituted to prevent recurrence of oral disorders.

Dental treatment must be performed with extreme care to prevent any injury to soft or supporting tissues, both pulpal and gingival. In the former, deep cavities may indicate indirect pulp capping procedures to prevent pulp exposure; in the latter, careful matrix placement must be done. Local infiltration anesthesia may be used, but only if necessary, and should be avoided if possible. When bleeding can be expected as a result of necessary dental treatment or for multiple dental procedures, hospitalization with plasma therapy or administration of the missing factor is indicated. The need for oral surgery should be determined carefully, in consultation with the hematologist, and when it is necessary, hospitalization with indicated supportive therapy is advisable.

Bleeding in the structures of the mouth and pharyngeal area can be troublesome and lead to complications additional to the difficulty in diagnosis because of extension of the bleeding. Thorough careful oral examination should be made in all such instances.

Similar precautions to avoid bleeding and poor gingival health should be observed in some of the metabolic disorders in which anemia with possible leukopenia and thrombocytopenia may be present, as in Gaucher's disease. In cyclic neutropenia oral signs occur during the periodically recurrent bouts of diminution in the numbers of neutrophilic leukocytes. They include inflammation of the tissues with possible ulceration in the gingivae and other oral mucous membranes. In time there is appreciable loss of periodontal bone, which may be more severe about those teeth that have been longest in the mouth, the first permanent molars and anterior teeth. Children with cyclic neutropenia should receive regular dental care, particularly conservative periodontal therapy, to maintain good oral health. It is important, however, that dental procedures, periodontal and restorative, be scheduled during the "well" periods, when there are remissions in the neutropenic condition.

Kidney Conditions

Prevention of infection in the oral cavity is essential in all patients with renal diseases. All necessary dental and gingival therapy is indicated to eliminate active caries and gingival inflammation and to attain a state of good oral health. Root canal treatment for nonvital teeth is not indicated; their removal with suitable antibiotic coverage is recommended. Local anesthesia should be used whenever possible and general anesthesia, if required, should be used only on an inpatient basis. After good oral health has been attained these children should be recalled regularly for maintenance care.

Varying degrees of enamel hypoplasia are seen occasionally, the result of disturbance in calcification in teeth whose crowns were developing during active periods of the specific conditions. Tetracycline discoloration of the teeth is also seen in those children for whom prolonged administration of tetracycline was used to control or overcome infection. If these dental conditions are not severe, there may be no need for correction; if the discolorations are extensive and appearance is markedly affected, corrective restorative procedures may be undertaken.

Mental Retardation

Many mentally retarded children are amenable to normal dental treatment, but when the retardation is severe, they may be excessively resistive to the dentist. Dentistry with preoperative sedation may be attempted; if this is not effective, general anesthesia is indicated for complete dental treatment.

The major needs for these patients are prophylaxis and periodontal treatment augmented by thorough instruction in toothbrushing and other home care procedures (instruction in these procedures must also be given to parents) and follow-up. A number of mentally retarded patients have excessive and extensive deposits of calculus that require scaling and subgingival curettage at intervals of two to three months. Other oral treatment needs are not unusual except in Down's syndrome (mongolism) in which mandibular prognathism and an enlarged tongue are seen frequently, and the lower anterior teeth are prone to loosening and early loss. These problems usually call for additional corrective procedures.

Dental morphology is affected in some forms of mental retardation. Again, for example, in Down's syndrome the dentition may be small and several teeth may be malformed (malformation of the cuspid has been reported most frequently). As a rule these aberrations require no treatment unless reconstruction is indicated to improve function.

In general, whether institutionalized or not, these patients should be exposed to dental care early. They usually respond favorably to the dentist's friendly attitude.

In some patients with severe mental retardation, other severe handicapping may increase difficulty in management. Many of them also may have extensive dental disease and breakdown; for these children extensive oral treatment may require the use of general anesthesia under suitable conditions.

Osteogenesis Imperfecta

An appreciable number of children with osteogenesis imperfecta have an accompanying dentinogenesis imperfecta. This condition also often occurs alone as an inherited non-sex-linked dominant characteristic affecting all the teeth of the primary and permanent dentitions. Along with the major sign of abnormal dentine formation, there is usually abnormal root formation. Enamel formation is normal, as are crown form and size. The normal appearance remains evident for a short time only, however, as severe darkening and attrition occur early, and the teeth may become worn down to gingival levels.

In osteogenesis imperfecta restorative procedures should be undertaken to prevent tooth loss, as extraction may be hazardous and cause fracture of the bone. Regular dental care is important. If pulp involvement by caries occurs, pulp management procedures such as pulpotomy and root canal therapy are recommended. Local anesthetics may be used as indicated.

Scoliosis

In forms of scoliosis in which a full body cast or Milwaukee brace that reaches to the lower jaw is used, special measures are required to prevent abnormalities in position of the teeth and in the mandible. In general there is a tendency for abnormality to occur as a result of abnormal pressures on growing bone; in the case of the Milwaukee brace there is constant pressure on the mandible over a long period of time. Depending upon the state of the patient's original occlusion, severe malocclusion with abnormal jaw shape may result. In these instances, the vertical dimension of the intermaxillary relationship becomes diminished as a result of the pressure, facial length is reduced, and the teeth are moved to abnormal positions.

Whenever the Milwaukee brace or a similar appliance is used, there is an absolute need to have an orthodontist in attendance to evaluate effects on the jaws and teeth, and to institute corrective therapy as indicated. Through the use of properly designed oral appliances these harmful effects can be prevented or lessened.

When scoliosis occurs as an accompanying feature of another condition, e.g., rickets or familial dysautonomia, the dentist should look for other dental and oral changes pertinent to those conditions.

SUMMARY

Dental care should be an essential component of the total care program for handicapped children. This can be accomplished readily for children admitted to hospitals by arranging for dental examination as part of the early screening procedure, with further scheduling as required. For ambulatory children regular dental care should be provided by family dentists; if this cannot be accomplished, these children should be sent for dental examination (and treatment) to the dental service in the facility where outpatient treatment is provided.

Most handicapping conditions require consultation with the physician in charge so that the dentist becomes aware of the extent and significance of the conditions and for collaboration on indicated precautionary measures.

Dental service for handicapped children should be based on the concept of complete dental care rather than palliative care, with emphasis on measures for preventive dentistry and good oral hygiene.

Treatment on this basis will result in maximum benefit to the handicapped. They will benefit from good oral health as their teeth contribute to good facial appearance, normal function, and the sense of cleanliness and well-being. They will benefit also from the general habilitation resulting from the interpersonal experiences of the dental situations and their new habits of oral health care.

Psychosocial Aspects

Chapter 22

Psychiatric Complications of Chronic Illness in Children

by *Robert L. Stubblefield, M D,*

    The incidence and prevalence of chronic illness in children and adolescents have been declining in the last 10 years. The gradual control of infectious diseases by vaccination and proper use of antibiotics has had a significant impact on chronic illness. The diseases with a strong genetic component, however, such as asthma, and the complications of physical trauma, especially from automobile accidents, continue to make a discussion of chronic illness a pertinent subject for review and discussion.

    Two important concepts should be considered in assessing and evaluating a patient with chronic illness and should prove to be useful in the development of management and rehabilitation programs. First, chronic illness inevitably produces a depressive reaction, with the usual phases of emotional shock, apathy and detachment, and the various regressive processes associated with mourning. Naturally, in chronic illness these responses are muted, disguised, and often appear in very subtle nonverbal and verbal communications. For example, a child with asthma who must be placed in a special institution away from his parents goes through the phases of grief, whereas the child who loses his parents abruptly has a more dramatic and visible reaction to the loss.

    Second, chronic illness has a negative effect on the child's self-esteem and personal self-image. It seems evident that the healthy child is presented with a series of frustrations and disappointments as he goes through the various developmental periods and that he masters many of these experiences by relying on the hope and expectation that he will be older, stronger, and better able to solve the particular problems. The child with a chronic illness, however, is likely to have more doubts about his skills, abilities, and potential

509

capacity to deal with the usual and expected developmental opportunities and problems that he will experience.

There are many factors that have a potential effect on the child's response to a chronic illness. Some of these factors are:

1. The nature of the chronic disease. For example, the presence or absence of an externally visible defect (such as extensive disfiguring burns).

2. The time of the establishment of the diagnosis. For example, the chronic process may be present at birth or it may begin at age three to five or later, and coincide with a critical incident period in the personality development.

3. The conscious and unconscious attitudes of the child's significant adult figures, usually the parents, about the cause, course, and prognosis of the condition. For example, the parents of a healthy son may become very anxious, ambivalent, competitive, or rejecting when a daughter develops unmistakable evidence of severe and chronic epilepsy.

4. The conscious and unconscious attitudes of the members of the health team, including the physician, nurse, various rehabilitation and special education personnel. For example, the subtle feelings of medical incompetence or hopelessness about the life expectancy of a child with chronic leukemia is usually conveyed to both the child and the parents.

5. The presence of pain, especially when increasing medication is required to control it. For example, a child with severe rheumatoid arthritis usually requires some analgesics, especially in later stages of the condition, and the perception of pain is usually interpreted as a signal to remain passive, to inhibit physical activity, and may lead to an uncooperative attitude in work with physical therapists.

Sociologists and social psychologists have made a number of interesting and useful observations about chronic illness, observations that are very valuable in assessing the psychiatric reactions. Kassebaum and Baumann noted several differences between acute illness and chronic illness.

> First, chronic illness by definition is not temporary, so that role expectations predicated on the assumption of the temporary nature of illness (for example, "motivation to get well") are clearly inapplicable without respecification. Also, since many chronic patients are ambulatory, incapacity for performance of other roles is often more partial than total.[13]

They also discuss several additional dimensions of the sick person's role, including the development of dependence and the tendency to use denial as a predominant psychological device. In addition, they state,

> ... sick role expectations are influenced not only by the patient's accustomed roles, but by the effects of his particular diagnosis on his capacity for performing them.[13]

THE INFANTILE PERSONALITY

Jurgen Ruesch has made a valuable contribution to our understanding of chronic disease. He suggested that

. . . the symptomology, personality structure, as well as social techniques of these patients pointed to a rather primitive level of organization. The common denominator then was identified as faulty or arrested motivation.[19]

He summarized his observations as follows:

Mature persons differ from the infantile personalities by having at their disposal suitable techniques for interpersonal relations and by having mastered problems of communication in terms of self-expression and self-extension, thus availing themselves of expressive signs which are derived from the somatic sphere, from action, and from verbal symbolization. In contrast, the infantile person does not possess the necessary techniques for social interaction and communication; hence life experiences cannot be integrated. In the absence of satisfactory interpersonal relations, communication is limited; signs used for self-expression originate in the somatic sphere or are related to action, and interpersonal relations on the level of verbal symbolization are rudimentary or nonexistent.

Personality disorganization and specific disability for interpersonal relations are factors which tend to expose the immature personality repeatedly to frustrating situations, the management of which is attempted by means of control rather than through mastery and adaptation. Inasmuch as operation through control is not likely to be successful in the long run, the infantile person is frequently confronted with emergencies. Although both mature and immature persons tend to handle emergency situations by means of physical symptoms, the mature person reverts only temporarily to somatic expression, while in the immature personality this type of expression persists.[19]

Although these were observations about adults, the implications for children and adolescents seem evident. In general, it seems that physicians and health personnel tend to expect too much age-appropriate behavior in the child who has a chronic illness, and these unrealistic expectations have a negative effect on the relationships with the patient.

DIAGNOSTIC CLASSIFICATION OF PSYCHIATRIC CONDITIONS IN CHILDREN AND ADOLESCENTS

Psychological reactions
    Anxiety
    Depressive states
Psychological reaction changes
Behavioral reactions
    Suicide
    Antisocial behavior (addiction)

Psychological Reactions

Anxiety. As Huxley described it, anxiety is the result of the constitutional inability to deal with stress, or the presence of excessive emotional stress, or a combination of the two factors. F. R. Hine has presented an excellent discussion of the processes that are involved in emotional conflict in a recent book, *Introduction to Psychodynamics.* He suggested that conflicts between internal needs and learned fears are usually visible in a

> ... dynamic triad of behavioral signs, 1) the emotions of distress; anxiety and depressive effect, 2) the inhibition of one particular area of overt interpersonal behavior and, 3) the inappropriate exaggerating of a contrasting or "opposite" area.[11]

Anxiety is best described as overconcern extending to panic and it is frequently associated with somatic symptoms. It is generalized, free floating, and overwhelming and "must be differentiated from the normal apprehension that occurs in realistically dangerous situations."[11] As an illustration, a child with moderate mental retardation, who possibly perceives the subtle rejection of his parents, continues over a long period of time to be fearful, have night terrors, and remain scattered and disorganized in his play habits and social relationships.

Often anxiety is seen in an admixture with other psychological defense mechanisms. Mattson and Agle describe the typical hemophiliac child, who must view every object such as a table or chair as a potential danger, who then develops counterphobic, "daredevil" types of behavior "and repeatedly exposes himself to dangerous activities in order to deny his fears of injury."[17]

Depression.   Depressive reactions are exaggerations of the common phenomenon of mourning with features of shock, disengagement, and denial. It is evident that the depth and intensity of the depressive response will be influenced by the child's personality strength, the parent's adaptive capacities, and the physician's skill, tact, and compassion in the diagnostic process, in the interpretation of findings, and in the management of the child.

Psychological Reaction Changes

These disorders are characterized by physical symptoms that are caused or partially caused by emotional factors; they involve a single organ system, which is usually under the control of the autonomic nervous system. Reactions may occur in skin, muscles, respiratory tract, cardiovascular system, gastrointestinal system, and in other organ systems. Anorexia nervosa, asthma, constipation, obesity, ulcerative colitis are classic examples of this type of psychiatric condition.

As an example, the child with chronic ulcerative colitis usually has episodes of diarrhea, with up to 30 to 40 bowel movements per day, and the stools contain mucus and blood. The child refuses to eat, becomes apathetic, anemic, and malnourished. Often, these children have had serious emotional deprivations or traumatic losses of significant parent figures; frequently, they are obsessive and perfectionistic, have unusual food habits, and are very dependent, almost clinging. George Engel and others have described the personality problems and management problems that are encountered with these patients.

Behavioral Reactions

Suicide.   As our knowledge about the incidence and prevalence of suicidal behavior expands, particularly through the efforts of the National Institute of Mental Health Studies in Suicide and Suicide Prevention, it is becoming evident that suicidal behavior is not a phenomenon that is confined to adults. Obviously, it is more difficult to assess the suicidal potential in children and adolescents than in adults, since the former have a more primitive personality structure and are less able to verbalize their affective states.

The data about suicide under the age of 10 are difficult to assess, and reports are often vague and inconsistent. Apparently girls make more suicidal attempts than boys, but boys outnumber girls in successful attempts by a three to one margin. In late latency and early adolescence it is difficult to obtain information about the frequency and intensity of suicidal fantasies and ruminations, and probably it is unwise to explore these ideas with children who have chronic physical illnesses. Excessive crying, loss of appetite, unusual fears about parents' health, and other symptoms may be viewed as signals for psychological testing (projective tests) and for discreet inquiries about the child's adjustment in school and at home. Muriel King has described the evaluation and treatment of suicide-prone youth recently and suggested several factors that deserve serious consideration by the physician: "disorganized families, marital discord, loss or threatened loss of parent or peer, abrupt behavioral change, particularly withdrawal."[14] It seems likely that disfiguring physical illnesses may play a prominent role in suicidal ideation in adolescence, when acceptance and involvement with peers and separation from parents become important.

In addition, in our rapidly changing, war-oriented society, with the dominant role of television in the education of the public, the increasing role of impulsiveness in some suicidal behavior should be acknowledged. The game of "chicken," or daring one's peers to perform some outlandish prank, is accelerated in our automobile- and drug-dominated society, and physicians should be alert to the impulsivity factor in patients with chronic disease (especially those with brain involvement) and in patients who are using medication.

Antisocial Behavior Disorders

There are several classifications of behavioral disorders that are encountered in children and adolescents. The most common are the hyperkinetic, the withdrawing, the overanxious, and the runaway reactions, and unsocialized aggression and group delinquency.

Hyperactivity.   The hyperkinetic or hyperactive reaction is described extensively in the literature and is encountered fairly frequently in clinical work with long-term patients. In childhood the symptoms and signs are overactivity, restlessness, distractibility, and short attention span. There are several causes of hyperactivity in children, including congenital hyperactivity, minimal brain damage, excessive frustration, and medication, and often more than one factor is present.

Bell, Waldrop, and Weller described an excellent rating system for the assessment of both hyperactive and withdrawn preschool children recently. Under hyperactivity they classified behavioral patterns as follows:

1. Frenetic play (ineffective, incomplete)
2. Induction of intervention (teacher must act)
3. Inability to delay (cannot wait his turn)
4. Emotional aggression (throws objects)
5. Nomadic play (wanders rapidly)
6. Spilling, throwing (food, water, etc.)[2]

This rating scale should be helpful in work with preschool and school age children. Patterns of hyperactivity seem, however, to be less prevalent in latency and in adolescence, even among children with chronic disease.

Runaway Reactions.   This is a DSM-II classification and is encountered occasionally with long-term patients, especially when they are rejected or fear rejection in a significant personal relationship with an idolized peer. Richard Jenkins and Galen Stahls recently reviewed the literature and identified several significant factors, especially an unpleasant home situation, harsh parents, overt rejection, overrestrictive parents, and economic deprivation. They suggest that this type of behavior, like a suicidal attempt, is "often a desperate plea for help." In children with chronic illness, the consequences of running away may be catastrophic, e.g., a 14 year old diabetic boy was found in a comatose state because he had "forgotten" to take his medication with him.[12]

Addiction.   In the last decade, the United States, and most of the nations in the world, have seen a phenomenal rise in the utilization of a wide variety of drugs and toxic substances that have mind-altering capabilities. The list is long (marijuana, heroin, hashish, hallucinogens, amphetamine, glue, alcohol) and the methods of administration are varied (oral, injection, sniffing). The literature is extensive and the effort to develop research, training, and service programs for diagnosis, treatment, and prevention of various addictive patterns of behavior has become a major national public health effort, especially in the last three years. Attempts are being made to classify people into such types as non-users of drugs, experimenters, episodic users, regular users, and addicts.

Efforts are also being made to identify people by describing their potential reaction to stress as adaptive, maladaptive, or dysfunctional.

The goals are to identify high-risk individuals early, to intervene actively, and to try to prevent the addictive states from developing. Unfortunately, the evidence seems to suggest that experimentation with drugs is drifting downward, into junior high schools, and even into elementary schools, especially in poverty and deprived metropolitan areas.

Probably children and younger adolescents with chronic physical illnesses are more likely to be in the groups that tend to be maladaptive or dysfunctional under stress. They may be pushed toward drug experimentation because they may be in a prolonged infantile dependency state, less able to develop cognitive and conative skills, more likely to experience partial or actual rejection by parent figures, or receiving medication for their illness or for control of pain.

It is not appropriate to review the significant literature in this large and complex field. Glasscote, Sussex, Jaffe, Ball, and Brill recently published a detailed analysis of the subject entitled "The Treatment of Drug Abuse, Programs, Problems, and Prospects."[8] In addition the National Institute of Mental Health has an extensive information service on alcohol and on drug addiction.

PSYCHOSES IN CHILDREN AND ADOLESCENTS

These disorders are characterized by (1) personality disintegration; (2) poor evaluation of reality; (3) inability to relate to others; (4) ineffective school performance; and (5) specific symptomatology including mood changes, bizarre behavior, delusions, and hallucinations.

Psychoses are usually classified as psychoses associated with impairment of brain function (examples — intoxication, metabolic disorders, degenerative disorders, infection, convulsive disorders, trauma, neoplasm) and psychoses without known brain impairment (examples — early infantile autism, symbiotic psychosis, atypical child, childhood schizophrenia).

The former conditions will require assessment of intellect, memory, affect; in brief, one must consider the history, neurological findings, and laboratory results, e.g., electroencephalogram. The latter are more diffuse and vague, and require long-term observation, careful history, and usually some observation of parent-child interaction. The literature is extensive. Many children with chronic illness and the resulting malnutrition and delay in maturation and growth are difficult to differentiate from those with psychoses without brain impairment, and, not infrequently, the psychotic process and the chronic illness exist concurrently.

DIAGNOSTIC PROCESS

The field of child psychiatry has spent much of its time and effort in establishing a workable diagnostic procedure that is not time consuming and repetitive. For the most part, these efforts have been unsuccessful, as it takes much time and effort to assess the biological, psychological, and sociocultural factors that are involved in the child, in his parents, and in his total environment. Anna Freud, Frederick Allen, Margaret Mahler, and many other authors have made significant contributions to the elaborate process that is the idealized diagnostic standard currently utilized by most child psychiatrists. Implicit in their work is a team concept, which includes most of the following participants:

1. Pediatrician — biological and developmental status
2. Social worker — assessment of parent's personality
3. Psychologist — assessment of intellectual, emotional, and psychological factors
4. Child neurologist — assessment of specific neurological condition
5. Special education consultant — evaluation of child's educational deficits, deficiencies, and potential educability

6. Child psychiatrist — direct observation of the child's play and attempt to synthesize the clinical data and formulate treatment plan

It should be noted that these roles are frequently shared, interchanged, or altered, especially where professionals have worked together in positions of mutual trust and mutual respect. Other personnel also make significant contributions to the diagnostic process, e.g., nurses, child care workers, and group therapists.

TREATMENT

Treatment of children and adolescents with chronic physical illness and a clinical psychiatric condition requires a systematic plan. An ideal treatment plan would include the following phases:

1. Accurate medical and psychosocial diagnosis

2. Planned intervention by biological, psychological, and social efforts

3. Careful assessment of the positive and negative effects of intervention

4. Periodic revision of the types, quality, and quantity of interventions, as continued clinical observations reveal appropriate alternative strategies.

The treatment strategies that are available for the physician today offer many more possibilities than existed even 10 years ago. The physician can consider several types of intervention and can find fairly appropriate methods to measure their effectiveness. In addition to the specific disease-related treatment, these interventions are available for him to try to modify the concurrent psychiatric condition:

Various types of psychotherapy
> Individual (to deal with anxiety and depression)
>> Supportive and directive
>> Expressive and exploratory
> Group therapy (to deal with peer groups with common problems, e.g., children with diabetes)
> Family therapy (to deal with family disorganization and misunderstanding)

Psychopharmacotherapy
> Major tranquilizers (phenothiazine)
> Minor tranquilizers (diphenhydramine, meprobamate, chlordiazepoxide)
> Stimulants and antidepressants (amphetamines)
> Anticonvulsants (hydantoin compounds)

Residential treatment
Day care
Special education

Case Examples — Psychotherapy

B. A., a 10 year old boy, developed a pattern of antisocial behavior that included episodic truancy, fire setting, and temper tantrums. He had been a healthy child of bright normal intelligence until the age of five, when he and his four year old brother were injured in a flash fire in their home. His brother's injuries were minimal, and the burned areas healed without visible scarring. The patient, however, had major scarring on his arms and face. At age seven he was hospitalized for surgery to permit him to use his arm naturally, and the operation was very successful. Patient initially was quite fearful and sad about entering the hospital, remained depressed about his condition, declined to cooperate with the hospital's visiting teacher, and dropped back one semester in school. Subsequently, he was alert, bright, active, began to play with friends, talked openly about his future ambitions. When surgery was suggested to produce a facial cosmetic improvement, he was enthusiastic initially and recalled the success of the previous operation. Abruptly, he became overtly competitive with his younger brother and developed the other parts of his antisocial behavior. When seen for psychiatric evaluation, he was tense, depressed, reluctant to play or talk with the therapist. It seemed unwise to schedule the proposed surgery because of the patient's uncooperative, erratic, and impulsive behavior. In the fifteenth interview he stated spontaneously, "My brother will get ahead of me at school," then began to talk fearfully, then openly about his resentment about his own misfortune, his brother's good fortune ("he didn't get burned at all"), and his real and secret fears of rejection by his father, who had blamed him (incorrectly) for the fire. With support and encouragement, the unreal aspects of his fears and anxieties about his long-suppressed fantasies were allayed and, subsequently, his erratic, impulsive behavior terminated. Thus, it seems to this observer that B. A.'s actual physical impairment was exaggerated and compounded by the unresolved symbolic meaning that he had attached to the frightening and traumatic experience in his earlier childhood, and that supportive psychotherapy, with minimal interpretation of preconscious conflicts, had permitted him to give up his regressive antisocial behavior.

M. C., age 11, was seen for evaluation because of "idle talk about suicide" and "too much competition with her stepmother." The diagnosis of severe and chronic asthma had been established by the time she was seven. For the most part, the medical routine had been successful without utilization of steroids, although she had been hospitalized on several occasions each year, beginning at age three. Her mother was a nurse, assumed much direct responsibility for her care, maintained an allergy-free environment, finally obtained an oxygen tank and kept it near the girl's bedroom. Unfortunately, the father and mother quarreled frequently in the child's presence, with the father assuming that M. C. "was faking, not really wheezing." When the mother was killed accidentally, the patient had a severe asthma crisis, had to be hospitalized in a special children's facility, became steroid dependent, and began to show signs of precocious puberty. When she was allowed to return to live with her father and new stepmother, she was elated and quite happy. Within two weeks of her return, her parents became concerned about the presenting symptoms and other regressive behavior. M. C. had a good relationship with the pediatric allergist, who had been the physician in charge for several years, so a plan was worked out for him to see the girl for regular interviews. Treatment plan called for supportive psychotherapy, uncritical acceptance of M. C.'s nostalgia for her mother, careful exploration of her rivalry with the new stepmother, and greater emphasis on her child needs (dependency, reassurance) rather than on her emerging premature adolescent fantasies. The allergist consulted each month with a child psychiatrist and reported consistent improvement in the child's mood and behavior.

The principles of pharmacotherapy have been described effectively by Eisenburg, Fish and other authors.[5a, 7a] It is evident that one cannot predict what new and more useful behavioral drugs will be available in the future, but one can be confident that newer drugs will be found and that indications and contraindications for the use of drugs to manage affective states will be developed in more and more precise ways.

In a similar manner, the effectiveness of various interpersonal interventions, or psychotherapies, will, in my opinion, continue to develop. The essential elements remain: compassion, time, and consistent theoretical framework for the therapist, and an increasing awareness of the child's thoughts and feelings. John Meeks has captured many of these concepts in his book, *The Fragile Alliance,* which is about psychotherapy with adolescents.[18] The challenges are in the sociocultural area, particularly with adolescents, as we live in a very rapidly changing cultural situation. Peter Blos has written extensively about modern adolescents and the opportunities and dilemmas that they face.[3] Finally, Robert Lifton has identified two very significant factors that need to be recognized in assessing children and adolescents with chronic physical conditions. He suggests that there are two general historical developments:

1. *Psychohistorical dislocation* is the break in the sense of connection men have long felt with the vital and nourishing symbols of their cultural tradition—symbols revolving around family, idea systems, religions, and the life cycle in general. In our contemporary world one often perceives these traditional symbols as irrelevant, burdensome, or inactivating; and yet one cannot avoid carrying them within and having one's self process profoundly affected by them.
2. *Flooding of imagery* is a phenomenon produced by the extraordinary flow of postmodern cultural influences over mass communications networks. These cross readily over local and national boundaries, and permit each individual to be touched by everything, but at the same time cause him to be overwhelmed by superficial messages and undigested cultural elements, by headlines, and by endless partial alternatives in every sphere of life. These alternatives, moreover, are universally and simultaneously shared—if not as courses of action, at least in the form of significant inner imagery.[16a]

CONCLUSION

I have suggested that childhood and adolescence are very turbulent experiences for most of the youth of our country. We can describe the processes, identify types of children and adolescents (adaptive, maladaptive, and dysfunctional), and assess some of the factors in the parents. Our problems in identifying sociocultural values and stresses are much more complex and deserve our careful attention. Finally, the psychiatric conditions that one encounters in children and adolescents with chronic physical illness require adequate diagnosis, proper treatment and management, and a constant search for hope and compassion.

References

1. American Psychiatric Association: *DSM–II Diagnostic and Statistical Manual of Mental Disorders.* 2nd Ed. Washington, D.C., 1968. (L.C. No. 68–26515)
2. Bell, R. Q., Waldrop, M. F., and Weller, G. M.: A rating system for the assessment of hyperactive and withdrawn children in preschool sample. Am. J. Orthopsychiatry, 42:23–34, 1972.
3. Blos, P.: *On Adolescence: A Psychoanalytic Interpretation.* New York, Free Press, 1962.
4. Bolian, G. C.: Psychiatric consultation within a community of sick children. J. Am. Acad. Child Psychiatry, 10:293–307, 1971.
5. Bryson, C., and Hingten, R.: *Early Childhood Psychosis: Infantile Autism, Childhood Schizophrenia, and Related Disorders.* Publication No. (HSM) 71–9062. National Institute of Mental Health, Rockville, Md., 1971.

5a. Eisenburg, L.: Psychoses: I. Clinical features. *In* Freedman, A. M., and Kaplan, H. I. (eds.): *The Child: His Psychological and Cultural Development.* New York, Atheneum Publishers, 1972, pp. 201–212.

6. Engel, G. L.: Studies of ulcerative colitis. Am. J. Dig. Dis., 3:315, 1958.

7. Eron, L., Walder, L., and Lefkowitz, M.: *Learning of Aggression in Children.* Boston, Little, Brown, and Co., 1971. (L.C. No. 72–145569)

7a. Fish, B.: Organic therapies. *In* Freedman, A. M., and Kaplan, H. I. (eds.): *The Child: His Psychological and Cultural Development.* New York, Atheneum Publishers, 1972, pp. 360–369.

8. Glasscote, R., Sussex, J., Jaffe, J., Ball, J., and Brill, L.: The Treatment of Drug Abuse — Programs, Problems, and Prospects. Joint Information Service, American Psychiatric Association, 1972. (L.C. No. 70–187294)

9. Greenfield, N. S., and Lewis, W. C. (eds.): *Psychoanalysis and Current Biological Thought.* Madison and Milwaukee, University of Wisconsin Press, 1965.

10. Group for Advancement of Psychiatry Committee on the Family. The case history method. In *The Clinical Study of Family Process.* New York, Mental Health Materials Center, 1970.

11. Hine, F. R.: *Introduction to Psychodynamics A Conflict-Adaptational Approach.* Durham, N.C., Duke University Press, 1971.

12. Jenkins, R., and Stahle, G.: The runaway reaction—a case study. J. Am. Acad, Child Psychiatry, 11:294–313, 1972.

13. Kassebaum, G., and Baumann, B.: Dimensions of the sick role in chronic illness. Chap. 10 *in* Jaco, E. G.; Patients, Physicians, and Illness. New York, Free Press, 1972, pp. 141–154. (L.C. No. 70 110520)

14. King, M.: Evaluation and treatment of suicide-prone youth. Ment. Hyg., 55:344–350, 1971.

15. Langer, J.: *Theories of Development.* New York, Holt, Rinehart, and Winston, Inc., 1969. (L.C. 69–13564)

16. LaVeck, G. D.: The acquisition and development of values: Perspectives on research. Report of a Conference, May 15–17, 1968, Washington, D.C. Bethesda, Md., National Institute of Child Health and Human Development, 1968.

16a. Lifton, R. J. (participant): The acquisition and development of values: Perspectives on research. Report of a Conference, May 15–17, 1968, Washington, D.C. Bethesda, Md., National Institute of Child Health and Human Development, 1968.

17. Mattson, A., and Agle, D.: Group therapy with the parents of hemophiliacs: Therapeutic process and observations of parental adaptation to chronic illness in children. J. Am. Acad. Child Psychiatry, 11:558–571, 1972.

18. Meeks, J.: *The Fragile Alliance: An Orientation to the Outpatient Psychotherapy of the Adolescent.* Baltimore, Williams & Wilkins Co., 1971. (L.C. No. 75–147080)

19. Ruesch, J.: The infantile personality. Psychosom. Med., 10:137–144, 1948.

20. Segal, J.: *The Mental Health of the Child.* Program Reports of the National Institute of Mental Health. P.H.S. Publication No. 2168. Rockville, Md., 1971.

21. Shaw, C., and Lucas, A.: *The Psychiatric Disorders of Childhood.* New York, Appleton-Century-Crofts, 1970. (L.C. No. 78–109164)

22. Sliden, R. H.: Youthful Suicide: A review of the literature. (Unpublished manuscript for Joint Commission on Mental Health of Children, Task Force III) University of California, School of Public Health, 11, 1967.

23. Smith, D. W., and Marshall, R.: *Introduction to Clinical Pediatrics.* Philadelphia, W. B. Saunders Co., 1972. (L.C. No. 71–186955)

24. Stuart, H. C., and Prugh, D. G. (eds.): *Healthy Child: His Physical, Psychological and Social Development.* Cambridge, Mass., Harvard University Press, 1960.

Chapter 23

Sexuality and the Handicapped Adolescent

by *Peter Blos, Jr., M.D., and Stuart M. Finch, M.D.*

Adolescence is that period of human life during which the individual must adapt to the new set of inner and outer conditions with which the stage of biological puberty confronts him.[4] It is a stage of human development that has a foundation in the past, certain phase specific tasks that must be met, and a goal in the future of adult psycho-sexual-social maturity. As is well known, this period presents each individual with many challenges that produce a wide range of emotional and behavioral repercussions.

Puberty, a biological event, ushers in the beginning of adolescence with its impact on body growth and change, intellectual capacities, and sexual urges and abilities. Masturbation, menstruation, seminal emissions, curiosity about one's own body and that of the opposite sex, and sexual experimentation in fantasy and actuality are part of being an adolescent. How each boy or girl responds to these challenges, however, is individual and based upon both genetic endowment and experience. Kinsey's report was one of the first to provide systematic data about some of the actual sexual practices of adolescents, and was followed by other extensive studies.[12] The preoccupation the adolescent has with his own body, how it works, and — because it is never perfect — what is wrong with it, has, of course, been known to writers of fiction for centuries.[11]

The handicapped adolescent has the additional delicate problem of including his defect as part of himself without overstating or understating the case. If the defect is a congenital one, he, his family, and the society around him have been struggling with this for many years. If the defect is recently acquired, not only must an adaptation be made but a mourning of the lost function, capacity, or body part must also take place. One of the many dangers

521

that lurk along the way is the propensity to hold a defect as cause for suffering, pain, and lack of achievement, when in fact it may not be.

Case History

George, a short-statured young man of 17, was referred for psychiatric consultation because of poor academic performance and rebellious behavior. He was an arrogant, suspicious, and resentful boy who tried to make the ensuing treatment a combative engagement and a constant test of his strength and will power. It rapidly became evident that his short stature was something he not only resented but tried to deny by aggressive acts. He drove faster and drank more, and bragged about his exploits with girls. Beneath this bravado, he was quite insecure and persistently attempted to prove his masculinity by reaction formation and counterphobic behavior. George's symptomatic behavior, however, was not caused by his short stature. Rather, his small size had important symbolic meaning for him and served as a nidus around which many concerns — intrapsychic and interpersonal — clustered.

There exists little in the pediatric and physical medicine literature regarding the sexuality of handicapped adolescents. Rusk remarks in his textbook, "of all the problems confronting the disabled patient probably least has been written about those concerned with sexual functioning."[20]

Barker et al. reviewed the literature on adjustment to physical handicap and formulated the

... somatopsychological problem as the relation between physique and behavior. This relation is concerned with those variations in physique that affect the psychological situation of a person by influencing the effectiveness of his body as a tool for actions, or by serving as a stimulus to himself or others.[1]

Wright, writing on the psychological aspects of physical disability, devotes a chapter to the adolescent. Here she discusses the social-psychological problems at great length, but in our opinion naively sees marriage and financial independence as the standards for gauging adulthood. In addition, she states, "There is no systematic evidence to indicate that young persons with disabilities have more troubles in heterosexual adjustments than other young people."[22]

Rutter's more recent epidemiological study of the Isle of Wight demonstrated that if one excludes children with neurological handicaps, the rate of psychiatric difficulty in handicapped and nonhandicapped children is roughly the same.[21] This study, however, includes only youngsters up to the age of 12½.

As far as we are aware, there has been no study that has investigated sexual practices or experimentation, sexual fantasies, intercourse, or masturbation among handicapped adolescents. Lesser and Easser in writing of the deaf child noted

... in our survey we have found that sex would appear to be a taboo subject despite the prominence of the role that sexual development has been given in the understanding of [child] development and in the psychoneuroses. Sexual difficulties were not even mentioned.... The educators of residential training institutes for the deaf were bewildered and shocked by [our] inquiry into such matters as childhood masturbation, sexual curiosity and sexual play.[14]

In the psychiatric and psychoanalytic literature there are some reports detailing the treatment or investigation of handicapped adults that look back at the role the particular handicap played in their youth, the effect on fantasy and behavior, and the reciprocating effect upon the family. In addition, there are a few case reports of the treatment of children with physical handicaps. There are even fewer case reports on the treatment of adolescents with handicaps. Lussier presents a particularly vivid descriptive case, which is summarized later.[16]

At this point several comments need to be made that underscore some of the parameters that ought to be considered in thinking about any handicapped adolescent and his or her sexuality. First, the word adolescent refers to a heterogeneous grouping of both males and females of a considerable age range. Clearly the sexual problems and dilemmas of a boy and a girl are different and must be considered and respected. Equally obvious, but often forgotten, is the fact that sexual problems confronting the recently pubescent (10 to 13 year old) boy or girl are very different from those that face the physically more mature late adolescents (19 to 20). The younger group may often not appear to have any problems of sexuality, since they are frequently denied even under normal conditions and may be evident only in masturbatory practices and fantasy.

Second, the title of this chapter implies knowledge of what is "normal" sexual adjustment for a normal teenager. The fact is we know little except the broad outlines, and our judgment of "normal" is much more an assessment of the sexual behavior or the absence of it in terms of the total personality within the context of the social-cultural environment. For instance, homosexual experiences among some pubertal peers may be within normal limits while with others they may be indicative of emergent disease. A heterosexual middle class college couple may indulge in heavy petting and mutual masturbation and be considered sexually normal, while for youngsters of the same age from the lower class, such restraint may indicate extreme sexual fears and tensions. To add to the complexity of definition we have a rapidly changing world in which it would be difficult to establish accepted modes of conduct. How the normal adolescent integrates his or her developing sexuality in this day of free sexual expression in the movies and literature, suggestive clothing, and semi or actual nudity, plus society's greater acceptance of out-of-marriage sexual relations is largely unknown. We think it is safe to say that the level of sexual stimulation is higher today, more nearly ubiquitous, and more socially accepted than it has been. What, if any, impact this may have on handicapped adolescents is not known. We do learn from many adolescents in psychotherapy, however, that their free and seemingly easier sexual behavior masks many of the same old doubts, fears, and morality conflicts that were evident in past years.

Third, the sexuality of adolescents has its roots in genetic endowment, early childhood experience, family mores, parental attitudes, and sociocultural patterns. It is not something that springs forth de novo at the onset of biological puberty. Suffice it to say, one's relationship to one's body and its functions, to the body of the opposite sex, and to one's peers, is grounded in one's relationship to parents, siblings, and other important adults. Love, respect for self and others, and consistent discipline all play important foundation-building roles.

Case History

Gertrude was first evaluated at age five when her pediatrician was concerned about her entry into school. She suffered from osteogenesis imperfecta congenita involving all four extremities. She also had a moderate facial disfigurement, including a flattened nose and a prominent lower jaw. She could walk only with the aid of crutches and braces, and to all outward appearances was physically unattractive and seriously handicapped.

Surprisingly enough, she proved, even at such an early age, to be friendly, very intelligent, and quite self-sufficient. She was the third of three children, with two normal brothers. Her father was a machinist and her mother a "housewife." The latter term hardly gives credit for the remarkable job she had done as wife and mother. She took the psychiatric referral in stride and gently but firmly insisted her daughter was not only ready for school but should be with physically normal children.

The youngster handled herself remarkably well during the interview with a psychiatrist. She spoke openly and freely about her braces and crutches, yet not in a complaining way. The doctor later queried the mother about the problems she must have faced in having a youngster with such handicaps. She responded that there were indeed many but she really had not considered the physical defects as much as Gertrude herself. Perhaps the mother's most revealing comment came when she was asked how and when she disciplined her daughter as compared to her other children. She thought for a moment and then answered, "I guess the same as the others. If she misbehaves, she gets the same spanking as they did." Here were a mother and father who accepted the child and did not react in a distorted fashion.

This youngster was followed periodically into her mid-teens. Plastic surgery had corrected some but not all of her facial disfigurement. She remained in public school, continued to be a friendly, outgoing girl, and was fully accepted by her peers. She was a youngster who was well liked by all her peers, had dates, and gave every indication of heading toward a "normal" sexual adjustment. In summary, Gertrude's parents loved and accepted her *with* her disabilities. She was, therefore, able to accept her disability, neither making light of it nor overemphasizing it, and she could feel herself worthwhile. Such children are not common, but indeed they are to be found.

Fourth, we must consider timing. In the development of the embryo, the effect of a noxious stimulus is determined by the point in the developmental sequence at which it is introduced. The same is true in psychological development. The point in the life history of the child and his family at which a handicapping disability occurs has important implications for, among other things, sexual development. There are certain stages of life when a youngster is psychologically particularly vulnerable to the effects of severe illness, long-term disability, or other severe stress.

For the purposes of discussion we have chosen to define "handicap" in a broad context. To facilitate our presentation we have made the following groupings: (1) The problem may be markedly visible as an overt body distortion (e.g., the result of cerebral palsy, amputation, congenital defect). (2) It may be visible but concealable (e.g., the colostomy in an ulcerative colitis case, hypospadias, cryptorchidism). (3) It may be completely invisible, but its effects perceivable to the patient and others (e.g., diabetes, rheumatic heart disease, epilepsy). (4) It may be one of others that do not fit well into the foregoing groupings but are fairly common (e.g., schizophrenia, mental retardation).

GROSS BODILY DISFIGUREMENT

In this group we would place those youngsters whose disability is obvious to themselves and others. Congenital deformity, crippling disease that distorts the body, loss of limb, or severe scarring are all handicaps that are evident not only to the individual but to the world around him. The distortion not only impinges on the body image of the damaged person but also influences how others in the world around him will act and react. Wright has described the social anguish that these young people experience and has drawn on numerous autobiographies for illustrative material.[22] But we know nothing of the authors' sexual lives and fantasies. Lussier's case of Peter is the only one we know of in which this aspect has been studied in an adolescent.[16] The following is a summary of that case.

Case History

Peter was 13 when he began psychoanalytic treatment that was to last for 20 months. (Continuing contact occurred for another 16 months.) He had been born with congenitally deformed shoulders to which were attached foreshortened arms, 8 inches in overall length. On the left, the elbow was absent. The hands bilaterally had three fingers and no thumbs. By 10 he could feed himself with knife and fork, but needed some help in cutting meat. He could partially dress himself, but not tie his shoe laces. He needed help on the toilet until 13 when slight pubertal growth of arms and shoulders made it possible for him to manage this aspect of self-care on his own. Scholastically, he did poorly, being only able to read a few 2 and 3 letter words by nine. His family consisted of his mother, who was emotionally crippled by guilt and shame over her son's handicap, his father who had been away in the service until Peter was seven and was now an engineer's mate, and a sister, Mary, who was normal and three years Peter's junior. The problems precipitating treatment were recurrent nocturnal enuresis and severe academic retardation. In addition, "as soon became clear during the analysis the fundamental problem was an emotional disturbance expressed in a continuous and inventive evasion of factual truth and the creating of a fantasy life of remarkable complexity and color. There were, too, some depressive tendencies . . . . Unexpected was the way in which Peter failed to exhibit either masochistic satisfaction, passivity, or self-pity. Dominant in his behavior was the active striving toward the achievement of his goals."

To cope with his physical deformity, Peter used primarily three psychological defenses: extensive denial of the reality of his handicap; a vivid fantasy world wherein his splendid exploits were achieved without note of his deformity; and reaction formation to strive to do as well as or better without artificial aids than those who had normal arms.

Peter's neurotic problems were not different in many ways from those of a physically normal neurotic boy except for the "permanent, unconscious need to compensate for the lack of normal arms." The sexualization of his fantasy life, which focused intensely upon such activities as bicycle riding, trumpet playing, and swimming, made it impossible initially for him to either think or undertake in any way the performance of these activities. He would have to avoid thinking of *his* bicycle or trumpet at night. "It makes me feel too hot and too excited and then it is hard to fall asleep." He had also learned to masturbate while lying on his stomach. But Peter was able to make the change from symbolic activity to real constructive action. The analyst assisted in the desexualization of these activities, and Peter was indeed able to learn to ride and even build a bicycle, to play the trumpet with performance level skill, and to swim with sufficient strength to earn a lifesaving certificate. Out of many grandiose, compensatory fantasies Peter had dared to try, to risk failure in these endeavors rather than to lapse into passivity and daydreaming. His analysis assisted in this important sublimation.

In connection with body images, it is important to note that Peter valued his arms and was insistent that they not be surgically removed so that a more efficient prosthesis could be fitted. His body was the way it was and he was going to make it work for him. At the same time, before the analysis, he had had to deny his handicap strenuously as a reality. The analytic work helped him to integrate his body as image and reality, which permitted invaluable ego synthesis and self-esteem and released considerable emotional energy.

This point concerning body image is important and should be stressed. Frequently the draw-a-person test is used to assess self-esteem and body image. Many times what is drawn is a figure that represents the ego ideal. This becomes evident when the patient is asked next to draw a picture of himself or herself. When these two pictures are very discrepant, stress is inevitable. Bender states:

Somatic diseases that distort the body structure cause an insult to the physical personality which the subject finds difficult to accept. This pathological process results in a discrepancy between the body structure and the body image constitutionally and socially acceptable to the patients. [This can lead to] behavioral discrepancies between what the body can do actually now and the behavior appropriate for and consistent with the body image.[2]

Peter demonstrated his struggle with this discrepancy when he was emotionally driven to action he was incapable of managing, e.g., jumping from the high diving board before he could properly dive or swim, as well as in his daring exhibitionistic compensatory fantasies.

Jacobson, in writing on the psychology of the exceptional, has described two types of women who have been severely physically handicapped since early childhood. The one "lives on spite, rebellion and worldly ambition" and the other "lives on self-sacrificing altruism, humble renunciation and acceptance of suffering." In the clinical examples provided in her paper one woman "refused to submit to the oedipal laws and was overtly rather uninhibited sexually" and the other "had renounced men and sex in general."[9] From the data provided one can only imagine the role of sexuality in their adolescence. The one was seductive, attractive, and charming and probably expected men to provide for her and succumb to her wishes. "In her adolescence her father's seductive overattachment to his daughter became so manifest that it drove her to an early marriage" that ended in divorce. Here sexual activity seemed to be used for, among other things, narcissistic and aggressive satisfaction with little regard for more mature gratifications and human relationships. The other woman, who had renounced sexual activity, was the opposite. Unconsciously, she "participated in her sister's 'worldly' pleasures as well as getting tremendous narcissistic gratification—spiritual as well as practical—from this masochistic position."[9] One can only imagine her as an adolescent of "angelic goodness" and "superior intelligence" who thereby caught people's interest and affection. Overt sexuality for her—as far as we can see from the material given—was denied on all fronts.

For these women, and for Peter, the physical handicap played an important role in the organization of their personalities in each stage of development. As Furman states in his description of analytic work with a six year old girl who was born with a blind and deformed left eye, "this little girl's deformity became involved in every stage of her development, making her psychological growth truly different and more complex." The task that faced the girl, her parents, and the analyst was "to delineate and restrict her difference from others to just the sightlessness of her left eye, [and restore] her self-esteem by limiting her damage to its proper reality proportions."[7] One of the psychological tasks of adolescence is to integrate sexuality as a part of the body and personality. Sexual behavior can be used to deny the defect or the defect can be used to deny sexuality. Reality and maturity lie somewhere in between.

CONCEALABLE BODILY DISFIGUREMENT AND DYSFUNCTION

This group contains a wide variety of disorders that range from severe handicap to minor cosmetic disfigurement without physical disability. The main characteristic of this group is that the defect is visible and palpable to the individual, but is concealable from others and can therefore remain a secret. In this category, for example, we would include such handicaps as permanent iliostomy or colostomy, congenital skeletal or genital deformities (e.g., cryptorchidism), large scars, pectus excavatum, certain eye problems, and skin blemishes.[3, 15, 17] As Niederland has pointed out, it is this secrecy that sets the group apart from those unconcealable malformations and handicaps of the previous section.[17] The "secret" has important implications for narcissistic development and the role of magic in fantasy and thought. In this regard, it is well to remember that "the secret" of a concealable deformity and its significant role in fantasy means that the secret may also be withheld from the doctor. In the everyday life of the adolescent this fear of having his defect discovered by peers often causes considerable difficulty around such familiar activities as using a public bathroom or a locker room. On the one hand the defect can be flaunted in an exhibitionistic albeit defensive manner or, as is more common, the youngster can go to great lengths to keep it concealed.

Case History

Andy was nine when he was brought for consultation because of hyperactivity, poor school work, impulsivity, and temper outbursts. He always felt cheated no matter what the circumstances. Medication for minimal brain damage and a special school setting had been of little help. He had been adopted as an infant, as had his older brother, Rupert, age 11, and a younger sister, Susie, age six. Andy had hypospadias with the urethral opening on the underside of the penile corona, and surgical repair had been deemed unnecessary. His brother had a congenital clubbed foot that had been operated on and placed in a cast several times. The sister had no congenital defects.

Andy was an attractive, outgoing, freckle-faced young lad who was beset by feelings of inferiority. He constantly wore a chip on his shoulder and would explode in rage at the slightest frustration, which he perceived as public evidence of his inadequacy. A look or an accidental push would be perceived as an attack on his masculinity. When his penile defect was discussed with him he became subdued and could not describe it or draw it, although he clearly knew he was different. His mortification that he could not urinate like other boys and that his urinary stream would often spray on his pants knew no bounds. In addition he was very fearful that others would find out about his defect.

Rupert, on the other hand, handled his congenital defect in quite another manner. He endured operations, pain, and casts with good-natured stoicism. He could talk about his clubbed foot fairly comfortably and understood his condition. He was not a behavior problem, had friends, and learned well at school. The parents felt he had made a good adaptation. In contrast they were dismayed, disappointed, and angry with Andy because he complained loudly and bitterly and felt more cheated than his brother who, they felt, had a more significant handicap and had had greater actual pain and suffering.

The contrast in the way these two adopted boys managed their handicaps is in part due to the fact that Andy had a "secret" that he wished desperately to keep hidden from others as well as from himself. Rupert, on the other hand, was forced by circumstance and marked visibility to acknowledge his handicap and to include it in his total self-concept and body imagery.

Parker reports a case that we would like to summarize as another example of a concealable defect.[18]

Case History

Julie had spina bifida with a meningocele associated with some neurological problems. The latter were evidenced in the impairment of muscular development of one leg and "sudden, unpredictable, uncontrollable evacuations of bladder and bowel." In her growing up years, Julie had managed, despite her handicap, to have good and pleasurable peer relationships. When accidents did occur on the playground, children could be casual and supportive and not reject her in disgust. Children became aware of the tumor, were curious, and would want to touch it. Since this made Julie uncomfortable she became more adept at keeping it a secret and few knew of it. In adolescence she had many friends, as well as boy friends with whom on occasion sexual play would occur. Later on, she had intercourse with several men and eventually had a relatively long affair. She was not promiscuous and could derive pleasure from her sexual activities.

Successful surgical correction occurred in Julie's early twenties and she sought psychotherapy for depression seven years later. Removal of the tumor and correction of the sphincter problems had not provided the emotional release she had expected.

In connection with her body imagery it is interesting to note that Julie had made the observation that "when drawing a human figure, she found it physically impossible not to put a bump on the back." In addition, she also became aware that she felt incomplete without her tumor, and a mourning of this loss had to occur.

From the data given, Julie's peer relationships, including those of a sexual nature, were not stunted or made maladaptive by her disquieting congenital defect. Nevertheless, Julie's defect, and its effect on sphincter control, placed a profound stamp on her adult thought processes and behavior, which Parker delineates quite convincingly. She also states:

Julie's development shows that when such internal [psychic] stability has been created by the maintenance of firm limits in the framework of love and consistency towards the child on the part of both parents, severe ego defects can be greatly mitigated.[18]

We would like to stress that the meningocele had been integrated into Julie's body image as a part of her reality even though it was concealable from others and was distasteful to her.

Andy, however, was caught between the wish to deny his defect, which was facilitated by its concealability, and the inevitable confrontation with reality whenever he had to urinate. Consequently, successful integration was impossible.

Ulcerative colitis with permanent iliostomy or colostomy is an illness that we have elected to place in this group since the presence of a new body stoma associated with an eliminatory prosthesis is both personally visible and concealable from others. This chronic illness can be a severe, debilitating, and at times fatal disease especially if onset is in childhood. It is a poorly understood disease, and because of its complex interrelated physical and mental aspects, a team approach to treatment has frequently been utilized. Psychiatrically speaking, studies have demonstrated that children with ulcerative colitis have a core depression often covered over with a defensive layer of compulsiveness. Psychotherapy, while probably not reducing the number of cases that eventually come to surgery, appears to decrease surgical mortality and improve postoperative adjustment. Surgically speaking, a sizable percentage of these cases undergo colostomy. This is especially true if conservative medical management has not been able to prevent extensive bowel damage or the disease has progressed for several years. In most cases, the rectum either is removed with the colon or, if left intact, continues to be involved with the disease and must finally be removed later. Thus, most of the cases coming to surgery end with a permanent iliostomy. Rarely the rectal stump is left in and remains healthy, and after three to four years a reanastomosis may be tried.

When surgery is recommended, one of the most frequently expressed concerns of parents and their adolescent child is about the effect surgery will have on the youngster's future sexual life. While it is customary for physicians to answer that there is virtually no impingement on sexual functioning, this is strictly true only from the physiological standpoint. What effect the temporary or permanent iliostomy will have on personality structure, narcissistic injury, body imagery, and the strain on the ego's capacity to cope is not easy to predict. For the adolescent who is coping with his own normal bodily changes and those of his peers, it is trying, to say the least, to integrate a permanent surgical violation of the body. If we add to this an "invasion" of bathroom activities into sexual activities that is created by the presence of the iliostomy, a youngster's coping powers may be sorely tested. Finally, add to this the frequent premorbid psychological problems of patient and family. Formidable adjustment problems can be expected and can include the area of sexuality. The following two vignettes serve to illustrate the healthy and unhealthy extremes of adaptation to ulcerative colitis.

Case History

Jean was 11 when she first had a thorough evaluation for what proved to be ulcerative colitis. She was an intelligent but quite compulsive girl from a rather rigid family who had few friends and seldom ventured from their home. The children, three in number, of which the patient was the oldest, had been raised under a strict authoritarian philosophy and had had little contact with peers. The family lived an isolated life, and when schooling began for Jean she was much upset by the various things she saw and heard. Bowel irregularities and food idiosyncrasies had existed for a long time, and when she first had bloody diarrhea she hid it from her parents. Finally it was discovered and brought to medical attention.

Jean's disease was considered to be sufficiently serious to warrant hospitalization in a psychiatric setting. She and her parents were initially resistant to the whole concept of any emotional contribution to her illness, but with the help of the pediatrician and the surgeon they were able to accept psychiatric hospitalization. The family, in spite of their rigidities, proved to be remarkably cooperative, and many positive changes occurred. The emotional climate did improve, yet the girl had to have a colectomy and an iliostomy. Following surgery she did well and was followed psychiatrically for some time as an outpatient.

As she became a teenager, she not only adjusted well to her iliostomy, but became a gregarious, attractive youngster with many friends. Four years postoperatively, the decision was made that her intact rectal stump and ilium were sufficiently free of disease to warrant a reanastomosis.

Interestingly enough, Jean, then 15, when offered this option was initially unsure if she wanted to undertake the surgical procedure. She was not fearful of the operation per se, but rather, in her remarkable adjustment to her iliostomy, wondered about changing her adaptation and risking a possible disappointment. She knew, at least intellectually, that there was a distinct possibility that the reanastomosis would not work. She recognized that her hopes might become unrealistically high and a disappointment would be hard to bear.

The main point to be made is that this girl had adjusted well not only to her iliostomy but to family, friends, and school. She did eventually decide to have the operation and in the ensuing three years has done well.

Case History

Jack serves as an example of a child with a chronic disease, in this case ulcerative colitis, who became a poorly adjusted teenager with little or no normal sex activity. He was 12 when the diagnosis was first confirmed. Unfortunately, neither he nor his parents could be convinced of any emotional contribution to his disorder. He was a markedly passive-aggressive youngster who literally used his colitis to get what he wanted. He would make demands of his parents and if these were not granted he would spend up to two or three hours on the toilet complaining loudly. He did not have severe diarrhea, but occasionally did have bloody mucus stools. He also had minor rheumatoid arthritis about which he constantly complained.

His parents were both hostile but in different ways. The mother dominated the family but overprotected her son. The father was passive-aggressive in many ways like Jack. Each parent complained about the problems of the other, which made for a stormy marriage.

Jack's disease progressed, and at 13 he underwent a colectomy with a resultant iliostomy. The postoperative course was stormy, and neither Jack nor his parents could adjust to the iliostomy and its care. The boy went slowly downhill, both physically and emotionally. He was very short and underweight from his long illness. He had a "moon face" from prolonged steroid therapy. He became increasingly infantile, demanding, and passive. His iliostomy care was poor and neglectful. He lost the few friends he had, had no contact with girls whatsoever, and began to miss more and more school. Jack was withdrawing on all fronts and becoming hostilely defensive. He thus became an individual who was increasingly difficult to reach and to whom one could not relate.

The role of the iliostomy stoma and the plastic bag in sexual fantasy and sexual play is not available to use in these case illustrations. Druss et al. do describe this kind of data and we would like to cite it to illustrate sexualization occurring. In their follow-up study of iliostomies following colectomy they were able to interview extensively four women out of a total of 41 respondents. What is of interest in their admittedly small and biased sample is: (1) the patient's use of the plastic bag as a masturbatory device; (2) the patient's observation of the stoma as an engorgeable organ that responded to stimulation (e.g., cleaning); (3) the conscious fantasy of the stoma being like a penis, and (4) the wish to show off and display the prosthesis. It should be noted that three of these women were more satisfied with their sexual life after the colectomy and, in general, all four were leading active, productive lives.

INVISIBLE DISABILITY OR DEFECT

This group comprises a number of well-recognized chronic disabilities that can afflict adolescents. We would include in this group such relatively common diseases as juvenile diabetes, asthma, epilepsy, hemophilia, kidney disease, and cardiac disease. There are three characteristics that these diseases have in common: (1) Nothing of the primary disease can be visually or palpably perceived by the patient or others as being "wrong" with his body. Generally the patient seems "normal" to others. What can be perceived sometimes by the patient are bodily signs that can serve as warning signals. For example, the aura of the epileptic, the early breathing difficulty of the asthmatic, the diabetic's perception of impending hypoglycemia or acidosis. Other visual perceptions are related to secondary effects of the disease such as barrel chest in asthma or side reactions to medications such as "moon face" secondary to steroid therapy, and lumpy and scarred skin secondary to insulin injection. (2) The characteristic manifestations of the disease often occur precipitously in a seemingly capricious and unpredictable way. (3) The life-threatening or life-curtailing characteristics of these illnesses pose perpetual adaptational problems.

Much has been written about the psychological impact of these diseases but little about how they have affected the sexual lives of adolescents. But the latter two of these three characteristics impinge on the adolescent just where it can hurt the most. His capacity for being in control of his own body is threatened. His ability to take care of himself and to be an autonomous individual is made more problematical. His need "to be like the others" in order to gain the group support he needs to differentiate himself from his parents and family is thrown into high relief. But it is hard to predict how a particular adolescent will react to a particular disease occurring in the context of a particular family at a specific time in his development. As we have stressed throughout this chapter, the development of the youngster's pre-illness personality, especially his ego coping capacities, and the parents' ability to cope with the stress and threat of their child's chronic illness are crucial factors in how well and in what way the adolescent manages his illness.

Juvenile diabetes is a not uncommon disability that often occurs before the age of six and demands proper control, which includes dietary restrictions and daily insulin injection. In addition, these diabetics are frequently "brittle" and present problems in medical management. Often "getting out of control," by becoming either hypoglycemic or acidotic, is unpredictable and the child, parents, and physicians search for precipitating factors. Unfortunately this search "for control" all too often focuses on the child or parent as being at fault for not carrying out management plans accurately. In any case, when the juvenile diabetic arrives at adolescence, the problems multiply. Many will deny the disease, try to lead a "normal life," and ignore medical advice. They will go to parties and eat as others do. They will "forget" their insulin as if to say "if I don't need (use) the medicine, I don't have the disease." All too often they show up in emergency rooms, usually in a coma. After such a crisis they may deny they had anything to do with precipitating the crisis. In psychotherapy, fantasies may be elicited of "drug (insulin) dependency," weakness, passive-aggressive rage at parents and the world for giving them this disease, and diabetes as a punishment for masturbatory or other "bad" activities. Body imagery also must incorporate reasonably correctly this chronic change in the body's function and needs. Kaufman and Hersher demonstrated how body drawings, discussions, and fantasy "about the nature of their pathophysiological processes and its effect on their internal organs" in five diabetic teenagers revealed clearly the complex interweaving of reality data regarding their illnesses and personal, idiosyncratic, primitive thought and logic.[10]

One of the ways in which an adolescent can strive against the feelings of being different, unacceptable, and damaged is by sexually acting out. The following case illustrates this.

Case History

Jane was four years old when the diagnosis of diabetes was established, and both dietary restriction and insulin were necessary to maintain adequate physiological control. She soon showed her resentment and unspoken anxiety via rebelliousness. Her parents, being quite compulsive, responded to this with attempts to oversee and regulate every aspect of her life. At home they were overzealous about her diet and yet made it plain that they did not appreciate the extra effort involved. If Jane went to a friend's birthday party, the hostess would be warned ahead of time about her condition and precise dietary limitations. As Jane reached adolescence she became increasingly resentful, rebellious, and hard to manage. She would often flout her diet and neglect to take her insulin. Repeated episodes of diabetic coma occurred despite warnings, threats, and instructions by her doctor and parents. Beneath this façade of bravado and devil-may-care attitude, Jane felt unloved and unacceptable.

In her early teens she began to become involved sexually with boys, and as her reputation spread many boys would indeed seek her out. She would always keep her diabetic condition a secret from them. Jane, through her sexual activity, could fulfill her unconscious longing for the attention she craved, the physical contact she desired, and the release of the bodily tension created by her profound sense of bodily inadequacy. In addition, she could maintain the illusion of being mature, grown-up, and independent.

In this case we see an example of sexual "acting out"; that is, the use of sexual activity repeatedly and unconsciously to prove the adequacy, worth, and desirability of one's body; to defend against chronic anxiety; and to retaliate against hated parents. It is, for both sexes in adolescence, unfortunately, not an uncommon form of defensive behavior that is difficult to modify because of its syntonic nature.

Epilepsy is another disease that lends itself to abundant misunderstanding and the development of fantasy. This is particularly true if it is idiopathic in nature and not caused by accident or injury. The "epileptic personality" is no longer a useful concept although it is surprising how the myths and folklore about this disease persist. In adolescence when so much is sexualized, this illness lends itself to much sexual fantasy. The uncontrollable rhythmic jerking of the body in a seizure followed by somnolence is easily confused with sexual orgasm. The fear may exist, either consciously or unconsciously, that masturbation or intercourse will, by its heightened level of ex-citement, precipitate a seizure. One type of defensive maneuver to avoid this whole issue may be the development of asceticism with strong intellectual in-terests.

Fraiberg has described in considerable detail the psychoanalytic treat-ment of an eight year old girl with epilepsy documented by electroencepha-lography.[6] In this case there were strong unconscious links between Nancy's aggressive and sexual feelings and the presence of seizures. She would mas-turbate in a particular and compulsive manner, but was anesthetic to genital sensation.

> With the recovery of genital sensation, the persecutory feelings in relation to mother disappeared from the picture and there was a marked diminution of seizures. At the same time spontaneity returned to her personality.[6]

Whenever the genital anesthesia returned on a hysterical basis, the same syndrome was reactivated.

Lest there be misunderstanding, we do not mean to imply that fantasies about sexuality are the only ones generated by epileptic disease, but rather that when such fantasies exist, they can have a profound influence on behav-ior. There is no doubt there is also a potential threat to such things as a sense of self-worth, the intactness of body imagery, especially the head, and fears of loss of control.

Asthma is a not uncommon handicap that may have its onset early in life or may not begin until adolescence. In some youngsters emotional factors may predominate, while in others allergic problems are primary. Whatever the mix of primary emotional or allergic factors, there is invariably a secondary emo-tional overlay. Again, this is an illness that impinges not only on the identified patient but on his family. Desensitization shots must be regularly given, fam-ily pets must be given away, certain foods may not be served any longer, and other, sometimes severe, household restrictions may be imposed. Not in-frequently conflicting advice has been given by different physicians, which can increase confusion and discord. The obvious difficulties of providing a "normal" childhood in this illness have their repercussions in adolescence. Overt rejection and overprotection are common and prove a difficult Scylla and Charybdis through which to chart a course. To make matters worse, these youngsters with intractable asthma often suffer serious damage to their pul-monary vital capacity, and their chest shape may become distorted. If pro-longer steroid therapy has been necessary, side reactions such as "moon face" complicate the emotional picture.

Case History

George was 14 when he was referred for residential psychiatric treatment, having been a severe asthmatic since the age of two. He had spent considerable time in pediat-ric hospitals and had developed many dependent and passive-aggressive character-istics. George was very small for his age, quite immature emotionally, and thoroughly unskilled in relating to peers as well as adults. He tried to be assertive by manipulating his parents and, with less success, his peers. In attempts to "improve his image" he openly boasted of many feats that clearly were impossible for him to accomplish. In psy-chotherapy, eventually he talked of his interest in girls, but it had a superficial ring and in reality he was unable to form a lasting relationship with any girl. During his psychiatric hospitalization he gradually improved his adjustment and the severity of his asthma diminished. However, he remained a frail, physically handicapped, and emotionally immature teenager.

SEVERE HANDICAPS THAT DO NOT FIT OTHER CLASSIFICATIONS

In this final group we have placed several chronic handicaps that perhaps have in common only the overwhelming disruption the disability produces on the entire personality and its environment. As examples we briefly discuss blindness, deafness, mental retardation, and schizophrenia. It is obvious that sexual fantasy life and behavior are only a single facet of the multitudinous difficulties with which these youngsters and their families must struggle. It is equally obvious that many determinants go into how such an afflicted youngster manages the biologically given sexual drive, and we are able to touch on only a few of them.

Blindness

Congenital blindness and deafness are sensory losses that profoundly affect the course of the individual's entire life. Blindness is usually detected by the physician or parents in early infancy, usually earlier than deafness. In either case it has a tremendous effect upon the parents who are confronted with dismaying prospects. They and their medical advisors are often completely unaware of the special needs of such an infant as well as of how to cope with their own overwhelming feelings of depression and guilt. In any case these specific congenital disabilities deny the infant the use of primary sensory modalities that are so important in the development of human relationships. When sight is absent, hearing and touching generally increase their importance as ways in which to relate to others and the world around. Many such children must spend years in institutions for the blind or the deaf for special education. Often, despite staff efforts to the contrary, they develop "institutional" personalities with extensive dependency attributes. For the adolescent, the sexual drive may manifest itself in autoerotic activities such as masturbation. Sexual play may occur between adolescents in such institutions, but often it is of an immature nature. The type of problem that confronts such youngsters in the sexual area may perhaps be exemplified by the practice of touching among the blind. To touch a person's face and hair as a way of establishing another's individuality may be permissible, but how to learn of sexual differences when to touch another's sexual body part is either prohibited or carries with it enormous stimulation? That youngsters and their families can negotiate this long and difficult maturational course is attested to by the fact that many of the congenitally blind have grown up, married, and led a normal sexual life. But we are rather ignorant of the vicissitudes that this entails and what toll must be paid.

Should blindness through accident or illness occur in childhood or adolescence, it is a psychologically traumatic event. Obviously bilateral blindness poses a much more serious problem than does blindness in which only one eye is involved. Here again prior personality development and coping capacities determine further psychological development. The individual must deal with this catastrophe in much the same way as with the amputation of any vital body part.Mourning for the lost part has to occur as well as a gradual incorporation of the defect in the body image. The danger is that the loss of vision may serve as a nidus around which latent psychological problems crystallize.

Deafness

Hearing loss or absence has a different isolating effect on the personality than the loss of vision. If it is of a congenital nature it is a major impediment to the development of speech, verbal thought, and conceptualization. The isolation from others is profound and results in some of the typical personality characteristics of the congenitally deaf child as listed by Lesser and Easser:

> Egocentricity, rigidity, impulsivity without accompaniment of anxiety or guilt, a paucity of empathy and a lack of realization of the effect of their behavior on others.[14]

Without direct evidence we can only suggest that with this kind of personality, satisfying sexual contact as part of a total human relationship must be unusual. Certainly for such an adolescent, the integration of sexuality into the personality is difficult. We would agree with Lesser and Easser that there is a rich vein of knowledge to be mined in the study of the perceptually handicapped both to increase our capacity to be helpful to those in need and to further our knowledge of man's adaptational plasticity.[14]

Mental Retardation

Mental retardation is a major handicap that involves up to 3 per cent of our population. In fact it is really a complexity of syndromes and ranges from the mild to the profound retardation that may be associated with physical difficulties. To facilitate discussion we will arbitrarily divide this group into three categories, severe, moderate, and mild, and limit our discussion of this large field to some problems the mentally retarded have with sexuality. The more severely defective often have associated physical disabilities and are most likely to be placed in institutions. Generally speaking, their sexual drives are manifested in immature and autoerotic behavior. They may rock or masturbate openly for long periods, or seek other self-induced sexual gratification. Their poor capacity for more than childlike relationships and their physical handicaps make sexual relations with partners unlikely. However, their at times open sexual displays do make for social management problems.

The moderately retarded youngster whose IQ is in the range of 50 to 75, has quite different problems. He is intelligent enough to know he is not as smart as others. While such a youngster usually lacks physical stigmata and on casual meeting seems normal, he knows he is different. He has been put into special classes, younger siblings have surpassed him in reading and writing abilities, and more often than not he has been labeled by other kids as dumb or stupid or called "retard." When he arrives at puberty he is socially and emotionally immature, and his endowment of sexual drive is usually less than that of other youngsters of his age. Often such youngsters are trusting and search for acceptance. When they do become involved in sexual activity, it is usually at someone else's instigation (for example, the recent movie "The Last Picture Show"). If the event offers some gratification without too much conflict, the attention is welcome and the activity is likely to recur. The obvious hazard for moderately retarded girls is that pregnancy is also likely to occur, in part because they can retain only a hazy notion of conception and contraception. For this and other reasons, some authorities have recommended sterilization or the insertion of an IUD in later adolescence.

The mildly retarded may be divided into two quite different groups. The smaller group is born or perhaps adopted into middle or upper class families in which the intelligence of parents or siblings is higher than their own. They are unable to perform up to expectations, which precipitates parental criticism and results in lowered self-esteem and often in behavior disorders. Only after some years may the problem be correctly diagnosed, and by then much character damage has occurred. In adolescence these youngsters may act out rebelliously in an aggressive or sexual manner with little conscious awareness of their unhappiness and its causes. The other group of mildly retarded is much larger in number, and they suffer from the multidimensional effects of poverty. They have had inadequate nutrition, nurture, and protection and have lacked appropriate stimulation over many years. Their tested IQ labels them as retarded but they are not much different from their siblings, parents, or peers. In fact their innate intelligence, at least as demonstrated by their ability to cope with a difficult environment, may be perfectly normal. This group tends to impulsive action, of an aggressive or sexual nature. It is debatable whether these young people are truly "medically" defective, but it is without question that they carry a heavy social handicap.

Case History

Barbara was 15 when she was first charged with prostitution. Ordinarily such charges would have been dealt with by the juvenile court, but Barbara had a long string of earlier offenses, so the circuit court was given jurisdiction. She came from a family of nine children who had been conceived by three different men. Her mother was an alcoholic and a parttime prostitute who had often been jailed and therefore could give little attention to her children. Barbara, as the oldest, frequently had to fill in to take care of her siblings. In addition, she had witnessed many of her mother's sexual escapades and at the age of 10 had been molested by one of her mother's boyfriends. As far back as she could remember, sex, violence, and stealing had been integral parts of her life. On the Stanford-Binet intelligence test, Barbara was mildly retarded, but her test results were such that the psychologist felt that she had more potential than the testing revealed.

It was unfortunate but hardly surprising that Barbara had little capacity for meaningful relationships. From infancy onward, meaningful adults had been unpredictably loving and markedly inconsistent. She had learned her lessons well—sex is to be sold, things are to be taken when needed, and angry feelings are to be expressed immediately on whoever or whatever is available. As with so many "mildly retarded," the presumed intellectual defect was not her biggest problem. Rather, she had built a primitive, poorly integrated personality and internalized a set of antisocial values all of which stood her in poor stead as a foundation for adult maturity. She was a truly handicapped adolescent.

Schizophrenia

Schizophrenia is a chronic disorder that comes in many forms and disguises. Whether one believes it is of organic origin, interpersonal origin, or both, it is possible to make a few generalizations about the schizophrenic's adolescent sexual adjustment. Whether the disorder begins early in life or at puberty, whether the symptoms have the classic features or lie in neurotic acting out behavior, multiple crippling neurotic symptoms or psychophysiological disorders, all these youngsters have a serious problem with human relationships and cannot get close to anyone. Sexuality for them is frequently fraught with danger, distortions, misperceptions, and mistakes. They may remain isolated from others and hide or deny their sexual drive, or have "strange" impersonal relationships with others of either sex. Rarely, a schizophrenic adolescent commits a serious or fatal so-called "sex crime." These are all badly damaged people with tremendous interpersonal handicaps.

Case History

At the age of five Dorothy, with a diagnosis of symbiotic psychosis, was admitted to a children's psychiatric residential treatment center. On admission she was an attractive but obviously seriously disturbed girl who frequently used neologisms and repeated TV commercials without apparent reason. In an indiscriminate manner she related poorly and inappropriately to everyone. During Dorothy's five year hospitalization, her mother divorced and remarried, retaining little interest in her daughter. Nevertheless, Dorothy did improve in many ways during her hospitalization.

She continued in outpatient psychotherapy for several years after her discharge. She had an extremely gifted therapist, and her relationship with him was vital but remained stormy. She gave every evidence of wanting literally to be a part or an extension of him and became furious with him whenever he went on vacation, was a few minutes late for an appointment, or even had to end the regular appointment.

In due time Dorothy became an extremely attractive adolescent. At first appearance her pulchritude attracted many boys, but all of them quickly lost interest. As a result of her therapy, she had built a "new" personality that in many ways was superior to her "old" one. But when the boys got to know her better, she was still lacking in warmth, depth, and spontaneity. She had literally learned a new type of behavior that, although more socially acceptable, left her an emotionally isolated cripple.

CONCLUSION

We have attempted to explore in this chapter the little known area of sexuality in the life of the handicapped adolescent. Sexuality has been broadly defined to include not only manifest sexual behavior but such concepts as body image, object relations, self-esteem, ego ideal, and reality testing, all of which influence sexual adjustment and behavior. The implication is that sexuality is expressed not only in sexual acts per se but also in one's capacity for human relationships and ability to play, work, and learn. "Handicap" has also been defined in a broad fashion to include any chronic illness of a physical or mental nature that serves to differentiate a youngster markedly from his peers. For purposes of exposition, handicaps have been separated into four groups: (1) handicaps that are visible and unconcealable both from self and others; (2) handicaps that are visible to oneself but concealable from others; (3) handicaps that are invisible to oneself and others; and (4) significant handicaps that do not fit the other groupings. Clinical examples have been presented in each group and we have discussed the many-faceted ways in which such an adolescent may react and adapt to the biological hormonal upsurge that occurs at puberty.

In the preparation of this chapter, we made several observations. Most startling was the paucity of data when the need for such knowledge seems so obvious. It is our speculation that this neglect is analogous to the neglect accorded, until recently, the phenomenon of death and dying. Both topics are difficult, threatening, and painful for all to discuss. In the area of the handicapped person's sexuality the future is difficult to predict except in regard to physiological functioning, and where this is clear, as in neurological impotence, the potential of talk seems bleak indeed. What must often happen, we think, is an unspoken collusion between doctor, patient, family, and peers to avoid references to sexuality or, if the question is raised, to "reassure" with generalities. It is easier to keep the focus on the admittedly difficult tasks of medical management, physical rehabilitation, and vocational training.

A question raised again and again in the literature was, "Is there a greater incidence of psychiatric disease among the handicapped than among the general population?" Pless and Douglas in their review felt that this issue is still not clear but believe that "a number of studies dealing with diverse individual disorders have strengthened the basis for the assumption that the chronicity of the disorder is of greater importance than its clinical attributes."[19] This concurs with our impression that *how* an adolescent incorporates his or her burgeoning sexuality into the totality of his personality has little to do with his *specific* handicap. We think that adaptation has much more to do with the time of onset in the specific patient's life, his previous psychological development, his capacities for coping with stress, the conscious and unconscious symbolic meaning of the handicap and how it was acquired, and his ability to come to terms with the handicap as well as the family's ability to master the trauma. As Kubie has said,

> Everyone carries from infancy and early childhood a residue of undigested experiences, of misconceptions, misunderstandings and misapprehensions about himself, about his body and about the world. Out of these undigested residues grow unconscious fears, unconscious guilt feelings, unconscious resentments and unconscious longings. Inevitably these underground streams are tapped by any profoundly moving experience.[13]

It is the reciprocal interaction between the handicap and this "underground stream" that determines the adaptation that is obtained.

The psychological study of the handicapped has for the most part taken homogeneous groups (e.g., diabetics, epileptics, amputees, dialysis patients) and tried to ascertain the presence of any psychiatric abnormalities — more particularly seeking to relate a type of disorder with a particular handicap. This has provided cross-sectional data. In the psychiatric and psychoanalytic literature there have been some treatment reports of individual patients with a specific handicap and we have summarized two such studies earlier. Here attention has been directed to the interplay of the three elements that Kubie has stated are part of any profound experience: "(a) the reality level; (b) the level of conscious fantasy and feeling and (c) the level of unconscious fantasy and feeling."[13] Thus we would like to see another question studied: "*How*, psychologically speaking, is a specific handicap dealt with over time by a particular individual and his family?" Perhaps the concept of "coping" might be useful in this regard. This question would get us away from the yardstick of normality, which is really only applicable to those who have an "average expectable environment," and an "average expectable endowment,"[14] and help us to focus on developmental processes. Then perhaps with some new knowledge, treatment of the handicapped might be facilitated. In the case of adolescence, the biological, hormonal upsurge causes rapid and widespread bodily changes that must be assimilated and integrated. If there are defects caused by genetics, accident, illness, or congenital malformations, these may only accentuate the struggle and prevent the integration of the self-image. Our task as psychiatrists is to convincingly provide the bridge from complex, individual dynamic understanding to concrete, helpful management recommendation. Much needs to be done here as well.

It is our hope that we have stimulated some to think and some to discuss more openly with their adolescent patients the trials, tribulations, and fears that their handicaps generate about sexual fantasy and functioning. For all concerned to deny that sexuality does indeed exist and is a problem for the handicapped adolescent is to deprive a youngster of desperately needed assistance. To choose what to say and when to say it may be difficult and will make the healthy adult feel uncomfortable, but the potentials are great. The possibilities we feel were hinted at in Lussier's case, which we summarized previously.[16]

We believe that mature sexual adjustment is possible for many handicapped adolescents as is attested by many who have achieved it. How they achieve it, what the vicissitudes of various aspects of the personality are, and how we may be of assistance deserve intensive study.

References

1. Barker, R. G., et al.: *Adjustment to Physical Handicap and Illness: A Survey of the Social Psychology of Physique and Disability.* New York, Social Science Research Council, 1953.
2. Bender, L.: Psychosis associated with somatic diseases that distort the body structure. Arch. Neurol. Psychiatry, 32: 1000–1024, 1934.
3. Blos, P.: Comments on the psychological consequences of cryptorchism: A clinical study. Psychoanal. Study Child, 15:395–429, 1960.
4. Blos, P.: *On Adolescence: A Psychoanalytic Interpretation.* New York, Free Press of Glencoe, 1962.

5. Druss, R. G., O'Connor, J. F., and Stern, L. O.: Changes in body image following ileostomy. Psychoanal. Quart., *41*:195–206, 1972.

6. Fraiberg, S.: The analysis of an eight-year-old girl with epilepsy. *In* Geleerd, E. R. (ed.): *The Child Analyst at Work*, New York, International Universities Press, 1967, pp. 229–287.

7. Furman, R. A.: Excerpts from the analysis of a child with a congenital defect. Int. J. Psychoanal., *49*:276–279, 1968.

8. Hartmann, H.: *Ego Psychology and the Problems of Adaptation.* Trans. by David Rapaport. New York, International Universities Press, 1958.

9. Jacobson, E.: The "exceptions" — an elaboration of Freud's character study. Psychoanal. Study Child, *14*:135–154, 1959.

10. Kaufman, R. V., and Hersher, B.: Body image changes in teen-age diabetics. Pediatrics, *48*:123–128, 1971.

11. Kiell, N.: *The Universal Experience of Adolescence.* New York, International Universities Press, 1964.

12. Kinsey, A. C., Pomeroy, W. B., and Martin, C. E.: *Sexual Behavior in the Human Male.* Philadelphia, W. B. Saunders Co., 1948.

13. Kubie, L. S.: Motivation and rehabilitation. Psychiatry, 8: 69–78, 1945.

14. Lesser, S. R., and Easser, B. R.: Personality differences in the perceptually handicapped. J. Am. Acad. Child Psychiatry, *11*:458–466, 1972.

15. Lipton, E. L.: A study of the psychological effects of strabismus. Psychoanal. Study Child, *25*:146–174, 1970.

16. Lussier, A.: The analysis of a boy with a congenital deformity. Psychoanal. Study Child, *15*:430–453, 1960.

17. Niederland, W.: Narcissistic ego impairment in patients with early physical malformations. Psychoanal. Study Child, *20*:518–534, 1965.

18. Parker, B.: A case of congenital spina bifida: Imprint of the defect on psychic development. Int. J. Psychoanal., 52: 307–320, 1971.

19. Pless, I. B., and Douglas, J. W. B.: Chronic illness in childhood: Part I. Epidemiological and clinical characteristics. Pediatrics, *47*:405–414, 1971.

20. Rusk, H.: *Rehabilitation Medicine.* 2nd Ed. St. Louis, C. V. Mosby Co., 1964.

21. Rutter, M., et al. (eds.): *Health, Education, Behaviour: Psychological and Medical Study of Childhood Development.* New York, Longman Group Ltd. [Wiley], 1970.

22. Wright, B. A.: *Physical Disability — A Psychological Approach.* New York, Harper & Row, 1960.

Chapter 24

Social Implications of Long-Term Illness in Children

by *Grace Fields, M.S.S.*

Many social problems of the handicapped child and family are sufficiently understood to justify an anticipatory or even preventive approach.
Which problems can be solved? Which can be diminished? Which must, for
the present, be merely coped with? Looking at the stresses experienced by
child and family in three areas, clues emerge for systematizing our knowledge
and refining our service patterns. These three areas concern the interaction of
the handicapped child and family: (1) with the treatment staff, (2) with each
other, and (3) with the world. This three-way division is a matter of emphasis
rather than precise separation. Implications for treatment pervade all sections.

THE HANDICAPPED CHILD AND FAMILY AND
THE TREATMENT STAFF

To identify and examine the mutual and separate stresses of the child and
family to be helped and those of the helpers, the primary observation area is
the health care system. This includes the physician's office, the large medical
complex with its wide spectrum of services and therapies, and the continuing
care programs in institutions or at home. These are where the handicapped
child and the treatment people meet.

One of the characteristics of this health care world is clear-cut definition.
There are precise names for ailments, specific remedies, exact procedures,
separate professional roles, definite places to go for definite services. There
are countable, definable ways of organizing time and personnel, appoint-

ments, clinic visits, and therapy sessions. There is always a beginning and an end.

In contrast, the problem being brought—whether the handicapping condition is juvenile rheumatoid arthritis, cerebral palsy, asthma, diabetes, or another disabling illness—is often a gnawing, endless, pervasive problem. The physical disability may have its crises, remissions, and periods of stabilization. The concomitant social problems, which often the child and family cannot distinguish from the physical problem, change. They do not necessarily parallel the crisis and success points of physical treatment.

Thus, people with a problem that is forever snatch intermittent solutions from a system as they pass through. Sometimes they feel trapped and detained. Sometimes they feel pushed out and rejected. Why is this so? Not because those in the system are indifferent to the nature of chronicity. Margaret Mead speaks of "too many needs for one human memory and one human brain to hold steady."[10] No one can be all things to all men, unless those men (even small ones and their parents) come and go in parade formation. At best, physicians, nurses, therapists of all sorts operate on a benign assembly line. The physician may complain because, since the medical work is done, the social worker should empty the bed so another patient can be admitted, his residents' learning be advanced, and more patients be helped. The social worker may complain because precipitate discharge takes no account that the mother is ill at home and that Johnny will soon be back in the hospital worse off than before if something isn't done about the home situation. They both know, however, that patients must move in and out of the hospital. It is not a commune. Dr. Morris Green identifies the nature and limitations of the health care transaction:

> While an acute illness can be managed and a helpful relationship can occur in an episodic encounter, a health care system organized to provide episodic care is usually not effective in such areas as growth and development, parent education, or behaviour stress.[3]

Within the health care system are experts in all these fields, and rehabilitation of children must of necessity take into account these and other psychosocial factors. The episodically geared system must develop some capability to respond differentially to nonepisodic need. Typical encounters between the health care system and the chronically ill child and his family reveal the meshing or missing of the system and the problem.

Sharing the Moment (and Years) of Truth

The news that a child is born congenitally handicapped, a feared diagnosis is confirmed, the results of an accident will be permanent—these moments, while most intensively shared by the physician and the family, are to a degree also an emotional transaction among the saddened parents, the child, and all related staff members. The place and people associated with emotionally laden news are significant. The system meshes with the need when those in it can resist the impulse to run or hide. To tolerate "being with" those in trouble without offering makeshift instant solutions requires professional maturity as well as commitment. New members in all professions require emotional as well as didactic support from their mentors until they can do this.

Ill-advised eagerness to spare parents pain can compound the tragedy. For example, the mother of a baby born with arthrogryposis was advised by her physician not to see the child since "it would only make her feel worse, and he would not live anyway." This boy is now 17 and still hospitalized despite dull normal intelligence and the ability to take care of most of his daily needs. Professional intervention was mobilized around the social situation when it was apparent the patient might be able to leave "the system." By that time parental patterns of denial and rejection were irreversible. The limitations thus imposed on the son and the guilt borne by such parents can only be conjectured.

However severe the disability, however limited the solutions, it is important for each family to have a chance to carve out, with the best help available, a sound plan for itself. Often the degree of disability cannot be accurately projected, and even if it can, absorbing the meaning of the professional formulations must be a step by step process for family and patient.

The chronically ill child and family need repeated episodes of service from many experts. An aggressive multidisciplinary projection of what can be offered, and when, is needed to connect child and family to their helpers in a rational, productive design.

The speech therapist's awareness of the feeding problems that will arise when a child begins to take solid food and their approximate timing may be as important in relation to follow-up as the knowledge that joint braces will need adjustment. At puberty, a child will have different privacy needs, and that this will have an impact on how bathing and dressing are to be accomplished can also be predicted. Helpful guidance may be offered by nursing personnel either at the hospital or in the community, but appropriate timing is critical. The first shopping trip when a physically handicapped child reaches the age of caring about appearance is an event with potential for either emotional growth and success or discouragement and withdrawal. If parents are given these check points to watch for, either in time periods or specific events, their sense of adequacy is reinforced.

"They said I'd need to come back now" sounds different from "They said I could come back if I needed to, but maybe I can manage on my own."

Thus the episodic system constructively serves patients with long-term problems. Clearly the system has or can develop the collective capability to delineate and project medical-social needs and matching service requirements. Whether it can locate and develop dependable connections with community-based services complementing those of the hospital is a challenging and sometimes frustrating issue. Wilma Gurney, speaking at the National Conference on Children Requiring Long-Term Hospitalization, called for a collaborative management network:

> Collaborative management cannot remain encapsulated within the hospital, but must be established within a network of community physicians, allied health specialists, and facilities. Such a network for collaborative management does not

just happen. It is purposefully developed, not only for provision of interim care, but for the purpose of preparing patients and families for the initial hospital care so that maximum benefit will ensue. . . . Too often those of us in medical centers are critical when communities lack the resources our patients need without taking the steps that would make those resources possible.[4]

Is not connecting the handicapped child and his family to a viable outside world as valid a treatment as ministering to them within the health care world?

The kind of work that St. Francis Hospital in Evanston, Illinois, did in connection with an educational program has implications for development of other interagency programs.

A committee made up of social workers, teachers, administrative personnel from the high school and from the hospital, and the director of the Visiting Nurse Association formulated a plan whereby the special services department of the high school would supply a teacher and teaching materials and the Evanston Recreation Department would provide facilities for the center.[17]

Goals — Common and Conflictual

When the treatment staff is engaged in diagnostic studies, evaluations, and intensive treatment processes they generally share common goals with family and child, and for the family there is a meshing of problem and solution. They are not alone with their problem; many wise and capable people are concerned. The time comes, however, when the achievable results have been achieved, and staff and family separate. Staff members may be moved by the tragic limitations a child must live with, or they may view the patient as lucky from the standpoint of relative disability. In any case, disengagement takes place. This is how professional persons are able to move on to the next "case." At best this disengagement is a loss for the family; at worst, it is experienced as rejection. Even the staff's assurance of being "available," even the clinic or doctor's appointment a few weeks hence does not hedge them against the loss of the tangible caring and sharing the experts in the system offered for the duration of their involvement.

Now comes the potential for conflicting goal setting. The staff's goal is as much independence for the child as possible; that means his parents will take him home and assure his place in the family, the school will make provision for his special needs, and, of course, there will be community-based recreation suited to his potential and limitations. Since this constellation of family and community capability may not be forthcoming, child, family, and staff goals may be dramatically or subtly in conflict. The family may wish there could be some more evaluations or treatment, since life was easier for all concerned when this was going on.

Long-term, intensive rehabilitation may put staff and family goals sharply out of phase.

Following spinal surgery for a malignant tumor, 12 year old Marie was placed by her loving and religious parents in a long-term care facility operated by devout members of their faith. She passively lay on her bed engaging in no greater physical activity than painting with her one good hand and arm on materials propped up for her. Both legs were paralyzed. On a return visit to the clinic, active rehabilitation was proposed and implemented. She became much more active, though she could move about only in a large electric wheelchair. In the course of a year of intensive rehabilitation, the whole family homeostasis was changed. Marie went home for occasional weekends; family activities were greatly modified for the other children as well as the parents so that Marie could participate.

When discharge was recommended, the family was cautious in accepting this, but ultimately undertook remodeling of the home to provide ramps and enlarged entrances so that Marie could get in and out. It was difficult for therapists whose heroic efforts had effected such dramatic changes to understand why the family moved so slowly in their preparations for taking Marie home. The active intervention of a social worker through-out this process assured the family time and support to change and regulate their defenses. When Marie was originally stricken the family had submitted to what they saw as God's will for their child and family. They saw themselves as supporting her and the other children through the process of her weakening and dying. Different plans and defenses were required when Marie's activity was greater and her life expectancy seemed improved. Their concern for the younger children was heightened at the thought of the patient being discharged home. In practical ways they felt overwhelmed by the burden of meeting the needs of all their children. They were also concerned about the greater emotional impact of Marie's death if she were a part of the family's everyday experience. When her malignant disease flared up and Marie quickly died, midway in preparations to go home, more adjustments were required of the entire family.

Without any question therapy improved life for Marie, and gave her a year she would not have had in terms of activity and stimulation. This same therapy complicated life for her family, and even though they were loving and devoted, their goals were at times out of phase with the health care system.

Families often cope with the helplessness of the handicapped child by relating to him as to an infant. Their gratifications are those experienced by a person on whom another is totally or largely dependent. Rehabilitation changes all this. Now the child has been enabled to be more independent. He must now be allowed to dress and feed himself, though these functions must be accomplished laboriously and slowly. The family has lost the earlier gratification of directly helping (we call it overprotectiveness), and a new basis of satisfactory coexistence must be carved out. Committed as staff members are to the maximum physical functioning of each person, it is apparent that the family or even the patient cannot always quickly and spontaneously espouse their goals of treatment. Clues for the resolution of goal conflicts emerge only as we recognize that they exist and inquire why. Then remediation can be offered at the appropriate point.

Communication and Coordination

Larry, a four year old boy with cerebral palsy, needed a series of surgical procedures interspersed with periods of intensive physical and speech therapy. This medical care had to be obtained many miles from his home. The physician in charge was aware of the emotional hazards for child and family, and unhesitatingly asked the mother to fly in and remain with the patient at what he saw as critical intervals within the treatment plan.

However, a serious breakdown in total coordination occurred. Larry had been away from home for 11 months. He had had several surgical procedures, and as he worked in physical therapy and with other staff people, the motivation theme became his wish to get back to his family to show brothers, sister, and father what he had learned to do. His functioning was imperfect, but dramatically better than when he had been at home. He wanted to demonstrate these gains to his family. The surgical timetable, however, called for another procedure, which would briefly immobilize the patient, after which it was projected that he would move forward to greater gains. Social workers, therapists, and others were concerned about the timing of the surgery, but the channel between them and decision making did not allow their convictions to be registered. The operation took place; Larry's mother flew in to be with him. The surgery done, the patient had no progress to show his mother. He was discouraged, regressive, and difficult to motivate.

The doctor then "got the message," and Larry went home for his much needed but now poorly timed visit without the skills he had wanted to exhibit to his family.

It is simplistic to blame the surgeon. We need to examine the system that connects surgeons and nurses and therapists and social workers. Whatever our interdisciplinary and interspecialty power struggles, the system must be considered our common servant. It must have the capability to accept orders derived from multiple expert perceptions of the patient's needs.

One of the most sobering features of the incident of Larry and his disjointed therapy and surgery is that it is recognizable and believable to anyone working in the health care system.

Douglas Brown says:

To combine managerial organizational efficiency with the humanitarian-egalitarian goals of the health field is one of the fundamental missions of the health care system.[1]

This mission is dependent on all of us in interdisciplinary work. How can we make each piece of our knowledge serve the interests of the patient and of the patient's family? Who should know it? How can this flow of knowledge be systematically directed? When it does not get through, can we identify and deal with the blockage? Are not breakdowns that are repetitive, classifiable, and predictable also preventable? Communication and persuasion are as vital in the medical complex as on Madison Avenue.

INTERACTION OF CHILD AND FAMILY WITH EACH OTHER

Erosion of the Parent Role

Any condition that disables the child assaults the parent-child relationship. Under normal conditions, parents for a time represent omnipotence and omniscience to their children. At best this role is not easily assumed by new parents though role expectations are clearly voiced by the infant who wants all needs met, all discomfort removed by the "parent people" who have charge of him. For the parent of the handicapped from birth child, the wise protector role is not attainable. Mother's kiss does not "make it all well."

In connection with her work with parents of handicapped children, Dr. Verda Heisler says, "When the powerlessness is experienced in relationship with one's own child, whom one is powerless to help, the pain is very deep."[5]

Whenever and however the disabling condition occurs, parents are diminished in their relative wisdom-power position.

Following an attack of encephalitis, five and a half year old Bryan spent 27 months in an intensive rehabilitation hospital. The pain this family felt at being displaced by the treatment staff comes through in excerpts from the social service record:

> In recent weeks Mrs. Doyle has begun to verbalize her feelings that she no longer is the important figure in Bryan's life. She feels that so much of great importance has happened to Bryan at the hospital that his "growing up" has been in a way taken out of her hands. As she puts it, Bryan was always her little baby and now he has become a little boy, but she has missed out on the experience of close contact with his daily growing and changing process.

It is significant to know that this mother felt she had "missed out" in spite of the fact that she and other family members visited often.

> Sixteen months after admission there had been some concern on the part of both staff and Mrs. Doyle around the fact that while Bryan was speaking freely to people here, he still was refusing to talk with his family. . . . A weekend visit schedule has been set up and Bryan spends every other weekend at home. This has helped considerably to alleviate some of Mrs. Doyle's feelings of being left out of Bryan's care. . . . He now [20 months after admission] talks readily with every member of his family, not only at home but when they visit him here. At present Mrs. Doyle is expressing concern around the fact that Bryan will not walk with his crutches when he is at home. . . . While she has some understanding of why Bryan may be refusing to walk at home . . . she also expresses honestly her feeling that it makes her "feel bad" when Bryan will perform correctly for strangers, but not for her. . . . She needs a good deal of support and reassurance from staff. . . . Mrs. Doyle also has some feelings she terms "jealousy" of staff. It is difficult for her to accept that this place has done things for Bryan that she as a mother has not been able to do.

> . . . As with speaking, Bryan ambulated at home at a much later date than he did here. He is now doing at home all the things he is able to do here. Mrs. Doyle has felt inadequate compared to staff in handling Bryan, and has been very apprehensive about taking him home, fearing he would regress.

Sharing the care of their child with others, parents may feel, "He doesn't belong to us any more." They may give him up to "others," and we call it rejection.

In the world of the specialist, parents themselves are often helpless "children." Clinical staff members then have the double responsibility of helping the parent with decision making and planning on the child's behalf and simultaneously reinforcing parent role fulfillment through other than traditional parent tasks. Crucial to this is recognition of the parent as a person with a particular set of needs and feelings, not all of which are related to the patient. Parents often comment with relief to social workers that they have at last been able to talk about *their* problems. "Parenting" may have come to mean little more than trying to fulfill assignments made by others. If the child improves, the parent feels it was what some wise person did or told him to do. If the child does not improve, the parent blames himself. Such parents need recognition and support individualized to their particular situation. This professional nurturing may reverse their sense of failure so that they can retain or recover their capacity to function with assurance.

Adjustment Tasks

The handicapping condition skews many processes and shifts many milestones. It also imposes its own progression of tasks. On the basis of work with parents of children handicapped by blindness, cerebral palsy, mental retardation, or disabilities in speech or hearing, Pauline C. Cohen outlined a progression of parent adjustment stages:

> 1. Experiencing a period of grief; 2. Acknowledging and learning to handle their anger; 3. Dealing with the anxieties aroused by the impact of the child's handicap on their usual adaptive patterns; 4. Making certain adjustments in their way of life that will affect not only the handicapped child but the total family unit.[2]

Leonard Shotland outlines a progression of "stress periods" commonly experienced around chronic handicaps:

> 1. The prediagnostic period, shot through with the suspicion, fear, doubt, blame, and guilt that accompany living with the unknown. 2. The diagnostic period, full of the hurt, anxiety, and mourning for a lost "wholeness" that follows the impact of learning the "facts." 3. The pre-school years when many of the child's disabilities show themselves more markedly and he begins to fall behind his peers. 4. The elementary school years; when it is necessary for the child to leave the family for a world that woefully lacks understanding. 5. Adolescence, when the burden of a future that is curtailed and limited must be faced. 6. Adulthood, when one *must* come to terms with that future.[16]

The progression of tasks varies for each family, and defenses workable today are unusable tomorrow, as noted in the case of Marie. The essential point to be borne in mind by the helpers of these parents and children is that their equilibrium is constantly having to absorb new "inputs." To know the work is with a "moving picture" will prevent "freeze frame" mistakes. The fact that parents have been given facts about the disease or instructions for care does not mean that they have absorbed them. It is important to understand that they cannot hear at certain times but may be able to hear at others. Help must be offered as a continuum that makes differential, timely support available when needed and when usable.

This has implications for the "collaborative management network." The knowledge common to the social worker in the health care field may not be so common to the one in the family agency or community mental health clinic. The educational role of the hospital in the community must be shaped and stimulated by the sensitivity and knowledge of many disciplines. While the broad implications for the hospital-based social worker are apparent, the explicit implementation will vary with the hospital and its community.

Achievement Problems

One of the legitimate rewards of being a parent is pride in the achievement of offspring. That Jane scored high in her classwork, that David made the Little League, that Doris has the lead in the school play—parents' exchanges on these topics can leave the mother and father of the handicapped child with little to say but much to feel. The physically impaired child scores low on the PTA achievement schedule operating in every neighborhood and in many social situations. Where can child and family look for the satisfaction they need from each other for the task done well, the recognition and status achieved, and mutual pride in accomplishment?

Actually the handicapped child may be making heroic achievements within the therapeutic value system, where physicians and nurses, psychologists and social workers, and physical and speech and occupational therapists count gains on a more precise and multifaceted scale. When the child is actively taking part in an institutional program parents can be infected with staff enthusiasm for Tommy's now being able to stand for 13 minutes in parallel bars versus eight minutes last week. But at home there is less definition of these accomplishments even if progress is being made. Infiltrating the value system of community centers, schools, and other agencies so that different but equal achievements of these children might be recognized is possible only if the knowledge of hospital people is communicated to other community institutions.

An intimation of these possibilities was given in an exhibit of children's artwork at Union Free School District No. 6 operating at Blythedale Children's Hospital. Below one drawing appeared in large letters, "Painted by Danny holding the brush in his mouth." Could this not happen at a school outside the hospital?

Mrs. Annette Ouellet, writing about her daughter born with multiple congenital defects, concludes:

> If your child has no feet, imagine your pride and joy in his first step. If he has no hand, how will you feel when he begins to feed himself with his artificial hand![12]

Must parents experience such pride alone? That other parents be acculturated to share these different but impressive accomplishments is not an unreasonable goal for a parent group in a family agency or community center. Hospital personnel can help with such goals by offering training and consultation to social agencies.

Family Problems

All relationships in the family with a physically handicapped child are subject to additional stress. If there is marital conflict, the child will almost certainly become central to that conflict. Either partner or both can blame the other for the condition. How it will be managed, what treatment will be gotten and where, resentment of time and money demands—all is fuel for marital strife. If, on the other hand, relationships are stable and gratifying, if communication between partners is open, the sorrow, planning, limitations, and satisfactions can be shared. Adjustments will be required, but equilibrium can be preserved or reestablished. Sheelhase and Fern, discussing the role of the family in rehabilitation, noted the usefulness to parents of sharing with other parents their concerns and the resolutions they have made from their own reactions to the disabling tragedy.

> There is demonstrable gain to the parent who can provide support to another during the stressful time that both are coming to a workable acceptance of their children's disability.[15]

Parents may be so overwhelmed with the grief of their child's limitations that they retreat into silence from each other and from the child himself. The expectation of "a miracle" may be held behind such barriers. Subtly this discourages the child from expressing his feelings, including his fears.

A study of parents of patients with rheumatic fever indicated that it was rare for a mother to have talked to her child about the illness.[6] The emotional costs of communication breakdowns between family members because of chronic disability are high.

Social work intervention will be most effective if offered on an anticipatory basis rather than after a breakdown has occurred. In addition to setting up a system for picking up such families for psychosocial counseling within the treatment facility, hospital-based social workers can well take the initiative in making similar linkages between private community-based physicians and counseling agencies, with consultation with such agencies if indicated. This may well be a matter of redeployment of time and skill rather than an additional social work burden since prevention of breakdown and better focused treatment is thus made possible.

Like the stress on marital partners, so the stress between handicapped and nonhandicapped siblings will be manageable or destructive depending on the emotional strength of the persons involved. Even siblings in homes with enough love, time, and money for everyone will feel different kinds of pain at different times because of the capability that is missing. Depending on the ages of children, the handicapping condition may give rise to different sorts of phantasies and problems, and the competitive demands of the handicapped and nonhandicapped children on parents are a mutual stress point.

Four college students, talking with Dr. Stanley Klein about their experiences as the brother or sister of a person with a disability, revealed a wide range of reactions. They spoke of feeling protective, the process of absorbing the "differentness," resenting others' attitudes, feeling guilty, feeling lucky, spontaneous affection and discomfort in association.[7]

In the Tropauer, Franz, and Dilgard study,

> School adjustment difficulties, learning problems, and delinquency in siblings were attributed by both patients and their mothers to the strain imposed by the chronic illness and its aggravating effect on family rivalries.[18]

The identification of a severely impaired child is an obvious signal for a

family emotional health check-up with active or "as needed" standby counseling built into the total care plan.

Growing Up Disabled

The long thoughts about growing up, life work, marriage, and children
are particularly complicated when a disabling condition must be translated
into life experience.

Dr. Verda Heisler refers to Jenny, the six and a half year old cerebral
palsied daughter of a couple in her treatment group. Jenny wanted to know
whether her mother would be there when she grew up, and asked if she
would walk and whether one could be a librarian in a wheelchair.[5]

Sharon, a nine year old girl with traumatic brain damage, had achieved independent physical functioning. As plans were being made for her discharge
from the hospital, Sharon's mother spoke to her social worker about her future
concerns. How will she handle puberty, menstruation, sexual awakening with
Sharon? Her impulsiveness and indiscriminate friendliness (medically assessed as symptomatic of her brain damage and acceptable in the protected
health care world) would be a problem in the community. She is trying to imitate her older brothers and sisters, and is talking about boy friends and marriage. Is marriage realistic for her?

A developmental task crisis predictably occurs with osteogenesis imperfecta patients at puberty. Bones are no longer fragile, and increased activity,
perhaps an attempt at walking, is indicated. Abruptly these previously highly
protected teenagers are confronted with the world. At a time when they are
hypersensitive about their body image, they must come to terms with deformities affecting both appearance and functioning.

A 15 year old boy with cerebral palsy, severely impaired both in speech
and physical functioning, complained to his social worker about feeling
pushed by his mother to intellectual achievement that he saw as futile since
his disability would block him from entering any vocation of interest to him.
He did not want to "achieve in spite of his handicap." The struggle to assert
himself seemed to him hopeless because of his physical dependency on
parents whose values and goals he was helpless to challenge even verbally.

The teenager's break away from parental domination, and the parents'
facilitation of this process is a staggering task for both when chronic illness
such as paraplegia, cerebral palsy, or osteogenesis imperfecta reinforces
dependency. When parent and child have not experienced the earlier gratification and certainty of the parent's ability to be the buffer and protector, developmental tasks due for completion many years before are superimposed on
the adolescent struggle for independence.

The physically impaired child, like all children, needs to get from the
world beyond his home affirmation of who he is and where he fits in with
others, peers, authority figures, and younger or weaker members of society.
Personality development is related to this absorption and identification.

What is feasible and possible with respect to vocation, education, marriage, and having children? It may be impossible to predict capabilities and
limitations of the patient and also of the society in which he must perform.

Uncertainty must therefore be part of planning, which needs to be both hopeful and realistic. Few families are able to handle this well alone.

INTERACTION OF CHILD AND FAMILY WITH THE WORLD

The visibly whole and the visibly impaired live together in a state of more intellectual than emotional acceptance. No longer is illness believed to be a scourge of God, but parents of physically defective children still suffer from chronic feelings of guilt.[8, 14] Mandelbaum and Wheeler say "residual feelings of anger and fear about the defective child remain in most of us—parents and professional people alike."[9] In a competitive, materialistic world, those who slow down the flow of traffic are troublesome. Just as no driver likes to be the cause or the victim of a traffic slowdown, the handicapped and the nonhandicapped are mutually frustrated by the impedimental condition.

The visibly whole in society are not without concern. Laws are passed to insure that theaters, schools, libraries, churches, and other public buildings take into account that not everyone is physically whole. Communities are surveyed with concern about access of the physically limited to museums, zoos, hotels, and theaters.*

Local and international groups committed to improvements through information, education, and political action are speaking out by and for the physically handicapped.† The wheelchair insignia, however, "the international symbol of access," is unfortunately still not seen as often as symbols of credit card acceptability. But at least one travel agency is owned by a quadriplegic and specializes in trips for the handicapped.‡

While the price of excluding those with the right to participate is becoming clearer and higher, competition and compassion are uneasy neighbors. The handicapped child and his family are products of and participants in this conflicting culture. Denial and acceptance struggle for mastery in the person and in the community. For both child and parent, it is difficult to face the world of close and distant relatives, close and distant friends, and the range of associates—shopkeepers, church people, bus drivers and riders, and delivery men—the entire community. These contacts will be played out differently by each family.

Annette Ouellet's strength can be felt when she says:

> It is not only undesirable, but nearly impossible to hide a disabled child away from the rest of the world. He will always be meeting new people. Therefore, it is important that he learn to accept and cope with unavoidable

---

*New York, New York—A Guide to New York City for Persons with Physical Limitations. Association for Crippled Children and Adults of New York State, Inc., 185 Madison Avenue, New York, N.Y. 10016, 1972.

†Rehabilitation International, U.S.A., 219 East 44th Street, New York, New York 10017, and Disabled in Action, 175 Willoughby Street, Brooklyn, New York 11201.

‡Travel Headquarters (Judd Jacobson), Box 382, Owatonna, Minnesota 55060.

questions and stares as early as possible. He may very well learn this acceptance before you do.

> In the months following my daughter's birth, I can remember how I watched people's faces on the street, in church or a department store. I was daring them to react to my child because she was different. But gradually, I do not know exactly when, I stopped watching for people to notice her anomalies. I became comfortable in my relationship with Michelle and if people stared, I was not aware of it.[12]

Not all parents make this transition. Robbins and Schattner in "Obstacles in the Social Integration of Orthopedically Handicapped Children" tell of parents complaining about "everyone gawking at him," of people staring with disgust, with morbid curiosity, staring and turning away.[13]

How well families cope depends not so much on the degree of disability of the handicapped member as upon the basic emotional health of the family. This involves the ability to use practical and attitudinal help.[16]

Our knowledge of crisis theory and intervention clearly implies that many families need ego supportive help at the point at which they face the world with the handicapped child, and that such intervention can significantly affect the future course of the adjustment of the child and family.

In this country, heavy burdens must be borne by the family with the handicapped child. Such parents need to be wiser, stronger, and wealthier than others to fulfill the same functions in relationship to their young.

We provide many services under a variety of auspices. There are federal, state, and local programs. Qualification for some is by disease or disability category, some by geographical location. In addition to tax supported programs and institutions, there are voluntary ones, administered broadly or narrowly in accordance with the philosophy of the sponsors. Foundations and associations espouse particular needs and are funded and render service in accordance with particular commitments. Some are research oriented and must, of that necessity, take a narrow focus. Private foundations may be both generous and idiosyncratic.

This individualistic pattern of offering service is played out in school and community, with variations according to county, town, or even neighborhood or school district. A community center may have a program for preschoolers for children with brain injury, but not for children with other diagnoses. Special schools provide an educational experience with an arbitrary chronological age cut-off though the handicapping condition may preclude or make difficult transit into college or a work situation. There are natural promotional points in education and recreation for nonhandicapped children, but "graduating" to greater challenge and opportunity is not a dependable expectation for the handicapped child. Even leaving a treatment setting may mean regression into a more constricted world.

A social worker's record notes a mother's search for help needed when her three and a half year old son with cerebral palsy would leave a children's rehabilitation hospital:

> In anticipation that George will be discharged home before he is of school age, his mother attempted to locate community resources that George could use for therapy and education. She was not able to locate an appropriate nursery

school facility since all of those she explored were either for severely retarded children or children without physical handicaps. Also, she was unable to locate any community based therapy programs. She had even made inquiries about where she could take formalized courses in physical therapy.

For such families, the ferreting out of educational and recreational programs is an endless struggle. The constant knocking on doors that the child is disqualified to enter activates and reinforces feelings of guilt and unworthiness on the part of both child and parent. Robbins and Schattner stated that:

> At present there is no one who takes responsibility for serving as a "broker" or "advocate" for physically handicapped children.[13]

While social workers and others may not agree with this assessment, there cannot be disagreement that the unevenness of availability, the fragmentation, and the cumbersome process of getting connections made between the services and the consumers is faulty. Considerably more than simple brokerage is involved, as affirmed by another incident in the life of Jenny, previously referred to:

> Some refuse to admit the handicapped child, while others will admit him but then limit him unnecessarily. This was true of a Sunday School teacher who admitted Jenny.... One Sunday morning when Paul [Jenny's father] went to ρick Jenny up at the time Sunday School ended, he found her sitting on her chair, where she had sat for an hour and a half watching the other children sprawled on the floor working with paper and crayons. She had tried to communicate to the teacher that she could lie on the floor and draw also, but the teacher had made no effort to understand what Jenny was saying and now used Jenny's speech defect as an excuse for not having known that Jenny could do this. It was only with reluctance that she agreed to help Jenny to the floor and remove her brace the next time she introduced this kind of play activity, but in time and through Paul's help, she became more comfortable with the responsibility of a handicapped child.[5]

There is a bit of Everyman in Jenny's teacher—fear, inability to "hear" what she cannot handle, and also the capability to change with the grasp of a new insight. Perhaps the incident is a microcosm of how the transactions between the visibly impaired and the visibly whole must be effected. The handicapped or their "brokers" must bear the burden of communicating their capabilities and their needs. The capability of the world of the nonhandicapped to pick up these signals and to open doors must be developed. Earl Schenck Miers, a writer-journalist who suffers from athetosis, tells of going to a restaurant in Chicago, which he had not visited for many months. The place was jammed, but without his asking, his meat came to him cut, a straw in his glass.[11] Doubtless he had initially explained these necessities. The concern of people in a busy restaurant, however, and the capability of the system to absorb and "remember" is impressive.

IMPLICATIONS AND FUTURE DIRECTIONS

In the universality and predictability of the problems of the handicapped child and his family are intimations of preventive action and solution finding.

Since these problems are played out in the health care system, the home, and the community, solutions must cut across those worlds. Out of its multidisciplinary nature and consequent multifaceted understanding of these needs is derived the hospital's leadership responsibility for finding solutions. Specific ways of exercising this capability are proposed:

Multidisciplinary Coordination, Recall, and Follow-up

The knowledge and skill in patient care of many disciplines has reached a level at which our treatment plans and follow-up systems can be improved to take into account more than surgery, medication, and brace measurements.

Recall points arrived at by interdisciplinary projection of time periods, developmental milestones, or particular events in terms of function are needed to determine the return schedule of children and their families. These return visits need to be multidisciplinary and directed at prevention as well as treatment. While the system would still render care episodically, the episodes could be more rationally timed, and children and parents would have a sense of more substantive support between care periods than is possible when they are charged to call on the treatment team "when needed," or "when the braces are outgrown."

Linkage of the Hospital with Other Community Institutions

Hospital people of many disciplines search out services related to their discipline. Patients and their needs are sometimes "matched" to available facilities more hopefully than realistically. Real linkage calls for collaboration between professionals based in different settings so that programs can be mutually influenced to serve effectively. In all specialties, professionals need to speak to each other not only about particular patients but also about the groups patients represent. Part of this dialogue might well take place in a "let's forget where we work" context. Members of the same profession can stimulate and monitor each other, as when a hospital-based nurse challenged a community nursing service about "closing their case." Because the child had been moved from one family member to another, the previous geographically based family-hospital-nurse service connection had been broken. The paper work showed why service had been discontinued, but the fact remained that a child with rheumatic heart disease had not received penicillin for three months. This was an imperative concern to nurses in both settings. Out of such recognition comes the stimulus to close gaps and retool old-fashioned systems.

Influencing and Stimulating the Community

Hospitals are perceived as strong and wise by other community institutions and people. Their capability can be used to strengthen or weaken the network of services needed prior to, subsequent to, or between episodes of hospital care.

The assumption of the community leadership and teaching role by the hospital in relation to family, child care, and other agencies that lack particular knowledge about handicapped children and their families is desirable though difficult. This is partly because strong, sometimes bureaucratic, institutions are not geared to the merging of their efforts. Furthermore, handicapped children and their families are difficult "cases." In this chapter, experiences of relatively strong families have been cited. Frequently, there is only one responsible parent; not uncommonly there is more than one handicapped child; parents are often older than average for the child's age; problems of poverty, poor housing, drugs, and delinquency coexist with or antedate the handicapping condition. This reality must be taken into account in organizing services to meet particular needs. Delivery is through a welter of other needs and demands.

While total solutions involve political, philosophic, and financial questions that seem remote from the clinical world of the specialist, putting together our collective capability in a compassionate orderly way is a reasonable goal. It is a goal that must be "owned" if we are to convey a sense of hope to those we help.

References

1. Brown, D. R.: Community health planning or who will control the health care system. Am. J. Public Health, 62:10:1336–1339, October, 1972.
2. Cohen, P. C.: Impact of the handicapped child in the family. Social Casework, 43:3:137–142, March, 1962.
3. Green, M.: The clinician's art: Some questions for our time. Pediatrics, 43:2:157–159, 1969.
4. Gurney, W.: Social aspects of long-term hospitalized children. Unpublished paper given at National Conference on Children Requiring Long-Term Hospitalization. Blythedale Children's Hospital, Valhalla, New York, 1968.
5. Heisler, V.: A Handicapped Child in the Family: A Guide for Parents. New York, Grune & Stratton, Inc., 1972.
6. Kennell, J. H., Soroker, E., Thomas, P., and Wasman, M.: What parents of rheumatic fever patients don't understand about the disease and its prophylactic management. Pediatrics, 43:2:160–167, 1969.
7. Klein, S.: Brother to sister/sister to brother. The Exceptional Parent, 2:1:10–15, June/July, 1972.
8. Korsch, B. M., Freemon, B., and Negrete, V. F.: Practical implications of doctor and patient interaction analysis for pediatric practice. Am. J. Dis. Child., 116:110–114, 1971.
9. Mandelbaum, A., and Wheeler, M. E.: The meaning of a defective child to parents. Social Casework, 43:7:360–367, July, 1960.
10. Mead, M.: In preface to Ayrault, E. W.: You Can Raise Your Handicapped Child. New York, G. P. Putnam's Sons, 1964.
11. Miers, E. A.: Why Did This Have to Happen? Chicago, The National Society for Crippled Children and Adults, Inc., 1957.
12. Ouellet, A. M.: Michelle: A long way to kindergarten. The Exceptional Parent, 2:1:31–33, June/July, 1972.
13. Robbins, H. W., and Schattner, R.: Obstacles in the social integration of orthopedically handicapped children. J. Jewish Communal Service, 45:2:190–198, Winter, 1968.
14. Schwartz, L. H., and Schwartz, J. L.: The Psychodynamics of Patient Care. Englewood, N.J., Prentice-Hall, Inc., 1972.
15. Sheelhase, L. J., and Fern, E.: Role of the family in rehabilitation. Social Casework, 53:9:544–550, November, 1972.
16. Shotland, L.: Social work approach to the chronically handicapped and their families. Social Work, 9:4:68–75, October, 1964.

17. Thomson, H.: Assisting patients with posthospitalization plans. J. Am. Hosp. Assoc., *47*:2:43–46, 1973.
18. Tropauer, A., Franz, M. N., and Dilgard, V. W.: Psychological aspects of the care of children with cystic fibrosis. Am. J. Dis. Child., *119*:424–432, 1970.

OTHER READINGS

Anonymous: Another sleepless night: A parent's viewpoint. Social Work, *18*:1:112–114, January, 1973.
Ayrault, E. W.: *You Can Raise Your Handicapped Child.* New York, G. P. Putnam's Sons, 1964.
Debuskey, M. (ed.): *The Chronically Ill Child and His Family.* Springfield, Ill., Charles C Thomas, 1970.
Green, M., and Haggert, R., Jr.: *Ambulatory Pediatrics.* Philadelphia, W. B. Saunders Co., 1968.
Juntti, M. J.: Problem solving in arranging for comprehensive home care. Nursing Forum, *8*:1:103–109, 1969.
Myers, B. A., Friedman, S. B., and Weinger, I. B.: Coping with a chronic disability. Am. J. Dis. Child., *120*:175–181, 1970.
Petrillo, M., and Sanger, S.: *Emotional Case of Hospitalized Children: An Environmental Approach.* Philadelphia, J. B. Lippincott Co., 1972.
Spock, B., and Lerrigo, M. O.: *Caring for Your Disabled Child.* New York, The Association for the Aid of Crippled Children, 1965.

Chapter 25

Administration of Hospitals Caring for the Long-Term Sick Child

by *Robert Stone, M.S.*

One of the consequences of improved control over acute illness in children has been the increased number and extended life expectancy of children with chronic or disabling conditions, and this trend can be expected to continue for some time. Improving the care for the long-term sick child, to better enable him to function in society, represents one of the great challenges in medicine for the future.

Due to the complex and multidisciplinary nature of providing care for such children, hospitals, rather than individual practitioners, play the predominant role in treating the chronically ill child. The nature of the medical institution giving this type of care should be reexamined carefully.

In the short-term care hospital, everything is geared to treating the patient quickly and discharging him to his home. The amenities of care are important, but not as important as dealing with the life-threatening situations. While this is understandable for the acutely ill child, the hospital can become a hazardous place for the child who must remain there for a prolonged period.

In a medical institution providing care for the long-term sick child, the central and paramount concept is to make the overall needs of the individual child more important than the needs of the staff or the institution. Humanizing and individualizing medical care is obviously important in all circumstances, but it is of critical importance in an institution where the child's participation in his care plays such a large role.

Traditionally, the chronic disease hospital has been located in the country and various benefits have been attributed to the bucolic setting. In recent years, the trend has been to make the hospital for acute illness more general, and pressure has been put on children's institutions for chronic diseases to move closer to the urban medical centers. Regardless of the decision on this matter, a few factors should be kept in mind. Children in the long-term care unit need a more "relaxed" environment. They should feel more like students at a residential school than patients in a hospital.

On the other hand, the physically isolated institution can soon become intellectually isolated. The chronically ill child should receive services from gifted and challenged medical personnel, and this can only happen if the hospital is in the intellectual mainstream. This usually means that the hospital should itself be a teaching center and in some way affiliated with a medical school. It is also important that the hospital have either in-house capability or, through agreement, ready access to a full range of medical services. This can be accomplished either through formal transfer and service agreements or through informal working arrangements that permit comprehensive care of the child.

The hospital for a chronically ill child can provide several forms of service; these are discussed separately:

FORMS OF SERVICE

Inpatient Care.   There are many situations in which the medical services required by the child necessitate hospitalization, but admission of a child to a hospital as an inpatient should be undertaken with caution. There are potential emotional hazards in separating a child from his parents, and this is particularly true with young children. There are, however, occasions when separation is not only necessary but in some cases highly desirable, as it gives both the child and the family an opportunity to restructure their relationships to each other.

Day Hospital.   The day hospital approach has been tried on a limited basis in the United States and to a greater extent in some European countries, notably in Great Britain. In such a program, the patient receives a wide variety of services from the hospital during the day, but goes home in the evening to be with his family and to sleep. For properly selected patients, it provides a good compromise between inpatient and outpatient services and can also be helpful as a transitional phase prior to the patient's discharge to his home, especially after long hospitalization or some complicated illnesses.

Night Hospital.   This is the corollary of the day hospital: here the patient spends his day in normal activity, but requires the support of a hospital at night. This approach is rare in pediatrics and should only be used in highly specialized circumstances.

Home Care.   The hospital-based home care program provides medical and hospital services in the home on an extramural basis. It has been found to be desirable in treating a wide variety of chronically ill patients, and may be used selectively in rehabilitation.

Diagnostic Outpatient Service.   In this service a patient is brought to the hospital or to a physician's office for diagnostic evaluations to help plan a management program. Ideally, the chronically ill child should be seen by various members of a team to provide a comprehensive picture of the child's illness.

This team should include medical, social, psychological, educational, recreational, and vocational personnel.

Outpatient Treatment.   This service provides treatment for a child on an ambulatory basis.

PHYSICAL SURROUNDINGS

In every instance and form of service, the general tone of an institution should convey a positive and hopeful outlook. The attitude of the child, his parents and the staff will all be influenced by a number of subliminal factors. For example, the colors used throughout the hospital are of great significance. Bold, bright, and cheerful colors help create an air of happiness and excitement in contrast with the coldness of the usual institutional colors. Thought should be given to the size of rooms and the type of furnishings. This building's primary purpose is to house children, not adults, and should be scaled accordingly. Room size and ceiling height should be judged from a child's view, including that of a child who is sitting in a wheelchair or lying on a stretcher. The number of children sleeping in a room is important. We have found that rooms with two and four beds are best since they encourage socialization with other children, which is useful in rehabilitation, yet avoid the sense of overcrowding and loss of personality that is felt in a large ward. Three children in a room should be avoided since almost invariably it ends up wi h two children siding against the third.

Patients should be encouraged to wear regular clothes during the daytime. A nightgown or pajamas, particularly a standard hospital nightgown, dehumanizes the child and makes him feel helpless and dependent, and even children with large casts can wear clothes that have been modified. Clothes should be kept in a locker next to each bed so that a child can learn to dress himself each day with minimal help from the staff.

Mobility is important. A child who is bedfast and in his room feels sick and dependent. All children who can walk should be given permission to do so as soon as possible after admission. The vast majority of children who are unable to walk can be given wheelchairs, stretchers, or other self-wheeling devices so they can move about the hospital on their own or with minimal assistance. Children should be encouraged to go, on their own, to school, to recreation programs, and to keep appointments for therapy and with other medical services.

MEDICAL SERVICES

It is frequently difficult to narrow the problem of a long-term sick youngster down to a single specialty in medicine. Patients with primary orthopedic problems may develop metabolic or psychiatric complications. In order to treat the whole patient, a team approach is necessary and must include a wide variety of disciplines. This is a considerable change from the usual organization of medical care for the acutely ill, and requires reorientation for physicians who have not previously worked in a team, for they must learn how to share responsibility for the care of the patient. Patient care is further complicated by the introduction into the team of other nonphysician professionals, all of whom have valid and important contributions.

It is obvious that one physician has to take prime responsibility for the overall management of the patient, and we have found that the physician most appropriate for this role is the pediatrician, who can see the overall needs of the child. Critical medical services include orthopedics, rehabilitation medicine, neurology, psychiatry, and dentistry. A large range of other specialized areas must also be available by consultation.

Nursing Services

The nursing service in any hospital plays a central and crucial role in patient care. In the long-term setting the attitude and approach of the nurses can do more toward rehabilitating or discouraging the rehabilitation of patients than any other single factor. Nurses who are anxious to maintain a traditional approach of protecting the patient and maintaining his dependency can be very destructive. On the other hand, nurses who can recognize the special needs of this type of child and can help him to improve his own self-sufficiency will make a major contribution to his rehabilitation.

This places great importance on the selection and direction of the nursing services. Nurses working in such a setting must be active members of the rehabilitation team, particularly in the planning of therapeutic goals for the child. A skilled nurse can convey encouragement to a child to undertake many activities in the knowledge that she is always there ready to provide help if it is needed.

The modern children's institution, with its encouragement of mobility and self-sufficiency of the child, inevitably brings with it some sense of disorganization and requires nurses who understand the needs of growing children for self-expression.

Nursing units for children should be for from 25 to 35 children. This will provide a balance between efficient operation and personalized care. Each unit should be staffed by a team consisting of professional nurses, practical nurses, and nurse-aides each assigned duties consistent with their ability and training. All members of the nursing team should be oriented to the philosophy of the hospital and the specialized needs of the long-term patient.

SUPPORTIVE SERVICES

Recreation

Play is the normal activity of children. This is so obvious that it is difficult to understand why so many health professionals dealing with children fail to plan for play activities in medical facilities. There seems to be an attitude that play is a frivolous and extraneous function in the hospital setting when exactly the opposite is true, as recreation is a useful and important component of the treatment of children, particularly in long-term care. A sophisticated play program can help relieve the fear and anxiety that all patients experience when receiving medical care. It encourages the child to see the hospital as a place where his needs and interests are understood, and this is particularly important in the field of rehabilitation, which requires the active participation of the patient.

Frequently, the long-term sick child has lost motivation. He sees himself and is seen by the people around him as helpless, requiring assistance in all matters. The development of skills in crafts and sports enables him to improve his self-image and subsequently his motivation.

Children who are sick for long periods of time are frequently denied opportunities to learn the give and take of play. They, as do all children, need to learn how to play. They must learn that there are rules that must be followed. They must learn how to win and how to lose. Controlled competition helps to sharpen skills and increase motivation. These are lessons that affect personality throughout life.

Play can also be helpful in achieving medical goals. By selective encouragement of play activities, a child can be induced to exercise a hand, strengthen a leg, improve gait balance, practice speech, or further any one of the many goals developed by the therapists.

To create a useful play service, the recreational therapists must be made integral and regular members of the rehabilitation team. As such they must be familiar with the goals of the other departments and must in turn provide other professionals with information and conclusions in the play program. A play group should consist of between 8 and 12 children of similar age and social development. Each group should be supervised by a professional recreation therapist, who should have an aide or volunteer to assist him. The number and variety of play activities that can be carried out with sick children are enormous and include: sand play, water play, ceramics, jewelry making, block play, dramatics, group singing, table games, sports, word games, and the like, the list being limited only by the imagination and desire to adjust staff needs to the needs of children.

A special word should be said for the use of the outdoors. Nature studies, campfires, cook-outs, sleep-outs, kite flying, gardening, and a host of other outdoor activities can all be part of a play program. The process of going outside is in itself useful in encouraging the child to think of himself as being well and useful rather than sick and dependent.

Dietary Service

Sensitive concern must be given to meal selection and preparation. Food that is tasteless, poorly served, or monotonous can become a major irritation. The children should have an opportunity to participate in the selection of meals. Unusual foods should be served occasionally. Tray favors and other decorative devices are particularly important in a long-term setting. It is not difficult to enlist the help of community groups in making such tray decorations.

Whenever possible, children should eat in a dining room and be encouraged to help themselves. A child who can learn to feed himself is well on his way to achieving important social goals. For this reason, it is useful to have speech, occupational, and physical therapists working with the children at lunchtime, to help them improve their feeding skills. The lunch hour thus becomes a therapy session with real and obvious gains for the child.

The grouping of children in a dining room requires some care. Obviously, one would want to put together children with common interests, but it is sometimes useful to put together children who have varying degrees of handicap. The ability of one child to help another is beneficial to both.

Education

It can be argued that the educational responsibility for children lies with the school system and not with the hospital. It is, however, clear that children who are hospitalized, and particularly those who are going to be in an institution for a long time, should not be deprived of their education.

It is not unusual to see youngsters with normal intelligence who are many years behind their peers educationally because no adequate educational provision was made for them during the time they were receiving medical care. Teachers of sick or handicapped children face special problems that require guidance and assistance from the medical team. One method of overcoming this problem is to establish a school, including a preschool nursery, in the hospital where all children regardless of age can receive full educational services. Teachers selected for such a school should be highly motivated and challenged individuals who look upon their work as an exciting opportunity to help a child catch up to or even excel his peers.

A fuller description of an educational program appears elsewhere in this volume. One special word of note should, however, be made on a children's library. Books and the world of information and fantasy that they carry are of special value to the disabled individual. Unfortunately, most hospitals have ill-equipped libraries for children, and all too frequently public libraries are constructed with architectural hazards that exclude the wheelchair-bound. The teacher and others working with the child can make an important contribution by opening up the world of books to a child with long-term illness. Books in a hospital library should be catalogued in accordance with standard library systems in order to help the child use a public library after discharge.

Religious Services

Religion plays a major and significant role in the lives of some children, and religious services and guidance should be available for all children who want it.

In a long-term setting this can become particularly important because a child is away from the home or family milieu and training. The child who will be in the hospital for a long time should be allowed to receive religious instruction if this is his desire and that of his parents.

Local or regional leaders of religious organizations are usually available to help in the planning and administration of services, education, and holiday observances — providing they are made welcome by the hospital authorities.

Volunteers

The use of volunteers as a service for providing extra care for patients is, of course, valid in any type of institution. With children who have a long-term illness, however, the role of the volunteer takes on an additional meaning. Very often this type of child requires individual attention, and even the most thoughtful and understanding staff of professionals does not have the time to provide this kind of help. A corps of intelligent and well-oriented volunteers can, in a wide variety of ways, be of great help to the young patients. Volunteers can also serve as a bridge of understanding to the community about the value of the handicapped to society.

Visiting

The entire concept of visiting and visiting hours should be viewed from the problem of parental relationships to the child with a long-term illness. All too often, there is a sense of incipient abandonment that pervades the relationship between the parent and such a child. Institutional prohibitions and restrictions on visiting only help to encourage the total dependency of the family on the institution and are to be discouraged.

Unlimited visiting does not create the enormous problem that its opponents project. There is really no reason why a child should not be visited by his parents, by his siblings of any age, by his friends and classmates from school, or even his pet dog or cat. Such an unlimited policy helps a child to believe that he has not been abandoned to the institution and that he is still an important and worthwhile member of his family to which he will someday return.

In addition to unlimited visiting wherever possible, regular home visits on weekends and holidays should be encouraged and prescribed by the medical staff. These visits help the child and the family to try out, in his home, newly made gains in rehabilitation. Although some hospital insurance carriers have difficulty in understanding the reason for such home visits and their obligation to continue payment during the day or two that the child is away, most governmental programs and insurance companies can understand this once they realize the therapeutic quality of the home visit. In all cases, they should be prescribed by the physician, and the bed should be retained for the patient during his absence.

FINANCING

As hospital care has grown in importance to all people, so has the mechanism for prepaid hospital insurance. Unfortunately, most hospital insurance systems presume that the patient will be in the hospital for a relatively brief period of time and do not cover long-term illnesses. As a result, the vast majority of patients who face a long-term illness are saddled with hospital bills well beyond their financial capacity. The institution that is involved in the treatment of the long-term sick has some special responsibilities and difficulties in helping to finance the care of its patients, and the hospital must act as the surrogate for the patient and his family in actively securing any insurance coverage that is available. The hospital business office must also help the family secure Title XIX (Medicaid) benefits when these are available and the patient is eligible. In some localities, Title V (Crippled Children's Program) money is also available and must be sought.

When the family has a generous major medical policy, this can be of great benefit. When there are no resources available, the hospital must develop a policy regarding the acceptance of patients without funds and find a source of income to make such a policy possible.

It is extremely important that the business office personnel be made sensitive to and aware of the problems facing parents of children with long-term illness. Frequently, these parents may never before have had to face the burden of an unsurmountable financial crisis such as that brought on by this hospitalization. A callous or demanding attitude can only result in further deterioration of the relationship between the parent and his child, neither of whom is responsible for the crisis.

The business office personnel must show a sincere and honest interest in trying to help the family secure whatever benefits to which they are entitled. If adequate financing is not available, the hospital must try to help the family work out a realistic payment program consistent with their ability, without pauperizing the entire family. Because of the long-term nature of the illness, a preadmission deposit probably serves no useful function and can only start the relationship between the family and the business office off on the wrong foot.

It is difficult to imagine that some mechanism for providing financial coverage of the catastrophically ill patient will not be available in the future. The inability of the prudent citizen to provide against the financial destruction caused by catastrophic illness makes some sort of governmental program inevitable. At present, the financial burden of catastrophic illness falls most heavily on the middle class, as the indigent sick are covered with Medicaid.

Payment to physicians for their services can generally fall into one of two categories. The first is the most traditional method of having each physician bill for his services directly on a fee-for-service basis. This presents some special problems in the treatment of the long-term sick child. Having a group of doctors working together as a team for the care of the patient makes individual billing impractical and inequitable. Moreover, a substantial percentage of patients can be considered medically indigent by the time they are seen in a long-term setting. Therefore, a more realistic approach would be to pay the physicians an annual fee or salary for all their services to all patients, and to include the cost of this medical component in the overall hospital charge.

SUMMARY

The treatment of children with long-term illnesses presents a current and growing problem. In addition to medical problems, these youngsters frequently have social, emotional, educational, recreational, and vocational needs. The hospital providing care for long-term sick children must be readjusted to meet their multiple needs.

This change in the nature of hospitalization for the long-term sick child has significant impact on all departments and on general hospital policies. A number of adaptations have been described in this chapter. It is of major importance that the child be encouraged to participate in normal activities such as education and recreation. The focus of his attention must be on his ability, not on his handicap.

Chapter 26

Vocational Planning
for the Handicapped Child

by *William M. Usdane, Ph.D.*

Vocational planning for the handicapped child rarely is found among the modalities and treatments available in hospitals or special education classes, homebound instruction, from parents, from peers in the neighborhood or in adjoining hospital beds, or within the home environment. In an entire issue of *Daedalus* devoted to Twelve to Sixteen: Early Adolescence, the 12 authors slight vocational planning even for the nonhandicapped.[21] For the younger as well as the young adolescent handicapped individual, little for his vocational planning is available in the professional literature.

Sidney P. Marland, Jr., United States Commissioner of Education, sees "the key to reform in contemporary American education . . . in the concept of 'career education.'" He is specific about his hopes:

> In the primary grades, children should learn more about the world of work and the various roles they might play in it. In the middle grades hands-on experience and practical observation of career areas that are of most interest should be provided.[14]

Recently, Jerome Bruner, writing on the continuity of learning, stressed the need for vocational planning:

> The decision to delay vocational or job decisions until comparatively late in the life cycle inevitably makes fuzzy one's definition of oneself as an adult. . . . The neuroses of the young are far more likely to revolve around work than around sex. Therefore . . . the first order of business in the transformation of our mode of educating is to revolutionize and revivify the idea of vocation or occupation.[4]

A recent pilot study of a new program in vocational planning involved two primary classes in North Carolina.[10] Children of primary school age were introduced to various occupational and social roles as a result of developing their own community structure. In consequence, a larger study is now contemplated. This effort stems from North Carolina's interest in the development and implementation of career education for children from kindergarten to grade 12. Unfortunately, there are not many studies analyzing the utilization of occupational education in the elementary school, especially on the primary grade level; those studies extant are concerned with the nonhandicapped individual.[9, 12, 16]

The status of guidance in the elementary school for nonhandicapped children shows 6041 counselors working in the 50 states, the District of Columbia, and the Virgin Islands.[22] None, however, is specifically trained in the field of special education or prepared to work with vocational planning for the handicapped child. In addition, while earlier studies noted that the training of elementary school counselors was little different from that of secondary school counselors, current studies present evidence that 23 states now have certification standards and requirements developed specifically for counselors at the elementary level.[15, 22]

Bruner's concern about the continuity of learning is far less visible for the handicapped child than for his normal peer. Although for more than 53 years the State-Federal program of vocational rehabilitation has responded to the needs of the disabled individual over the age of 16, there has been little assistance available for the handicapped child or young adolescent to prepare him vocationally.

Rehabilitation facilities throughout the United States, comprising vocational evaluation centers, comprehensive rehabilitation centers, and sheltered workshops, exist for the vocational planning and rehabilitation of the severely disabled adult. His vocational planning includes outreach, counseling, assessment and evaluation, training, and follow-along placement. And since Public Law 83–565 was passed in 1954, there has existed an innovative and creative program of research and demonstration geared to providing an imaginative cutting edge for the future of the rehabilitation of the severely disabled adult.

These rehabilitation facilities, however, have never been fully realized as educational institutions for work study programs affording vocational planning assistance for the handicapped child. Nor have the research and demonstration projects (now numbering over 2000 completed efforts) been analyzed to see what significant contribution they can make to vocational planning for a younger disabled group.

VOCATIONAL PLANNING PROCESSES FOR THE HANDICAPPED CHILD

Vocational planning for the handicapped child can be approached from the standpoint of five processes: (1) the socialization process — development of social skills, (2) the evaluation process — development of vocational awareness and skills, (3) the exploration process—the resource room, (4) the ambulation process—development of travel skills, and (5) the counseling process—concern with reality approaches in preparation for future community and occupational adjustment.

Obviously not exhaustive, these five vocational planning processes are conceived as an initial baseline of habilitation activity. Their relevance to the medical, psychiatric, educational, social, psychological, and other aspects is assumptive. Other chapters cover those facets of the total habilitation process.

These processes have in part been obtained from an analysis of a large number of final reports stemming from the applied research and demonstration program of the Rehabilitation Services Administration legislative research mandate. These vocationally oriented projects conducted by universities, rehabilitation facilities, and in some cases, special education schools often included populations of both young adults and adults.[17] Discussion with special education professionals, while the author was Chairman of the Department of Special Education and Rehabilitation Counseling, State University of California at San Francisco, provided additional observations on which these five processes are based.

The Socialization Process—Development of Social Skills

One of the chief demands made by business and industry of any applicant is, "Can you work with others successfully and in the general interests of production, achievement, and your own self-advancement?" Work skills themselves are useless if they cannot be encompassed with social skills within the work setting. Although the author has supported the work sample approach in preference to the psychologically standardized test as most appropriate in the assessment and evaluation of the handicapped individual, the work sample alone and by itself does not provide the proper information.[18] The socialization process surrounding the work assessment provides a baseline of information about the individual as well as presenting a work "role" to the handicapped child.

This process, a mix of work and social skills, is described often in the final reports of completed projects. While the essential intervention in the conduct of the demonstration has been a vocational evaluation based upon job samples or work evaluation trials, the evaluators constantly noted the presence or lack of social skill as one of the better predictors of future vocational success either in training classes or on the actual job itself.[1, 19, 20]

The process of socialization is also a predictor of later vocational adjustment. It is especially relevant to the adolescent with cerebral palsy, the orthopedically impaired youngster, and also the educable mentally retarded adolescent.

The discussion in this chapter concerns the youngster who is derailed from his regular track of growth and development. Loneliness is everywhere present, despite the warmth and attention of medical, nursing, and other professional staff members. Because of frequent hospitalizations his educational discontinuity includes periods of loneliness.

Toward the last years of her life, Frieda Fromm-Reichmann began to write about the psychiatric concept of "loneliness," especially related to long-term institutionalization.

> A young woman with a right-sided hemiplegia, mental retardation, and traumatic epilepsy from birth came to the hospital at the age of seventeen. She had learned to do all types of needlework with her left hand with considerable skill, and she was evidently accustomed to being commended for it by everybody who saw it. The first time I saw her doing some elaborate embroidery, I turned it to the reverse side, which did not look at all tidy. I commented that one who had her obvious skill could certainly improve the appearance of the reverse side. Many years later, after she had succeeded in making great progress in improving her life and her personal relationships under modified psycho-analytic therapy, she volunteered the information that her success was due to my initial remark about her embroidery. This had convinced her that she was not just being patted on the back and made her believe that I had confidence in her potentialities for growth and maturity.[5]

In long-term hospitalization or extensive special education classwork of the young child, the best preparation for any vocational planning can initially spring from group discussions concerning work, vocations, and occupational information about the work of the hospital—but always involving the development of social skills. These social skills, should lack of mobility preclude future transport to and from regular employment, would still be of inestimable value to the handicapped person in using the telephone or the future picture phone and writing letters.

Many research demonstration projects found that preparation for the initial job interview for the young habilitant had been inadequate. Practice in social skills and group relationships had often been omitted from the training period. The personal adjustment training program within the rehabilitation facility included consideration of social skills only shortly before referral to regular employment. The job interview itself, always a trying incident in the life of the normal person, becomes a nightmare to the habilitant. Without the awareness and early recognition of the importance of social skills to interpersonal relationships on any job, the best of vocational planning and job preparation may not sustain future employment.

The Evaluation Process—Development of Vocational Awareness and Skills

Vocational assessment and evaluation at best must afford a series of graded situations in which the individual can progressively advance under optimal environmental conditions. There should always be appropriate anxiety, during the assessment or introduction to areas of employment, to propel him forward and maintain his interest throughout the lengthy process of vocational evaluation. Any introduction to the choice of occupations must be flexibly concerned with the handicapped person's identification with the various ways of earning a living. Our culture is work-oriented.[3] Such cultural identity can be achieved through the development of vocational awareness and skills. Regular school has been far more successful with this concept than the vocational guidance and counseling movement within the habilitation process. Although Ira Gordon in his book, *The Teacher as a Guidance Worker,* stresses the teacher's role in serving as a front-line counselor, his concern is more with interpersonal counseling problems than with occupational introduction and vocational assessment.[11]

The inclusion of occupational information, as well as skill with prevocational evaluation on the part of the teacher, in vocational planning with the handicapped child will lead to these outcomes: (1) It will increase the later predictive value of the various types of work sample approaches now existing in rehabilitation settings. (2) It will expand the direction and focus of current conservatively operated sheltered workshops. (3) It will involve the physician and other medically oriented staff members vocationally in a more meaningful and supportive manner. (4) It will provide the family with more realistic and appropriate occupational expectations. (5) It will recommend needed changes in vocational rehabilitation legislation with regard to lower age levels, staffing arrangements, and earlier vocational planning for the handicapped child.

The lack of occupational information for youngsters in the regular grades exists concurrently with the same problem for the handicapped child. Bennett points up the concern youngsters have about their vocational future, documenting her research on the SRA Junior Inventory responses to the question: "I'd like to know what I'm going to be when I grow up." She found that their concern remained constant from Grades 4 through 8, and she obtained a 40 per cent response for each grade.[2] Dr. Walter Lifton, formerly with Science Research Associates, noted the early age at which attitudes and values about the world of work arose. He found that the emphasis on vocations in career planning should be replaced, and that instead, the elementary grades should be utilized as a laboratory about the world in order to widen the youngster's experiences.[13] The world of television, for example, is stocked with different types of jobs, notwithstanding the emphasis upon crime and delinquency as a way of life. Use of this medium to portray a variety of life-styles could be easily worked out. Manpower needs in the correctional rehabilitation field, for example, are as demanding as those within the health and social science areas.

Dr. Lifton at times asked elementary school teachers to consider which occupations they could use as illustrations to increase classroom learning. They were asked to list only those jobs in which they knew training requirements, salary levels, and job opportunities; their answers were compared with the Dictionary of Occupational Title (Department of Labor) categories. He found that professions led the list by far, followed by some sales and clerical tasks. But skilled trades were little noted. Actually their job distribution was in almost exact reverse to the distribution of jobs resulting from census data. In the primary grades, there is always a heavy emphasis upon service occupations. This emphasis shifts in the upper grades to the professions, usually without including the skilled and semiskilled areas. In other words, from both teachers and the tests used, youngsters received a skewed picture of the importance and types of jobs available.

School texts and books for early primary grades offer a partial view of the true picture of the world of work. Recently, the Office of Economic Opportunity in one of its inner city projects attempted to broaden the youngster's exposure to a larger variety of work opportunities.

There has been divergence in the field as to what constitutes a work sample. The author has witnessed many work sample approaches that seem to be unrelated to actual work and are contrived tool and equipment exercises. Such a so-called work sample is neither actual work nor a sample of real work, but continues the ambiguity factor in the testing situation. In other instances, the work sample must represent a completed work assignment recognizable as such by the disabled child.

As Gellman states:

> The field of vocational rehabilitation has long recognized the need for adequate predictive indexes of vocational potential. The field has vacillated about the use of standardized tests, non-standardized tests based on factorial analysis of a wide variety of job tasks, and work samples.[8]

Of the TOWER system, he states:

> Its virtues of a strong reality orientation, close simulation of work demands, and the observance of work behavior in a controlled situation are somewhat qualified by its disadvantages of being expensive, time-consuming and conceptually as much a training technique as an evaluative procedure.[8]

Dr. A. H. Edgerton, Professor of Education at the University of Wisconsin, reporting on the results of the National Guidance Evaluation Studies, indicated that 78 per cent of the games children play deal with occupations. He noted that two out of five people in this study had reached the age of 30 to 35 and were working in areas that reflected hobbies they reported when they were in Grades 3 to 6.[6]

Edlefsen and Crowe, Washington State University, conducted a study of teenagers' occupational aspirations in four school districts of the State of Washington: Dayton, Highline, Kelso, and Longview. Questionnaires were administered in the classroom anonymously. The students were told that the survey would provide information useful to the community and the schools as well as increasing the knowledge important in the development of young people as responsible members of American society. Results showed that:

1. Actual work experience in the field was the paramount reason for the student's interest in his preferred occupation.

2. There was more preference for the higher and middle status jobs than for the blue collar occupations. Children whose fathers were in the higher and middle status occupational groups expressed overwhelming preference to enter the same occupational groups as their fathers.

3. Though the higher status jobs were preferred by more respondents than any other group of occupations, students were rather doubtful that they would actually enter these occupations.

4. Students with definite college plans exhibited uncertainty about their occupational choice.

5. Students living in towns preferred a type of work involving people. Students living on farms preferred a type of work involving things.[7]

The December 1967 issue of *The Personnel and Guidance Journal* concerns itself with articles covering theories of vocational choice, realities confronting elementary school guidance, factors related to inconsistent career preferences, and some unresolved issues and conflicts regarding the legitimacy of elementary school counseling. A practical solution to some of these issues and conflicts might be found in the "resource room."

The Exploration Process — The Resource Room

The elementary or junior high schools can develop a resource room. Rather than being identified as only a prevocational area, or scheduled for occupation therapy, such a room can be identified as a meeting ground for a variety of needs: social, vocational, and educational. It should not be arranged like a regular school room, since the exploration process should afford optimal opportunity to offset loneliness, and include the mobility process that is discussed later. In the resource room occupational films could be shown, group meetings held (elections, committee work, group interchange), and there could be exposure to actual work situations.

Developmental tasks geared to occupational skills and based upon actual work samples could also be available within the resource room. As defined by Havighurst, a developmental task is

> . . . a task which arises at or about a certain period in the life of the individual, successful achievement of which leads to his happiness and to success with later tasks, while failure leads to unhappiness in the individual, disapproval by the society of his peers, and difficulty with later tasks.[12a]

Whether the interest developed is based on reality or on someone's tentative theory is not important. Most of all, the youngster will have some feeling of maintaining the level of accomplishment with his peers who are in regular schools. Obviously, the resource room for the disabled child is an important part of the community in which he lives, involving work, family, friends, and recreation. The resource room *should be* identified with all those *substitutes of reality,* or extensions of his real experiences that will help the vocational aspects of his special education classes. The resource room should provide an opportunity for the development of social skills independently of, or concurrently with, the increased awareness of occupational goals.

The Ambulation Process — Development of Travel Skills

There is need, from a vocational standpoint and for community adjustment, for journeys to investigate the school, vocations connected with a hospital, the resource room for peer relationships and vocational assessment, and school areas with which the child may be able to have some type of occupational identification and accomplishment. Ease in travel expands freedom of mind, body, and spirit. To lie encompassed in bandages, cases, or other limiting body image cages can foster frustration, loneliness, and passivity.

Assessment within the habilitation or rehabilitation process normally requires some level of mobility. Movement from one bench to another in a variety of actual work samples, utilization of training classes, or even possible travel within the employer's establishment should be a part of evaluation. Several workshops and rehabilitation centers are now utilizing anywhere from 10 to more than 30 employers in regular business and industry as extensions of the evaluation process. These employers act as evaluators, with a liaison relationship with the rehabilitation facility, for a week. Several demonstration programs in Seattle, St. Louis, New York, and other cities have experimented successfully with this innovation in vocational and psychological evaluation. Especially observable are the social skills of the disabled individual as he relates to the regular employers during this evaluation.

In long-term hospitalization, every effort must be made to bring the handicapped child into different environments even in the hospital. He can feel that he is making progress in achieving within different hospital settings. In addition, the movement itself could have a meaning and enhance his perception of progress. Travel through the various departments involving different occupations would be desirable in exposing the child to vocational training possibilities as well as career goals. Trips through the kitchen, departments in which the laboratory work is done, the x-ray department, and certain paramedical occupational settings could be followed by group discussion among several of the patients led by themselves. Later, reports could be given to those who were unable at that time to take part in the conducted tour. Occupational reports could be a part of scrapbooks, to which professional staff members of the hospital could also make contributions.

There are also games concerning vocations and occupational training that could be included in the resource room and mobility activity. One encyclopedia has introduced a vocational game that appears throughout the volume. The game is designed to help children see how their interest persists from one industry to another, and gives them a chance to think about work activities on several hundred jobs (Our Wonderful World, Spencer Press, 1957). A social studies series on the third grade level focused on "working together" includes skilled trades among many examples (McIntire, A., and Hill, W., Chicago, Follett Publishing Company). There is also an unpublished course materials series for the Chicago elementary schools on vocations, grades 7 and 8, for students who may not be continuing into high school.

From the resource room, there could also be prepared a mobile occupational unit containing booklets, games on occupations, information, and material geared to the educational levels of the special education classroom. Films and slides concerning a number of occupations are plentiful and can be obtained through the Washington Office of the American Personnel and Guidance Association or the National Education Association Council for Exceptional Children, both in Washington, D.C.

The Counseling Process — Concern with the Here and Now

Strangely enough, there has been little mention of the guidance and counseling process until now. The one-to-one relationship normally takes place in traditional counseling. But for the handicapped child, there is far more need for the group process to equalize the many medical one-to-one relationships during the treatment process. While he may not specifically recognize problems in his vocational preparation, he will appreciate the opportunities for group discussion about occupational areas of interest and the training that must precede the actual job in the real world. Should his interests be more crystallized and include specific types of training and jobs, the resource room could be utilized for visits from individuals representing those jobs of interest to the individual youngster. Both the Kiwanis and Rotarian organizations can contribute members who are glad to discuss the background of their occupations with special education classes. These representatives should be chosen carefully for their capacity to relate to youngsters rather than for their lecture competency.

Again, the focus should be on the immediate vocational concerns or occupational plans of the handicapped child. The counseling process can grow out of the child's questions about the occupational fields under discussion. Long-range plans for education and training are obviously understood, but the "here and now" frustrations might best be resolved in part by group counseling sessions that have meaning and can be substitutes for outside trips to business and industry—a part of many school curricula. This type of counseling, concerned with the immediate queries of the youngsters, can also promote the development of communication skills. Ease with new acquaintances and practice in discussion with other young adults afford positive reinforcement of a feeling of accomplishment.

The resource room, incidentally, can be utilized for the writing of letters requesting information about various types of occupations. Actual letters requesting job interviews can be worked out with the local Rotary Club and Kiwanis groups. The Lions Club has in the past provided business addresses of its members for letters of request for job interviews. The job interview can be conducted as practice in and a measure of both social skills and knowledge of what it takes to be appropriately trained for certain specific jobs.

Many employers have been interested in providing time to interview long-term hospitalized adolescents concerning the nature of different types of occupations. This exercise becomes a job interview sample, and builds into it social skills, communication skills, and a meaningful experience. This particular exercise can also mix peers from the regular school system, if nearby, with the special education group. Barring medical contraindications, and under circumstances that are helpful, even the long-term hospitalized child might carry on a correspondence with a "buddy" in his regular school class. In certain instances, visits from schoolmates could be arranged at intervals when they would advance the progress of the patient. The visits, however, should involve activities within the resource room rather than in the patient's room.

The five processes that have been described provide a baseline for vocational habilitation. These concepts must parallel the advance of bioengineering research in miniaturization of prostheses and orthoses, the continuing achievement of transplants, transducers, muscle implants, and externally powered equipment. We must be prepared with early innovation and ingenuity in vocational planning with the handicapped child.

References

1. An Investigation Into Methods of Obtaining and Using Actual Job Samples in a Work Evaluation Program. SRS Demonstration Project, RD-412, Vocational Guidance and Rehabilitation Service, Cleveland, Ohio, 1968.
2. Bennett, M. E.: *Guidance in Groups.* New York, McGraw-Hill Book Co., 1955.
3. Borow, H. (ed.): *Man in a World at Work.* Boston, Houghton Mifflin Co., 1964.
4. Bruner, J.: Continuity of learning. Saturday Rev. Educ., 21–23, March, 1973.
5. Bullard, A.: *Psychoanalysis and Psychotherapy: Selected Papers of Frieda Fromm-Reichmann,* Chicago, University of Chicago Press, 1959.
6. Edgerton, A. H.: Report: National Guidance Evaluation Studies. University of Wisconsin, Madison, Wis., 1959.
7. Edlefsen, J. B., and Crowe, M. J.: Teenagers' occupational aspirations. Washington State Univ. Bull., No. 618, July, 1960.
8. Gellman, W.: The principles of vocational evaluation. Rehabil. Literature, 105, April, 1968.
9. Ginzberg, E., and others: *Occupational Choice, an Approach to a General Theory.* New York, Columbia University Press, 1951.
10. Golden, L., and McKinney, J. D.: Frank Porter Graham Child Development Center of the Child Development Institute, University of North Carolina, Chapel Hill, N.C. (Pilot Study) 1972.
11. Gordon, I.: *The Teacher as a Guidance Worker.* New York, Harper & Row, 1956.
12. Gunn, B.: Children's conceptions of occupational prestige. Personnel Guidance J., 42:558–563, February, 1964.
12a. Havighurst, R. J.: *Human Development and Education.* New York, Longmans, Green & Co., 1953, p. 2.
13. Lifton, W. M.: *Working with Groups.* New York, John Wiley & Sons, 1961.
14. Marland, S. P., Jr.: Career Education—a new priority. Science, 176:585, 12 May, 1972.
15. Nitzschke, D. F.: Preparation programs in elementary school guidance—a status study. Personnel Guidance J., 43:751–757, April, 1965.
16. O'Hara, R. P.: The Roots of Careers. Elementary School J., 62:277–280, February, 1962.
17. *Rehabilitation, 1971.* Social and Rehabilitation Service, Department of Health, Education, and Welfare, Washington, D.C. 20201.
18. Rosenberg, B., and Usdane, W. M.: The TOWER system: Vocational evaluation of the severely handicapped for training and placement. Personnel Guidance J., 149–153, October, 1963.
19. Social Inference Training of Retarded Adolescents at the Pre-Vocational Level. SRS Demonstration Project RD-1388, University of Kansas Medical Center, Kansas City, Kan., 1968.
20. Training Guide for Vocational Habilitation. SRS Demonstration Project RD-1525, Jewish Employment and Vocational Service, St. Louis, Mo., 1966.
21. Twelve to sixteen: early adolescence. Daedalus, Fall, 1971.
22. Van Hoose, W. H., and Kurtz, M.: Status of guidance in the elementary school: 1968–69. Personnel Guidance J., 48:381, January, 1970.

Chapter 27

Education for the Handicapped Child

by *Frances P. Connor, Ed.D.*

It is clear that children in hospitals are there to receive the medical ser-vices necessary for their well-being and improved function. Educators, how-ever, in the hospital setting, serve an important role in fostering and main-taining childhood activities through as productive a learning environment as possible. Thus, the teacher qualified to work in a hospital needs to know normal child development and the kinds of activities children generally pur-sue since, in the hospital, special education is in a continuum with regular school instruction. Education should be designed to fill the gap that exists for children who need unusual assistance to learn, work, and play at their capacity, whatever it may be.

Every child has a right to an education. Neither age nor intellectual abil-ity or disability should be reason for denying a child a quality education while he is hospitalized and after. Rather, it is an opportune period for teachers to be creative and systematic in reaching specific stated objectives for each of their pupils. In the hospital setting, the program can be planned to provide enrich-ment, normalize development, prevent secondary disabilities, assess the pupil's educational remediation, and evaluate his program. Such individu-alization of instruction fosters experimentation in use of materials, methods, and curriculum.

A child does not develop entirely within himself (as noted by Dewey as early as 1902), i.e., his development requires an experience of what is really wanted. It is the adult who selects the stimuli, especially for very young children, and thus the direction of the student's learning. The more opportu-nity children are given to apply workable behavior structures in a variety of selected situations, the more easily they will emerge with the ability to mod-ify their own actions and to cope with their environment.

INFANT EDUCATION

Young children learn and demonstrate cognitive development within the first few weeks of life, and even Jensen, who reported genetic bases for intellectual differences, has supported early education for hospitalized children. He found that the only supportable upward shifts in IQ associated with environmental factors were related to "young children whose initial social environment was deplorable to a greater extent than can be found among any children who interact with other people or [are] able to run about out of doors." For those children, he suggests that a shift to good environmental circumstances can boost the IQ 20 to 30 points, and in extreme cases as much as 70 points.[14]

The implications for children confined to bed, in halo and hoops or large body casts, on stretchers, or using wheelchairs seem to be great. All hospital staff members need to find ways for individual children to move about, to reach out to and receive responses from other children. Education penetrates all of the child's life in the hospital; it cannot be left to teachers alone.

Children can learn at much earlier ages than was previously considered possible. Lipsett and others, for example, have demonstrated that newborns will suck harder and faster—or kick harder and faster—in order to regulate the brightness of a picture projected on the wall.[19] It appears that the infant actually seeks out pleasurable stimulation of many kinds rather than responding only to physiological needs such as hunger, pain, or thirst. In an educational sense, therefore, educators can use the newborn's curiosity to encourage activity that will promote specific kinds of learning through the use of body parts, which when employed according to a designated plan will provide the desired response.

For example, a baby who needs to exercise his left leg might do so in order to see an attached set of lights flash or hear bells ring. The child thus regulating a desirable sensory stimulus through specially designed rigging in his crib will be learning while enjoying the results of prescribed motion. Not to be overlooked is the educational potential of purposefully selected and placed mobiles and commonplace objects placed in a crib, on a mat or tray, or on the floor within reach and sight or sound of a child, particularly if he can manipulate or control them.

An infant needs to be fondled. Physical handling is a necessary factor in the physical, cognitive, linguistic, social, and emotional development of infants, but consistency of handling and personal attachments are critical to such development. Solkoff suggested that premature children who were handled and stimulated were healthier and more active and brighter, and demanded more stimulation than those who were not handled and that the effects were stable over time.[27a] According to Dennenberg, puppies that were handled had "grandpuppies" that were superior to the descendants of puppies that were not handled.[8] The implications of the existing results seem to point to the need for systematically designed and very early educational intervention for children with limited ability to reach out for or to obtain the necessary physical contacts because of confinement or medical or therapeutic devices that separate the child from normal relations with adults and peers.

A young child's sustained attention to stimuli is probably the most critical factor in his cognitive as well as other development. Kagan and his associates conducted a longitudinal study of attention, cognition, emotion, and temperament in 180 infants at 4, 8, 13, and 27 months of age. They concluded that a developmental sequence of processes exists that governs the use of attention.[15a] For example, primary attention gainers in the first month are the major stimulus contrasts and movement; by two or three months, moderate differences in schema and the event attract attention. By the end of the first year, teachers and other staff members need to be prepared to engage the child's more active kinds of information processing, including generation of hypotheses that relate events to the schema. The child's progress in cognitive and linguistic development particularly depends upon the quality of the experiences in which he can apply his rapidly developing skills.

There can also be too much stimulation in the early development of children. Cronback and others have pointed to the confusion that results when a young child cannot process the excess visual and auditory stimuli that occur in some children's artificial environments.[7] For the same reason Caldwell suggests taking the very young child from the booming, buzzing confusion to which some youngsters are exposed.[2] Again what is called for is properly selected materials, carefully placed for specific child use in learning. Well-meaning professional workers, each performing his designated and traditional role can work to the child's detriment.

To promote maximum child development, educators need to exploit the decision making abilities of very young children. Rheingold and Echerman, among others, support the hypothesis that a child with a strong internal locus of control will do better than one dependent upon external forces for control.[25a] Coleman has related locus of control and achievement. He emphasized that the child can learn structural arrangements through planned tactual and other sensory experiences.[2a] The emphasis on developing internal control does not militate against the use of behavior modification. External reinforcers are clearly indicated for improving certain types of behavior, especially in establishing functional patterns in deficit areas.[19]

Piaget, along with most theoreticians and practitioners concerned with human growth, agrees that an organism needs information in order to adapt and develop.[23, 24] This information as it applies to the adaptive process can be considered in terms of (1) the quantity of information available at any one time, (2) its quality, i.e., content or meaning, and (3) the context in which it appears. While each of these factors is of critical importance to all teachers, including the instructors of chronically ill or hospitalized children, there are other factors for consideration. Each child presents challenges to his teachers because of the constellation of variables that affect his learning and educational functioning.

DIFFERENTIAL EDUCATIONAL ASSESSMENT

Because of the wide range of individual variations found in hospitalized populations, teachers develop their differential diagnoses from their own evaluations as well as from information from other professional workers. It is anticipated that a differential educational diagnosis will provide some specific guides for instructional programming. The assessment data assist the teacher in determining the most appropriate setting for the child's learning (determining and modifying available school placement, whether classroom or ward), selecting the content (skills, knowledge, understanding) the child should acquire in his school program (curriculum), determining the barriers to his learning and the gaps in its content (educational deficits), and identifying the teaching strategies to be employed (methods and materials).

There are several approaches to the clarification of educational problems, which can be classified as: (1) a basic screening test battery, (2) analysis of test results, (3) a task analysis curriculum and evaluation, and (4) diagnostic or prescriptive teaching. Each of these approaches is described briefly.

Basic Screening

In the basic screening approach, the teacher samples the child's function in specific areas. Within his repertoire of formal tests, the special education teacher can obtain samples of the child's functioning on specific measures. Among the general data that have proved helpful in educational planning are the child's listening vocabulary, nonverbal intelligence, ability to apply inflectional rules of language through oral response, gross motor coordination and balance, laterality, skill in developing integrated written and oral composition, speech production levels, hearing acuity, auditory memory (digit span), visual function (employing a Snellen Chart test for myopia, the Plus Sphere test for hyperopia, the Titmus test of near and far point fusion and eye muscle balance, and the Frostig test of visual perception), and visual discrimination assessments. These measures serve the limited purpose of determining how, at a particular time, the child functions in an educational setting. Also easily administered by the teacher are the Wide Range Achievement Test (WRAT), which provides results of tests of word recognition, spelling, and arithmetic, and The Southern California Test of Motor Accuracy, which identifies the pupil's preferred hand. Used also by teachers are the Peabody Picture Vocabulary Test, A Psychoeducational Inventory of Basic Learning Abilities,[30] Psychoeducational Evaluation of the Preschool Child Using the Haeusermann Approach,[13] and the Gates-MacGinitie Reading Tests. The results provide a basis for designing a program of educational intervention, and the implications for cross disciplinary information sharing and planning are enormous.

Analysis of Test Results

The second diagnostic approach being used by teachers is one requiring considerable interdisciplinary confidence and respect. Psychologists are increasingly willing to share the results of subtests of standardized instruments such as the Wechsler Intelligence Scale for Children (WISC), which provides information about the child's performance in tests of information, comprehension, arithmetic, similarities, vocabulary, digit span, picture completion, picture arrangement, block design, object assembly, and coding. The Test of Auditory Perception (TAP) includes test performance in auditory discrimination, recognition, memory, and comprehension. From the Illinois Test of Psycholinguistic Abilities (ITPA), teachers can receive information on how the child performs in receptive and expressive processes (vocal and motor) including auditory decoding (listening), visual decoding (understanding visually presented materials), vocal encoding (verbal expression), motor encoding (motor expression), auditory vocal association (verbal association), visual motor association (visual association), auditory and visual memory, and visual closure. Such data assist in establishing a differential diagnosis of the abilities and disabilities of each child and serve as a basis for a language training program. The use of such information in education programming is described by Karnes with concrete suggestions for teachers in their work with handicapped children.[16]

The results of the WISC and other tests were formerly given to the teacher as a global or full scale score that had little meaning to those responsible for educational planning. However, when the profile of subtests is combined with the results of other highly specialized evaluations, teachers can clearly see areas of strength and weakness as they relate to sensory-motor development, communication, and academic achievement. The teacher can then identify areas of adequate and more than adequate performance as well as areas in which major training efforts must be made. While such a profile does not specify a parallel curriculum, a teacher can see the child's relative levels of performance. Cross disciplinary planning may be particularly important to the child's improved function when, for example, scores on similarities and object assembly are much lower than those on information, vocabulary, or digit span (auditory memory).

Most teachers receive some cues for program planning to strengthen the child's ability to note similarities in toys, household objects, or pictures and help him see relationships through jigsaw puzzles, making decorations for a party, simple carpentry, or preparing a salad from fruits or vegetables selected on the basis of similarities in color, shape, or general texture. These ordinary activities are seen as such by the child, but from the teacher's viewpoint the learning objective has been specified and is being realized. Practice for test taking is not what is recommended or suggested. Rather, the teacher is making use of available information provided by the psychologists, therapists, and other specialists.

Task Analysis

The third approach to differential educational diagnosis is curriculum based and task oriented. This kind of profile requires that the teacher have a step by step breakdown of the school tasks to be performed by the children in a usual program. In this task analysis, the teacher describes specifically what constitutes function at designated spots in the continuum of accomplishments required for successful performance.

For example, for each substep noted in the task analysis of each of the usual school activities to be developed are (1) clear written descriptions, (2) indication of the child's already learned behavior upon which the teacher can count as a base, and (3) specific activities, comfortable for the child, that can be employed to promote his progress to the next higher or parallel subskill essential for learning the task. All too often adults start instruction at a level beyond the child's level of development. The concept of time, as related only to numerical symbols on the face of a clock, is a case in point. Note that reference to the clock per se is at advanced stage, level four, in the five-point scale presented in Table 27–1 (one of the 190 items of *An Experimental Curriculum for Young Retarded Children*).[5]

Teachers and other hospital staff members need to become aware of possible deterrents to learning by systematically observing the factors operating in the school setting. Intensive and extensive interaction among staff members concerned with the child in the hospital will be helpful in selecting, modifying, and using equipment and materials of various shapes, sizes, and colors in order to assure the elimination of as many barriers to learning as possible. Utilization of hospital-related measuring devices (thermometers, vials), generally used equipment (braces, casts, urinals), personnel in the environment (physician, therapist, social worker, nurse), and related coping problems (death, cubicle-mates, pain, loneliness) will undoubtedly attract increased attention and promote concept development, problem solving, and other avenues of learning.

Such information is helpful in determining whether a child will function only, or better, in a one-to-one relationship with an adult, with another child, with a few children; at very close range or at a distance; using large materials or small; in an active, highly diversified classroom or in a quiet and isolated small area. Thus, the teachers have the bases for formulating teaching hypotheses.

When a teacher formulates questions about the relationships between a child's level of function and the activities planned for school, he is forced to test his hypotheses through careful and systematic observation of how and when the pupil responds to the stimuli presented.

Diagnostic and Prescriptive Teaching

The fourth approach might be called diagnostic or prescriptive teaching. Many educators are attempting to refine this process. Usually it combines elements of the three previously mentioned. Haeussermann, an early pioneer, actually shifted her testing emphasis from a test of intelligence to an assessment of educability. She modified the test items and materials to assure the child's being able to demonstrate his capacity. Most *child* advocates have questioned whether testing procedures that fractionate the global behavior of disabled children are appropriate to serve as the base for teaching children with complex experiential and other learning deficits.

The most productive portions and aspects of tests can form a repertoire to be applied flexibly and selectively, and interpreted systematically through a clinical reporting system. The report, rather than being quantitative, is an organized, highly structured but communicating document describing and integrating test results to depict interrelationships and relevance to school function. In addition, specific educational recommendations are developed for each child. They focus directly on the areas in which the child needs remediation and development. For example, for a pupil who needs to clarify his body image, to improve spatial organization, and to establish laterality and directionality, very specific school activities can be designed and prescribed to upgrade function. Descriptive assessments and recommendations can be employed not only during hospitalization but also later when he is at home or in the school he will attend upon discharge.

The teacher in the hospital needs to be encouraged to observe behavior systematically and study the child on a continuing basis. He can then make general behavioral observations of the child in school and set up a preliminary program of specific tasks with tentative hypotheses about the way the child will respond. When he closely observes the child as he performs the tasks about which the tentative assumptions have been made, he modifies the tasks or the program so that the child can do what he knows how to do as he learns the next more difficult function or task. In other words, the teacher studies the child's actual responses to the remedial efforts made and enables the pupil to use that which he knows well as he attacks new academic and social problems.

SCHOOLING IN THE HOSPITAL

Several factors are influencing current emphasis on the education of school-aged children in hospitals. Cross disciplinary planning, intervention, and evaluation in the educational process are gaining acceptance for a number of reasons. First, it has become increasingly clear that no one professional group can provide the basic elements of a comprehensive education for handicapped children. In most hospitals, such integrated intervention is more feasible than in other settings in which special education takes place. There is also awareness that the multiple learning disabilities of many hospitalized children call for educators competent in many areas in their own field of special education. These pupils may have difficulties in physical coordination and sensory acuity, perceptual functioning, short-term and long-term memory, language reception and expression, and cognitive functioning.

With the change of emphasis in cross disciplinary and cross categorical function each professional worker continues to extend his knowledge and skill in his own field; he also shares his role with others who might either be in a better position psychologically or physically to work effectively with the child and his family, or be able to integrate the learning of two or more areas into a single activity; he extends his own role to incorporate the traditional functions of his colleagues from other professional groups; and regardless of

TABLE 27-1 CONCEPTS OF QUANTITY: TIME*

THE FIVE LEVELS OF THE CURRICULUM ITEM

		RATING		
1. now	2. after a while versus tomorrow	3. activity schedule	4. activity in relation to clock position	5. awareness of telling time

DEFINITION OF THE TERM: BEHAVIOR UNDER OBSERVATION

The child's utilization of the daily activity structure. The time unit here was the school day; observed was child's ability to plan his own activities in accord with orderly allotments of time.

DESCRIPTION OF BEHAVIOR OBSERVED AT EACH LEVEL

Child followed plans for now; acted in accord with materials and resources immediately available (e.g., used paper, crayons, and table space for a drawing activity). Child did not defer activities on own initiative.	Child put away materials in anticipation of another activity; or continued with an occupation on hearing that another activity would be ready next, soon, after while.	Child acted according to "adjacent" activities (e.g., music was followed by work period; free play was followed by clean-up, then juice; juce was followed by roof play or projects.	Child noticed clock hands in conjunction with an activity; attended to clock position for activity transitions.	Child used clock as clue for change in activity.

PROGRAMMING

PREDICTABLE (INTERNALIZED) BEHAVIOR USED IN PROGRAMMING FOR NEXT LEVEL

Acts on immediate clues.	Defers or changes activity.	Knows two plus consecutive activities: handles transition.	Includes clock symbol in activity.	Undertakes an activity because of clock symbol.

TEACHING PROCEDURES TO ESTABLISH READINESS FOR NEXT LEVEL

Planning activities: a) teacher planning tangible: setting out, showing materials for immediate and next activity, treating sequence as a double activity. Verbal: setting out materials for immediate activity and describing next activity. b) child planning: asking child to choose next activity while he completes first activity or asking him to choose next activity before he begins the first one.	Verbal attention to transitions. a) "Warning signal" "In ___ minutes we must get ready for juice." b) Teacher planning: "You can start putting these things away, as we want to have juice and go to the playground." Conversational reviews of schedules (e.g., "We have had music and finished our handwork. Now it is time for free play.")	Verbal focus on a) Planning activities: arrangement of whole day's schedule. b) review on summary of day's activities (e.g., "When your mother asks you what you did today, what will you tell her?"). c) symbols: picture or print charts. Verbal attention to clock at transitions ("Look at that clock! We must get ready to ___").	Use of play clock, setting hands in correct position for a major group movement (e.g., time to go to roof). Gradual increase in clock symbol sequences: "The clock says it is time for handwork." "The little hand is pointing to 10. That means get ready for the roof."	Verbal attention to limits. There is not enough time to get out the blocks. Handwork: making clocks with moveable hands. Verbal attention to numerals and little hand. Review of daily schedule, with related clock times. Leading to beginning time-telling.

*From Connor, P., and Talbot, M.: *An Experimental Curriculum for Young Mentally Retarded Children*. New York, Teachers College Press, 1964.

who provides the specific service, he retains responsibility for assuring superior intervention from his professional area.[12]

The teacher's role is to promote his pupil's cognitive development through differentiating colors, shapes, sizes, and the functioning of objects. To be able to do this, a child must be able to communicate his choice of an object to represent the category to which it belongs. In a cross disciplinary training program, the nurse, therapist, or teacher might position the child so that he can reach for and more easily visually track a desired toy. Usually the child in school is forced to sit in his chair with his legs and feet directly in front of him under the table. In such a posture, the handicapped child might find it difficult to perform usual school tasks. With direct instruction from a physician or therapist, a teacher can learn to modify the physical environment to assist the child in maximum use of a prosthetic device or to place him in a position to foster functional movement or prevent physical deformities. Thus, the teacher is carrying out the tasks of a therapist while facilitating the pupil's school performance. In such situations, although the professional role may be transferred for a given time in a specific situation, the accountability still belongs to the person professionally qualified in the area. This kind of cross disciplinary approach will help the young child to build his hospital relationships gradually rather than face the challenge of communicating with and pleasing an inordinate number of adults in the full range of treatment and services.

The concept of controlling the degree and kind of stimuli a child encounters appears to apply to the number of persons involved as well as other aspects of his environment. Blank and her colleagues have concluded that disadvantaged young children, for example, benefited more from a program directed toward assisting the child in cognitive development, conceptualization, and relating to adults than from usual undifferentiated enrichment experiences.[1] Apparently, exposure to usual nursery and kindergarten materials and activities cannot be depended upon to facilitate learning in a child who is unable to process the information. Indeed, it might extend the actual deprivation and isolation of the child, particularly in the captivity of the hospital environment.

The lower a child's stage of decision making and problem solving, the more dependent he is upon the directions necessarily imposed by the adults in his world. Obviously, effective problem solving requires synthesis and integration of information. To facilitate their own development and use of these processes, children usually employ verbal communication skills, the prerequisite sensory-motor, visual and auditory perceptive development, and the perceptual-motor skills that lead to higher level cognitive function.

Thus, it would appear that in a trust-laden school environment, the hospitalized child should be inspired to and rewarded for even minimally intelligible speech responses and production, especially as he attempts to express feelings and explain his actions. For some children conversation boards, cue cards, and code systems are helpful. To utilize most school materials, the child needs some understanding of motor skills and awareness of his body in space as it relates to the usual childhood movements. The relationships between gross motor and eye-hand coordination, sensory discrimination, and language need to be understood by the teacher as he fosters self-motivating and self-directing creative child behavior. Van Witsen has systematically developed and empirically tested perceptual training activities that are designed to be modified and adapted for use by teachers in a variety of instructional relationships.[31]

If the education program is to promote the total growth and development of the young hospital patient, teachers need to take cognizance of his handicaps. It is proposed that for effective special education, the elements of the three major domains of human development be incorporated into the teaching situation to cultivate freedom for growth while the child is in the strange environment of the hospital. Among the intellectual processes to be spotlighted are cognition, perception, memory, divergent production, convergent production, and evaluation.[10] The pertinent *sensory-motor* factors include precision, coordination, control, vocalization, speed, and strength.[16a] Steps in the *affective* domain as suggested in 1950 by Erikson include trust, autonomy, initiative, duty, accomplishment, and identity.[9] Maritain described the function of education as liberation of the learner.[21] Such liberation of the long-term or chronically ill or disabled child should permit him to move about, to explore, to receive impressions, to process the information, to respond, and to express his reactions. Teachers' efforts, therefore, must be directed toward the child's sequential development with emphasis on specific elements of instruction, some of which differ from general education. Unusual cues, demonstrations, prompts, and adaptations will be removed gradually as autonomy becomes evident.

The teacher's responsibility rests in instruction, which includes the selection of the content to be learned, the materials through which the child can best learn the content, the setting most appropriate for instruction, and the instructional methods and sensory channels through which maximum learning is realized for the individual child.

Teachers are becoming increasingly systematic in their instructional roles as members of a hospital team. Lazarus's conceptualization of these roles offers a base for teacher function.[18] The following identified roles reflect the view of the teacher as a processor of information:

Observer.   The teacher as observer: (1) uses an observational schedule to record normal and deviant behavior, (2) records 10 minute samplings efficiently so that any teacher can translate findings for analysis, and (3) applies a behavior analysis technique to determine tentative hypotheses of developmental levels of a child.

Recorder.   The teacher as recorder: (1) administers tests to refine hypotheses, group screening, and individual tests and (2) designs informal tests for group or individual assessment of specific competencies.

Analyzer.   The teacher as analyzer: (1) compiles a summary of behavioral and cognitive aspects of a child's behavior from observations and records (description) and (2) is able to set up a profile of these competencies (assessment).

Transducer.   The teacher as transducer: (1) participates in interdisciplinary conferences and interprets findings to others, (2) assimilates into his analysis information and observations from other disciplines, and (3) synthesizes this feedback and amends his own analysis.

Transcoder. The teacher as transcoder: (1) sets up tentative objectives for instruction of the child, including short-term and long-term goals; (2) analyzes tasks; (3) analyzes media (e.g., materials for instruction); and (4) decides on modes of instruction to attain the goals.

Transmitter. The teacher as transmitter: (1) sets up the physical environment for effective instruction; (2) communicates by appropriate verbal and nonverbal transaction; (3) selects and competently uses methods and media in presentation of the concept or skill to be learned; (4) instructs individuals, small (2 to 6), and large groups; and (5) involves each child in the instructional transaction.

Evaluator. The teacher as evaluator: (1) uses "feedback" from all the preceding functions to recast any and all approaches; (2) uses media for self-study and self-criticism (e.g., tape recorder, film, videotape, computer assistance; and (3) shares his success and failure in teaching-learning experience during group evaluation with colleagues in allied disciplines.

Taxonomy of Instructional Treatments

Determining the specific program for the child is the task of each professional group and each individual. Piaget agreed that an organism needs information in order to adapt and develop.[23] This information as it applies to the adaptive process can be considered in terms of: the quantity of information available at any one time, its quality (i.e, content or meaning), and the context in which it appears.

Of recent interest is the Taxonomy of Instructional Treatments currently being tested by Tannenbaum and his colleagues.[29] Some of the principles upon which it is based are the following:

1. Teachers respond to the behavior of individual children, rather than function in a predetermined manner to a specific program for children with a diagnosed learning disability.

2. Instructional processes appropriate for the child are not a mirror image of the psychology of the child; i.e., understanding the child is not synonymous with understanding how to teach him.

3. Engagement of the child's attention is central to the instructional process.

4. Each learner has a favorite receptive style, and there is a set of mechanisms best suited to engage him at a given moment. Therefore, the teacher's instructional diagnosis provides information on the most comfortable and receptive stimuli for the instructional moment in time.

5. The teacher's instructional role is to achieve a "good fit" between the pupil's functional capacity and preferred learning style on the one hand and the organization of content and strategy on the other. Attainment of this match ("good fit") is defined as individualized instruction.

The ultimate goal, however, is to move the pupil from individualized to personalized instruction in which engagement (attention) control is maintained even through hitherto receptively unfavorable strategies. Individualization implies the identification of the best "wavelength" between the transmitter (teacher) and the receiver (pupil), while personalization involves the improvement of reception on an increasing number of wavelengths.

The two-step process toward individualization and then toward personalization is facilitated by the Taxonomy of Instructional Treatments, an operative model of the kaleidoscope of instructional behavior. The taxonomic approach offers a model to study the teacher as a transmitter and to examine his storehouse of instructional strategies and resources. Central in the instructional process is the child's attention or engagement. If attention is to be aroused most effectively, a combination of content, communications channels, and strategies for the instruction is required. For the teacher to employ these in appropriate combinations, he will need a large array of "bits" of information regarding the alternate combinations.

It appears that information processing is a delicate, complicated task, even when all the relevant "bits" are available to the teacher. When they are not, the task is almost impossible except through trial and error.

When, for example, a child's response pattern is erratic and unpredictable, it is possible that no combination of instructional stimuli produces optimal engagement on successive trials. The teacher then needs to be adroit enough to shift from one strategy to another, swiftly but smoothly. This requires that his arsenal of strategies be both abundant and systematically organized.

This new taxonomic approach takes into account the teacher's function in organizing content, in transmitting instructional stimuli through any of the pupil's receptive sensory modalities, in eliciting responsiveness through any of the pupil's expressive channels of communication, and in mastering the total range of instructional modes (styles) and methods (pupil grouping arrangements) available to be utilized.

For such a system teaching materials must be categorized according to: (1) content (level and sequence of knowledge or skill), (2) children's receptive channels, (3) children's models of expression, and (4) teaching styles to be employed and teaching method in which the material can be useful.

Through intelligent application of such a classification, teachers need not move directly from diagnosis of a child's functional capacity to the selection of appropriate instructional materials. Rather, the taxonomy provides them with an intermediate step. After the diagnosis, the teacher determines the content and the strategy and then seeks materials to fit the contextual and strategic requirements.

The only interchangeable part of the taxonomic model is content. Any substantive material, factual or behavioral, can be plugged in, but it must be organized as a pyramid of successive layers of concepts, each resting on a simpler, more fundamental stratum. To promote personalization of instruction with flexibility and variety, the teacher will vary the mode or method or both as appropriate to extend attention and the child's information processing.

As indicated earlier, teachers need to secure information about the stimuli that are most comfortable and readily acceptable by the child in the teaching process; i.e., those that foster and prolong the child's attention. Essentially, then, the content to be learned remains constant while the teacher varies the packages and the means of presenting them in response to the child's behavior. The teacher must make decisions regarding the content and the strategies to be employed; the more handicapped the child and the more options that will be eliminated, the more important it is that the teacher really know and use all the strategies that stimulate a child's behavior.

Modes and Methods

It behooves us to identify the possible varieties of modes and methods that constitute the teacher's instructional resources.

Thus far, the "How of Instruction" shown in Table 27–2 has been described as including four main headings: Instructional Setting, Instructional Modes, Communication Input, and Communication Output.

Instructional Settings.   The instructional settings (classroom groupings that provide the child with various instructional settings to which our attention can be directed in planning instructional strategies include:

1. Teacher–Total Class: A prescribed grouping of students in attendance that day involving task interaction between teacher and students.

2. Student Self-Instruction: A student working alone on an instructional task that is teacher-initiated and teacher-prescribed.

3. Teacher–Subgroup: Fewer than the total number of students in attendance that day being involved in a teacher-prescribed task that requires task interaction between the teacher and students (excluding teacher-student setting).

4. Teacher–Student: A one-to-one instructional interaction between the teacher and the student.

5. Student–Student (parallel): Two students working in close proximity on teacher-prescribed tasks, possibly sharing material or equipment with no physical or verbal interaction between the students intended.

6. Student–Total Class; A student is assigned to instruct all attending class members in a teacher-prescribed task.

7. Student–Subgroup: A student is assigned to instruct fewer than the total number of attending class members in a teacher-prescribed task.

8. Student–Student (tutorial): A two-student grouping based on an inequality of skills in which the more skilled student functions as tutor to the less skilled one.

9. Student Self-Directed: A student, with teacher approval, working alone on a self-initiated and self-prescribed instructional task.

10. Student–Student (interactive): Two students working on a teacher-prescribed task involving the sharing of material or equipment and requiring either social or task-oriented interaction between them.

11. Group Self-Instruction: At least three students cooperatively involved in a teacher-initiated and teacher-prescribed task.

12. Group Self-Directed: A least three students cooperatively involved in a group-initiated and group-prescribed task that has the teacher's approval.

TABLE 27-2 RESEARCH AND DEMONSTRATION CENTER TAXONOMIC INSTRUCTION PROJECT, TEACHERS COLLEGE, COLUMBIA UNIVERSITY: THE HOW OF INSTRUCTION (Strategy)*

Instructional Setting	Instructional Mode	Communication Input	Communication Output
1. Teacher-Total Class	1. Exploration	1. Visual	1. Oral Response
2. Student Self-Instruction	2. Problem Solving (divergent)	2. Auditory-Visual	2. Motoric Response (marking and writing)
3. Teacher-Subgroup	3. Testing Recall	3. Auditory	3. No Response
4. Teacher-Student	4. Problem Solving (convergent)	4. Motoric (haptic, tactile, kinesthetic)	4. Oral-Motoric (marking and writing)
5. Student-Student (parallel)	5. Exposition	5. Auditory-Motoric	5. Motoric Response (gestures and movement)
6. Student-Total Class	6. Game Competition (standard)	6. Visual-Motoric	6. Oral-Motoric Response (gestures and movement)
7. Student-Subgroup	7. Game Competition (player)	7. Auditory-Visual-Motoric	
8. Student-Student (tutorial)	8. Game Competition (field)		
9. Student Self-Directed	9. Game Competition (team)		
10. Student-Student (interactive)	10. Role Playing		
11. Group Self-Instruction	11. Programmed Response		
12. Group Self-Directed	12. Patterning		

*From Tannenbaum, A. J.: *The Taxonomic Instruction Project: A Manual of Principles and Practices Pertaining to the Content of Instruction.* Report to the U.S. Office of Education, 1969 (revised, 1973). Reprinted with permission.

†A distinction between extrinsic and intrinsic auditory input is being made. Whenever the purpose is a self-monitoring auditory input, the letter "I" will follow the appropriate number.

Instructional Modes. The second category for instructional variables, called instructional modes (i.e., the manner of instruction or the types of format and style that provide a varied presentation of materials), most often include the following twelve items:

1. Exploration: Involves an open-ended task that does not necessarily culminate in a product.

2. Problem Solving (divergent): Involves discrimination of relevant and irrelevant data and manipulation of relevant data in order to reach an indefinite set of responses.

3. Testing Recall: Involves the student's ability to retrieve facts either immediately or after a lapse of time.

4. Problem Solving (convergent): Involves discrimination of relevant and irrelevant data and manipulation of relevant data in order to reach a predetermined set of responses.

5. Exposition: Involves the teacher or a student as the central figure in transmitting instructional content to an essentially passive audience.

6. Game Competition (standard): Requires striving by the participant or participants to meet a performance standard that is imposed by any of the following: the teacher, the nature of the game itself, or the participant's inherent competitiveness.

7. Game Competition (player): Requires two participants to compete with each other to be the winner of the activity.

8. Game Competition (field): Requires the participants to strive against a field of others, all of whom are seeking to be the only winner in the game.

9. Game Competition (team): Requires that the participants be divided into teams, each team becoming the unit of competition that seeks to be the winner of the activity.

10. Role Playing: Involves play acting in which the content and the assumption of roles can be either preplanned or spontaneous.

11. Programmed Response: Involves extensive exposition, small sequential learning steps, and immediate student feedback.

12. Patterning: Involves the teacher, or a student, as the central figure in transmitting instructional content (verbal or nonverbal) to an audience that replicates the content immediately.

Communication Input. The communication input category, the student's sensory channel selected by the teacher for transmission of information, includes seven:

1. Visual: Reception of instructional stimuli through the sense of sight.

2. Auditory–Visual: Reception of instructional stimuli through the senses of hearing and sight.

3. Auditory: Reception of instructional stimuli through the sense of hearing.

4. Motoric (haptic, tactile, kinesthetic): Reception of instructional stimuli through the sense of touch in the palm (haptic), or fingers (tactile), or through the sense of movement and tension in muscles, joints, and tendons (kinesthetic).

5. Auditory–Motoric: Reception of instructional stimuli through the

senses of hearing and touch (haptic, tactile), or internal body movement (kinesthetic).

6. Visual–Motoric: Reception of instructional stimuli through the senses of sight, touch (haptic, tactile), or internal body movement (kinesthetic).

7. Auditory–Visual–Motoric: Reception of instructional stimuli through the senses of hearing, sight and touch (haptic, tactile), or internal body movement (kinesthetic).

Communication Output.   The communication output (the channel of expression noted or selected by the teacher and utilized by the student to communicate a response) consists of six identified possibilities:

1. Oral Response: Vocal expression in reaction to instructional stimulus.

2. Motoric Response (marking and writing): Marked or written expression in reaction to instructional stimulus.

3. No Response: No overt expression in reaction to instructional stimulus.

4. Oral–Motoric (marking and writing): A combined vocal and motoric (marked or written) expression in reaction to instructional stimulus.

5. Motoric Response (gestures and movement): Gestures or movement in reaction to instructional stimulus.

6. Oral–Motoric Response (gestures and movement): A combined vocal and motoric (gestures or movement) expression in reaction to instructional stimulus.

In using the Taxonomy model, the teacher makes decisions in planning for instruction: three for content (basic skills, subskills, and level of difficulty) and four for strategy (communication input, communication output, instructional mode, and instructional method). The model itemizes and codes all the alternatives available to the teacher in making each of these decisions. By placing the selected code numbers in appropriate cells on the Taxonomy chart, he reveals his instructional plan for a given child, a total class group, or a subgroup.

By no means is such a model designed to mechanize instruction; rather, it furnishes a way to select systematically certain instructional modes and methods and tie them into the child's means of communication. Through it teachers can respond to children and permit them the alternatives inherent in their individuality.

This approach to systematic teacher assessment of the child's modal preference and attention was considered by Kuffler.[17] She emphasized the need to determine the mode to which the child gives, not exclusive, but prior attention. Without recognition of the individual modal strategy and accommodation of the pedagogical patterns to the child's needs, unnecessary academic achievement deficits will result. For example, she suggests that the extensive use of verbal description and definition in mathematics may serve the non–spatially oriented child with a good memory for serially ordered sound, but is weighted against the visually spatially oriented pupil. It is for this reason that the earlier described educational assessment and subsequent instruction are critical. With comprehensive codification, school materials can be categorized and selected on the basis of a child's learning style. The content is then built into the materials.

Curriculum Content

In selecting content to be learned, the teacher in a hospital has a unique opportunity to focus on a number of options that will be available to his student. Since the chronological ages, intellectual abilities, experiential backgrounds, physical and medical problems, and overall prognoses are among the variables that force individualization of instruction, they also require special learning situations. Probably the most important dictum upon which the teacher acts is the one articulated by a 10 year old hospitalized boy who told a group of teachers, "Please don't think we can't do anything, but give us work at our own levels."

Several major factors are operating as curriculum plans are made:

1. Each child should be prepared to participate at his home school upon discharge from the hospital.

2. Curriculum content should enable the development of a variety of knowledge and skills that will increase academic as well as nonacademic performance. The latter may well be the vehicle through which the critical qualities of self-concept, unique competencies, and community participation might emerge.

3. Curriculum content should begin with areas of student knowledge and skill and build on those.

4. Curriculum content should be organized in terms of basic skills, subskills, and levels of difficulty for each of the students.

5. The curriculum content should incorporate the affective aspects of the child's life in the hospital, his family relationships, and the process of returning home.

6. Curriculum development requires systematic identification and recording of specific objectives for each child, the means by which the objectives are expected to be met, and the performance criteria that will signify accomplishment of the objectives.

7. Curricula for the hospitalized should include continuing education for infants and usual school-aged children and youth as well as training and retraining as appropriate for postschool populations.

8. Curriculum planning and implementation require cross disciplinary cooperation in planning, implementation, and evaluation.

Preparation for Participation at the Home School

The point of departure for such preparation is awareness of the educational placement options available upon leaving the hospital school. The Cascade of Educational Placements as presented by the Educational Policies Commission of the Council for Exceptional Children (1973) is shown in Figure 27–1.

It is generally agreed that handicapped children benefit most from attending school with their "normal" peers. Although a wide range of organizational patterns is necessary and available to disabled children, the more satis-

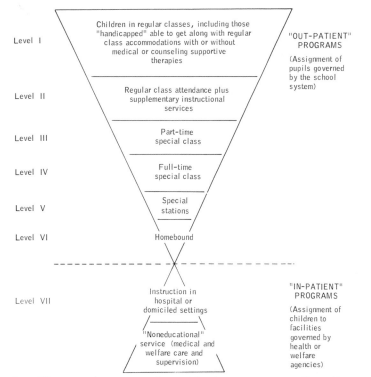

Level I — Children in regular classes, including those "handicapped" able to get along with regular class accommodations with or without medical or counseling supportive therapies

Level II — Regular class attendance plus supplementary instructional services

Level III — Part-time special class

Level IV — Full-time special class

Level V — Special stations

Level VI — Homebound

Level VII — Instruction in hospital or domiciled settings

"Noneducational" service (medical and welfare care and supervision)

"OUT-PATIENT" PROGRAMS (Assignment of pupils governed by the school system)

"IN-PATIENT" PROGRAMS (Assignment of children to facilities governed by health or welfare agencies)

Figure 27-1   The cascade system of special education service (from Deno 1968). The tapered design indicates the considerable difference in the numbers involved at the different levels and calls attention to the fact that the system serves as a diagnostic filter. The most specialized facilities are likely to be needed by the fewest children on a long-term basis. This organizational model can be applied to development of special education services for all types of disability. (From Council for Exceptional Children. Education Policies Commission: Organization and administration of special education. Exceptional Child., 37:431, January, 1971.)

fying and satisfactory his relationships are with age peers, the better will be the total development of the handicapped child.

Implied, of course, is direct contact between the educational personnel in the hospital and in the child's home community. In some instances, it is advisable to obtain the textbooks used by the home school and, if possible, arrange visits from former or future classmates. These visits will motivate the patient to incorporate the content of this instructional material into the hospital school program. Special remedial work can be initiated without embarrassment or undue attention to academic deficiencies. Progress can be made at the child's own rate and be as intensive and extensive as possible for him. He can consider the highly individualized instruction as a vote of confidence in his ability to master the tasks through his own efforts, thus enhancing his own expectation and sense of internal control.

Academic and Nonacademic Learning

Personal study has revealed unnecessary academic retardation among crippled and health-impaired children who have been hospitalized or homebound or attended school in special classes. Aware of the pupil's achievement and deficits in learning processes as well as content, the teacher is in a unique position to increase academic achievement levels.

If education is to encourage the child's active rather than passive participation in his own learning, however, the hospital classroom and after-school program needs to be project-product oriented. Particularly recommended are teacher-student developed work contracts that are monitored by both parties. In such an arrangement the objectives are clear, adult guidance is available, and the product is a tangible completion of the agreed-upon task. The open-classroom arrangement and the individualization concept seem to be appropriate for the wide age and grade range of hospital school grouping.[27]

As a child acquires knowledge related to a particular "extracurricular" activity, hobby, or game, he is enhancing his potential community group membership. For example, a fine chess player, activity organizer, news editor, or expert score keeper will be welcome in a hometown recreation center. Such an entree will facilitate personal and social adjustment as well as acquisition of other skills.

Curriculum Base

In the personal teacher-student relationship possible in a hospital, there seems little excuse for not being able to arrange content that builds directly upon what the child already knows and the skills that he can perform easily. It is in the application of established knowledge and skill that the child can perceptually reform previous points of view by a process that moves backward and forward, continually correcting initial errors and those arising subsequently.[24] As the child himself participates in his own learning and in self-evaluation, he can see his own progress and build upon his internal control rather than depend upon externally regulated conditions for his achievment. He can, for example, more easily read material of interest and of use to him than he can manage similar written or printed vocabulary that is not within the realm of his experience. In other words, stress in reading and writing will be on meaningful language rather than on rote vocabulary. Again, the hospital personnel need to devise means of incorporating the vocabulary and content taught in the child's home school into the program in this special setting.

As Mallison reported in her study of educational therapy, "Standards of work are important. There is rarely any justification for permitting children to do things less well than they are capable of doing, in each work session."[20] She notes, however, that the more functional the academic work and the more consistent its level with the child's ability, particularly for those with limited experiential background or major learning disabilities, the more likely will be the pupil's continued growth in academic skills and acquisition of information.

The teacher's objectives include upgrading the child's functions in deficit areas, e.g., the tasks to be performed are designed to strengthen auditory or visual memory, body image, or directionality if these are the areas of dysfunction. For example, small and large form puzzles with which the child enjoys playing are made available to him. The teacher's objective is to promote the development of the child's ability to see relationships of parts to a whole, to provide experiences in motor coordination, and to enable the pupil to combine visual and kinesthetic dimensions as he uses special colors, shapes, weights, and content. For the child, however, it is challenging play.

Content Organization

Systematic organization of content into basic skills requires the identification of decision-making parameters. Table 27–3 presents an early attempt to describe language arts content for reading for retarded learners as part of the Taxonomy of Instructional Treatments.[29]

Affective Aspects of the Curriculum

The need for teacher concern that the affective qualities of the teacher-pupil and pupil-pupil relationships be present throughout instruction is increasingly evident as educators take their professional accountability seriously. It is clear that systematization and productivity need not preclude humanism. Teachers are cognizant of the value of their manipulation of reinforcement systems and are making efforts to apply the results of substantial study.[12b, 32, 33] Without losing the opportunities for teacher-pupil transactions in exchange of ideas, reward systems can be employed that are attractive and yet subject to alteration and extinction as workable patterns of enhanced child behavior develop.

An explicit guide for dealing with some common problems encountered by hospitalized children highlights curriculum content relevant to their life, which is often fraught with severe stress, separation, death and other loss, physical pain, limitation, and disfigurement.[22] The inclusion of mental health concepts as part of the child's learning about himself, his family, and his fellow patients, and developing self-concept will help him recognize and cope with inevitable problems concerned with hospitalization.

Behavioral Objectives

Instruction geared to specified objectives is employed by teachers of handicapped children. Their approach takes several forms. Objectives are identified for teacher performance as well as for child learning and achievement. As Snyder describes the process, the following outline serves as the organizing scheme:

What is to be accomplished?
By whom?
When and for how long?
Under what conditions?

TABLE 27–3 RESEARCH AND DEMONSTRATION CENTER TAXONOMIC INSTRUCTION PROJECT, TEACHERS COLLEGE, COLUMBIA UNIVERSITY: THE WHAT OF INSTRUCTION*

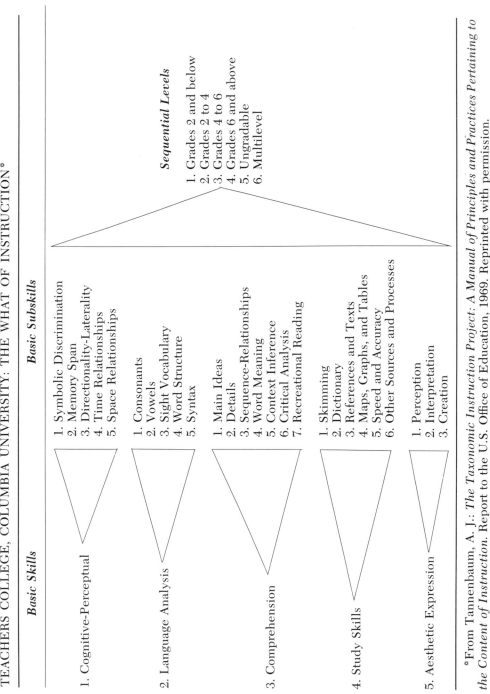

Basic Skills	*Basic Subskills*	*Sequential Levels*
1. Cognitive-Perceptual	1. Symbolic Discrimination 2. Memory Span 3. Directionality-Laterality 4. Time Relationships 5. Space Relationships	1. Grades 2 and below 2. Grades 2 to 4 3. Grades 4 to 6 4. Grades 6 and above 5. Ungradable 6. Multilevel
2. Language Analysis	1. Consonants 2. Vowels 3. Sight Vocabulary 4. Word Structure 5. Syntax	
3. Comprehension	1. Main Ideas 2. Details 3. Sequence-Relationships 4. Word Meaning 5. Context Inference 6. Critical Analysis 7. Recreational Reading	
4. Study Skills	1. Skimming 2. Dictionary 3. References and Texts 4. Maps, Graphs, and Tables 5. Speed and Accuracy 6. Other Sources and Processes	
5. Aesthetic Expression	1. Perception 2. Interpretation 3. Creation	

*From Tannenbaum, A. J.: *The Taxonomic Instruction Project: A Manual of Principles and Practices Pertaining to the Content of Instruction.* Report to the U.S. Office of Education, 1969. Reprinted with permission.

With what tools or materials?
To what extent or degree of accuracy?
Judged how?
Any special features?

For workable objectives, a checklist includes the following questions:

Is the objective pertinent to the problem?
Are the events or behaviors externally observable?
Are they measurable or countable?
Is the objective feasible? Can it be met?
Is it publishable, in the sense of being public?
Is there a clear criterion for performance level?
Is there a stated time frame for its completion?[28]

This process assures a child oriented, teacher directed program with publicly stated objectives. Children too can be involved in the development of objectives; they can participate in the preparation of performance contracts through which they state the objectives for a designated instruction period.

Through these means, a functioning program of individualized instruction can be realized; an open classroom environment can become a workable reality.[27] The necessary internal control and self-monitoring can be applied for increased school learning and accomplishment.

Education as a Continuum

Hospitalized children create a demand for well-organized, self-directed, creative, knowledgeable teachers. They range from the most severely and multiply handicapped to the least disabled; from short-term to long-term patients; from newborns to preschoolers to school-age children and youth to adults desirous of reeducation, remediation, or raising their educational levels. The need for a variety of educational specialists is inherent in this instructional setting.

For some groups such as infants and adults, professional preparation programs are not as yet adequate in either quantity or quality. Particularly critical is the need for highly competent specialists to assume responsibility in subject matter fields. Required also is knowledge of the pupil as a growing organism and as one with unique problems.[6]

Materials and Equipment

The child makes early responses to his world. Early sensory training dictates the selection and availability of stimuli to promote desired behavior. Although no formula as yet exists to guide in the determination of optimum degree and kind of stimulation for each child, sensitivity to the effects of the environment on learning is emerging.[7] The materials selected should promote the student's action in the anticipated direction and should lead to reinforcement for the child of his appropriate response. For severely disabled children it is necessary to modify and adapt materials and equipment to permit as much active and self-directed participation as possible.

Of particular interest in infant and toddler education are two especially designed program innovations.[15] The first is the use of a confined space into which several small children are placed. Their bodies touch each other, and the responses to various textures (skin, hair, clothes) and to physical contact in this free environment have proved profitable. Systematic observations are made by an unobtrusive adult sitting in a corner of the area. Participating children improved in awareness and peer interaction and social, verbal, and motor activity.

The second training vehicle is a "sensory story" through which contrasting stimuli and situations on a turntable with four scenes involved in a child's day in the hospital are presented. As the story is told, and retold, children touch the materials relevant to the situation; they move them and dramatize to the extent that they are able. It is an opportunity for the adults to listen to children as they express their thoughts and feelings through various means of communication.

Also effective is the Fun House at the same hospital. The details of its design are available from Dr. Margaret Jones, Professor of Pediatrics at the University of California in Los Angeles. In general it consists of varitextured surfaces on a center bowl into which children can climb from stairs and ramps that they mount and then descend. On the walls are selected stimuli that can be easily attached and removed. Entrance to the Fun House is voluntary and for children only. Increased physical movement, problem solving, socialization, vocalization, exploration, and experimentation have been evident.

Modifications of materials and equipment will permit the use of the hospitalized child's own action while learning even though he must remain in a prone position, in a wheelchair, or in another confining device. In a cooking activity, for example, children learn to read and write recipes, follow directions, experiment, solve problems, and integrate sensory experiences. Motor planning requires an integrative process. But, for the child, he is creating a product he will enjoy and can share.

Home and community contacts are to be encouraged as much as possible. With the increasing number and kinds of vehicles equipped to accommodate the nonambulatory child, well-planned and carefully executed field visits are possible. At all costs the vision of the hospital as a place of isolation and confinement must be dispelled.

The activities of daily living as learned in other hospital departments can be utilized by the child in the school as he gains independence in his individual program. The total hospital environment needs to be mobilized to focus on the child's overall development as well as his acquisition of precisely identified knowledge and skills.

CONCLUSION

The setting of goals, specification of objectives and the means by which they are to be achieved, and evaluation of the effectiveness of staff and child effort are not the responsibility of any one discipline, nor can they be accomplished without a multidisciplinary effort. More teams of specialists who are interested in child development must be trained. The involvement of family members, particularly parents, in a primary programmer role has positive potential both for in-hospital programs and in subsequent community adjustment. Knowledgeable and participating parents can develop skills that will enable them to obtain necessary information and service for their children. In today's world of rapidly changing societal and cultural values, the role of advocate for the disabled is a continuing one for all professional workers concerned with these children.

References

1. Blank, M., et al.: Individual teaching for disadvantaged kindergarten children: A comparison of two methods. J. Special Education, pp. 207–219, Fall, 1972.
2. Caldwell, B. M.: What is the optimal learning environment for the very young child? Am. J. Orthopsychiatry, pp. 8–21, 1967.
2a. Coleman, J. S.: *The Adolescent Subculture.* New York, The Free Press of Glencoe, Inc., 1966.
3. Connor, F. P.: *Education of Homebound and Hospitalized Children.* New York, Teachers College Press, 1964.
4. Connor, F. P.: Education of children with chronic medical problems. *In* Cruckshank, W., and Johnson, G. O. (eds.). Englewood Cliffs, N.J., Prentice-Hall, 1967.
5. Connor, F. P., and Talbot, M.: *An Experimental Curriculum for Young Mentally Retarded Children.* New York, Teachers College Press, 1964.
6. Connor, F. P., Wald, J., and Cohen, M.: *Professional Preparation of Education of Crippled and Other Health Impaired Children.* New York, Teachers College Press, 1971.
6a. Council for Exceptional Children. Education Policies Commission (M. Reynolds, Chairman): Organization and administration of special education. Exceptional Child., 37:431, January, 1971.
7. Cronback, L. J.: Heredity, environment and educational policy. Harvard Educational Rev., pp. 338–347, Spring, 1969.
8. Dennenberg, V. H.: Critical periods, stimulus input and emotional reactivity: A theory of infantile stimulation. Psychol. Rev., pp. 335–351, 1964.
9. Erikson, E. H.: Growth and crises of the "Healthy Personality." *In* Senn, M. (ed.): *Symposium on the Healthy Personality.* New York, Josiah Macy Jr. Foundation, 1950.
10. Guilford, J. P.: Three faces of intellect. Am. Psychol., August, 1959.
11. Gordon, R.: A nursery school in a rehabilitation center. Children, 1:145–148, July-August, 1966.
12. Haynes, U. (Project Director) et al.: *Collaborative Infant Project.* U.S. Office of Education Grant No. 42–039–1. New York, United Cerebral Palsy Associations, Inc., 1971.
12a. Haeussermann, E.: *Developmental Potential of Preschool Children.* New York, Grune & Stratton, 1958.
12b. Hewitt, F.: *The Emotionally Disturbed Child in the Classroom. A Developmental Strategy for Educating Children with Maladaptive Behavior.* Boston, Allyn & Bacon, 1968.
13. Jedrysek, E., Klapper, Z. S., Pope, L., and Wortis, J.: *Psychoeducational Evaluation of the Preschool Child—a Manual Utilizing the Haeussermann Approach.* New York, Grune & Stratton, 1972.
14. Jensen, A. R.: How much can we boost I.Q. and scholastic achievement? Harvard Educational Rev., pp. 1–123, Winter, 1969.
15. Jones, M. H., Barrett, M. L., Olonoss, C., and Andersen, E.: Two experiments in training handicapped children. *In* Clinics in Developmental Medicine No. 33. *Planning For Better Learning.* Philadelphia, J. B. Lippincott Co., 1969, pp. 108–122.
15a. Kagan, J.: *Change and Continuity in Infancy.* New York, John Wiley, 1971.
16. Karnes, M. B.: *Helping Young Children Develop Language Skills.* Washington, D.C., The Council for Exceptional Children, 1968.
16a. Klausmeir, H. J.: *Learning and Human Abilities.* New York, Harper & Brothers, 1961.
17. Kuffler, P.: Modal preference—a key to idiosyncratic learning. *In* Wolff, P. H., and MacKeith, R. (eds.): *Planning for Better Learning.* London, Spastics International Medical Publications, William Heinemann Medical Books Ltd., 1969, pp. 49–57.

18. Lazarus, P.: *An Experimental Evaluation of a Two-Year Extended Reading Readiness Class Program.* New York, 1969.
19. Lipsett, L.: Learning in the human infant. *In* Stevenson, H. W., Tess, E. H., and Rheingold, H. L. (eds.): *Early Behavior Comparative and Developmental Approaches.* New York, Wiley, 1967, pp. 225–247.
20. Mallison, R.: *Education as Therapy: Suggestions for Work with Neurologically Impaired Children.* Seattle, Special Child Publications, 1968, p. 65.
21. Maritain, J.: *Education at the Crossroads.* New Haven, Yale University Press, 1957.
22. Petrillo, M., and Sanger, S.: *Emotional Care of Hospitalized Children.* Philadelphia, J. B. Lippincott Co., 1972.
23. Piaget, J.: *Psychology of Intelligence.* (Translated by Piercy, M., and Berlyn, D. E.) London, Routledge and Kegan Paul, 1947.
24. Piaget, J.: Comments on Vygotsky's critical remarks concerning *Language and Thought of the Child* and *Judgment and Reasoning in the Child.* Cambridge, Mass., M.I.T. Press, 1962.
25. Plank, E. M.: *Working with Children in Hospitals.* Cleveland, Press of Western Reserve University, 1962.
25a. Rheingold, H. L., and Echerman, C. O.: The infant separates himself from his mother. *Science, 168:*78–83, 1970.
26. Robertson, J.: *Young Children in Hospitals.* New York, Basic Books, Inc., 1959.
27. Silberman, C. E.: *Crisis in the Classroom, the Renewal of American Education.* New York, Random House, 1970.
27a. Solkoff, N., Yaffee, S., Weintraub, D., and Blase, B.: Effects of handling on the subsequent developments of premature infants. Dev. Psychol., *1:*755–768, 1969.
28. Snyder, T.: *Professional Preparation of Education of the Crippled and Other Health Impaired: Competency-Based Programming.* New York, Teachers College Press, 1973.
29. Tannenbaum, A. J.: *The Taxonomic Instruction Project: A Manual of Principles and Practices Pertaining to the Content of Instruction.* Report to the U.S. Office of Education, 1969 (revised, 1973).
30. Valett, R. F.: *Effective Teaching—A Guide to Diagnostic-Prescriptive Task Analysis.* Belmont, Cal., Fearon Publishers, 1970.
31. Van Witsen, B.: *Perceptual Training Activities Handbook.* New York, Teachers College Press, 1967.
32. Ward, M. H., and Baker, B.: Reinforcement theory in the classroom. J. Appl. Behavior Analysis, pp. 323–328, Winter, 1968.
33. Whelan, R. J., and Haring, N. G.: Modification and maintenance of behavior through systematic application of consequences. Except. Child., *32:*281–289, January, 1966.

Index

In this index page numbers in *italics* refer to illustrations; those followed by (t) refer to tables. The abbreviation vs. indicates differential diagnosis. Drugs are indexed under the generic name only.